THE
STRUGGLE
FOR
EUROPE

William I. Hitchcock was born in Fukuoka, Japan, in 1965, the son of a US Foreign Service officer. He now teaches history and international relations at Wellesley College in Wellesley, Massachusetts. He received his BA from Kenyon College in 1986 and his Ph.D. from Yale University in 1994. He is the author of *France Restored: Cold War Diplomacy and the Quest for Leadership in Europe* (1998), and co-editor, with Paul Kennedy, of *From War to Peace: Altered Strategic Landscapes in the Twentieth Century* (2000).

THE
STRUGGLE
FOR
EUROPE

THE TURBULENT HISTORY OF
A DIVIDED CONTINENT
1945–2002

·

WILLIAM I. HITCHCOCK

P

PROFILE BOOKS

This paperback edition published in 2004

First published in Great Britain in 2003 by
PROFILE BOOKS LTD
58A Hatton Garden
London EC1N 8LX
www.profilebooks.co.uk

First published in the United States in 2003 by
Doubleday

1 3 5 7 9 10 8 6 4 2

Book design by Gretchen Achilles

Printed and bound in Great Britain by
Bookmarque Ltd, Croydon, Surrey

A CIP catalogue record for this book is available from the British Library.

ISBN 1 86197 463 9

FOR LIZ

ACKNOWLEDGMENTS

.

THIS BOOK HAS BEEN in the works for many years, and I wish to thank a number of people and institutions who gave me support and encouragement throughout.

I first conceived of the idea for the book while teaching at Yale University, where I encountered many outstanding students who wanted to know more about Europe and its recent past. In pressing me for details, they sent me back to the library to widen my own understanding of the continent's rich history. My former colleagues at Yale, especially Paul Kennedy and John Lewis Gaddis, consistently gave me support and never deterred me from such an ambitious undertaking.

I owe a great debt to the Wellesley College history department, which welcomed me onto a superb team of scholars and teachers and has provided a warm, collegial environment in which to work. In particular, I thank the recent departmental chairs: Lidwien Kapteijns, Guy Rogers, and Nina Tumarkin. I wish to acknowledge the kind assistance of Thelma Pellagrini, our departmental administrator, and research assistance from Diane K. Morgan and Grace D. Kim. Finally, the beneficent Office of the Dean of the College intervened with financial support at a critical moment.

A number of friends kindly agreed to read parts of the manuscript and gave me enormously helpful comments. I must thank in particular Jeffrey Auerbach, Matthew Connelly, Mary Sarotte, Andrew Shennan, Jeremy Varon, and Paul Wink, all of whom took precious time away from their own work to help me with mine.

Many kind souls have given me aid and advice over the past few years, far too many to name here. But I must mention two—my friend and former colleague Timothy Naftali, and my agent Susan Rabiner—who offered me wise counsel in the early stages of this book that had a dramatic impact on its overall shape. Gerald Howard of Doubleday and Peter Carson of Profile Books read draft chapters throughout and gave me swift, unerring, and detailed comments. The book has been immeasurably improved by their wisdom and experience.

I could not have completed this project without the constant, unwavering support of my wife, Elizabeth R. Varon. While I struggled with Europe, she managed to write a book of her own, teach hundreds of keen students, raise two beautiful children, and keep our household together, all with exquisite grace and humor. She is incomparable, and I owe her everything.

And so this book is for her.

CONTENTS

.

PART FOUR: UNITY?

THE
STRUGGLE
FOR
EUROPE

© Orbis, 2002

INTRODUCTION

·

A LITTLE MORE THAN a year after the end of World War II, Winston Churchill, Britain's former prime minister and now leader of the Conservative opposition, gave a speech to an audience at Zurich University, in Switzerland. His description of Europe at that time captured the sense of desperation many Europeans felt as they faced the immense task of postwar reconstruction. "What is the plight to which Europe has been reduced?" he asked. "Over wide areas a vast quivering mass of tormented, hungry, careworn, and bewildered human beings gape at the ruins of their cities and homes, and scan the dark horizons for the approach of some new peril, tyranny, or terror. Among the victors there is a babel of jarring voices; among the vanquished a sullen silence of despair." Churchill was right: the months after the close of the war were among Europe's worst. Though the killing had mercifully stopped, Europeans faced the devastation of their continent, the collapse of their national economies, and the staggering human toll. Perhaps 40 million people on this continent were killed between 1939 and 1945—on average, 18,500 deaths a day for six years. Could Europe ever recover from such a horror, or were its days of vitality and civilization gone forever? Was this the start of some new Dark Age, as Churchill put it, "with all its cruelty and squalor"?

Europe did not stay down for long. Half a century after Churchill spoke, Europe, the great continent that stretches from the Urals to the Irish Sea, from Norway's Arctic fjords to Malta's sun-baked beaches, has prospered beyond anyone's wildest dreams. At the start of the twenty-first century, Europe is richer, freer, and more stable than at any time in its long history. The continent that gave the world both absolute monarchy and totalitarianism is now almost entirely democratic, and those few holdouts—mostly the former

Soviet republics—are isolated. Europe is economically united in ways once unimaginable: twelve European states now share a common currency that is governed by a single European Central Bank. The fifteen states that make up the European Union (EU) churned out a staggering $9.9 trillion in GDP in 2001—surpassing even the United States. The former Communist-bloc countries are busily preparing to join the EU and will do so within a decade. Of the world's six largest economies, four are European: Germany, France, the United Kingdom, and Italy. And above all, Europe is at peace. This is no small achievement for a continent that in its modern history has rarely known any period longer than a generation during which the scourge of war was absent. During the past fifty years, Europe did not languish in the valley of darkness but moved slowly and steadily into the "broad, sunlit uplands" that Winston Churchill had famously hoped for in the bleak early years of the war. How did this extraordinary transformation happen?

This book sets out to answer that question. It does not offer an encyclopedic account of each European country, but instead focuses on the principal conflicts, debates, and political actors that have done the most to give Europe the shape it has today.[1] Although each of the sixteen chapters that follow investigates one period, theme, or country in depth, the book places particular stress on four interrelated factors that help explain Europe's improving fortunes over the past five decades.

First, Western Europe had a good Cold War. Between 1945 and 1990, Western Europe profited from the American military and economic commitment to Europe. The division of Europe into rival blocs, though a tragedy for many Germans and virtually all Eastern Europeans, nonetheless provided a sense of cohesion and purpose to the states of Western Europe. The constant lurking threat of the Soviet Union, its willingness to use military force to protect its sphere of influence, and its sponsorship of large Communist parties in the West spurred Europeans to make common cause with the United States. At times the United States played up the Soviet threat to assure a greater degree of cohesion; but most Western European governments needed little persuading. They had seen Stalin's barbarity up close since the mid-1920s and had no desire for the Soviets to extend their reach farther into Europe. Europeans embraced the US security commitment in the form of the North Atlantic Treaty Organization (NATO) in 1949, and European leaders steered their sometimes unwilling publics toward closer economic cooperation with once rival nations; the cornerstone of the European Economic Community (EEC) was laid in 1950, a time of profound Cold War tension. These institutions bound Germany to Western Europe, contributed to Europe's economic

expansion, and gave Europe a structure that has continued to provide prosperity and security well after the end of the Cold War.

A second factor in Europe's success was, paradoxically, the very intensity
of the war. World War II, despite its destructive impact on the landscape and
peoples of Europe, had in the long run a positive effect on the European economy. By leading to the destruction of so much industrial equipment, rolling
stock, and rail lines, roads, bridges, harbors, and buildings, the war forced
Europe to rebuild its industrial capacity anew. The reconstruction effort provided an opportunity for European industry to retool along modern lines just
at the moment when the American model of industrial production was laying
roots in Europe. Reconstruction on so massive a scale required new institutions and new leadership, which in Western Europe were fortunately at hand.
A talented class of civil servants emerged from the war, prepared to inaugurate ambitious state investment in the economy. Political leaders were equally
keen to encourage growth as a means to bolster social stability at a time when
the European Communist parties were at their most popular and powerful.
The prospect of social upheaval obliged Western European governments to
consider reconstruction not as a luxury but as an emergency effort, requiring
the full mobilization of national and international resources. Here again, the
presence of the United States in the early years was crucial, for not only did
the Americans provide a certain amount of aid, but they encouraged the
process of trade liberalization that allowed the Europeans to bolster their internal economies by trading with one another. The result was a confluence of
factors leading to rapid economic growth and modernization: a new ideology
of expansion that was touted by the United States, new state investment in industry, swift reestablishment of multilateral trade in Europe, and a well-
educated workforce eager to reap the rewards of peaceful labor after a
generation of war and depression.

Alas, Western Europe's riches were inaccessible to those beyond the Iron
Curtain. Eastern Europeans enjoyed no general trend of rapidly rising incomes and productivity. To taste the fruits of prosperity, they would have to
fight for them. And they did. Thus, a third explanation for contemporary
Europe's success is that many Europeans over the past half century fought and
died in the name of a free, democratic, and just Europe. Just as a history of
World War II would be incomplete without detailed attention to the underground resistance movements, so must the history of postwar Europe feature
the long, patient struggle against Communist repression and injustice. In virtually every Eastern-bloc country, resistance to Communist ideology seethed.
This resistance was not terribly effective, nor could the East European dissi-

dents alone have toppled the Soviet-controlled regimes. Dissenters in the Eastern bloc needed and relied upon intermediaries, that peculiar breed of Communist "reformers" who worked from the inside to effect change. Thus, the policies of leaders such as Wladyslaw Gomulka of Poland, Imre Nagy of Hungary, Alexander Dubcek of Czechoslovakia, and especially Mikhail Gorbachev of the USSR inadvertently stoked the flames of resistance.

These embers were kept burning by the courageous efforts of thousands of dissidents who circulated banned publications, met in small groups, and smuggled their literary work to the West. Occasionally they took to the streets and engaged in open conflict with the Communist regimes, as in East Berlin in 1953, Budapest in 1956, Prague in 1968, Gdansk in 1970 and 1980; but more often they simply tried to sustain the sinews of an oppositional life that could counteract the dehumanizing banalities of Communist rule. Figures like Lech Walesa and Vaclav Havel and their many colleagues kept the fight for human dignity alive, and profited from the openings provided by the reformers. This stubborn resistance was one of modest victories and small-scale heroics; yet seen in its fifty-year sweep, it is the more admirable for its persistence and the totality of its final victory. For the Berlin Wall did not collapse magically in 1989. It fell because it had been fatally undermined by many courageous sappers; the power of the charge they laid was strong enough to reshape the history of Europe.

The events of 1989, though revolutionary, were remarkably free of violence and bloodletting, and this is consistent with the overall pattern of political evolution in Europe since 1945. Here lies a fourth factor of Europe's success: during the past half century, the continent has avoided the pitfalls of violent revolution and moved toward democratization along a path of moderation and compromise. At various moments when revolution seemed at hand, conciliation won out instead. In the fluid 1945–49 period, the possibilities of radical social change urged by the heterogeneous left-wing groups that emerged from the wartime resistance were fended off by social conservatives, market liberals, Christian Democrats, and their generous American benefactors. In the 1960s, when students and workers challenged this order, elections returned conservative parties back to parliament with enhanced majorities. In the 1970s, as the authoritarian regimes in Spain, Portugal, and Greece collapsed, they were ushered out not at the end of a bayonet but by the conservative elites who had served the previous regimes and now sought an orderly transition to market democracy. And in the 1980s, the revolutions that did take place in Eastern Europe avoided bloodshed because the leaders of the opposition movements spoke the language of power sharing rather than power seizing. In this instance, it should be recalled that Vaclav Havel was elected president of Czechoslovakia in December 1989 by a parliament made up of Communist Party members.

Obviously, this propensity for reform rather than revolution—of gradual healing rather than radical surgery—has its faults. Europe never had the kind of housecleaning that many wished for, nor the bold experiments in social justice and economic equality that many clamored for in 1945, 1968, 1974–75, and 1989. In the immediate postwar days, most European countries effected only modest purges of wartime collaborators before losing the taste for it. Figures who had been prominent in Nazi Germany, Vichy France, and Fascist Italy made the transition to postwar life without undue difficulty. Likewise in the mid-1970s, many servants of Franco's Spain and Salazar's Portugal later served in the democratic successor governments. After 1989, former Communists remained in political life in Eastern Europe. With the exception of a few high-profile cases in Germany, there was no post–Cold War settling of accounts. These continuities angered critics of European public life, who assailed the basic conservatism of European politics. Yet in a continent that suffered through two world wars in a generation, Europeans were prepared to accept a certain degree of continuity—even at the expense of complicity.

Europe, despite the progress of the past fifty years, still faces many serious problems, which this book examines in their historical context. First there is what we might call the persistence of division. For all its talk of unity, contemporary Europe remains divided along lines of race, ethnicity, cultural identity, and wealth. Racial violence has beset most European states at various times over the past half century, and the picture seems, if anything, to be worsening. The appeal of far right, xenophobic, anti-immigrant, anti-Semitic groups has increased since the late 1980s. National governments, and the European Union itself, have condemned this violence but also tacitly legitimized it by imposing new regulations on immigration that serve to keep foreigners out. The fires of ethnic conflict, largely dormant in Europe for much of the Cold War, exploded in Yugoslavia in 1991 and have yet to be fully extinguished, despite a decade of war and the subsequent well-meaning reconstruction efforts of the international community. The picture has improved somewhat in Northern Ireland, where a fragile peace process has been kept alive—just—since 1998; but Basque terrorism persists in reaping a grisly harvest of death and destruction. Nor have the states of Europe achieved economic equality between themselves: the newly liberated countries of Eastern Europe remain far behind their wealthy neighbors in per capita GDP, in living standards, and in economic opportunity.

Alongside these social, ethnic, and economic divisions looms another serious problem: the future of Europe's democracy. To be sure, universal suffrage is the norm in Europe, and voter turnout has consistently run at about 80 percent over the past fifty years—a record that shames the United States. Nonetheless, it is undeniable that in contemporary Europe there is a certain malaise in the political sphere. On the national level, this may reflect the evolution of political consensus between left and right: Europe's Social Democratic parties jettisoned their Marxist baggage long ago, while Christian Democrats and even Thatcherites accepted the need for the welfare state and a significant role for government in the public life of the nation. Most parties of both right and left support integration in the European Union. Now that Communism is dead and gone, there are few alternatives in European public life, which may explain why parties on the margins—especially on the far right—consistently attract modest support.

But the real problem for European democracy lies on the transnational scale, in the European Union. European integration promoted growth, modernization, and productivity, and broke down the national barriers that in the past constrained European economic expansion. But integration was a process conceived and driven by elites, who never subjected their ideas to the voting public. The European Union has come into being as the product of international bargaining by government leaders; the public never asked for it, and when called on to ratify European treaties—albeit rarely—European voters often show significant skepticism toward the erosion of national sovereignty. This is not because they oppose the EU on the merits: French producers like having access to German markets, Spaniards like the development aid, Italy likes the influence the EU gives it, Germans like being liked, and most Eastern Europeans are eager to join. Rather, the hesitation toward Europe comes from the impression that it is unaccountable, too cumbersome, and beyond the reach of the average voter. As the EU takes on wider powers over the daily lives of Europe's citizens, the public will demand greater direct control over its actions and policies. Unless the EU responds promptly to these demands, the divide between Europe's institutions and its peoples will grow, threatening to undo many of the hard-won accomplishments of the past fifty years.

It is easy to suggest that these problems will prove insuperable. A casual glance at the European press reveals the serious concerns about future economic growth and unemployment, about democratic accountability, about race, ethnicity, and immigration, and about the generally disappointing performance of the current political class. Indeed, so great have been the debates between Europeans, so conspicuous the failures, so petty the squabbling, that some scholars, and indeed many Europeans, are unwilling to acknowledge the degree of Europe's success over the past half century.[2] Yet Europe has met far greater challenges before. This book shows that the path Europe has traveled has not been straight and easy, but a rocky, crooked, and perilous one. Since 1945, this continent has seen its share of heroes and villains, periods of high hopes and profound disillusionment, times of peace and war, of courage and cowardice, of honesty and deceit. But in the end, this is the story of a struggle against adversity and a triumph over the odds.

Winston Churchill, speaking to his Swiss audience in September 1946, never doubted the capacity of Europe to rebound from the war. Though the continent still lay in ruins, he believed that Europe could rebuild and establish the foundations for a new European civilization. Churchill asked his listeners that day to imagine a new Europe, rising out of the rubble of the old, that offered a future of decency, human dignity, fairness, prosperity, and above all, peace.

> Why should there not be a European group which could give a sense of enlarged patriotism and common citizenship to the distracted peoples of this turbulent and mighty continent, and why should it not take its rightful place with other great groupings in shaping the destinies of men? . . . If Europe were once united in the sharing of its common inheritance, there would be no limit to the happiness, to the prosperity and glory which its four hundred million people would enjoy.[3]

PART ONE

AFTERMATH

■

In American public memory, the end of World War II is usually associated with grainy newsreel footage depicting delirious Europeans waving American flags, welcoming US Army tanks into Italian and French towns, tossing flowers in the air, reveling in the taste of freedom after many years of war. These scenes are often accompanied by still photos of GIs embracing women of all varieties in a testament to the basic humanity and fraternity of the United States. The war was over; now it was time for love.

The view from Europe was never so rosy. In East and Central Europe, the end of the war on 8 May 1945 meant little except that the bombing came to an end; the killing went on, as Soviet troops rampaged through Poland and Eastern Germany and triggered a massive program of ethnic cleansing in Eastern Europe that led to the death of another 2 million ethnic Germans and the expulsion of perhaps 12 million people from their homelands. Germany swarmed with refugees of all sorts: POWs, forced laborers, emaciated survivors of concentration camps, all grouped generically by the Allies under the term "displaced persons." Foreign armies of occupation dominated the landscape, whether American, Russian, British, or French, and their leaders hastily convened meetings to lay out the future political organization of Europe. They

briefly nursed the illusion that they could carry the spirit of wartime cooperation over into the peace. These hopes died quickly as the occupation powers
vied to impose their own ideological priorities on this conquered land. The
moment of liberation had been electrifying. But once the bunting and the
flowers had been swept up, the town squares were empty again and the battered residents went back to the grim task of burying their dead and mourn-
ing the death of Europe.

Among the greatest problems Europeans now faced, beside the task of
daily survival, was order: what political system would these war-scarred nations now adopt? During the war, many in the European resistance movements had spoken longingly of the need to rebuild post-Hitler Europe along
lines of socialism, egalitarianism, and democracy, sweeping away the vestiges
of aristocracy, oligarchy, Fascism, monarchy, and other forms of government
that were variously blamed for starting the war. The old order had demonstrably failed; surely now it was time for something new?

In Britain, a remarkable political experiment did take root. In July 1945,
the Labour Party took over the reins of government and initiated a broad program of social and economic reform that did much to define the welfare state
of the postwar years. With brisk efficiency and a notable lack of political acri-
mony, the government launched a massive project for the renovation of
Britain. There would be homes for heroes, free health care, full employment,
nationalization of industry, enlightened government, a people's Britain. The
legacy of these times remains contested today: did Labour go too far, or not
far enough? True, the British people had made sacrifices during the war that
now must be made good; but did the sudden beneficence of the state crush the
entrepreneurial spirit and erode the very toughness that had helped Britain
win the war?

Across the Channel, other Europeans could only envy the swift, decisive
actions of the Labour government. In France and Italy, the optimism of the
liberation dissipated very quickly as the political parties on the left and right
quarreled with one another. Elections offered little clarity, as the voters too
were equally divided between Communism, socialism, and Christian Democracy. The Cold War served to make these political divisions sharper and
eroded the middle ground.

Intellectuals began to doubt the motives of their American liberators. One
noted French writer, Simone de Beauvoir, left an evocative record of her growing anxiety toward the United States. After a visit to the United States in 1946,
she returned home alarmed. Americans, she wrote, "approved of all Truman's
speeches. Their anti-Communism bordered on neurosis; their attitude to-

wards Europe, toward France, was one of arrogant condescension. . . . I heard students, teachers and journalists seriously wondering whether it would not be better to drop their bombs on Moscow before the USSR was in a position to fight back. It was explained to me that in order to defend freedom it was becoming necessary to suppress it. The witch-hunt was getting under way." Back in France, she saw American soldiers in a restaurant. She recalled that once, "we had loved them, these tall soldiers in khaki who had looked so peaceful; they were our liberty." Now they represented "our dependence and a mortal threat."[1]

These were not just the carpings of alienated intellectuals. Throughout the late 1940s, Western European society was profoundly divided by the problem of how to rebuild the political life of the continent. Strikes, street brawls, open conflict with the police, industrial action, trade union militancy, all were at their peak in this period. Nor was de Beauvoir entirely wrong when she declared that "the Americans were secretly occupying France." Through the vehicle of economic and military aid, as well as the continuing presence of large numbers of US military personnel across the continent, the United States had made it clear that it intended to remain engaged in European political life. The 1948 elections in Italy, when the CIA channeled funds to the pro-American Christian Democrats, was only the most clumsy example of American influence in Europe at this time.

However, de Beauvoir's line of attack on the United States, echoed in the writings of hundreds of other European intellectuals then and later, missed a crucial part of the overall picture. The Iron Curtain was quite real, and behind it a decidedly nasty form of political order was being imposed that could very well have been visited upon France, Germany, and Italy, were it not for those tall US soldiers in khaki. De Beauvoir failed to see—did not wish to see—the nature of the "people's democracies" being erected in Eastern Europe under Soviet coercion. Taking advantage of the brief popularity of Communism in the region—the Red Army, after all, had chased out the Nazis—the Soviet Union worked with astonishing cleverness to manipulate the political settlement in Eastern Europe. Communist Party members, many trained in Moscow during the war, seized control of the ministries of interior, justice, and defense; they edged out non-Communists either by swallowing them into the Communist Party, as with the socialists, or exiling them to the fringes of power, where they could be labeled wreckers, saboteurs, and foreign agents. Through adroit use of propaganda, intimidation, and repression, the Communists in Eastern Europe took control of the levers of power, which they would not relinquish for forty-five years. Here, distressed intellectuals did not publish memoirs and go on the lecture circuit; they wrote forced confessions and went to prison.

These, then, were not joyful years. Daily bread was in short supply, politics offered only strife and division, and an ideological contest between the superpowers severed the continent in half. In the late 1940s, the European "miracle" seemed an improbable dream.

CHAPTER ONE

GERMAN MIDNIGHT:
THE DIVISION OF EUROPE,
1945

•

THE SPRING OF 1945

THE WAR IN EUROPE ended officially on 8 May 1945, a date that marks the death of the Third Reich and the birth of a new Europe. To those present, however, death seemed far more apparent than renewal. Hitler's armies had laid waste to the continent, murdered millions of people, waged ideological warfare upon the nations of Europe, and undertaken a horrific plan to exterminate Europe's Jews. There was nothing in the smoldering cinders to suggest that the future held anything but toil and pain.

In the early years of the war, Germany had been spared the sort of destruction that the Wehrmacht so readily inflicted upon other countries. The chief victims then had been Poland, the Soviet Union, the Low Countries, France, Greece, and Yugoslavia. By 1943, however, Germans began to get a taste of the sort of suffering other Europeans knew well. In the last year and a half of the war, the Allied bombing offensive exacted a terrible toll against German cities, taking over a million lives. In July 1943, for example, bombers from Britain's Royal Air Force struck the industrial city of Hamburg, a major port on the North Sea. Incendiary bombs created a firestorm that ultimately engulfed eight square miles, killing 45,000 people. From November 1943 to March 1944, the RAF and US Army Air Force concentrated on Berlin, leaving the city in ruins but doing little to bring the government closer to surrender. In February 1945, just three months before the end of the war, Allied bombers launched a massive air assault on the city of Dresden. This ancient capital of Saxony, once called the Florence of the Elbe for its magnificent baroque architecture, possessed little heavy industry. Following an assault by some eight hundred RAF bombers and 311 American B-17s, the city was swallowed by fire, and over 50,000 people were incinerated. By the end of the war, most of Germany's major industrial cities in the Western part of the country were completely shattered. Ninety percent of the buildings in Düsseldorf, the major city of the industrial Ruhr Valley in Western Germany, were uninhabitable. Nearby Cologne lost 72 percent of its buildings, and 95 percent of its population had fled the city.

Vengeance came not just from the skies. It also came at the hands of the occupying armies, particularly the Soviet Red Army. Recent scholarship now puts the Soviet death toll during the Second World War at the staggering figure of 25.5 million. In the era of total war, civilians died in greater numbers than combatants: the Soviet Union suffered 8.6 million military and 16.9 million civilian deaths.[1] Most of the civilians died as a result of the exterminationist occupation policies imposed by the Germans in Ukraine and Belorussia, where the population was enslaved and starved to death. It should come as no surprise that after four years of ferocious war between Russia and Germany, the victorious Red Army was primed to return the favor in equal measure. Russian soldiers were urged on by their commanders to behave as brutally as possible. In January 1945, as his vast army was about to cross onto German soil, Soviet marshal Georgi Zhukov, victor of Stalingrad and soon to become the commander of the Soviet zone of occupation in Germany, exhorted his men to crush the Germans without pity:

> The great hour has tolled! The time has come to deal the enemy a last and decisive blow, and to fulfill the historical task set us by Comrade Stalin: to finish off the fascist animal in his lair and raise the banner of victory over Berlin! The time has come to reckon with the German fascist scoundrels. Great and burning is our hatred! We have not forgotten the pain and suffering done to our people by Hitler's cannibals. We have not forgotten our burnt-out cities and villages. We remember our brothers and sisters, our mothers and fathers, our wives and children tortured to death by Germans. We shall avenge those burned in the devil's ovens, avenge those who suffocated in the gas chambers, avenge the murdered and the martyred. We shall exact a brutal revenge for everything.[2]

Sadly, it was the weak and defenseless, the villagers and townspeople of Eastern Germany, who first felt the impact of the Soviet army. Pumped up with Zhukov's rhetoric, Soviet soldiers unleashed a campaign of terror in the Eastern German lands of Pomerania, Silesia, and East Prussia that was barbaric even by the standards of an already ghastly war. Not only were Germans abused, terrorized, and driven off their land, but they were murdered in large numbers, and women in particular were made into targets of abuse. German women were raped in unimaginable numbers, then often killed or left to die from their wounds. Some women's bodies were found raped, mutilated, and nailed to barn doors. Hundreds of thousands of women have given testimony to the rapes they endured at the hands of the Russians; historian Norman Naimark has estimated that as many as 2 million may have been sexually assaulted. Worse, most women were victims of repeated rapings; some were raped as many as sixty to seventy times.[3]

With cruel irony, this outburst of violence seemed to confirm the wartime fulminations of Joseph Goebbels, Hitler's propaganda minister, that the Russians were inhuman beasts. One member of an anti-Nazi cell in Berlin, a woman named Ruth Andreas-Friedrich, has left a vivid account of the sense of shock and fear that these assaults left upon German people. Writing in her diary on 6 May 1945, she observed:

These days have become dangerous to many. Panic prevails in the city. Dismay and terror. Wherever we go, there is pillaging, looting, violence. With unrestrained sexual lust our conqueror's army has flung itself upon the women of Berlin.

We visit Hannelore Thiele, Heike's friend and classmate. She sits huddled on her couch. "One ought to kill oneself," she moans. "This is no way to live." She covers her face with her hands and starts to cry. It is terrible to see her swollen eyes, terrible to look at her disfigured features.

"Was it really that bad?" I ask.

She looks at me pitifully. "Seven," she says. "Seven in a row. Like animals."

Inge Zaun lives in Klein-Machnow. She is eighteen years old and didn't know anything about love. Now she knows everything. Over and over again, sixty times.

"How can you defend yourself?" she says impassively, almost indifferently. "When they pound at the door and fire their guns senselessly. Each night a new one, each night others. The first time when they took me and forced my father to watch, I thought I would die."

... "They rape our daughters, they rape our wives," the men lament. "Not just once, but six times, ten times and twenty times." There is no other talk in the city. No other thought either. Suicide is in the air ...

> "Honor lost, all lost," a bewildered father says and hands a rope
> to his daughter who has been raped twelve times. Obediently she goes
> and hangs herself from the nearest window sash.[4]

For a generation of Germans, then, the spring of 1945 would forever be linked
with the image of a grime-encrusted, battle-scarred Russian soldier, boots on,
forcing himself upon a German woman.

We must stretch our imagination to place these scenes of raped and tortured women into a broader whole, one even more grisly when considered in
its full scale. In the months after the war's end, all of Europe was crawling with
disoriented people, moving in all directions, most of them crossing into or out
of Central Europe. In a continent overrun with armies, the face of war did not
belong to the soldier but to the refugee.

The displaced persons (DPs), as they were clinically termed, numbered
about 13 million in the summer of 1945. Among these were 10 million foreign
workers who had been shipped into Germany from all across Europe to provide slave labor for the German war machine. They now began to drift home,
though without any easy means of transportation. Millions of prisoners of
war and concentration camp survivors joined this flood. The bulk of these
people passed through massive refugee camps established by the United
Nations Relief and Rehabilitation Administration (UNRRA). This organization provided relief—albeit very limited—to an astonishing array of nationalities. In addition to millions of West Europeans, who found it on the whole
fairly easy to return to their nations of origin, UNRRA gave shelter to
Russians, Poles, Balts, Yugoslavs, and Central European Jews, for whom the return home was made more difficult by the broken transport networks and the
far greater war damage.

UNRRA did not exist simply to provide a meager plate of soup. Its purpose was to bring some sense of order to the massive population flows.
UNRRA established demarcation lines all across Germany and set up assembly centers where DPs could be collected and sorted and classified. The DPs
were given a cursory medical examination, deloused, and issued ration cards.
Security checks were made in order to prevent the escape of wanted enemy
nationals from Germany. Then the DPs were sent on their way, the goal being
to get them out of Germany, and out of UNRRA camps, as soon as possible.

Life in the UNRRA camps was terribly hard. Every sort of accommodation was used for housing people, including barracks, concentration camps,
schools, factories, barns, stables, and tents. DPs interned in such facilities were
looked after by a skeletal team of Allied soldiers, doctors, and orderlies, who

attempted to establish at least some basic order. German POWs were used to dig latrines and build temporary shelters. Supplies were requisitioned from the local German population, though the Germans themselves were already in bad shape. DPs were provided with meager rations of potatoes and soup, and were lucky to receive fifteen hundred calories a day—barely enough to survive. The official British history of this period acknowledges the failings of Allied policy toward the DPs:

> For the individual displaced person the actuality of conditions in the centers fell sadly short of the hopes and excitement that had filled him when he knew the war was over and that he had been liberated from his Nazi masters. Accommodation was often damaged and squalidly patched up with salvaged or improvised material. Water, electricity, and sanitation were scarce. In the circumstances of the time such conditions were inescapable. They were better than those of many Germans, but in all these respects displaced persons were frequently worse off than they had been under the Nazis.[5]

Perhaps the most tragic group among Europe's woeful refugees were the Soviet DPs. While the French, Italians, and Poles were on the whole eager to get back to their homes, many Soviet citizens were anxious about the fate that awaited them upon their return. They had good reason to worry, as Stalin viewed DPs, as well as Soviet POWs, with great suspicion. They had spent time abroad, had worked for the enemy, had betrayed their nation and their ideology. Nonetheless, thousands were forcibly repatriated to the Soviet Union under an international agreement between the Allied powers. Soviet displaced persons would be sent back, the agreement had said, "regardless of their individual wishes." Under this agreement, some 2 million Soviet DPs were repatriated from the Western portion of Germany under Anglo-American control; to these may be added another 3 million in Eastern Germany already in Russian hands. Upon their arrival in Soviet-held territory, DPs were sorted into categories, and anyone considered to be politically suspect or in any way a potential threat to the regime was simply liquidated. Of the 5 million returning Soviet citizens, only about one-fifth were allowed to return to their homes and families. The rest were sent to forced-labor camps or executed.[6]

Alongside these bedraggled refugees, another of Europe's tragedies now unfolded, generated not by the war itself but by the territorial changes instituted at the war's conclusion. At the Yalta Conference in February 1945, the three great powers—the United States, Britain, and the Soviet Union—agreed that the postwar territory of Germany would be considerably diminished. Poland was granted control of Pomerania, Silesia, and half of East Prussia—some 40,000 square miles, with a prewar population of 9 million Germans. (This transfer of territory would compensate for the loss of 70,000 square miles of eastern Poland that was to be incorporated into the Soviet Union.) The tentative deal struck at Yalta was confirmed at the Potsdam Conference of July–August 1945, where Roosevelt's successor, Harry S. Truman, lifted his initial objections to the plan in the interests of maintaining good US-Soviet relations.

In light of these territorial changes, the millions of Germans in these eastern lands now under Polish control instantly became targets of vilification and abuse at the hands of Polish authorities. The same was true in Czechoslovakia, where hundreds of thousands of Germans, especially in the west of the country, were targeted for expulsion. In a gruesome echo of Nazi policy toward the Jews, Polish and Czech authorities rounded up Germans in internment camps or simply placed them on rail cars and shipped them into Germany, there to be dealt with by the already overwhelmed occupation authorities. The numbers involved in this immense transfer of population are not exact, but German authorities have estimated that some 11.7 million people of German descent were expelled from the lands of the old German Reich, from Poland, Czechoslovakia, and other countries such as Hungary, Romania, and Yugoslavia. Many of these Germans had fled voluntarily from what they rightly expected would be a marauding Red Army. The rest were forcibly expelled. The expulsions were accompanied by intense violence, the revenge of Poles and Czechs upon the ethnic Germans who for the six previous years had so cruelly treated them. Over 2 million of these expellees were killed or went missing during this ghastly chapter of ethnic cleansing. All of this was undertaken with the tacit approval of the great powers. To make matters worse, about two-thirds of these Germans flooded into Western Germany, there to be added to the already large numbers of refugees. Despite losing a quarter of its territory, Germany's population grew by 17 percent—and this in a country already ground into rubble by six years of war.[7]

So to the hungry of Berlin, the raped women of Eastern Germany, and the multinational flood of refugees—to this collective portrait of tormented Europe add the saga of the *Volksdeutsche,* the ethnic Germans, who were now forcibly uprooted, packed onto cattle cars with doors nailed shut, and sent westward.

IMPOSING ORDER: THE CONFERENCES OF
YALTA AND POTSDAM

Onto this chaos the victorious Allies sought to impose some semblance of order, though the precise nature of that order had yet to be defined. This issue
brought US president Franklin D. Roosevelt, Soviet leader Joseph Stalin, and
British prime minister Winston Churchill—the Big Three—together at the
Yalta Conference in February 1945. Yalta occupies a special place in historical
accounts of the Second World War, and for good reason. It was the last meeting of the three great leaders of the coalition that had defeated Hitler. Within
two months of the conference, Roosevelt was dead, and in July 1945 British
voters ousted Churchill from office. It also marked the last time that these
three countries convened as allies, working together in a spirit of compromise.

Yalta, located on the southern coast of the Crimean Peninsula, in the
Ukraine, was an exceedingly awkward place for a conference. The British and
Americans had agreed to it only because Stalin refused to leave the Soviet
Union. For the aged and infirm Roosevelt, the trip was arduous. The visitors
had to fly into Saki, a city some ninety miles away. From there they drove to
Yalta along bumpy, unpaved roads through countryside only recently liberated from the Germans. All along the route, Red Army sentries stood at attention, posted at fifty-yard intervals—a powerful testament to the sheer size of
Stalin's army. The conference was held at the Livadia Palace, built in 1911 as
the summer residence of Tsar Nicholas II. The retreating Germans had thoroughly looted the place, obliging the Russian hosts to truck in loads of furniture from Moscow hotels. The surrounding area, the guests were told, had not
yet been cleared of mines.[8]

The three leaders came to Yalta with specific priorities in mind, and each
knew he would have to compromise somewhat in order to achieve them.
President Roosevelt had one short-term aim: to bring Russia into the war
against Japan. His broader goal, however, concerned the shape of the postwar
order. FDR long nourished the hope that the great powers, by which he meant
the Big Three and China, would work together to keep order and peace in
their areas of the globe. This was a view based not on the Old World idea of
spheres of influence, which he believed had led to war both in 1914 and 1939.
Rather, Roosevelt thought he could persuade his great-power Allies to join a
new, international organization in which, working in consultation with the
nations of the world, they would be able to adjudicate world affairs. Of course,
specific interests and regional security would have to be recognized; but the

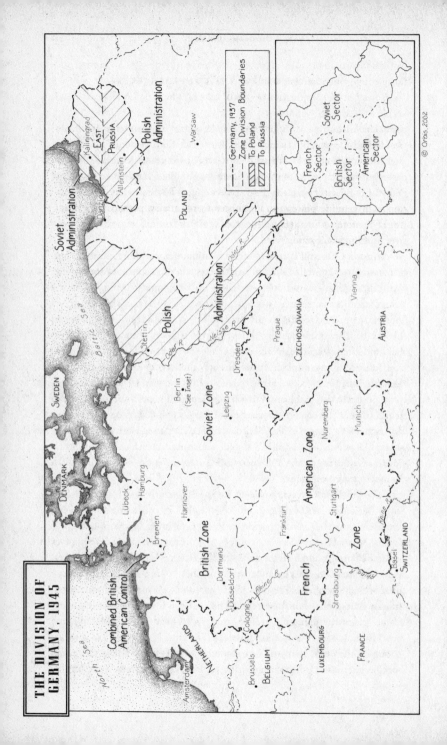

THE DIVISION OF GERMANY, 1945

Legend:
- Germany, 1937
- Zone Division Boundaries
- To Poland
- To Russia

© Orbis, 2002

Soviet Administration

EAST PRUSSIA
Kaliningrad
Allenstein
Danzig

Polish Administration
Warsaw
POLAND

Polish Administration
Stettin
Oder R.
Neisse R.
Oder R.

Baltic Sea
SWEDEN
North Sea
DENMARK

Lübeck
Hamburg
Bremen
Hannover

Berlin (See Inset)
Soviet Zone
Leipzig
Dresden
Prague
CZECHOSLOVAKIA
Vienna
AUSTRIA

Combined British-American Control

British Zone
Dortmund
Düsseldorf
Cologne
Rhine R.

NETHERLANDS
Amsterdam
Brussels
BELGIUM
LUXEMBOURG
FRANCE
Strasbourg

French Zone

American Zone
Frankfurt
Nuremberg
Munich
Stuttgart
Rhine R.
Basel
SWITZERLAND

Inset:
French Sector
Soviet Sector
British Sector
American Sector

world body would provide an arena for the prompt settlement of disputes and the encouragement of cooperation.

Roosevelt had another reason for supporting the creation of what would become the United Nations. In 1945, American public opinion was divided about its postwar role. Would the United States remain an influential player in world affairs, or would it return to a policy of isolation, withdrawing as it did after the First World War? If Europe swiftly relapsed into a pattern of nationalist rivalry and spheres of influence, Americans might wash their hands of the Old World. By contrast, if the great powers crafted an international organization with genuine powers to administer world affairs, perhaps Americans would be more willing to engage themselves in the process of postwar reconstruction and stabilization.[9]

Winston Churchill also favored the creation of a world organization, but he placed less faith in its ability to exert real power. He was a man bred in the nineteenth-century world of balance-of-power diplomacy. In his formative years, tsarist Russia had been one of Britain's greatest rivals, chiefly for influence in Central Asia. But now, in the hands of a cynical dictator and a powerful new ideology, Soviet Russia, he believed, presented a grave new menace to Europe. Churchill knew that Britain alone was powerless to stop this expansion. Indeed, he recognized its inevitability in October 1944, when, in a meeting with Stalin in Moscow, he offered his infamous "percentages" agreement to the Soviet leader, exchanging Russian control of Romania and Bulgaria for British control of Greece, with Hungary and Yugoslavia to be split evenly. This kind of cynical grab for territory was just what FDR wanted to avoid, at least publicly. But it reflected Churchill's belief that Britain should itself have a sphere of influence in the Mediterranean, from which it could more readily contain any future German revival. While attempting to come to an understanding with Stalin over influence in Europe, Churchill also wanted, through gentle persuasion, to bring the United States to share his suspicious views about Soviet expansionism, thereby encouraging the Americans to help contain the Soviet Union.[10]

The positions of the American and British leaders are fairly easy to determine because of the vast archival record available to scholars. Yet the intentions of Stalin are far harder to know, and recently released material from Russian archives has not fully clarified our picture of this inscrutable man. Stalin certainly thought of himself as a disciple of Lenin, charged with bringing to fruition the world Communist revolution that had started in Russia in 1917. He understood history in Marxist terms, and believed that the capitalist world order would soon collapse due to its internal contradictions. The Second World War, he thought, signaled the beginning of that collapse and opened the way toward a new socialist world order. But socialism could triumph only if the Soviet Union remained strong and secure. The country had suffered terribly in the war, its people killed in vast numbers, its industry shattered, its land mauled by German depredations. If the Soviet Union was to become the engine of a world Communist revolution, it would need time to recover and marshal its resources.

Stalin's foreign policy in 1945, then, was a rather defensive one. It focused on winning a territorial and political settlement that would provide Russia with security from any future attack from the West, whether from Germany or another capitalist power. In practical terms, this goal required Stalin to insure that in Eastern Europe the political order was friendly to Soviet interests. Given the presence of the Red Army all across this region, his goals seemed well within reach as the leaders convened at Yalta.[11]

As the conference unfolded, there proved to be ample opportunity for compromise. The three leaders readily agreed that Germany, once defeated, would be divided into four zones of occupation (one for each great power and one for France), and these four occupiers would work together through an Allied Control Council to run the country. The main message with respect to Germany was that Nazism and militarism were to be utterly purged and defeated and that Germany's future would lie entirely with the Allied victors. Other issues, however, required more haggling, and after a week the three leaders produced an agreement on a broad range of issues. Roosevelt received Stalin's support for the world organization. The future UN would have a Security Council of five powers, each armed with a veto—thereby insuring that the UN could not enforce any decision without the full cooperation of all the great powers. Stalin also agreed to enter the war against Japan; and he proved willing to sign a Declaration on Liberated Europe that stated that the Allies would encourage, in liberated or former Axis territories, the creation of governments that were "broadly representative of all democratic elements in the population." To this end, the Allies would support the holding of free elections at the "earliest possible" time.

From Roosevelt's point of view, these were significant successes, and indeed, the American delegation thought Yalta a marvelous success. The president, upon reporting to the Congress after his return to Washington, was met with a standing ovation. Yet Roosevelt had to pay for these Soviet concessions, and he paid in Polish coin. Poland was the issue that most concerned Stalin at Yalta, because this country was crucial to Soviet security. Though the Red Army occupied Poland at the time of Yalta, the issue of what kind of government Poland would have had not been settled. Roosevelt and Churchill supported the members of the Polish government in exile, based in London, who were pro-Western and wary of Soviet intentions. Stalin argued that the Committee of National Liberation, based in Lublin and made up entirely of Communists, was far more representative than the London group, and in any case the Soviets had already recognized this committee as the provisional government of Poland. Stalin was intransigent on this issue. He would not allow the London Poles to share power on an equal basis with the Communists. Roosevelt and Churchill, of course, had no leverage to force Stalin to budge. Nor did they really believe that Stalin would ever agree to relinquish control of the country that played such a big part in his geopolitical aims.

Instead, they meekly asked that at least a few of the London Poles be included in the Lublin committee and that Stalin sign the Declaration on Liberated Europe. At least this way the West would have the moral high ground if Stalin should renege on his promises for free and prompt elections. FDR did not want the issue of Soviet influence in Eastern Europe, which was already a fait accompli, to block an agreement on his pet project, the United Nations. Conversely, Stalin agreed to these cosmetic changes in the Polish provisional government because it gained for him and his Polish allies the legitimacy of recognition from the other great powers. The United States and Britain now had sanctioned the territorial and political arrangements in Eastern Europe that Stalin believed best for Soviet security.[12]

Despite the hopeful rhetoric of the conferees and the atmosphere of cooperation and compromise, Yalta marked a dark moment for Central Europe. At this conference the great powers jointly acknowledged the Soviet Union's control over Eastern Europe. From now on, this part of Europe would be subject to Moscow's control. Yalta has long been vilified as a sellout of Poland and Eastern Europe. This charge does not accurately capture the significance of Yalta. Rather, the conference revealed the dominating position of the Soviet Union in Eastern Europe, a position won after four years of brutal war; and it revealed the limited ability of the Americans and British to challenge that dominance. Roosevelt sought to make a virtue of necessity: instead of opposing the Russians, he hoped to work with them in bringing peace and stability to a war-torn continent through a great-power compromise. Unfortunately, FDR gave a hostage to fortune by declaring after Yalta that the agreements reached there would "spell the end of the system of unilateral action, the exclusive alliances, the spheres of influence, the balance of power, and all the other expedients that have been tried for centuries and always failed."[13] Yalta had achieved nothing of the sort. There is no shame in that: diplomacy based upon idealism alone has never worked. But FDR complicated matters by insisting that Yalta marked the start of a new era of diplomacy. When it turned out that this was not the case, and that the Russians wanted to behave in their sphere as they wished, Americans felt that they had been betrayed.

Franklin Roosevelt, the architect of the Yalta accords, died on 12 April 1945, leaving behind a complex, perhaps even contradictory set of agreements on postwar Europe. His successor, Harry S. Truman, a neophyte in world affairs, wanted to continue Roosevelt's policies but discovered that these policies were not clear. Did Yalta acknowledge a Russian sphere of influence in Eastern Europe, or did it establish democracy and sovereignty as the guiding principles of government in postwar Europe? Upon coming into office, Truman, like many Americans, took the text of the Yalta Declaration on Liberated Europe at face value and insisted that the Russians live up to their agreements to let the Eastern Europeans determine their own political future. There was ample evidence in Poland, Romania, Bulgaria, and Austria that the Russians since Yalta had been moving swiftly to consolidate the control of local Communists and to oppose the restoration of non-Communist political parties. But Truman also wanted to continue Roosevelt's legacy in foreign affairs, one that placed importance on cooperating with the Russians in establishing peace in Europe. Although at the end of April he expressed his frustration and disappointment to Stalin's foreign minister, Vyacheslav Molotov, about Soviet actions in Europe, Truman acquiesced in Soviet control of Poland when he offered US recognition of the almost entirely Communist—and Soviet-backed—Polish government on 5 July.[14]

The Yalta deal, one crafted by his predecessor, bound Truman to grant Soviet control in Poland. But it had said little about postwar Germany, and here Truman was determined to make his mark. Precisely because Poland had been written off by the Americans and British, it was essential that Germany not be surrendered so easily. Following the defeat of Germany on 8 May, the Big Three planned to meet again to discuss the postwar treatment of their vanquished enemy. As Stalin, Churchill, and Truman convened in mid-July 1945 in the town of Potsdam, a suburb of bombed-out Berlin, they knew that the very future of Europe was at stake.

What awaited them in Berlin was shocking. On 16 July, Churchill toured the ruined capital, stopping at the chancellery, Hitler's seat of government, long enough to explore the building and Hitler's bunker, where just ten weeks earlier the Führer had committed suicide. He was duly stunned by the chaos he saw, but Churchill had seen his share of bombing damage in the streets of London during the German blitz in 1940. For Harry Truman, the scenes of devastation were something altogether new. "I never saw such destruction," he recorded after mutely riding through the city. After the tour, Truman returned to his official headquarters at 2 Kaiserstrasse, a villa in the Berlin suburb of Babelsberg. He would learn many years later that the house had been requisitioned by the Russians a few months earlier and that the female occupants of the house had been brutally raped there in front of all the members of their family.[15]

The Potsdam Conference was a long and difficult meeting, with none of the bonhomie of the Yalta gathering. At the start, there did appear to be grounds for compromise: the Soviets and the Anglo-Americans wanted Germany to be treated as a single unit, not dismembered or broken up into two or more states. The Americans and British believed that dividing Germany would cripple the country's economy, promote irredentism in the German successor states, and create a power vacuum in Central Europe that might invite Russian interference. Further, if the four powers could cooperate in Germany, then the overall relationship in Europe and beyond would be strengthened. The Soviets too wished to see Germany remain united. They believed that since the German Communists were so quickly establishing themselves in Berlin and the Soviet zone, there was every likelihood that they would be able to exert influence across the country; a unified political system would create the best conditions for eventual Communist control of Germany.[16]

Despite this initial consensus on keeping Germany united, however, the Potsdam Conference did a great deal to insure that postwar Germany would be reestablished on starkly divergent principles in the Eastern zone and the three Western zones. This was so because the Potsdam agreement granted to the occupying powers the responsibility and the right to effect a social and political reformation of Germany. The occupiers agreed not just to eradicate Nazism and militarism from Germany but to rebuild its political institutions, rewrite its laws, control and restructure its education, and decentralize its government. Since the Soviet Union and its three Western partners held competing and even mutually exclusive political beliefs, there was bound to be disagreement on how best to implement this charge.

On economic grounds, too, Potsdam set out contradictory principles. Germany was to be treated as an economic unit, but the occupation powers would be able to seize from their own zones reparations in the form of industrial and agricultural equipment. The Russians chose to thoroughly loot and pillage the Eastern zone, ripping the heart out of the territory under their control. The Americans and British, fearful of having to pay for the cost of feeding hungry Germans, resisted such rapacious reparations policies. As the four occupiers continued to haggle in their zones about how to enforce unity, they continued to pursue strictly zonal policies, putting into place governing structures that reflected their own objectives in Germany.

Like Yalta before it, the Potsdam Conference left a contradictory legacy. The Big Three agreed to govern Germany as a single unit. Yet at the same time, they insisted that each occupying power maintain full control over its own territory. As with Yalta, the Americans chose to stress that Potsdam had established the principle of unitary control, and when this policy proved impossible to fulfill, they blamed the Russians and claimed full justification for establishing their own policies in the Western zones of occupation. The Russians, in the meantime, did not concern themselves with Western hand-wringing. For them, Potsdam was a continuation of Yalta: it confirmed the idea that Eastern Europe and Eastern Germany lay within the Russian sphere of influence, and that the social and political transformation there would be undertaken in accordance with Soviet interests. Without hesitation, the Russians began to construct in their zone the core of what they hoped would one day be a united, socialist Germany.[17]

THE SOVIET OCCUPATION:
TRANSFORMING GERMANY

For Joseph Stalin, the Soviet occupation of Eastern Germany offered an unrivaled opportunity to institute a form of government that would protect and perhaps advance Soviet interests and ideology. As he had said to the Yugoslav partisan Milovan Djilas in the waning days of the war, "whoever occupies a territory also imposes on it his own social system. Everyone imposes his own system as far as his army can reach. It cannot be otherwise."[18] This conception of the Soviet role in Germany was followed to the letter. The Soviet authorities in Germany, and the German Communists who worked closely with them, sought to undertake a social and economic transformation of Germany consistent with their own belief that capitalism had spawned Nazism and must therefore be replaced.

But with what? And how? The contradictory impulses visible in Stalin's foreign policy—its emphasis both on a Communist revolution across national borders and on the search for Soviet national security through the creation of a sphere of influence—appeared in Soviet policy toward occupied Germany. The Russians adopted two general goals: first, to reestablish the German Communist Party (KPD) as the principal agent of a popular, radical reconstruction of the country; and second, to plunder the resources of the Soviet zone as a means of aiding Soviet internal reconstruction and insuring that even a revived Germany could not threaten the Soviet Union again. The latter objective, which entailed the massive deindustrialization of Eastern Germany, created resentment toward the Russian occupation and badly hurt the efforts of the KPD to create a popular Communist regime in the wake of the Nazi defeat. This basic contradiction could be resolved only by force and coercion, and thus from the very start of the Soviet occupation, Communism established itself through the subversion of the democratic process it claimed to promote.[19]

On 6 June 1945, the Russians proclaimed the Soviet Military Administration in Germany (SMAD), and Marshal Zhukov took command of it. But the Russians did not plan to govern Germany directly; rather, they delegated this role to a team of German Communists carefully prepared for the job. Since 1933, when Hitler came to power, German Communists had been on the run, ruthlessly persecuted by the Nazis. They had fled the country, some to Western Europe, many to Moscow. (Those who remained usually wound up in concentration camps.) During the war, the Russians worked with these German émigrés to create a core of loyal Communists who would reestablish the party inside Germany following Hitler's defeat. In late April and early May 1945, the Soviets flew three "initiative groups" of German Communists into their homeland, where they were to begin the work of rebuilding political and economic life along Communist lines.

The most important of these groups was the one sent into Berlin under the command of Walter Ulbricht—the man who would run the future East German state until 1971. Born in Leipzig in 1893, Ulbricht was active in the German trade union movement during World War I. He was elected to the Reichstag as a Communist deputy in 1928 but fled the country in 1933, first taking refuge in France, then fighting with the Communists in the Spanish Civil War, finally reaching Moscow in 1940. Colorless, humorless, he was the model Communist apparatchik: disciplined, tireless, and fiercely loyal to Moscow. With him he brought ten other well-trained lieutenants, and they established headquarters in the Lichtenberg neighborhood of Berlin.

Ulbricht and the SMAD adopted a subtle strategy for exerting Communist control in the zone. Rather than overtly using the power they possessed to impose a Soviet single-party system in Eastern Germany, the Russians allowed for the reestablishment of the prewar political parties in their zone. By showing themselves to be tolerant of diverse political views, the Russians hoped to create a groundswell of support for the KPD and the other major left-wing party, the Social Democratic Party (SPD). On 10 June, the SMAD issued an order allowing the SPD and the two center-right parties, the Christian Democrats and the Liberal Democratic Party, to re-form. Of course, these parties had been profoundly affected by the experience of the war, and shared a general view that unbridled capitalism was a destabilizing factor in political life. The state, they all agreed, should exert much more control over the economy through nationalizations of industry, and Germany must not return to the political structures of the failed prewar Weimar Republic. In this atmosphere, it is no surprise that the left-wing parties, the KPD and the SPD, were genuinely popular and seen as agents of major reforms. The KPD sought to promote its popular image as a party that favored a parliamentary democracy, cooperation with other parties, and a united national effort of reconstruction. In its first public platform of June 1945, the KPD made no reference to socialism or to Marx, and even went so far as to state that it believed that "imposing the Soviet system on Germany would be wrong."

However, the KPD strategy was duplicitous. The party did not intend to institute genuine democracy but wanted to use the reestablishment of the non-Communist parties as cover for its gradual consolidation of control over all the important institutions in the Soviet zone. For example, the Communists carefully controlled the newly formed trade unions to insure that the leadership was securely in Communist hands; the same was true of the farmers' organizations set up in 1945. Socialist members shared power in these organizations but voting rules were structured to insure Communist dominance.

The Communists also took a hostile attitude toward the grassroots resistance organizations that had sprung up in Germany in the last year of the war—even though these groups were entirely sympathetic to the public stance the KPD had taken on many issues. One of the members of Ulbricht's group was twenty-three-year-old Wolfgang Leonhard, a German who had spent the previous ten years training in Moscow. Filled with enthusiasm for the Communist project, he arrived in Berlin expecting these "anti-Fascist" resistance groups to be a valuable asset to the KPD. Leonhard saw that these small groups were working independently to restore basic services in Berlin, clear rubble, and improve supplies, and were doing so in alliance with Communists, socialists, and Catholics—just the position the KPD had urged. Ulbricht, however, ordered Leonhard to break up these groups. Leonhard obeyed, but recalled his distaste for the job. "These people," he wrote, "had banded together, despite all previous divergences of outlook, in a common struggle against Hitler, and a close cooperative spirit united them. Now, with the destruction of fascism, they wanted to carry on the work together for a new Germany in a vigorous anti-Fascist organization." Precisely because of their independence, their commitment, and their ability to work across party lines, these groups were seen as a threat to the gradual Communist strategy of exerting control over the political and economic life in the Soviet zone. All across the Soviet zone, dozens of similar groups were shut down. The KPD had no interest in a grassroots revolution, sparked by forces it could not control.[20]

The assault on the grassroots anti-Fascist groups undermined support both for the KPD and for the Soviet occupation authorities, as did two other components of the Communist transformation of the Soviet zone. The KPD initiated a broad program of land reform, expropriating huge tracts of land from wealthy agrarian elites. Land reform figured high on the list of priorities of the Communists. The landowning class had long been demonized as militarists, Nazi supporters, and reactionaries; their antipathy to the farm laborer placed them in the category of class enemy to the socialist movement. In September 1945, the SMAD ordered that every estate over a hundred hectares (about 247 acres) be confiscated from its owners, broken up, and redistributed to landless peasants and to the many millions of homeless expellees coming from the east. Property owners were driven off the land, beaten, often killed. By 1948, some 2.7 million hectares (about 6.6 million acres) of land had been redistributed.

Yet despite the apparent appeal of such a policy, the land reform was a disaster. The new farmers, many of them inexperienced, had no tools, equipment, animals, or fertilizer, all of which had been seized by the Russian occupation authorities for shipment to the Soviet Union. As a result, agricultural production plummeted, aggravating an already chronic food shortage. In villages across the zone, peasants decried the land reform experiment. The KPD, which had hoped to bolster its image in the provinces through land reform, instead won only scorn and resentment.

A similar pattern played out with respect to Soviet policies toward dismantling German industry. The Russians understandably sought to make Germany pay for the destruction it had wrought inside the Soviet Union during the years when the German army had occupied Soviet territory. At Potsdam, the Russians had demanded reparations amounting to $10 billion, most of which was to be seized from the Soviet zone. The Russians took this task seriously, and briskly dismantled thousands of German factories, plants, and businesses all across the zone. By the end of 1945, they had carted off 4,339 German enterprises, more than a quarter of all productive capacity in the zone. Soviet policy hurt the KPD badly. Just as the party was attempting to win over Germans to its platform of socialist reconstruction, the Russians were stripping the country bare, leaving it unable to address the zone's most basic needs. Even when, after 1946, the Russians slowed their dismantling of factories, they still demanded that reparations be paid in kind out of German production. These demands deprived the Germans of the fruit of their own labor, thus deepening hostility toward the occupiers and worsening the public image of the SMAD's principal agent, the KPD.

Due to these kinds of counterproductive policies, the KPD's fortunes—so rosy in May 1945—began to dim somewhat. While many Germans still supported a radical reconstruction of their country and wanted to see the economy and the political structure overhauled, the Communist Party was increasingly identified with a foreign occupation power, a power that had shown little interest in the welfare of the German people. As a result, by the end of 1945 the SPD, a socialist party but one not directly identified with Moscow, gained increased support in the Soviet zone. The German Communists, in conjunction with authorities in Moscow, developed a clever strategy to nip this challenge in the bud. They proposed that the two parties of the left, the KPD and SPD, unify, thereby creating a single workers' party, all the more able to carry out the transformation of Germany that the working class demanded. From December 1945 through February 1946, KPD officials, as well as high-ranking Russian occupation authorities, carried out an intensive campaign to persuade the SPD leaders to fold their party into the KPD. Initially these overtures were met by sharp resistance from the SPD, but after three months of persuasion, pressure, intimidation, jailings, and blackmail, the SPD leadership submitted. In an astonishing and utterly undemocratic move, they agreed in April 1946 to join the KPD in creating a Socialist Unity Party (SED). Few believed that this party was anything more than an expanded version of the KPD. In less than a year, the Russians and their loyal German Communist allies had crafted in the Soviet zone a powerful political tool that could reshape Eastern Germany in the Soviet image.

THE AMERICAN OCCUPATION: RESTORING GERMANY

Just as the Soviet Union's policy in Germany reflected a particular set of ideas and interests, so too was the American occupation of its zone in Western Germany framed by a governing set of ideological principles. The United States was hostile to tyranny, to militarism, to economic autarky, and to monopoly capitalism that concentrated too much national wealth in too few hands. Nazi Germany had manifested all of these traits, and it was no accident that the United States government had seen Hitler's Reich as a threat to its national interest and to those European nations that shared its political beliefs. Once Germany was defeated, Americans believed that the country ought to be recast in the American image, with a free market economy, a democratic political system, tolerance for diverse points of view, a decentralized federal government, and an open trading system that was integrated with its neighbors.

At the same time, however, Americans quite naturally felt that Germany must be made to pay for its conduct during the war. Germany had to be purged of its Nazi leaders and institutions, shorn of its military and industrial capacities, made to suffer a reduced standard of living, obliged to pay reparations to the countries it had damaged, and generally stigmatized as having been under Hitler a menace to Western civilization. In both Soviet and American policy toward Germany, then, there lay a basic contradiction between the desire to punish and the desire to resuscitate, between the desire to destroy and the desire to rebuild. Unlike the Soviets, however, the United States quite quickly overcame its vengeful instincts. Within six months of the end of the war, the leading American policy makers had concluded that punishing Germany would ill suit the American design to reestablish democracy and a free market in Germany and Europe.

In large part, American occupation authorities shifted from a policy of punishment to one of restoration of Germany because they could see that the Russians, in their zone, were establishing a rival political system, one that, if not contested, could threaten American efforts to build a democratic German state. While there was, in the summer of 1945, a wide range of opinions within the US government about how to interpret Russian actions and policies in Germany, most Americans agreed that Communism as a governing system was a direct threat, both to their own political values and, more important, to the interests of Europe as a whole. Communism was bound up in the minds of American policy makers with Joseph Stalin's tyrannical regime, and while the American public still considered "Uncle Joe" a likable figure and sympathetic ally, official opinion harbored few illusions about Stalin's political philosophy. Truman and his advisers believed that if Germany were allowed to fall under the sway of Communism, it would provide Russia with a massive geopolitical and ideological lever to pry the rest of Western Europe away from the Anglo-American sphere of interest. If this were allowed to happen, the sacrifices of the war would have been in vain. So like the Russians, American officials viewed Germany as the vital testing ground of their political beliefs. If they failed in their efforts to transplant their political system in Germany, then American power in Europe and across the globe would be drastically weakened. For Americans, the stakes in Germany could not have been higher.

Although the United States government had long planned to occupy defeated Germany and knew that it would face a major challenge in rebuilding a stable, nonthreatening state in the heart of Europe, surprisingly little detailed planning had been done to prepare for the postwar occupation. The general lines of policy had been set out at Yalta and Potsdam: Germany was to be demilitarized, the Nazi Party and all its adherents were to be removed from public life, the great industrial cartels that had helped Hitler's war machine were to be broken up, and the bureaucracy was to be decentralized in favor of stronger local and regional government.[21] JCS 1067—the directive delivered in April 1945 by the US Joint Chiefs of Staff to the American military occupation forces in Germany—portrayed the German people as having been guilty of crimes against the world and a menace to civilization. As a consequence, they were to be treated harshly, their living standards reduced, and their economic assets used in the rebuilding of the rest of Europe. JCS 1067 stressed the importance of de-Nazification, reeducation, and the gradual establishment of democracy in Germany.[22]

The task of implementing this directive fell to the deputy military governor, Gen. Lucius D. Clay. The overall commander of the occupation until November 1945 was Gen. Dwight Eisenhower, and he was succeeded by Gen. Joseph T. McNarney. Both men delegated the day-to-day running of the occupation to Clay, an engineer by training and a man who had never commanded soldiers in battle. Clay was fifty years old and had served overseas only once, in the Philippines; he knew little about German history, politics, or language. In October 1945, Clay declared the establishment of the Office of Military Government, US (OMGUS), in the city of Frankfurt, and took command of a staff of some 12,000 people, charged with the wholesale reconstruction and reformation of Nazi Germany. General Clay quickly discovered the difficulties he faced in carrying out JCS 1067. He could not restore order, stability, and democracy in Germany while also stripping the country of its economic infrastructure and jailing all previous members of the Nazi Party. It was only a matter of time before he began to circumvent his orders.

American efforts to de-Nazify Germany typified the swift evolution in policy from punishment to restoration. The United States believed that a stable Germany could not be established until Nazism and its adherents had been thoroughly purged from German society. Twenty-two of Germany's leading Nazis were put on trial at Nuremberg in a much publicized, yearlong proceeding. This trial established the notion that certain internationally accepted standards of civilized behavior had been violated by the Germans, and that the Nazis had waged a criminal war and pursued an inhuman policy of genocide. The greatest achievement at Nuremberg, however, was not the convictions it rendered but the accumulation by the prosecution of a massive body of evidence that established in clinical detail every aspect of the Nazi regime. To this day, the Nuremberg documents constitute an essential source for historians of Germany's criminal behavior during the Second World War.[23]

But once these leading figures were swept away, a major problem remained: how to treat the millions of Nazis and ordinary Germans at the lower ranks who had carried out the orders of their leaders and who had made the Third Reich such an efficient machine of war and destruction. JCS 1067 stipulated that "all members of the Nazi party who have been more than nominal participants in its activities, all active supporters of Nazism or militarism and all other persons hostile to Allied purposes will be removed and excluded from public office" and from positions of influence in private enterprise. Extirpating Nazism from German society was a legitimate goal. Yet the JCS directive, broadly defined, could easily include most Germans who had ever supported the war effort. Clay thought that to remove them all from positions of influence in Germany would compromise recovery efforts; worse, it would also open up their positions to those who had opposed Nazism within Germany—many of whom were Communists, labor leaders, and working-class activists. They might be uncooperative in rebuilding a capitalist, market economy in Germany. The broader goal of rebuilding Germany along American economic principles served to restrain the de-Nazification program.

The numbers tell the story of the limits of the American de-Nazification effort. After an extensive investigation through the use of questionnaires, the US occupation authorities declared that some 3 million Germans were subject to penalties for their wartime actions. Most of these had occupied positions of influence in the economy, in the administration, in schools and universities, and in the professions. In August 1946, General Clay granted an amnesty to those born after January 1, 1919, on the argument that the younger generation had been more impressionable and therefore less responsible than their elders for Nazi practices. Another amnesty in December 1946 cleared those with low incomes, on the ground that they could not have profited from rapacious Nazi economic policy. Yet still some 2 million Germans remained to be tried for their wartime activities. In June 1946 the American occupation authorities transferred the responsibility for de-Nazification to German legal authorities—a controversial action but one deemed important in fostering German self-government. Yet the German record in de-Nazification was not a strong one: of the 2 million suspects, only a million were charged, and of these, only 1,549 were found to have been major offenders. A much larger number, some 500,000, were fined or given light prison sentences for their actions, but overall, the process of rooting out Nazis from German society and making them pay for their crimes had fallen well short of the initial intentions of the occupiers. The de-Nazification exercise revealed that Americans were more interested in restoring order, stability, and productivity in Germany than in transforming German society.[24]

A similar pattern of moderation is visible in US efforts to restructure the German economy. JCS 1067 had stated that Clay and his team would "take no steps (a) looking toward the economic rehabilitation of Germany, or (b) designed to maintain or strengthen the German economy." This passage, Clay's staff believed, had been composed by "economic idiots," and Clay promptly ignored it.[25] On the other hand, he did initially pursue a policy of breaking down the centralized cartels in German industry that were seen as contrary to American free market ideas. American officials considered the German cartels and monopolies as having been agents of the Nazi state, engaged in a systematic effort to shut out US companies in world markets while using US technology to advance their own war preparations. Moreover, German monopolies had damaged the smooth flow of international trade, thereby worsening the effects of the depression and hastening the drift toward war. Thus, at Potsdam the occupying powers agreed that "the German economy shall be decentralized for the purpose of eliminating the present excessive concentration of economic powers as exemplified in particular by cartels, syndicates, trusts and other monopolistic arrangements."

But what, in practice, did this mean? Were all big businesses in Germany to be broken up? Or should deconcentration be limited just to the leading firms such as chemicals giant IG Farben (which among other things manufactured the Zyklon-B pellets used in the Nazi gas chambers), arms merchant Krupp AG, and the steel cartel Vereinigte Stahlwerke, companies that had so openly and efficiently backed the German war effort? The New Dealers in the Roosevelt administration, many of whom had been instrumental in the antitrust campaigns of the 1930s, hoped for a radical dismantling of German big business, but their influence waned rapidly after FDR's death. By the summer and fall of 1945, Clay was being pressured by many circles in the United States and people on his own staff to moderate his decartelization policies on the grounds that a rapid industrial recovery in Germany would not only encourage stability there but would enhance the prospects for American business interests, which looked forward to reestablishing ties to Europe. As a result, American decartelization stalled, and in the end only a very moderate economic restructuring was undertaken. Even in the case of Farben, toward which US opinion was unanimously hostile, the original plans to break it up into fifty smaller units were modified substantially. In 1952, Farben was broken down into four core companies, Hoechst, Bayer, BASF, and Casella, the first three of which occupy a dominant place in today's pharmaceuticals market. The German steel industry too was moderately treated, with firms such as Thyssen and Krupp today among the world's largest.[26]

While efforts to purge Germany of Nazism and to break up its powerful industrial conglomerates produced only modest results, the American authorities did make progress in establishing the basic institutions for democratic government. At Potsdam the four occupying powers had agreed that no central government would be established, and this made it easier for each power to proceed to form local government bodies in its own zone. Even this task was exceedingly difficult, however. Americans could not use personnel who had served the Nazi regime; and even when they did identify local personalities to act as mayors and clerks, the town halls themselves were in a shambles and their records destroyed. Still, the OMGUS authorities pressed ahead, outlining new regional and state (Land) governments. The leading posts in the new state governments were given to Catholic centrists from the Christian Democratic Union (CDU), to the nonclerical, conservative Free Democratic Party (FDP), or to Social Democrats. (US appointees sometimes occasioned embarrassment, as when the conservative Catholic minister-president of Bavaria, Fritz Schäffer, had to be removed from office for opposing de-Nazification policies.)

The restoration of German political life in the three Western zones did have a distinctly conservative bent to it. As in the Soviet zone, grassroots democratic movements that had sprung up in opposition to Hitler were quickly pushed aside. Instead, the US granted licenses initially only to four political parties, the CDU, the FDP, the Social Democratic Party (SPD), and the Communist Party (KPD). By restricting political activity, the occupation authority could more readily control the evolution of German democracy. In January 1946, in the first round of local elections—held in towns of less than 20,000 inhabitants—the CDU and SPD emerged as the leading forces in the US zone; this pattern was readily encouraged by the occupation regime. Further elections were held in 1946 that led to the formation of constituent assemblies to draw up state constitutions. The building blocks for German self-government, at least within the Western zones, were slowly being put into place.[27]

THE IRON CURTAIN

Taking the cases of de-Nazification, decartelization, and government administration into account, it is clear that beneath the rhetoric of punishing and transforming Germany, the US administrators had concluded that Germany had already suffered enough during the war, and that their duties should be to allow the Germans to reconstruct their society under American supervision and tutelage. US officials hoped that German recovery could be achieved in harmony with the Soviet Union, but their desire to work in unison with the Russians was far weaker than their passion for instituting a particularly American conception of government and economic order in that part of Germany they controlled. Thus, a profound difference of ideology between the US and the USSR predetermined a conflict of interests in Germany. However, the specific issue that brought that conflict out into the open, and led to the formal division of Germany, was reparations and the treatment of the German economy.

At the Potsdam Conference, the United States, Britain, and the USSR agreed to allow each occupation power to withdraw from its own zone whatever reparations it wished. But since the industrial heartland of Germany lay inside the British zone, far to the west, it was agreed that the Russians would be given 25 percent of whatever industrial equipment and goods were left over after the reestablishment of a German peacetime economy. While Russians believed that reparations from Germany were their rightful due after the horrific loss of so much blood and treasure, the United States quickly came to the conclusion that stripping the Western zones of reparations would damage Germany's prospects for reconstruction. During his trip to the Potsdam Conference in the late summer of 1945, President Truman had seen for himself the extent of the physical damage Germany had experienced during the war. The implications of Germany's collapse were immense, as the president's advisers repeatedly told him. Without a productive economy, Germans could not feed, clothe, and shelter themselves, nor could Germany's immense natural resources, especially coal, be exported to help fuel Europe's industries and heat its hearths. "Unless we do what we can to help," said Truman in a public address upon his return to America, "we may lose next winter what we won at such terrible cost last spring. Desperate men are liable to destroy the structure of their society to find in the wreckage some substitute for hope. If we let Europe go cold and hungry, we may lose some of the foundations of order on which the hope for worldwide peace must rest."[28] This sentiment ran directly counter to the Russian insistence on reparations.

President Truman and his many advisers who shared his view about reparations were strongly supported by the British government. Although Winston Churchill had been voted out of office in July 1945, his deep distrust of the Soviet Union and its ideology still reigned in the British Foreign Office, where the veteran labor activist and anti-Communist Ernest Bevin had taken control. Bevin said he knew all about Communists from his days of fighting them for control of the British labor movement: he considered them un-scrupulous and utterly untrustworthy. More to the point, however, Britain was in 1945 totally broke and could not afford the cost of running its own zone of occupation. Bevin wanted to see German industry restarted quickly so the German people could feed themselves, instead of relying on handouts from an impoverished Britain. Bevin insisted that no further reparations be siphoned out of the British zone to meet Soviet demands. What is more, he pushed the US government to fuse its zone with the British one, in order to ease the costs of the occupation and speed up economic recovery.[29]

The US government by the start of 1946 was increasingly warm to Bevin's ideas because it too had gone through a significant change in outlook toward the Soviet Union. The rather hopeful if naïve tone of FDR's policy toward Uncle Joe now ceded place to a far harsher, simplistic, and aggressive stance. In February 1946, a foreign service officer named George F. Kennan, then serving in the American embassy in Moscow, wrote a long cable to the State Department about Russian foreign policy that was widely distributed. It of-fered the comprehensive interpretation of Russian motives that had been lack-ing in Washington. Kennan characterized the Soviet Union as "a political force committed fanatically to the belief that with [the] US there can be no perma-nent modus vivendi, that it is desirable and necessary that the internal har-mony of our society be disrupted, our traditional way of life be destroyed, the international authority of our state be broken, if Soviet power is to be secure." The Soviet leadership believed, according to Kennan, that Soviet security was possible only if the United States was entirely defeated as a political system. Kennan was somewhat in advance of opinion within his own government, but not by much. His arguments were powerful and quickly set the tone of a new reading of Soviet actions in Germany.[30]

Moreover, his opinions were given immediate credibility when Winston Churchill, the venerated British prime minister and now leader of the Conservative opposition in Parliament, came to Harry Truman's home state of Missouri on 5 March 1946 to deliver an address at Westminster College. He too painted the Soviet Union in the darkest possible terms:

A shadow has fallen upon the scenes so lately lighted by the Allied victory. Nobody knows what Soviet Russia and its Communist inter-national organization intends to do in the immediate future, or what are the limits, if any, to their expansive and proselytizing tenden-cies . . .

From Stettin in the Baltic to Trieste in the Adriatic, an iron curtain has descended across the Continent. Behind that line lie all the capitals of the ancient states of Central and Eastern Europe. Warsaw, Berlin, Prague, Vienna, Budapest, Belgrade, Bucharest and Sofia, all these famous cities and the populations around them lie in what I must call the Soviet sphere, and all are subject in one form or another, not only to Soviet influence but to a very high and, in some cases, increasing measure of control from Moscow.

There was some irony in Churchill's criticism of Soviet policy, for it was he who in 1944 had agreed with Stalin on Soviet influence in precisely these countries. Nonetheless, Churchill's Olympian rhetoric captured the terms of debate and cast the Soviet Union as an expansive, totalitarian state, bent on spreading Communism and instability into Western Europe. President Truman, who sat on the podium as Churchill delivered these remarks, had read the speech beforehand. He found it "admirable" and told his guest that "it would do nothing but good, though it would make a stir."[31]

This hardening of the American view of Soviet motives in Europe immediately affected Germany. The Americans now refused to entertain Soviet demands for reparations from the Ruhr industries. Instead, Clay blamed the Russians (and the equally unhelpful French) for blocking joint four-power control of Germany. In May 1946 he announced a halt to all reparations deliveries from the US zone to the east. In July, after consulting with Bevin, US secretary of state James F. Byrnes announced the formation of a single "bizone"—the result of fusing the US and British zones of occupation. Here was the future West German state in embryo. And to cap off this quite sudden shift in US occupation policy, Byrnes, visiting the German city of Stuttgart, delivered an address to an assembled group of German dignitaries on 6 September 1946 in which he stated that the time had come for the German people to be granted control of their own affairs, to feed, clothe, and shelter themselves, and to open Germany's markets for trade to Western Europe. If these priorities could be achieved with Soviet cooperation, so much the better, but the general policy was no longer up for discussion.[32]

The Soviet Union observed these American initiatives with growing alarm. The Soviet ambassador to the United States, Nikolai Novikov, cabled his interpretation of postwar US strategy, arguing that the US had broken its promises made at Potsdam to undertake the transformation of Germany:

In Germany, the United States is taking measures to strengthen reactionary forces for the purposes of opposing democratic reconstruction . . . The American occupation policy does not have the objective of eliminating the remnants of German Fascism and rebuilding German political life on a democratic basis, so that Germany might cease to be an aggressive force. The United States is not taking measures to eliminate the monopolistic associations of German industrialists on which German Fascism depended in preparing aggression and waging war. Neither is any agrarian reform being conducted to eliminate large landholders, who were also a reliable support for Hitlerites. . . . One cannot help seeing that such a policy has a clearly outlined anti-Soviet edge and constitutes a serious danger to the cause of peace.[33]

There was a kernel of truth to what Novikov wrote. The United States had slowed down its de-Nazification and its decartelization plans, had restructured a German political system that favored centrists, and sought to restart the German economy so that it would be integrated into the rest of Western Europe. Indeed, in the pursuit of its aims in Germany, the United States did press ahead with policies that were substantially different from those agreed to at Potsdam, and undoubtedly speeded the division of the country.

It is not enough to rest content with that conclusion, however. For while the *motives* of the United States in consolidating its hold on Western Germany were in some general sense similar to those of the Soviet Union—to enhance security and advance its own political ideology—the *means* by which these goals were to be achieved differed starkly. The United States substituted electoral democracy where there had been tyranny; it restored the free market where there had been autarky; it instituted new social, civic, and political institutions that would allow over time the full expression of an independent, post-Hitler Germany. America's goals in Germany and in Europe as a whole, then, were to be attained with the full cooperation of the great majority of Europeans, precisely because Europeans came to share those goals. Surely this explains the swift postwar reconciliation between West Germany and the United States. Despite friction and clashes of culture over the next fifty years, Americans and Western Europeans could look to, and celebrate, a shared body of values that they deeply cherished. By contrast, the Soviet occupation of Eastern Germany and the rest of Eastern Europe saw the imposition of a vastly unpopular political and economic system, a system that could be kept in place over the subsequent decades only by force, and that bred a deep-seated fear and resentment toward the Soviet Union. Germany in 1945 was wholly defeated, but in retrospect we can see that only the Western two-thirds of the country was liberated as well.

CHAPTER TWO

BUILDING JERUSALEM:
THE LABOUR GOVERNMENT IN BRITAIN,
1945–1951

∙

PEOPLE'S WAR, PEOPLE'S PEACE

THE BAD NEWS STARTED COMING in at ten on the morning of 26 July 1945, when Winston Churchill was still in his bath. Capt. Richard Pim, an aide to the prime minister, carried in an early report about the general election results: the Labour Party had won ten seats over the Conservatives. Churchill was "surprised if not shocked," and hurried down to the Map Room of 10 Downing Street, from which he had directed Britain's war effort for the previous five years. There, the news grew worse, until at one, the BBC confirmed that the Labour Party had won a landslide victory, taking 393 seats in the House of Commons and leaving the Conservatives with 213.[1]

Churchill was soon joined by his wife, Clementine, his daughters Mary and Sarah, and a core of close friends and advisers. "Everyone looked dazed and grave," remembered Mary, and the group sat through a gloomy and depressing lunch. "But not for one moment in this awful day did Papa flinch or waver." Indeed, by all accounts, Churchill showed remarkable poise, and at seven in the evening he drove to Buckingham Palace, where he submitted his resignation to King George VI.

Still, the blow fell hard. "The next few days were, if anything, worse than that dreadful Thursday," wrote Mary.

After years of intense activity, for Winston now there was a yawning hiatus. The whole focus of power, action, and news had been transferred to the new Prime Minister. The Map Room was deserted; the private Office empty; no official telegrams; no "red boxes." True, letters and messages from friends and from countless members of the general public started pouring in, sweet and consoling, expressing love, indignation, and loyalty. But nothing and nobody could really soften the blow.[2]

Lord Moran, his doctor and confidant, asked him the day after the election if he planned to take a holiday. "There is no difficulty about holidays now," Churchill replied wistfully. "The rest of my life will be holidays. . . . It is a strange feeling, all power gone. I had made all my plans; I feel I could have dealt with things better than anyone else. This is Labour's opportunity to bring in Socialism, and they will take it. They will go very far."[3]

What explains this extraordinary turn of events? To subsequent generations, nurtured upon the stories of the pugnacious, resilient Churchill, the man who led Britain in its "finest hour," who offered only "blood, toil, tears, and sweat," and who more than any other man was identified by the public as the source of Britain's strength against the German onslaught, this summary ejection from office at the moment of his greatest triumph remains hard to fathom. Certainly, few contemporaries believed the Conservatives would lose the election. The general consensus was that the party would have its majority reduced, perhaps to a margin of somewhere between thirty and eighty seats. Even Churchill's successor, Clement Attlee, thought that with a great deal of luck, the Conservative majority would be trimmed to forty seats. Instead, Labour now enjoyed an absolute majority of nearly 150.[4]

Labour's victory revealed the profound effect upon citizens of six years of wartime sacrifice and privation. The war years had a certain leveling effect, creating an atmosphere of selflessness, unity, and camaraderie that had obvious political utility for the Labour Party. The war also legitimated ideals long nourished by Labour about the role of the state in improving the welfare of the average citizen. At a time of national crisis, the government cleverly mobilized all its resources to improve the lives of the many citizens who were working on behalf of the war effort. It was easy to suggest, as Labour did, that these powers ought now to be applied to the task of postwar social reform. Thus, the vote in 1945 was more a repudiation of the policies of the depression-wracked 1930s than it was a statement about Churchill. The war further boosted the party's fortunes by bringing into public view a new crop of moderate, reforming Labour leaders who shared power with Churchill in the wartime coalition; here, they demonstrated their capacity for sound and efficient government, dispelling any fears of the consequences of socialists in power. Finally, Labour's victory at the polls owed something to the miserable electoral campaign led by Winston Churchill himself, during which he quite openly rested on his laurels as war leader, revealing ignorance and a certain disdain toward the domestic issues that his Labour rivals now championed.

Unlike every other country in Europe that fought Hitler, Britain never faced occupying troops on its soil, nor, after September 1940, any real threat of a German invasion. The British people experienced the war with their political and civic institutions intact, indeed strengthened by the trial of war. Nonetheless, the war brought widespread suffering on the home front, especially from aerial bombing. Between June 1940—the defeat of France—and June 1941, when Hitler broke his pact with Stalin and invaded Russia, Britain faced Germany alone, bereft of allies. Though the Germans were unable to destroy Britain's air power during the Battle of Britain (10 July–7 September 1940), they delivered a humiliating defeat to the British Expeditionary Force in France, which had to be plucked off the beaches of Dunkirk in late May and ferried back to England. Hitler then tried to break Britain's will to fight by pulverizing London and other industrial centers. London was bombed every night from 7 September to 2 November 1940. Buckingham Palace was struck twice, though it was the working-class East End and the dockyards that were heaviest hit. The pounding continued well into 1941, with massive raids in March, April, and May. On 10 May, London suffered its worst raid ever: 1,436 people were killed, Westminster Abbey and the Tower of London were damaged, the House of Commons destroyed. Rubble blocked a third of London's streets. Other cities—Belfast, Birmingham, Bristol, Cardiff, Coventry, Liverpool, Southampton—absorbed punishing hits, though of the 60,000 civilians killed during the war by German bombs, half lived in London. At the height of the blitz, 177,000 people were sleeping in London's Underground, putting into public view the most private of habits. Some 1.3 million city dwellers were evacuated and sent to live with sometimes unwilling and often shocked country folk, who encountered for the first time the ill-clad, undernourished, and bad-mannered inhabitants of Britain's tenements. The classes were mingling, though under duress.[5]

Despite Dunkirk and the blitz, morale remained rock solid in support of both the war and the Churchill government that was conducting it. In fact, blame for the failure of Dunkirk was laid at the doorstep of the "guilty men" of the previous government, led by Neville Chamberlain, who had allowed Hitler to rearm while leaving British troops ill equipped for war.[6] And the air raids had the effect of solidifying national unity and blurring, at least for a while, the lines of class antagonism that so defined British society. The blitz was awful to live through, with thousands of civilians killed, homes destroyed, their inhabitants uprooted and made homeless; yet at the height of the bombing, Gallup polls showed that 80 percent of the public were confident in

British victory. Citizens not enrolled in the services flooded into voluntary organizations such as the Air Raid Precautions, the Auxiliary Fire Service, the
Women's Voluntary Service, and the Home Guard, which had over a million
and a half new recruits in 1940 alone, including many World War I veterans.
British society quickly and willingly mobilized itself for war.[7]

This loyalty, to be maintained, had to be rewarded. In the short term, this
meant intensive government intervention into the workings of society, to insure that resources were fairly shared and that all who served the country were
in turn cared for. Rationing of essential goods was swiftly instituted; clothes,
food, and even labor were controlled by the government; school meals were
improved and offered free of charge; milk was subsidized, taxes were raised,
prices controlled. These were the features of "war socialism." But to soften the
impact of wartime austerity, the government also needed to promise postwar
prosperity, or at least propose serious plans to achieve it; and when the cabinet discussed postwar social reform, the conversation took place entirely in
the idiom of the left. Cooperation, mutual aid, solidarity: these were the values that would help Britain win the war, and they were themes that the labor
movement had promoted since its founding.[8]

Actually, it was a Liberal, Sir William Beveridge, who authored the principal piece of social legislation to emerge from the war. Beveridge was a lifelong technocrat who had worked as a civil servant before the First World War
and then ran the London School of Economics from 1919 to 1937. Asked in
June 1941 to chair a committee that would investigate Britain's system of social insurance—that is, unemployment relief, sick benefits, and pensions—
Beveridge seized the opportunity and proposed their total overhaul. His
report, called "Social Insurance and Allied Services," appeared on 1 December
1942 and introduced a comprehensive plan for social security that went far
beyond the hodgepodge of temporary expedients then in place. Beveridge saw
unemployment compensation and old-age pensions—the ostensible subject
of his study—as components of a much larger scheme to insure a minimum
standard of existence for all citizens. He sought to integrate unemployment
benefits with a plan to provide universal medical care through a national
health service, a plan for children's allowances to poor families, and a government commitment to a policy of full employment. By insuring jobs, offering
free medical care, and assisting families with the cost of raising children, the
government would not merely correct unemployment but also improve the
productivity of workers and strengthen the bond between the citizen and his
government. Beveridge had drafted the first blueprint of the welfare state.

The report, widely distributed by a Ministry of Information eager to cap-
italize on its morale-boosting potential, set the terms of debate on social pol-

icy for the rest of the war. It was not, however, warmly welcomed in all quarters. Churchill and his chancellor of the Exchequer, Kingsley Wood, thought it too costly and were reluctant to declare their commitment to it. Labour backbenchers in the House of Commons demanded a strong government endorsement of the plan, however, and in February 1943 broke the wartime truce of party politics by voting on a resolution in favor of the plan. By not openly and fully embracing the Beveridge proposals, Churchill gave the appearance of opposing them. The immense popularity of the Beveridge report—polls showed 86 percent of the public favored its implementation—assured Labour of a ready election issue in the postwar elections.[9]

Another reason for Labour's victory lay in the successful record the party leadership established during the war, and indeed even before the war. The group of ministers that took power in 1945 were highly experienced, and most were over sixty: hardly a revolutionary vanguard. The public that voted them into power knew them as pragmatic, effective, reform-minded leaders who could deliver on their promises for postwar social reform just as they had delivered during the war. The leader of the Labour Party since 1935 was Clement Attlee, who, though usually overshadowed by some of his more outspoken colleagues, was a critical element in Labour's success. He was a quiet, unassuming figure of moderate socialist views who did his work with a minimum of fanfare. He grew up in a happy, devoutly Anglican upper-middle-class family in the London suburbs. He went to Haileybury school and Oxford University, then studied law and briefly practiced it. His socialist and Christian convictions led to his involvement in a boys' club in Stepney, part of London's impoverished East End. In 1907 he moved into that neighborhood, joined the Labour Party, and threw himself into social work amongst London's poor. Upon the outbreak of war in 1914, he voluntarily enlisted, was wounded twice, and left the army with the rank of major. He returned to his work in Stepney, became involved in local politics, served two years as mayor, and in 1922 was elected to Parliament.

In the years before World War II, the Labour Party emerged as a powerful force in British politics, eclipsing the Liberals as the chief opposition to the Conservative Party. The path to power was nonetheless a rocky one. There were periods of exhilaration, as in 1923, when the Labour Party won 191 seats and formed its first government; and moments of despair, as in 1931, when the party was nearly wiped out, clinging to a mere forty-six seats. It was in the wake of this election, when many of Labour's leading lights lost their seats, that Attlee became the party's deputy leader; and in 1935, on the eve of a national election, he was elevated to party leader. Through it all, Attlee earned a reputation as a modest, hardworking man, a team captain if not the star player. He served as a binding agent in the Labour movement, holding a disparate group of factions together and keeping them focused on returning the party to power.

He burnished his reputation during the war, first by supporting the creation of a national coalition with Churchill's government in 1940, then by serving loyally as Churchill's deputy for the duration of the war. Most important, Attlee had a great degree of influence over the home front. He chaired the Lord President's Committee, which he turned into the chief decision-making body for domestic policy. As Churchill's number two, he toured the country, visiting bombed cities and towns and speaking about the new Britain that would emerge from the war. He depicted the war as a battle against Fascism abroad and poverty, unemployment, sickness, and squalor at home. He paid special tribute to the men and women working in war-related industries like coal mining, aircraft production, and shipbuilding. Behind the scenes, he was effective in pushing reconstruction priorities on Churchill, who had no interest in such issues. He insisted on the creation of a Ministry of Reconstruction and the development of plans for reform in housing, education, pensions, and industrial development. While Churchill was winning the war, Attlee was preparing to win the peace.[10] It has always puzzled historians, as it did Attlee's contemporaries, how such an unprepossessing figure could unseat Britain's heroic wartime leader. Attlee, with a thin, reedy voice, a slight bearing, and a bald pate, appeared to merit Churchill's comment that he was "a sheep in sheep's clothing." The politician and diarist Harold Nicolson wrote that Attlee was, "compared to Winston, like a village fiddler after Paganini."[11] Yet as we shall see, "poor Clem" had a greater hand in the shaping of contemporary Britain than his illustrious wartime colleague.

Of course, Attlee alone could have achieved little. His party emerged from the war in such strong political shape chiefly because of the enormous success of the rest of the Labour team in running the home front during the war. Two men in particular were vital to Labour's reputation. Herbert Morrison served as home secretary throughout the war and developed a national reputation as a man of immense energy and efficiency, coupled with the common touch. The son of a police constable, he grew up in the East End of London, working as a grocer's assistant. He joined the Labour Party at age twenty-two and entered into local politics in London. He rose to become leader, between 1934 and 1940, of the London County Council, a municipal administration with huge responsibilities and resources. It was he who engineered the evacuation of hundreds of thousands of Londoners in September 1939, and again in 1940. In October 1940, at the height of the blitz, Churchill made him home secretary, in recognition both of his administrative skills and of his popularity with London's working class. Alongside Morrison and Attlee there stood the colossus of Ernest Bevin. A hulking, 250-pound man with a rich West Country accent, Bevin was in 1940 one of the most powerful union leaders in the country. After the First World War, Bevin founded the Transport and General Workers' Union, which became the largest in Britain. During the war he was made minister of labor and served as the critical link between Churchill and the labor movement. Only a man with Bevin's credentials could have forced upon the working classes the demands that the war made necessary. Bevin, armed with the Emergency Powers (Defense) Bill of 22 May 1940, oversaw the state direction of the labor supply for the duration of the war while winning the support of the country's unions in the process. Generally considered to be on the right of the Labour movement, he brought about the practical application of state management of labor that he had long advocated as a union leader. In Attlee, Morrison, and Bevin, Labour possessed three of the most talented, successful, and powerful politicians in Britain, and they dominated the home front throughout the war.[12]

Labour's victory at the polls in 1945 was predicated on the social and political transformations during six years of war, though Churchill did his party little good during the brief election campaign itself. Parliament was dissolved on 5 June, and polling took place exactly one month later. The differences between the parties were stark. Labour possessed great confidence in its ideological appeal to the voters. The party's manifesto, *Let Us Face the Future*, declared that "the Labour Party is a Socialist Party, and proud of it. Its ultimate purpose at home is the establishment of the Socialist Commonwealth of Great Britain—free, democratic, efficient, public-spirited, its material resources organized in the service of the British people."[13] By contrast, Churchill offered only invective. On 4 June, he made his first radio broadcast of the campaign. It was a disaster. Churchill failed to concentrate on the Conservative Party platform but instead painted a lurid picture of Britain under socialist government.

> Socialism is, in its essence, an attack not only upon British enterprise, but upon the right of the ordinary man or woman to breathe freely without having a harsh, clumsy, tyrannical hand clapped across their mouths and nostrils. . . . Socialism is inseparably interwoven with Totalitarianism and the abject worship of the State. . . . I declare to you, from the bottom of my heart, that no Socialist system can be established without a political police. . . . No Socialist Government conducting the entire life of the country could afford to allow free, sharp, or violently-worded expressions of public discontent. They

would have to fall back on some form of Gestapo, no doubt very hu-
manely administered in the first instance.[14]

It was an unfair attack, and all the more perplexing in that Churchill had
worked so closely and effectively with Labour's leaders for five years. The reference to the Gestapo was especially disgusting. Attlee gave a calm and dignified response the following day, saying that he agreed that "people should have
the greatest freedom compatible with the freedom of others. But there was a
time," he went on, "when employers were free to work little children 16 hours
a day. I remember when employers were free to employ sweated women on
finishing trousers at a penny-halfpenny a pair. There was a time when people
were free to neglect sanitation so that thousands died of preventable diseases."
Churchill could expect this sort of reply from Labour's leader, but even his
daughter Mary, then working in a desk job in the RAF, expressed her misgivings about Churchill's attack. "Socialism as practiced in the war," she gently
chided him, "did no one any harm, and quite a lot of people good. The children of this country have never been so well fed or healthy, what milk there
was, was shared equally, the rich didn't die because their meat ration was no
larger than the poor; and there is no doubt that this common sharing and feeling of sacrifice was one of the strongest bonds that unified us." Churchill's
physician, upon hearing the broadcast, wrote in his diary, "for the first time
the thought went through my head that he may lose the election."[15]
    Churchill had no doubts: everywhere he went, he was met by adoring
crowds and enthusiastic cheers. But these were for the war leader, not the
party leader. Harold Macmillan, a future Conservative prime minister who
lost his seat in 1945, was quite right in his assessment when he wrote that the
election was lost before it had begun. Churchill, uninterested in domestic policy and ill at ease on ground Labour knew well, could not use his prestige to
persuade the public that he and his party offered the best chances for postwar
reform in Britain. The Conservatives as a party were still identified with the
depression years of the 1930s, with Neville Chamberlain and appeasement,
and with an outdated ruling-class ethos. It was time for a change.[16]

THE ECONOMIC CONSEQUENCES OF THE WAR

On 28 July, two days after the election results had been announced, Clement
Attlee met with the new Labour parliamentary delegation, now 393 strong.
The atmosphere was electric and the party greeted its leader with thunderous
applause. Attlee, true to form, showed little emotion, declared his intention to

move immediately in pursuing Labour's agenda, and then departed on a plane for Berlin, where he was to replace Churchill at the head of the delegation to the Potsdam Conference. Upon his return, he declared to the country that "it is right for a short time that we should relax and celebrate the victory" over Germany and Japan. "But I want to remind you that after we have had this short holiday we have to work hard to win the peace as we have won the war."[17] These words were well received in the country as a whole, whose mood was optimistic and determined. Surely a nation that had defeated the Germans could provide housing, schools, and hospitals for its people.

The new government faced a serious problem, however, that would condition and constrain all its decisions over the next five years: the country was broke. Britain had expended about one-quarter of its national wealth in fighting the war. It had developed a huge trade deficit during the war as imports soared and export industries were retooled for military production. Much of the imports was paid for by aid from the United States in the form of Lend-Lease, by selling Britain's overseas assets, and by borrowing from other sterling countries in the Empire. By the end of the war, Britain had debts of 3.5 billion pounds (about $14 billion). With this massive burden, it was going to be difficult to pay for the continued imports of food and raw materials the country would need after the war. Worse, the United States was bound by law to cut off Lend-Lease aid as soon as the war ended, thereby leaving Britain without external aid.

On 13 August 1945, John Maynard Keynes, who had spent the war as an adviser to the Treasury, submitted a memorandum to the cabinet that painted an alarming picture of Britain's financial position. Alive to the probability that the United States would cut off Lend-Lease aid soon (as it did on 21 August), Keynes wondered how Britain would survive over the next few years. Britain's industry had been focused on war-related production for six years, and the nation was dependent upon imports to feed itself. It would take time to retool the export industries and earn sufficient foreign exchange to pay for imports. Keynes estimated that Britain would have a shortfall in its financial needs of some $5 billion in the coming three years. (This assumed that Britain would be able to avoid repayment for some time of the $15 billion debt.) "Where on earth," he asked, "is all this money to come from?" Without massive US aid, he concluded, "we have not a hope of escaping what might be considered, without exaggeration . . . a financial Dunkirk."[18]

Keynes, the bearer of these bad tidings, was dispatched to Washington in September to negotiate either a grant or a loan to Britain. The memories of the Anglo-American alliance had already begun to fade in Washington, however. Only with great difficulty did Keynes persuade his American interlocutors that America's own interest in an open, free market trading system would be put in jeopardy if Britain's economy collapsed and had to fall back on imperial preference and protectionism. Grudgingly, the Americans offered a loan of $3.75 billion, at 2 percent interest, to be paid back in installments over fifty years. (To this the Canadians added a loan of $1.25 billion.) The Americans insisted, however, that Britain reduce its tariffs and make its currency freely convertible for dollars in one year, a condition that, as we shall see, had disastrous consequences.[19]

The loan negotiations created much rancor in Britain, whose financial weakness was due to its sacrifices in a war fought on behalf of the democracies. Now, the wealthiest country in the world was reluctant to assist its great wartime ally in its hour of need. The *Economist* caught the tone of the country when it declared that "we have, at present, no real option but to accept the American offer. . . . [But] we are not compelled to say we like it. And we do not. . . . Our present needs are the direct consequences of the fact that we fought earliest, that we fought longest, and that we fought hardest. In moral terms we are creditors; and for that we shall pay $140 million a year for the rest of the twentieth century. It may be unavoidable; but it is not right."[20] The Americans, with a new president and a Congress clamoring for a swift exit of US troops from Europe, did not show great magnanimity. It is remarkable to think that just two years later, in much-changed international circumstances, the Truman administration would call for US aid to Europe of over $20 billion in the form of the Marshall Plan. Despite British disappointment over the size of the loan, and the American insistence that it be paid back with interest, the aid did alleviate for a short period the worst anxieties of the new government. The country could meet its immediate needs and begin the process of reconstruction. The historian Kenneth Morgan has concluded that without the loan, the entire Labour program of 1945–51 "would not have been possible."[21]

The American loan, which became available in July 1946, did not bring Britain's financial troubles to an end. Despite some encouraging signs that the British economy was on the mend by the end of 1946—exports had reached their prewar level, public investment in industry was moving ahead rapidly, and unemployment remained low—there was a great crisis looming on the horizon that was not fully anticipated by the Labour leaders. Britain, an island nation with few raw materials, needed massive imports to meet the demands of consumers and industry. These materials, however, were in short supply around the world, which had yet to recover from the ravages of war. Only North America, and especially the United States, could export such materials, and so Britain had to find large quantities of dollars to pay for US imports.

The American loan, which was expected to last until 1951, started to dwindle as the British sucked in imports from the United States. In 1946, Britain imported six times as much as it exported to the United States, opening up a huge dollar gap. Worse, American prices increased by about 45 percent during 1946 and early 1947, forcing Britain to part with still more precious dollars. Britain had to rely on US imports because the country faced a coal shortage, due to inadequate manpower, and a grain shortage, due to a failure of continental agriculture to rebound from the war. In mid-1946 the government actually introduced a bread ration, something never done during the war. On top of these difficulties, the government had done little to reduce its still-massive overseas commitments, which included the cost of maintaining an occupation army in Germany (and paying for imports to feed the Germans), administrative costs in the colonies, and British military garrisons in places such as Palestine, India, Egypt, Singapore, and Malaya. The cost of remaining a great power now seemed beyond reach.

Britain's fragile economic recovery in 1946, then, was a house of cards. It had been bought at the price of a large dollar deficit, which was temporarily covered by the US loan. By the end of 1946, Britain had a trade deficit of almost 300 million pounds, or $1.2 billion.[22] When the winter of 1946–47 hit, Britain's economy could not take the strain. At the end of January 1947, heavy snow fell across the country, and then the worst freeze since 1881 set in. The Thames froze, as did all the northeast ports from which coal was shipped. Coal supplies, already in short supply, could no longer be transported. Factories had to be closed, power generators could no longer produce electricity, homes went unheated, and workers had to be laid off. In March 1947, 15 percent of the labor force was idle. With such a drop in industrial production, Britain's export industry could not keep up with its targets, and dollar imports increased. The government had drawn down $500 million of the American loan in the first quarter of 1947, and this nearly doubled, to $950 million, in the second quarter. By the middle of the year, Britain had already consumed over $2 billion of the original $3.75 billion loan, and yet could still not fulfill the basic needs of the country.

In mid-July 1947 the crisis reached the critical point. The terms of the American loan, it will be recalled, had required Britain to make the pound sterling convertible—that is, freely exchangeable for dollars—one year from the start of the loan, or 15 July 1947. This meant that countries holding sterling balances—and there were many countries that did, due to Britain's massive wartime debts—could freely convert their pounds to dollars. At a time when the British economy appeared so weak and its exports were lagging, most holders of sterling thought it wise to trade their sterling for dollars.

These dollars had to be paid out by the British treasury, which in turn had to draw down further on the US loan. Within six weeks, Britain's dollar reserves were facing total exhaustion. On 20 August, with American approval, the British government suspended convertibility of sterling, thus stanching the outflow of dollars. By September, Britain had spent $3.3 billion of a loan expected to last until at least 1951.[23]

The convertibility crisis marked a new stage in the Labour government experience. Before the summer of 1947, the government had seemed to be negotiating rather well the rocks and shoals of postwar reconstruction. It had moved ahead with nationalization of industry, worked hard to revive exports, and made sure that demobilization did not lead to large-scale unemployment as it had done after World War I. In the wake of the 1947 crisis, however, the government faced an ugly truth: it was overburdened and unable to meet the country's basic needs. Britain maintained a vast military apparatus overseas that it could not afford, and the country remained dependent upon imports for which it could not pay. The apparent normality of the first postwar year was abruptly shattered. In 1947, following its withdrawal from Greece, Britain would also begin its exit from India and then Palestine. At home, a new wave of severe cuts in imports plunged the country into a period of austerity that rivaled the war years. The consequences of the Second World War now began to register upon the people.

Attlee's solution was to appoint Sir Stafford Cripps as chancellor of the Exchequer. Cripps, who came from a family of high church Tory lawyers, had never fit in well in the Labour Party. Devoutly religious, he publicly urged Britons to adopt Christian precepts of duty, charity, good works, and faith as the best preparation for the task of reconstruction. His monastic lifestyle—he was a vegetarian, teetotaler, and bathed only in cold water—established Cripps as the public conscience of the government, a man willing not simply to impose an austere regime on the public but to abide by one himself.[24] From his ascendancy to the chancellorship in November 1947 until his resignation due to ill health three years later, Cripps oversaw a successful turnaround of Britain's economic fortunes, earning universal plaudits. Consider, for example, the difference in tone of two editorials in the *Economist,* a magazine cool at best toward Labour. In February 1948, in a panic-stricken editorial, it declared that "Britain faces bankruptcy." With reserves nearly wiped out, "the spectre of starvation and mass unemployment is now alarmingly close." By the end of the same year, however, the economy had gone through "an almost magical change," with exports booming and the current account in modest surplus. "By far the greatest individual share of praise," the magazine wrote, "attaches to Sir Stafford Cripps and the small circle of his intimate advisers. Not only has he shaped policies and tenaciously defended them, he has also provided the essential moral foundation."[25] How had he done it?

There were four critical elements behind Cripps's success. First, he improved the machinery of government and instituted efficient planning methods. Cripps was the government's earliest advocate of planning, by which he meant not the totalitarian state control of all aspects of industry but the use of state powers to control certain aspects of production, like the allocation of labor and raw materials, and the establishment of targets that both state and industry would work toward in a collaborative, rather than coercive, fashion. Second, Cripps relied on the continuation of wartime controls over the economic activity of the country. The government maintained the rationing of food, clothing, furniture, coal, and tobacco, and continued to control prices of most consumer goods. It also controlled allocation of raw materials like coal, steel, and lumber, which were channeled into the export industries. Most important, Cripps maintained tight control over imports, 90 percent of which were bought under government contract or through private licensed traders. This control was vital in the effort to redirect purchases away from the dollar area, so as to ease the dollar drain. Between 1947 and 1948, Britain sharply cut its imports from the dollar area by 30 percent while increasing its overall exports in the same period by 25 percent. By the end of 1948, Britain had finally balanced its trade accounts, although it was still running a large deficit with the United States. This was offset by a third factor, the arrival of $682 million in Marshall Plan aid in 1948 and $1.13 billion in 1949, which allowed Britain to cover its dollar deficit.[26] And finally, in September 1949, the treasury undertook a 30 percent devaluation of the pound, lowering its value from $4.03 to $2.80. This was designed to boost exports by making them cheaper, but was spurred on by the slowdown of US growth, which had led to a slackening of demand for British goods. Taken together, these measures brought about a significant improvement in Britain's economic performance, so that by 1950 the country had weathered the worst of the postwar crisis.[27]

For all their technical content, these decisions about imports, exports, controls, and currency rates had a direct impact upon the lives of British people. The war had, after all, raised expectations about a new and better lifestyle. As the writer Susan Cooper later recalled, people in 1945 hoped for a "release from the long grinding privations of wartime life which had done much to put the Labour Government so resoundingly in power; release from the small, dull, makeshift meals, from darkness and drabness and making do, from the depressing, nerve-aching, never-ending need to be *careful*."[28] It was not to be. Instead, wartime rationing of basic consumer goods continued in large measure until 1949, and ration books were not discontinued until 1954. Nor was the record during that time one of gradual improvement. A comparison of the basic weekly rations in 1945 and 1951 shows little change at all:[29]

	July 1945	October 1951
Butter	2 oz.	3 oz.
Bacon and ham	3 oz.	3 oz.
Cheese	2 oz.	1½ oz.
Margarine	4 oz.	4 oz.
Cooking fat	1 oz.	2 oz.
Tea	2 oz.	2 oz.
Sugar	8 oz.	10 oz.

To supplement these meager commons, the government bought large quantities of expedients like whale meat and an evil-smelling, tinned South African fish called snoek, to be made available to the public at bargain prices. Both were widely reviled and used chiefly as cat food.

Bread was rationed between July 1946 and July 1948, and even what bread there was looked gray and mealy. Britons had to adjust to whole wheat bread, which used more of the grain and was actually more nutritious; few liked it. In the midst of the 1947 convertibility crisis, the minister of food, John Strachey, cut the butter and meat ration and had to acknowledge in the House of Commons that the average daily intake of calories would now drop to twenty-seven hundred—not desperate, and twice what the average Frenchman was getting, but seven hundred calories below the recommendations of the British Medical Association. Alongside these privations, the black market thrived. Gasoline, food, clothing, soap, and luxuries like watches, alcohol, and nylons all could be procured at a cost from a "spiv," a skulking figure on the street corner who slyly alerted passersby to his illicit wares. This "age of austerity," as it was known, naturally provided the Conservatives with much political fodder. The chairman of the Conservative Party, Lord Woolton, declared that "every piece of rationing is an admission of failure." By 1950, the British people had endured rationing for ten years. The Conservative Party slogan that year was "Set the People Free."[30]

HOMES FOR HEROES

Of course, the government would have been perfectly happy to set the people free, but had made a calculated decision to insist on austerity so that resources could be mobilized for exports and for the creation of a new network of benefits and services on which its reputation, finally, would stand. Tightening of belts was to be repaid by the creation of the welfare state. What is remarkable about the Labour government—and the source of much later criticism—was that despite the massive economic crisis that it faced at least until the middle of 1948, it spared no effort in creating a vast, comprehensive, and expensive system of social services that was designed to provide every Briton with a basic modicum of health, education, and insurance against poverty. The government had won the election by promising to implement the Beveridge Report, and that is what it set out to do.

The first wave of legislation enacted by the new Parliament concerned nationalization of industry. The Labour Party argued that if the state could assume control of key industries, it could better guide scarce resources, assure fair wages and decent labor conditions, encourage efficiency and retooling, and improve labor relations. In a broadly popular move, the government placed one-fifth of the country's productive capacities under the control of the state. With amazing speed the government proclaimed the nationalization of the Bank of England, civil aviation, telecommunications, coal, railways, road haulage, and electricity, gas, iron, and steel.

Yet this was no radical redistribution of the nation's wealth. The owners of these industries were all well compensated by the government. The state instituted national boards to govern each industry, and many former owners now served on the boards. Nor were the unwashed factory laborers to be vaulted into positions of leadership. As Stafford Cripps said, "from my experience there is not as yet a very large number of workers in Britain capable of taking over large enterprises. . . . [U]ntil there has been more experience by the workers of the managerial side of industry, I think it would be almost impossible to have worker-controlled industry in Britain, even if it were on the whole desirable."[31] Labour was initiating not a workers' democracy but a new synthesis of capitalism and socialism, the "mixed economy" that emerged as the dominant model for all of Western Europe in the subsequent half century.

Nationalization was not terribly controversial. Labour's record on public housing and medical services provoked much more debate. Furthermore, the man tasked with both areas of policy was Aneurin Bevan, a fiery left-wing partisan, a Welsh miner and superb orator who never lost a chance to score political points against the Tories. Unlike the dignified technocrats Attlee and Cripps, Bevan was a radical, a threat not only to the opposition but to many members of his own party as well, whom he challenged to stay true to the principles of socialism.

Housing, or its absence, emerged as the leading domestic issue in the

minds of the public: 41 percent placed it at the top of the list. The war destroyed 200,000 houses in Britain and left three and a half million damaged.
Repairs and upkeep had been postponed due to lack of materials. On top of
this, the population had increased by 1 million during the war, and birth rates
were on the rise. Everyone agreed on the need for a massive house-building
program, and Labour rashly promised swift action: "Five million homes in
quick time," declared Ernest Bevin during the 1945 campaign. But the skilled
labor force was scattered, with many still in the services; there was a terrible
shortage of timber and the dollars needed to buy it; and the brick industry in
1946 was running at one-fifth its prewar level. In the face of such problems,
the government clearly could not meet public expectations, and relied heavily
on the use of prefabricated homes until the materials and labor for permanent
homes could be organized. In the meantime, desperate families—almost
50,000 people—squatted in disused military camps across the country, and
the government did nothing to stop them. The government did manage to
build over a million houses by 1951, which, given the terrible economic troubles of the country at this time, was quite an achievement, though well below
its initial goals.[32] The houses that did get built, moreover, were spacious—
Aneurin Bevan insisted on the generous (and later reduced) allocation of
1,000 square feet of floor space—and hugely popular with the families that
lived in them. The future Labour Party leader Neil Kinnock grew up in one
such house after the war. "It was like moving to Beverly Hills," he recalled.
"People used to come just to look at it."[33]

Alongside his heavy responsibilities for housing, Bevan also crafted the
centerpiece of the Labour government's social policy: the National Health
Service (NHS). As with most initiatives between 1945 and 1951, the war had
paved the way for rapid improvement in the system of public health benefits.
The Churchill coalition, in 1944, proposed a National Health Service based on
the twin principles that every citizen in the country had a right to the best
medical facilities available and that these services should be free. Bevan started
by proposing the nationalization of all hospitals, which gave the government
total control over the system and brought them into one unified structure.
The real problem was with the doctors and their lobbying arm, the British
Medical Association. They feared a loss of autonomy, a weakened relationship
with patients, and of course, an inability to charge fees to paying customers
who wished to have special treatment. Bevan wisely decided to give the BMA
what it demanded, but not before a great deal of invective from the doctors,
who accused Bevan of seeking dictatorial control over the medical profession.

Bevan took immense pride in the fact that "despite our financial and economic anxieties, we are still able to do the most civilized thing in the world—put the welfare of the sick in front of every other consideration."[34] These were noble words, but very quickly it became clear that the government had massively underestimated the cost of the NHS. Bevan assumed that free health care would mean a healthier public, and therefore fewer trips to the doctor. He did not consider the natural human impulse to take full advantage of a free service. Consider the testimony of Mrs. Claire Bond of Leeds, recorded by the historian Paul Addison: "When the National Health Service started, oh it was fantastic. My mother and dad had been having problems with their teeth for ages, and I think they were the first at the dentist, as soon as he opened, they were there for an appointment. And instead of having just a few teeth out, they had the complete set out. And free dentures."[35] They were not alone. In the first year of operation, eight and a half million people sought free dental treatment, and over 5 million pairs of free spectacles were dispensed. Doctors wrote 187 million prescriptions in the first year alone. Overnight, the NHS became the second largest item in the national budget, following only the military. In its first nine months, the NHS overran its budget by more than 50 million pounds. By 1951 it cost more than 400 million pounds a year to run. The chancellor of the Exchequer, then Hugh Gaitskell, insisted that a small charge be imposed on prescriptions for teeth and glasses; Bevan refused, saying it would undermine the principle of free service that lay at the heart of his Health Service. On 23 April 1951, Bevan resigned in protest. Since then, Bevan has gone down in history as the architect of the most enduring institution of the welfare state. The NHS epitomized the new relationship Labour had formed between the citizen and the state. The citizen gave his loyalty and his taxes; the state now had an obligation to provide health and welfare. Some have seen these measures as "perhaps Britain's finest hour."[36] They also became a source of immense controversy and criticism as the years wore on.

THE IMPORTANCE OF BEING ERNEST

Labour was radical at home, but in international affairs, the Attlee government pursued a hawkish foreign policy that did much to set the Cold War under way. When he became foreign secretary, Ernest Bevin was sixty-four years old and not in good health. He suffered from angina, heart disease, sinusitis, liver and kidney trouble, and high blood pressure. He was overweight, smoked and drank too much, and never exercised. His doctor, upon examining him in 1943, said that there was not a sound organ in his body. Bevin soldiered on, however, serving for six years in his job, enduring the physical hardships of constant travel, lengthy negotiations, long working hours, and endless social functions. Upon his death in April 1951, he was widely hailed as one of Britain's greatest foreign ministers.

Despite the economic constraints facing the country, Bevin laid out an ambitious three-part strategy: to lead Europe toward recovery while ensuring that the continent was free from the dominance of either Germany or Russia; to restore and improve the Empire; and to secure the material and if possible political support of the United States in pursuit of the first two objectives. Bevin and his advisers in the Foreign Office believed that the Soviet Union presented the chief obstacle to British and European security. In fact, as recent research has revealed, they came to this conclusion much sooner than their American counterparts. The British saw Russian actions in Central and Southern Europe, the Eastern Mediterranean, and the Middle East as directly threatening to British interests, just as they had seen German and Italian threats to these regions before 1939 as detrimental to their international position. Flush from the victory over Germany, British leaders—in both the Conservative and Labour Parties— were determined not to delay in confronting Russia as they had delayed in confronting Hitler. British statesmen felt that they had earned the right to shape postwar Europe, and a temporary balance-of-payments problem could in no way deter them from this objective.[37]

Though a lifelong trade unionist, Bevin maintained a hostile attitude toward the Soviet Union. During his days as a labor organizer, he had developed an abhorrence of Communists, who throughout the 1920s and 1930s sought to infiltrate and take over his union. Never a doctrinaire socialist, he was a patriot, an earthy, proud, and keenly intelligent man who believed profoundly in the survival of the British Empire and in its power for improving the world. Almost from the day he took office, he—like Churchill—harbored deep suspicions about Soviet policy in the postwar world. There were members of the Labour government, notably Prime Minister Clement Attlee, who were disposed toward a more conciliatory attitude toward Russia. Bevin was not, and fit right in with the prevailing view in the Foreign Office that the postwar world would not be stable or peaceful unless the Western powers declared to the Soviet Union with firmness and resolve precisely where their interests lay.[38]

Excluding for the moment the Far East and Africa, there were three theaters in which Russian actions unnerved Bevin. First was Southeastern Europe. Churchill's "percentages" deal of October 1944 had recognized the Soviet position in Romania and Bulgaria, while allowing Britain predominance in Greece; Yugoslavia and Hungary were supposed to be divided evenly. With a powerful Communist government under Josip Tito now established in Belgrade, there was nothing Britain could do in Yugoslavia. But these losses made Britain's position in Greece, its anchor in the Mediterranean, all the more important. The second major area of British interest was the Middle East, which included a broad arc of territory running from Egypt northeast into Palestine and the Levant, Jordan, Iraq, and Iran. These countries covered the land and sea routes to India, and Iran alone produced more oil in 1945 than all of the Arab countries combined; moreover, Britain didn't have to pay for it in dollars. Finally, Britain maintained a large military presence in occupied Germany, though at least here Bevin had the advantage of working alongside the United States in confronting Soviet designs. What is striking, therefore, about Labour's early foreign policy is not its weakness but its ambition and massive scope. It was with some sense of exasperation that Bevin told the House of Commons in November 1945 that "all the world is in trouble and I have to deal with all the troubles at once."[39]

Given such a vast web of strategic commitments running from the Atlantic to the Indian Ocean and beyond, it was likely that the British would encounter friction at key points of contact with the largest and most powerful nation in Eurasia, the Soviet Union. Stalin's determination to test British resolve made such friction certain. Tension first flared up in Iran, where the British and Russians had, in 1941, divided and jointly occupied the country; a great deal of military supplies were subsequently delivered to the Russians by the Allies through Iran during the war. The deal stipulated that both powers would withdraw at war's end. The British did; the Soviets did not, and instead demanded oil concessions. In November 1945 they took advantage of a leftist secessionist movement in Azerbaijan to challenge the Iranian government and establish a bridgehead in the country.

At the same time, Russia placed immense pressure upon Turkey—which had stayed neutral during the war—to allow Soviet naval bases along the vital straits connecting the Black Sea to the Mediterranean. The Turks, as well as the United States and Britain, opposed any such concessions, but Stalin manufactured a huge campaign of intimidation by massing troops on Turkey's border and encouraging the separatist ambitions of the Kurdish people in eastern Anatolia. By the spring of 1946, the Russians had more than half a million troops in Romania and 150,000 in Bulgaria; both American and British analysts expected an invasion of Turkey. Bevin saw a carefully orchestrated plan at work: "Russia is seeking," he told a group of journalists in an off-the-record chat on 1 January 1946 "to get one paw down the back of Turkey . . . [through

Iran] and the other paw through the Straits so that there would be a grip on Turkey, and Turkey would become virtually a satellite state with her foreign policy controlled by Russia."[40]

British observers saw Iran and Turkey as part of a pattern of Soviet expansion. In March 1946, the British ambassador in Moscow, Frank Roberts, sent a series of long cables to London, summarizing his view of Russian strategy. Like the American chargé George Kennan, who had sent his "long telegram" to Washington the previous month, Roberts now believed that the Soviet Union was determined to challenge British influence throughout the world, but especially in the Empire and the Near East, areas not directly of interest to the United States. Britain therefore faced "with doubtful American backing constantly increasing Soviet pressure in the whole zone vital to British security between India and the Dardanelles." The Soviets would push until they were stopped. "It is becoming uncertain," he wrote, "whether there is, in fact, any limit to Soviet expansion."[41]

Thanks to Stalin's aggressive tactics, American officials now agreed. President Truman called the Soviet pressure on Iran "an outrage if ever I saw one," and when on 6 March 1946 the US State Department received word that Soviet tanks were moving on Tehran, Truman directed US ships to the Persian Gulf. In a stunning about-face, Stalin announced in April his decision to withdraw his troops from Iran, but then stepped up pressure on Turkey in August. Once again, Truman ordered his military planners to draw up war plans. Only when a highly placed Soviet spy—Donald Maclean, one of the infamous Cambridge Five working in the British Foreign Service—informed Moscow of Washington's determination to fight for Turkey did Stalin relent. The affair pushed the British and the Americans together when it had been Soviet strategy to divide them. Foreign Minister Vyacheslav Molotov later realized that the Iran-Turkey crises were a mistake. "We should have been very careful. But we threw a bad scare into them."[42]

The affair brought little joy to Bevin, however, for he realized that only American power had saved Iran and Turkey from invasion. This lesson was reinforced in Germany, where the British again concluded—sooner than the Americans—that four-power control was hopeless. The huge financial strains of the occupation, however, forced Bevin to search for a solution that would allow some resurrection of the German economy, at least so the country could feed itself. Britain's financial weakness pushed Bevin to seek in July 1946 a fusion of the Western zones of occupation. When this bizone emerged in January 1947, Britain's influence in Germany necessarily slipped somewhat, as the Americans now shouldered a larger share of the occupation costs.[43] In

Iran, Turkey, Germany, and elsewhere, American economic and military power supplanted British influence.

In India, the British were still in control of events—barely. Here, the Labour government, especially Attlee, was determined to "transfer power"—a telling phrase intended to denote a deliberate policy of withdrawal—to Indian authorities by 1948. In the end, pressure from Gandhi pushed the date up to August 1947. This transfer was depicted as a success story for British colonialism: Britain had assisted in the material and political development of India and could now withdraw on good terms. Indeed, independent India promptly joined the Commonwealth. Of course, the breaking away of Muslim Pakistan, and the wave of massive sectarian violence this precipitated, tarnished the withdrawal. Yet Labour could look to the dissolution of the Raj more with pride than bitterness.

Palestine presented a stark contrast. Here the structural weakness of Britain's overseas position was brutally laid bare. Britain had administered the territory since the collapse of the Ottoman Empire in 1918, under a League of Nations mandate. The British government had made a number of contradictory statements about it, including the 1917 Balfour Declaration, in support of a Jewish homeland (not a state) in Palestine, and the 1939 white paper that recognized Arab predominance in a unitary Arab Palestine. By the end of World War II, Britain had come to see Palestine as a vital component of its Middle Eastern position. Yet world opinion had become strongly sympathetic to Jewish demands for a state, as small recompense for their sufferings in the Holocaust. Bevin, in one of the worst misjudgments of his career, steadfastly opposed the creation of a Jewish state and even an increase in Jewish immigration to Palestine. It would weaken his efforts to solidify British relations with the Arab world, he felt. Many in the US State Department concurred with Bevin's strategic outlook and urged a compromise: a "binational" state with power-sharing structures for Arabs and Jews. This solution was endorsed by a committee of British and American public figures in April 1946, which also called for an increase of the Jewish immigration quota to 100,000. Bevin refused. "If we put 100,000 Jews into Palestine tomorrow, I will have to put another division of British troops there," he said in June 1946. "I am not prepared to do it."[44]

Bevin's narrow strategic calculus blinded him to the larger moral imperative at work here. The Jews had earned statehood. The world knew it, and the Zionists would fight for it. In July 1946, they blew up the British headquarters in the King David Hotel in Jerusalem, revealing the extreme measures they were willing to adopt to expel the British. In essence, the Jews dared the British to engage in a long campaign of persecution, arrest, and imprisonment—even execution—of Jewish fighters in Palestine only a year after the liberation of the concentration camps. President Truman, for one, thought such a policy political suicide, aside from its moral repugnance. He urged a policy of partition on Bevin, who angrily resisted American interference. Instead, Bevin grimly held on, keeping some 100,000 British soldiers and police in Palestine, at a cost of 40 million pounds a year. It could not last. In July 1947—just at the start of the convertibility crisis—British authorities in Haifa turned away a boatload of forty-five hundred Jewish refugees. In an act of unconscionable insensitivity, the British rerouted the ship—the *Exodus*—back to Germany. The reaction was ferocious. Within a month, a special UN committee urged a policy of partition, leading to a Jewish state. The UN as a whole did the same in November. The British, now going bankrupt, had incurred the wrath of world opinion, had been insensitive to Jewish appeals, and had strained relations with America. Palestine had been an unmitigated disaster, and in September 1947, the British announced their intention to withdraw.

By the start of 1947, British economic troubles had become so acute that the country could not maintain any presence at all in Greece, a country that, just eighteen months earlier, Bevin had declared was crucial to the defense of the Middle East and the Empire itself. Greece was in the midst of a bitter civil war that grew out of the wartime struggle between the Communist-dominated resistance and the promonarchy government in exile that the British had supported during the war. The British stationed as many as 80,000 troops in Greece in 1946 but could not sustain them. In February 1947, the cabinet decided to cut off all aid to Greece and Turkey after the end of March. Bevin pleaded with Washington to take over responsibility for these strategically crucial states. The United States did, and on 12 March President Truman announced a new aid package, dressed up in a strident anti-Communist speech that declared it "the policy of the United States to support free peoples who are resisting attempted subjugation by armed minorities or by outside pressures." The president went on to say, in a speech that became known as the Truman Doctrine, that "if Greece should fall under the control of an armed minority, the effect upon its neighbor, Turkey, would be immediate and serious. Confusion and disorder might well spread throughout the entire Middle East."[45] The United States had now committed itself to defend an area of traditional British hegemony. It was a dubious victory for Bevin. America had agreed to defend British interests only because Britain could no longer do it herself.

By the spring of 1947, Bevin's foreign policy was in tatters. His hope for a reassertion of Britain's great-power status had been dashed, and British dependence upon American power now made plain. In just a few short months, however, Bevin revealed how effective British leadership could still be, despite the country's weakness—or perhaps because of it. In January 1947, George C. Marshall, the renowned chief of staff of the US Army during the war, took over the State Department. His introduction to Soviet diplomacy came at a meeting of foreign ministers in Moscow, where the Russians sought to slow down Anglo-American efforts to revive the German economy. Marshall was deeply discouraged by the experience and left Moscow feeling that Stalin intended to drag out disagreements over Germany until the German, and perhaps European, economy completely collapsed, making these countries easy pickings for a campaign of Communist subversion. Marshall, upon reaching home, recounted his impression of Europe's troubles to an American radio audience on 28 April 1947. "The recovery of Europe has been far slower than expected," he said. "Disintegrating forces are becoming evident. The patient is sinking while the doctors deliberate. So I believe that action cannot await compromise through exhaustion. New issues arise daily. Whatever action is possible to meet these pressing problems must be taken without delay."[46] Paired with the Truman Doctrine, this assessment suggested a major shift in American thinking toward Europe. The continent now had to be revived economically, and German resources had to be used to do it, even if that meant shattering the Potsdam agreements and moving ahead on the basis of a divided Germany.

Bevin welcomed this shift in American attitudes. He had come to this same conclusion much earlier, and now saw it as his role to assist the United States in effecting the recovery of Western Europe, not through piecemeal aid packages such as the Americans had relied on so far but through a coordinated assault on the causes of economic instability in Europe. His views ran parallel to those of a growing cadre of American policy makers who now believed that Europe could not recover economically without a broad, coordinated recovery program, backed by American aid. On 5 June 1947, George Marshall delivered his famous commencement address at Harvard University in which he reviewed Europe's economic breakdown and declared it in America's self-interest to help. Of course, the United States had already channeled some $9 billion to Europe, and this had done little good. Now, the Europeans had to develop a plan:

> There must be some agreement among the countries of Europe as to the requirements of the situation and the part that those countries themselves will take in order to give proper effect to whatever action might be undertaken by the government. It would be neither fitting

nor efficacious for this government to undertake to draw up unilaterally a program designed to place Europe on its feet economically. This is the business of the Europeans. The initiative, I think, must come from Europe.[47]

Marshall's speech was little more than a statement of American good intentions. As yet, policy makers in Washington did not have any idea how to put them into effect. This is why Bevin's role was so crucial in the formation of the Marshall Plan. He seized on the phrase in Marshall's address that "the initiative must come from Europe." For a man as zealous as Bevin to secure US support for European recovery, these words amounted to an engraved invitation for swift action. "I assure you," he told American journalists two years later, "it was like a lifeline to sinking men. It seemed to bring hope where there was none. . . . I think you understand why, therefore, we responded with such alacrity and why we grabbed the lifeline with both hands."[48] Bevin immediately contacted the French foreign minister, Georges Bidault, and together they agreed to prepare a joint plan for American aid. They also agreed that the Russians must be asked to participate in drawing up a response to the US offer, though both Bevin and Bidault hoped the Russians would refuse. In fact, the Russians did decide to send a large delegation to Paris in late June, to meet with the French and British. Recently available evidence from Russian sources suggests that the Soviets were genuinely intrigued by the prospect of securing American aid for themselves and their satellites, but feared that the Marshall Plan was a Trojan horse for a US takeover of Europe. They would participate in it if they could dominate it and, as the Soviet ambassador to Washington wrote in a cable to Moscow, "hinder the realization of the American plans for the subordination of Europe and the creation of an anti-Soviet bloc."[49] Bevin anticipated this and quite clearly hoped to provoke the Russians to walk out of the Paris Conference. When Molotov insisted that the Americans state precisely how much money they were willing to commit to Europe, Bevin shot back that "debtors do not lay down conditions when seeking credits from potential creditors." Later, the Russians refused to allow any examination of their economy as a prerequisite to a request for aid; on 3 July, they walked out. Bevin was relieved at Soviet intransigence, for the failure of the conference could be pinned on the Russians, while he and Bidault could get on with drawing up a plan.[50] This they did, hammering out during the month of August a sixteen-nation proposal to the United States for a massive four-year aid program. This was the basis for what became the European Recovery Program, through which the United States would spend some $12.5 billion on

European recovery. Bevin's swiftness in responding to Marshall's speech and his readiness to thwart the Russians had been critical. Bevin, though not the father, was the midwife of the Marshall Plan.

For all of Secretary Marshall's public assurances that his plan was, as he put it in his speech, "directed not against any country or doctrine but against hunger, poverty, desperation, and chaos," the effect of the plan was to speed up the division of Europe, a process that had already been under way in Germany but that now spread to the rest of the continent. The Russians, for example, moved immediately to forbid their own client states from participating in the Marshall Plan, though Poland and Czechoslovakia desperately wished to do so. It increased Soviet suspicions of American activities in Germany, where the Russians now became completely inflexible. It also gave a considerable shot in the arm to Bevin's own diplomacy. Since the Americans had staked their credibility on the success of European recovery, they might be persuaded to back that effort with more than money.

Bevin now set his sights on a security pact to insure that if there were a war with the Russians, the Americans would not sit out the first two or three years of it, as they had done twice before in the century. Of course, he did not put it so brazenly to the Americans. On 15 December 1947, Bevin told Marshall he wanted to see the formation of "a western democratic system comprising the Americans, ourselves, France, Italy, etc., and of course the Dominions. This would not be a formal alliance but an understanding backed by power, money, and resolute action. It would be a sort of spiritual federation of the West." In a formal paper, Bevin proposed the creation of a Western Union, including not just the core Western European countries but old foes like Germany, Spain, and Portugal, as well as all the Scandinavian countries. This, he believed, was the only way "to call a halt to the Soviet threat."[51] This proposal was well in advance of American ideas. In the midst of seeking a congressional commitment of many billions of dollars for Europe, the State Department did not want to begin lobbying for a military alliance as well. The Americans responded by giving Bevin their blessing but refusing any outright support for his alliance scheme. This came as a blow to Bevin, who realized that without American membership, any European security system would be a hollow shell.

At this point, Bevin's vision for a Western alliance was given a huge and quite unintentional boost by events in Prague, where the Communists in the Czech government, with the tacit support of Moscow, forced President Edvard Benes to accept a Communist-dominated administration. Nervous Westerners immediately labeled this the Prague "coup." Bevin contacted the US ambassador in London and called for immediate talks on ways "to prevent the extension of the area of dictatorship." Georges Bidault announced his own support for such a program to the American ambassador. On 17 March 1948, Britain, France, Belgium, the Netherlands, and Luxembourg signed the Brussels Pact, a mutual defense agreement, and Bevin again urged the United States to join in a broader Atlantic security system to "inspire the necessary confidence to consolidate the West against Soviet infiltration." The alternative, Bevin pointedly declared in a memo to the US State Department, "is to repeat our experiences with Hitler and to witness the slow deterioration of our position."[52]

The Europeans were positively begging for an assertion of US military power into Europe to defend them from what they perceived to be a determined Soviet campaign of expansion. If there were any doubts, the Russians dispelled them by blockading Berlin in June 1948, cutting off road and rail travel into the city in retaliation for the Anglo-American introduction of a new currency in their zones of occupation. The blockade was a massive miscalculation. It made heroes of the Berliners, triggered a daring and successful airlift operation to provision the city, and gave Bevin yet another opportunity to plead for a formal military commitment from the United States. In mid-July 1948, the Western powers began exploratory talks on the creation of a Western alliance. The result, in April 1949, was the North Atlantic Treaty Organization (NATO), a military alliance of twelve European and North American countries. Once again, Bevin's determination, his drive, his vision, and the bungling tactics of the Soviets had persuaded the Americans to give military backing to the economic community envisaged by the Marshall Plan. NATO was an expression of transatlantic solidarity, a pact between the United States and Western Europe that underscored a common set of values and governing principles. More than any other single individual, Ernest Bevin deserves to be considered its chief architect. It is no small irony that a socialist trade union leader emerged as the chief agent for the extension of US economic and military power to Europe after the Second World War.[53]

For all these successes, Bevin must also be saddled with one enormous failure: his policy toward European integration. Bevin had never stopped thinking of Britain as a country on an altogether different plane from the rest of the continent. The French were weak, divided, unreliable; the Italians were still kept at arm's length; the Germans Bevin continued to despise: "I tries 'ard, but I 'ates 'em," he told the commander of the British occupation forces.[54] In May 1950, the new French foreign minister, Robert Schuman, announced a proposal for the pooling of the coal and steel resources of the Western European states and the creation of an impartial high authority to govern their use. The Schuman Plan was a brilliant compromise struck between Germany and

France, intended to insure swift recovery and expansion of German coal and steel production while offering France the assurances of international control of those resources. All the potential members naturally looked to Britain to join; Bevin refused, claiming that the scheme would limit Britain's sovereignty over its national economic policies and weaken links to the Commonwealth.

The pattern of British distrust and disregard for continental plans of integration was thus struck in 1950 by the man who had done so much to ensure Europe's economic and military security. In the end, this was a colossal misjudgment, as great as his mistake in Palestine. For Britain was in fact much less imperial than Bevin believed, and far more European. Over the next decade, Britain's trade would reflect this, shifting ever more toward Europe and away from the Commonwealth. But by staying out of the Schuman Plan and affecting aloofness from European integration, Britain lost any say in the shape of the emerging European Community. By the early 1960s, when the British Empire had withered to a mere shadow, Britain was left without a toehold in Europe and without an empire. All that remained was a distinctly second-class position in the Anglo-American "special relationship"—not quite what Ernest Bevin had envisioned when he boldly took office in July 1945.

The first five years of the Labour government witnessed enormous accomplishments. The government weathered the worst of the postwar economic crisis, launched the welfare state, nationalized many key industries, and tied the United States to a Europe-centered alliance. The election of 1950 rewarded the Labour Party with an increased number of votes compared to 1945 (13.2 million versus 11.9 million), but the Conservatives too increased their support, mostly among middle-class constituencies lost in the previous election. Labour's once-formidable majority was reduced to five seats. The government limped on for another eighteen months with no mandate for major legislation and no inclination to pursue it in the face of the economic crisis that erupted in mid-1950. Upon the outbreak of war in Korea, in June, world commodity prices soared, triggering another balance-of-payments crisis; at the same time, the government initiated a large and unsocialist rearmament program. In October 1951, Winston Churchill, now a wheezing relic, led the Conservatives through a quiet electoral campaign that resulted in a narrow victory: 321 seats against Labour's 295. Here was a clear statement of the country's centrist ambitions.

Indeed, the Conservatives left much of Labour's work intact. The Beveridge consensus was now universal, while the two leaders of economic policy in the opposing parties, R. A. B. Butler and Hugh Gaitskell, lent their names to a neologism: "Butskellism" implied a common governing philosophy of moderate social reform and progressivism. From 1951 to 1964, Britain continued to grow and expand. The age of austerity was replaced with an age of affluence. Neither party had a real answer for what followed: three decades of industrial decline, a bloated public sector, chronic balance-of-payments difficulties, inflation, unemployment, and troubled industrial relations. Alongside these domestic troubles, British governments watched anxiously as the continental Europeans, working ever more closely together, eventually overtook the British economy, with Germany, France, and Italy all outproducing Britain by the end of the 1980s.

These woeful developments were often laid on Attlee's doorstep. Despite the fact that the Conservatives held power for seventeen years between 1951 and 1979, Margaret Thatcher could see all of Britain's troubles as starting with the Labour victory of 1945. "No theory of government," she sneered in her memoirs, "was ever given a fairer test or a more prolonged experiment in a democratic country than democratic socialism received in Britain. Yet it was a miserable failure in every respect." The Attlee legacy for her consisted of too much state control, too many taxes, too much nationalization and economic planning, too many welfare benefits. Labour championed "the virtues of dependence."[55] The Attlee government has been cursed for raising public expectations about the power of government to meet the needs of the people, while failing to adapt the economic infrastructure to meet those demands. From the glittering New Jerusalem promised by Attlee emerged, in the words of one critic, "a dank reality of a segregated, sub-literate, unskilled, unhealthy and institutionalized proletariat hanging on the nipple of state maternalism."[56]

Were things so bad? As the historian Kenneth Morgan—himself sympathetic to Labour—has argued, national income doubled in Britain between 1948 and 1976. The standard of living for everyone rose as consumer products of all sorts became a reality; take-home pay rose; vacations became routine and longer; education, housing, health care, and social insurance all improved.[57] Placed alongside the record of the 1920s and 1930s, these were significant achievements. The fact that other countries did as well and some better hardly makes the postwar experience of Britain a failure, nor does it mean that the Labour government of 1945–51, which largely laid out the framework of postwar society, bears responsibility for British failings. On the contrary, there is a striking resonance in certain respects between Margaret Thatcher's rhetoric of the 1980s and themes invoked by Labour leaders in the late 1940s: the need for national regeneration through hard work, duty, sacrifice, Christian ethics, patriotism, idealism, honesty, integrity. The difference between the two positions was over the role of the government in adapting these principles to policy, and here Labour had an absolute faith—too great, in retrospect—in the power and wisdom of government to do good. Placed in its historical context, this confidence in the political process marks the Attlee years. It not only separates them from the later decades of political apathy in most Western democracies but also brings out the deep contrast between Britain in the late 1940s and the rest of Europe, where political institutions were far weaker, where consensus was absent, where economic life remained stalled, and where democracy itself was under siege.

CHAPTER THREE

DEMOCRACY EMBATTLED: FRANCE, ITALY, AND WEST GERMANY, 1944–1949

·

PLUS ÇA CHANGE: FRANCE, 1944–1950

IN JUNE 1940, Charles de Gaulle was an unknown brigadier general in the French army and an undersecretary of defense in the government of Paul Reynaud. The German invasion in May left his country defeated, demoralized, and in a state of shock. The French government settled on a policy of armistice, and fled Paris for Bordeaux. De Gaulle instead hopped on a transport ship to London. It was an ignominious exit. Four years later, de Gaulle was a world-renowned figure, the undisputed leader of Free France, and the only man with the credibility to govern the country.

This astonishing transformation of de Gaulle's fortunes had not come about easily. It began with his famous broadcast of 18 June 1940, on the BBC, calling on all French men and women to join him in continuing the fight against the Germans. That few heard his appeal, and that only a handful did join him in London, meant nothing to de Gaulle. Through a combination of political skill, mulish determination, vanity, and patriotism, de Gaulle by 1943 had won the respect of the internal resistance within France, which strengthened his bid for recognition from the Allies as the sole leader of the French exiles. Roosevelt and Churchill, who disliked the headstrong Frenchman, found that they needed him as a rallying point for French opinion. Churchill compared him to Joan of Arc, and resented his "arrogant demeanor." "The Cross of Lorraine," Churchill quipped about the symbol de Gaulle adopted for the Free French, "was the heaviest cross I have ever had to bear."[1] They continued to treat him with disrespect throughout the war, annoyed at his apparent ingratitude toward his allies and at his insistence on being treated like the leader of a sovereign nation—when in fact he had no army, no navy, no money, no government, and no capital city. The Allies kept him out of the planning for the invasion of French North Africa in October 1942, and General Eisenhower briefed him on the 1944 Normandy invasion only two days before it took place. Nonetheless, de Gaulle earned Churchill's grudging respect. Churchill claimed to have recognized in him a "man of destiny" and likened him to the medieval constable of France who commanded the French king's armies.[2]

Part of what made de Gaulle both compelling and exasperating to his contemporaries was his ability to shape his mission in powerful, though often inflated, rhetoric. Deprived of the normal tools of statecraft, de Gaulle instead had to rely upon words. "Such was my task!" he said later of his goals in 1940. "To reinstate France as a belligerent, to prevent her subversion, to restore a destiny that depended on herself alone. . . . It was the entire French people, as it stood, that I would have to rally around me. Against the enemy, despite the Allies, regardless of terrible dissensions, I would have to constitute around myself the unity of lacerated France."[3]

Unity became the keynote of his public rhetoric, during both the war and the liberation. France, he claimed, had always been united in its determination to resist the German occupation. He chose to ignore the profound ruptures in French society that had existed before 1939 and that had been exacerbated by four years of a near civil war. In August 1944, in his first speech in the liberated capital, de Gaulle acclaimed the historic unity of the country and spoke with certainty about the French people's determination to stand shoulder to shoulder during the last stages of the war and during the period of recovery. From the balcony of the Hôtel de Ville on 25 August, he declared:

> In the present situation, the nation would not allow national unity to be disrupted. The nation well knows that to conquer, to reconstruct and to be great, all Frenchmen are needed. The nation well knows that the sons and daughters of France—all the sons and daughters except for a few unhappy traitors who gave themselves over to the enemy and who are tasting or will taste the rigors of the law—yes! all the sons and daughters of France must march towards France's goal, fraternally hand in hand.[4]

In these and other public remarks, de Gaulle offered a narrative in which France had been betrayed, first by the weak politicians of the Third Republic, then by the "few unhappy traitors" of the Vichy regime. Throughout the war, Frenchmen remained loyal, resisting the German occupation in their hearts if not in their deeds. Vichy, never legitimate, could now be plucked off the body politic like a nagging parasite.

De Gaulle wove this elegant tapestry out of palpable falsehoods. Vichy's leader, the octogenarian Marshal Philippe Pétain, had received his powers legally in 1940 and remained popular through 1944. The Vichy government was hardly the work of a "few"; with much popular acclaim, Vichy undertook a transformation of the political culture in France that found many willing participants. Not the least of Vichy's appeal to many Frenchmen was its profound anti-Semitism. And as for national unity, this was wishful thinking on de Gaulle's part. Despite the surge of unity around him that August, the war experience left the French nation shattered, a broken picture window of a hundred brittle, threatening shards.

The jockeying for power under way in Paris in the fall of 1944 belied de Gaulle's rhetoric of national unity. De Gaulle himself stood at the head of a jury-rigged provisional government, made up of members of the external resistance and various Gaullists that had gathered first in London and then in Algiers. It still did not have the recognition of the Allied governments and did not gain it until October 1944. De Gaulle faced a great challenge in asserting his authority in liberated France, as many in the internal resistance still contested de Gaulle's claim to supremacy. The resistance included citizens from all walks of life and of every political persuasion, though its most effective militants had been Communists. In the last months of the war, the resistance emerged as an organized military force, loosely grouped into the Forces Françaises de l'Intérieur (FFI), whose command structure was dominated by Communists. As the FFI liberated towns and villages across France, usually after the Germans had withdrawn, they established Comités de Libération (CDL), many of which were run by local Communists, but all of which were in any case highly autonomous, proud of their efforts, and suspicious of Gaullist control. Only reluctantly did the FFI allow itself to be amalgamated into the regular armed forces.

More troubling still for de Gaulle was the prospect of a massive outpouring of vengeance toward those who collaborated with the Germans. Even before the Normandy landings, the resistance had begun to liquidate some of the more notorious Vichyites, especially among the hated Milice, Vichy's thuggish police force. The FFI, whose members had spent the war years in France and knew all too well who had given aid and comfort to the occupier, targeted many local profiteers, informers, and petty tyrants for revenge. Historians now place the summary executions at about 10,000, a figure far lower than one might expect in a country immersed in civil war for four years. For women accused of "horizontal collaboration" with the enemy, local bands of partisans devised a nasty form of public humiliation: women were stripped of their clothes, their heads were shaved, and then they were paraded through the streets of towns and villages, often under a torrent of blows from onlookers.

Most members of the resistance believed that France needed some kind of purge of collaborationists. Even politically moderate underground activists like the writer Albert Camus argued that "since 1939, we have truly learned that not to destroy certain men would be to betray the good of this country. France carries within itself a diseased body, a minority of men who yesterday brought France sorrow and who continue to do so today. . . . [The purge] is the only chance left us to keep France and Europe from becoming a desert of mediocrity and silence where we could no longer want to live."[5] In fact, the purge was short-lived and ineffectual. By September 1944, de Gaulle's officials arranged for mass roundups of suspects, chiefly to protect them from being shot by outraged resistance bands. From then on, the purge became less and less severe, until it degenerated into a charade. A special high court tried 108 of Vichy's leading ministers; of these, forty-four were released, fifteen given the public wrist slapping called "national degradation," and twenty-two given prison sentences. Only eighteen were condemned to death, but of these ten had already fled the country. Only three Vichy-era leaders were actually executed. Overall, 160,287 cases of collaboration were examined by the end of 1948, of which half were dismissed. Only 7,037 (4 percent) received the death penalty, and of these only 767 people were executed. The purges quickly became a symbol of the postwar order: in the interest of national unity, the ugly truths of the wartime past were to be swept quietly under the rug. This moderation served de Gaulle's objective of assuring a swift consolidation of power, but it also met with the silent assent of the *notables* within the bureaucracy, the schools, churches, business and industry—indeed, of the many thousands who had during the war years made such compromises with the Vichy regime as they felt necessary to survive.[6]

Though de Gaulle managed to suppress a serious purge, he could do little to compel unity from the political parties that now sought power. The Communists were the most powerful, best-financed, and most experienced political grouping in France in late 1944. They emerged from the war with a reputation for effectiveness and determination against the German enemy, a renown they exploited by referring to themselves as "the party of the 75,000 murdered"—an exaggerated reference to German reprisals against Communist resistance fighters. The Communists had no interest in a seizure of power that could too easily lead to open conflict with the US Army and strengthen proponents within the American government who wanted a military occupation of France. After all, the Parti Communiste Français (PCF) had an excellent chance of taking power through the ballot box, and already occupied high posts in de Gaulle's provisional government.

The non-Communist resistance also nourished fond hopes for a major political role in postwar France. During the war, the resistance formulated a political ethos that emphasized national renewal, reform, and a program of reconstruction that would make over France's antiquated political institutions, assure social justice, break the hold of monopolies and cartels over the economic life of the country, and extirpate all vestiges of the collaborationist regime erected by Vichy. But the resistance was itself the result of a grand compromise of diverse people, joined together in a common struggle against Nazism and French collaborationism. With these threats removed, the wartime unity swiftly dissipated and the prewar political parties soon returned to the field.

The Socialists, who called themselves Marxists, refused to merge into a single working-class party with the Communists because they saw themselves as progressive but not revolutionary. They also believed that the path to power lay in working alongside the Communists in a coalition rather than in a united, single party in which their leadership might be pushed aside. The center of the political spectrum was dominated by the Mouvement Républicain Populaire (MRP), a Christian Democratic party whose leadership featured many Catholic resistance leaders opposed to the Marxist ideology of the left. The MRP had close connections to de Gaulle through its leader, Georges Bidault, who entertained the hope that de Gaulle would openly declare his support for this Catholic party and lead it to victory over the Communists and Socialists. It was not to be: de Gaulle affected an above-party stance that weakened the MRP and forced it to compromise with the left.

The first national election for a Constituent Assembly, in October 1945, revealed the deep divisions within the electorate. The PCF emerged with 26 percent of the vote, the MRP with 25 percent, the Socialists with 24 percent, the right with the remaining quarter. Though half the country now supported explicitly Marxist parties, the absence of unity between the Communists and Socialists, and the hostility of the MRP toward unifying with the still-tainted far right, assured complete paralysis in the new Assembly, whose sole purpose was to draft a new constitution. The PCF wanted a powerful unicameral Assembly and no executive; the Socialists wanted at least a weak executive as a check on the Assembly; the MRP wanted a second legislative house like the Third Republic's Senate, and a stronger executive. The parties' inability to agree on the shape of the country's new political institutions led an exasperated de Gaulle to attempt a bold and ultimately foolish political ploy: on 20

January 1946, he resigned from the presidency of the provisional government, hoping that the shock would lead the country to demand his return to power and the promulgation of a constitution with a powerful executive—him—and a weak parliament. He miscalculated. Like his English wartime counterpart, Winston Churchill, de Gaulle was seen as an able warrior ill suited for the tasks of domestic reconstruction. His departure from office brought a close to the war years in France and marked the start of a new era of political instability and fractiousness that was not ultimately resolved until 1958—when de Gaulle once again used war and national crisis to vault back into power.

With de Gaulle gone from the scene, French politics returned to its prewar patterns. The major parties, all implacably opposed to one another, nonetheless had to try to build coalitions to govern. For a little over a year, the three major parties, the PCF, the Socialists, and the MRP, shared power in a tripartite regime that failed to create anything like the legislative dynamism visible in the Labour government across the Channel. Far more time was spent on political maneuvers than on serious reform. In the eyes of many young resistance fighters, the spirit of the resistance that had led so many to die in the interests of building a new France had been betrayed. When the Fourth Republic constitution was finally put to a national referendum in October 1946, only 36 percent of the public voted in its favor; 31 percent opposed it and 31 percent abstained. The Fourth Republic was born, but the labor was difficult and the health of the child not at all promising.[7]

The new republic inherited massive problems born of the war years. Jean-Pierre Rioux, the leading historian of France in these years, has tallied up the damage the country faced at the war's end. Most of the country had been scarred by war damage, and a quarter of the nation's buildings lay in ruins. A million families were homeless, and in April and May 1945, France had to find room for a wave of returning prisoners of war, political prisoners, and forced workers—almost 5 million people flooding back into the country. The food distribution system had broken down since the transport network—railways, roads, and bridges—was destroyed. Less than half the nation's railways were intact, and rolling stock was sadly depleted. On top of this, the coal-producing facilities of the country were stopped dead. In 1945, French mines could produce only 40 million tons of coal, compared to a figure of 67 million in 1938. In addition, the 23 million tons France imported every year before the war, mostly from Germany, were unavailable because of the vast damage to Germany's coal production. Thus, France lacked the vital fuel needed to stoke factories, fire train engines, and heat homes. French finances were a mess too, with inflation rampant, an outgrowth of the German policy that had required Vichy to pay for the costs of the occupation by printing money. Added to this,

France was living off imports, had exhausted her foreign currency reserves and therefore faced a chronic trade deficit. Like the British, French leaders had to go hat in hand to the Americans for stop-gap aid, winning a loan of over a billion dollars in 1946.[8]

The government, deeply divided by the party loyalties of its leading ministers, failed to articulate a coherent national strategy to tackle these problems. Of course, there were initiatives, like nationalization, that reflected the wartime consensus that the state must oversee key industries so as to insure that the wealth of the nation was not siphoned off by the much-derided oligarchs and trusts that were considered largely responsible for the failure of France to defend itself from economic collapse and German invasion. Coal mines, the gas and electricity industries, insurance companies, most large banks, the Renault automobile works, Air France, and the local and national railways all were taken under control of the state, on the dual argument that the state would manage them more efficiently and in the interests of the working class. The result, as in Britain, was twofold: nationalization opened up a great opportunity for innovation in management but also created a massive burden on the state, which now had to finance and administer this vast public sector. Alongside these reforms in management, the government passed new legislation for social security, requiring both workers and employers to contribute to schemes for health insurance, unemployment benefits, and maternity allowances.

It is indicative of the feebleness of France's postwar political institutions that the most imaginative and successful plans for the restoration of economic activity emerged not from within the government but from outside it. In mid-1945, Jean Monnet began a lobbying effort for the creation of a planning agency that could oversee the economic modernization of the country and place France on the road to recovery. Monnet, raised in Cognac by parents in the brandy business, trained as a lawyer and served in the League of Nations in the 1920s. Unlike many of his compatriots, Monnet had a good war. After France's defeat in 1940, Monnet went to London, where he worked on behalf of both the French and British armies to secure American matériel. He developed close contacts in the US government and acted as an informal liaison between Roosevelt, Churchill, and de Gaulle. He became director of the French Supply Mission in Washington, negotiating US aid for the Free French army, and he worked out the Lend-Lease package for France in February 1945.

Monnet admired the US and British way of doing business. He wished to see France adopt the corporatist style of state management that encouraged business, industry, and labor to cooperate rather than compete. Monnet was deeply discouraged by the bureaucratic infighting of the French ministries, and in November 1945 urged de Gaulle to create a new economic planning agency under the guidance of "one person, surrounded by a small group of energetic men from outside the administration," who will have "all the necessary powers" needed to institute real economic reforms.[9] Monnet wanted, like his British counterparts, to drag France out of its economic doldrums by kick-starting industry and boosting exports. This could not be done without an overhaul of the productive apparatus of the country. The solution, he believed, was to create a Commissariat Général du Plan (CGP) to lay out a national modernization program in consultation with the support of all sectors of the economy. The result was the approval of the Monnet Plan in January 1947. Over the next five years, the plan succeeded in taking major economic decisions out of the hands of the politicized ministries and turning that power over to a small, talented coterie of technocrats who, in conjunction with employers, industry, and unions, worked to set production targets, channel public investment, give tax breaks, and coordinate distribution of raw materials, especially coal, into key industries. Monnet's CGP led the way toward a major new program of public investment and modernization that enabled France to boost production of coal, steel, cement, heavy machinery, electricity, railways, tractors, and agricultural fertilizers. By 1952, France had met or exceeded the 1929 level of production in these areas. More important, Monnet had fashioned a new model of state-managed industrial strategy that went way beyond anything contemplated in prewar France and that would serve as the country's economic blueprint for the next thirty years.[10]

Yet these positive results were still in the future. At the time that Monnet's plan was just taking root, the political situation in France took a serious turn for the worse. As in Britain, the economic situation during the winter of 1946–47 was desperate. The harsh weather destroyed the grain harvest; stocks grew low, and the bread ration had to be reduced to 250 grams in the early spring. Meanwhile, prices continued to soar, rising some 90 percent between January and July. Workers, whose weekly pay packets brought them less and less, began to take action. In the Renault factories, a strike unfolded in April 1947, and there were massive demonstrations on May Day all across the country. Workers had begun to lose faith in the ability of the Communist-controlled Confédération Générale du Travail (CGT), the country's largest labor federation, to extract real wage increases and cost-of-living improvements from the government. The PCF began to fear that, as a member of the tripartite coalition government, it would begin to lose favor with its rank and file. On 4 May 1947, the PCF refused to support a vote of confidence in the Assembly on the government's economic policy. The following day, the premier, the Socialist Paul Ramadier, revoked the portfolios of the Communist

ministers in his government. The PCF could no longer be both a party of opposition and a party of government.

While Ramadier was chasing the Communists out of the government, another important story was unfolding on the other side of the political spectrum. Charles de Gaulle, cooling his heels since his departure from office in
January 1946, decided to return to politics. On 14 April 1947, he announced
the creation of a new political party, the Rassemblement du Peuple Français
(RPF). This had as its aim to promote, "over our divisions, the union of our
people in the effort of reform and renovation of the state." De Gaulle invoked
the mythical unity of the French people at a time when the country was deeply
divided. The RPF was clearly a right-wing party, but it also presented itself as
a party of order, tradition, and hierarchy against the chaos of French politics.
This call struck a chord, and the RPF succeeded brilliantly in the municipal
elections of October 1947, capturing over 36 percent of the vote, greater than
even the PCF's 30 percent.

The ejection of the Communists from the government in May 1947 and
the creation of the RPF together marked a major development in the history
of postwar France. Two mass movements, one on the left and one on the right,
now stood outside the government and were working to weaken and discredit
the parties that remained. They, in turn, forged a new centrist coalition, called
the Third Force, composed of the Socialists, the MRP, and the right-wing
Radicals and Independents. The non-Communist Third Force, though fragile,
was a much more appealing partner for the United States, which now began
to channel aid to France so as to fend off a collapse of the country. At the same
time, the PCF, out of government and frustrated by the failure of its parliamentary tactics since 1944, decided to turn toward a policy of open confrontation with the government.

LIBERATION AND RESTORATION:
ITALY, 1943–1948

The liberation of Italy started earlier and took much longer than that of
France. The Anglo-American invasion of Sicily began on 10 July 1943; the
country was not free of German troops until late April 1945. Things moved
quickly at first. It took Allied troops just six weeks to clear Sicily of Germans,
and in early September, British and American forces jumped over to the mainland to begin driving up the boot of Italy, reaching Naples by the end of the
month. Then, a hundred miles south of Rome, the Allies hit the Gustav Line,
a forbidding German defensive barrier that stopped the liberators in their

tracks, cut the country in half, and turned the Allies into occupiers of Italy's southern half. For the next two years, the armies of Germany, the United States, and Great Britain churned through the country, leaving Italy a smoldering ruin.

It might have worked out differently but for the bungling of the Italian king, Victor Emmanuel III, and his military chief, Marshal Pietro Badoglio. On 25 July 1943, the king, in an attempt to save his skin, ousted Mussolini from power and sought a separate peace with the Allies. He prevaricated over the terms of the surrender, however, while the Italian army melted away and the Germans began pouring troops into northern Italy. On 8 September, the king and the Allies announced that Italy had surrendered to the Allies. The Germans, having anticipated this, seized Rome, and General Eisenhower was forced to scratch an airborne invasion plan to capture the capital. Instead, the king and the marshal were forced to flee the invading Germans, and placed themselves under the protection of the British and Americans. The Germans captured and deported half a million Italian soldiers. They also rescued Mussolini from the jail in which the king had incarcerated him and placed him at the helm of a new puppet government in the northern, German-occupied half of Italy, now to be called the Italian Social Republic. In October, the impotent king redundantly declared war on Germany.

Liberation brought little relief to the people of southern Italy; they exchanged one occupier for another. The official British history of the Italian occupation recounted the social problems in Naples, where the British set up the headquarters of the Allied Military Government. Food was in very short supply, the water mains cut off, and the aqueduct destroyed by German sabotage. The sewers were badly damaged; there was no electricity; the ports needed to be cleared; and the whole distribution network for food and supplies was shattered due to lack of transportation. In circumstances like this, officials feared an epidemic of typhus, which was averted only by delousing virtually everyone in the city with heavy dustings of DDT. Malaria and smallpox also broke out. Both civilians and the troops suffered especially from venereal disease, despite a system of regularized and licensed prostitution; Allied hospitals were treating thirty-five hundred patients a month for VD alone. A British intelligence officer, Norman Lewis, has left a vivid memoir of Naples under Allied occupation. "It is astonishing," he wrote in late October 1943,

> to witness the struggles of this city so shattered, so starved, so deprived of all those things that justify a city's existence, to adapt itself to a collapse into conditions which must resemble life in the Dark Ages. People camp out like Bedouins in the desert. There is little food,

water, no salt, no soap. A lot of Neapolitans have lost their possessions, including most of their clothing, in the bombings, and I have
seen some strange combinations of garments about the streets, including a man in an old dinner-jacket, knickerbockers and army
boots, and several women in lacy confections that might have been
made up from curtains. There are no cars but carts by the hundred,
and a few antique coaches such as barouches and phaetons drawn by
lean horses. Today at Posilipo I stopped to watch the methodical dismemberment of a stranded German half-track by a number of
youths who were streaming away from it like leaf-cutter ants, carrying pieces of metal of all shapes and sizes. Fifty yards away a well-
dressed lady with a feather in her hat squatted to milk a goat.[11]

The overriding problem was the lack of food. In Rome—which was finally
taken by the Allies in June 1944—the daily bread ration under the German occupation had been fixed at a hundred grams, about three thin slices. The Allies
tried to increase this to two hundred grams but had difficulty sustaining even
that low figure. It was not for lack of trying. In June–July 1944, the Allies
shipped 10,000 tons of flour, grain, sugar, olive oil, and soap into Rome alone,
though one in three truckloads wound up on the black market. There were
just too many mouths to feed: the city was swollen with 200,000–300,000
refugees, fleeing the fighting in the north. Allied armies were reluctant to use
valuable military trucks for civilian uses, and so the food problem persisted
throughout the last years of the war. "In these circumstances," wrote the official British historian, "the general enthusiasm with which Rome had welcomed her liberators soon began to wear a little thin; the comment was not
infrequently heard that Rome had been better off under the German occupation."[12]

In fact, life under German occupation in the north was decidedly worse
than life in the south. After the events of the summer of 1943, an Italian resistance emerged, slowly at first, made up of small bands of young men and
women, many on the run from German forced-labor roundups or military
service on behalf of Mussolini's puppet regime. The Italian resistance in the
north was cut off from the south, where the Allies were already installing new
political structures. Instead, the partisan bands slowly developed a political
culture of their own, chiefly under the influence of the Communists, who
styled themselves Garibaldi brigades, and the non-Communist resistance in
the Justice and Liberty group, which soon emerged as the Action Party. These
bands worked together in a loosely coordinated Committee of National
Liberation for Upper Italy (CLNAI), which was based in Milan. It developed

close contacts with the Committee for National Liberation in Naples and then Rome, which was acting as a provisional government. Over the last two years of the war, this resistance grew to include 100,000 partisans.

Their fight was a desperate one, under horrific conditions and savage German reprisals. When a partisan attack on a German troop column in Rome on 23 March 1944 killed thirty-two soldiers, Hitler ordered that the civilians be made to pay at the rate of ten Italians for every German killed. Field Marshal Albert Kesselring, in overall command of this theater, promptly gave the order, and 335 Romans were rounded up, driven to the Ardeatine caves outside the city, and shot. But he did not stop there. In June, Kesselring offered a gruesome pledge to his trained killers: "The fight against the partisans must be carried on with all means at our disposal. I will protect any commander who exceeds our usual restraint in the choice and severity of the methods he adopts against the partisans." This was an open invitation to his junior commanders to commit atrocities, and many obliged. In the early fall of 1944, the SS stormed through northern Italy, killing 360 civilians at Santa Anna di Stazzema in Lucca; 107 civilians at Vallà; 53 in San Terenzo; 108 at Vinca; and so on. On 29 September, two regiments of SS soldiers entered the small town of Marzabotto, near Bologna; 147 people who had taken shelter in the village church were dragged out into the cemetery and shot. The priest was among them. Over the next two days, the Nazis scoured the town and the nearby villages, burning as they went. The final tally was 1,830, including five priests, two nuns, and over a hundred children.[13] In these circumstances, it is not surprising to find that many Italians set aside ideology and banded together in a widespread resistance movement, united by a deep abhorrence of Fascism, both in its German and its Italian manifestations. This experience of occupation, resistance, and war, as historian Paul Ginsborg has noted, "gave rise to a myth of solidarity which was to be as potent and enduring as that of the Blitz in London."[14]

As in France, the story of postwar Italy is one of disappointment over the failure of this wartime unity and idealism to endure into the peace.[15] The resistance, a spontaneous, courageous popular movement in response to foreign occupation, could not compete on the political plane with the older, more savvy parties that emerged as the chief players in Italy at the end of the war. The dominant political force was the Italian Communist Party (PCI), which throughout the war ran a strong underground organization, despite longtime persecution from Mussolini's government, dating back to the 1920s. In fact, such was the strength of the Communists in the north that many landowners and industrialists feared that in the wake of the German departure, the Communists would stage an insurrection, taking power by force. The *grande paura,* or great fear, of 1945, however, was based on an exaggerated assessment of Communist plans. In fact, the strategy of the Communist Party in Italy emerged as moderate to a fault, angering many militants, who believed that the PCI had missed a great chance for a national uprising of the working classes in 1945.

The PCI's moderate strategy was devised by the party's leader, Palmiro Togliatti. One of the founders of the Italian Communist Party in 1921, Togliatti had to leave Italy to avoid arrest. He made his way to Moscow, where in the 1930s he rose to become vice secretary of Stalin's agency for fomenting Communist revolution, the Comintern. He returned to Italy in March 1944, and to the surprise of many in his own rank and file, swiftly declared his intention to back the Allied-sponsored government in the south. This required an oath of allegiance to the king, which he promptly took. Working under Stalin's orders, Togliatti adopted the same strategy taken by Maurice Thorez in France: to ally in a popular front with the democratic parties, assure the liberation of the country, and establish the credibility of the left as a major power broker in the postwar government. This position was also based, as in France, on an honest appraisal of the facts on the ground: the American and British armies occupied the country, and an armed leftist insurrection would trigger a prompt military response. Instead of an insurrection, then, Togliatti prepared his party for the gradual assertion of Communist power through the parliamentary system and the ballot box.[16]

Togliatti had reason to be optimistic about the chances of the PCI to control the fate of postwar Italy. Not only was the resistance largely dominated by the PCI, but the Italian Socialist Party (PSI) under Pietro Nenni offered strong support to the PCI. Unlike the Socialists in France, who kept their distance from their Marxist brethren, Nenni proved a willing ally, and marched in lockstep with the Communists. This lent instant credibility to Togliatti because the PSI was Italy's oldest political organization, with roots stretching back to the days of the nineteenth-century Risorgimento. Further, the calls for wide-reaching reform were championed by the one non-Communist political party that emerged from the resistance, the Action Party, formed chiefly by democratic socialists who wanted to see postwar Italy completely restructured in the wake of the Fascist experience.

The chief political rival of the left was the Christian Democratic Party. It was founded in July 1943, mostly by anti-Fascist Catholics who had been part of the prewar Partito Popolare, disbanded by Mussolini in 1926. It was both overtly Catholic and deeply anti-Communist. Its leader, the man who would dominate Italian politics until 1953, was Alcide De Gasperi. Sixty-two years old in 1943, he had been the last leader of the Partito Popolare. He was born in the Trentino before the First World War, when that region had been under Austro-Hungarian control, and attended the University of Vienna. He served between 1911 and 1918 in the Austrian parliament. After the war, when the Trentino reverted to Italy, De Gasperi joined the Partito Popolare and was elected to parliament in 1921. His reputation as a strong anti-Fascist led to his arrest in 1927, and after a two-year prison term he took shelter under the protective arm of the Vatican, working in its library for the duration of the war. Because it did not participate in the resistance, his party could not have mounted an effective challenge to the Communists had it not been for the open support of the strongly anti-Communist Pope Pius XII. In the summer of 1944, the pope urged the 2 million–strong lay Catholic organization Azione Cattolica (Catholic Action) to support the newborn Christian Democrats, and instructed parish clergymen to speak out on behalf of De Gasperi's party. As historian Paul Ginsborg has noted, this transformed the political status of the party: "In a country where so much of the popular culture and belief was indissolubly linked with the Catholic church, the Vatican's overt espousal of the Christian Democrat cause contributed enormously to De Gasperi's eventual primacy in Italian politics."[17]

In the spring of 1945, the Allies, with considerable help from the partisans under the CLNAI, liberated the north and pushed the Germans out of the country. The CLNAI now laid claim to the fruits of the heroic struggle against the German occupiers and demanded a leadership position in the first postwar government. More radical than the CLN in Milan, with which it had tenuous and strained relations, the CLNAI thought of itself as a revolutionary political force, the *vento del nord* (wind from the north) that would sweep away the stuffy political atmosphere of Rome, clarify the goals of the reconstruction period, and energize the masses.

In June 1945, in recognition of the role of the CLNAI in the armed struggle, the CLN named Ferruccio Parri, the head of the Action Party and former supreme chief of the partisan forces, as leader of the provisional government. Though not a Communist, Parri was a renowned and respected partisan leader who garnered wide support from many political parties. Yet he had no experience in running a government, especially at a time when the common enemy that had cemented the resistance was no longer present and all the parties were scrambling for power. The dependence of Parri upon the major parties was signaled by his distribution of posts. The Socialist leader, Nenni, became vice premier; De Gasperi became minister of foreign affairs; and Togliatti was given the Justice Ministry: a careful balancing act that insured stalemate. In an atmosphere characterized by chaos, hunger, retribution, strikes, inflation, and political division, the Parri government proved unable to cope. The state had too little authority to impose itself on the hundreds of thousands of armed, angry, and possibly insurrectionist partisans, POWs, and refugees wandering across the countryside and into the big northern cities. Leading elites began to call for a show of force by the government and a re-assertion of state control. Instead, Parri found himself without the means to control the country, with a weak police force and no mandate to push serious reform. His proposals for an income tax and a widening of the purge of the civil service, for example, were quashed by the Christian Democrats. The gov-ernment, attacked from all sides for its failure to improve the situation, fell on 24 November 1945. This marked the end of the "resistance era" in Italian pol-itics. From now on the wind from the north became a weak and ineffectual current, unable to blow away the old forms of government.

The parallels with France are illuminating. In both cases a leading resis-tance figure, claiming to represent the interests of the state above party poli-tics, formed the first postwar government and found that the political parties merely used him as a cover to pursue partisan ends. Both Parri and de Gaulle therefore resigned (within two months of each other), both decrying the role of the parties. Of course, Parri was a man of the left and de Gaulle of the right. But the effect was the same: their departures signaled an end to the political unity and possibilities of the war years. The resistance was finished as a polit-ical force in both countries by the end of 1945. Indeed, most of the men who dominated politics in both countries in the postwar decade—Robert Schuman, Antoine Pinay, and Henri Queuille in France, and De Gasperi and Togliatti in Italy—were not members of the internal resistance during the war.

On 10 December 1945, Alcide De Gasperi formed his first government. Upon his arrival in power, De Gasperi exploited his close relations with the Anglo-American military authorities. Italy won a $450 million aid package from the UNRRA, while De Gasperi's reputation benefited from the closing down of the Allied Military Government on 31 December. De Gasperi con-solidated his control by replacing resistance appointments with functionaries from the Christian Democratic ranks, including civil servants with experience during the Fascist period; he also ended the purges, leaving Italy with a worse record than France in addressing the legacy of the Fascist years. (In fact, the PCI supported De Gasperi here; the amnesty of June 1946 was promulgated by Justice Minister Palmiro Togliatti). Despite his conservative program, his forcefulness contrasted with the drift of the Parri government and placed the Christian Democrats in a good position for the national elections of 2 June 1946. This was the first free national election since 1924, and the first in which women voted.

In this initial test of the new party, De Gasperi won a major victory. The

Christian Democrats garnered the support of industrial and agricultural elites, white-collar workers, the middle class, small businessmen, state employees, and the rural poor in the south. It was not lost on left-wing observers that these had also been Mussolini's strongest supporters. As in France, the party won strong support from women, who accepted the argument that the damage to family order and tradition wrought by the war had now to be repaired. Stressing anti-Communism, family values, and a restoration of a liberal economy, the Christian Democrats emerged as Italy's largest party, winning 35 percent of the vote. The Socialists took 20 percent, and the Communists 19. (Simultaneously, the electorate voted by 54 to 45 percent to abolish the monarchy.) Yet this was by no means a guarantee of Christian Democratic preeminence. In October 1946, the Socialists renewed their "unity of action" pact with the Communists. Unlike their French brethren, the Italian Socialists sought to create a single working-class party. Together, the two parties commanded 219 seats in the assembly—more than the Christian Democrats' 207. The coalition that emerged in July 1946 under De Gasperi incorporated the three large parties in an uneasy and tenuous alliance.

Between the summer of 1946 and the expulsion of the Communists from De Gasperi's government in May 1947, Italy drifted, a victim of the inability of the leading parties in the coalition to agree on a common strategy for reconstruction. The government's economic policy was characterized by a laissez-faire approach, under the guidance of Treasury Minister Epicarmo Corbino, an old-school liberal who wanted to remove the state from the workings of the economy. In part, this was a reaction against the heavy-handed role of the state in the economy during the Fascist period, but Corbino's policies also appealed to the industrialists, who were pleased to avoid the wave of nationalizations evident in Britain and France. Instead, they were encouraged to get exports going again, and the state did everything it could to help by keeping wages low and tightening the money supply in order to avoid inflation and so make Italian exports affordable. These policies were undertaken without US pressure, and in some cases against the advice of American technical experts. Well before the advent of the Marshall Plan, Italy became a bastion of laissez-faire economics. By contrast, the Communists pressed for substantial increases in wages and in the money supply, and a larger role for the state in administering the economy and providing jobs. These were demands that, as we have seen, had been adopted with widespread consensus in Britain and France. In Italy, however, Corbino's approach was uncompromising, and may in fact have been designed deliberately to trigger a crisis in the governing coalition. It worked. The Communists launched personal attacks on Corbino in the press. In September 1946, Corbino responded by publicly declaring that

Italy was in the midst of a battle between the forces of reconstruction and the forces of chaos, and that it was time for a confrontation with the Communists.[18]

Prime Minister De Gasperi, according to the chargé d'affaires at the US embassy in Rome, "sympathized wholeheartedly with Corbino's desire to have a showdown with the Communists." The time was not yet ripe—Italy was still negotiating a final peace treaty at the Council of Foreign Ministers, and De Gasperi did not want to antagonize the Russians—but he did feel that there was no way to reach a long-term agreement with the Communists in the government. De Gasperi therefore remained at the helm of a government torn by internal dissension, unable to solve the economic crisis. Frequent strikes and demonstrations broke out in the fall. In October 1946, 20,000–30,000 people tried to storm the Interior Ministry in Rome in protest against job layoffs. The police fired into the crowd, killing two and injuring 119. In November, De Gasperi feared that a wheat shortage would force him to cut the bread ration further, with disastrous political consequences. In local elections in November, the Christian Democrats suffered serious losses, as many of their right-wing supporters deserted them for smaller parties that refused any cooperation with the Communists. The Vatican now began to put pressure on De Gasperi to break definitively with the PCI and the Socialists.[19]

De Gasperi faced a difficult choice. If he expelled the left-wing ministers from his coalition and replaced them with men from the right, he would certainly face a major outburst of public disorder that could lead to open revolt in the country. It would antagonize the Soviets, and De Gasperi seriously feared the possibility of an armed Yugoslav intervention in the north. On the other hand, if he delayed a clean break, his support on the right and from the Vatican would continue to weaken; the center-right would then fracture, and the united left might take power legally. The only way De Gasperi would take the risk of an open rupture with the left was with greater American economic support. In January 1947, his government began a major campaign to win it.

In the first week of that month, De Gasperi visited the United States, in a carefully choreographed public relations campaign designed to demonstrate US support for the prime minister and his country. In visits to Washington, New York, and Cleveland, De Gasperi met with politicians, Catholic Church officials, and the leaders of the Italian-American community. Behind the scenes, he and his team pleaded for more aid, especially increased supplies of wheat and coal. He also urged the US government to approve a $100 million loan from the Export-Import Bank, which had been proposed months earlier but had not yet been approved. This loan, the Italians explained, "had attained very great significance in Italy," and De Gasperi's position "would be seriously jeopardized if he should return to Italy without a loan." Secretary of State Byrnes was sympathetic and told De Gasperi that he thought "that the greatest political pressure was being brought to bear at this time by the Communist Party to bring Italy within the orbit of Russian influence." After two weeks of negotiations, De Gasperi returned home to announce the approval of the $100 million loan. Italy, a defeated Fascist state just two years earlier, was now an American ally.[20]

Events moved quickly in the spring of 1947. De Gasperi arrived home to find that one of his coalition partners, the Socialist Party, had split apart: a moderate minority under Giuseppe Saragat seceded and formed a new Social Democratic Party. This served De Gasperi well: the left was now smaller and, shorn of its moderate members, could more easily be tarnished by its loyalty to Moscow. In February, the crisis over Turkey and Greece roused the American government to assert its strategic interest in the Mediterranean, and in early March the Truman Doctrine announced a major new financial commitment to countries that were fighting Communist subversion. This allowed the Italian government to argue that its own problems were as grave as those of Greece and Turkey and that it needed more aid to insure stability. The Communists played into De Gasperi's hands. On 11 March, Togliatti announced in the assembly that his party might have to take "direct action" to protect the interests of the working class. The breakaway Socialists meanwhile reported that their members had been the subject of intense abuse and intimidation from roving bands of "Red Squadristi." These moves thoroughly alarmed the State Department. On 25 April, Acting Secretary of State Dean Acheson told the US embassy in Rome that he was now considering a long-run stabilization plan for Italy that would go well beyond the piecemeal approach of UNRRA and the Export-Import Bank loan.[21]

Both the US government and De Gasperi had reached the conclusion that it was time to face the Communist challenge head-on. US ambassador James C. Dunn told the State Department that as long as the Communists remained in the government there could be no prospects for stability in Italy. Dunn urged Marshall to make a strong statement of support for De Gasperi's government. At the same time, De Gasperi met discreetly with Dunn to ask about the prospect of future American aid in light of a reshuffling of the cabinet. Dunn made no direct guarantees. He said that the United States was "deeply interested in the Italian situation" but that the Italians themselves had to "put their house in order" before further aid could be guaranteed. Here was an open hint of American aid following an expulsion of the Communists from the government. On 12 May, De Gasperi resigned, triggering the political showdown he had expected for over a year.[22]

Was there a quid pro quo between the United States government and De Gasperi, promising American aid in exchange for the expulsion of the Communists from the government? The Italian left has always assumed so, and while there is no direct evidence of a specific deal, it is clear that since his visit in January to the United States, De Gasperi was working to deepen Italo-American relations, secure more aid, and win a strong US declaration of support for the anti-Communist parties in Italy. Certainly, the actions of the Italian ambassador, Alberto Tarchiani, left no doubt about his aims. A long-time anti-Fascist and a founder in the 1920s of the anti-Mussolini group Justice and Liberty, Tarchiani was strongly anti-Communist and kept up steady pressure on US State Department officials for more aid, placing Italy's problems squarely in a Cold War context. While De Gasperi schemed to form a government without the Communists, Tarchiani begged Marshall for more US aid, arguing that without it, De Gasperi would fail in his efforts, "and a period of uncertainty and disorganization will ensue with eventual Communist success and tragic effects on Italy." Tarchiani relayed De Gasperi's direct appeal: could he "count on the moral support of the United States and on additional financial help to enable Italy to meet its financial necessities this year if he undertook to head a new government"? Back in Rome De Gasperi told Dunn he needed "new and substantial evidence of economic aid" if his efforts to govern without the left were to succeed. Dunn's report to the State Department makes the degree of US-Italian collusion clear: De Gasperi "said that if he had this new substantial support he was ready to take up the battle against the parties of the extreme left."

The Americans reacted swiftly. On 20 May, Secretary Marshall informed De Gasperi that the United States would make a strong public pledge of support for his government, would undertake new commercial and trade agreements, and would mobilize "every source" of available economic assistance. Ten days later, De Gasperi formed a one-party government. For the first time since the liberation, the PCI was not in power, and De Gasperi had to rely on the votes in the assembly of the far right, neo-Fascist, and monarchist parties. Just six days later, the United States did more than offer additional aid to Italy. Speaking to the graduating class of Harvard University on 5 June 1947, George Marshall announced a major new initiative for the coordinated recovery of the European economy, to be funded by the United States.[23]

Two things emerge from this political crisis. The American records make clear that the Italians, like the French and the West Germans, had learned a valuable lesson by the middle of 1947: the threat of Communism worked to galvanize American action and win economic aid. At the same time, however, this was not empty rhetoric on the Italians' part. It is apparent that the United

States did not play the dominant role in bringing about a break with the Communists: De Gasperi did. It was an Italian leader, backed by his own deeply anti-Communist party, who sought to break what he saw as an unnatural coalition with the secular, Marxist, and revolutionary PCI. The Cold War was not imposed upon unwilling Italians by an imperialist America. The Italians quite willingly brought it on themselves.

FRANCE AND ITALY BETWEEN COMINFORM AND CIA: MAY 1947–APRIL 1948

Of course, that is not how the Soviet Union saw it. The sharp response over the Greek and Turkish crises in late 1946 had been followed in March 1947 by the bellicose Truman Doctrine. In May, in what appeared to be a coordinated assault on the left in Italy and France, the Communist ministers in both countries had been dismissed from their posts. Three weeks later, in early June 1947, Secretary Marshall announced a plan for American aid to Europe, and then insisted that aid recipients must open their accounting books to US officials. The Soviets read these actions as deliberately aggressive, part of a broad campaign on the part of the United States to consolidate its hold on Western Europe but also to weaken Soviet influence in the East as well.[24]

As of early 1947, the Communists in Eastern Europe had not fully consolidated their control of national governments. For Stalin, the Marshall Plan came at a moment of turmoil and vulnerability within the Eastern bloc. In Poland, considerable resistance emerged in response to the seizure of power by the Soviet-backed Polish Workers' Party, and it was only with massive intimidation, vote fraud, and persecution that the Communists secured their hold on the government by February 1947. In Hungary, a vote in November 1945 gave the Communists only 17 percent, whereas the centrist Smallholders Party had won 57 percent. It was not until May 1947 that the Communists, who controlled the secret police, managed to pressure the non-Communist parties into leaving office. In Czechoslovakia, with its strong democratic tradition and popular non-Communist president, Edvard Benes, the Communists shared power in a coalition government and by early 1947 had still not consolidated their hold over the country. The Communist leader there, Klement Gottwald, spoke of a "Czech road to socialism," and the government in July 1947 declared its interest in receiving Marshall aid.

At the other end of the spectrum, Yugoslav leader Josip Broz Tito had shown too much comradely ardor. Not only did he swiftly consolidate his own power in Yugoslavia, but he threatened to carry Communist insurrection into

Greece in 1946–47, even after Stalin had decided to give up Greece to the West. Tito also began to plan for a federation with Albania and Bulgaria and set himself up as a rival power center within the Communist movement. The expulsion of the Communists from the coalitions in France and Italy in May, followed so soon by the Marshall announcement, sharpened Stalin's anxiety: the United States, he now believed, had begun an economic and political campaign to weaken Communist control in Europe, both East and West. It was time for concerted action.[25]

Stalin responded to this crisis with swiftness and force. He directed the leaders of eight of Europe's Communist parties (including the French and Italian) to join the Russians at a conference in the Polish spa town of Szklarska Poreba, near the Czech border. Here, from 22 to 28 September, in carefully choreographed meetings, two of Stalin's most loyal deputies, Georgi Malenkov and Andrei Zhdanov, imparted a new line to their European protégés. They dispensed with the language of the wartime alliance, replacing it with a ferocious and unstinting attack on postwar American foreign policy. Zhdanov opened the conference by stating that the world had been divided into camps—one imperialist and antidemocratic, the other anti-imperialist and democratic. The Americans had become "openly expansionist." They were busily rearming the defeated Fascist states of Germany, Italy, and Japan; they were amassing an atomic arsenal; and they were using economic aid to constrain the independence of European states. In this they were aided by willing dupes of the so-called left, like Ernest Bevin and French Socialist leader Léon Blum. The Marshall Plan, declared Zhdanov, was the first stage in "the American plan for the enslavement of Europe." It was aimed directly at the East European states and was a brazen ploy to bribe them into subservience to American dictates. The only way to fend off such blandishments was to unite in a disciplined bloc of anti-imperialist states, bound by "loyal, good-neighborly relations."[26]

No less harsh than Zhdanov's treatment of the United States was the denunciation of the French and Italian Communist Parties. Using as a mouthpiece the Yugoslav delegate Milovan Djilas, the Russians decried the failure of the PCF and PCI to respond with sufficient violence to their expulsion from the government. They had been the victim of a calculated plot to destroy the Communists, yet they had done nothing to challenge the reactionaries. The events of May 1947 showed the entire postwar strategy of cooperation with the bourgeois parties to be a sham. The West European Communists must forget about achieving power through the ballot box. "Parliament is only one of the forms of struggle," declared Djilas. The French and Italians must now prepare for an open assault on the government. Zhdanov agreed. It was time for "a serious reorientation" by the PCF and PCI. The French and Italian delegates knew what this meant. French Communist leader Jacques Duclos declared that his party was "developing forms of struggle that are not parliamentary." His party, he said, would "mobilize the people for the struggle against American imperialism." The Italian delegate also promised "a wave of demonstrations, land-seizures, economic and political strikes," and an effort "to overthrow the De Gasperi government."[27] As a final gesture of solidarity, the delegates agreed to the formation of a new agency, the Communist Information Bureau, or Cominform, to coordinate the offensive against American imperialism.

The creation of the Cominform marked an open declaration of war on American policy in Europe. The results were immediately visible in France. Within six weeks, the PCF organized a wave of strikes across France that crippled the economy and brought the country to a standstill. Of course, there were ample reasons for strikes: inflation was out of control, bread was still being rationed, and the government appeared ineffectual. But the PCF stage-managed an intense outburst of strike activity that lent the work stoppages the flavor of insurrection. The strike wave started in France's second largest city, Marseilles, where most factories and all public services were closed by 11 November. The next day, large crowds stormed the law courts and the town hall, where they beat up the mayor. Storefronts, cafés, and nightclubs were vandalized and looted as 40,000 strikers roamed the streets. A few days later, the miners in the northern part of France followed suit, and the French government called in the army, which cleared the mines of strikers only after firing shots into their ranks. By the middle of the month, 3 million people were on strike across the country. The American ambassador's sources told him that the Communists were working under the direct orders of Moscow. The president of France, Vincent Auriol, feared that if the Communists did not seize power, de Gaulle's right-wing RPF might do so instead. "We are on the edge of the abyss," he confided to his diary.[28]

The situation in Italy, which had been unstable since the spring, also grew worse in the wake of the Cominform meeting. In November, the Communists triggered strikes all across the country, attacked right-wing party headquarters and newspapers, laid siege to police stations, town halls, and prisons. In the first three weeks of the month, twenty-one people were killed in rioting, and several hundred wounded. On 28 November, Communists stormed the prefecture in Milan and ordered a citywide strike. American observers heard rumors that the Communists planned to stage an armed insurrection in northern Italy and possibly call in Yugoslav armed support.[29]

Like the Soviets, Americans now viewed France and Italy together as the chief theater of the Cold War. While the newly established CIA concluded in a September 1947 study that the USSR was "unlikely to resort to military aggression," it nonetheless believed that "the greatest danger to the security of the United States is the possibility of economic collapse in Western Europe and the consequent accession to power of Communistic elements." The Soviets sought to establish hegemony "by political and economic means" and would do so by "conspiratorial rather than by military means." The Americans decided to fight fire with fire. On 17 December 1947, the National Security Council gave the CIA the authority to undertake "covert psychological operations designed to counteract Soviet and Soviet-inspired activities."[30]

In France, American efforts to block Communist activities were significantly aided by elements of the American labor movement, which had been fighting its own battles against Communist subversion of its unions. In Europe, the American Federation of Labor (AFL) channeled financial aid and strategic advice to the non-Communist French unions and strongly urged them to split off from the Communist-dominated Confédération Générale du Travail. On 19 December, non-Communist labor leaders split the CGT and created Force Ouvrière, a non-Communist union. The US ambassador in France called this "the most important event that has occurred in France since the Liberation," for it showed that the Communists could be beaten by the workers themselves.[31] The new union was aided not least by the growing disenchantment with the strikes among the rank and file and the perception that the CGT, once proudly independent, was now under the thumb of Moscow. But US aid helped too. The AFL representatives in Europe, Irving Brown and Jay Lovestone, personally transferred tens of thousands of dollars in mid-1947 to the non-Communist labor movement in France, and promised much more. The State Department gave the AFL's actions its warm support, and probably funded them through the CIA's European network.[32]

In Italy, the US undertook a far greater degree of intervention, organizing an extensive program of economic, military, and political support for De Gasperi. The Truman administration used the strikes as leverage with Congress to pass emergency "interim" economic aid for both France and Italy in December 1947. The US Army planned for the transfer of 50,000 rifles, 5,000 pistols, and 20,000 submachine guns to the Italian armed forces. In February 1948, the National Security Council urged the president to use whatever resources, "and if necessary military power," to prevent Italy "from falling under the domination of the USSR either through external armed attack or through Soviet-dominated Communist movements within Italy."[33]

The elections of 18 April 1948 put American policy in Italy to the test. A Communist victory at the polls, thought US officials, would place Italy under

Moscow's orders and probably wreck the Marshall Plan in the rest of Europe. The United States government, in close cooperation with De Gasperi, intervened heavily in the election campaign. It pressed the Vatican, which needed little encouragement, to declare Communism incompatible with Catholicism. The Vatican in turn urged American Catholic leaders to step up private aid to the Christian Democrats, and as the election neared, Pope Pius XII himself denounced Communism in sharp terms. The church, from the pope down to the parish priests, swung its immense power behind the De Gasperi government. The American government prevailed upon prominent Italian-Americans to generate financial aid for the non-Communist parties; Italian-American press magnate Generoso Pope—the publisher of New York City's *Il Progresso*—headed up a letter-writing campaign through which over a million Americans urged their families and friends back in Italy to oppose Communism. The US government shipped thousands of newsreels to Italy detailing the benefits of American support, and increased Voice of America broadcasts. At the same time, George Marshall, in mid-March 1948, declared that if Italy went Communist, Italians would get no further aid. Alongside these public efforts, the US government channeled significant covert aid to both the Christian Democrats and the breakaway Saragat Socialists. The efforts paid off. On 18 April, the Christian Democrats received 48.5 percent of the vote, while the united Communist-Socialist ticket won only 31 percent— down 9 percent from just two years earlier.[34]

The victory of the right in Italy in 1948 was not won simply by American aid. The Czech coup of February galvanized anti-Communist opinion in Italy, and the intervention of the pope probably weighed far more heavily on the average Italian voter than the US-funded broadsheets of the Christian Democratic Party. Nonetheless, American officials read the election results as a thundering vindication of their tactics in Europe. From now on, publicly touted US economic aid would be accompanied by covert aid in the pursuit of US interests. Indeed, just two months after the election in Italy, the National Security Council approved NSC 10/2, which called for a new program of covert operations to thwart Communism around the globe. The NSC, with the Italian experience clearly in mind, created the Office of Policy Coordination, nominally under CIA control. Reflecting the confidence of the US government in such covert activities, the OPC soon ballooned into a worldwide operation. By 1952 it had a staff of some 6,000 people and a budget of $82 million. The United States concluded that with the right tools, Communism could be defeated in Europe.[35]

FROM BERLIN TO BONN: THE BLOCKADE
AND THE ORIGINS OF WEST GERMANY

Events in France and Italy served to reinforce the American perception that the Soviet Union was on the offensive in Europe. In the Western zones of Germany, still under direct Allied military occupation, the United States and Britain resolved to move quickly in consolidating political and economic institutions that would bind Germany to the West. Secretary of State George Marshall and his successor, Dean Acheson, sought to create facts on the ground that would condition any future talks on German unification. In the first few months of 1948, the American occupation authorities, seconded by the British, laid out the groundwork for a West German government. They expanded the range of responsibilities of German authorities; they slowed the dismantling and decartelization of German industry; and they significantly scaled down the dimensions of the de-Nazification project. In March, the US and British authorities introduced new restrictions on the political activities of the German Communist Party and began a systematic purge of the German bureaucracy and police of all Communists. Having accepted the breakdown of four-power control in Germany, the three Western occupation powers called a conference in London to plan for the creation of a West German government in the three Western zones. The conference opened on 24 February 1948, just as events in Prague were reaching a climax. Nothing could have served American purposes better, for now even the once reluctant French could see that the Russians were a far greater threat to Europe's security than a much weakened and constrained Germany.[36]

In March and April, while the conferees in London outlined a comprehensive German settlement for the Western zones, the Soviets showed their displeasure at being excluded by tightening their hold on the city of Berlin. The capital, it must be recalled, lay 110 miles deep in the Soviet zone. Though the city, like Germany, had been divided into four occupation zones, Western access to the city was at the forbearance of Soviet authorities. In the spring, Soviet interference with rail and road traffic into the city increased. General Clay, the head of the American occupation authority, cabled his superiors in Washington with dire prognostications. "For many months," he wrote on 5 March, "based on logical analysis, I have felt and held that war was unlikely for at least ten years. Within the last few weeks, I have felt a subtle change in [the] Soviet attitude which I cannot define but which now gives me a feeling it may come with dramatic suddenness."[37] Just at the moment when American officials feared a Soviet subversion of Italy, this was strong stuff. It triggered a sudden war scare in Washington and led the Americans to press all the faster to shore up the German state.[38]

With Soviet intimidation in Berlin as a backdrop, the three Western powers worked feverishly in London to frame the institutions of a new German state. In June 1948, they released their plan. They would allow the Germans to call a Parliamentary Council, which would devise a new German constitution, albeit under Western guidance. To appease France, the occupiers declared that the powerful industries of the Ruhr would be placed under an international authority that would monitor production of coal and manufacturing of steel, and insure strict German compliance with all disarmament requirements. Although the Germans pretended to object to these conditions on their sovereignty—both the Christian Democratic and the Social Democratic leadership denounced the London agreements—they were in fact delighted at the prospect of regaining real autonomy in their own political affairs. The London agreements, everyone knew, marked the start of a new West German state. As a crowning gesture, General Clay announced on 18 June 1948 the introduction of a new currency, the deutsche mark. America was declaring Germany's independence of Soviet control.

This move provoked a swift Soviet response. On 24 June the Russians cut electricity to the Western zones of Berlin and blocked all rail, canal, automobile, and pedestrian traffic into and out of the city. Berlin and its 2.5 million people were being held hostage. What did the Russians hope to gain by this assertion of strength? Clearly, they did not want war with the United States. But the formation of a West German government was a direct provocation, and was read by the Russians as part of a new US campaign of militarism in Europe, designed to shore up the bases of Western strength in Germany for an eventual assault on Soviet-held territory. Berlin was an obvious lever to use to respond to Western initiatives. It was a canker in the Soviet zone, an annoying aberration, and a reminder of the Russian failure to complete their consolidation of power in Eastern Germany. Stalin in January 1948 told Yugoslav Communist Milovan Djilas that "the West will make West Germany their own and we shall turn Eastern Germany into our own state."[39] But that meant getting the Western powers out of Berlin. Stalin, perhaps due to faulty intelligence that underestimated Western resolve, believed that the right amount of pressure might get the Western powers to abandon Berlin.[40]

This proved a major misunderstanding of Western thinking, which by June 1948 had hardened into an implacable hostility toward Soviet actions. The Anglo-American response was swift and clear. Although the precise means to defend Berlin was as yet unclear, President Truman and Foreign Minister Ernest Bevin were both determined that they must remain in Berlin at all costs. On 26 June, Bevin told the press that "we intend to stay in Berlin," and he secretly asked the Americans to send a fleet of B-29s, capable of carrying atomic bombs, to Britain to demonstrate this commitment to the Russians. (The planes were sent—without their atomic payload—in July.) The same day, President Truman—in a move that was never anticipated by the Russians—ordered a massive airlift to supply the city until a solution to the problem could be resolved. This was a temporary expedient; little did he know that the airlift would last for nearly a year, until May 1949.[41]

The airlift itself was a masterpiece of logistics and courage. Berlin needed 2,000 tons of foodstuffs a day—flour, cereals, meat and fish, potatoes, sugar, coffee, milk, fats and oils—to survive. One American C-47 could only carry 2.5 tons. How could Berlin be saved? And what about raw materials like coal, oil, and gasoline that fueled the city's gasworks, sewer plants, and factories and heated homes? Power stations alone needed 1,650 tons of coal a day to produce electricity. Worse, Allied aircraft were restricted to flying into Berlin on three narrow bands just twenty miles wide, over Russian-held territory. Tempelhof Airport was smack in the middle of the city, among tall blocks of apartments, and frequently fog-bound. There were not nearly enough pilots, air traffic controllers, mechanics, and personnel to handle the massive influx of aircraft. On 26 June, the first day of the airlift, C-47s and RAF Dakotas managed to bring just eighty tons of food into the city. At that rate, Berlin would soon starve.

But with astonishing speed, the airlift picked up steam. Ground crews worked regular sixteen-hour shifts, and sometimes stretched to twenty-four. Airmen, when they were not flying, slept in hastily built Nissen huts on airfields in a deafening roar of aircraft engines. The US Air Force and the RAF scrambled to get every available plane into action. On 8 July, 1,117 tons of supplies reached Berlin, and by mid-July a steady stream of fifteen hundred tons was reaching Berlin daily. The figures rose throughout the summer as the Americans brought in larger aircraft, the C-54, which could carry ten tons, and the airlift procedures were formalized.

Perhaps even greater than the material resources supplied by the airlift was its morale-boosting impact. Just three years earlier, American and British aircraft had rained down tons of lethal bombs on the German people; now they were risking war to supply the captive city with daily bread, milk, coal, and basic supplies. Further, the blockade allowed Germans to feel that they were now on the side of liberty. The popular socialist mayor of Berlin, Ernst Reuter, declared to a packed stadium of 50,000 Berliners on the day the blockade began that "we shall apply all the means at our disposal and repel to our utmost the claim to power which wants to turn us into slaves and helots for a political party. We lived under such slavery in Adolf Hitler's empire. We have had enough of that."[42] On 9 September, some 300,000 Berliners staged a giant rally at the Reichstag to protest Soviet restrictions, and a handful of youths climbed to the top of the Brandenburg Gate and tore down the Soviet flag.

In the end, US and British aircraft delivered 2.3 million tons of food, fuel, and supplies into Berlin. In April 1949, the month before the end of the block-ade, 7,845 tons reached Berlin—a figure unimaginable in the difficult days of July 1948.[43] Seventy-three Allied airmen were killed during the airlift, and five Germans. The blockade marked a new era for German-American relations and created a groundswell of favorable public reaction toward the Western powers that had been sorely lacking since the end of the war. In the meantime, the Russians, anxious to avoid an open conflict, did nothing to interfere with the airlift—refraining even from jamming radar, for example. Instead they watched glumly as public opinion swung increasingly against the Soviet pres-ence in Eastern Germany, while Ernst Reuter, General Clay, and President Truman took on the mantle of saviors of the West. For the Russians, the air-lift was a propaganda and diplomatic fiasco. After a year, Stalin had had enough and finally ended the blockade on 12 May 1949. He did so in exchange for a Western agreement to reopen discussions in the Council of Foreign Ministers on Germany's status. This meeting, held in Paris during June 1949, produced no agreement and revealed that all the parties had taken firm and inflexible positions on the division of Germany.[44]

In the meantime, the blockade had galvanized opinion in the West and in Germany itself. The NATO alliance, only a gleam in Ernest Bevin's eye at the start of 1948, was born in April 1949. Many Europeans, once reluctant, now embraced the American military presence in Europe and welcomed the US commitment to defend Europe from Russian attack. The Berlin blockade sig-nificantly contributed to this Western solidarity. For the West Germans them-selves, many of whom felt reluctant about taking the first step toward statehood and thereby formally dividing the country, the blockade steeled their courage. On 1 September 1948, in its first meeting in the sleepy provin-cial town of Bonn, the Parliamentary Council elected Konrad Adenauer as its president and began the laborious task of crafting a constitution for the new state. On 23 May 1949, this document went into force as the founding docu-ment of the Federal Republic of Germany. A new West German state was born. In August 1949, the Germans held national elections, and the Christian Democrats won 7.36 million votes, nudging out the Social Democrats, who won 6.93 million. On 15 September 1949, the new German Bundestag, meet-ing in the new capital city of Bonn, elected Konrad Adenauer as federal chan-cellor.

Little known in 1949, Adenauer became, after Adolf Hitler, the most important German of the twentieth century. He was born in 1876 in Cologne, the capital city of the Rhineland. He made his career in the Catholic Center Party, and rose to become mayor of Cologne in 1917. He served as mayor during the tumultuous days of the Allied occupation after the First World War, when France and Britain maintained soldiers along the Rhine to insure against renewed German militarism. It was sometimes said in this period that Adenauer favored the detachment of the Catholic Rhineland from the eastern, Prussian-dominated, Protestant Germany. As mayor he opposed the Nazis, refusing to fly the swastika flag when the newly appointed chancellor, Adolf Hitler, came through Cologne in February 1933. Adenauer was swiftly run out of his job and fled Cologne, spending the war years in quiet though anxious retirement. (He was twice arrested under the Third Reich, in 1934 and 1944.) At war's end, his conservative, anti-Nazi, Catholic credentials made him a natural leader of the reborn Catholic party, now to be called the Christian Democratic Union (CDU). Yet he also had personal qualities that made him successful. Like his contemporary and later friend Charles de Gaulle, he was immensely egotistical, proud, headstrong, and deeply patriotic. Aware of the limitations of his position as a politician in an occupied country, he also understood how to turn the occupation to Germany's advantage. He insisted on following the American lead in building up close ties to Germany's old nemesis, France; he pursued a free market approach to economic policy; and he was willing to acquiesce in a divided Germany provided that the Western powers accepted their responsibility of defending Germany from Soviet pressure.

These policies were not universally praised in Germany. Many citizens resisted the division of their country and disliked Adenauer's pro-Western, free market policies. His formidable political enemy, the socialist leader Kurt Schumacher, once derisively called him "the chancellor of the Allies." It was taken as an insult, but in fact, Adenauer's chief legacy was the bond he built between the Federal Republic and the West, at a time when this policy was considered by many on the left to be a betrayal of Germany's independence, unnecessarily provocative to the Russians, and destined to drag out the division of the country. But Adenauer, like his Italian and French counterparts in the Christian Democratic parties that now dominated European politics, believed that a close relationship with the United States did not threaten Europe's autonomy. It would, on the contrary, promote it, by offering security, stability, and the opportunity for prosperity—all things that a war-weary, hungry, deprived, and battered Europe had every right to expect.

CHAPTER FOUR

BEHIND THE IRON CURTAIN:
COMMUNISM IN POWER,
1945–1953

.

ON 10 MARCH 1948, the shattered, lifeless body of Czechoslovak foreign minister Jan Masaryk was discovered on the pavement below his bedroom window. To this day it is unknown whether Masaryk, the son of the country's founder and at the time the only non-Communist member of the Czechoslovak government, was murdered or took his own life. The Communist-controlled Interior Ministry declared it a suicide and closed the books on the case. Masaryk's demise quickly became an apt metaphor for the violent death of democracy in Eastern Europe as a whole. Was it a case of murder or suicide?

Writing in 1951, the English historian Hugh Seton-Watson argued that the seizure of power by Communist parties after 1945 followed a three-stage process. First, Communist and non-Communist parties established genuine coalitions, converging on a common short-term program of reform and reconstruction. In this stage, the Soviets tolerated and indeed encouraged such pluralism in order to demonstrate to their Western Allies their commitment to democracy, but at the same time the Soviet authorities and the Red Army worked diligently to place Communist Party members in positions of influence throughout the bureaucracy, the police, and the army, and deeply penetrated the non-Communist opposition. In the second stage, with Communists in control of the levers of power, these coalitions were broken up. Non-Communist opposition parties were intimidated, their newspapers closed, their members arrested, their meetings broken up by bands of Communist thugs. In Poland this began as early as 1945; in Hungary this started in 1947, and in Czechoslovakia in 1948. Finally, in the third stage, the Communists would declare the formation of a united front of working-class parties, ban the opposition, and totally crush any dissident activity. A basically Stalinist and totalitarian model was now imposed. This stage was reached in Yugoslavia in 1945 but usually did not appear until late 1948 in the rest of the region.[1]

Seton-Watson's analysis, which was subsequently supported and extended by leading Western scholars, lent academic authority to the emerging view among political leaders in the West that the Soviet Union followed a single blueprint to create a series of client regimes in their sphere of influence.[2] Scholars today still acknowledge the overriding importance of the Soviet Union, its army, and the secret police in determining the political outcome in Eastern Europe. But we also know more about the degree of complicity of the East European Communists themselves in forcing their countries down the tragic path toward totalitarian rule. Rather than focus simply on the actions of the Russians, who naturally sought to create friendly and in fact subservient regimes in the East, we can now incorporate the motives, ideas, and behavior of local Communists into a broad picture of the early postwar years.

Before we consider national cases, however, it is critical to recall the devastating impact of the Second World War on this region, especially in its social and political dimensions, for here lies the prerequisite to the swift establishment of Communist rule. In the West, the domination by Communists of the resistance enhanced their political appeal and legitimized their claim to power in postwar coalitions. In the East, however, with the significant exception of Yugoslavia, the Communists were not the leading source of resistance to the German occupation. In the interwar years, Communists had been ruthlessly persecuted in Eastern Europe, where many states maintained deep anti-Soviet attitudes. In Poland, in fact, the massive underground state and army that emerged during the war was anti-Communist and became more so as the war neared its conclusion. In Czechoslovakia there was only a modest underground; and Hungary, Bulgaria, and Romania were dominated by authoritarian, anti-Communist, anti-Semitic regimes that led them to ally with the Axis powers. Unlike Western Europe, then, in the East Communism had no traditional base on which to stand in the postwar period. That would have to be created artificially in the wake of the war.

In this effort, the Communists were aided by the transformations in social and political structures wrought by the war. Whether occupied by the Germans (like Poland, Yugoslavia, and Czechoslovakia—or in Albania's case, by Italy), or allied with the Axis in a firm and dependent embrace, like Hungary, Romania, and Bulgaria, the states of Eastern Europe were violently and harshly treated by six years of war and exploitation. As historian Jan T. Gross has outlined in an important essay, there are many ways in which the Second World War opened the way to a rapid seizure of power by the Communists after the war. Perhaps most striking was the effect of the dramatic population losses: in Poland, for example, 6 million people were killed during the war—3 million of them Jews exterminated by the Nazis. After the war, some 7 million or so Germans were expelled from East Prussia, Pomerania, and Silesia—territory incorporated into the new borders of Poland. Both the Jews and the ethnic Germans had formed a large part of the urban merchant class and intelligentsia, and their loss opened up new avenues of social mobility that Communists could use to promote their partisans. Another legacy of the German occupation was economic. German exploitation of the economies of Eastern Europe sped up industrialization and enhanced the power and authority of the state to direct the economy. Finally, the war worked to break down civil society—the network of community, civic, and religious institutions that knit the largely rural communities of Eastern Europe together. In the midst of chaos, confusion, and refugee flows, the only plausible source of authority—however compromised—was the central state bureaucracy. War therefore served to strengthen the role and widen the responsibilities of the state, a fact that the Communists were only too happy to exploit.[3]

These are general patterns, however, and we must consider each country on its own terms. In particular, we must avoid the temptation to assume that the Communist success in Eastern Europe was in some way inevitable. It was not. Rather, it was the result of a series of choices made by the Russians and their European proxies to seize power through an often violent subversion of democracy. The deck was, of course, stacked in favor of the Communists. But Communism came to power not simply because the Russians insisted on it. In each of the four cases examined here—Poland, Hungary, Czechoslovakia, and Yugoslavia—European Communists themselves engaged in an ideological and social revolution that had deep local roots and was based on significant support among the people. As with Masaryk, the death of democracy in Eastern Europe involved both murder and suicide.

MASTERS OF THE HOUSE: POLAND, 1943–1947

If there was any country toward which Stalin's postwar plans were clear, it was Poland. Having annexed half the country in 1939, in connivance with Hitler, Stalin made it clear throughout the war that he intended to keep his spoils of war. He never budged from this position. Moreover, the only kind of Polish government that he would allow to be created after the war was one that accepted this annexation, that played a role as a buffer state against Germany, and that was obedient to Soviet leadership. For Stalin, Poland could have no future independent of the Soviet Union. Despite these strong and consistent views on the Polish question, the establishment of Communism in Poland was a messy affair. There were three complicating factors: the Polish government in exile, based in London, was violently anti-Russian and unwilling to compromise with Moscow. The Western Allies themselves, though quite willing to acknowledge Russia's dominant position in Poland, still held out for at least the trappings of democracy and constantly badgered Stalin about Poland. And finally, the massive underground military organization called the Home Army, created to fight the Germans, came to view the Russians as an equal menace. Loosely under the London regime's orders but capable of acting alone, the Home Army presented the most serious threat to Stalin's plans for a Communist triumph in Poland. Once Stalin had rid himself of these problems, he still faced the fact that Communism was unpopular in Poland, which meant that only the use of force would keep Poland in his grasp.[4]

The London-based government in exile, since July 1943 led by Peasant Party leader Stanislaw Mikolajczyk, had little power when faced with the Red Army and the determination of Stalin to create a Communist Poland. Stalin sought to isolate and then ignore these exiles, and he used a cynical pretext to break off relations with them. In April 1943, the German army announced that it had discovered a mass grave of forty-four hundred Polish officers in the Katyn Forest, near the recently captured Russian city of Smolensk. The Germans suggested that the men had been murdered by the Soviets. Indeed, their whereabouts had been unknown since their capture, along with 11,600 other officers and 180,000 soldiers, by the Russians during the 1939 invasion of Poland. The Poles in London called on the International Red Cross to investigate, whereupon Stalin severed relations with the London Poles, claiming that the Germans had done the dirty deed and that the Poles had defamed the Soviet Union. (It was not until 1990 that the Russians acknowledged that the Soviet secret police, the NKVD, had indeed murdered the 15,000 Polish officers; Stalin wished to crush any possible Polish resistance to the Soviet occupation of the eastern part of the country.) By cutting off relations with the London Poles, Stalin could now proceed to create a rival, and more pliable, Polish government on his own terms.[5]

His path was made considerably easier by the Allies. Both Winston Churchill and Franklin Roosevelt sympathized with the Poles, who they saw as gallant and rather tragic, but Churchill especially felt that they were too unwilling to compromise and that they antagonized the one nation in Europe, the USSR, that seemed to be able to defeat the Germans in pitched battle. Churchill did not wish to damage Allied relations over Poland. As early as December 1943, at the Tehran Conference, Churchill expressed to Stalin his satisfaction with the idea of moving Poland westward and creating a government there that was "friendly to Russia." He said he "was not prepared to squawk" about the Russo-Polish frontier. As a result of these assurances, Stalin told the Polish Communists that "the alliance will not break up over Poland" and that the process of consolidating Communist power there could go ahead unchecked.[6]

But Stalin's real problem lay in Poland itself. For since 1939, a massive Polish underground—virtually a separate state—had emerged in response to the dual German-Soviet occupation. That occupation was unspeakable in its severity: in both German- and Soviet-occupied Poland, Poles suffered a reign of terror, the mass destruction of their cultural, civic, and religious institutions, the dispossession of their property, forced emigration and resettlement, and the imposition of foreign ideologies and political rule. The Germans, of course, undertook a systematic destruction of Polish Jewry in their half of Poland and then extended this assault eastward after their invasion of the Soviet Union in June 1941. In response, Poles undertook to create a parallel underground state, complete with universities, a massive underground press and publishing apparatus, religious and civic institutions. The key to this underground was, however, the Home Army, which eventually grew to include some 350,000 partisans as well as experienced officers and recruits from the Polish army. Despite communication difficulties, the Home Army, under the leadership of Gen. Tadeusz "Bor" Komorowski, was in close touch with the London Poles.[7]

In order to take on this formidable underground apparatus, Stalin needed to create a rival source of power within Poland. After the German invasion of the Soviet Union, the Russians gathered together in Moscow a band of Polish Communists, which they formed into an "initiative group" and parachuted into Poland in December 1941. In conjunction with Communists already in Poland, they then formed the Polish Workers' Party.[8] The Communists banded together in underground and partisan units designed to rival the Home Army, and in December 1943 they declared the formation of the National Council for the Homeland, a Communist front organization that claimed to be the sole representative of the Polish people. In addition to these Communist political structures, the Russians created a rival Polish army under their control, staffed by the many Poles in the Soviet Union who willingly wished to help defeat the Germans. Under the direction of Gen. Zygmunt Berling, this force eventually attained a strength of six divisions and saw action in Ukraine and Belorussia. On 22 July 1944, as Russian forces, along with Berling's troops, crossed the new Russo-Polish border, the National Council announced the creation of the Polish Committee of National Liberation, quartered in Lublin. All of the committee's fifteen members were Communists or sympathizers. This committee immediately recognized Soviet claims to the eastern lands of Poland the Russians had occupied in 1939; in return, the Soviets transferred administrative authority to this committee, and the committee carried out land reform and nationalization, and began to publish newspapers and propaganda. On 31 December 1944, the committee declared itself the provisional government of Poland and won instant Soviet recognition.

Of course, all of these actions alarmed the Home Army and the London government, but without strong support from the Western Allies, their chances of turning back the Communists were limited. Still, they tried. From the fall of 1943, the Home Army engaged in a war on two fronts, against the Germans and the Russians. In November 1943, the Home Army issued plans for an uprising in the wake of the German withdrawal, designed to forestall a Soviet occupation. Operation Tempest, as it was called, did inflict damage on the retreating Germans, but led to a massive disaster in Warsaw in August 1944. General Komorowski believed that the Home Army had to capture Warsaw if it was to stand a chance in asserting Polish autonomy against the Russians. If Poles could liberate their capital, much as Frenchmen liberated Paris in the same month, their struggle would gain legitimacy and world attention. Komorowski anticipated that the advancing Red Army, then a few miles away from Warsaw, would in any case chase off the Germans, and the sovereign Poles would greet the Russians upon their arrival.

On 1 August 1944, some 37,000 Home Army soldiers rose against the German garrison in Warsaw and succeeded in taking most of the city. The rising was greeted with great enthusiasm by the 1 million city residents. But the Germans ordered a counterattack on the city starting on 25 August, and gradually crushed the uprising, using far better equipped soldiers as well as dive bombers, artillery, and tanks. The Soviet offensive, meanwhile, mysteriously stalled just outside Warsaw. There may have been military factors that mitigated the Soviet advance—the Germans had indeed begun a general counterattack—but Stalin's refusal to allow US and UK aircraft to use Russian air bases to organize drops to the Poles revealed that the Soviet leader accepted the defeat of the Home Army in Warsaw with equanimity and most likely a considerable degree of perverse pleasure: the Germans were doing his dirty work for him. The Poles held out until 1 October, when Komorowski surrendered to the Germans. Fifteen thousand insurgents were killed, and perhaps a quarter of a million civilians died as well. Over 80 percent of the city was turned into rubble.[9]

Not only did the Warsaw uprising fail, but it had a devastating political impact on the London Poles. They now looked incompetent and weak, and the entire Tempest strategy had clearly failed. The Communists used the failure of Warsaw as a propaganda tool, declaring that by failing to coordinate with the Russian liberators, the Home Army leadership had betrayed its soldiers and the nation.[10] In London, Mikolajczyk was shaken by these attacks and thought it was now time to attempt some sort of power-sharing compromise with the Communist-led Committee of National Liberation before they had completed their seizure of power. In this he was bitterly opposed by those in the exile coalition government, and so he resigned his position as premier and took his Peasant Party out of the government. The London Poles were now leaderless and irrevocably split. Stalin could not have planned it any better.

In the meantime, the Committee of National Liberation began a sustained effort to root out the Home Army and the supporters of the London-based government. Stalin personally urged the adoption of tougher tactics, telling the Polish Communist leadership that "the abolition of a whole class is not a reform but a revolution and cannot be executed with the full majesty of the law."[11] The Communists did not disappoint. From the fall of 1944, the Home Army was declared an illegal organization and its members ordered either to submit to the authority of the committee or to face the consequences. In an effort to save the Home Army members from retribution, Komorowski's successor, Gen. Leopold Okulicki, ordered the army disbanded in January 1945. The Home Army soldiers, who had endured six years of foreign occupation and fought for their country's liberation, were now labeled bandits and reactionaries and were hunted down throughout the forests of Poland. In addition, the Polish secret police, under direct control of the NKVD in Moscow, rounded up thousands of politically suspect people, interned them, deported them, or liquidated them. The general secretary of the Polish Workers' Party, Wladyslaw Gomulka, quite openly acknowledged the need for repression to crush "the reactionaries and their lackeys." In the three years after the end of the war, some 30,000 Poles may have been killed in a wave of Communist repression, and some 45,000 arrested and tried for offenses against the regime between 1945 and 1949.[12]

The Western powers chose not to challenge Stalin's consolidation of power in Poland. At Yalta in February, the United States and Britain agreed to Stalin's territorial demands, asking only that Mikolajczyk and a few token non-Communists be taken into the provisional government and that the Poles be allowed to hold "free and unfettered" elections. Stalin agreed and the United States gave diplomatic recognition to Poland on 5 July 1945. Stalin, it seems, did not fear the prospect of elections. For one thing, they could be easily rigged. But he also believed that the Communists in Poland had a real chance at taking power with the support of many Poles. In November 1945, Stalin met with Workers' Party leader Gomulka and revealed that he had considerable confidence in the future of the party. He urged Gomulka to go ahead and hold elections in the spring of 1946. Stalin told Gomulka that the success of the Communists in liberating the country and in restoring an independent army and state and financial institutions would earn them widespread support. Stalin chided Gomulka, who was perhaps less sanguine about the prospects of the Communists at the polls. "The arguments are right there at your feet and you don't know how to make use of them," Stalin declared. "With good agitation and a proper attitude, you may win a considerable number of votes. You have to stop being so diffident."[13]

Perhaps Stalin's analysis was not so far off the mark. After all, six years of war and terror had created a widespread demand for a swift return of normal conditions to Poland. Fear of future conflict—whether internal, between Mikolajczyk and the Communists, or external, between a non-Communist Poland and her giant Soviet neighbor—engendered resignation on the part of much of the population. As Polish historian Krystyna Kersten has noted, Poles experienced a wide range of emotions in 1945, but the overriding desire was for peace, stability, and a restoration of the basic norms of existence. Poles wanted the reconstruction of the economy, of schools, health services, and civic institutions. Here, the Communist-dominated government could deliver. The land reform, for example, which broke up the landed estates and distributed their acres to peasants, was genuinely popular in a country whose economy was overwhelmingly agricultural. Further, the Communists exploited the former German territories now under Polish control, doling out land and industrial resources to loyal supporters. Gomulka himself ran the Ministry of Recovered Territories. Clearly, it made sense to come to terms with the regime and benefit from its patronage. Thus, the membership of the Polish Workers' Party began to grow by leaps and bounds, reaching 300,000 by April 1945, and half a million by the start of 1947.[14]

Patronage and passivity were hardly adequate, however, to insure the Communist hold on power. Violence and terror would have to be employed. Despite the agreement at Yalta that the Poles be allowed to hold free elections "at the earliest possible time," and despite Stalin's urgings, national parliamentary elections were not held until 19 January 1947. In the run-up to these elections, the government used its considerable powers to destroy the vestigial non-Communist opposition, most of which had rallied around Mikolajczyk's Peasant Party. Adopting tactics that would become familiar throughout Eastern Europe, the government closed down branches of the

Peasant Party, disrupted its meetings, cut off radio access, cut its paper allocation, arrested its members, barred many of its candidates from electoral activity on the grounds of their "Fascist" wartime past, and of course rigged the
ballot counting. Ballots were unsealed and immediately examined—in the
presence of each voter—by electoral boards that were staffed exclusively with
Communists. In addition, the government deployed the Polish army in
Protection-Propaganda Brigades to distribute political material and intimidate voters. The results were a foregone conclusion. The government announced that the pro-Communist parties received 80 percent of the vote, the
Peasant Party only 10. It was just a matter of time before the non-Communist
political leaders themselves were placed in jeopardy. In October 1947,
Mikolajczyk learned that he was about to be arrested and tried for subversion
and treason; he was certain to receive the death penalty. On 24 October, sympathetic Poles smuggled him out of the country and into the Western zone of
Germany. The Communist seizure of power was complete.

How had they done it? Obviously, the occupation of the country by the
Red Army had given the country's Communist forces an unrivaled advantage
over their opponents within the country. But the Polish Communists believed
in what they were doing. In prewar Poland, bourgeois democracy had opened
the way to authoritarian rule and contributed to the deterioration of relations
with Germany and the Soviet Union. It had failed to alleviate poverty, to improve the economy, or to soothe ethnic tensions. Communism, by contrast,
offered *answers:* it dictated that capitalism would fail, that socialism would triumph, that Fascism would be crushed, that the working class would finally receive its due, and above all that the fraternal Soviet Union would provide
peace and stability against imperialist aggression. Bankrupt as these claims appear over half a century later, they held out considerable appeal in a country
that had been subject to six years of unimaginable horror.[15]

It is cruelly ironic that the Communists who espoused such views would
soon find themselves victims of the very ideology they served. The case of
Wladyslaw Gomulka is instructive. By all accounts a ruthless Communist, he
had been a member of the party since 1926, had studied in Moscow at the
International Lenin School, and done time in Polish prisons in the 1930s for
his political activities. Rather than flee to Moscow when the war broke out, he
stayed in Poland and fought the Germans, spearheading the formation of the
Communist underground movement. He became general secretary of the
Polish Workers' Party in November 1943 and vice premier of the Soviet-
backed provisional government. He was instrumental in crushing the Peasant
Party, and in a 1945 speech to Polish political leaders of diverse party back-

grounds, he declared that the Communists "will never hand over power once it has been taken. . . . We are the masters of the house."[16] And yet this same man showed a surprising independent streak. He opposed forced collectivization of agriculture, criticized the Cominform's rigidity, and believed he could chart a Polish path to socialism that maintained Polish independence. In May 1945, he sharply criticized the harsh and oppressive tactics used by the Soviets and by the Soviet-controlled police, which he felt alienated the population from the Communist party. Gomulka, perhaps like many of his party brethren, saw himself as both a Communist and a patriot. It was precisely this sort of "nationalist deviation" that Stalin abhorred and that would soon lead to Gomulka's arrest and imprisonment.[17] Stalin placed no value in expressions of ideological solidarity. He wanted control and power, and required that even the Communists, his natural allies, be reduced to submissive puppets. The Polish Communists would soon find what it meant to be a part of the Soviet bloc.

TOWARD THE PRAGUE "COUP"

Unlike Poland, where Stalin clearly aimed to establish a Communist regime, Soviet policy toward Hungary and Czechoslovakia was less clear and did not take definitive shape until 1947. Indeed, precisely because Stalin placed such a high priority on controlling Poland while maintaining the alliance with the West, he did not press his hand elsewhere. The Communist parties in both Hungary and Czechoslovakia showed marked restraint by comparison to Poland, and a functioning democracy emerged in both countries that allowed Hungarians and Czechs to think that they might well avoid the fate of the Poles.

It was not, alas, to be, and the reason for the eventual rise of Communism to power in these two states lies chiefly in the international politics of the postwar period up to 1947. Before about February 1947, Hungary remained a pluralistic democracy; Czechoslovakia held out for a year longer. By early 1947, Stalin's ideas about cooperation with the West had sharply changed. He became far more suspicious about Western intentions in Eastern Europe, just as the West was becoming much more concerned about Soviet challenges in Western Europe and the Near East. The announcement of the Marshall Plan in June 1947 was the critical turning point for both of these countries, for after Marshall's Harvard speech, Soviet control and interference rapidly increased, leaving no doubt that Stalin saw the Marshall Plan as a direct threat to his informal rule in Eastern Europe. He would have to resort to more overt methods of coercion to protect Soviet interests. It is sobering to consider that one of America's most selfless and farsighted gestures—the creation of the European Recovery Program, or Marshall Plan—contributed directly to the Communist seizure of power in Eastern Europe.

Hungary's fortunes at war's end did not look good. The country had allied with Hitler, thereby insuring that it would be harshly treated by the postwar settlement. The country lost a million people in the war, or one-eighth of the population. Some 40 percent of its national wealth was destroyed, and its capital city, Budapest, was cruelly mangled by the prolonged German-Soviet battle for the city in the winter of 1944–45. As a former enemy, Hungary was obliged to accept an Allied Control Council, which acted as the de facto government. In practice, this council, though jointly chaired by American, British, and Soviet representatives, was dominated by the Russians, who after all had thousands of soldiers on Hungarian territory. The head of the ACC was in fact Marshal Kliment Voroshilov, one of the Soviet Union's leading generals and a close military adviser to Stalin since the 1920s. The ACC allowed the formation of a four-party coalition called the National Council, but insured that key ministries—such as agriculture, which oversaw radical land reform—stayed in Communist hands. Yet mindful of the need to preserve Allied unity, the Soviets proved remarkably restrained in Hungary, allowing a high degree of pluralism, freedom of political life, the press, and religious expression.

To their shock, the Communists did not accrue any political credit from the Hungarians for these successes. In October 1945, in the municipal elections in Budapest, the Communists and Social Democrats, standing on a joint ticket, won only 42.8 percent of the vote, while the peasant-based Smallholders Party won 50.5 percent—an outright majority. This, despite the fact that the Communist Party leader, Mátyás Rákosi, had personally guaranteed Voroshilov a Communist victory. The next month's national parliamentary elections were worse. On 4 November 1945, the Smallholders won 57 percent of the vote, and the Communists, now standing alone, won only 17 percent. It seems odd that the Communists were so optimistic. Rákosi himself had told the Russians in May 1945 that public opinion toward the Soviets had been much affected by Soviet dismantling of machinery and factories, while Soviet military analysts in Hungary bemoaned the "arbitrariness, pillage and violence on the part of certain Soviet soldiers." Public opinion toward the Soviets, the analysts noted, "could be described as negative."[18]

Still, by previous agreement, the four major parties governed by coalition, and so the Communists remained in the government despite their losses at the polls. In fact, at Soviet insistence, the Ministry of the Interior was given to a Communist, László Rajk, although the Smallholder leader, Zoltan Tildy, became president and Ferenc Nagy, another Smallholder member, was named premier. On 1 February 1946, Hungary was proclaimed a republic.

The votes in the fall had been an unpleasant surprise, and the Soviets were determined to see the Communists improve their position in Hungary, by hook or by crook. The only restraint on Soviet action was the ongoing conference with the Western powers to draw up a peace treaty between Hungary and the Allies. If the Russians proved cooperative, they could win better terms, which is precisely what happened. The United States and Britain largely let the Soviets determine Hungary's fate during negotiations in 1946 and 1947. The final peace agreement, signed in February 1947, allowed the Russians to keep their forces in Hungary, though the Allies had long since decamped. It was clear that the United States and Britain viewed Hungary as within the Soviet sphere of influence, and not worth a confrontation.

As soon as the treaty was signed, which all but guaranteed Soviet dominance, pressure on the non-Communist parties intensified. On 25 February, Soviet authorities arrested the executive secretary of the Smallholders Party, Béla Kovács. In May 1947, the Soviets announced that Kovács had fingered Prime Minister Nagy as a co-conspirator in a plot against the republic. Nagy, then on vacation in Switzerland, was told that he must never come back to Hungary and must resign his office. Since the Russians were holding his infant son and using him as a hostage, Nagy acquiesced, and the Smallholders as a party were ruined. Nagy was replaced by a Communist, Lajos Dinnyés. And in July, Hungary was blocked by the Russians from participating in the Marshall Plan.

In the wake of the Marshall Plan announcement and the Cominform meeting, the Hungarian Communists pursued what Rákosi famously called "salami tactics": the slow slicing away of unwanted elements from the body politic. Although the Communists could win only 22 percent of the vote in relatively free elections in August 1947, they hardly needed the seal of legitimacy to gain power. At the September 1947 meeting of the Cominform, Hungarian representative Mihály Farkas boasted that whereas the French and Italian Communists had failed to defeat the larger Christian Democrats, the Hungarians had "attacked and smashed" the Smallholders.[19] They did so through coercion. Rajk made the Interior Ministry a Communist fiefdom and turned his security police into a private force on behalf of Communist interests. The army, too, was entirely in the hands of Communists. Moreover, the Communists penetrated the other parties, placing secret agents in positions of influence from which they then called for subordination to the Communist

Party. In March 1948, the Social Democrats were forced to dissolve their party and join with the Communists in a "unified" Hungarian Workers' Party. In July 1948, the Communists pressured Tildy to resign the presidency and had him replaced with a fellow-traveling Social Democrat named Arpad Szakasits. With the opposition crushed, the triumphant Workers' Party could claim that in elections in May 1949, it had won 95 percent of the vote. The era of totalitarian rule had arrived.[20]

If anything, the Communist takeover in Czechoslovakia was still more tragic than in Hungary, if only because for a brief period it seemed as if the Czechs might have crafted a workable balance between the Communists and the democratic forces of the country. Unlike Poland and Hungary, Czechoslovakia possessed a democratic heritage: its republic had been a model state between 1918 and its dismemberment after the Munich Conference of 1938. In this tolerant environment, the Czechoslovak Communist Party had attracted about 10 percent of the vote in national elections. The Czechs had no longstanding enmity toward Russia, as the Poles had, and indeed the Soviet government denounced the Anglo-French deal with Hitler to surrender Czech territory to the Germans in 1938. During the war, therefore, the president of the Czechoslovak government in exile, the widely respected democratic leader Edvard Benes, worked diligently to keep open his contacts with Moscow and to assure Stalin of Czechoslovakia's recognition of Soviet predominance in Central Europe after the war. Jan Masaryk privately gave this policy a neat tag line: "I'd rather go to bed with Stalin," he said, "than kiss Hitler's behind."[21] In December 1943, Benes signed an alliance treaty with the Soviet Union. The Poles had tried full-fledged resistance to Soviet takeover and failed miserably. Benes would try accommodation, compromise, and neutrality in an effort to maintain his country's sovereignty.[22]

Benes's policy required close cooperation with the Czech Communists who had taken up residence in Moscow during the war. Klement Gottwald and Rudolf Slansky, the two dominant figures in the Czech Communist Party, were quite open to these overtures, chiefly because Stalin insisted that they work with Benes to create a broad front of diverse parties. A united coalition, Stalin knew, would reassure the Western powers that despite his actions in Poland, the Soviet leader was prepared to allow a multiparty settlement in Czechoslovakia. The Communists were pleased: they would profit from their agreement to work with Benes, who was very popular, while also taking advantage of their close association with the Soviet Union, which had liberated the country in 1945 and whose ideology promised major reform.

Thus, unlike the Poles, the Czech Communists embraced a genuine multiparty democracy in which they believed they could come to power through the ballot box. Benes, the Communists, and the leaders of Czechoslovakia's other parties met in Moscow in March 1945 and hammered out an agreement on a National Front government that would be established once the country was liberated. On 4 April 1945, before Czechoslovakia had been completely swept of Germans, this coalition government unveiled itself and its program in the eastern Slovak town of Kosice. The Kosice Program spoke warmly of the Soviet Union, declared the government's intention to maintain a close alliance with Moscow, and promised to maintain close relations with Poland, Yugoslavia, and Bulgaria on the "basis of Slavic brotherhood." At the same time, the program was devoid of heavy-handed Marxist rhetoric, and indeed promised only a moderate program of economic reform and nationalization, of the kind found in the platforms of virtually all European parties in 1945, both in the East and in the West. Above all, it assured the people that their political rights would be protected and that elections would soon be held. The terrible conflict in Poland between Mikolajczyk and the Communists had been successfully avoided by Benes's flexibility. As Benes described his policy, "we want no trouble between the East and West. . . . We shall do everything in our power to try to interpret them to each other."[23] This openness to socialism was widely popular in Czechoslovakia. Here, as throughout Europe, bourgeois democracy was much discredited by its failure to stop Hitler in the 1930s. Many shared the view expressed in May 1945 by the leading Catholic party's newspaper: "As we renew our economic and social life it is impossible to return to the capitalist system which prevailed here during the first twenty years of our republic. This war put a period at the end of the capitalist era. We stand on the threshold of a new economic and social order."[24]

For all the outward appearances of cooperation, however, the Communists did not remain quiescent. For one thing, they held eight seats in the cabinet and controlled the Ministries of Interior, Information, Education, Agriculture, and Social Welfare—the vitally important levers of state control at a time of political fluidity. The prime minister was Zdenek Fierlinger, a Social Democrat who had spent the war in Moscow and was in all but name a Communist. Even the head of the army, Gen. Ludvik Svoboda, was a fellow traveler. As in Poland, the Communists controlled the land reform, breaking up large estates and distributing small parcels of land to farmers and peasants. And the Communist-controlled Ministry of Agriculture oversaw the transfer of some 1.7 million Czech farmers into the Sudetenland after the Germans had been expelled. The Communists naturally took credit for this massive improvement in the fortunes of the peasants.

Under Vaclav Nosek, the Ministry of the Interior developed a formidable array of repressive tools. In June 1945 he abolished the old security apparatus and formed a new State Security Guard, with branches responsible for police work, border patrol, and intelligence. The members of the security services were recruited from Communist ranks and from the wartime underground. A 1947 decree placed the entire system under the direct control of the Ministry of the Interior—which in turn was always held by a Communist. The Communists deeply penetrated the local and state bureaucracy as well. At the first Cominform meeting in September 1947, Rudolf Slansky was able to declare that 140,000 Communists were working in national committees that monitored the workings of the economy throughout the country. He also acknowledged that "the high command of the armed state-security units" were Communists. "The leading positions in the internal intelligence service are also in our hands." He stated that "nearly a third of all the generals" in the army were party members. By March 1946, the Czechoslovak Communist Party had over 1 million members and had considerable influence over the 3 million members of the trade union movement as well.[25]

While consolidating their hold on the state, the Communists maintained an outward appearance of moderation. They remained deferential toward the church; they adopted nationalist slogans that appealed to the anti-German and anti-Hungarian sentiment in the country; they declared their support for democracy and the new constitution; and Communist Party leader Klement Gottwald went out of his way to stress that his party's policy was to find "a Czechoslovak road toward socialism," rather than hewing to a model imposed from outside. In the 1946 electoral campaign, the party's platform sounded no more radical than any socialist party in Western Europe, complete with declarations of respect for private property and for the rights of small and medium-sized entrepreneurs.

In these circumstances, it is hardly surprising that in the free elections of May 1946, the Communists outpolled their rivals, winning 38 percent of the vote across the country, while the National Socialists (a progressive, anticlerical party) won 23 percent, the Populists (Catholic) 20 percent, and the Social Democrats 15 percent. The Communists had naturally done well among the industrial workers, but they also polled strong support from the traditionally conservative peasants, who now flocked to the party most identified with land reform. Though they were short of the hoped-for majority, the Communists had won a plurality in a free election. Edvard Benes remained president of the republic, but Gottwald assumed the premiership with all the trappings of legitimacy.

Yet did the Communist victory in 1946 necessarily mean the advent of totalitarian rule by 1948, as in fact happened? The evidence suggests that the Czech Communists were content to remain the dominant party in the state and had no plans for the elimination of all rival parties. They continued to up-hold the National Front coalition and initiated a two-year economic plan that assumed some degree of Western economic aid and open trade relations with the West. In April 1947, Benes and Masaryk both told the US ambassador in Prague, Lawrence A. Steinhardt, that the Soviets were not interfering in Czech affairs. In June, the ambassador told the US State Department that the Communist seizure of power in Hungary would not be followed in Czecho-slovakia and that Communist influence was, if anything, waning.[26] Czechoslo-vakia, despite the predominance of Communists in the government, appeared to be emerging as that rare thing in Central Europe—a bridge between East and West.

It is therefore crucial to reflect on the course of events in Czechoslovakia after the 5 June 1947 announcement of the Marshall Plan. When the United States made its offer of assistance to Europe, it did so without restriction. Any country was welcome to participate in the program, including the Soviet Union. The Czechs, whose economy badly needed aid, received encouraging word from Moscow that they would be allowed to prepare a report as a basis for discussions on receiving American aid. Foreign Minister Jan Masaryk nonetheless trod very softly, declaring in late June that "we are for any action if its aim is to unify Europe, but we are against any action that aims at divid-ing it." On 1 July, Masaryk announced his government's favorable reaction to the American proposals, and on 7 July, the cabinet voted unanimously to par-ticipate in the Marshall Plan and to attend a meeting of all aid recipients scheduled for 12 July. This decision took some courage, because by then the Czechs knew that Molotov had walked out of the Paris meetings with the French and British. Molotov had rejected the condition posed by the Ameri-can plan, namely, that the countries involved be prepared to share informa-tion about the state of their economies.

In an effort to reassure the Soviets that their decision to participate in the Marshall Plan was in no way a repudiation of the Czech-Soviet friendship, however, Masaryk and Gottwald traveled to Moscow on 9 July for a meeting with Stalin. It was an unpleasant experience. Meeting in the middle of the night in the Kremlin, as was Stalin's habit, the Soviet leader made it clear in di-rect terms that the Czech attitude was unacceptable. The Marshall Plan was an American effort to create a Western bloc and isolate the Soviet Union, he said, and the other "friendly" states like Poland, Romania, and Yugoslavia had now decided to reject American aid. He continued:

> The Soviet government has therefore been surprised by your decision
> to accept this invitation. For us it is a matter of friendship. . . . We

consider this matter basic and our friendship depends on it. If you go
to Paris you shall demonstrate your willingness to cooperate in the
action of isolating the Soviet Union. All the Slavonic states have refused, not even Albania feared to refuse, and therefore, we think you
should reverse your decision.

Benes at that very moment was in Prague, bedridden, just having suffered a
stroke. He could offer no organized resistance to the Soviet demand. Masaryk,
stunned, argued that at least the Czechs should be allowed to save face by attending the 12 July meeting and then walking out after the first day. Stalin refused. The Czech cabinet met and approved the reversal of the decision.
Czechoslovakia had been forced to bend to Stalin's will. Jan Masaryk later declared that he "went to Moscow as the Foreign Minister of an independent
sovereign state; I returned as a lackey of the Soviet Government."[27]

The Soviet insistence that Czechoslovakia reject Marshall's offer of aid
immediately radicalized Czech politics. The Communist Party, which of
course now publicly denounced Marshall's offer of aid as "imperialist aggression," was revealed to be nothing more than a mouthpiece for Moscow.
Whatever Gottwald's personal intentions—and again, the evidence suggests
that before July 1947 he was willing to work in coalition with the non-
Communists—the party had to follow Stalin's dictates. The Cominform
meeting in September left no doubt on this score, and as we have seen, it was
there that the Soviets insisted on abandoning the strategy of coalitions with
bourgeois parties and "crushing the reactionary forces" in Europe. For the
Czech Communists, the time for confrontation was at hand.

Now events followed the pattern visible in Poland and Hungary. Communist propaganda spewed forth from the Ministry of Information, casting
aspersions on all non-Communist politicians and parties. Three democratic
ministers, including Masaryk, received mail bombs, which fortunately were
discovered before they exploded. The police and trade unions were mobilized
to intimidate rival political organizations. In fact, it was the Communist abuse
of the police that triggered the final crisis. Interior Minister Nosek had begun
a purge of non-Communist police officers, and the democratic parties in the
cabinet demanded their reinstatement. When Nosek refused, the democratic
ministers, who together outnumbered the Communists, resigned en masse on
20 February. In France and Italy, this move had been the preliminary to a re-
formulation of governments that excluded the Communists. This is what the
ministers hoped Benes would now do. He did not. Instead, the Communists
staged immense rallies across the country, mobilized the police, unions, and

army leadership, and declared that they would resort to violence if they were not given control of the government.

Benes was caught on the horns of a dilemma. He could reject the demands of the Communists, overrule the results of the 1946 election (in which they had freely won a majority), and court civil war and Soviet intervention. These were serious concerns: there were 250,000 pro-Communist demonstrators in the streets of Prague, and the Soviets had sent Deputy Foreign Minister Valerian Zorin to the city to "confer" with Gottwald. Or Benes could concede to the Communists and let Gottwald form a Communist-dominated government. Either way, democracy in Czechoslovakia would be ruined. The frail and elderly Benes, in a decision that forever tarnished the reputation of this good man of peace, relented, and offered Gottwald what he wanted. On 25 February, Gottwald was again named prime minister, and he formed a new government staffed with Communists and Social Democratic fellow travelers. Foreign Minister Masaryk was left in place, a sop to Western opinion, but in fact quite powerless to control foreign affairs. By their precipitate resignations, the democratic ministers enabled Gottwald to take power by constitutional means. There was no coup in Prague; there was only a turbulent but legal transfer of power to Communist hands.[28]

STALIN'S HIGH NOON

The Czech flirtation with the Marshall Plan, combined with his growing fears of American policy in Germany, shocked Stalin into adopting a ruthless plan for the immediate consolidation of Communist rule in Eastern Europe. Fearful that any deviation from strict Stalinist rule would open the door to American subversion, Stalin initiated a wave of repression in 1948 that crashed across the region with great violence. His goal was to insure total, unswerving obedience to Moscow. His tool was terror.

Of course, Stalin was no neophyte in these matters. Stalin had been engaged in a war on his own people since the early 1930s. His insistence on imposing collectivized agriculture led to the deaths of perhaps 6 million people in 1932–33, most of them in the Ukraine. Despite his enormous power, Stalin's paranoia led him to see scheming "oppositionists" on all sides. Starting in late 1936, he ordered his security service, the NKVD, to purge the country of all hostile elements. His former colleagues from the revolutionary days, such as Lev Trotsky, Grigori Zinoviev, Lev Kamenev, and Nikolai Bukharin were disgraced, accused of conspiracy, and murdered; all their followers were done in as well. But the Great Terror was much wider than that: all potential sources of opposition to Stalin's control had to be destroyed. Local party chiefs, factory directors and managers, middle-class city dwellers, and anyone suspected of economic sabotage—"wreckers," they were called—were rooted out and destroyed. The entire high command of the Red Army was also exterminated. And ordinary people suspected of harboring anti-Stalinist sentiments—whether farmers, peasants, workers, or wives of Old Bolsheviks— were dispatched to labor camps, or worse. Between 1937 and 1938, at least 700,000 people were executed by the NKVD. To this one can add the hundreds of thousands, perhaps millions, of deaths in the gulags, or state-run concentration camps, during the 1930s.[29]

The show trial became Stalin's favorite method to humiliate and destroy those around him. Suspects, many of them devoted Stalinists who had dedicated their lives to carrying out his orders, were brought up on charges of conspiracy against the state and forced to confess to elaborate plots of subversion. The historian Robert C. Tucker has asked why Stalin needed not just the murder of his enemies but also their abject confessions. He has suggested that Stalin's use of deceit, lies, and conspiracy as the basic tools of governing led him to assume that all those around him worked on the same pattern: his own duplicity convinced him that others were equally duplicitous. In Stalin's warped mind, it seemed only natural that those who appeared most loyal were in fact the most treacherous.[30]

The results of Stalin's Terror were spectacularly successful: by 1939, Stalin's power was absolute and the country gripped by fear. The war against Germany suited Stalin's domestic political objectives, as it focused the nation's attention on a very real enemy (for once) and allowed Stalin to expand his already impressive security apparatus. This was bad news for anyone who might conceivably be considered a threat to the regime. In 1945, there were 1.4 million people in Stalin's labor camps and colonies, a number that rose to 2.5 million by 1950. To this we may add 2.5 million non-Russian settlers—Volga Germans, Crimean Tatars, Kalmyks, and half a million Chechens—whom Stalin had deported from their homelands during the war; 600,000 Ukrainians, Balts, Greeks, Armenians, Georgians, Moldavians, Jehovah's Witnesses, and Jews that Stalin had exiled to Siberia between 1945 and 1953; and some 300,000 people held in common prisons. If ever there was a police state, Stalin's Soviet Union was it.[31]

Stalin knew no other form of governance but terror, and he now applied this system to his new satellites in Eastern Europe. His first target: the dynamic, independent-minded Communist leader of Yugoslavia, Josip Tito. During World War II, Tito emerged as the most successful resistance leader in

Europe. In the face of both German occupation and a civil war, Tito's Communist partisans overcame Yugoslavia's complex ethnic divisions to form a genuine mass underground movement that by 1944 had established nominal control over much of the country and established a democratic, grassroots revolutionary movement. At a time when Stalin was urging European Communists to form fronts with bourgeois parties, Tito, by spearheading the resistance to the Germans and by promoting federalism and power sharing among the country's ethnic groups, had rallied widespread support for his political and ideological goals. Indeed, such was his battlefield success against the Germans that he was also embraced by the British government. Tito was able to make much of the fact that the partisans liberated their own country without the help of the Red Army. By 1945, Tito alone held sway in Yugoslavia.

There were, of course, advantages for the Soviets in having such an effective Communist ally. The Yugoslavs, it will be recalled, were appointed as the enforcers at the September 1947 Cominform meeting, designated to point out the failings of the French and Italian parties for their misguided faith in parliamentary coalition. But Stalin was not simply interested in ideological affinity. He wanted subservience, and Tito, because of his undisputed power within his own country, never adopted the sycophantic, timid attitude of other Communist leaders toward the Soviet Union. In the context of the shifting Soviet stance in mid-1947 toward the Western powers, a series of low-grade irritants in Soviet-Yugoslav relations took on new significance.

In August 1947, the Yugoslavs and Bulgarians signed a treaty of friendship and mutual aid without consulting Moscow, a move that earned Stalin's swift rebuke. Then disagreements about Yugoslav-Albanian relations surfaced. Since 1946, Tito had been working on a plan to tie Albania into a Yugoslav federation; Stalin, not opposed in principle, nonetheless feared that the Yugoslavs were trying to set themselves up as the dominant power in the Balkans. When Tito proposed to send troops into Albania, the Russians summoned a Yugoslav delegation to Moscow in February 1948 and censured the wayward brethren for failing to consult with the Soviet Union on international questions. At the same meeting, Stalin and Molotov demanded that Yugoslav support for the Greek Communists, then fighting a civil war, be curtailed. Stalin said he had "grave doubts" about the partisans' chances of success there, and therefore "we should rethink and terminate the guerrilla movement. The Anglo-Americans will spare no effort to keep Greece" in the Western sphere. Stalin seemed to be implying that by aiding the Greek Communists, Tito was aggravating East-West relations in the pursuit of regional influence.

Despite these warnings, two weeks later the Yugoslav leadership reassured the Greek partisans of their continued military support. On 1 March 1948, the

Yugoslav Communist Party Politburo passed a resolution criticizing the Soviet Union for its unwillingness to consider Yugoslav national interests, its delay in supplying arms and economic aid, and its dictatorial pressure tactics. This resolution, transmitted to Moscow by Soviet informants, triggered an immediate reaction against these "sham friends" of the Soviet Union. On 18 March, citing various Yugoslav acts of "mistrust," the Russians ordered the withdrawal of all Soviet civilian and military personnel from the country. The crisis was now out in the open.[32]

There is no fury like that of a dictator scorned. In a sharp exchange of letters between March and May 1948, the Soviets accused the Yugoslavs of all manner of transgressions, including slanderous remarks about the Red Army, spying on Soviet advisers in Yugoslavia, criticism of alleged Soviet "great-power chauvinism," and (ironically) a failure to follow democratic procedures in the Yugoslav Communist Party. The Yugoslavs protested, declaring their love of the Soviet Union, but also stating that "no matter how much each of us loves the land of Socialism, the USSR, he can in no case love his country less." This was just the sort of nationalist deviation that so annoyed the Russians, and occasioned yet another round of nasty catcalls, in which the Soviets declared that since the Yugoslavs would not admit their errors, as good Marxists must, they were not good Marxists. Only a man as firmly entrenched in power as Tito could have had the courage to refuse to acknowledge the error of his ways. Instead, he threw the charges back at the Soviets and courted expulsion from the Cominform, which duly took place in June 1948.[33]

Is this what Stalin had intended all along? Or had the conflict with Tito gotten dangerously out of hand? Not only had Stalin now lost a valued ally, but the Soviets had been shown up as powerless to enforce their will upon this recalcitrant leader. It now became critical to the integrity of the Soviet bloc that any other potential Tito be eliminated before another national challenge to Soviet hegemony arose. The Cominform meeting of June 1948 provided an excellent stage to test the remaining satellites, and indeed, the parties vied to outdo one another in their condemnation of Yugoslav treachery. Perhaps no one enjoyed the process as much as the French and Italian delegates, who only a year earlier had sat in glum silence as the Yugoslavs hammered away at them for their bourgeois failings.[34] Yet Stalin was not content. Someone would have to pay for Tito's acts of defiance, and the first target to appear in Stalin's crosshairs was another charismatic Communist who, like Tito, had spent the war organizing his country's resistance to the Germans rather than attending seminars in Moscow: Poland's Wladyslaw Gomulka.

Gomulka had always presented a problem for Stalin. A ferocious partisan leader and underground organizer, he maintained strong nationalist convictions that in Stalin's eyes took on Titoist overtones. On 3 June 1948, in the midst of the Soviet-Yugoslav dispute, Gomulka delivered a speech to a gathering of Poland's leading Communists. He took as his subject the history of the Polish workers' movement. The thesis of the lecture was that the Polish Communist Party in the interwar years had made certain mistakes: it had not stressed Polish independence and nationalism enough. This had made it less popular than the Socialist Party, which had done so.

Why did Gomulka make the speech? Was this a coded affront to Stalin? A secret signal of support for Tito? Scholars differ as to Gomulka's motives, but it seems unlikely that a man as carefully attuned as Gomulka to Communist-bloc politics could have been ignorant of the import of his words. True, these were themes that Gomulka had lectured on before, and that even a few months earlier would not have merited any notice at all. In the context of the Yugoslav dispute, however, his speech took on the appearance of a direct challenge to the strict Marxist interpretation of history.[35]

Boleslaw Bierut, Gomulka's rival in the Communist leadership and now president of Poland, immediately seized on this and demanded that Gomulka retract the statement. Working on direct orders from Moscow, Bierut severely criticized Gomulka, demanded an admission that his views were wrong, and insisted that he give up his post. Gomulka refused. The Polish Politburo therefore increased the pressure on Gomulka and drew up a list of charges under the general rubric of "rightist-nationalist deviation." The indictment now reached back into the war years and claimed that Gomulka had shown "capitulationist" tendencies by seeking an accommodation with bourgeois parties— even though at the time this was Stalin's policy! After the war, the indictment continued, Gomulka had opposed collectivization of agriculture and favored the rich farmers, or kulaks. In 1947, Gomulka had shown hesitation about the formation of the Cominform; and now his view of the Yugoslavs was far too forgiving. These charges were woven together to suggest a persistently anti-Marxist, nationalist stance. In the context of Tito's challenge to Soviet domination, these few flickerings of independence took on immense significance.

At the party plenum of late August 1948, Bierut leveled these charges at Gomulka, and Gomulka offered contradictory and insincere apologies. But the blood was in the water and the party leaders now swarmed, piling on lengthy criticisms of their former leader. By the last day of the plenum, Gomulka conceded that he had been overcome by "alien influences" and that he would engage in serious self-criticism. On 3 September Gomulka was removed from his post as secretary general of the party. Gomulka was not arrested—yet. For the time being, the Polish leaders were content to use Gomulka as a national whipping boy, a convenient target of abuse in the party's rhetorical diatribes.[36]

His counterparts in Bulgaria, Hungary, and Czechoslovakia would not be so lucky. The Bulgarian leadership was an easy target for Stalin. Under Georgi Dimitrov, a former chief of the Comintern, the Bulgarians had been working closely with the Yugoslavs since the end of the war to establish a Balkan federation. In light of the Soviet rift with Tito, this pro-Yugoslav attitude appeared treasonous. Moreover, an attack on the Bulgarian leaders would offer an easy way to secure denunciations of Tito. Dimitrov, who genuinely admired Tito, was an old and dying man by 1948; others would have to be found and used to unmask the Titoist conspiracy. The search for a Bulgarian Tito turned up Traicho Kostov, a devout Stalinist who had actually mistrusted Dimitrov's plans for a Balkan federation. Kostov had been a founder of the Bulgarian Communist Party. His devotion to his cause was such that, when he was arrested by the Bulgarian police in 1924 for his Communist activities, he attempted suicide rather than betray his comrades. His leap from a fourth-story window merely left him with two broken legs, however, and he remained a cripple for the rest of his life.

His physical disabilities did not stop him from party work, and during the war Kostov toiled in the Bulgarian underground against the Germans. He emerged from the war as the number two man, after Dimitrov, in the Bulgarian Communist Party. This devout Communist would appear an unlikely threat to Stalin's control of Southern Europe. Yet it was precisely the nature of Stalinism that the most effective, loyal, and determined Communists be destroyed, so that they could be replaced by weak, terrified, and sycophantic stooges. Fabricating charges against Kostov required little effort for the Soviets. As head of the Bulgarian economic ministries after the war, Kostov had resisted Soviet efforts to secure unfair purchasing agreements of Bulgarian products: an act easily transformed into sabotage by the Soviets. In March 1949, Kostov was removed from the Bulgarian Politburo and charged with nationalist deviations and fostering anti-Soviet attitudes. On 10 June, Kostov was arrested, and after four months of nonstop torture, he agreed to confess to his participation in a plot sponsored by Tito and American agents to surrender the Balkans to the control of the Anglo-American imperialists. Still, Kostov proved a tough nut to crack. During his show trial of December 1949, which had been carefully scripted beforehand, Kostov suddenly broke away from his memorized text and declared his innocence to the courtroom. He was dragged away by the guards, and the judge proceeded to read the confessions Kostov had made under torture. Kostov and the other ten defendants—mostly, like Kostov, dedicated Communists who had worked on economic matters—were all found guilty on 14 December 1949. Kostov alone was given the death penalty, and two days later he was hanged.[37]

In the summer of 1948, just as the assaults on Gomulka in Poland and Kostov in Bulgaria gathered momentum, the Soviet security apparatus determined that Hungary would provide another stage for a piece of Stalinist theater. The task was made quite simple by the fact that of the five most powerful members of the Hungarian Communist leadership, three—Mátyás Rákosi, Ernö Gerö, and Mihály Farkas—were active members of the Soviet secret police. Only one had not spent the war in Moscow, under the close supervision of the Soviet NKVD: Interior Minister László Rajk. Worse, Rajk had fought in Spain during the Spanish Civil War. In Stalin's eyes, veterans of this war, who had come from across Europe to fight against Franco's Fascist forces, had been hopelessly compromised by their exposure to American, British, French, and Trotskyist agents of subversion, who Stalin had assumed were active among the heterogeneous leftists fighting on behalf of the Spanish Republicans. Despite the fact that Rajk was a loyal Communist and had masterminded the destruction of the democratic parties in Hungary, once he had been targeted by Stalin as a conspirator, his fate was sealed.

Arrested on 30 May 1949, Rajk was subjected to merciless torture by the Hungarian secret police. Rajk, it was now declared, had been recruited by the French intelligence service in the late 1930s, and was then enticed to work for the Americans. His year in a German concentration camp in 1944–45 was used as evidence that he had also been recruited by the Gestapo to betray the Hungarian underground. And of course, prominent in this catalogue of treachery was the most important charge: that Rajk was in league with Tito in a plot that would restore Hungary to the capitalist bloc.

In Hungary as elsewhere, there were virtually no prisoners who refused to confess to the charges leveled at them. From the accounts of those that survived the process, we have learned what torture can do to the human mind: all resistance is broken, all dignity is destroyed, all sense of loyalty or honor is crushed by the rubber truncheons, the fire hoses, the starvation diets, the sleeplessness, the mock executions, and so on.[38] Few can resist for long. And so we find dozens of once-proud, determined, indeed zealous and fanatical Communists reduced to shivering zombies, willing to sign any document, admit to any charge, name any name, just so that the pain will cease. By the time Rajk and seven other defendants took the stage in the Budapest show trial in September 1949, they were all broken men, quite willing to admit that they had been recruited by French and American agents in the 1930s, had been in touch with US spymaster Allen Dulles and the Yugoslavs during the war, and had conspired to assassinate the Hungarian Communist leadership. In the carefully scripted words of the prosecutor, Rajk and his "gang" had sought the "introduction of a bloodthirsty dictatorship on the fascist pattern, the betrayal of the independence of the country, and colonization on behalf of the imperialists." The violence of the language used by the prosecutor in calling for the death penalty is worth noting: "the head of the snake which wants to bite us must be crushed. . . . The only defense against mad dogs is to beat them to death."[39]

On 15 October 1949, despite his abject and pathetic confessions, László Rajk, the mastermind of the Communist seizure of power in Hungary in 1947 and one of the most ruthless Communists of his generation, was hanged. He was hardly the last victim of the purges. The secret police continued to hunt down suspects, especially among the former Social Democratic Party, then the army, and later engineered another purge of the Communist Party itself. In 1952, Col. Ernö Szücs, deputy head of the Hungarian secret police and one of the architects of the purges, pleaded with Moscow to end the murderous cycle of violence. He was immediately arrested and hanged. Only Stalin's death, in March 1953, finally brought Hungary's torment to a close.

By the time the Soviets and their security operatives turned their attention on Czechoslovakia, they had raised the process of torture, confession, and show trial to a fine art.[40] Czechoslovakia had two features that made it especially troublesome for Stalin: it had a large prewar Communist Party, made up of a variety of leftists, Trotskyists, Spanish Civil War veterans, and Jews; and the Czech Communists had governed up to February 1948 in a coalition with the "imperialist" camp of Benes and Masaryk. In October 1949, Soviet advisers arrived in Prague to take command of what was now planned to be a massive purge of the Czech government. The arrests began with Eugene Loebl, the Czech deputy trade minister, then moved on to Otto Sling, a leading party bureaucrat; Vladimir Clementis, the minister of foreign affairs; his deputy Artur London; and Karel Svab, the deputy minister of national security. Despite their impeccable Communist credentials, they were all compelled to confess to treasonous activities on behalf of the Western imperialists.

The most surprising—and surprised—victim of the Prague purge, however, was Rudolf Slansky himself, the general secretary of the Czechoslovak Communist Party. He was arrested on 24 November 1951. Why Slansky? Stalin wanted to show that the conspiracy had reached the very top of the Communist hierarchy; then the vast sweeping out of underlings could be much more easily justified. Besides, Slansky was a Jew. And what stands out from the Czech purge, beyond its massive scope and unprecedented cruelty, is its official usage of anti-Semitism. Of the fourteen leading defendants at the show trials of November 1952, eleven were Jewish. This was no coincidence.

Stalin himself, of course, was an anti-Semite, and Jews had been a special target of the Great Terror of the 1930s in the USSR. Jews, in the code words of the day, were "rootless" and "cosmopolitan," and therefore a potential fifth column; they were also bourgeois and capitalist, and therefore hostile to socialism. In 1948, after the state of Israel turned overtly toward the Western powers in the Cold War, Stalin again gave anti-Semitism a prominent role in Soviet official rhetoric, and a widespread assault on Jews and Jewish culture got under way within the Soviet Union. Stalin did not have to press anti-Jewish sentiments upon his East European proxies. Throughout the region after the war, anti-Semitism remained widespread, as if the Jewish catastrophe at the hands of the Nazis had never happened. In Poland, members of the shattered Jewish community continued to suffer the seizure of property, public abuse, discrimination, and worse: in the city of Kielce, on 4 July 1946, a mob abetted by local militiamen stormed through the Jewish quarter and killed forty-one Jews. One estimate placed the number of Jews killed in Poland since the end of the war at eight hundred. In Czechoslovakia, anti-Jewish feeling was widespread, and in 1949, some 15,000 Jews—out of the 55,000 Jews that had survived the war in that country—emigrated to Israel. Clearly, the association of the defendants in the Czech purge trials with a Zionist conspiracy was designed to fan the flames of an already burning hatred of Jews.[41]

Thus, during the Slansky trial, Zionism was placed alongside the other now-familiar trespasses like Trotskyism, Titoism, and bourgeois nationalism, and Slansky's Jewish origins were made a central element in the case. It was only natural that Israeli diplomats in Prague were also at the heart of the conspiracy, for they had assisted in preparing a plan for the economic sabotage of the Czech economy and bilking Czech citizens of their wealth—a charge likely to resonate at a time when Jews, having been despoiled of their property by the Germans, were seeking restitution through the courts. In his summation at the trial, the state prosecutor depicted Jews in terms that might have been drawn from the speeches of Heinrich Himmler, were it not for the patina of Marxist rhetoric:

> Zionist organizations have always been linked with world capitalism by a thousand ties. As such they have always been a dangerous enemy of the liberation struggle of the working class. . . . The Zionist agents in Slansky's conspiratorial center served, by their criminal activities, the efforts of American imperialism to dominate the world and to

unleash a new war. . . . Their cosmopolitanism and their Jewish bourgeois nationalism are indeed only two sides of the same coin, minted in Wall Street.[42]

In private, the Jewish defendants met even more gruesome expressions of hatred. Artur London recalls that during his interrogation, one of his jailers shrieked at him: "We'll get rid of you and your filthy race! You're all the same! Not everything Hitler did was right, but he destroyed the Jews, and he was right about that. Too many of you escaped the gas chamber. We'll finish what he started."[43]

Alongside these accusations of Zionist treachery, the Prague victims were charged with other crimes against the state, such as Slansky's collaboration with Benes, his contacts with Western agents, his cooperation with Tito, and his widespread sabotage of the economy. The defendants played their roles in the trial perfectly, reciting their memorized texts, agreeing to every charge placed before them. The death sentence was duly pronounced upon Slansky and ten other defendants, and none of them appealed. On 3 December 1952, they were hanged. So completely had the process broken Slansky that as the noose was placed around his neck, he said to his executioner: "Thank you. I'm getting what I deserved."[44]

It may puzzle contemporary readers that the defendants appeared so docile during their public confessions. Survivors of the process have explained why this was so. Apart from the degrading physical tortures that each victim experienced, and apart from the sleeplessness, the exhaustion, and the use of drugs to subdue the prisoners, most defendants confessed willingly because they had been mentally shattered by the process. Eugene Loebl recalled in his memoirs an explanation he was given by his jailhouse tormentor, one Captain Kohoutek. Beatings and physical torture, Kohoutek told Loebl, were to be used only in criminal cases, when information was needed quickly. "Quite different methods had to be used in preparing political trials," he said. Kohoutek told him that "they could not risk anyone retracting during a public trial; thus in these cases there was no point in forcing a confession by using physical force. Pain passes and the confession will be withdrawn. The interrogators had to break those concerned and they must be so conditioned that they would not dare to withdraw their confessions, even if invited to do so by the prosecutor himself." In the end, Loebl too confessed. "I did not even toy with the idea of retracting later; in fact I did not even feel sorry or ashamed that I had given in, that I was lying. It is not easy to explain that state of mind."[45]

What purpose did this assault on leading Communists serve? Stalin imposed terror on Eastern Europe, just as he had done within the USSR, in order to sweep away any vestiges of the dynamic Communists who had seized power in the confused and turbulent years just after the war. He now wished to dispense with these revolutionaries and install in their place a leadership gripped by fear, held in place by terror, and unswervingly loyal to Moscow. To obtain this objective, he needed not just to destroy his enemies but to bring them to surrender unconditionally to a system premised on Stalin's omniscience, his benevolence, his wisdom. The purges and the show trials were not simply about punishment, therefore, but about conversion. In his novel *1984*, George Orwell chillingly articulates this deeper motive that lay behind the show trials. As his central character, Winston Smith, lies strapped to a table in an interrogation chamber, his tormentor, O'Brien, explains:

> We are not content with negative obedience, nor even with the most abject submission. When finally you surrender to us, it must be of your own free will. We do not destroy the heretic because he resists us; so long as he resists us, we never destroy him. We convert him, we capture his inner mind, we reshape him. We burn all evil and all illusion out of him; we bring him over to our side, not in appearance, but genuinely, heart and soul. We make him one of ourselves before we kill him.[46]

Perhaps this is a fitting epitaph for the Stalinist era in Eastern Europe.

PART TWO

BOOM

.

If the immediate postwar years had been marked by shortages, long lines, Cold War anxiety, and political division, the 1950s, at least in Western Europe, offered a welcome contrast. This was the decade of the boom, a time of unprecedented material prosperity and political equilibrium. Just a decade after the end of the war, Europeans found themselves awash in goods, from farm products to durable goods like televisions, automobiles, refrigerators, and washing machines. Unemployment all but disappeared, incomes rose, and Europeans began to let out their belts for the first time in a generation.

What explains this swift recovery? American aid in the form of the Marshall Plan certainly helped, though its overall impact remains controversial. In strictly monetary terms, Marshall aid constituted a mere fraction of total spending on reconstruction by the European recipients. Yet its impact spilled over into the political sphere and helped boost the political fortunes of the parties that had embraced the American relationship in the first place: the Christian Democrats and nondoctrinaire socialists, who, along with various parties on the right, combined to give European politics a distinctly liberal, free market orientation. These parties in turn worked to free up European trade, improved mutual relations between the once warring states in Europe, and acted in concert on behalf of a Europe-wide recovery. They were re-

warded for their successes: as long as the boom persisted, Christian Democrats and centrists of varied stripes dominated the political landscape of
Western Europe. Europeans, no less than the free market Americans, had discovered the value of the "politics of productivity."[1]

As Europe boomed, the colonial empires went bust. This was not by
chance. A principal rationale for empire had been national rivalry: British
control of, say, Malaya, Singapore, and Burma served to defend India and
counterbalance the French, German, and American positions in China,
Indochina, and the Philippines. By the 1950s, India was independent, the
Japanese and Germans were allies and had no colonial ambitions, and the
French were also winding down their Empire. Empire had never paid, and by
the mid-1950s, European states were trading far more with one another than
with their colonies. Only the Cold War rivalry with the Soviet Union provided
a justification for a continued European colonial presence, but precisely for
this reason, the United States displaced the Europeans in most of the strategic
points of conflict around the globe. Even colonial war, which had once made
the careers of junior officers and offered outlets for jingoism, had lost its lus-
ter. The British attempt to invade Egypt and seize the Suez Canal in 1956,
along with the French army's atrocities against Muslim insurgents in Algeria,
won these countries little but shame and humiliation. Most Europeans were
quietly relieved to see the era of empire come to a close.

There would be no decolonization in the Soviet empire, however. After
Stalin's death, in 1953, the Soviet leadership did inaugurate a thaw of sorts.
The worst excesses of Stalinism were ended, the slave labor camps mostly
emptied, the economy opened up; and even Stalin himself was denounced by
his charismatic successor, Nikita Khrushchev. But there was no end to the
Cold War, and no freedom for the states under Soviet control. In East Berlin
in 1953 and in Hungary in 1956, Soviet troops used force to suppress open
challenges to Communist control. Lest there be any doubt that the Soviet bloc
would remain intact, Khrushchev allowed his East German satrap, Walter
Ulbricht, to erect a wall in Berlin in August 1961, sealing the last hole in the
Iron Curtain and thereby putting on display the obscene nature of the Soviet
system.

Despite the prosperity of the West, some Europeans chafed under the
hegemony of the two superpowers and desired to end it. No leader was a more
articulate and determined critic of American dominance than Charles de
Gaulle, who became president of France, for the second time, in 1958. De
Gaulle wished to use Europe's newfound prosperity to counter America's
global role. Didn't the Old World still have something to teach the new? De
Gaulle tried to forge political and military institutions that could check US

power, bolster Europe's world presence, enhance East-West dialogue, and of course, promote France's own claims to grandeur. He failed, mainly because few Europeans liked de Gaulle any more than they did America. And what de Gaulle misunderstood was that Europeans, especially young ones, had grown less interested in issues of global rivalry and influence. They were starting to ask, what kind of Europe has the boom brought us? By the time of de Gaulle's departure in 1969, the seeds of a new revolution had begun to sprout.

CHAPTER FIVE

THE MIRACULOUS FIFTIES

·

BY 1949—after six years of war and four years of a difficult peace—Europeans began to see reassuring signs that their battered continent was on the road to recovery. Industrial production had just about reached prewar levels; politics had settled down somewhat since the turbulent crisis year of 1947; the cafés and boulevards were full once again, although in every country most food-stuffs were still being rationed. Even tourists, after a ten-year hiatus, began to return to European capitals, where they encountered swarming construction crews amidst the rubble, rapidly rebuilding city squares, churches, schools, and town halls. Europe was on its way back.

If these trends looked auspicious in 1949, few could have predicted just how fast and how far Europe's recovery would proceed. The 1950s forever changed Western Europe. In 1949, European manners and morals, the rhythms of life, the patterns of industrial, labor, and social activity would have been quite familiar to a man born in 1870. But within a decade, these cher-ished patterns were forever altered as the first wave of postwar modernization crashed over Europe, sweeping away many old, no doubt venerable, but anti-quated habits.

The greatest impact, and the easiest to measure, was felt in the industrial sectors of the economy. Europe in the decade of the 1950s grew at a pace never seen before or since. Industrial production in West Germany and Italy tripled between 1949 and 1963; that of France expanded at almost the same rate. Even the smaller economies like Austria, Greece, and Spain showed impressive growth rates. In virtually every category of the European economy, from pro-duction of raw materials, steel, and iron to chemicals, electronics, and au-tomobiles, the progress was breathtaking. Between 1950 and 1960, steel production, that all-important index of industrial might, doubled in the six countries that made up the European Economic Community (EEC): Germany, France, Italy, Belgium, the Netherlands, and Luxembourg. German production, reaching 34 million tons in 1960, accounted for almost half of the EEC total. Far from being the dependent weaklings of 1945, Europe's leading nations by 1960 had emerged as economic powerhouses.

Europe's agricultural productivity improved as well. France in 1929 produced 9.1 million metric tons of wheat, the highest level between the wars. This figure was cut almost in half during World War II and reduced to a shockingly low 3.2 million tons in the bitterly cold year of 1947. But by 1949, wheat production had climbed back up to prewar levels, and in 1959, French farmers grew 11.5 million tons of this all-important crop. Barley harvests increased five times between 1946 and 1959; the maize crop increased tenfold between 1949 and 1959. Butter and meat production both tripled between 1945 and 1960. By the start of the 1960s, French consumers were awash in high-quality agricultural produce after almost a generation of shortage and hunger. In West Germany, the other agricultural giant in Western Europe, a similar pattern was visible: wheat production doubled between 1949 and 1960, as did the production of barley. The German sugar-beet crop grew by a factor of three in the 1950s. The smaller states, too, sharply improved productivity. The Dutch almost tripled their milk production between 1945 and 1960; the Danes more than doubled their output of meat; the Greeks and Spaniards produced ten times more cotton in 1960 than they had in the mid-1940s.[1]

Another index of Europe's expansion was the increase of its external trade. In 1950, France imported just over a billion francs' worth of goods, and exported about the same. By 1960, both imports and exports had increased three times in size. West Germany's increase was still more astonishing: in 1950, the Federal Republic of Germany imported 11.4 billion marks of goods and exported about 8.4 billion. By 1960, Germany sucked in 42.7 billion marks' worth of imports and sold 47.9 billion marks of exports—a fourfold increase in imports and a sixfold increase in exports within a single decade. Even Italy, with a much smaller economy, showed impressive growth, tripling the value of both imports and exports between 1950 and 1960. Further, the EEC Six were trading ever more with one another. In 1953, about one-quarter of all EEC imports came from within the community, a figure that rose to just over a third by 1960. Likewise, EEC exports went increasingly to member countries—from 28.6 percent to 34.5 percent over the same seven-year period. Not only was Europe becoming more productive, but it was becoming more interdependent as well.[2]

Alongside these impressive indices of industrial and agricultural growth are figures that suggest Europeans began to enjoy luxuries on a scale once unimagined. In 1950, there were 1.7 million private cars in France; within ten years, there were 5.5 million, and this figure would double again by 1966. West Germans too experienced a love affair with the automobile. In 1950, there were barely half a million private cars in the Federal Republic. In 1960, there were 4.4 million, and Germany reached 10.3 million by 1966. As in 1950s America, the automobile in Europe became the leitmotif of the decade: fast, clean, modern, and a way out of the time-worn patterns of rural life. When not driving, Europeans could watch television, a distinctly postwar form of entertainment. The number of TVs in France soared from 4,000 in 1950 to 1.9 million a decade later. In Italy in 1953, virtually no one owned a TV set, but within a decade there were over 4 million of them. The growth of German viewership was even faster: Germany had only 2,000 sets in 1953, but 8.5 million in 1963.[3]

These dazzling statistics reveal that the miracle of postwar European economic expansion, while spread out over half a century, was most heavily concentrated in the decade of the 1950s. This chapter lays out some general explanations for this boom. It also points to the various ways that Europeans responded to such sudden riches. For after a generation of war and instability, Europeans found that the transition to prosperity posed its own problems. For some, of course, the decade ushered in the much-feared prospect of Americanization—the creation of a homogenous, assembly-built Europe, a Europe made the American way. But for many more, the 1950s were a decade of unprecedented material comfort, opportunity, and genuine liberty after so many years of harrowing fear and privation. Prosperity also encouraged Europeans to look beyond the animosities of the recent past and consider new common institutions that might bind up this fractured continent. The fifties allowed Europeans, for the first time in a generation, to look beyond mere survival and to lay out the shape of a future European home.

THE MARSHALL PLAN AND THE GREAT BOOM

Americans have long believed that they are in some sense the authors of Europe's stunning postwar economic success story. Few US government programs have had as good a press as the Marshall Plan, the program that delivered some $12.3 billion to Europe between 1948 and the end of 1951. Secretary of State George Marshall himself has attained a saintlike stature in histories of the period. The fiftieth anniversary of the plan, in 1997, produced a new flood of studies and conference reports underscoring the wisdom of the plan and its architects. The text of an exhibit arranged by the United States Library of Congress captured the predominant tone:

> The plan was the boldest, most successful, and certainly the most expensive foreign policy initiative ever attempted in peacetime. A milestone in the growth of US world leadership, the Marshall Plan has had far-reaching consequences. In the short run, it relieved widespread privation and averted the threat of a serious economic depression. In the long run, it enabled the West European nations to recover and maintain not only economic but political independence. It also paved the way for other forms of international cooperation such as the Organization for Economic Cooperation (OECD), the North Atlantic Treaty Organization (NATO), and today's European Union.[4]

American policy, then, saved Europe from chaos and starvation and laid the groundwork for Europe's postwar success. As one Marshall Plan official put it in his memoir, "I think that Marshall Plan dollars did save the world."[5]

We now know, thanks to the detailed research of numerous scholars working in the archives of Western European states, that the Marshall Plan did not save Western Europe.[6] In narrowly economic terms, the contributions of the Marshall Plan to Europe's industrial recovery were small, and in fact a significant recovery was already under way before Marshall aid arrived in Europe. What Marshall aid did do was allow European states to continue along a path of industrial expansion and investment in heavy industry down which they had already started, while *at the same time* putting into place a costly but politically essential welfare state. Marshall aid allowed European governments to move with some confidence to effect a transformation in Europe's economic life, away from the cautious, deflationary 1930s to the Keynesian, high-investment strategies of the 1950s. In this sense, Marshall aid gave Europeans choices that they might not otherwise have had. Marshall aid allowed the Europeans to save themselves.

George Marshall made his Harvard speech in June 1947—a time of acute economic and political crisis in Europe. He had just returned from the Moscow Council of Foreign Ministers, which had deadlocked over how to treat occupied Germany. The British economy was in a tailspin, reeling from the impact of sterling convertibility, which had been required by the terms of the American loan. The French government, having expelled its Communist ministers from the cabinet, now faced a new round of strikes and direct actions that threatened to lead to open insurrection. And across the continent, a desperate shortage of bread, coal, and animal feed left Europeans without the means to feed themselves or their livestock. Marshall, no alarmist, could be excused for thinking that Europe was headed for complete collapse.

Yet the European Recovery Program (ERP), as the Marshall Plan was officially known, did not become law until 3 April 1948; and aid did not start arriving in Europe until May and June of that year. In the full year since Marshall's dire warnings of imminent collapse, Europe did not implode, but in fact began to turn itself around. By the end of 1947, both Britain and France had reached or surpassed their prewar levels of industrial production. Italy, Belgium, and the Netherlands, among others, would do so by the end of 1948. Even when the slower performance of divided and occupied Germany is factored in, Europe had matched its prewar industrial production by mid-1948—just about the time Marshall aid reached Europe.

INDICES OF INDUSTRIAL PRODUCTION, 1946–1950
(1938 = 100)

	1946	1947	1948	1949	1950 (2nd Q.)
Total	77	87	101	115	126
Total excluding FRG	95	106	120	129	139
Austria	46	55	85	113	132
Belgium	91	106	114	116	116
Denmark	103	119	133	141	161
France	79	95	111	122	125
FRG (West Germany)	29	34	51	75	90
Greece	55	69	76	90	106
Ireland	112	120	132	144	166
Italy	75	93	99	105	119
Luxembourg	86	109	145	139	141
Netherlands	74	94	113	126	137
Norway	100	115	124	132	147
Sweden	139	142	151	157	169
Turkey	135	153	154	161	NA
Britain	106	114	128	137	148

SOURCE: United States, *Tenth Report to Congress of the Economic Cooperation Administration,* 1951, table A–1, 97.

Once Marshall aid began, it remained a small fraction of the total gross national product (GNP) of the recipient countries. In its first year of operation, from July 1948 to June 1949, Marshall aid represented 2.4 percent of

Britain's GNP, 6.5 percent of France's, 5.3 percent of Italy's, and only 2.9 percent of West Germany's. The country with the highest figure was Austria, where Marshall aid amounted to 14 percent of GNP in this year. These are not paltry sums, yet they remain small enough to suggest that Marshall aid alone was not the decisive factor in Europe's recovery after World War II.[7]

These figures can be used to argue that Marshall aid was not necessary at all, and the British economic historian Alan Milward has made that argument.[8] But the impact of overall American aid in the eight years or so after the end of the war in Europe should not be underestimated. It is too often forgotten that the United States undertook a massive program of foreign aid well before the Marshall Plan took shape. The United Nations Relief and Rehabilitation Administration (UNRRA) provided some $2.5 billion in aid to Europe, mostly to Greece, Italy, Poland, Yugoslavia, and Czechoslovakia. Much of this aid came in the form of food, textiles, clothing, and shoes. Though it was under UN control, the United States and Britain paid for virtually all of it. Alongside UNRRA aid, the United States gave extensive loans and credits to European countries, with some $4.4 billion going to Britain, $1.9 billion to France, and another $1.7 billion going to Germany, Greece, the Netherlands, and Italy. UNRRA aid and US loans and credits up to the fall of 1947 totaled $11.2 billion, almost as much as the total aid delivered under the Marshall Plan. The economic recovery under way before the arrival of Marshall aid, then, was built upon these grants and credits, which allowed the purchase of food and of raw materials like coal and oil.[9]

Yet to limit the analysis of US aid to its dollar value alone is to miss the point. From its inception, the Marshall Plan aimed to do much more than simply feed and clothe Europeans. The ERP sought to recast the foundations of Europe's economy. As Marshall himself said in his Harvard address, "any assistance that this government may render in the future should provide a cure rather than a mere palliative." The ERP committed the United States to a restructuring of the way Europe worked, traded, and produced. Marshall aid, it was hoped in Washington, would provide the leverage the US needed to cajole and perhaps compel Europeans to lower tariff barriers, pursue sound fiscal policies, stabilize their currencies, increase intra-European trade, and above all maximize their productive potential. These were ambitious goals, and though none was fully achieved to the extent that American policy makers might have liked, the huge shift in European attitudes toward expansionist economic policies, lower tariff rates, and transnational European cooperation suggest that the Marshall Plan profoundly marked the entire dialogue of European reconstruction.

France offers an example of a country that desperately needed the aid the

Marshall Plan offered, and used it to support an ambitious program of industrial investment and expansion. Like much of Western Europe, France was showing impressive signs of industrial recovery soon after the war, with industrial output surpassing prewar levels in 1947. Moreover, the government had pledged itself to the Monnet Plan, a state-designed plan to channel investment into key sectors of the economy like steel and coal production, railway and transport, cement, housing, and agriculture. But industrial recovery required raw materials, machinery, vehicles, and coal in order to stay on track, so France was obliged to import vast quantities of these goods, as well as foodstuffs. With its export industries still recovering, France had little foreign exchange with which to pay for these goods, and so faced an alarming trade deficit of some $2 billion in 1946, $1.3 billion of which was with the United States. As French exports picked up in 1947, the trade deficit diminished slightly, but the deficit with the United States remained over $1 billion in 1947 and 1948. Before Marshall Plan aid, the only way to cover the cost of imports was through stopgap US loans, and from the liquidation of gold assets and foreign investments. France sold over $1 billion of its gold reserves in 1946 alone, and by the fall of 1947, the French treasury held a mere $445 million in gold and dollar reserves. France would soon be down to its last US nickel. Without dollars, France could no longer import goods from America, and its program for industrial recovery would have to be curtailed. In such a scenario, unemployment would worsen, consumer goods would be cut back, and the political situation, so fragile in mid-1947, might take a turn for the worse. In December 1947, the Truman administration, already primed to do battle with Communism in Europe, found it relatively easy to win $284 million of "interim aid" from the Congress, slated to cover the French import program before Marshall aid arrived.[10] The French crisis of 1947 showed that political stability was dependent upon maintaining the flow of raw materials into Europe so that the impressive recovery begun in 1946 could be maintained.

The effect of Marshall aid, when it did come in mid-1948, was to provide France with the funds to cover the dollar deficit, which in turn allowed the French government to continue to invest in the Monnet Plan. France did not use its Marshall credits chiefly to purchase food; rather, some 67 percent of Marshall aid in France was used to obtain raw materials vital for continued industrial production, like coal, oil, and cotton, as well as for purchasing machinery and vehicles. As a result of this strong commitment to heavy industry, French industrial output continued to climb throughout the Marshall Plan period: in 1951, it exceeded by 42 percent the level of 1938. Exports began to pick up, so that by 1950 France was exporting almost as much as it was importing (though it continued to have a large deficit with the United States).

Marshall aid was also used in France to help cover some of the national debt, which, because of an inefficient tax system, France could not do by internal revenues. This eased, though it did not cure, the constant inflationary problems that France faced in this period by limiting the amount that the treasury had to borrow to cover the debt. On strictly economic grounds, then, the Marshall Plan in France proved a major success.[11]

Yet the impact of Marshall aid was greater even than its dollar amounts suggest. Marshall aid redounded to the benefit of the centrist, anti-Communist coalitions that held the fragile Fourth Republic together. This was no easy task, as the government had to contend with a challenge both from the far left and from the Gaullist Rassemblement du Peuple Français, which reviled what it saw as a growing dependence upon the United States. The Third Force, made up of Christian Democrats, Socialists, and Radicals, needed to deliver industrial recovery as well as increased wages, social security, and health benefits. Marshall aid allowed these promises to be met.

In Britain and Italy, the record was more modest, but impressive nonetheless. Britain received the largest amount of Marshall aid, at some $2.8 billion. Yet the British economy was much larger than that of any other recipient, and Marshall aid amounted to no more than 2 percent of GNP overall. It was even smaller than the American loan of 1946. By 1948, the British economy was well on its way toward viability, with exports having recovered well, thanks to the heavy demand in Europe and the colonies for British manufactured goods. By 1948, Britain had reached a current account balance. Unlike France, Britain did not have an urgent political need for aid, as it was not facing a Communist challenge from within. Nonetheless, British officials still wanted Marshall aid, and felt it would provide the critical margin during a time of economic fragility. Because the government had pursued such a severe restriction of imports, the British people were constantly short of foodstuffs, a point the Conservative Party ceaselessly emphasized in its attacks on Labour. British officials thus planned to spend much of the Marshall aid on staples like wheat, tobacco, maize, barley and oats, meat and bacon, cotton, and edible oils and fats. Overall, 30 percent of Marshall aid in Britain was spent on foodstuffs, compared with only 10 percent in France. A large portion of the remaining sum was spent on paying down the national debt.[12] Such was the basic health of the British economy that Marshall aid was stopped in December 1950. Without it, Britons would have been hungrier than they already were in 1948–50, but the country would have survived.

Italy's experience in the Marshall aid period was altogether different from that of Britain and France. Italy, after all, was a former enemy and a defeated power. The effort to regain international standing and domestic legitimacy preoccupied the Christian Democratic governments that dominated Italian politics after the expulsion of the Communists in May 1947. The government of Prime Minister Alcide De Gasperi therefore sought to distance itself from the statist, interventionist economic policies of the Fascist period, as well as the sharp inflation that Italy had suffered in the last years of the war. De Gasperi outlined no urgent state-financed program of national recovery, as Monnet had done in France. Instead, De Gasperi followed the lead of his ultraorthodox budget minister, Luigi Einaudi, in attacking inflation first and restoring the stability of the currency. Einaudi wanted to balance the budget and trade deficit not through increased production but with sharp cuts in government expenditure—precisely the opposite of the approach taken in France. For De Gasperi, this was smart politics: it appealed to the middle and upper classes in Italy, who were gratified at the appearance of sound money policies and now rallied firmly to the Christian Democrats. The working class, which bore the brunt of these deflationary policies in the form of higher unemployment, were in any case already hostile to the De Gasperi regime.

The Italian government therefore looked upon American aid with some caution. Of course, the aid itself was welcome, especially the large quantities of bread grains, oil and coal, cotton, and machinery that the ERP provided between 1948 and 1951. At the same time, however, Einaudi steadfastly refused to accept American advice on using Marshall aid to kick-start the Italian economy. Fearful that a large state-financed investment program would aggravate inflation, the Italian government during the Marshall Plan period undertook to finance only reconstruction efforts, and put little investment into new manufacturing capacity. This they left to the private capital markets, which were still moribund. Unlike the French government, which had pumped huge sums into heavy industry—and was suffering high inflation because of it—Italy restricted public investment, a policy that slowed expansion and contributed to unemployment. Large quantities of the "counterpart" funds—the lire that the Italian government earned from selling Marshall Plan goods in Italy—were merely put in the bank to bolster Italy's reserves and strengthen the currency; too little of the aid made its way to industrial modernization. Only after two years of wrangling with the Americans did Italian officials agree to begin shifting counterpart funds into public works projects, industry, and agriculture. Moreover, Italy did not lay out a long-term plan for recovery until 1955—three years after the end of the Marshall Plan and a decade after the advent of the Monnet Plan in France. Italy during the Marshall Plan period offers little support to the legend of an American rescue of postwar Europe. Italians took the aid but failed to use it well—and the Americans discovered to their surprise that they had little leverage to compel Italy to do so.[13]

And yet the statistics reveal that Italy, no less than France or even Germany, enjoyed skyrocketing rates of growth from the mid-1950s onward. What explains Italy's economic boom? The Italians did it their way. While Italy's public investment effort was small compared to other Western European economies', the private sector revived anyway, if half a decade later than some competitors. By the mid-fifties, Italy had made impressive strides in producing high-quality durable goods like automobiles, refrigerators, washing machines, and typewriters that formed the basis for a strong export industry. Here, Italy's battle against inflation helped, because prices remained stable and Italy's goods were affordable. And at just the very moment that Italy's export industries recovered, the EEC began to reach agreements on reducing tariffs as part of the gradual process of European integration. By 1958, the six EEC countries had formed a common market, with no tariffs between their states—boosting sales of Italy's high-quality, well-priced durable goods. Between 1958 and 1963, Italy's exports grew at an average annual rate of 14.5 percent, while the GDP grew at about 6.3 percent per year in the same period. The EEC helped considerably, reducing tariffs and encouraging intra-European trade: Italy sent 23 percent of its exports to EEC countries in 1955, but this figure rose to 40 percent by 1965.[14]

Alongside the improvement of Italy's exports came the swift growth in what might be called the quasi-national sector of the economy. Despite the general mistrust of the De Gasperi government for the economic policies of the Fascist years, certain corporatist structures were in fact carried over into the postwar period. Most prominent was the innocuous-sounding Institute for Industrial Reconstruction (IRI), founded in 1933 as an autonomous industrial cartel, designed to be entirely free of bureaucratic meddling. IRI held a controlling interest in dozens of industries, especially steel, engineering, shipbuilding, electricity, and telephones. By 1948, IRI employed 216,000 people. Yet IRI was not a nationalized firm; it was financed largely through private capital and operated beyond the reach of the administration. This was an invitation to corruption, patronage, and inefficiency, and these problems did emerge in the late 1960s. But during the fifties, IRI served as a sort of central nervous system for Italian industry, combining the benefits of direct control with the flexibility of the free market. Likewise, the advent of the National Agency for Hydrocarbons (ENI), under the determined leadership of Enrico Mattei, revealed how the Italian state encouraged the growth of the public sector while trying not to interfere with the "invisible hand." When in the late forties large deposits of methane gas were discovered in the Po Valley, De Gasperi allowed Mattei to form ENI to develop the new resource. Using profits from the gas industry, Mattei created a vast empire that expanded into petrochemicals, motels and highways, rubber production, engineering and construction, textiles, and even nuclear power. Rather than rely on a state-planned and -financed industrial strategy, as the French did, the Italian state offered patronage and tax breaks to well-placed Christian Democrats like Mattei and allowed them to do what they wished, so long as production, investment, and employment increased. Flourishing in an atmosphere of monetary stability, low taxes for business, and low interest rates, these industrial cartels served to bolster the economy without large commitments of capital from the state treasury. This was hardly a recipe for structural reform, but in the short term, the strategy was immensely effective in boosting production.[15]

Even this brief summary reveals that it would be wrong to assign too much credit for Europe's postwar recovery to the Marshall Plan of 1948–51. Benevolent and effective as it was, the Marshall Plan did not in itself provide the resources that triggered the swift economic recovery visible in the 1950s. Yet its impact was nonetheless significant. For it was the US government that ceaselessly urged Europeans to pursue national strategies of recovery that stressed exports, lower tariffs, and high investment in technology and new industrial plant. American planners believed that the lessons of the war years were clear: tariffs slowed growth, hurt productivity, hindered expansion and employment, and contributed to political instability. The Marshall Plan sprang from the belief that stability and peace required economic expansion; and while the sixteen different governments that received Marshall aid might quibble over which national economic strategy suited its needs best, none of them disagreed with this basic premise. It is in this general sense of transforming the mentality of the major states of Europe that the Marshall Plan had its greatest impact. If the United States did not "save" Europe in the 1940s, it certainly helped Europeans chart out a path to a new era of peace and prosperity.

WIRTSCHAFTSWUNDER

For all the breathtaking improvement in the economic position of France, Britain, and Italy during the 1950s, it was Germany that most exemplified the European miracle. Few missed the irony here. Germany had brought catastrophe to Europe not once but twice in the first half of the twentieth century. In 1945, it looked as if Germany had paid a heavy price for its savage aggression. At war's end, the country was a desolate wasteland of rubble, its reputation

forever stained by Nazism. Its land was occupied and then divided by the victorious powers, its political future looked clouded and uncertain, its streets
were choked with refugees, its people morose, exhausted, traumatized.

But Germany did not remain down for long. In the ten years between
1948 and 1958, West Germany—the two-thirds of the former Reich lucky
enough to have been occupied by the Western Allies—passed through a
transformation so great, so swift, that it soon came to be called the
Wirtschaftswunder, or economic miracle. In the 1950s, industrial production
tripled and unemployment sank from over 10 percent to less than 4. Exports
increased so much—sixfold—that by 1960 the Federal Republic of Germany
exported 10 percent of the world total, more than Britain and second only to
the United States. Between 1950 and 1960, the GNP increased at an average
annual rate of 7.9 percent. What caused this extraordinary growth?

GERMAN ECONOMIC DEVELOPMENT, 1950–1960

Year	GNP % Change	GNP Per Capita (DM)	Cost of Living Increase %	Percent Unemployed	Trade Balance (Billions DM)
1950		1,602		10.2	–3.0
1951	10.9	1,921	7.7	9.0	–0.1
1952	9.0	2,174	2.1	8.4	0.7
1953	7.9	2,328	-1.8	7.5	2.5
1954	7.2	2,486	0.2	7.0	2.7
1955	12.0	2,834	1.6	5.1	1.2
1956	7.0	3,100	2.5	4.0	2.9
1957	5.8	3,337	2.0	3.4	4.1
1958	3.3	3,528	2.2	3.5	5.0
1959	6.9	3,757	1.0	2.6	5.4
1960	8.8	4,252	1.4	1.3	5.2

SOURCE: Karl Hardach, *The Political Economy of Germany in the Twentieth Century* (Berkeley: University of
California Press, 1980), 162; B. R. Mitchell, *International Historical Statistics: Europe, 1750–1993* (London:
Macmillan, 1998), 167.

Certainly much credit should go to the architect of Germany's economic
policy during the 1950s, Ludwig Erhard, who was named director of economic affairs in the Anglo-American bizone in 1948 and then Konrad
Adenauer's minister for economic affairs in 1949. Not initially a political man,
Erhard had pursued an academic career in Bavaria before the war. His antipathy toward the Nazi regime led him to develop contacts with the wartime
resistance to Hitler. But he sat out the war in an economic institute in
Nuremberg, sketching plans for the postwar German economy. Erhard

strongly advocated a return to liberal free market ideas. In his view, the German economic experience since 1918 had been a complete disaster. Under the Weimar Republic, the government had pursued contradictory aims, intervening heavily in the economy while allowing cartels to swallow up whole sectors of the industrial economy. Nazi economic policy was worse: with no respect for the rule of law or for the rights of individual producers and consumers, the Nazis had broken the contract between the state and the citizen. The regime had looked upon industry as a tool to pursue its political and military ends, rather than as an integral part in the creation of a stable society. If Germans wished to have a free society in the wake of Hitler, argued Erhard, they had first to allow a free economy, unburdened of state controls. Of course, the less fortunate should be cared for, but this could be accomplished only if the society as a whole prospered.[16]

Initially, these ideas made little headway in the political discourse of postwar Germany. Few Germans looked to capitalism as the answer to their troubles, and many saw it as the principal cause of the economic instability and war that had beset the continent since 1914. Surely a new order, based on social justice, fairness, and the distribution of wealth, offered the best means to avoid renewed class and national conflict. The popularity of the Social Democratic Party in West Germany reveals how widespread these views were. Indeed, even the German Christian Democrats issued a platform in February 1947 that called for the socialization of heavy industry and banks, and declared that "the time of unlimited power of private capitalism is over."

But what should replace it? The occupation period offered no obvious alternative. The Western occupying powers strongly disagreed with one another over economic matters, with the British favoring a policy of nationalization of industry and heavy state control, and the French generally fearful of any industrial recovery in Germany at all. The Americans at first were bound by their Potsdam commitments to reduce German industrial strength by dismantling factories and controlling production. As a consequence, Germany's recovery lagged far behind that of other European states. As East-West relations soured, the Western Allies grew increasingly concerned that to delay German recovery would fatally hinder a return to political stability and create further resentment toward the occupation.

By the start of 1948, it had become clear to the occupiers that the key to a swift revival of German economic activity was a new currency. During the war, the Nazi leadership pumped reichsmarks into the economy, with heavily inflationary effects. By 1945, with German industry at a standstill, there were far too many old marks chasing very few goods. The currency's value collapsed and Germans fell back on bartering and the black market. In 1948, the

Western powers—the Russians would have none of it—agreed to withdraw all the old bills and replace them with a new deutsche mark, at about a ten-to-one ratio. Thus, some 90 percent of the currency was withdrawn from circulation overnight. The new bills, printed in the United States and secretly shipped to Germany, were introduced on 20 June 1948. The effect was immediate. The new currency had genuine purchasing power, which gave people an incentive to find work and earn a living. Workers returned to their jobs, absenteeism dropped, and productivity surged. The black market disappeared, as those who had goods to sell would now exchange them for the new currency. Shops filled up with goods that hitherto had been hoarded or stashed away. Factory managers could now look forward to earning hard currency for their goods instead of the worthless reichsmarks. The ethos of the moment changed entirely, from one of survival and barter to one of working and earning. At the same moment as the new currency appeared, Economics Minister Ludwig Erhard took the bold step of abolishing rations and price controls on most consumer goods, demonstrating his strong faith in the power of the free market to meet consumer demand, which after a decade of war and chaos was now at a fever pitch. The first step toward recovery had been taken.[17]

Suddenly it seemed that the death certificate issued to German capitalism had been premature. Certainly Erhard saw it this way. In his new post he pursued a swift liberalization of the economy, an end to controls, and a restoration of the enterprising spirit that he believed would lead Germany and Europe back to prosperity. Erhard is often credited with the creation in Germany of the "social-market economy" (a term actually coined by his junior colleague Alfred Müller-Armack). Though later German governments embraced the idea of capitalism with a conscience, Erhard himself placed far greater emphasis on the "market" element of the phrase than the "social." As he wrote in his 1957 testament of faith, Wohlstand für Alle (Prosperity for All), "only by firmly rejecting socialist dogmas, of whatever complexion, and by affirming a free economic order, can mounting prosperity and genuine security be achieved." The social-market economy did not mean "granting a man complete security from the hour of birth, and protecting him absolutely from the hazards of life." In such a case, citizens would fail to develop "that full measure of energy, effort, enterprise, and other human virtues which are vital to the life and future of the nation." The role of economic policy, Erhard believed, was to create opportunities for each citizen to improve his own standard of living through work, thereby lessening the need for social welfare. "Economic success is the basis and cause of all social progress," he insisted. "The Welfare State," by contrast, "must finally spell poverty for all."[18]

The results of Erhard's policies seem to offer full vindication for a man

once vilified by the German left as the "patron saint of hoarders and profiteers." By 1957, the improvement in Germany's economic position was so remarkable that he could laugh at the Social Democrats, who, he declared in a
speech to his CDU colleagues, "were constantly prophesying that our economic policy would lead to bankruptcy." Instead, these "blinkered demagogues" could only offer a socialist policy "that brought disaster in every
country in which it had been tried." By contrast, his own policies, which
stressed open competition, monetary stability, low taxes, reduction of tariffs,
and abolition of controls, offered an ever-improving standard of living for the
German people. Given Germany's record of success, Erhard's hubris is perhaps understandable; for he rejected the notion of a German economic miracle. For him, Germany's success was "anything but a miracle. It is the result of
the honest efforts of a whole people who, in keeping with the principles of liberty, were given the opportunity of using personal initiative and human energy."[19] Yet economic historians have been quick to point out that Germany
profited from a very unusual *convergence* of factors that created just the right
circumstances for Erhard's policies to succeed. Not least of these was American aid.

Erhard pooh-poohed the role of Marshall aid in Germany's postwar recovery. In Erhard's memoirs, the commander of the US occupation force,
Gen. Lucius Clay, appears as a distant supernumerary, a man who "stood behind me endorsing my orders."[20] But this is to overstate the case. The currency reform, after all, was an American plan. Moreover, as soon as it was
implemented, Germans went on a buying spree, drawing in vast quantities of
imports from abroad and contributing to a massive trade deficit. As in Britain
in 1946 and France in 1947, it was Germany's own recovery that triggered a
payments crisis. Here, American aid proved vital. Even before the Marshall
Plan aid arrived, Germans were receiving large US grants of emergency aid
through the GARIOA program (Government and Relief in Occupied
Areas)—aid that totaled $1.6 billion by the end of 1950. On top of this,
Marshall aid started flowing in mid-1948. US aid from both programs covered
a great deal of Germany's import needs: 70 percent in 1946–47, 65 percent in
1948, and 43 percent in 1949.[21] In addition to helping Germans pay for their
imports, the Marshall Plan gave a kick start to industrial recovery through the
use of counterpart funds. The German government sold US-financed goods
to consumers, and then placed those marks in a separate account. These
funds, still controlled by Washington officials, were then reinvested into industries that badly needed an influx of capital, such as electricity, coal mining,
agriculture, housing, railways, and shipping. Once new US-backed capital
started to flow into certain industries, the private capital markets in Germany

soon followed suit. German money followed American money, and the result was a swift restoration of German industrial production—so swift, in fact, that the Germans were running a trade surplus by 1951. US aid, though modest in size—Germany received only half the aid given to Britain and France— had a very significant ripple effect. As the historian Charles Maier has deftly put it, Marshall aid acted "like the lubricant in an engine—not the fuel—allowing a machine to run that would otherwise buckle and bind."[22]

In addition to Marshall Plan aid, Germany profited from an immense pool of labor, the product of the postwar migration from the Eastern zone at the end of the war. Some 9 million refugees had poured into West Germany in the early postwar years, and they were joined by another 3.6 million who fled East Germany between 1950 and 1962. By 1960, about 23 percent of the FRG's population had not lived there before the war. At first this presented a terrible burden on the occupying powers, whose resources were already strained. But in the boom conditions of the early fifties, these mobile and mostly skilled workers were a godsend. Moreover, the desire to work deeply affected the climate of labor relations. Labor unions showed remarkable restraint. Although they did succeed in pressuring the government in 1951 to pass legislation mandating worker-management codetermination (*Mitbestimmung*) on the boards of some major industries, the unions shied away from direct action. In 1955, Germany lost only five days for every hundred workers to strikes, while France lost twenty-five and Italy sixty-one. Clearly, the rank and file had no interest in slowing down a boom that had so dramatically improved their economic fortunes.[23]

Yet if there was any one single theme that characterized the German economic boom in the 1950s, it was the astonishing increase in Germany's foreign trade. Germany had been the engine of the Central European economy before the war, but in the postwar period, Germany reconfigured its trading patterns. Instead of exporting coal and textiles, as it had done in the nineteenth century, Germany now specialized in machine tools, engine and vehicle manufacturing, chemicals, and electrical engineering. German-made machines were the best in Europe and were in heavy demand throughout the decade. By 1958, 40 percent of Germany's total output was devoted to its export industries. The increase in German exports had political implications, for Germany began to displace American and British exports to Europe, thus underscoring the common economic ties between the continental West European nations, and Germany's dominant position in Europe. Economics Minister Erhard put a good face on this new discovery of Germany's power. He said in 1957 that "it was the historic task of the Federal Republic . . . to underpin, to strengthen, and to defend the free economic order of Europe with the full weight of German trade."[24] A noble aim, no doubt. Yet this was a remarkable claim. Germany, which from 1933 to 1945 had aimed at enslaving all of Europe in the interest of tyranny, now appointed itself the defender of European freedom and prosperity. How did the rest of Europe feel about Germany's "historic task"?

THE ADVENT OF EUROPEAN INTEGRATION,
1950-1957

It wasn't that Europeans had started to *like* the Germans. They hadn't. Rather, during the 1950s Europeans figured out how to control them. Starting in 1950, a number of key leaders and their advisers in France, Germany, Italy, and the Benelux countries began crafting a new political and economic structure for Europe designed to harness and contain Germany's economic power while limiting Germany's political role. It was not an easy process. One cannot do away with decades, even centuries, of national rivalry and suspicion overnight. But in the shadow of the Cold War, Europe's leaders concluded that their nations could prosper only as a whole, and not singly. They agreed that to pursue joint aims required a new ethic of international relations, a new spirit of sacrifice and compromise. It is quite wrong to depict these leaders as pan-Europeans, as if somehow they had stopped caring about their own country's interests. On the contrary, it was because they sought to advance their countries' national interests that they aimed to craft a new cooperative regime that might bolster interdependence and mutual reliance. This paradox lies at the heart of the experiment called European integration.

There were really four principal authors of European integration, at least as it emerged in the early 1950s: German chancellor Konrad Adenauer; French foreign minister Robert Schuman; the American secretary of state, Dean Acheson; and the French economic adviser and international statesman Jean Monnet. The role played by these men and, of course, by the governments they represented was critical to the success of the European project. Without their commitment to a Europe based on cooperation, balance of power, equality, and common security, the history of the continent after World War II would have much more closely resembled the pattern of politics in Europe following World War I: a continent of suspicious, competitive, fractious states, whose governments had little public support and whose peoples sought solutions through extremism and conflict rather than moderation and compromise.

Adenauer's role cannot be underestimated. This crafty Rhinelander—the

Germans called him *der alte Fuchs,* the old fox—became Germany's first post-war chancellor in 1949, soon after the three Western occupying powers had agreed to restore limited sovereignty to the newly formed Federal Republic. Yet Adenauer's new state was hardly independent. It was still occupied by hundreds of thousands of American, British, and French soldiers; its economy was still subject to a web of controls and restrictions imposed by the Allied powers; it had no army and no control over foreign affairs or security matters; and Adenauer himself still had to answer to the three high commissioners—the American John J. McCloy, the Englishman Gen. Sir Brian Robertson, and the Frenchman André François-Poncet. The continuing Allied presence put Adenauer in an awkward position. He knew that the FRG's security and economic success depended upon a close and cooperative relationship with the Western powers, yet he also feared that continued restrictions on German independence would encourage a revival of German nationalism. Adenauer's archrival, the powerful Social Democratic leader, Kurt Schumacher, denounced him for his pliant attitude. Schumacher was a ferocious opponent. A Berliner and ardent socialist who had lost an arm fighting the Russians in World War I and then lost a leg as a result of his incarceration in Dachau under the Third Reich, he wanted Germany united, all foreign occupiers out, and a return to the German people of their full sovereign rights. It was a potent message with considerable appeal, rooted as it was in the belief that Germany's rightful place was between East and West, with a foot in both worlds. But Adenauer believed that Schumacher's plan could be bought only at the price of long-term subservience to the Soviet Union. The chancellor envisioned an alternative scenario. He would make West Germany a model democracy, an economic powerhouse, a staunch supporter of European federation, and a close ally of the Western powers. The Eastern zone would be welcome into the FRG, but on terms laid down by the West.

Adenauer could not make this bold policy work unless he was given strong backing by his Western partners. He had to show the West German public that a policy of cooperation with Europe and the United States—a *Westpolitik*—had clear benefits for them. This is why Adenauer was so infuriated by the continued restrictions on German sovereignty. In 1946, the occupiers had identified some 744 companies, factories, and firms that were to be dismantled, ostensibly as a way of reducing Germany's ability ever to threaten its neighbors. Although the dismantling policy had been somewhat scaled back by 1949, major steel, coal, and chemical plants awaited destruction under Allied orders, even as the US was channeling Marshall Plan dollars to Germany in order to rebuild the country. In the Bundestag in September 1949, Adenauer made an open appeal to the occupation authorities to end the dismantling. "If the German people," he declared, "is to be integrated into the cultural and economic life of Europe, the majority of Germans must be convinced that the three Western powers really want this. But I think it must be said that it is precisely the unjustified destruction of German assets that causes doubts among large parts of the German population."[25] He was quite right: the Germans would not commit themselves to the West until the West demonstrated its goodwill toward the Germans.

Goodwill toward Germany remained in short supply, however, especially in France. In the first years after the war, French leaders had welcomed the division of Germany and seemed inclined to pare down the Western portion still further by removing the industrial belt of the Rhineland and Ruhr Valley from German control altogether. The French also annexed the coal-rich Saarland, a German region adjacent to Lorraine. Although the French had been pressured to moderate their annexationist plans, they continued to demand some kind of international oversight of Germany's powerful coal and steel industries. French politicians and spokesmen from across the political spectrum could find rare unity on the subject of keeping the German economy under careful control and insisting on a permanently demilitarized, subservient state. When one considers that the Germans had invaded France three times within one lifetime—in 1870, 1914, and 1940—French suspicions seem amply justified.

Yet at the start of the 1950s, the East-West conflict seemed to be taking a sharp turn for the worse, dwarfing the continuing tensions across the Rhine. The Prague coup of 1948 had come as a shock to Western Europe, apparently revealing the long reach of international Communism. The Berlin blockade of 1948–49 also led Western governments to anticipate war with the Russians, in which case the divided, unarmed Western powers would be sorely unprepared. In September 1949, the Soviets tested their first atomic weapon, and in October 1949—in the same month that Mao Zedong proclaimed the People's Republic of China—the Soviets announced the creation of the German Democratic Republic. By the spring of 1950, both the US and British military establishments were pressing their governments to rearm West Germany. Five years after destroying the German Wehrmacht, the Anglo-Americans now contemplated reviving this potent force and turning it upon the Russians.

The French were horrified, and not least the mild-mannered foreign minister, Robert Schuman. Not well known outside of France, and still too often ignored in histories of European integration, Robert Schuman played the decisive role in breaking a deadlock between the Western powers on the problem of Germany. Schuman was born in Metz at a time when this city was under German control, as it had been since Germany seized Alsace-Lorraine in 1871.

As a student in Luxembourg, he grew up in two worlds, one French, one German. He served in the German army reserves in World War I and spoke French with a German accent. After the war, when his native Lorraine reverted to French control, he became active in Catholic politics and ran for parliament. He served briefly in the Vichy government as minister for refugees but soon severed relations with Pétain's regime and joined the resistance. He emerged from the war as one of the few right-wing politicians whose reputation had not been damaged by wartime collaboration, and when his party, the MRP, emerged as the leading player on the right of French politics, Schuman's place was secured. He served as finance minister, prime minister, and, most important, as foreign minister from July 1948 until the end of 1952. These were crucial years, when the basic framework of both European integration and the Western alliance were laid. This tall, stooped, quiet man, a lifelong bachelor with a balding pate, played a crucial part in these deliberations.

Schuman believed that France's long-term interests would best be served by a policy of cooperation and integration with Germany. In light of the sharp deterioration of East-West relations, it was clear that Western Germany must play a part in buttressing Europe's economic fortunes: it had to be brought into Europe's fold. But this was no easy task to accomplish, given the still-burning hatred many French harbored toward the Germans. Schuman gambled that giving Germany limited concessions, such as allowing Germany to join the newly established Council of Europe and rolling back the harshest of dismantling measures, would send a signal to Konrad Adenauer—a fellow Christian Democrat—that France did seek to build a new partnership, albeit one in which the Germans played second fiddle to France. It was a delicate balancing act, however: domestic politics constrained both men in their pursuit of compromise. The French National Assembly reproached Schuman for giving Germany too much autonomy too quickly (and some parliamentarians called Schuman "the Boche" behind his back), while Adenauer's critics in the Bundestag demanded faster movement on recovering Germany's full sovereignty.

Without strong European institutions that could control Germany, Europe's future would always remain unsettled. In the late 1940s, the problem seemed urgent. As German public opinion chafed under the continuing Allied occupation, prominent German politicians—including members of Adenauer's cabinet—spoke out openly against the Western powers and blamed them for Germany's unemployment problems. The Germans were becoming restless. Reports in the press told tales of underground fraternities of former Wehrmacht soldiers, harboring strong Nazi sentiments and plotting to return to power. One deputy in the Bundestag publicly cast doubt on the

Holocaust. For all of Adenauer's genuine commitment to *Westpolitik,* the German public did not seem to be following his lead. It was a vicious circle: as long as the Germans misbehaved and publicly denounced the occupation, the French would insist on still more restrictions against Germany's freedom of action—which would in turn generate further German resentment.

Here, the US secretary of state, Dean Acheson, deserves recognition for his efforts to break the logjam of Franco-German relations. American policy was premised on the idea that European unity would strengthen the continent, help contain the Soviets, increase prosperity, and boost the confidence of the European public at a time of high anxiety. But Britain had shown no desire to enter into binding agreements with the continent. Acheson believed that France had to take up the cause of a united, integrated, and cooperative Europe. To persuade France to do so proved immensely difficult, and Acheson labored long and hard on the problem. In October 1949, just as Adenauer had begun his campaign against Allied dismantling, Acheson stepped up his direct appeals to Robert Schuman, urging him to adopt a new course in his policy toward Germany. In a personal letter to the Frenchman, Acheson asked Schuman to consider how the Western powers could best develop "a Western European community in which the Germans can assume an appropriate position as a reasonable democratic and peaceful nation." He continued:

> Now is the time for French initiative and leadership of the type required to integrate the German Federal Republic promptly and decisively into Western Europe. . . . I believe that we shall probably never have any more democratic or more receptive atmosphere in Germany in which to work than we have at the present moment. Unless we move rapidly the political atmosphere will deteriorate and we shall be faced with much more difficult and dangerous personalities in the German Government. The 1920s teach us that we must give genuine and rapid support to those elements now in control of Germany if they are to be expected to retain control.

Acheson recognized that he was asking a great deal of Schuman: to trust the Germans, to believe in their commitment to the Western community, to slow dismantling and ease Allied restrictions as a means to win over German public opinion. For Acheson, it made sense "to advance to the Germans a political credit which they have not yet fully earned. In this way, we could make more certain that the developments which we much desire will take place in Germany, since by our action we could strengthen those forces in Germany upon whom we must rely." Acknowledging the limits of a policy imposed by

Washington upon unwilling Europeans, Acheson declared that the future of Europe "depends on the assumption by your country of leadership in Europe on these problems."[26]

Acheson's exhortations made an impression on Schuman. What motivated Schuman to take up Acheson's challenge, however, was not altruism but fear. Starting in early 1950, as the two countries continued to wrangle over dismantling and the limits on Germany's sovereignty, French leaders began to get wind of discussions within the American and British military establishments on rearming the Germans and even enrolling them as full-fledged partners in the NATO alliance.[27] The idea was alarming. Not only did it represent a provocation to the Russians, who might use it as a pretext to invade Western Europe, but it was far in advance of French public opinion, which would never abide such a scheme. It would also tilt the balance of power in Europe in Germany's favor, for in addition to having a powerful economy, the Germans might soon possess a new, American-supplied army as well. What use would Germany have then for European cooperation? French officials in the Foreign Ministry were stumped by the problem. The Americans were urging France to trust Germany yet were simultaneously talking about rearming this once-formidable foe. At the same time, Britain was unwilling to provide any counterweight to Germany inside a unified Europe. So what was France to do? Obstruction and loud complaint had not worked. That approach merely alienated the Germans further and exasperated the Americans. Perhaps Acheson had been right: perhaps now was the moment for bold French leadership.

Certainly Jean Monnet thought so. Monnet, the ever-creative, energetic director of the French economic recovery agency, believed Schuman had to make the first move. In early May 1950, he urged Schuman to take a political gamble that might cut the Gordian knot of Franco-German relations. Monnet proposed that France and Germany, and any other willing state in Western Europe, pool their coal and steel industries, placing them under the international, binding control of a high authority. In a stroke, Monnet believed, the long wrangle over Germany's coal and steel production would be swept away. Germany would enter on equal terms into a novel arrangement with France, signifying a joint partnership in a program of industrial expansion. French anxieties would be eased because German industry, should it expand rapidly, would pull France and the rest of Europe along with it. The high authority would "contain" Germany: by controlling coal and steel—the sinews of power in the 1950s European economy—it would in effect preside over a new balance of economic power in Europe, eliminating, as Monnet put it to

Schuman, "the supremacy of German industry, whose existence creates fear in Europe." But it would do so in a constructive framework rather than through a humiliating military occupation. It would offer an olive branch to Germany but placate French anxieties over German recovery; and it would please the Americans, who had been urging Schuman to take just such a bold step. On 9 May 1950, Schuman announced the plan that would carry his name, and laid the cornerstone of the new Europe.[28]

Adenauer leapt at the chance; here was the gesture of solidarity and equality that his *Westpolitik* required. Acheson, too, was buoyant, and the US ambassador in Paris, David Bruce, hailed the plan as "the most constructive thing done by the French government since the Liberation." The response in Britain, by contrast, was hostile and peevish. Ernest Bevin seethed with anger at having been ambushed in this way; the Foreign Office felt France had "behaved extremely badly in springing this proposal on the world at this juncture without any attempt at consultation." The British feared that France and Germany were reviving an old dream of a Franco-German cartel in Europe, one with profound implications for Britain's own economy. Britain refused to join in subsequent talks on plan, opposed in principle to a scheme in which decision making would be placed in the hands of a supranational body that was, as Clement Attlee put it, "utterly undemocratic and responsible to nobody."[29]

British objections moved few in Paris. From the start of the Marshall Plan, the Labour government had been openly resistant to any moves toward European federation, and would have certainly blocked Schuman's plan if it had been given the opportunity. Schuman knew perfectly well he would anger Britain, but the alternative course of drawn-out, acrimonious negotiations on Allied occupation policy had brought Western European relations to the point of crisis. Britain had already abdicated its responsibilities as the leader of continental Europe; in 1950, France cautiously assumed that burden. It was a bold and courageous decision for a country profoundly unsure of itself, with a still-fragile economy and a divided body politic. Yet it also marked a turning point in postwar European history. From 1950 onward, France and Germany pursued a common policy of economic and political cooperation that drew their countries over time into an intimate embrace unimaginable at war's end. At the same time, Britain, its eyes lingering too long and too fondly upon its fading Empire, missed the great chance that destiny briefly offered: the leadership of Europe.

The Schuman Plan came into being as the European Coal and Steel Community (ECSC), and had six members: France, Germany, Italy, Belgium, the Netherlands, and Luxembourg. The ECSC placed the coal and steel sectors of these states under a common, supranational authority whose purpose was to rationalize and modernize production, making the industry more efficient while removing decision making from the hands of national governments. It started operations in August 1952, headquartered in Luxembourg, and with Monnet as its first chairman. The ECSC was Europe's first concrete experience in integration, and the results were mixed. National antagonisms, the result of centuries of economic rivalry, quite naturally persisted. The Belgians and the French proved loath to close down failing and outmoded coal mines; the West Germans complained about the continuing protectionism practiced by France; and the range of operations affected only a single sector of the European economy, one that was itself in decline as new forms of energy, especially oil and nuclear power, came into operation. But the ECSC laid a foundation on which the next forty years of progress was based. The high authority, made up of nine members, with France, Germany, and Italy having two members each, had wide powers over the coal and steel industry. It was balanced by a Council of Ministers whose purpose was to moderate any sudden burst of supranational enthusiasm by the high authority. There was also a Common Assembly of seventy-eight members, in practice a powerless body but a symbol of optimism that the ECSC might spawn European political institutions. And there was also the Court of Justice, which could rule on the legality of high authority decisions—establishing the principle of a common body of European laws. For a group of nations that just ten years earlier were fighting one another in history's most destructive war, these were remarkable achievements.

The ECSC proved that real power sharing could work in Europe, and encouraged the member states to continue down the path of expanded cooperation. This road was rocky and the cart was frequently overturned. Between 1950 and 1954, the West European states were embroiled in a long, painful, and ultimately fruitless debate about German rearmament and how best to effect it while not recreating a sovereign German army. The proposal by the French for a European Defense Community (EDC), in which Europeans would serve in international units under common command, was finally defeated by the French themselves, who realized after much soul-searching that they would rather keep their army intact than share one with the Germans.

The EDC fiasco, however, did not squelch new proposals for widened economic integration. The Benelux countries, themselves united in a customs union since 1948, pushed especially hard for the creation of a customs union between the ECSC members—eliminating barriers to trade between the members and instituting a common external tariff. They found considerable support from Germany, whose economy was oriented toward exports. But when, in the spring of 1955, Belgian foreign minister Paul-Henri Spaak raised the proposal for the establishment of a common market between the Schuman Plan Six, the idea was met with misgivings in France. France had a long tradition of protectionism, and many French business leaders feared the adverse consequences of a sudden rush of open competition with the more dynamic German economy. Yet there were also modernizers, who argued that in order for France to keep up with Germany economically, and to profit from the already visible postwar European boom, the country had to make itself more competitive, and this could be done only by submitting itself to the cold shower of international competition. By 1956, these forces were in the ascendant, and the dynamic French premier, the Socialist Guy Mollet, embraced the position of the modernizers. In March 1957, the six ECSC members agreed to a framework for the eventual establishment of a customs union. But this was more than a treaty about trade. The European Economic Community that came into force in January 1958 committed its members "to promote throughout the Community a harmonious development of economic activities, a continuous and balanced expansion, an increase in stability, an accelerated increase in the standard of living, and closer relations between the members states." These were broad political goals, and indeed, the EEC built upon the Schuman Plan's original architecture, creating a Commission, a Council of Ministers, a Parliamentary Assembly, and a Court of Justice to carry out the tasks of further cooperation across a wide range of fields.

The EEC did not create a new Europe overnight. In economic terms, it did achieve some notable success. By 1961, most internal tariff barriers were substantially reduced, while trade within the EEC grew at twice the pace as trade with nonmembers. By the start of the sixties, the EEC formed the world's largest trading bloc. Adenauer, Schuman, Monnet, and Spaak, with the generous assistance of the Americans, laid out a new model for Europe. It focused on growth, expansion, improved living standards, and the reduction of national differences. Walter Hallstein, the German who became the EEC Commission's first president, made it plain that the EEC was not simply about bean counting: "We are not integrating economies," he said. "We are integrating politics."[30] But a Europe that was bigger, stronger, more productive, and built not on national and cultural principles but economic ones did not appeal to everyone. Indeed, across the decade of the fifties, amidst the celebrations, the rising indices, and the growing profits, one hears muffled grumbling and dissent: what has become of our Europe?

CONTENDING WITH THE COLD WAR

"I must say it's pretty dreary living in the American age—unless you're an American of course. Perhaps all our children will be Americans. That's a thought isn't it?" Thus Jimmy Porter, the antihero of John Osborne's 1956 play, Look Back in Anger, characterized his era: a stifling, boring existence under the shadow of American-engineered prosperity. He wasn't alone: for many intellectuals, writers, and critics, the 1950s were a grave disappointment. Rather than reviving radical traditions of change and reform, the era of reconstruction had suppressed them, replacing an ethic of revolution with one of Cold War, materialism, and social order. "Our victory had been stolen from us," thought Simone de Beauvoir, one of France's leading leftist voices. By whom? By the bourgeoisie, by the moneyed classes, the forces of reaction, aided and abetted by the Americans. Indeed, these years in the early fifties were for de Beauvoir "the darkest of my life." The Americans, she felt, were invading Europe, propping up ex-collaborators in power, rearming the Germans, helping to put down the left and the workers, and preparing for war against the Russians. "There was no place left for those who refused to become part of either of the two blocs."[31] These were common complaints across the political spectrum: de Gaulle was making the same argument from the right. The new Europe was becoming less European as America exercised hegemony in the political, economic, and cultural spheres. This critique of American political and cultural priorities was most vocal—and remains most visible—in France, yet it appeared across Europe in this decade, a result of Europe's anxiety about ceding world leadership to a young, politically immature country obsessed by the threat of Communism.

McCarthyism and the Red Scare of the early 1950s shocked even pro-American Europeans. The US ambassador in Paris, Douglas Dillon, told his superiors in Washington that Senator McCarthy's attack on suspected Communists in the United States was "the greatest single cause" of a loss of French confidence in America. The French press, according to the US embassy, featured alarming headlines such as "McCarthy Dominates American Political Scene—Prestige of Wisconsin Senator Grows Constantly Before Weakness of President." Said one dispirited embassy official in 1954: "American prestige in France . . . has dropped to the lowest point we can remember." The execution of Julius and Ethel Rosenberg, in 1953, caused particularly sharp outbursts in Europe; left-wing writer Jean-Paul Sartre declared that America "had rabies" and that Europe must cut all ties with this beast or "we shall be bitten and infected next." The message was the same from Italy, where Prime Minister De Gasperi, staunchly pro-American, told US ambassador Clare Booth Luce that the execution of the accused spies had allowed the Communists to make great inroads into public opinion, especially since calls for clemency had been raised across the political spectrum. In Denmark, "the prestige of the United States" was "sharply diminished" by McCarthyism, and Danes had grown anxious about the country's strident anti-Communism; while Norwegians wondered at the failure of President Eisenhower to denounce McCarthy. Europeans had every right to ask why a nation so manifestly unbalanced in its political judgments should deign to lay down a moral code for Europe.[32]

The NATO alliance, too, came under considerable attack in France from leftist and centrist critics who saw it as provocative to the Russians, unnecessarily tying Europe to America's military objectives. Of course, the Communists were against it, claiming that NATO was a vehicle to continue Hitler's war against Russia. But even the moderate newspaper *Le Monde* came out against American policy in the Cold War, calling on Frenchmen to reject the choice between Soviet and American imperialism, which were readily equated. Only a third of the *non-Communist* French voters supported the North Atlantic Treaty in 1950. A survey of West European opinion carried out in 1952 found widespread approval of America's generous economic aid but little support for its military policies, especially the rearmament of West Germany. In the ECSC countries, 57 percent of the public worried "a lot" or "somewhat" about war breaking out, yet this made them more resistant to increased military aid, which was seen as likely to trigger war. Throughout the 1950s, polls showed that a third to one half of the public in Britain, France, and Italy wished to remain neutral in the Cold War; only in West Germany did a consistent majority side with the United States. Americans saw such criticism as disloyal. But as Harold Nicolson told an American acquaintance, Europeans were not anti-American; it was just that they were "frightened that the destinies of the world should be in the hands of a giant with the limbs of an undergraduate, the emotions of a spinster, and the brain of a pea-hen."[33]

There were times when the critique of America's Cold War strategy spilled out into the streets. In 1952, the French Communist Party staged a massive rally against the appointment of U.S. Army general Matthew B. Ridgway as supreme allied commander of NATO's forces. Ridgway, they claimed, had ordered the use of biological weapons against Chinese and North Korean troops while commanding US forces in Korea. (This was a blatant piece of propaganda engineered by the Chinese.) On 28 May, 15,000–20,000 protesters hit the streets of Paris, carrying placards with anti-American slogans and denouncing the general as a "microbial murderer" and "Ridgway the plague!"

The French interior minister ordered a brutal suppression of the demonstration, and over seven hundred people were arrested, including the leader of the French Communist Party, Jacques Duclos. In the melee, a dozen policemen and two hundred protesters were injured.[34]

A more sustained protest movement developed in Britain and West Germany in response to the increasing nuclearization of Europe. In September 1954, American-controlled nuclear weapons were deployed to Britain, followed by the stationing of nuclear weapons and components in West Germany (1955), Italy (1957), France (1958), Turkey (1959), the Netherlands and Greece (1960), and Belgium (1963). There were almost 3,000 American nuclear weapons in Western Europe by 1960.[35] These weapons remained under the command of the US military, but the British and French were developing their own nuclear arsenals. In October 1952, the British exploded their first atomic bomb over Australia's Monte Bello Islands, and in 1957 tested a hydrogen bomb. France went nuclear in 1960. In Britain, these events spurred the creation of the Campaign for Nuclear Disarmament in January 1958. It was spearheaded by the mathematician and philosopher Bertrand Russell, the playwright and journalist J. B. Priestley, Canon John Collins of Saint Paul's Cathedral, Michael Foot of the Labour Party, and the historian A. J. P. Taylor. Priestley made a ringing declaration in the magazine *New Statesman* in favor of unilateral nuclear disarmament. "Alone, we defied Hitler; and alone we can defy this nuclear madness into which the spirit of Hitler seems to have passed," he wrote. The CND grew into a national movement, with 270 local chapters by the end of 1958; during Easter 1958, thousands of protesters marched fifty-two miles from Trafalgar Square to the Atomic Weapons Research Establishment at Aldermaston. This became a yearly pilgrimage, with 150,000 marchers making the journey in 1962.[36]

The West German government's effort to acquire its own nuclear forces in 1957 provoked a sharp reaction, not only from the Soviet Union, which threatened to seize Berlin in retaliation, but from within the FRG as well. Adenauer and his defense minister, Franz Josef Strauss, in private contacts with President Eisenhower, received initial support for their objectives. In response to public statements to this effect in early 1957, a number of top German scientists, including four Nobel laureates, issued a public call for the renunciation by West Germany of all nuclear weapons, and the cause was a central theme in the SPD's electoral campaign in 1957. In March 1958, a national movement called Kampf dem Atomtod (Struggle Against Atomic Death) emerged, and half a million Germans took part in over a hundred antinuclear demonstrations. That April, 150,000 people protested in Hamburg.

The campaign won the solid backing of the German trade union federation as well as prominent writers and artists.[37] Though not framed in explicitly anti-American terms, these protests revealed the growing frustration across Europe with the military priorities of the Cold War.

Alongside the Cold War critique, Europeans took aim at America's economic hegemony. Here there was much grist for the mill. Between 1950 and 1963, US investments in Europe surged from $2 billion to $8 billion, with most of the increase following the creation of the EEC. Between 1958 and 1963, US companies poured into Europe, with 300 starting operations in Belgium, 250 in the Netherlands, 600 in France, and over 1,000 in Britain. By the mid-1960s, US businesses in France controlled 40 percent of the petroleum market, 65 percent of the production of films, 45 percent of synthetic rubber production, and 65 percent of the production of farm machinery and telecommunications equipment. American capital also pushed Europeans out of the most technologically advanced sectors, especially in the emerging electronics and computer industries. By 1967, US companies owned about $14 billion in fixed capital in Europe.[38]

Was America trying to use its economic muscle to create a new culture of consumption geared to American products and tastes? To some observers, it appeared so. For example, in 1946 Washington used its economic leverage to insist that in return for American aid, France lift import quotas on American films, a move that seemed to suggest a government-sponsored plot to ruin France's historic film industry. The result was a sharp reduction in the number of French films as Hollywood blockbusters began to displace the home-grown product. When in 1947 the British Labour government tried to impose a 75 percent customs tax on new films entering Britain, Hollywood halted all exports of films to Britain, forcing the government to rescind the tax within a few months. By 1951, 61 percent of the movies showing in Western Europe were American. The appearance of Coca-Cola stirred up widespread protest in Europe, not from consumers, who quaffed down tons of the stuff, but from wine manufacturers, business interests, and left-wing intellectuals who readily identified Coke with the United States. In Belgium and Switzerland, the drink was challenged with lawsuits that focused on its caffeine content; in Denmark, the brewing industry managed to have the beverage banned briefly; in Italy and Austria, the Communists handed out pamphlets claiming that Coke could turn your hair white and ruin children's teeth. In France, the left-leaning Catholic paper *Témoignage Chrétien* saw the American effort to sell Coke in France as part of a broader invasion, as "the avant-garde of an offensive aimed at economic colonization against which we feel it's our duty to struggle." The French Communist newspaper *L'Humanité* asked, "Will we be Coca-colonized?"[39]

For all the gnashing of teeth over the advent of Americanization in 1950s Europe, many of Europe's most prominent and talented minds nonetheless believed the Soviet model of totalitarianism posed far greater dangers to Europe. Gathering under the rubric of the Congress for Cultural Freedom (CCF), writers and artists from across Europe, many of them personally acquainted with Hitler's and Stalin's methods, wanted their compatriots to see the Soviet Union for what it was: a brutal system of repression and savagery— not the shining scientific utopia many leftists in Western Europe continued to claim. The CCF held its inaugural meeting in West Berlin in June 1950. Made up mostly of members of the non-Communist left, the congress sought to energize liberalism by exposing the fallacies of the Communist sympathizers who for a generation had excused Soviet atrocities on the grounds of revolutionary necessity. In light of Soviet actions in Eastern Europe, the congress advocated a political and intellectual stance against totalitarianism and in favor of liberty. At last, said the Hungarian-born author Arthur Koestler at the inaugural meeting in Berlin, "freedom has seized the offensive!"[40]

The congress was inevitably written off as a front for American imperialism. Indeed, in the mid-1960s it was revealed that the congress had been aided by secret CIA funding. But this support was unknown to its participants, whose anti-Communism was based on an abhorrence of Soviet repression, which for them posed the same threat to Europe as Nazism had once done. The congress's board included the German philosopher and anti-Nazi Karl Jaspers, the American theologian Reinhold Niebuhr, and Bertrand Russell. German Social Democrats Carlo Schmidt, Ernst Reuter, and Willy Brandt were supporters, as were the Italian socialist writer Ignazio Silone, the progressive American liberals John Kenneth Galbraith and Arthur Schlesinger Jr., and the French sociologist Raymond Aron. Many were disillusioned former Communists, like Stephen Spender and Koestler, who wrote of their break with Communism in a famous volume of essays called *The God That Failed* (1949). The congress sponsored many journals across Europe, including *Encounter* and *Soviet Survey* in London, *Preuves* in Paris, *Der Monat* in Berlin, *Tempo Presente* in Rome, and *Cuadernos* (in Spanish and published in Paris). Although officially nonpartisan, the journals combined fiction, essays, and reviews with sharply worded commentary on contemporary politics. In *Encounter,* the American coeditor Irving Kristol explained that liberals must be at the heart of the anti-Communist movement. "It is a fact," he wrote, "that Communism today rules one-third of the human race, and may soon rule more; and that it is the most powerful existing institution which opposes such changes and reforms as liberalism proposes. Why, then, should not liberals, and liberals especially, fear and hate it?" In a later issue, Raymond Aron ridiculed the French Communist sympathizers, especially his old schoolmate Jean-Paul Sartre, who insisted that the Soviet system was the only one available that offered the prospect of revolutionary change. For Aron, the West since the end of the war had shown that "there is no incompatibility between political liberty and wealth, or between free markets and a higher standard of life." The Soviet Union, by contrast, had transformed its revolution into "long-term despotism," and held no appeal for those who valued liberty and well-being.[41]

This debate between those who still clung to the revolutionary possibilities of the liberation and those who accepted the facts, and opportunities, of a divided Cold War Europe typifies the 1950s. The debate was not resolved in that decade—though the Soviet invasion of Hungary in 1956 did much to shock even the most myopic of sympathizers. Indeed, the debate was not concluded until the very end of the Cold War. But in retrospect, we can see certain patterns that emerged in the 1950s that came to characterize West European society for the next half century: the willingness to embrace the free market, to accept the Cold War as at least a semi-peace that Europe had not enjoyed for a generation, and to get on with a life that had been so frequently interrupted by war. The 1950s in Western Europe, then, was not the decade of Sartre but the decade of Erhard; not the decade of revolution but of stability and prosperity. Indeed, as life became better on the continent, Europeans grew increasingly willing to give up one of their most cherished possessions: their empires.

CHAPTER SIX

WINDS OF CHANGE:
THE END OF THE EUROPEAN EMPIRES

.

PATTERNS

IF ONE CENTRAL THEME of the 1950s in Western Europe was economic expansion, the other was the dissolution of the European colonial empires. In fact, the two phenomena were closely linked. As Europe grew richer, its states increasingly bound together by economic and political ties, the colonies shrank in importance. They no longer offered economic benefits or strategic assets, and still less did the colonies enhance the prestige of a home country. After the war, colonialism became a tarnished ideology, associated with oppressive regimes of the type the Western allies had just vanquished. And the colonized peoples, armed with the language of national self-determination that Europeans had taught them, now forcefully expressed their desire not to be ruled by foreigners, and proved willing to fight for their independence. By the late 1940s, it was obvious that the days of empire were over.

And yet decolonization was not easy. Britain and France especially had closely woven up their national identities with their colonial empires, and numerous institutions, from the military to the business community to the government services, considered a break with the imperial past to be a renunciation of the national ideal itself. In some places, the Cold War militated in favor of resisting nationalist demands in the colonies, especially when, as in Indochina, these demands were expressed in the language of Marxism, or when, as in Egypt, a failure to retain political and military influence was believed to benefit Soviet interests. Nor were economic factors absent from the pressures to hang on to the colonies: Britain and France were entirely dependent upon imported oil, and in an era of economic boom, these supplies had to be guarded. The Middle East, as a result, remained hotly contested territory. Finally, there were those millions of European settlers who had made their homes in the colonies. They thought of the colonies as home, and had no wish to depart. The result of these competing forces was a swift dissolution of empire that, despite its inevitability, provoked violence and in some cases lengthy, costly, and tragic wars of national liberation.

The most striking element of the story is the speed with which the whole process occurred. After three centuries of colonial rule, the empires dissolved in little more than a decade. There are a number of reasons for this, though the principal factor was the transforming effect of the Second World War upon Europe and the colonized peoples themselves. In Asia, the Europeans, who had long trumpeted their own civilization as superior in moral and technological terms, were defeated by a dynamic, and for a time unstoppable, Asian power. The Japanese seized control of French Indochina, drove the Dutch out of Indonesia, swept the Americans out of the Philippines and the British out of Singapore, Malaya, Burma, and Hong Kong. The once-omnipotent Europeans suddenly looked feeble. These defeats in Asia in turn made India all the more valuable as a source of imports of raw materials, and indeed the British encouraged the mobilization of the Indian economy to aid in the production of chemicals, automobiles, and even light tanks. But at the same time, Indian nationalist leaders took advantage of Britain's difficult circumstances to press their claims for independence, triggering in August 1942 a "Quit India" protest demanding an immediate end to British rule. Britain tried a carrot-and-stick approach, arresting Mahatma Gandhi and the nationalists while offering a promise of postwar independence in exchange for keeping India in the war on the Allied side. Britain in the end held on to India only by force, inflaming nationalist opinion in the process. Even in Africa, where Britain and France continued to rule during the war, the populations suffered higher taxes, inflation, conscription of labor, mobilization for war, and in the case of North Africa, the imposition of large numbers of foreign troops. The war experience thus humbled the Europeans while further stimulating colonial nationalism.[1]

Another factor that worked against the continuation of empire was the anticolonial stance of the United States. Americans viewed themselves as hostile to colonies, though the United States had at various times behaved like a colonial power in places such as Puerto Rico, Guam, Cuba, Haiti, and the Philippines. During the war, President Franklin Roosevelt compelled Winston Churchill to join him in promulgating the Atlantic Charter in August 1941, which called for free trade and self-government for the world's peoples—ideas directly contrary to the imperial project. There was little altruism in it: the

Americans wished to break Britain's imperial trading bloc, which effectively shut the US out of lucrative markets in the Middle East and Asia. In order to mobilize the American public for war, FDR had to make his case that this was a war for freedom and liberty, and not a campaign to perpetuate European colonialism. Churchill resisted any implication that Britain was planning to wind down its empire. "I have not become His Majesty's Chief Minister in order to preside over the liquidation of the British Empire," he roared in 1941. But as Britain grew more reliant upon the United States in its war effort, so too were the British obliged to conform at least to the rhetoric of imperial reform. During the early Cold War, American officials began to moderate their anticolonialism, as they could see the benefits of European partners holding strategic positions in the global struggle with Communism. Thus, the United States heavily bankrolled the French military operations in Indochina. Yet Americans always maintained an outward stance of anti-imperialism, and sometimes, as in Palestine, Algeria, and Egypt, encouraged the British and French to put an end to their colonial pretensions.

Economics, too, worked against empire, though here the lessons emerged only slowly. Imperial governments always claimed that empire paid: colonies were sources of cheap raw materials and markets for manufactured goods from Europe. The British and French expected the colonies to continue to be economically valuable in the period of postwar reconstruction, especially because it was hoped that they could produce raw materials that otherwise would have to be bought from the United States using scarce dollars. The British launched the Colonial Development and Welfare Act in 1945, and the French invested in their colonies through a new, state-sponsored Investment Fund for Economic and Social Development (FIDES was its French acronym). Both countries pumped resources into the colonies in the hope that this would bring them greater benefits in the form of raw materials and protected markets for their own manufactures. This policy was also dressed up in the usual progressive rhetoric. Labour's colonial secretary, Arthur Creech-Jones, declared such postwar schemes essential to getting "the colonial peoples to stand on their own feet"; anything less would "betray the peoples and our trust."[2]

By the mid-1950s, however, the costs of colonial development were beginning to outweigh the economic benefits. European economic recovery was by then well under way, and the dollar shortage was over. Commodity prices, sky high during the Korean War, dropped to all-time lows, and the inefficient production efforts of the colonies were no longer viable. Colonial development plans for roads, bridges, hydroelectric works, mechanization of agriculture, and so on proved far too costly and never returned on the investment made in them. In Niger, for example, the French tried to promote the production of cotton. By 1961, after spending 44 billion francs, the scheme produced a mere 1,000 tons of cotton out of a projected 300,000 tons. The British spent 40 million pounds between 1945 and 1951 on a plan to grow peanuts in Tanganyika (later Tanzania), without paying heed to warnings about the inappropriate environment, the lack of labor, and the cost of production and transport. The plan failed miserably. The colonies, evidently, were not going to fuel Europe's economic recovery.[3]

Of course, the Europeans did not simply choose to leave the colonies; they were encouraged to do so by nationalist movements. In some cases, these were weak, fledgling groupings of colonial elites who presented no military threat to the Europeans; but in places like India, Palestine, Indonesia, Malaya, Vietnam, Egypt, Algeria, Cyprus, and the Gold Coast (Ghana), dynamic leaders backed by ideologically coherent political and sometimes military organizations presented Europeans with a serious challenge. Not only did the British, French, Dutch, and Belgians have to face the onerous task of waging colonial warfare, but they had to do so in the name of an imperial creed that was no longer relevant to Europe's changed circumstances in the 1950s. Colonial wars, frequent enough in this decade, were never popular in the home countries and merely drained resources away from the more pressing tasks of modernization. It was with considerable relief that the Europeans cut the ties that bound them to their former colonial charges.

Still, if the reasons for withdrawing from empire were so compelling, why did the Europeans not go sooner? Why fight colonial wars at all? This remains a difficult question to answer. Certainly European leaders, and many in the general public, took some time to register the lessons of the war years. Despite the trauma of the war at home—and perhaps because of it—European political leaders continued to insist that Europe was still capable of guiding colonized peoples toward self-sufficiency and improvement. The sense of colonial mission still held fast. Decolonization was accepted as a necessary and inevitable process, but it was hoped that it could be carried out deliberately, with Europe's dignity in tact. Winston Churchill, leader of the Conservative opposition in parliament, excoriated the Labour Party's swift withdrawal from India, saying that it was dishonorable, chaotic, and certain to lead—as it did— to massive sectarian violence between Muslims and Hindus. Speaking in the House of Commons, he said, "It is with deep grief I watch the clattering down of the British Empire, with all its glories and all the services it has rendered to mankind. . . . But at least, let us not add—by shameful flight, by a premature, hurried scuttle—at least let us not add, to the pangs of sorrow so many of us feel, the taint and smear of shame."[4]

Churchill's views were widely shared. In many official circles, decolonization was planned as a triumphant recessional, an orderly departure from the field after a job well done. In this scenario, the transfer of power would be undertaken on European terms, with designated native elites as the beneficiaries. In a number of cases, this pattern did in fact hold true, especially in black Africa. But in other cases, the flood tide of nationalism would not flow in the orderly channels cut for it by the Europeans. Across the globe, the outburst of anti-European sentiment, fueled by centuries of poverty, repression, and often a good dose of revolutionary Marxism, overwhelmed the best laid plans for colonial devolution. The end of empire would not, after all, unfold on the parade ground but in the jungles and swamps of tropical Africa and Asia.[5]

BRITAIN'S IMPERIAL RETREAT

Why, after so many years of jealously guarding India, its "jewel in the crown," did the British government decide to give it up without a fight in 1947? Partly because India had developed political institutions to which power could be transferred; partly because Labour had long supported Indian independence as an expression of its enlightened colonial policy; partly because Britain could no longer afford to keep military and colonial officers in India; and mainly because it was evident that India was preparing in any case to seize independence, whatever the British authorities did. Prime Minister Attlee sought to make a dignified exit, and moved to resolve the Indian problem quickly. The problems he encountered derived not so much from the resistance of his countrymen to giving up control of India as from the deep divisions within Indian society that jeopardized the smooth transfer of power. The Congress Party of Jawaharlal Nehru and Mohandas K. Gandhi, which had worked for so long to achieve independence, had to contend with the Muslim League. Its leader, Mohammed Ali Jinnah, argued that Britain must not simply hand India over to the Hindu-dominated Congress leaders but must protect the rights of India's Muslims by allowing them their own state, Pakistan. The Congress leaders, speaking on behalf of the majority Hindus, rejected the partition of India, and so the British were left to work out a plan that would grant independence to a unitary India while recognizing minority rights. It was a thankless task: while the British were willing to hand over power, the Indians could not agree who should take it.

Attlee would not be deterred, however, and declared in February 1947 that the Indians would have to overcome the problem of forming a transitional government themselves; the British would leave, he said, no later than

June 1948. He then sent a new Viceroy, Lord Mountbatten, to India to help establish a unitary government for India to which power could be transferred. But by now there was little chance of reconciliation between Hindus and Muslims, as the prospect of independence had radicalized both sides. Violence broke out all across the country. Mountbatten and the Congress leaders could now see that India would have to be partitioned, and the sooner the better to avoid total chaos. Thus, Mountbatten announced that the transfer of power would take place on 15 August 1947—almost a year earlier than envisioned by Attlee—and that the Muslims would get their state. He decided that any delay would only intensify communal violence while leaving the British with the responsibility for quelling it. That fall, there was a brief but intense period of violence amidst huge refugee flows, as some 9 million Muslims fled into West and East Pakistan and an equally large number of Hindus moved into India from these same areas. This opened Mountbatten and Labour to the accusation that their "scuttle" in India contributed to the hundreds of thousands of deaths that resulted from communal violence. In fact, Mountbatten was wise to get Britain out quickly, for by 1947 there was nothing that could have been done to resolve the religious split; delaying independence may only have prolonged the clashes that did occur after August 1947.

Prime Minister Attlee, and many others since, considered Britain's decolonization of India a great success. Speaking to the House of Commons, Attlee described the transfer of power there as "not the abdication but the fulfillment of Britain's mission in India, a sign of strength and vitality of the British Commonwealth."[6] The white man's burden, it seemed, had been duly shouldered by Britain, and now India was deemed strong enough to carry the load. This was a paternalistic way of viewing the Indian endgame, predictable rhetoric from a British leader. True, India remains the world's largest democracy, committed to electoral government and individual rights before the law. Yet these are hardly the legacies of British rule, which was based on force and subjugation. Rather, it is a testament to the Indian people themselves that despite the way in which Britain exercised imperial rule, they looked to Britain and the West for political inspiration, clinging to principles that the Raj had honored only in the breach.

What made the exit from India comparatively easy was that the British had a sophisticated, bourgeois political elite with which to deal, an elite that was eager to keep a democratic India closely linked with Britain after independence. In Malaya, the British encountered an entirely different set of local circumstances. Malaya was rich in natural resources such as rubber, tropical oils, and tin, and strategically valuable in extending British power into Southeast Asia. But it had no coherent governing structure, and when in the late 1940s the British tried to create a unitary state, tying together the independent territories on the basis of racial equality between Malays, Chinese, and Indians, they ran into stiff opposition. Malay elites refused to share power with the dynamic Chinese entrepreneurial class and mobilized in defense of their traditional rights. Ironically, then, an effort by Britain to encourage national coherence had only stimulated ethnic division and reaction against British policy. In response, the Chinese-dominated Malayan Communist Party, with the example of the swift British departure from Palestine and India in mind, began a political and military campaign against both the British and the Malay aristocracy that had thwarted Chinese ambitions on the peninsula.

In the face of attacks on British personnel in Malaya by the Communists, the British declared a state of emergency in June 1948 and undertook a long-running battle against the Communist insurgency. Contrary to Communist expectations, the British decided to fight it out in Malaya. Unlike Palestine and India, where the nationalist parties were genuinely popular and non-Communist, Britain could not conceivably concede independence to a Communist faction in the Cold War atmosphere of the late 1940s; nor did they feel it right to do so on political grounds, as the majority of Malaysians did not support the Communists. Further, Malaya's trade surplus with the United States meant that the colony was a dollar-earning asset, filling up the Bank of England with scarce American currency. The British thus decided upon a policy of colonial warfare instead of colonial retreat. Initiating a policy that both the French and Americans would try in Indochina, the British tried to undermine the Communist guerrillas by resettling the poor Chinese settlers who, encamped on the fringes of the jungle, had been the chief source of manpower and foodstuffs for the rebels. One-quarter of the total Chinese population of Malaya was resettled into four hundred new communities. In addition, British air power was employed to destroy guerrilla encampments and drop leaflets promising amnesty for those who surrendered. In the urban areas, especially Kuala Lumpur, the British-Malay nexus cooperated to root out and destroy Communist infiltration. All of this enormous expenditure of resources by Britain was driven not by the desire to remain perpetually in control of Malaya but by a determination that it should be London alone that decided on the terms of the transfer of power. The British, with the insurgency under control by 1954, brokered a compromise between elite Malays and non-Communist Chinese leaders that led to national elections in July 1955. With the newly formed government in the hands of conservative, moderately nationalist, probusiness elites, the British were able to declare the Federation of Malaya in August 1957. For the British, this was a remarkable success story: they had fended off a Communist insurgency and forged a new political coalition of pro-Western interests to which power could be transferred. But it was a strategy that worked because of the ethnically and commercially stratified nature of Malayan society. It was not a model (as the French discovered) easily adopted in settings where the colonized were united in hatred of the colonizer.

It would be wrong to suggest that because the British left India and Malaya on their own terms, they were always in control of events during the process of decolonization. Palestine alone offers evidence of how determined nationalists could challenge British rule. So too does the rise of politically powerful nationalism evident in tropical Africa—a part of the continent to which both British and French colonial administrators had turned particular attention in the 1950s. For Europe, tropical Africa loomed large as a source of valuable products, such as metals like copper, tin, cobalt, and gold; rubber and palm oil; and foods such as rice, cocoa, coffee, and peanuts. But increased development and exploitation of colonial resources placed greater pressure on African populations, and also triggered increasing concentrations of people in urban areas and workers' camps. Mining settlements in the copper belt of Northern Rhodesia and the Belgian Congo employed tens of thousands of Africans, as did the extensive network of timber and plywood mills in Nigeria. The city of Lagos more than tripled in size between 1910 and 1950. As laborers gathered together under intensified pressures, in an atmosphere of scarcity of consumer goods and disappointed expectations heightened by the rhetoric of the Allied powers during the war, a heady brew of discontent quickly fermented. In civic groups, labor unions, tribal associations, and youth movements, most of which had been approved if not encouraged by the Europeans themselves, the new language of nationalism spread rapidly.[7]

The first stage in what turned out to be a sprint toward African decolonization began in the Gold Coast (Ghana after 1957). Here was a case of a colony that, because of its relative prosperity due to commercial cocoa farming, and its high levels of schooling and health services, had expected better treatment from Britain than it got after the war. British controls on foreign trade frustrated the African commercial elite, while a severe shortage of consumer and capital goods from Europe had led to marked inflation. In January 1948, nationalists launched a boycott of European products in protest, and on 28 February, two thousand ex-servicemen marched on the governor's residence, angered that their demobilization bonus had not been paid. A small detachment of two white officers and twelve African police fired into the demonstrators, killing two and wounding four. The confrontation triggered three days of rioting in Gold Coast's capital, Accra, as youths stormed into European offices and businesses, setting fire to the headquarters of the United

Africa Company (controlled by the Anglo-Dutch conglomerate Unilever). The unrest spread into the countryside, and after a month, twenty-nine people were dead and 237 injured. The business district of Accra was destroyed. The British authorities blamed the riots on the political machinations of the United Gold Coast Convention, a nationalist group of elites, businessmen, and lawyers established in 1947. Its general secretary, the London-educated Kwame Nkrumah, was clapped in irons and labeled a Communist—an act that instantly vaulted Nkrumah to hero status. Soon released from prison, he launched a new political party in June 1949, the Convention People's Party, whose slogan was "Self-Government Now," and worked tirelessly to mobilize support for this objective among the urban working class and agricultural laborers. He argued that the only way for the Gold Coast to secure its economic prosperity was to break the hold of European business and colonial interests upon the country. When he announced a general strike in January 1950, he was again arrested, and again his status as the leader of the opposition to British rule was enhanced. To the chagrin of the colonial administration, elections held in February 1951 resulted in a landslide victory for the CPP, and Nkrumah was summoned from his jail cell to become the first prime minister, albeit still under British administrative control.

This was a momentous transformation. Gold Coast had gone from model colony to rebel almost overnight. But the British could justify their now swift devolution of power to Nkrumah as Attlee had done in India: the advent of coherent political parties, a constitution, and fair elections were the legacies of British imperial rule, and now Nkrumah had adopted these forms of governance as his own. Nkrumah seemed determined to show that he was worthy of the new responsibilities he had sought. "I am a friend of Great Britain," he declared upon his assumption of power. "We will remain within the British community of nations. I am a Marxist Socialist and an undenominational Christian. I am no Communist and have never been one. I come out of jail and into the assembly without the slightest feeling of bitterness. I stand for no racialism, no discrimination against any race or individual; but I am unalterably opposed to imperialism in any form."[8] Perhaps because of such statements, Nkrumah was able to persuade the British to revise the 1950 constitution and accelerate the process of devolution of power. Britain could hardly refuse: the political institutions Nkrumah now presided over were solid and legitimate, and the government revenue, boosted by the soaring price of cocoa, rose 50 percent between 1951 and 1957. The British tested Nkrumah by insisting on not one but two more elections, in 1954 and 1956, which his party won handily. On 6 March 1957, the Gold Coast became the independent state of Ghana.

The independence of Ghana now led British colonial officials to accept a new logic in Africa: independence could not be delayed, and indeed it ought to be granted swiftly so as to preserve a modicum of control over the process. In Nigeria, which was ethnically far more heterogeneous, British officials nonetheless sped up the process of political devolution, using a federal model with local autonomy for the diverse regions of the country; independence followed in 1960. Sierra Leone was granted independence the following year, and Gambia, with almost no resources or political coherence, was granted independence in 1965. In East Africa, the process was delayed somewhat by factors not present in the West. In Kenya, a large white settler population resisted a swift British withdrawal, and they had to be placated. At the same time, a tribally based peasant revolt of the Kikuyu, known as Mau Mau, required Britain to send almost a full division of soldiers and paramilitary police to Kenya to quell the unrest. As in Malaya, the British insisted on creating order before they would dissolve their colonial ties. In 1963, Jomo Kenyatta, leader of the Kenya African National Union, won national elections and led the country to independence in December of that year. On balance, the British experience of decolonization in Africa was a successful one: it was swift, done with an earnest desire to promote viable African successor states, and carried out with a marked absence of violence. Given the high hopes maintained in London in 1945 for an expanded colonial role in Africa, it is a credit to British colonial officials, and a testament to the moderation of African nationalist elites, that independence, once only a distant prospect, was settled on so swiftly. By the early 1960s, almost all formal British rule in Africa was ended.[9]

A TALE OF TWO CONTINENTS: FRANCE IN AFRICA AND INDOCHINA

Like the British, the French handled their withdrawal from colonial rule in tropical Africa well. This is remarkable, given their catastrophic experience in Indochina and Algeria. Why did the French pursue such divergent policies in Africa and Asia?[10] French thinking about Africa had been shaped by the war experience: parts of Africa had rallied to de Gaulle in 1940 and lent him legitimacy as the source of opposition to Vichy until 1942, when North Africa was liberated by the Allies. In 1944, de Gaulle convened a summit in Brazzaville, capital of the French Congo, and spoke grandly about conferring rights and privileges upon the African elites that had shown such solidarity with France. For the French, it was only natural that Africans would wish to continue their political evolution under French tutelage, and so full independence was not yet on offer. Thus, the French Union, established in 1946—a Francophone counterpart to the British Commonwealth—allowed African representatives to participate in politics through a system of electoral colleges that would send representatives to France. African political elites thus worked closely with the major parties in Paris, especially the Communist and Socialist. Through this mechanism, African political elites worked as intermediaries between the French government and the colonies, channeling the generous handouts to clients back home. With a smaller educated class and far less economic development, French tropical Africa accepted this system as a workable short-term settlement. Further, because these African elites were obliged to converge upon Paris to participate in the political process, they were able to build up political alliances that crossed national boundaries. The Rassemblement Démocratique Africain (RDA), under the leadership of the moderate socialist and Ivory Coast premier Félix Houphouet-Boigny, worked closely with the French Socialists and built up political ties that extended French influence in West Africa for many decades after independence. It also gave African elites a useful lobbying presence in Paris, and undercut the birth of national political parties such as had sprung up in Ghana. In 1956, having seen that British Africa was beginning to move toward independence, the French introduced a new "framework law" *(loi cadre)*, which promised to devolve political power upon handpicked political successors in West Africa. When de Gaulle came back to power in 1958, he pressed ahead with this process, eager to show the world that France, despite the fiascoes in Indochina and Algeria, could handle decolonization well. In typical Gaullist fashion, he placed before the African colonies a choice, to be voted upon via referendum: either they could remain in a new French Community, and thus continue to receive French economic and military aid while exercising control over their own internal affairs, or they could have independence immediately, but forgo French beneficence. It was an index of how complicit African and French elites had become that all the French African colonies but Guinea opted to stay in the Community. The French continued to channel large sums of development aid to black Africa and created a common African currency for its protégés, pegged to the French franc. By the early 1960s, with French political and economic ties firmly ensconced among African elites, formal colonial control had become irrelevant, and France was able to gain international credit for granting political independence to its African charges.

The story was far less happy in Indochina.[11] There, the French fought a ten-year colonial war that cost France dearly in lives, money, and prestige. The Vietnamese, of course, would pay a far higher price, but they were fighting for national liberation, and in the end, they won it. Why did France fall into this colonial trap? At the start of the Indochina War, France fought simply to defend its claim as an imperial power. French leaders believed they would be able to create a workable settlement there that maintained French hegemony while surrendering limited autonomy to Indochinese political institutions. They fought, then, because they believed they would win. But after 1950, the war in Indochina changed from a colonial struggle to an international one: it became, along with Korea, an active front in the global Cold War struggle. Neither France and its Western supporters, especially the United States, nor the Vietnamese Communists and their Chinese backers could accept defeat or even compromise. The stakes had become too high, and the French raison d'être in Indochina was soon swallowed up by the ideological imperatives of the great powers. This point is borne out by the fact that the war continued for twenty years after the French withdrew in 1954.

In 1945, the French had no intention of ending their rule in Indochina. Though during the war the Japanese had dismantled the French colonial administration there, the new French government was determined to reassert its claim after Japan's defeat. With British assistance, French troops under the command of Gen. Philippe Leclerc arrived in Saigon in September 1945. The political situation was highly unstable. The Vietnamese Communists had hoped to profit from the weakness of France by proclaiming the independence of the country. On 2 September 1945, Ho Chi Minh, the charismatic leader of the Vietnam Independence League, or Viet Minh, did so, declaring the establishment of a provisional government and the creation of the Democratic Republic of Vietnam. Ho Chi Minh had worked diligently to secure his power base in northern Vietnam during the war, and he possessed a significant following among the peasants. But the French pursued a divide-and-conquer strategy, seeking out moderate nationalists, Catholics, and other non-Communist groups that feared Ho's Communist movement. They also prevaricated by engaging in negotiations with Ho about some sort of compromise or transition to autonomous rule. He was invited to Paris in July 1946 to discuss the future of Indochina within the French Union, yet all the while the French military was working to restore its control over the major cities in both the northern and southern parts of the country.

By the time Ho returned to Vietnam in October 1946, his strategy of negotiation had failed. It needed only a spark to set off an explosion against the French, and the French themselves provided it. In the fall of 1946, the Vietnamese complained to the French about their tight control of the custom duties and shipping traffic in the port of Haiphong, over which the French had imposed a virtual blockade. When the French navy on 20 November seized a Chinese junk heading into the harbor, Vietnamese shore batteries opened fire. On 23 November, the French high commissioner, Adm. Thierry d'Argenlieu, who had been looking for some sort of incident to demonstrate French power, ordered the commander of French troops in Haiphong to reply. He sent an ultimatum to the Vietnamese: evacuate the city within two hours or face attack. When, inevitably, the demand was refused, the French navy and air force shelled the port and the city, with ghastly results. Conservative estimates by the French military suggested 6,000 Vietnamese killed, though the exact figure remains unknown. Attacks by both sides erupted across the country. When the French demanded the disarmament of the Viet Minh militia on 19 December, the Vietnamese responded by cutting off Hanoi's electricity and water and launching machine gun and mortar attacks at French targets across the city. The French eventually reestablished control of the city, but Hanoi had become nothing more than an armed camp in a north that was totally hostile to the French presence. The Indochina War had begun.

The French strategy in Indochina now followed two parallel axes: one military, the other political. With its military commitment to Indochina limited by financial weakness at home and the need to keep French troops in occupied Germany, as well as in other French overseas territories, France could not take on a major offensive against the Viet Minh. Instead, it followed a static, defensive course, holding on to urban enclaves around Hanoi, Hue, and Saigon, while sending patrols into the countryside during the day and relinquishing control there by night. This passivity gave Ho Chi Minh and his ever-expanding military force the opportunity to strike where and when they chose, usually against small patrols and remote outposts. At the same time, the French worked to shore up an alternative political force in Vietnam to counter Ho's claim to national leadership. They enrolled the former emperor of Annam, Bao Dai, as the leader of a new nationalist coalition, upon which they now conferred limited autonomy. Ho denounced Bao Dai as a puppet and quisling.

In late 1949, the French war in Indochina significantly changed its character. In October, the Communist armies of Mao Zedong emerged victorious from the Chinese Civil War and proclaimed the People's Republic of China. This placed Indochina squarely on the Cold War map, and the United States now began to take a strong interest in the French war effort. American officials feared that the Chinese might now reach out to the Communist forces in Vietnam, and then seek to extend their control into Southeast Asia, via Burma, Malaya, Indonesia, Japan, the Philippines, and possibly into India. Overlooking the deep local roots of the Vietnamese liberation movement, the Americans instead viewed the Viet Minh as merely one part of a global

Communist campaign controlled from Moscow. The Soviets in fact encouraged this belief by recognizing, in January 1950, the Viet Minh government of Vietnam. The following month, the United States responded by offering formal recognition of the Bao Dai government and promising to support it with economic and technical assistance. The United States had put its big toe in Indochinese waters.

But could French troops and American aid to Bao Dai really create the grounds for a free, pro-Western Vietnam? By 1950, Ho Chi Minh possessed an organized, regular army of over a hundred thousand troops; his regulars controlled two-thirds of the countryside, his movement was popular, and China had begun a massive effort to supply the Viet Minh. In October 1950, at Cao Bang in northeast Vietnam, the Viet Minh forces for the first time fought an extended conventional engagement with the French army, and annihilated some 6,000 French troops. This came hard on the heels of the North Korean invasion of South Korea in June 1950, and these dual crises led the United States to make the war against Communism in Asia its top priority. The Americans in 1950 began sustained military aid to the French that by 1952 covered a third of the cost of the French war. In return for their largesse, the Americans expected the French to accept American military advice and badgered the French government for more aggressive action in Vietnam. In 1953, the French appointed Gen. Henri Navarre to take over command of the war. He planned to bolster the Vietnamese national army, place more French troops on the ground, and mass them together for a decisive blow against the Viet Minh strongholds in northwestern Tonkin. A long, drawn-out conventional battle, he reasoned, would work to France's advantage.

In early 1954, the French constructed a garrison at the village of Dien Bien Phu, at the crossroads of the main routes into Laos. Navarre hoped to lure the Viet Minh into an offensive against 12,000 elite, well-equipped troops. The French high command sent foreign visitors, government ministers, and the press to see this "jungle Verdun," a redoubt that it claimed was impregnable. The military leader of the Viet Minh forces, Gen. Vo Nguyen Giap, willingly accepted the challenge the French had presented. For weeks, tens of thousands of Vietnamese men and women carried food and ammunition into the surrounding hills, using trucks and bicycles to transport their loads. They invested their position with heavy artillery and, crucially, antiaircraft batteries. Giap then moved five divisions—some 50,000 soldiers—into position around the garrison. When on 13 March 1954 the Vietnamese attacked, they quickly captured two distant French outposts whose purpose was to guard the French airfield. This meant the garrison, from the start of the campaign, had no means of supply except for parachute drops. For almost two months the

Viet Minh hammered away at the besieged French. The French military leadership pleaded with the Americans for air support, and possibly the use of tactical nuclear weapons, but US president Dwight Eisenhower rejected the idea, not wishing to engage American prestige in a war that obviously was going nowhere. In early May, the Viet Minh stormed the camp and overwhelmed the determined but vain French resistance. Three thousand French soldiers died in the battle, and the rest were taken prisoner. The Viet Minh had suffered far more, losing perhaps 10,000 killed. But they had done the unthinkable: they had defeated a great power on the field of battle, on ground chosen by the French.

The blow to the morale of the expeditionary force, and to the government, was incalculable. Within three months the French had agreed to a political settlement at a conference in Geneva. Vietnam was to be partitioned along the seventeenth parallel, a division that was meant to be temporary. It was agreed that elections, scheduled for 1956 and supervised by an international commission, would unify the country and determine its political makeup. The Viet Minh agreed to the deal under heavy pressure from China, which feared that a continued war in Indochina would soon draw the United States in. They urged Ho to accept a temporary partition that would buy time for the consolidation of the north before the eventual unification of the country under Communist control. That plan seemed plausible, given the absence of any political legitimacy of the mini-state the French left in the south, now under the control of a Catholic nationalist, Ngo Dinh Diem. But with their departure from Vietnam, the French gladly turned over the job of preserving South Vietnam to the nation that had claimed all along to have the right answers for nation building in Southeast Asia: the United States.

The cost in lives of the Indochina War is easy enough to tally up: 20,000 French soldiers, 11,000 Foreign Legionnaires, 7,000 Africans, 30,000 Indochinese soldiers killed fighting on behalf of the French Empire. Perhaps 200,000 Vietnamese died fighting the French. But the larger logic here is difficult to follow: why did France fight in Vietnam, and what did the war cost in moral and political terms? In 1946, when France commenced its military campaign against the Vietnamese forces, the dominant attitude among the political and military elite of the country still reflected the suppositions of the nineteenth century. Great powers naturally possessed colonies, and colonies in turn gave great powers legitimacy. For a country that had been so humiliated by the defeat of 1940, and whose claims to great-power status frequently aroused derisive hoots in Washington, London, and Moscow, the reassertion of imperial authority was no less important than economic reconstruction at home. For French elites in the late 1940s, restoring France meant not simply boosting exports but regaining that critically important asset that all great powers must possess: credibility. Yet the French faced an enemy that was more talented, more determined, more militarily prepared, and more popular than any other nationalist movement ever to challenge a colonial power. It was France's great disadvantage to be fighting for its reputation against an enemy it had no hope of defeating. Thus, France did lose more than a colony in Indochina: it lost its claim to great-power status. This lesson registered clearly among the other nations of the world, and especially among the national liberation movement in North Africa, which took heart from France's defeat. The great shame of it was that this lesson did not yet register in Paris, where a dejected, disgusted, and embarrassed political elite resolved simply to fight the next colonial war with greater force and determination.

HUMILIATION AT SUEZ

British observers of France's woes in Indochina occasionally congratulated themselves on how well they were managing their transition from imperial rule to a new association of nations under the British Commonwealth. After India and Palestine, Britain had regained the momentum in colonial affairs, squashed a number of nationalist uprisings, invested heavily in colonial development, and begun to lay the groundwork for an orderly withdraw from colonial commitments while protecting British global economic interests. Indeed, it was precisely the apparent success of British decolonization up to 1956 that encouraged the Conservative government to believe that it could continue to play a large role in the Middle East even after formal colonial control had been removed. This somewhat complacent notion of decolonization was rudely shattered in July 1956, when Egypt's leader, a dashing thirty-six-year-old army officer named Gamal Abdel Nasser, nationalized the Suez Canal, thus placing a choke hold on Europe's oil supplies and directly challenging Britain's continued influence in the Middle East.

The Suez Canal was far more than an international waterway. Since its construction, in the 1860s, it had become a highway of world trade and a critical tool in Britain's ability to maintain a global economic and naval presence. Over a third of the ships that transited the canal each year were British, and the British government held a 44 percent stake in the Suez Canal Company, making it the largest shareholder. Some 70 percent of Western Europe's oil passed through the canal. More broadly, the canal, Gibraltar, and Malta formed a chain of outposts that projected British influence all across the Mediterranean and into the Middle East, assuring the country of a sphere of influence and a rough parity with the two superpowers. The canal was the keystone of Britain's design for influence in the postcolonial world.[12]

The crisis of 1956 did not erupt overnight. During the early 1950s, the British government, with Anthony Eden as its foreign minister, had been negotiating with the Egyptians for a withdrawal of the British military presence in the canal zone that it had maintained since the Second World War. It was consistent with British colonial policy at this time to replace formal control with economic aid and partnership, and so Britain agreed in 1954 to evacuate its massive military base near the canal. This expression of goodwill, it was hoped in London, would open up a new avenue of Anglo-Egyptian cooperation. The British offered Nasser significant economic aid for building a dam along the Nile at Aswan. However, Britain could not fund the project alone, and Eden, now prime minister, appealed to the United States for help. The United States, fearful that Nasser might become a Soviet client in the Middle East, agreed. But Nasser did not play the role the Anglo-Americans had assigned him. Instead of demonstrating his gratitude for the financing of the dam project, Nasser continued to hurl epithets at the British for their colonial pretensions in the Middle East. He championed the cause of Arab unity, pressured the Jordanians to rid themselves of their British military advisers, and worked to sabotage the Baghdad Pact, a regional security arrangement between Britain, Iran, Iraq, Turkey, and Pakistan that Eden saw as essential to his Middle East policy. In light of Nasser's truculence and his earlier agreement to receive a shipment of Czech arms, the United States on 19 July 1956 reneged on its financial offer and the Aswan Dam project collapsed. Nasser's response was swift: a week later, he declared the canal to be under Egyptian national control.

The crisis that now unfolded cast many Britons back to the days of 1938, when Britain, faced with Hitler's aggressive designs on Eastern Europe, appeased the German dictator rather than resist him. In February 1938, the handsome young foreign minister, thirty-nine-year-old Anthony Eden, resigned over the issue and joined with Winston Churchill as a critic of Neville Chamberlain's government. In 1956, Eden was prime minister and Nasser looked to him every bit as menacing as Hitler. Eden intended to show that Britain had learned the lessons of appeasement: aggression must be checked early and with firmness. In drawing this conclusion, Eden was supported by the majority of his advisers, who like Eden read the Suez crisis through the lens of World War II. Harold Macmillan, then chancellor of the Exchequer, referred to Nasser in his diary as "an Asiatic Mussolini." The press used similar parallels, and even Labour's leader, Hugh Gaitskell, said in the House of Commons that this "was all very familiar. It is exactly the same thing that we encountered from Mussolini and Hitler."[13] By attaching this stigma to Nasser, the British raised the stakes of the crisis to enormous heights. Eden's colonial secretary, Alan Lennox-Boyd, wrote to the prime minister that "if Nasser wins or even appears to win we might as well as a government (and indeed as a country) go out of business." The top civil servant in the Foreign Office, Sir Ivone Kirkpatrick, laid out a nightmare scenario:

> If we sit back while Nasser consolidates his position and gradually acquires control of the oil-bearing countries, he can . . . wreck us. If Middle East oil is denied to us for a year or two our gold reserves will disappear. If our gold reserves disappear the sterling area disintegrates. If the sterling area disintegrates and we have no reserves we shall not be able to maintain a force in Germany or, indeed, anywhere else. I doubt whether we shall be able to pay for the bare minimum necessary for our defense. And a country that cannot provide for its defense is finished.[14]

Eden did not need these voices to spur him on; even before Nasser had seized the canal, he declared that he wanted Nasser "destroyed—not removed, destroyed."[15]

The crisis over the canal seemed to all the British players one in which the very survival of the nation was at stake. But was it? Why should it concern Britain who owned the canal, so long as passage through it was assured? Surely a compromise solution that did not further inflame Arab opinion could be found. This was the position of the United States, which, while displeased with Nasser, did not want to push the Arab world into the Soviet camp by using force to topple him. US secretary of state John Foster Dulles and President Eisenhower both strongly believed that the use of force against Nasser would "make bitter enemies of the entire population of the Middle East and much of Africa."[16] The United States adopted the high ground and called the parties to a series of conferences that would focus on the use of the canal and the creation of some sort of international agency to monitor it. These meetings proceeded during August and September, but the British considered Dulles's ideas as failing to insure British access to the canal, while Nasser saw them as a means to perpetuate Western control of Egyptian territory. They failed to resolve the dispute, and by mid-October, Eden was as determined as ever to reclaim the canal and topple Nasser.

Eden, however, needed a pretext for invading Egypt, especially since Nasser had not stopped a single British ship from passing through the canal since nationalizing it in July. This is where France played a vital role. The

French government, also a shareholder in the Suez Canal Company, had been equally outraged by Nasser's behavior and was just as prone to resort to specious analogies from the 1930s. Worse, Nasser's pan-Arab rhetoric and his antipathy to the Western powers had inflamed the liberation movement in France's most important colonial possession, Algeria. The Egyptian leader had been sending arms to the rebels and training their cadres. The French therefore proposed an ill-considered plan, which they sprung on the British in a secret meeting at the prime minister's country residence, Chequers, on 14 October. Israel, still in a state of war with Egypt since 1948 and constantly engaged in border disputes and raids, should be prevailed upon to attack Nasser. Britain and France would intervene, ostensibly to separate the warring sides; in the process, the canal zone would be occupied, the Egyptian army and air force destroyed. Nasser would be so humbled by the defeat that his ouster would naturally follow. Eden was noncommittal but left his French visitors with the impression that he thought this a promising plan. On 22 October, the French arranged for the Israeli prime minister, David Ben-Gurion, to travel to a secret meeting in the Paris suburb of Sèvres with the British foreign minister, Selwyn Lloyd, and the French foreign minister, Christian Pineau. There, a protocol was worked out. Israel would attack Egypt on the evening of 29 October. The next morning, the British and French governments would call on Egypt and Israel to stop military action and withdraw their forces from the Suez Canal zone, and Egypt would be told that it must accept an Anglo-French occupation of the canal zone so as to insure freedom of passage through it. It was understood that Egypt would refuse this condition, whereupon Anglo-French forces would attack Egypt early on 31 October.[17]

When this daft scheme was put into operation, it fooled no one: world opinion rightly saw this as Anglo-French-Israeli collusion to destroy Nasser and seize the canal. The Israelis swept through the Sinai Peninsula while the British and French bombarded Egyptian airfields. On 2 November, the General Assembly of the United Nations approved a declaration calling for an immediate cease-fire, and the United States and the USSR both voted in favor, leaving Britain, France, and Israel totally isolated. Yet Eden and his cabinet decided to go ahead with the plan, and on 5 November, French and British paratroops landed in Port Said; they were followed the next morning by a large naval landing. The objective was to secure control over the canal zone.

The American reaction to an invasion in direct contravention of the UN and in defiance of repeated warnings from President Eisenhower was furious: Ike exploded in a torrent of foul language that reflected his long life spent in soldiers' barracks. He was angry not only because he felt this was a colossal strategic mistake that would turn the Arab world against the West. It also provided an excellent cover for the simultaneous Soviet invasion of Hungary, which started at precisely the same moment. Worse, it gave the Soviets a pretext for interfering in the Middle East. On 5 November, Marshal Nikolai Bulganin issued letters to the Western powers and Israel that denounced the invasion and declared the Soviets ready to "crush the aggressors" and possibly even use nuclear weapons to do so. Eden had expected a hostile American response, but no one in the British cabinet anticipated just how far the United States would go in making its displeasure known. Eisenhower and Dulles ordered all American officials to cut off contact with their British counterparts and raised the prospect of oil sanctions against Britain and France. Most important, the United States refused to support a suddenly vulnerable pound sterling. In light of Britain's diplomatic isolation and the likely economic damage that an oil embargo from the Arabs and the United States would cause, currency traders now rushed to cash in their pounds for dollars. British currency reserves plummeted, dropping by $57 million in September, by $84 million in October, and by an alarming $85 million in the first week of November alone. Britain would soon be bankrupt unless the Bank of England could get a short-term loan from the US Treasury or the International Monetary Fund. Eisenhower refused. There would be no American financial support until the Suez invasion was reversed.[18]

Faced with the imminent collapse of the pound, Eden telephoned French premier Guy Mollet in Paris on 6 November and told him that Britain would agree to a cease-fire and stop its offensive in Egypt. Mollet was shocked and urged Eden to give the operation at least a few more days. He knew that without Britain, France could not continue the invasion. Eden said the decision had already been made. By extraordinary coincidence, Mollet was at that very moment engaged in conversations with German chancellor Konrad Adenauer about the formation of the common market. When Mollet, totally deflated by Eden's call, returned to the room where Adenauer was waiting, the German chancellor bucked him up by denouncing the Americans and British as unreliable. Instead, he declared, "Now is the time to build Europe."[19] It was a fateful statement, for it would mark the start of a new relationship between Germany and France that was deeply marked by the American pressure and British submission in this vital week of November 1956.

At first, Eden thought that agreeing to a cease-fire, which he did late on 6 November, would win back American goodwill. It did not. Eisenhower insisted not simply on a cease-fire but that all British and French troops be removed from Egyptian soil, and replaced by a UN force, before any aid was granted. When the currency reserves continued to be depleted even after the cease-fire, Eden was forced to relent: Britain simply did not have the economic strength to resist a long-term run on the pound without American help. On 3 December, Selwyn Lloyd put a brave face on and declared in the House of Commons that the invasion had been a success, had stopped an Egyptian-Israeli war, and also "unmasked Soviet plots in the Middle East."[20] Britain was therefore prepared to withdraw its troops. Within a week, the IMF approved a $561 million loan to Britain. The Americans, who had punished a recalcitrant ally, now rewarded an obedient one.

The Suez crisis did not make Britain weak. Like an X ray during a long-postponed visit to the dentist, it revealed the frailty of Britain's world position. In 1940–41, Britain held out for two years—alone—against the mighty German war machine that dominated the continent. In 1956, a much weaker Britain could not last a week without American help against a Third World country. Never had the ability of the United States to influence Western European choices in world affairs been so evident. Of course, there were many in Britain who vented some spleen at this apparent betrayal by the United States. But many more drew the obvious lesson of the affair: Britain was now, and had been for some time, a second-rate power that had been masquerading since 1945 as a great one. In the future, only a careful alignment with American policies and global objectives would insulate Britain from similar humiliations.

Certainly Eden's successor thought so. Harold Macmillan took over the premiership after Eden, who was gravely ill and deeply humiliated, resigned. Macmillan was a thirty-year veteran of British politics and the Conservative Party. He had served in the army in the First World War; had a seat in Parliament throughout the interwar years, where he opposed his party's leadership on appeasement; and had been assigned to North African affairs during World War II. A hugely successful housing minister in the early 1950s, he also led the Foreign Office and treasury. Macmillan departed sharply from Eden's foreign policy. He realized that decolonization now must be completed quickly—and within four or five years, virtually all formal British possessions were granted independence. In Macmillan's view, as he told the South African parliament in 1960, "the wind of change is blowing through the continent. Whether we like it or not, this growth of national consciousness is a political fact [and] our national policies must take account of it."[21] Macmillan would try to take Britain into the European Economic Community, making an application—later rejected by France—to join in 1961. And Macmillan accepted the reality of Britain's financial weakness, which meant dependence upon the United States in the realm of security and defense. Britain sought American technical know-how to develop a nuclear arsenal, and in 1957 a new phase of nuclear sharing was initiated by Britain and the United States. In 1962, the United States agreed to sell Britain Polaris submarine-launched missiles as well. The Anglo-American special relationship prospered under Macmillan, who was constantly consulted on world affairs by Presidents Eisenhower and Kennedy. But he could never hope to act as their equal. He had become a trusted adviser and counsel, a Greek vizier in a Roman world.

In Paris, French leaders drew starkly different lessons from the Suez crisis. Unlike their sometime allies across the Channel, the French public largely supported the military intervention at Suez, and Prime Minister Mollet was if anything strengthened in his position by the events. The blame for the failure was laid squarely at the feet of the British and Americans. The operation, in the view of the French, could have been a success and could have delivered a real blow to Arab nationalism in North Africa, if only Britain had not knuckled under to American pressure. Now it was apparent that neither of the "Anglo-Saxons" could be trusted to help protect French interests. Mollet responded in two ways. He immediately took up Konrad Adenauer's challenge to "build Europe" as a counter to the Anglo-Saxons, agreeing to break the stalemated negotiations with Germany on the making of the European Economic Community. Within four months, the Treaty of Rome, creating a new economic bloc in Europe, would be signed. He also ordered that the research effort to create a French-built atomic weapon be accelerated. The French were determined to build an arsenal on their own, without American technological support; in 1960, with the testing of the first French atomic bomb, they realized their ambitions.[22]

Hard as it was for the British to swallow the bitter pill of Suez, they surely drew the more appropriate conclusions. After all, Britain was not a great power and did need a close alliance with the United States to insure its security. France, by contrast, now hoped to free itself of what it saw as a constraining Western alliance that did not serve French interests. Even before Gen. Charles de Gaulle returned to power in France, this spirit of defiance against Anglo-American leadership in Europe brought French leaders to challenge the institutions of the Western alliance and to consider a new European architecture that would limit its influence on the continent. Most tragically of all, perhaps, the French Fourth Republic ignored what Macmillan rightly called the "wind of change" and pressed ahead with its colonial war in Algeria. For France, the real lessons of Suez would be learned not in Paris but in Algiers.

THE LAST STAND: FRANCE IN ALGERIA,
1945-1962

At the very moment that the Suez story was unfolding, France found itself engaged in yet another bloody colonial war, this time in Algeria. This war, unlike the conflict in Indochina, struck deep into the heart of French national identity. It tore the country apart, immobilized its political institutions, alienated the army, and finally led in 1958 to a bloodless coup d'état by a disaffected general who since 1946 had been seeking to reclaim power in France: Charles de Gaulle.

Why such passion for Algeria? While Indochina remained for most Frenchmen a distant and unknown land, Algeria lay just four hundred miles south of Marseilles, the large southern port city of France. Acquired in 1830, Algeria was France's largest possession, with immense potential as a colony of settlement and trade. It was formally integrated into French territory, unlike its neighbors Morocco and Tunisia, which were acquired later and given only protectorate status. (This made them easier to relinquish in 1956.) Algeria's economy, especially its wine production, was closely integrated with the mainland. Its cities became European in appearance and architecture. During the Second World War, Algiers had been the home to France's wartime resistance government for almost two years, and an ethic of Algerian solidarity with France had been encouraged ever since by propagandists. Most important, a large French settler population—over 1 million by the 1950s—had been living in Algeria for almost a century. "Algeria is France," said the prominent young Socialist politician François Mitterrand in 1954; and virtually all Frenchmen agreed.[23]

The great majority of Algerian Muslims, however, did not. From their perspective, French rule in Algeria had brought nothing but disaster. The French settlers had appropriated most of the cultivatable land. They exploited Algerian labor for work on large export crops such as wine and grain. In the 1930s, over 75 percent of the population was classified as poor or very poor. Nor had the French brought enlightenment to their subjects: in 1954, 85 percent of Algerian men and 95 percent of women were illiterate. The Second World War aggravated the economic situation by cutting off Algeria from its markets in France. The wine, grain, and livestock industries collapsed, leaving an impoverished, unemployed proletariat of 10 million Muslims governed by an increasingly anxious French colonial elite.

Algerian nationalism, then, had numerous wellsprings. The French themselves gave the Algerians the means to express their dissatisfaction. In the wake of World War I, the French government, in keeping with its rhetoric of limited colonial self-government, approved a law giving limited political rights to those Algerian men who had become sufficiently French in their habits and attitudes: these were the *évolués* of French colonial parlance. Patronizing though this attitude was, it did allow the creation of an elite-based nationalist movement in Algeria, which by the 1930s had engaged the French authorities in a dialogue about political reform. These nationalist liberals, whose outstanding leader was Ferhat Abbas, were basically pro-French in outlook: they argued that French principles of equality, liberty, and justice should be extended to Algerians so that Algerians could fulfill their rights as French citizens. But France failed to take up the offer of a reformed, progressive Algeria and denied the liberals their hope of an assimilated Algeria. Instead, the more radical groups in Algeria began to call for a complete break with France and an expulsion of the colonizer from the country.

Again, the Second World War did much to aid Algerian nationalists. By laying France low and reducing French authority in the Empire to a shadow of itself, the war made France look weak and vulnerable. When Frenchmen in Algeria celebrated the day of the German surrender on 8 May 1945, Algerians instead staged a protest against the prospect of a return to French rule. In the city of Sétif, a small march turned violent and an Algerian mob killed twenty-one European settlers. Fearful that this action might signal a national rising, the French military responded with stunning ferocity, sending units into cities and towns across the country to arrest and often shoot protesters, and even using air and naval assaults to bombard the area around Sétif. Over a hundred Europeans died during this month of insurrection; Algerian deaths are unknown, but have been estimated at between 6,000 and 8,000.[24]

The French had made it clear that they would use force to remain in Algeria. They also attempted to coopt the liberal elite by offering some political reform, notably the right to participate in a colonial legislature dominated by European settlers. This might have worked in the 1930s, but after Sétif, Algerians would not be bought off quite so easily. They rejected power sharing as inherently undemocratic, a ruse to perpetuate minority French rule over 10 million Muslims. For a small but growing group of nationalists, it seemed that armed insurrection would be the only way to get the French out of Algeria. On 31 October 1954, a new revolutionary organization calling itself the Front de Libération Nationale (FLN) issued a manifesto declaring its intention to win national sovereignty and destroy the colonial system in Algeria. The next day, All Saints' Day, the FLN launched a national insurrection. But the FLN had a mere 3,000 operatives, and only half of them had guns. The French swooped down on them ruthlessly and contained the uprising within a matter of a few weeks. Nonetheless, the FLN had a strategy that Ho Chi Minh knew all too well: it sought to engage the French in a military struggle that would over time radicalize Algerians and drive them to take up the cause of independence. This blood-soaked strategy proved its effectiveness in August 1955, when FLN militants attacked a small European mining settlement near the city of Philippeville. Seventy-one European civilians, including a five-day-old baby, were slaughtered. In response, the French military went on a rampage, killing by some estimates as many as 12,000 Muslims in the subsequent repression. The spiral of violence continued its lethal ascent.[25]

The FLN soon took the war into the city of Algiers itself. On 30 September 1956, three young pretty Muslim girls, dressed in Western clothes, set out into the streets of the capital. Zohra Drif was headed for a popular café called Milk-Bar, on the place Bugeaud, where European families and their children often stopped for a refreshing afternoon ice cream. Zohra's friend Samia Lakhdari walked to another café, the Cafétéria, on the rue Michelet, this one a hot spot for young couples who came to listen to music, dance, and have a few drinks. Djamila Bouhired made for the main Air France office. Each woman carried a bag under her arm in which she had placed beach towels, bikinis, suntan oil, and a small bomb set to a timer. The timers were synchronized to explode at six-thirty in the evening, just when these public locations would be busiest. The girls, who in their Western garb raised no suspicions, all made it to their targets. They placed their bags under tables, well out of public view, and casually walked back out into the streets. The bomb at the Milk-Bar ripped apart the crowded café, sending shards of plate glass into the patrons. One died and some thirty, including children, suffered serious injuries. The bomb at the Cafétéria killed two and injured sixteen. The third bomb failed to detonate.[26]

The calculations of the FLN were certainly correct in one way: these terrorist strikes, and the hundreds like them that erupted in Algiers that fall and winter, brought down the full wrath of the French military establishment upon the FLN. On 7 January 1957, the French governor general, Robert Lacoste, called in the army's Tenth Paratroop Division, fresh from the sands of Suez, to retake the city and restore order. The FLN had not perhaps anticipated just how successful the French army would be in carrying out its appointed task. Ever since Dien Bien Phu, the army had been smarting at its humiliation by the Viet Minh. Then they had been forced to accept another capitulation in Egypt. But in 1957, the French government gave the military carte blanche to restore control over its wayward colony. Paris had sent almost half a million men, mostly conscripts, in a powerful gesture of determination to hold on in Algeria. The army now had its chance for redemption.

The parachutists' commander, Gen. Jacques Massu, engaged in a brutally successful campaign of urban warfare. Through mass arrests, intensive police actions across the city, the sealing off of the Muslim quarters, and a sophisticated intelligence operation, Massu slowly penetrated and destroyed the FLN network in Algiers. This victory came at a high price, for it soon became known that Massu and his soldiers had engaged in widespread use of torture in interrogating FLN suspects and sympathizers. It is hard to fathom that a country in which memories of the German occupation and its many barbarisms was still fresh could subject others to similar treatment. Yet there is ample evidence of the practice in Algeria. One of the fullest and most gruesome accounts appeared in 1958, in a book by Henri Alleg called simply *La Question*. Alleg was a European Algerian and Jewish; he was a Communist and the editor of the *Alger Républicain* newspaper. On 12 June 1957, under suspicion of sympathizing with the FLN, Alleg was arrested and imprisoned for a month, during which time he underwent repeated interrogations under torture. His book recounted the various practices used upon him by his captors, including the use of electrodes placed on his ears and chest and in his mouth; the constant beatings; and the use of water forced into his lungs to induce the sensation of drowning. The mattress in his cell was stuffed with barbed wire. Desperately thirsty, he was given only salt water to drink. Finally he was given drugs to make him speak.[27]

By 1958, though the French military seemed to be winning the war in Algeria, the French public was growing deeply troubled and ashamed at the methods being used. Although the accusations of torture did not in themselves bring about a conversion of the public to the cause of independence, it did contribute to the growing disillusionment not only with the war but with the political system that was waging it. As early as 1955, Claude Bourdet, a leader of the wartime resistance and editor of *France Observateur*, asked: "Is there a Gestapo in Algeria?" By 1957, center-left publications like *Temoignage Chrétien, Esprit,* and most important, *L'Express* had joined in a chorus of criticism. *L'Express* was edited by Jean-Jacques Servan-Schreiber, a man who had served in the army in Algeria and wrote a moving account of his experiences. His magazine became a forum for leading politicians and intellectuals to declare their opposition not so much to a French Algeria as to the means being used to maintain it. In March 1957, a prominent general in the army resigned his commission after his tour of duty in Algeria and published a letter in *L'Express* declaring that France was losing sight of "the moral values that up to now have made for the greatness of our civilization and our army."[28] The weak and divided Fourth Republic, under assault now from within, could not long fend off such attacks.

Algeria presented the French political establishment with an awkward paradox. The army had carried out orders to retain control of the country. But in the late 1950s, in the context of a global winding down of empire, the old colonial models could not be revived. Paris had to loosen the bonds to Algeria even as it fought to strengthen them. So the government moved along an axis of compromise, while the army and the settlers, drawing confidence from their military success, became more rigid. In late April 1958, Pierre Pflimlin, a member of the Christian Democratic Party who was known to favor discussions with the Algerians, was called on to form a government. His appointment came at a moment of intense international pressure upon Paris. In February of that year, French aircraft had struck at FLN encampments inside neighboring Tunisia, and it looked as if the Algerian war might soon ignite the rest of North Africa. This led the United States and Britain (a sign of the post-Suez realignment) to make an offer to negotiate a settlement of the war—something the French army felt it had made unnecessary. On 13 May 1958, the date scheduled for Pflimlin to take office, the settlers prepared for a national strike and a demonstration against any policy of compromise. What happened next was a virtual coup that, within three weeks, would bring the former president Gen. Charles de Gaulle back to power in France and mark the end of the Fourth Republic.

Toward the end of the day on 13 May, the crowd that had gathered in central Algiers to protest against Pflimlin made its way toward the main government headquarters. Riot police and the army stood aside as hundreds of settlers stormed the building. Immediately it became clear that this was no outburst of mob violence but the coordinated act of a handful of settler leaders, army officers, and Gaullist political figures who had been active in Algiers for six months, waiting for just such a moment. These men turned to General Massu and asked him to lead a Committee of Public Safety—a term associated with the revolutionary dictatorship of 1794. Massu agreed, thereby bringing the army and the settlers into a conspiracy against rule from Paris. Two days later, the head of all French forces in Algeria, Gen. Raoul Salan, appeared to throw in his lot with this colonial revolution by giving a speech that he ended with the cry *"Vive la France, vive l'Algérie française, vive de Gaulle!"* This was an ambiguous remark, but it was seen in Paris as a veiled threat from the army: de Gaulle must be given the reins of power peacefully, or else he would be installed by force. De Gaulle, in a move of extraordinary audacity, released a public statement: "I am ready to assume the powers of the Republic."[29]

The settlers and the army sought to use de Gaulle to keep Algeria French. De Gaulle sought to use the army to gain power. De Gaulle would have to achieve his goal first. In order to speed up this process, the army began to lay plans for an airborne invasion of Paris, dubbed Operation Resurrection. De Gaulle was fully apprised. Just to show that they were not bluffing, the paratroopers on 24 May launched an airborne assault on the capital city of Corsica and seized it. Paris, it seemed, might be next. The National Assembly was ringed with tanks, but the problem was the loyalty of the troops inside them. In a healthy political system, perhaps de Gaulle's threats would have led to a galvanizing of popular opinion against such undemocratic machinations. But the Fourth Republic had given France two divisive colonial wars and an ever-changing carousel of second-tier political leaders. It was a reviled political order that had few defenders, and de Gaulle was a man who, for all of his right-wing tendencies, remained the hero of 18 June 1940: a man above party, the savior of France. The political class in Paris began to waver: perhaps a legal transfer of power to de Gaulle might be better than an open conflict with the army. On 29 May, President René Coty called de Gaulle to the Elysée Palace and asked him to form a government. On 1 June 1958, de Gaulle presented himself to the National Assembly, a body he had heaped scorn on for over a decade, and was elected premier by a vote of 329 to 224.[30] He would act as the undertaker of the Fourth Republic. Within three months—and with overwhelming public support—he promulgated a new constitution that placed great power in the hands of the head of state. He then began a ten-year reign as the unchallenged leader of his own Fifth Republic.

But what of Algeria? Now that the settlers had done their part in this conspiracy, what would de Gaulle do for them? Depending on one's politics, the endgame that de Gaulle played in Algeria may be seen as the brilliant management of an explosive crisis in which he brought France to accept the inevitability of Algerian independence—or as an unscrupulous betrayal of his word, his honor, and his most loyal supporters. This scenario has a familiar ring to it, for indeed, it followed the script of the 1944–45 period. Then, de Gaulle was brought to power by a dynamic resistance movement that believed he would adopt their agenda as his own. Instead, he immediately sidelined them and cut them out of power. De Gaulle would be beholden to no one. Likewise in 1958, as soon as he had taken up the reins of power, he kept the army and the diehards at arm's length. None of the coup plotters were given posts in his new cabinet; the military men were fobbed off with minor posts. De Gaulle alone would tackle Algeria.

De Gaulle is a man who excites much controversy, but it seems incontestable that France was lucky to have him in 1958. He was the only man in the country with the moral and political authority to resolve the Algerian crisis in a way that averted civil war or a military seizure of power in Paris. Though it came as a nasty surprise to the army and the settlers, de Gaulle, once in power, appeared to favor self-determination for Algeria. But the path to sovereignty was not a direct one in de Gaulle's thinking.[31] He hoped, at least for a while, to salvage some kind of link between France and Algeria, like the ties that he hoped would bind West Africa and the metropole even after independence. Thus, instead of withdrawal from Algeria, de Gaulle adopted a strategy seen before in this decade: colonial development and political reform combined with continued military operations. In October 1958, he announced a new major modernization plan for Algeria, to bring French technology and investment to Algerian agriculture, industry, schooling, housing, and public works. This allowed him to placate the army, which saw this step as a sign that Algeria would stay French, while appearing to be a progressive in colonial matters. At the same time, he called for a cease-fire with the FLN— a *"paix des braves,"* he called it—which was a tacit recognition of their struggle. He hoped that he could work out a unique settlement that, while delivering autonomy to Algeria, would keep France closely linked to the political and economic life of this North African country.

But this was too little, too late. The FLN had no incentive to give up their military struggle, for it had brought such astonishing results: the radicalization of the Algerian people, a near civil war in France, and the international condemnation of France. They could sense, too, that de Gaulle might be pushed into accepting full independence, if only the pressure could be kept up. Ironically, it was the army and settlers who did more to pressure de Gaulle than the FLN. In September 1959, de Gaulle outlined a new policy offering "government of Algerians by Algerians . . . in close union with France." It was a public demonstration of support for a negotiated solution with the Algerian rebellion, and the army was aghast. In January 1960, General Massu criticized de Gaulle in an interview with a German newspaper, and the president called him back to Paris and revoked his command. Right-wing settlers, supported surreptitiously by elements of the army, responded by staging a general strike in Algiers, during which barricades were thrown up across the city and violence against Muslims intensified. The city stood, once again, in defiance of Paris. On 29 January, wearing his general's uniform, de Gaulle went on television and radio and broadcast an appeal to the rebels. Showing his mastery of rhetoric and his canny sense for the power of his own personality, he denounced the insurrection, declaring that "no soldier must, under penalty of a serious offense, associate himself, even passively, with the insurrection." He stated that the uprising was the work of usurpers bent on destroying France itself. As he concluded his speech, he shifted to a lighter, almost nostalgic tone, drawing on the immense reserves of respect that the French public still held for the man. *"Eh bien, mon cher et vieux pays,"* he sighed. "Here we are to-gether, once again, facing a harsh test." If he were to give in to the insurrection in Algiers, the country would be lost: France would become "only a poor broken toy adrift on a sea of chance."[32] The effect of his speech was electric: it galvanized the French public behind his policy of self-determination for Algeria, it rallied the mass of the army inside Algeria, and it isolated the far right in Algiers, who had hoped to wring from de Gaulle concessions for their position. The barricades melted away and de Gaulle once again remained in control.

Having shown that the army could not challenge him, he moved more confidently toward resolution in Algeria. He now accepted, as he wrote to his son, that it was time to finish with "the myth of French Algeria which merely disguises the desires of the settlers to maintain their domination over the Muslims."[33] In the spring of 1960, he secretly opened talks with the FLN leaders, and while these soon stalled, the dialogue had been started. In November he publicly referred to the prospect of a future Algerian republic—an "Algerian Algeria" instead of a French one. He then placed his policy before the French voters in a referendum in January 1961. Seventy-five percent of the voters supported de Gaulle's efforts to negotiate a settlement with Algeria that would give Algerians the right to determine their own political future. The referendum, and de Gaulle's now evident support for a swift withdrawal from Algeria, led to one last desperate attempt by the army in Algiers to challenge rule from Paris. In April 1961, four generals carried out a putsch and declared that Algeria was now under their direct military control. But the army was not united, and de Gaulle, again using the medium of television to rally opinion behind him—he famously cried *"Françaises, Français, aidez-moi!"*—managed to deflate the rebel generals. Within forty-eight hours, their few supporters had deserted them. The army had played its last card in Algeria.

The Algerian tragedy still had one more bloody act to play, however. De Gaulle pressed ahead with negotiations in 1961 with the representatives of the FLN, but it was slow going. He wanted to keep control of the Sahara, where French companies had discovered oil, and he wanted assurances of safety for the Europeans left behind after independence. The negotiations dragged on, and it was not until March 1962 that a final agreement was reached: France would give up any claim to territory in Algeria but retain some rights of exploration and production in the Saharan oil fields. In July 1962, de Gaulle proclaimed the independence of Algeria, trying to take some credit for the liberation that the Algerians had won for themselves. In the meantime, the die-hard settlers and a few right-wing allies in Paris formed a secret underground organization, the Organisation Armée Secrète (Secret Armed Organization), which launched terrorist attacks against Algerians and proindependence Europeans. They not only struck across Algeria, but even brought their bombing campaign into mainland France, including numerous assassination attempts against de Gaulle himself. The OAS was not fighting for anything except revenge; their actions were simply the last cry of a dying colonial elite. The settlers, fearful of being abandoned in a country no longer theirs, prepared to flee. In 1962, almost a million French Algerians, some of whom could look back upon a hundred years of family history in Algeria, abandoned their homeland, destroying schools, factories, farmland, and public works as they left. It was a final act of spite against the Muslims they once claimed to rule in the name of civilization.

From one perspective, it appears that France was liberated from Algeria just as Algeria freed itself from French control. The immense sums spent on fighting could now be channeled back into modernization at home. True, the war had led to the destruction of the Fourth Republic, but also to the creation of a much stronger political edifice at home. And after Algeria, France could pursue a policy of selective engagement in world affairs, using economic leverage to hold the Francophone community together. These gains, however, had come at a terrible cost. The French lost 13,000 soldiers killed in action; perhaps 350,000 Algerians died—and at least half of these were killed by the FLN itself. The French left behind a shattered Algerian economy, with 3 million people having been displaced from rural villages. The cities began to grow as many young people from the countryside sought a new life in urban areas. And ironically enough, many of them, starting in the mid-1960s, would decide to leave their newly independent country altogether and seek their fortunes in—of all places—France.

CHAPTER SEVEN

HOPE BETRAYED:
THE KHRUSHCHEV YEARS,
1953–1964

.

AFTER STALIN

ON 28 FEBRUARY 1953, Joseph Stalin spent the evening at the Kremlin in the company of his closest colleagues: Lavrenti Beria, Georgi Malenkov, Nikita Khrushchev, and Nikolai Bulganin. They watched a movie together and then drove to Stalin's dacha at Kuntsevo, near Moscow. There the Soviet leaders ate and drank throughout the night, finally breaking up at five o'clock in the morning on the first of March. Throughout that day, as guards and secretaries busied themselves with the work of the leader's household, there was no sound from Stalin's quarters. It was not until late in the evening that one of his guards summoned up the courage to check on the boss. Upon entering his room, he found Stalin on the floor, alive but cold and immobile. Sometime during the course of the day, Stalin had suffered a brain hemorrhage.

What happened next is a subject of some controversy. Given the paranoia and fear that pervaded Stalin's entourage, and the particular animus that Stalin maintained toward doctors, Stalin's guards did not call for medical help but instead contacted Malenkov, who in turn informed Beria and Khrushchev of Stalin's seizure. In his memoirs, Khrushchev says that they all rushed to Stalin's dacha only to learn that the guards had put him back into bed, where he was sleeping soundly. Khrushchev therefore went home, but was woken in the middle of the night by another call from Malenkov, who said that Stalin's condition was worsening. The leadership again convened at the dacha and ordered doctors to the scene. At the very least, this delay in getting medical attention suggests a high degree of incompetence among the Kremlin leaders. But Stalin's daughter, Svetlana Alliluyeva, has suggested there were more nefarious motives at work. In her view, Stalin's underlings deliberately stalled in order to hasten his death, with Beria in particular demanding that no doctors be called to the scene. Why should they have delayed so? Certainly Beria had the most to gain by Stalin's death. As the head of internal security he had amassed immense power within the Soviet system and may have been positioning himself to succeed Stalin. Yet Beria's very power had begun to attract the suspicion of Stalin, who might well have purged him had he lived any longer. Another plausible explanation for the delay and confusion is also the most human: Stalin's lieutenants were terrified. Either Stalin might live, and so blame them for his illness, or he would die, thus triggering a leadership struggle that all of them knew could end in their own liquidation. The moment was one of extreme tension and anxiety for this small clique of subordinates. Khrushchev later explained his emotions: "I wasn't just weeping for Stalin. I was terribly worried about the future of the Party and the future of the country. . . . This could be the beginning of the end."[1]

Stalin finally succumbed on 5 March 1953. That date closed the chapter on thirty years of Soviet totalitarianism. After Stalin, the Soviet system remained repressive, unjust, a crude experiment in human misery. But it also moved sharply away from the worst excesses that Stalin had engaged in: mass extermination, the gulag system, vast purges predicated on the personal paranoia of one demented leader. Indeed, with Stalin out of the way, his successors seem genuinely to have hoped for a new start for the Communist movement, both at home and within the Soviet empire in Eastern Europe. But who would lead the revolution onward to this new beginning? The question of succession had first to be settled.

Within hours of Stalin's death, the chief Kremlin leaders gathered to establish a new "collective leadership," signaling that the era of one-man dictatorship was over. Yet among the inner circle, a new pecking order emerged, as Malenkov and Beria seemed to be amassing great power in their own hands. Malenkov, a longtime bureaucrat and Stalinist toady, became chairman of the Council of Ministers, or head of government. Beria took control of a newly consolidated security apparatus that now included both external and internal security. Khrushchev became head of the party, a powerful position from which he immediately began to scheme against Beria.

Since 1938, when he became head of the Soviet political police, the NKVD, Beria oversaw the vast terror apparatus of Stalin's Russia, controlling intelligence activities and domestic security, as well as the gulag system of slave labor camps. During the war he proved a ruthlessly efficient administrator, organizing the evacuation of industry to the East during the German invasion, and after 1945 he headed the atomic bomb project, using coercion to wring from scientists a full-scale commitment to the production of a Soviet atomic weapon. Like Stalin, he was from the Soviet Republic of Georgia, and he built a close relationship with his master based on a common cultural heritage as well as a pathological distrust of others and willingness to use violence to achieve their aims.[2] By the time of Stalin's death, Beria was probably the most powerful and dangerous man in the Soviet Union.

Beria did not wish to replicate Stalin's regime, however, and instead sought to enhance his own power and influence in the country by initiating widespread reforms that ran directly counter to the policies Stalin had imposed. Beria wanted to be the architect of de-Stalinization and solidify his power through popular acclamation. He moved with surprising swiftness. Three weeks after Stalin's death, the ruling council, or Presidium, issued an amnesty that freed perhaps a million of the 2.5 million prisoners incarcerated in the gulag. A week later, Beria's ministry made public certain documents showing that the so-called doctors' plot—in which an alleged cabal of Jewish doctors had schemed to assassinate leading Soviet personages—had been fabricated, presumably by Stalin himself. Beria also initiated wide reforms in the Soviet republics, insisting that new leaders with knowledge of the languages and culture of the non-Russian nationalities be installed as regional governors and that the murderous Russification program that had led to forced deportations be curtailed. Beria was moving fast—perhaps too fast—to put an end to the Stalin era.[3] His policies were reckless and not well thought out, and provided an opportunity for his enemies in the leadership, especially Khrushchev and the ardent Stalinist Vyacheslav Molotov, to confront and indeed destroy him. For not only did Beria's proposed reforms have implications within the Soviet Union. In the closely connected world of Communist-bloc politics, they created an immediate ripple effect, first evident in East Germany. There, a slowly simmering crisis erupted just three months after Stalin's demise, and to the shock of the Soviet leadership, the challenge to Communist control was not directed by the imperialists in the West but by East German workers themselves.

17 JUNE 1953: THE BERLIN UPRISING

The anti-Communist uprising that exploded East Germany in mid-June 1953 was long in the making. As the Western half of Germany, under Adenauer, openly embraced a policy of integration with Western Europe, the leadership of the GDR sought a corresponding boost to its "construction of socialism." At the Second Party Congress of the Socialist Unity Party (SED) in July 1952, the East German leadership announced a series of new directives to speed up the socialization of the country. The party ordered that production of industrial goods and heavy machinery be expanded at the expense of consumer goods; that workers' productivity be increased by raising production quotas; that agricultural collectivization be intensified; that private industry, trade, and small businesses be subjected to crushing taxes and reduced rations; and that a new wave of purges and arrests be imposed upon the "wreckers and saboteurs" within the country.

The result of these policies was a sharp deterioration of an already bad economic picture in the GDR. The harvest in the fall of 1952 was a disaster, as farmers left the land in droves and the collectivization program destroyed the distribution network. As a result, shortages of foods, especially fats and sugar, were widespread, and rations had to be cut even further. Coal and electricity were sporadic during the winter of 1952, and on top of this, the increased repression led to an upsurge of arrests across the country. East Germans responded to these hardships by rushing to the exits. Over 180,000 people fled the country in 1952. In the first half of 1953, another 225,000 refugees registered at emergency reception centers in West Germany. The SED perversely reacted to this flight by intensifying its propaganda against the West and, on 28 May 1953, increasing work quotas for industrial workers by 10 percent.[4]

The East German leadership badly misjudged the timing of these initiatives. For in the wake of Stalin's death and the rise of a collective Soviet leadership determined to ease such Stalinist practices, the SED found itself in serious disfavor in Moscow. There, reports had reached the Council of Ministers about the terrible economic conditions in the country and the failure of the Ulbricht regime to grapple with the refugee crisis. Further, the Soviet leaders, especially Beria and Malenkov, had begun to entertain the idea of pressing ahead with a plan for the reunification of Germany, the calling of all-German elections, and the neutralization of that country. Ulbricht wanted a Stalinist East Germany; the new Soviet leadership seemed to be contemplating a unified and neutral German state.

The division over German policy can be seen in the remarkable memorandum of 2 June 1953 entitled "On Measures to Improve the Political Situation in the GDR," in which the Soviet Council of Ministers sharply criticized the "incorrect political line" of the East German leadership. The memo declared that some half million refugees had fled the country as a result of the GDR's misguided efforts to intensify the construction of socialism. The East Germans were told to halt the collectivization drive; to stop the attacks on small farmers and businesses; to increase the production of consumer goods; and to moderate the use of excessive police powers. Then the East German leadership was summoned to Moscow, where the New Course was presented in uncompromising terms. Back in Berlin, the Soviet high commissioner, Vladimir Semenov, demanded an immediate announcement of the reversal of SED policy. On 11 June 1953, the SED official organ *Neues Deutschland* duly carried a communiqué admitting the mistakes of the regime in trying to build socialism too quickly, and announcing wholesale reversals of its previous policies.[5]

It was inevitable that this retreat by the SED leadership would embolden the public to demand still greater change. In light of the fact that these reforms had come at the express demand of the Soviet Union, it appeared that the Ulbricht regime, already loathed by the people, had also lost its great-power patron. When Ulbricht, in spite of this broad reversal, refused to revoke the recently imposed rise in work quotas for industrial workers, calls for strikes and protests against the government sprang up all across the country, and especially in Berlin. On 16 June, construction crews working on the Stalinallee—a main thoroughfare in East Berlin—organized a demonstration against the work quotas, and called for a general strike and protest the following day. Throughout the night, news of the demonstration spread. By 10 A.M. the next day, 60,000 protesters had jammed the streets in the government quarter of the city, and some demonstrators even crashed the gates and entered government buildings. Protesters tore down propaganda posters, set fire to kiosks, overturned cars, and attacked East German policemen. Some ransacked apartments of prominent SED party officials. Berlin was not alone: across the country, in 350 cities and towns, perhaps as many as 500,000 people went out to protest against the GDR's leadership, demanding that it resign and that free elections be held immediately.

The events of 17 June presented the Soviet and East German leadership with a difficult dilemma. Clearly, the protests were gaining momentum and might put the GDR in jeopardy; yet a military crackdown would undo the work that the reformers in the Kremlin had hoped to achieve by initiating the New Course in the first place. Still, Soviet authorities believed the strike might end in a national uprising. In particular, as Soviet reports on the events of 17 June show, the local military forces feared a Western-backed invasion of Berlin by "bands of provocateurs" and perhaps even Western military forces in support of the strikers.[6] Further, the East German police, lightly armed, proved ineffective in stopping the protesters. In the early morning of 17 June, the Soviet Second Mechanized Army, including the six hundred tanks of the Twelfth Tank Division, entered Berlin. At 10:30 A.M., the SED leadership was evacuated to the Soviet Control Commission in Karlshorst, on the edge of town, and at 1 P.M., martial law was declared in Berlin and much of the GDR.

The Soviet forces established control quickly in Berlin, but in other large cities, like Magdeburg, Dresden, Görlitz, and Leipzig, the clashes between demonstrators and Soviet forces were lethal. In Magdeburg, Soviet military authorities estimated that 15,000 demonstrators had hit the streets, and fifty people were killed or wounded in clashes with Soviet forces. By midday on 18 June, only sporadic resistance remained, and the Soviets were in firm control of the country. By the count of the Soviet military, 209 people had been killed or wounded across the GDR.[7]

Was this really a lost opportunity in the Cold War, a moment when the German people, both East and West, might have seized their own destiny from the hands of their occupiers? The answer is clearly no. For all the drama in the streets, the events of 17 June revealed that the Cold War order was set in place and that no great power wished to challenge it. Of course, the East German and Soviet authorities, in after-action reports, fulminated against Western intelligence operatives and the "very active role of the American military in the disorders in Berlin." The Soviet commander in Berlin claimed in a report to Moscow that the whole affair was "prepared by the three western states and their accomplices" in West Berlin. In fact, there is no evidence whatsoever of Western involvement in the Berlin uprising. On the contrary, American leaders, fearful that the Russians would use the events in Berlin as a pretext to launch an aggressive strike against West Berlin, insisted on restraint and caution among their personnel in the capital city. The US radio network in Berlin, though it did report on the events in the city, did not issue any call for a general strike and in fact called on Berliners to respect the orders of the East German and Soviet police. This caution was consistent with the American effort since Stalin's death to avoid any provocative move or initiative that might alarm an unstable and untested Soviet leadership. CIA director Allen Dulles could report to President Eisenhower that his organization "had nothing whatsoever to do with inciting these riots." The United States not only accepted the Cold War division of Europe but now sought to squelch any open challenge to that order that might result in a broader conflict between the great powers.[8]

The Russians, in their own way, drew the same lesson. The Cold War order that Stalin had crafted, whatever its faults, had the great merits of stability and predictability. Beria's attempt to solve the German question by releasing East Germany from the socialist bloc, or coming to terms with the West on a neutral and united Germany, now looked like a madcap scheme, certain to plunge Central Europe into chaos. Khrushchev now cleverly seized on the Berlin affair to unseat his fearsome rival. Khrushchev won over the malleable Malenkov to his view that Beria was dangerous and unstable; Molotov, the arch-Stalinist, agreed that Beria's East German policy had been reckless. Minister of Defense Bulganin had already fallen out with Beria over the GDR, and so readily fell in line behind Khrushchev.

In a ploy as deft as anything that Stalin might have arranged, Khrushchev staged a meeting of the Presidium of the Council of Ministers at which Beria would be confronted and arrested. On 26 June 1953, in the Kremlin, the leadership gathered, with Beria suspecting nothing. Khrushchev took the floor as soon as the meeting opened, and launched an attack on Beria, claiming that he had worked for British intelligence before the war. He denounced Beria's policies in the non-Russian republics, as well as his handling of the amnesty for prisoners. "No honest Communist would ever behave the way he does in the Party," thundered Khrushchev. Bulganin and Molotov followed with similar denunciations. Malenkov, visibly upset and panicky, pressed a secret button, upon which Marshal Zhukov, the great general and now a member of the Presidium, burst into the room with a band of soldiers, leveled a weapon at Beria, and shouted, "Hands up!" He was smuggled out of the Kremlin so as not to alert his own loyal security troops. On 23 December, after a lengthy hearing replete with all the mendacity and double-talk of a Stalinist show trial, Beria was shot.[9]

Beria's demise marked an important turning point in Soviet and European history. We cannot know whether, had Beria survived, he might have pursued a policy of liberalization in the Soviet sphere, or if his de-Stalinization plans were simply part of a ploy to secure his own power base within a system he sought to extend. But Beria's ouster had important consequences for the GDR. For now Beria's New Course had to be totally repudiated. Walter Ulbricht, the man lately reviled by the Soviet leadership for his disastrous rule, won a reprieve. Soviet policy reverted to its pre-Beria form, and all talk of slowing the imposition of socialism was cut off. Ulbricht now received strong support from Moscow, and those SED party members who had used the New Course as a platform to launch criticisms of him were purged. Some 6,000 arrests were made, and the security services strengthened to deal with internal unrest. The GDR emerged from this tumultuous summer a more repressive state than ever. Ulbricht, a Stalinist of the old school, remained in control of the GDR until 1971.

Germans on both sides of the divide looked back on 17 June as a missed opportunity.[10] Of course, all public memory of the event was suppressed in the GDR, though periodic grumblings on that date revealed that in private the uprising held an important place in the minds of East German citizens. The West Germans made far more of it, declaring that day a national holiday and renaming the avenue that ran up to the Brandenburg Gate "17 June Street."

The holiday honored a courageous German challenge to Soviet rule, and offered a poignant testimonial to the captive Germans under Soviet control. More than anything, however, for all Germans 17 June was a date tinged with failure: the failure of reform, of revolution, and of reunification.

KHRUSHCHEV AND DE-STALINIZATION

One man turned 17 June into a triumph: Nikita Khrushchev. This man of peasant origins and no formal education emerged from the GDR crisis and the succession struggle as the dominant player in the Kremlin; within a year, the collective leadership had vanished and Khrushchev alone ruled. Yet Khrushchev was not a cut-rate Stalin. He marked out, in his turbulent period at the helm of the Soviet state, a distinct style and program that possessed great promise. He sought to revive Lenin's dream of a socialist system and to return to the revolutionary roots of the Soviet state. He believed ardently in the possibilities of socialism and in the historic opportunity available to the Soviet Union to bring it to life. Khrushchev was born in 1894 in Kalinovka, a Russian village near Kursk, about a hundred miles from the Ukrainian border. His family's poverty forced him to find work in the vast coal mines of the Donets Basin in southeastern Ukraine, and here he toiled among the industrial proletariat. After Lenin seized power in 1917, Khrushchev was elected chairman of the local Union of Metal Workers. He openly supported the Bolshevik Revolution, and during the Civil War he became a political commissar in the Red Army. In 1929 he went to Moscow as a representative of his union to study at the Industrial Academy. There he met Stalin's wife, Nadezhda Alliluyeva, who connected him to Stalin himself. Khrushchev then moved swiftly up the ranks, soon rising to the number two post in the Moscow party. By 1939 he was a member of the Politburo. Just before and during the war, he oversaw the Ukraine on Stalin's behalf and also acted as Stalin's political emissary to the military command during the Stalingrad campaign. He proved himself loyal, capable of great brutality, and above all a survivor. During his career, Khrushchev's colleagues consistently underestimated him. He was fat, with a jolly, hail-fellow-well-met style. He had an earthy wit and made much of his peasant background, peppering his conversation with folktales and aphorisms. He had an oblong head with thin, close-cropped white hair. His eyes were narrow, and his smile, which was frequent, carried a hint of menace. Richard Nixon said of him that "he was a man of great warmth and totally belligerent." By all accounts, he was also a dedicated

Communist, formed in the crucible of revolution, civil war, and the desperate struggle with Nazi Germany.[11]

His ideology drove him to attempt to return the Soviet Union to its Leninist roots, to rid the country of the aberration of Stalinism and revive the revolutionary dynamism of the 1920s. But how could a country deformed by thirty years of totalitarianism be healed? At the very least, Khrushchev took initiatives to increase the supply of consumer goods and improve the life of the ordinary citizen—a concern Stalin had never shown. Khrushchev curbed the abuses by the police agencies so common in Stalin's time and presided over a large-scale amnesty of millions of gulag prisoners. He staked his authority upon economic production, and here he had, by Soviet standards, some significant successes. In the Khrushchev years, the economy grew at 5–7 percent per year. The output of consumer goods increased by 60 percent in the same period, and shoppers could buy things in department stores undreamed of a decade earlier. By 1968, 50 percent of Soviet households possessed a television and a quarter had refrigerators. Heavy industry saw important progress, as iron ore, steel, and tractor production doubled in the decade after 1955; oil production tripled. In the area of agriculture, Khrushchev considered himself an authority, and implemented huge efforts to increase crop production. Given the neglect of agriculture in the Stalin years—there were fewer cattle in the USSR in 1953 than in 1914!—this wasn't difficult. But despite efforts to decentralize decision making, increase investment in agriculture, expand cultivation into the steppe of Kazakhstan, and pay better prices for farm produce, production increased only modestly. Cereal production went from 82 million tons in 1952 to 132 million tons; milk and meat production did not quite double in the same period. Khrushchev was saved politically by large wheat harvests in 1956, 1959, and 1960. But these were short-term gains. Soviet agriculture remained inefficient and technologically backward, and hopelessly ill-equipped to compete with the burgeoning farms of Western Europe and the United States. Even so, in placing so much emphasis on the consumer, the peasant, and the citizen, Khrushchev's reign signaled a marked shift from the days of Stalin.[12]

In foreign affairs he also made a series of moves that broke with the Stalinist pattern. In June 1955, he traveled to Belgrade and publicly reconciled with Tito. His visit was an admission that the Russians had been wrong about Yugoslavia: there were in fact various roads to Communism and the USSR did not have a monopoly on Communist authenticity. Of course, this had ramifications: if Tito could pursue his own national road, could not others in the socialist bloc? In the same year, Khrushchev signed a treaty with the Western powers that recognized Austria's neutrality and removed all occupying forces from that country. Khrushchev was not always conciliatory. In response to the entry of West Germany into NATO in 1955, the Soviets created the Warsaw Pact organization, a military alliance of the socialist-bloc nations. He also pleased the Soviet military by insisting on modernization of the armed forces and the massive increase of the Soviet nuclear arsenal. And in November 1955, Khrushchev undertook a tour to India, Indonesia, Burma, and Afghanistan— nonaligned Third World nations that might be receptive to his message of dynamic socialism.

Khrushchev delivered his boldest stroke in February 1956 at the Twentieth Party Congress of the Communist Party of the Soviet Union. Before a packed hall of some fourteen hundred delegates, Khrushchev launched a direct and devastating attack on Joseph Stalin's thirty-year reign. His short-term objective was tactical, no doubt: he wished to reassure his colleagues and the country that while he had emerged as the dominant leader of the Soviet Union, he would not attempt to rule through terror, as Stalin had done. But Khrushchev also wished to plot a new course for the USSR. He declared his intention to return to the principles of Lenin, to the dynamic revolutionary ideas that Stalin had forsaken. In his four-hour speech, which was interrupted frequently by applause from the no doubt astonished listeners, Khrushchev systematically tore down the imposing edifice of Stalin's carefully constructed legacy. He revealed that Lenin himself had thought Stalin unworthy of the leadership of the party because of his cruelty and paranoia. He condemned the great purge of the 1937–38 period and denounced the use of torture to extract confessions. He ridiculed Stalin's wartime leadership, declaring that Stalin's refusal to take advice led to numerous military disasters. Khrushchev also mentioned the foolishness of Stalin's break with Tito, which had only weakened the socialist camp and alienated a powerful ally. Yet it was Stalin's character that Khrushchev focused on. Stalin had sought "to transform him[self] into a superman possessing supernatural characteristics akin to those of a god." Stalin demanded "absolute submission to his opinion," and those who opposed him were subject to "moral and physical annihilation." Stalin, according to Khrushchev, had originated the concept "enemy of the people," which "made possible the usage of the most cruel repression, violating all norms of revolutionary legality, against anyone who disagreed with Stalin." Instead of following Lenin's precept of educating the people, he "abandoned the method of ideological struggle for that of administrative violence, mass repressions and terror."

Of course, Khrushchev's speech was full of half-truths and significant omissions. It made no mention of Lenin's own use of mass terror during the

Civil War and in the early twenties. It omitted mention of the dedicated service that Khrushchev and many other leaders had given Stalin for thirty years, or of the purges he himself had conducted in the Ukraine on Stalin's behalf. Nor did it explain how and why Lenin's state had lent itself so readily to the totalitarian course Stalin pursued. Rather than examine the system itself, Khrushchev attacked Stalin as an aberration of Lenin's ideal; all that was needed now was to rid the system of Stalin's ghost and "restore completely the Leninist principles of Soviet Socialist democracy." Here was Khrushchev's recipe for success.[13] It was vintage Khrushchev: bold, brave, and reckless, with little sense for the consequences that this remarkable speech would have on the Communist world. Almost immediately, the text was circulated to foreign Communist parties, from which it made its way to the Western media. The implications for the Soviet bloc were enormous, for Khrushchev had, by toppling Stalin, also placed into question the viability of Stalin's empire in Eastern Europe.

GOMULKA'S RETURN

The country that first took up Khrushchev's implicit challenge to de-Stalinize socialism was Poland.[14] This is not surprising, for Poland had always maintained a strong national identity and a distinct hostility toward Russia, even while its leadership had been Stalinist since the 1948 ouster of that maverick Communist Wladyslaw Gomulka. Gomulka, though purged, avoided the fate of many other Eastern European leaders, who had been branded Titoists or nationalists during the show-trial period; he merely landed in jail, having recanted nothing and maintaining his reputation as an ideologically committed though independently minded Communist. His release from detention in December 1954 signaled that the Polish leadership, then under the control of Edward Ochab and Boleslaw Bierut—the very men responsible for Gomulka's imprisonment—had picked up the signals from Moscow that a thaw was in the offing. When in May 1955 Khrushchev mended his fences with Tito, Gomulka's former liability became an asset; it was now acceptable to pursue a national road to socialism. A cultural awakening occurred in Poland that saw a burgeoning underground press; and in 1955 the world youth festival, attended by jazz-mad youngsters in blue jeans, opened in Warsaw. These trends were given a boost by Khrushchev's February speech; indeed, Bierut, an old-school Stalinist, died in Moscow soon after hearing it. In April 1956, the government amnestied some 40,000 prisoners, many of whom had served in the Home Army during the war.

By the summer of 1956, Poles began to press for more rapid measures of de-Stalinization. In late June, a wildcat strike erupted into a major uprising in the city of Poznan, as workers rioted against food shortages, inadequate housing, low wages, and the incompetence of their managers. The protesters carried signs declaring, "Bread and Freedom" and "Russians, Go Home." As the march grew, shots were fired into the crowd by the Polish security forces; over fifty marchers died. The country was deeply shocked by these events, and workers across the country began to form strike councils that placed at the top of their list of demands the return to power of a man they saw as independent and honest: Wladyslaw Gomulka.

This problem presented the Polish Communist leadership with a difficult dilemma: could they rehabilitate a man once discredited as a dangerous rightist without posing a direct affront to the Soviet Union? And what path would Gomulka take the country down if he were indeed restored to the post of party leader? Gomulka made it plain that he would accept the position as head of the Polish Workers' Party only if the Russians agreed to withdraw their military advisers from the Polish armed forces. He also insisted that Marshal Konstantin Rokossovsky, the Polish-born Soviet officer who had been installed as Poland's defense minister, be removed from his position on the Politburo. These demands made it certain that if the Central Committee of the Polish party named Gomulka as its leader, the Russians would sharply object and perhaps use force to block Gomulka's return. Despite the resistance of a minority of old Stalinists in the party, on 17 October the Politburo decided to admit Gomulka as a member, and set the date of 19 October when the full plenum would meet to elect the first secretary. All now expected the post would go to Gomulka.

These events were watched with grave concern in Moscow. Khrushchev was afraid that Poland might soon spin out of control and that Gomulka might use anti-Soviet feelings to unite the country. As Khrushchev put it in his memoirs, "The situation was such that we had to be ready to resort to arms. . . . The Soviet Union was being reviled with abusive language and the [Polish] government was close to being overthrown. . . . We decided to send a delegation to Poland and have a talk with the Polish leadership."[15] At 7 A.M. on 19 October, therefore, a large and uninvited group of Soviet leaders, including Khrushchev himself and, significantly, Marshal Ivan Konev, commander in chief of the Warsaw Pact forces, arrived at the airport in Warsaw. At the same moment, Soviet forces already stationed in Poland were put on high alert. Khrushchev stepped onto the tarmac and deliberately snubbed the waiting Gomulka, instead greeting Marshal Rokossovsky in a gesture of contempt for the civilian leaders. He then turned to Ochab and Gomulka, shouting at them about their treacherous activities and giving them a stern dressing down. When Gomulka tried to reply, Khrushchev threatened him, stating, "We are ready for active intervention."

But Gomulka was a tough old salt and was not impressed by Khrushchev's bluster. Adopting a tone unthinkable in Stalin's day, Gomulka stood his ground:

> I understand it is possible to talk in an aggressive tone, but if you talk with a revolver on the table you don't have an even-handed discussion. I cannot continue the discussions under these conditions. I am ill and I cannot fill such a function in my condition. We can listen to the complaints of the Soviet comrades, but if decisions are to be made under the threat of physical force I am not up to it. . . . I believe that what we propose will strengthen the [Polish-Soviet] friendship. Any other form of resolution to these affairs will only strengthen the anti-Soviet campaign.[16]

Here was a direct warning: if the Russians used force in Poland, they would be met with determined resistance. With that, Gomulka left the airport and returned to the party plenum. There, just three hours after facing down Khrushchev, Gomulka was elected to the post of first secretary of the Polish Workers' Party. Meanwhile, Khrushchev went to the Soviet embassy and met with his generals and with the collaborator Rokossovsky, who knew the state of the Polish armed forces as well as anyone. His report was not encouraging. The anti-Soviet feeling in the army was high, he said, and few units could be relied on to use force against their own people. If Gomulka was going to be stopped, Soviet troops would have to do the job, and that would be a messy affair indeed. As Khrushchev put it to his colleagues, "finding a reason for armed conflict now would be very easy, but finding a way to put an end to such a conflict would be very hard."[17]

Yet Khrushchev's anxiety about Gomulka proved ill-founded. Gomulka was no radical; in fact, Stalin had probably been right in thinking that he was something of a Titoist. Though opposed to the abuses of Stalinism, Gomulka was strongly in favor of good relations with the Soviet Union, believed in the continued monopoly of power by the Polish Workers' Party, and remained a devoted Communist. He said as much to Khrushchev, who, ever the romantic, was moved. Gomulka spoke with "such sincerity that I believed his words," Khrushchev later said in his memoirs.[18] By the end of Khrushchev's visit to Warsaw, in fact, the Soviet leader had become convinced of Gomulka's good faith, and agreed to the removal of Soviet military advisers and the hated

Rokossovsky. Gomulka had won the day, and on 24 October he was cheered by 300,000 delirious Poles outside the Palace of Culture in Warsaw. Poland had faced down the Soviets. But if Gomulka won the trick, Khrushchev may have played the wiser hand. He avoided an armed confrontation with Poland, which would have led to disaster and surely triggered his own downfall. He saw that a national Communist like Gomulka could be a strong asset to the Soviet bloc, a showcase for his brand of de-Stalinization. And Gomulka himself proved a loyal subordinate, ruling his country with an iron fist until 1970. Khrushchev could be excused for thinking that the Polish solution was not a bad one at all.

BLOOD IN BUDAPEST

Things did not go as smoothly in Hungary. The Hungarian Communist leadership, which had imposed an especially brutal regime upon the country after 1948, was hit hard by the death of Stalin and the subsequent thaw in the socialist bloc.[19] Hungary had recently staged one of the most obscene purges, in which former Communist party leader László Rajk, among others, had been executed following an elaborate and mendacious show trial. The engineer of Rajk's demise, Mátyás Rákosi, had held a tight grip on the country since then, but in the spring of 1953, the signals from Moscow indicated that a new collective leadership model must be pursued and the cult of the individual leader discarded. Rákosi was obliged therefore to give up his post as premier, while remaining head of the Hungarian Workers' Party. The new premier as of July 1953 was a moderate Communist named Imre Nagy, who had spent the 1930s and the war years in Moscow (where he informed for the NKVD on the Hungarian émigré community in Moscow). He was known as a critic of collective agriculture and an advocate of an increase in consumer goods. Soviet premier Malenkov in particular supported him as the man best able to initiate the New Course in Hungary, which badly needed one, as its economy was in a disastrous state and its people angry and restive.

Nagy did not last long in his new post. Mirroring the unstable nature of Soviet politics in this period, the Hungarian leadership too was caught in a fierce battle between Nagy and Rákosi, between a thaw and a hard line. Rákosi, a wily Stalinist of the old school, managed to sabotage Nagy's efforts to initiate the New Course, and Nagy was ousted in April 1955. But by expelling the reformer from the premiership and declaring a return to Stalinist principles, Rákosi enhanced still further the appeal of Nagy in the eyes of the country as a man of integrity who supported the cause of change and progress. Like

Gomulka in Poland, Nagy loomed as a potent symbol of the promise of de-Stalinization. The longer he remained out of power, the greater became the force of the demands calling for his return.

In Poland, the party leadership and the Soviets themselves eventually acquiesced in Gomulka's return to power, a move that pleased the Polish public, soothed the country, and left Poland securely committed to the Warsaw Pact. The Hungarian case followed another course, far more tragic and bloody. Following Khrushchev's rapprochement with Tito and the Twentieth Party Congress speech, Rákosi's position became untenable. An old-school Stalinist simply had no credibility in the light of the revelations about Stalin that Khrushchev had made. When Rákosi responded to the Poznan riots in Poland in late June 1956 by banning student organizations and announcing a new round of "stern measures" against the "antisocialist" forces, the Russians became alarmed that his harshness might stir up a revolt in Hungary just as Poland seemed ready to burst. In mid-July, therefore, the Soviet Presidium sent Anastas Mikoyan to Budapest to persuade Rákosi to retire from office for reasons of "hypertension."

Rather than turn to a genuine alternative, however, the Russians insisted that Rákosi be replaced by Ernö Gerö, an associate of Rákosi's who had no reputation as a credible reformer. Gerö tried to shore up his position as an advocate of the New Course by rehabilitating the murdered Rajk and staging a huge public reburial of the slain comrade on 6 October 1956. This ceremony, however, brought hundreds of thousands of mourners into the streets in silent protest against the regime and its abuses—Rajk's trial being the most prominent of them. Gerö confided to Soviet ambassador Yuri Andropov that his gesture had failed: "The reburial of Rajk's remains has dealt a massive blow to the party leadership, whose authority was not all that high to begin with."[20]

In this period of high tension, Hungarians were watching events in Poland carefully. When, on 19 October, the Polish party brought Gomulka back as first secretary, Hungarians interpreted this—as did many Poles—as a huge defeat for Soviet imperialism and a triumph of Polish nationalism. The Polish nation, it seemed, had broken the hegemonic grip of the Soviet Union on Eastern Europe. However, the Hungarian party, far less independent and more servile to the Soviets than its Polish counterpart, had no intention of replacing Gerö and installing a Gomulka-like figure as an emblem of reform. The public was forced to take matters into its own hands.

On 22 October, a meeting of students, intellectuals, and factory workers was held at the Technological University in Budapest and adopted a wide-ranging list of demands, including the removal of Soviet troops from Hungary—precisely the demand Gomulka in Poland had won from the

Russians—and the replacement of Gerö with Imre Nagy. They also called for the "reexamination" of Hungary's relations with the Soviet Union, the holding of multiparty elections, freedom of press and assembly, and the prompt removal of the massive statue of Stalin that still stood in central Budapest. In addition, the students expressed their solidarity with the Poles, who they saw as leading a genuine independence movement from Soviet control. A mass demonstration on 23 October led to an outpouring of anti-Soviet rhetoric, and spontaneous demonstrations popped up across the city. In the evening, a group of iron workers managed to cut through the massive metal legs of the statue of Stalin, toppling the grotesque memorial.

Gerö handled the crisis with supreme ineptness. He went on the radio and declared that imperialists and class enemies were trying to undermine the power of the working class—this, when perhaps two hundred thousand people stood in the streets denouncing his regime. He also secretly contacted the Soviet ambassador and requested the use of Soviet troops to restore order in the city. Hearing Gerö's broadcast, a crowd that had gathered outside the city's central radio broadcasting offices attempted to storm the building, and at this moment—about 9 P.M. on 23 October—the Hungarian security police fired into the unarmed crowd. The demonstration had become a revolution.

Nikita Khrushchev, confronted with a near uprising in Poland and now a full-blown revolt in Hungary, faced the prospect that the entire socialist bloc might be coming unraveled. He was determined not to let Hungary slip away, and almost immediately upon learning of the situation in Budapest, decided to use force to crush the rebels. The Soviet Presidium met on the night of 23 October and agreed to allow Soviet troops stationed near Budapest to be used to restore order in the city. These were joined by Soviet units from Romania and the Ukraine. By early morning on 24 October, 30,000 Soviet troops had entered the country, bringing with them over a thousand tanks. But the appearance of Soviet soldiers only provoked the citizens of Budapest to defend the city. Bearing Molotov cocktails, as well as thousands of rifles taken from the barracks of army units that had rallied to the side of the rebels, Hungarians defied the Soviet troops and chaos continued to grip the city.

The Russians were in a bind. Without a cooperative and effective Hungarian government in place, restoring order would be impossible. They needed Hungarian collaborators to give their military suppression domestic and international legitimacy. On 25 October, with the city still engulfed in flames, the Hungarian Communist leadership, with Russian approval, dismissed Gerö and put Imre Nagy in control of the government. The gamble was that Nagy, as prime minister, could use his popularity with the people to stem the rebellion, as Gomulka had done in Poland. But Nagy, as it turned out, was no Gomulka. Less resolute, uncertain of his strategy, and subject to the emotional pull of the obvious anti-Soviet feeling in the streets, Nagy drifted from a position favoring a restoration of Communist control to one of open defiance of Soviet authority. He began to press upon the Russians a compromise solution in which Hungary would pursue socialism but only in a neutral framework, possibly outside the Warsaw Pact. This, accompanied by a Soviet withdrawal of forces, might salvage the situation in Hungary, thought Nagy. Without such compromise, Nagy told the Russians, the uprising would only intensify.

He seemed to be right. On 28 October, the Soviet Presidium met and learned that over 350 Hungarians had already been killed and that Soviet losses had reached six hundred dead. According to Presidium member Mikhail Suslov, who had just flown in from Budapest, "the popular view of our troops is bad and has gotten worse."[21] The following day, the KGB chief in Moscow reported that the rebellion had spread to the countryside, that prisons were being stormed, that Hungarian security police were being lynched and burned in grisly reprisals, while armed bands were now hunting down prominent Communists and shooting them in the streets.[22] Mikoyan, in Budapest, confirmed these pessimistic reports on 30 October: "The political situation in the country is not getting better," he wrote to Moscow; "it is getting worse. . . . The party organizations are in the process of collapse. Hooligan elements have become more insolent, seizing regional party committees, killing communists. . . . The factories are stalled. The people are sitting at home. The hooligan students and other resistance elements have changed their tactics and are displaying greater activity." Worse, the Hungarian army, according to Mikoyan, had "adopted a wait-and-see position. Our military advisors say that relations between the Hungarian officers and generals and the Soviet officers in the past few days has deteriorated. There is no trust as there was earlier."[23]

On 30 October, the Presidium began to think that it might have to defuse the situation through compromise rather than force. The Presidium hoped that a declaration announcing the USSR's willingness to discuss troop withdrawals and respect for the sovereignty of each socialist state would help stem the rebellion.[24] Events in Budapest had gone too far for such a palliative to work, however. On 28 October, Imre Nagy ordered the Hungarian army to cease firing on the insurgents and announced major concessions to the demands of the revolutionaries, including the abolition of the secret police. The following day, students seized the Interior Ministry and began rifling through the vast collection of secret files. On 30 October, Nagy, now fully committed to siding with the forces of national revolution, announced the end of the one-party state in Hungary and the revival of multiparty democracy. This opened the way to the formation of a coalition government made up of members of the once-outlawed non-Communist parties. On 31 October, in his boldest and perhaps most reckless move, Nagy declared the Hungarian government's intention to withdraw from the Warsaw Pact. With Soviet troops on the run and the Soviet leaders backtracking, Nagy and the Hungarian people seemed to think that their revolution had triumphed.

It was not to be. The rapid pace of events in Budapest shocked the Soviet leaders and led them to turn once again to the use of the military to put down the rebellion and keep Hungary securely in the socialist camp. On 31 October, Khrushchev and the Presidium agreed to launch a full-scale military invasion of Hungary. Not least in Khrushchev's mind, as he revealed at the meeting, was that if Hungary should be lost, then the imperialist powers would see this as a great victory. Britain and France were at that very moment engaged in an invasion of Egypt, which Khrushchev naturally assumed was backed by the United States. A socialist defeat in Hungary and Egypt would be far too humiliating to bear. Further, he worried that if the unstable situation in Hungary was allowed to continue, it would be just a matter of time before other Warsaw Pact states, especially Hungary's neighbors Czechoslovakia and Romania, also tested Russia's resolve to control the socialist bloc. In the wake of the success of the forces of nationalism in Poland, Hungary would have to be shown that there were limits to what Moscow would allow in the era of de-Stalinization.[25] At the conclusion of the meeting, Khrushchev gave the order for Operation Whirlwind: the repression of the Hungarian revolution by over 60,000 Soviet troops.

The operation was carried out with systematic brutality and an efficiency that had been conspicuously absent so far on the part of the Soviets. During 1–3 November, Soviet troops made a great show of leaving Budapest, declaring their intention to allow Hungary to pursue its neutral policy. Moreover, Soviet and Hungarian officials continued negotiations until the night of 3 November on the question of Soviet troop withdrawals. Meanwhile, Soviet marshal Zhukov had alerted twelve divisions of the Red Army, which were on the move from the Ukraine and Romania. In Moscow, Khrushchev and the Presidium met secretly with Janos Kadar, a Hungarian Communist who was a leading member of Nagy's cabinet. They decided that as soon as the invasion began, Kadar would be installed at the head of a "revolutionary" government.[26]

At 4 A.M. on 4 November, Budapest residents heard the shattering sound of Soviet artillery shells being launched into the city center. Soviet troops moved swiftly to capture the radio broadcasting stations and munitions de-

pots; they surrounded the Hungarian army barracks in the city and disarmed
the troops. They occupied all the bridges across the Danube, and then seized
the parliament building. The troops were met with fierce but sporadic and un-
coordinated resistance. Nagy himself wavered, uncertain how to respond. He
ordered Gen. Béla Király, chief of the National Guard, to tell his troops to hold
their fire, hoping this was all a big misunderstanding. "We cannot undertake
war against the Soviet Union," he told the exasperated and confused general.[27]
Just past five in the morning, Nagy did go on national radio to declare that "at
daybreak Soviet forces started an attack against our capital, obviously with the
intention to overthrow the legal Hungarian government. Our troops are fighting. The Government is in its place." But that was not the case, for Nagy himself then fled to the Yugoslav embassy, leaving his government in disarray.
Around noon, Zhukov radioed back to Moscow that most of the city was under his control, with the exception of a few strongholds in the southeastern
part of the city.[28] Kadar, meanwhile, announced the formation of a "revolutionary worker-peasant government" that would "put an end to the excesses
of the counter-revolutionary elements," as he now labeled the demonstrators.
Kadar's new puppet government also announced that it had "requested the
Soviet Army Command to help our nation smash the sinister forces of reaction and restore order and calm to the country."[29]

In the end, it took the Soviets only a few hours to take Budapest. Underground bands of resisters held out for a few days, and longer in the countryside, making pathetic appeals on their radios for outside help. "Civilized
people of the world!" said one broadcast on the afternoon of 4 November.
"Listen and come to our aid, not with declarations but with force, with soldiers, with arms! Do not forget that there is no stopping the wild onslaught of
Bolshevism. . . . Light is failing. The shadows grow darker every hour over the
soil of Hungary. Listen to our cry. . . . SOS! SOS!" Throughout the afternoon,
weak and crackling radio signals carried such messages out onto the airwaves,
where they died quietly, unheard.[30]

Was there in fact any chance that the international community would
come to Hungary's aid? In a word, no. Of course, there were genuine expressions of outrage and horror at the Soviet invasion. At the United Nations, US
ambassador Henry Cabot Lodge made a valiant effort to win condemnation
of the Soviet action, but was thwarted by the repeated Soviet veto of any motion of censure. Worse, the UN was in the midst of treating the Anglo-French-
Israeli invasion of the Suez Canal, and so the Western powers, who were of
course assumed to be in collusion over that invasion, had no moral high
ground from which to launch denunciations of the Russians. The Russians
treated the debate with their usual perversity, declaring that "interference by

the United Nations and by the Western countries in the Hungarian events might only lead to complications and it goes without saying that such interference would be unlawful and contrary to the principles of the Charter."[31] Even had the UN been able to overcome Soviet stonewalling, the United States had no intention of getting involved in the Hungarian crisis. Since 23 October, the US government had been sending the Russians reassuring signals that it did not wish to tempt Hungary to break away from the Soviet orbit. President Eisenhower had enough on his plate, including the Suez crisis and a presidential election scheduled for 6 November. A week after the crisis was over, safely reelected, Ike told the press that while he was sorry about the fate of the Hungarian people, "the United States does not suggest . . . that a defenseless population start an open revolution against a power which it is not capable of defeating."[32] Eisenhower's words reflected the degree of consensus that the superpowers now shared about the division of Europe. A divided Europe, Ike believed, was a stable Europe. A Hungarian Revolution was not in American interests, whatever he might say about defeating the ideological threat of Communism. Given Western apathy toward the Hungarians, it is clear that there was never a chance for any sustained Western response to Soviet oppression.

But does that mean that the suppression of the Hungarian Revolution of 1956 was a success for the Soviet Union? Certainly Khrushchev believed it was. In his eyes, Nagy had been a puppet, a tool of "the imperialistic forces of the world, especially the United States." Khrushchev's deeply held ideological beliefs informed his view of the events in Hungary. He believed that the Hungarian Communists had come under attack by an international counterrevolutionary conspiracy. "Our goal in Hungary," he wrote later, "was to support progressivism and to assist the people's transition from capitalism to socialism. The enemies of socialism had the opposite goal: wherever a socialist way of life had been achieved, they wanted to liquidate it, to suppress the working class, and to restore capitalism." In order to save socialism and to stave off subversive forces elsewhere in the socialist bloc, the Soviet Union had no choice but "to help the Hungarian people to crush the counterrevolutionary mutiny."[33]

It is precisely this sort of twisted logic that makes the Soviet regime and its leadership so incomprehensible to historians. Could Khrushchev have believed such an argument? In the streets of Budapest, workers, students, soldiers, writers all belied these Soviet efforts to give the invasion legitimacy. The working class in particular drove the revolution, with workers' councils sprouting up all across the country. They staged a revolution and then proved quite willing to die for it: in the ten days from 23 October to 4 November, at least 2,000 Hungarians died and perhaps many more. They went down fighting: some 640 Soviet soldiers were killed and 1,251 were wounded. Tens of thousands of Hungarian civilians were injured. Then there were the postinvasion reprisals. According to latest estimates, some 35,000 people were investigated for their activities during the revolution, and 22,000 of them were sentenced to jail terms. About three hundred revolutionaries were executed.[34]

Nagy was among them. Having fled to the Yugoslav embassy during the Soviet invasion, Nagy and his colleagues presented an awkward problem to the newly installed Kadar regime. Tito, ever on the lookout for an opportunity to enhance his position as the leader of national Communism, brokered a deal: Nagy would be given a written letter of safe conduct from Kadar and be allowed to return to his home, where he would desist from political activities. Kadar agreed, eager to defuse the crisis; but no sooner had Nagy stepped out of the embassy than he was abducted, flown to Romania, and imprisoned. In June 1958, after yet another show trial, he was shot, probably on Khrushchev's orders.

THE WALL

The crises in East Germany and Hungary lay bare Nikita Khrushchev's puzzling, contradictory policies. Here was a leader who took great risks to depart from the orthodoxies of Stalinism. He tried to reinvigorate the Communist movement by reclaiming its earlier dynamism and promise for a better future. But his idealism and romanticism ran up against a stubborn fact: Eastern Europeans did not like Communism, whether Lenin's, Stalin's, or Khrushchev's brand. This Khrushchev could not accept, and so he, like all his predecessors, fell back on the one means of governance he truly understood: force. The hopes raised by the Twentieth Party Congress speech now lay in tatters amidst the ruins of Budapest. Instead of a newly inspired Communist bloc, Khrushchev faced a sullen, dispirited group of states held in place by force and fear.

Nor did the prospects for the socialist bloc appear to be improving. No sooner had the Hungarian crisis been resolved than Khrushchev faced what he saw as a new and profoundly disturbing problem: the growing disparity in power between the two German states. Since 1953, when Walter Ulbricht had been left in control of the country despite his inept handling of the uprising, the GDR had floundered. Its economy was in a tailspin and the still-open border between East and West Germany—mandated by the Potsdam agreements and the four-power control of Berlin—allowed East German citizens to observe firsthand the sharp divergence of fortunes between East and West. As the West boomed, the East Germans were going bust. Worse, Ulbricht, who had come out of the 1953 crisis with his power enhanced, had intensified his efforts to build socialism in the GDR by forcing the pace on collectivization, seizing private property, and enforcing strict obedience to the ideological tenets of the SED.

As a result, the refugee problem that had triggered the 1953 crisis persisted, and hundreds of thousands of East Germans continued to leave the country each year. Their reasons for leaving were not hard to find. Many wished to be reunited with family members already in the West; others sought better economic opportunity; farmers in particular fled the harassment brought on by collectivization. But there was also an explicitly political dimension to their flight. A West German study analyzed 2,810 refugees from the month of July 1961 and found that the most common reason given for leaving the GDR was the pressure to join in political organizations, including working as an informer for the state security services.[35] Not only was this constant outflow embarrassing, but for Khrushchev it presented a reminder of the basic instability of the socialist bloc. When given a chance, people wanted to leave the harshness of the East and flee westward. How much longer could the GDR survive such hemorrhages?

To make matters worse, the West Germans in Khrushchev's eyes had become far more aggressive in their stance toward the East since their admission into NATO in 1955. Konrad Adenauer's Federal Republic had never recognized the legitimacy of East Germany and continually emphasized its objective to unify all Germans in a liberal democratic state. Adenauer had made it the keystone of his government: a strong West Germany would act as a powerful magnet force to the East Germans and draw them into accommodation and perhaps unification along Western lines. Thus, Adenauer took great pride in the economic accomplishments of the FRG, as well as in the new rearmament program started in 1955. Here, the Western powers seemed to be egging him on. In the mid-1950s, the Eisenhower administration began to discuss the prospect of supplying the new West German army with nuclear weapons. As early as December 1955, Eisenhower had told his staff that the United States must "not be stingy with an ally," and should "give our NATO allies the chance to use some of our modern weapons." By the spring of 1957, Adenauer had agreed to begin a program of developing an atomic arsenal for the Bundeswehr (the FRG's army), and told the Soviet ambassador as much. The NATO commander, Gen. Lauris Norstad, declared in public in February 1958 that "atomic weapons were absolutely indispensable" for defending West

Germany; by 1960, the president publicly acknowledged his interest in sharing atomic weapons with the Germans.[36]

These developments deeply worried Khrushchev and many of his advisers, who came to believe that the West might launch a combined economic and military offensive against the socialist bloc. In particular, they worried that Poland, already unreliable, might succumb to West German blandishments and try to defect from the Warsaw Pact in exchange for massive German aid. The West Germans would then insist on prompt unification with the GDR, and NATO would soon be encamped right on the borders of the Soviet Union. If the Russians objected, the West Germans could fall back on an arsenal of atomic weapons. These fears sound exaggerated today. But the events of 1956 had deeply shaken the Soviet leadership, which felt defensive and vulnerable. As far as Khrushchev was concerned, "the situation throughout Eastern Europe was highly unstable," and the West Germans seemed only to be aggravating the problem.[37]

How could Khrushchev manage to restore some sense of balance between the two Germanys? How could he increase the power and legitimacy of his fledgling East German state and deter the West Germans from any rash actions? Of course, the Soviets could increase economic aid to the GDR, but there was a limit to what the Russians could send, given the needs of the rest of the bloc. In any case, the West Germans were so far ahead in economic terms that there was little point in trying to match their productivity. Instead, Khrushchev devised a plan that he hoped would score a political victory over the West, increase the prestige of the East German state, and bolster the morale of the entire socialist bloc. These motives lay behind his 27 November 1958 ultimatum to the Western powers on an issue that would dominate the headlines until 1961: Berlin.

Berlin, Khrushchev later declared, was like "the testicles of the West: every time I want to make the West scream, I squeeze on Berlin."[38] Located one hundred miles inside East Germany, Berlin was still an open city under four-power occupation. This meant that American, British, and French soldiers and civilians operated freely deep inside the East German state; it also meant that the overflowing shopwindows, the cars, the theaters, the cafés of West Berlin were on view every day to those East Germans who crossed over into the Western part of the city. For Khrushchev, and especially Ulbricht, this anomaly was thoroughly annoying, and might serve to weaken the already fragile East German regime. Khrushchev's November ultimatum to the Western powers declared that this situation must end. The Western powers must recognize the legitimacy of the GDR—which they had not yet done—

and surrender their rights in Berlin. If they did not do so within six months, the Soviet government would simply turn over its sector to the East German government, and allow Ulbricht to do what he wanted with the city. The implication was that if the Western powers did not get out of Berlin, then the Soviets would allow the East Germans to cut off all access into West Berlin, isolating the city and triggering another Berlin blockade.[39]

Historians now know that Khrushchev did not seek to start a military conflict with the West over Berlin. On the contrary, his aim was to remove what he saw as a dangerous irritant in East-West relations, and to insure that the status quo of a divided Germany was openly accepted by the West. "We were simply asking the other side to acknowledge that two irreconcilable social-political structures existed in Germany," he wrote later, "socialism in East Germany and capitalism in West Germany. We were asking only for formal recognition of two German Republics."[40] Khrushchev did not want war; he wanted stability and recognition. In fact, when the Western powers agreed to open up negotiations on Berlin and Germany in the spring of 1959 in Geneva, Khrushchev quietly forgot about his six-month ultimatum, which lapsed in May 1959. Instead, in September 1959, Khrushchev traveled to the United States and met with Eisenhower at Camp David. The crisis seemed to have abated, and Khrushchev, despite periodic outbursts about Berlin being "a bone in his throat," seemed unwilling to push the crisis any further. In May 1960, he told the East Germans that "we are realists and we will never pursue a gambling policy. Under present conditions, it is worthwhile to wait a little longer and try to find a solution for the long-since ripe question of a peace treaty with the two German states."[41] Khrushchev had triggered the Berlin crisis in order to win a German settlement that enhanced stability in Central Europe; his instincts now told him to be patient, and he might just get what he wanted.

But as in the previous crises in the Eastern bloc, Khrushchev found that he was not entirely in control of events. For one thing, Khrushchev's 1958 ultimatum, with its implied threat to close off the last exit to the West, prompted thousands of East Germans to flee the country. In 1959, 144,000 left, and the next year some 200,000 more followed. Between 1949 and 1961, at least 2.6 million East Germans had fled the GDR into West Germany, and about 50 percent of them were under twenty-five years old. For the GDR, this exodus presented not only a public embarrassment but a serious material problem. Since 1954, 17,000 engineers, 16,000 teachers, and 3,300 doctors had fled the country.[42] When Walter Ulbricht met with Khrushchev on 30 November 1960, he said that while the GDR could not match West Germany's economic performance, "we must improve the position of doctors and the intelligentsia and some workers, since the situation in West Germany is improving faster." To do so, the GDR needed more Soviet aid, more raw materials, as well as $50 million in hard currency and sixty-eight tons of gold. But Khrushchev balked at this and declared such sums "inconceivable." "We don't have much gold, and we must keep it for an emergency." This position infuriated Ulbricht. Khrushchev had failed to follow up on his ultimatum and now refused to supply the GDR the resources it needed to keep its people from fleeing the country. It was an intolerable situation, one Ulbricht felt would endanger his very regime. In January 1961, Ulbricht wrote to Khrushchev a letter that would have been unthinkable in Stalin's day, in which he demanded action on resolving the "abnormal situation in West Berlin."[43] Khrushchev's policy seemed to be backfiring. Instead of winning assurances from the West that the status quo would be recognized, his initiative on Berlin seemed to have exacerbated the GDR's political and economic difficulties, and led the East German leadership to make ever stronger demands for Soviet action.

Khrushchev hoped that election of John F. Kennedy to the US presidency in November 1960 might allow him to win a resolution of the Berlin problem and appease his insufferable East German ally. Kennedy was young, untested, and after the disastrous CIA-backed invasion of Cuba at the Bay of Pigs in April 1961, in need of a foreign policy victory. Perhaps a peace treaty with East Germany and a new settlement on Berlin would appeal to the new president. Yet Khrushchev had a funny way of asking for favors. Meeting with Kennedy at a summit in Vienna in June 1961, Khrushchev laid into the American leader, barking at him that socialism was on the march, that the Bay of Pigs invasion was an imperialist fiasco, and that the West must recognize the GDR or risk war. He then issued another ultimatum: if the West did not agree to a permanent German settlement, then Berlin would be turned over to the East Germans. Kennedy was surprised by Khrushchev's aggressive attitude, but in light of his recent failure in Cuba decided that he could not show any weakness in handling the Russians. On 25 July 1961, Kennedy went on national television and told a now highly anxious American public that "we cannot and will not permit the Communists to drive us out of Berlin, either gradually or by force." West Berlin was, Kennedy declared, "a showcase of liberty, a symbol, an island of freedom in a Communist sea." As such, the city had become "the great testing place of western courage and will." He then went on to outline plans to increase the defense budget, call up the reserves, and undertake a massive program of civil defense. "If we do not meet our commitments to Berlin," he concluded, "where will we later stand?" Kennedy had turned

Khrushchev's bid for Berlin into a test of strength between the two super-powers and made it clear the United States was willing to go to war if the Russians infringed on American rights in West Berlin.[44]

The Berlin crisis was going from bad to worse for Khrushchev. His original goal had been to win recognition from the West for the East German state, thereby creating a stable and secure Eastern bloc. Instead, his war of words had now led to a renewed flight by the East Germans to the West, a loss of confidence by the Ulbricht regime in its Soviet patron, and a threat to go to war from the United States. Khrushchev desperately tried to backtrack, declaring publicly that "there should be a conference; let us not create a war psychosis, let us clear the atmosphere, let us rely on reason and not on the power of thermonuclear weapons." He also made a particular point of saying that "any barring of access to West Berlin, any blockade of West Berlin, is out of the question."[45]

These assurances may have been welcome to the Americans, but for Ulbricht it seemed as if Khrushchev had once again lost his nerve and would fail to help stem the tide of refugees. "If the present situation of open borders remains," he told the Soviet ambassador, Mikhail Pervukhin, "collapse is inevitable." He now proposed to take far more drastic action: the erection of a barrier around West Berlin that would stop the refugee flow. Kennedy's 25 July speech had insisted only that the Western powers' access to *West* Berlin be maintained; it had said nothing about the rights of the GDR to maintain its own border with West Berlin. On 31 July, Ulbricht met with Khrushchev in Moscow and proposed taking advantage of this loophole by sealing off the access into West Berlin from the GDR, while leaving open the roads into the city from West Germany. This would keep the East Germans in while not blockading West Berlin. Khrushchev had no alternative now and agreed to allow Ulbricht to build a barrier cutting off the Soviet sector of Berlin and the GDR from West Berlin.[46] Khrushchev saw this as a stopgap: it would help the East German regime survive by cutting off the flow of refugees, but it was a technically legal measure that would not prompt a war with NATO.

On the morning of 13 August 1961, East German workers, supervised by the military, launched Operation Rose: the erection of a barbed-wire fence along the border between the Soviet sector of Berlin and the three Western sectors. The reasons the GDR gave for building the wall were laughable: a government decree that day stated that the barrier was intended "to interdict the hostile activity of the revenge-seeking and militaristic forces of western Germany," which was intent on continuing "the predatory policy of German monopolistic capital and its Hitlerite generals." East Germans saw it rather differently. For them, it came as a shocking surprise, dividing families from one

another, cutting neighborhoods and even apartment blocks in two, and leading many desperate Berliners to attempt escape across the hastily strung-up
barbed wire. Buildings that lay athwart the new dividing line became escape
routes for some, but these were soon boarded up. Some panic-stricken residents leapt from rooftops into nets held by West Berlin firemen. But within a
few weeks, the Eastern side of the wall was turned into a heavily guarded strip,
studded with watchtowers, that ran over a hundred miles around the island of
West Berlin. The purpose of the wall was, of course, not to keep West Berliners
out of East Germany, but to imprison the remaining inhabitants of the concentration camp known as the German Democratic Republic.

At a minimum, Khrushchev got what he wanted out of the Berlin affair.
The GDR now controlled its borders; the refugee crisis had been stopped and
Ulbricht appeased; and the Western powers, by allowing the East Germans to
maintain the wall, tacitly acknowledged the existence of the GDR. But he had
wanted much more. "It was my dream," he wrote about the affair later, "to create such conditions in Germany that the GDR would become a showcase of
moral, political, and material achievement—all attractively displayed for the
Western world to see and admire."[47] Instead, the GDR became a prison, supervised by a hard-line Stalinist regime. For that, Khrushchev had risked war
with the West. His colleagues began to weary of this kind of brinksmanship.
After Berlin, Khrushchev undertook a reckless adventure in Cuba, placing nuclear missiles on the island. When the United States again turned the crisis
into a showdown, Khrushchev backed down and withdrew them. For ten
years, Khrushchev had led the Soviet Union on a precarious path. He
attempted to dismantle Stalinism and revive the revolutionary ideas of
Marxism, but then used Stalinist methods to crush the genuine revolutions in
East Germany and Hungary. He sought stability and coexistence with the
United States, but used inflammatory language and nuclear threats to pressure
the United States into recognizing Soviet interests. His colleagues could bear
no more. In October 1964, Khrushchev was ousted from power by a ring of
Politburo members led by Leonid Brezhnev.

It would take some months before the Western powers decided to accept
the existence of the wall. At issue was the question of whether access into West
Berlin from West Germany, and into East Berlin by American, French, and
British officials, would still be allowed. After a few tense moments, including
a twelve-hour face-off between Soviet and American tanks in late October, it
became clear that the East Germans and Soviets would continue to respect
Western rights to enter East Berlin, while keeping the wall sealed against East
German citizens. The Berlin Wall squared with the Cold War consensus that
had emerged in the 1950s: a divided Europe was a stable one. Peace required

respect for the spheres of influence of the two superpowers. The Americans had followed this principle in 1953 and 1956; it was entirely within character for them to accept the erection of the wall in 1961. "It's not a very nice solution," said President Kennedy to his aides. "But a wall is a hell of a lot better than a war."[48]

It also gave the West a marvelous propaganda coup that it was not slow to exploit. Vice President Lyndon Johnson went to West Berlin on 20 August 1961, accompanied by Gen. Lucius Clay, the hero of the 1948 airlift, to show US solidarity for the beleaguered citizens of that city. And in June 1963, President Kennedy made a dramatic visit to the city. As his motorcade traveled from Tegel Airport through the city, 2 million delirious Berliners cheered him on. Before the West Berlin city hall, he made one of the most memorable speeches of his life, and Berliners never forgot it:

> There are many people in the world who really don't understand—or say they don't—what is the great issue between the free world and the Communist world. Let them come to Berlin. . . . Freedom has many difficulties and democracy is not perfect. But we have never had to put a wall up to keep our people in, to prevent them from leaving us. . . . Freedom is indivisible and when one man is enslaved, all are not free. When all are free, then we can look forward to that day when this city will be joined as one and this country and this great continent of Europe in a peaceful and hopeful globe. When that day finally comes, as it will, the people of West Berlin can take sober satisfaction in the fact that they were in the front lines for almost two decades. All free men, wherever they may live, are citizens of Berlin. And therefore, as a free man, I take pride in the words, "Ich bin ein Berliner."[49]

The tone was defiant, and the three-quarters of a million onlookers erupted in euphoric applause. The United States, it was clear, would protect the island outpost of West Berlin. But the theatrics of the speech obscured the obvious fact that the Americans had acquiesced in the building of the wall and in the Soviet bid to enhance the legitimacy of its East German client. The wall, by shoring up the GDR, insured that Germany would never be reunited until the wall came down. For Konrad Adenauer, who had staked his political career on the promise of German unity, this was a bitter pill to swallow. It seemed as though the Americans had given in and accepted a divided Europe, as indeed they had. In such circumstances, perhaps it was time for West Germany to distance itself from Washington and its priorities and to go in search of a more dynamic foreign policy that placed Europe and its interests first.

CHAPTER EIGHT

THE GAULLIST TEMPTATION: WESTERN EUROPE IN THE 1960s

•

THE DECADE OF DE GAULLE

THOUGH THE CIRCUMSTANCES of his return to power in 1958 were murky, Charles de Gaulle presented himself—and was received by his countrymen— as the savior of France. It was a role he had played well during World War II, and he reprised it with skill. His ability to handle and resolve the Algerian war massively increased his prestige, so that by the start of the 1960s, de Gaulle possessed enormous political capital. He could begin his long-held ambition to make France into the nation he believed it should become. His efforts had a major impact on the political, economic, and diplomatic position not just of France but of Europe as well. By calling for a greater role for France in world affairs, he created an opportunity for other European states to join him in claiming a particular destiny for Europe, possibly even breaking with the bipolar world order imposed on the continent by the superpowers. He spoke with passion about the need for Europe to cut the leading strings that tied it to America and for the great states of Europe to resume their rightful place alongside the superpowers. De Gaulle seemed intent not simply on remaking France but on restoring Europe itself to greatness.[1]

Thus began a great struggle in this decade over the shape of the "new Europe." Would it emerge from the prosperous fifties as a community of economically robust sovereign states, working in concert to assert their independence from the overweening power of the United States? Or would Europe remain a small band of cautious, consensus-driven nations, eager to remain in the good graces of its superpower patron, earnestly working to avoid backsliding into competition, rivalry, and war? De Gaulle's willingness to challenge

American hegemony, to question sacred truths about the Atlantic alliance and the dollar-centered global economy, struck a chord among many Europeans. But finally, they did not embrace de Gaulle's vision. The stability of the post-war years had been too hard won to be gambled away in a risky gesture of contempt for American leadership. De Gaulle made his mark nonetheless. Europe would never look to America with quite the same reverence after de Gaulle. The superpower that had saved Europe lost its moral appeal in Vietnam. Its nuclear monopoly ended as France and Britain developed their own nuclear weapons. Even America's once dominating economic position came under siege by the end of the decade. De Gaulle fell short of his ambitions to dethrone the United States from its dominating position in Europe, but the 1960s—really the decade of de Gaulle—saw a marked decline in the moral and political influence America had once enjoyed in Europe. The Old World, it seemed, was staging a comeback.

Before de Gaulle could take on the Americans, he had to get France's house in order. Since resigning from the presidency in 1946, de Gaulle had been fulminating about the weakness of the Fourth Republic and the failures of its political leaders to defend French interests in the global arena. De Gaulle wished to see France flex its muscles again. His first priority, therefore, was to sweep away the decrepit structures he identified as responsible for France's woes. Under the Third and Fourth Republics, the head of state was elected by the parliament and played a secondary role in political life. De Gaulle's animus toward the rabble in the National Assembly knew no bounds. In laying out the constitution of the Fifth Republic, de Gaulle sought to push the Assembly to the margins of political life. He believed that a strong executive must be given the powers to rule the country, to nominate his ministers and promulgate laws. His new constitution gave the president the power to call for a national referendum on any issue, thereby creating a special mechanism to allow the executive to circumvent the parliament if he chose and take his case to the people. The president was given the right to dissolve the National Assembly. All issues of foreign and defense policy were strictly reserved to him. And most important, the president could, in times of national emergency, assume special powers under article 16 of the constitution, and govern by decree. By contrast, the powers of the National Assembly were sharply curtailed. All political initiative passed to the head of state. The French people were thrilled. On 28 September 1958—a mere four months after he took power—the electorate overwhelmingly approved the founding text of the Fifth Republic. De Gaulle now ruled supreme in France.[2]

Though de Gaulle's broader goal was to improve France's prestige in the world, he understood that whatever power France might exercise would derive from economic strength. The Fourth Republic had made impressive strides, as the economy grew at a brisk 4.5 percent per year between 1949 and 1959; but the finances of the French government were a shambles. There was high inflation—the impact of heavy military spending during the Algerian war—and the French franc had become one of the weakest currencies in Europe. The country had a huge trade deficit, which drained away currency reserves; and the government had run up large budget deficits. Nothing remained of the last loan from the IMF. "On every single score," de Gaulle wrote later, "we were on the verge of disaster."[3]

De Gaulle tackled the situation using his new constitutional powers. His finance minister, Antoine Pinay, and his economic adviser, Jacques Rueff, administered shock treatment. The franc was devalued 17.5 percent; taxes were raised on businesses, high incomes, alcohol, and tobacco; prices for public-sector services like oil, gas, electricity, transport, and coal were raised; and a new loan was floated that raised 300 billion francs and kept the treasury solvent. These were all policies no Fourth Republic government could have adopted without upsetting the deputies in the National Assembly. De Gaulle, by contrast, faced little opposition. In addition, the new government liberalized trade with its European neighbors. This had been stipulated in the Treaty of Rome of 1957, but the French had been dragging their feet, afraid of the adverse internal consequences of a rush of international competition. Given de Gaulle's hostility toward the institutions of the new Europe, this move may have seemed a surprise. But de Gaulle's team believed that if France was to get out of the economic doldrums, it must embrace open markets. On 1 January 1960, France sharply reduced its tariffs on trade with the EEC countries and with the United States. The effect of these measures on French growth rates was marked: from 1959 to 1970, French gross domestic product grew at an annual rate of 5.8 percent, a rate not matched by any European country, including Germany (4.9 percent), Italy (5.5 percent), and Britain (2.9 percent).[4]

De Gaulle's government built on the Pinay-Rueff reforms by pursuing an aggressive industrial and modernization strategy for the country. In the 1940s and 1950s, the state had played a large role in jump-starting the industrial sector by investing heavily in key sectors, like steel, coal, cement, transport, electricity, and housing. De Gaulle's team now wished to pressure the private sector to assume more direct responsibility for modernization and technological improvements. This was in keeping with the overall goal of preparing the French economy for global competition in the EEC. The government therefore encouraged a rationalization of French industry, urging the private sector to consolidate through mergers. In banking, chemicals, cement, automobiles, textiles, and steel, mergers began to reshape industry along the lines of large,

multinational corporations that would have the muscle to compete on the
world stage. Companies like the Banque Nationale de Paris, Renault, the oil giant ELF, and the aluminum manufacturer Pechiney began to take on truly
world-class proportions. The days of the tradition-bound small family firm
were over. The state also pursued modernization plans in the publicly owned
sectors, like oil, coal, and aeronautics, and laid out a state-sponsored plan for
the development of a computer industry. The hard work paid off: the French
economy grew at unprecedented rates in the 1960s, and by 1965 France had
become the world's fourth largest exporter, behind America, Germany, and
Britain. De Gaulle, for all his old-school bluster about tradition, proved willing to break with the venerable ways of French business. If France was to be
great, it would become so by succeeding in the global marketplace.

With the economy strong, the colonial wars winding down, and his own
powers at home uncontested, de Gaulle might well express some satisfaction.
"In the year of grace 1962," he wrote in his memoirs, "France's revival was in
full flower. She had been threatened by civil war; bankruptcy had stared her in
the face; the world had forgotten her voice. Now she was out of danger. The
State had succeeded in rescuing her by virtue of a complete change."[5] Having
gotten France's house in order, de Gaulle began to lay a plan for the restoration of French global influence. But France could not become great alone.
Even de Gaulle knew that. He needed allies. And to the world's great surprise,
he began his search for a partner not in Washington or London but in Bonn.

THE GENERAL AND THE GERMANS

In 1958, the year of de Gaulle's return to power, Konrad Adenauer was an unhappy man. At the age of eighty-two, in his tenth year as chancellor, he still
dominated West German politics. Yet he faced two problems that threatened
not only his own hold on power but the very success of the West German experiment. First, his parliamentary opponents, the Social Democratic Party, remained implacably opposed to his policy of *Westpolitik*—the integration of
the FRG into the Western alliance—which they saw as certain to perpetuate
the division of Germany. They wanted to see Germany reunited, even if this
meant withdrawal from NATO and a neutralization of the country. Adenauer
steadfastly rejected this argument. He deeply mistrusted the Russians and believed that a neutral Germany would become a satellite state of the Soviet
Union. He hoped that East Germany might one day be rejoined with the
Federal Republic, but his first priority, as he wrote privately in February 1958,
was "the protection of the Federal Republic's freedom. . . . Our main goal

must be to secure irrevocably the liberty of our fifty-two million people." Only then could he worry "about the liberty of the seventeen million on the other side of the Iron Curtain."[6] Once West Germany was strong, confident, and secure, it could negotiate on better terms with Moscow about the prospect of reunification.

Adenauer's second concern was the Americans. Despite the strong commitment of the United States to the economic recovery and security of Europe and especially Germany, Adenauer continued to fear the possibility that the Americans might be manipulated by the wily Nikita Khrushchev into striking a deal to end the Cold War. In this scenario, the superpowers would agree to end the division of Europe, reduce nuclear armaments, and reunify Germany, thereby making NATO unnecessary. Adenauer's *Westpolitik*, the raison d'être of his Christian Democratic party, would then be shattered. Adenauer sincerely believed that the Americans could not be counted on to protect West German interests forever; they would be tempted at some future point to end the East-West conflict by resolving the German problem. Adenauer planned to prepare for this eventuality by making West Germany as strong as possible both economically and militarily so that unification, if it ever took place, would be on Western terms. Adenauer did not wish to weaken the ties between Germany and America, but he wanted to reinforce them by creating a stronger European structure that could not be dictated to by Washington.

Given his views about the Americans, then, it is no surprise to find that Adenauer and Charles de Gaulle soon developed a strong rapport. They were both men of an earlier age in which Europe had towered over America in military and economic might. (Adenauer was already forty-one years old when America entered the First World War in 1917; de Gaulle was twenty-seven.) They had only slowly adjusted to the reversal of fortune that found Europe dependent upon American goodwill. But since the 1950s, Europe had recovered its footing, and it was time to place the US-European relationship on a more equal plane. To be sure, Adenauer worried that de Gaulle might prove too much of a nationalist to accept an integrated Europe, and might work to break up the Western alliance. Yet upon their first meeting, most of these fears were dispelled.

De Gaulle went out of his way to win over the octogenarian chancellor, inviting him in September 1958 to visit him at his country home in the small village of Colombey-les-Deux-Eglises, about 120 miles southeast of Paris. This was an honor that had never been extended to any foreign visitor, and demonstrated de Gaulle's sincere desire to reassure Adenauer that the policy of Franco-German friendship, started by de Gaulle's predecessors, would be continued. Adenauer arrived on a Sunday morning, 14 September, and the men engaged in a wide-ranging discussion for two and a half hours, joined only by an interpreter. Adenauer was immensely relieved to find that de Gaulle had no intention of undoing a decade's worth of patient diplomacy that had brought about good relations between France and Germany. The two men commiserated about American hegemony in Europe, and de Gaulle went even further, suggesting that it was time to put the Anglo-Saxons on notice that Europe did not need them at all. De Gaulle told Adenauer that he opposed British entry into the EEC, and would probably withdraw from NATO before long. France, declared de Gaulle, wanted "political independence commensurate with my country's position."[7] Adenauer was not unduly alarmed by this language. In fact, he seemed rather pleased that de Gaulle was ready to act as Washington's chief critic, expressing publicly the criticisms Adenauer could now keep to himself. Provided that de Gaulle would allow the institutions of the EEC to remain in place, Adenauer saw de Gaulle not as a threat but as a powerful ally in building a strong Europe that was unafraid to face America eye to eye.[8]

Of course, there were many differences between the two countries, which the personal relationship between de Gaulle and Adenauer could not bridge. Germany was strongly committed to European integration; was equally committed to NATO and the American presence in Europe; and wished to strengthen, not weaken, the institutions that held this fledgling Europe together. De Gaulle's ambitions were framed more squarely in national terms. He accepted the terms of the Treaty of Rome because he could see that easing protectionism in France would stimulate competition and help the economy. But he loathed the institutional structures of the emerging European community. He did not want important decisions affecting national economic policy to be taken by a powerful supranational commission. He steadfastly opposed British entry into the EEC and considered NATO a hindrance to French military independence. On those grounds, he moved forward with the construction of a French nuclear weapons program.

Events continued to press Adenauer and de Gaulle closer together, however. In November 1958, Soviet leader Nikita Khrushchev made his first ultimatum concerning Berlin: the Western powers must recognize the East German state and give up their rights in the divided city. For Adenauer, Khrushchev's demand assaulted not just Allied rights in West Berlin but the legitimacy of the West German state itself. The crisis emphasized the provisional nature of the postwar settlement. Adenauer's chief fear was not Russia but America: the United States might concede to Soviet pressure tactics, give in on Berlin, and repudiate the very logic of Adenauer's *Westpolitik*. Thus, he was appalled by the tepid response of the Americans, who, Adenauer believed, seemed to be looking for a way to appease Khrushchev. Significantly, de Gaulle publicly denounced the Soviet chicanery over Berlin and lent strong support to Adenauer during the crisis.

With the Berlin crisis as a backdrop, de Gaulle and Adenauer continued to meet frequently. In June 1960 they held an important conference at Rambouillet, the imposing château some twenty-five miles southwest of Paris that French monarchs and heads of state had often used as an official retreat. Here, de Gaulle began in earnest to seduce Adenauer away from the integrated, supranational Europe and the US-centered alliance system that had developed since 1945. The Treaty of Rome of 1957, the founding document of the EEC, created four new institutions designed to govern relations between the six signatory states: the Commission, the Council of Ministers, the Assembly, and the European Court of Justice. Although the Council of Ministers contained national representatives and was supposed to act as the main coordinating body between the six EEC states, it was the Commission that quickly emerged as the most dynamic component of the new community. The Commission was the supranational executive branch of the EEC structure. It could initiate new policy and also had the responsibility of insuring that agreed treaties were enforced. The nine commissioners were not representatives of their states and indeed took an oath of loyalty to the EEC. Under the leadership of its first president, Walter Hallstein (a German), the Commission became an active force in European politics.

This was precisely the reason de Gaulle despised it. In a memo written on the eve of the Rambouillet talks, de Gaulle wrote that "supranational organisms . . . tend inevitably and abusively to become irresponsible superstates."[9] Further, by focusing on the narrow technical aspects of interstate relations, the EEC structures ignored the true foundations of power in the world: an attitude of confidence, authority, and dignity that only the nation-state can provide its people. He posed the problem thus in a press conference in early September: "What are the pillars on which Europe can be built? In truth, they are the States, States that are certainly very different from one another, each having its soul, its history and its language, its glories and ambitions, but States that are the only entities with the right to give orders and the power to be obeyed. To fancy one can build something effective in action, and acceptable to the peoples, outside or above the States, is a chimera."[10] Instead of a supranational Europe, de Gaulle proposed an *Europe des patries*, a Europe of nations, that would concert together in common cause while allowing the flame of national identity to burn in the hearts of Europe's citizens. The French president did not end there. He also told Adenauer that he wished to see NATO similarly reformed. Its structure, which placed overall command in the hands of an American supreme commander (SACEUR), was unacceptable, and power to command armed forces must be returned to the states.

De Gaulle's plans to reshape both the EEC and NATO, if they had come to fruition, would have changed the shape not just of contemporary Europe but perhaps also of the Cold War. De Gaulle was asking for Adenauer and the other EEC states to rethink the architecture of postwar Europe. His objective was to make Europe not simply stronger but also more ambitious in world affairs. He wanted a Europe that did more than enrich itself, but used its power to end the Cold War, to end the interference of the United States and Russia in European affairs, and to recover the leadership in world affairs that history had assigned it for the previous five centuries. De Gaulle was smart enough to know that France could not aspire to such visions alone, but as part of a dynamic confederation of states, Europeans might once again dare to dream.

Tempting—yet the Gaullist design for Europe did not finally rally Konrad Adenauer. At Rambouillet, Adenauer tried to appease de Gaulle, saying that he shared the Frenchman's view that the powers of the EEC Commission might need to be curtailed. Adenauer was anxious that any direct refusal to de Gaulle would alienate him altogether from the common Europe. Privately, however, he expressed anxiety about de Gaulle's animosity toward NATO. Adenauer had always been profoundly anti-Communist and deeply suspicious of the Russians. At the very moment that the Berlin crisis was reaching its most intense phase, Adenauer had no intention of breaking apart the Western alliance. Furthermore, his own political party and his chief advisers pressed him to reject de Gaulle's ideas, which, they argued, represented a complete repudiation of the chancellor's own *Westpolitik* and the ideal of integration that the Christian Democrats stood for. Thus, Adenauer decided to delay: he would agree to hold additional talks on de Gaulle's ideas about a "Europe of nations." But he told his advisers in late September 1960 that "I have completely lost confidence in General de Gaulle."[11]

De Gaulle was not deterred. Throughout 1961, he pressed Adenauer and the other EEC states to join him in reshaping the community into a union that had more political power but fewer supranational characteristics. After summit meetings in February and July 1961, the EEC, with Adenauer's tepid support, agreed to allow a Frenchman named Christian Fouchet, then de Gaulle's ambassador to Denmark, to convene a panel that would give concrete shape to de Gaulle's ideas. Fouchet unveiled a draft treaty for a "union of states" in November 1961. The Fouchet plan proposed four institutional components: a council made up of heads of state (not technocrats); a permanent secretariat (based in Paris, not Brussels); a European assembly of members appointed by national legislatures; and four intergovernmental committees that would concert on issues of foreign affairs, defense, commerce, and culture. This appeared to be a major widening of the European project, and de Gaulle tried to sell it as the realization of true European political unity. Yet he could not hide his real objective: to destroy the power of supranational institutions that might constrain the decision-making powers of national leaders. "It is only the States that are valid, legitimate, and capable of achievement," he said in May 1962, in a press conference about the Fouchet plan. "There cannot be any other Europe than a Europe of States, apart, of course, from myths, stories, and parades."

De Gaulle was wrong: there was another Europe apart from the states, and it was encapsulated in the EEC and its constituent parts. Here, the ideal of integration had triumphed, and it was an ideal that attracted most of the political leadership in Western Europe. Integration meant surrendering some sovereignty in return for mutual cooperation, stability, and a balance of power in Europe. De Gaulle's Fouchet plan, by contrast, offered a return to state sovereignty and its corollary, that the larger states would have more political clout. Though Konrad Adenauer might have been tempted by such a vision, the smaller states, the Netherlands, Italy, Belgium, and Luxembourg, rejected it. They had no interest in sacrificing an integrated Europe, even with its restrictions on sovereignty, for French hegemony in Europe. The Fouchet plan never rallied the EEC states and was quietly forgotten. De Gaulle felt let down by Adenauer, and the much heralded Franco-German marriage was not consummated.

Despite the failure of the Fouchet plan, de Gaulle continued to believe that France and Germany in tandem could dictate terms to the rest of the continent and forge a powerful force in world affairs. As de Gaulle put it in May 1962, "there is an interdependence between Germany and France. On that interdependence depends any hope of uniting Europe in the political field as also in the defense or economic fields. On that interdependence depends, consequently, the destiny of Europe."[12] These sentiments, de Gaulle knew, were designed for public consumption. Adenauer had in fact derailed de Gaulle's "Europe of nations." But both leaders wished to show the world that their two countries, old antagonists, had overcome their history and forged a new partnership. In July 1962, Adenauer was welcomed to France on a state visit enhanced by Gaullist gestures: a military parade of six hundred French and German tanks, and a joint Mass in Reims cathedral. In September, de Gaulle took his turn as the guest of the Germans, toured the country, and ended his speeches by declaring, in German, "Long live Germany! Long live Franco-German friendship!" These sentiments were given concrete expression in the Franco-German Friendship Treaty of 22 January 1963, which committed both countries to deepening cooperation in military, economic, and cultural spheres.

Yet by 1963, the bloom was off the rose. The German political class, defying Adenauer, had decided that de Gaulle was a threat to NATO and to an integrated Europe. De Gaulle himself rudely confirmed these suspicions when, two weeks before signing the Friendship Treaty, he announced that he would veto Britain's application to join the European Economic Community. If he could not have a Gaullist Europe, he would certainly not have a British one. The German Bundestag, piqued, ratified the Friendship Treaty only after appending a preamble that declared Germany's enduring commitment to NATO, to the unification of Europe, and to friendship with the United States—a direct rebuke to the Gaullist design. And Adenauer himself was hurt by his four-year flirtation with Gaullism. In October 1963, under intense pressure from his own party, he resigned after fourteen years as chancellor. He was succeeded by Ludwig Erhard, the wizard of Germany's economic revival and a man who immediately undertook to repair German-American relations, which had been frayed by the Adenauer–de Gaulle minuet.

De Gaulle's bid to reshape Europe had failed, and at great cost. By 1963, the French president was widely mistrusted by his European partners and by the United States. He had threatened to break up NATO, to slow integration, and to push the Americans out of Europe. And worst of all, he had in the process slapped down the outstretched hand of an old friend, Britain, a country that had finally decided to cast its lot with its European neighbors, only to face public rejection. It was an insult of historic consequences.

SUPERMAC AND RAMROD

Harold Macmillan became Britain's prime minister in January 1957 upon Anthony Eden's resignation in the wake of the disastrous Suez affair. He was sixty-three, a man born in the high Victorian age. He had gone to Eton and Oxford, served in the First World War as a captain, and remarkably—given the death rates for officers—survived Loos, Ypres, even the Somme. Wounded four times, he carried shrapnel in his body for the rest of his life. He worked briefly in the family publishing business but was soon drawn to politics. In the 1930s he emerged as one of the Conservative Party's leading young figures, forming an alliance with the antiappeasers Churchill and Eden that would last into the 1950s. During the Second World War, Macmillan again served with distinction, this time in a civilian capacity, at the Ministry of Supply, then the Colonial Office, and most important, as British representative to the Allied Headquarters established in Algiers in late 1942. It was here that he crossed paths with two later world leaders, General Eisenhower and General de Gaulle. After the war, he helped the Conservatives rebuild the party in the wake of the 1945 Tory defeat, and in 1951 found himself serving in the cabinet again, first as housing minister, then defense minister, foreign secretary, and chancellor of the Exchequer. He has been much criticized for his stance during the Suez crisis, when he urged Eden on in his attack on Nasser, only to jump ship and oppose the military operation once launched. Still, there were few men better qualified or more experienced than he to become prime minister; and despite his Edwardian air, his stooped figure, his limp wrist and shuffling gait (the result of his war injuries), Macmillan soon became one of Britain's most popular prime ministers.

Upon taking office, Macmillan worked hard to restore the international and economic position of Britain, which had suffered so much during Eden's last year in office. He immediately shored up the "special relationship" by meeting with his old wartime comrade President Eisenhower at a conference in Bermuda in March 1957. There, he won Ike's agreement to sell Britain sixty Thor intermediate-range nuclear missiles. This was to be the centerpiece of Britain's own nuclear deterrent force (but one that could be used only with permission from Washington). Macmillan burnished his reputation as a world statesman by traveling to Moscow in 1959 to meet Khrushchev, where they discussed arms control. And on the home front, too, the news was good. The British economy showed signs of improvement under Macmillan's stewardship, as interest rates were lowered, industrial output increased, exports expanded, the trade balance moved into the black, and taxes were lowered. Despite signs of inflation, the British consumer went on a buying spree and the country as a whole felt a sudden burst of affluence. Macmillan won plaudits for his efforts, and was transformed into "Supermac"—a brawny, caped crusader—by the cartoonist Vicky. After only two years in office Macmillan led his party to a thumping electoral victory in October 1959 that gave the Conservatives a hundred-seat majority in the House of Commons.

Yet there were a number of major problems looming that preoccupied Macmillan for the rest of his term in office and did much to deflate the high expectations he had raised. In the area of the special relationship with Washington, the promised benefits of nuclear sharing pointed up Britain's dependence upon the United States. Even with US technology, the British proved unable to build their proposed long-range missile, Blue Streak. Macmillan had to go back to the Americans, who now offered Skybolt instead—a long-range guided missile launched from aircraft. It was an embarrassment that the British "independent" nuclear deterrent, the key to a great power's status, was so obviously dependent upon America. The point was excruciatingly driven home when in December 1962 the Americans announced that they would abandon construction of the Skybolt missile system, which didn't work.

Although an outraged Macmillan managed to secure from President Kennedy a commitment to provide Britain with sea-launched nuclear missiles—Polaris—instead, the affair revealed Britain to be totally reliant on the Americans for access to the nuclear club.[13]

Another problem that persistently nagged Macmillan was the state of the British economy. For all the apparent good news in the late fifties, Britain's economic position, relative to its newly affluent European neighbors, looked anemic. In the period 1950 to 1962, Britain's share of world trade dropped from 25 percent to 15 percent, while Germany's share rose from 7 percent to 20 percent. In the 1950s, British GDP doubled, but Germany's and France's tripled.[14] Britain had failed to invest in new manufacturing plant, while the continentals, rebuilding afresh and adopting new methods of economic planning, were by the start of the 1960s reaping the benefits. In the area that had always been the most dynamic of the British economy, manufacturing, the rate of growth on the continent could only be envied.

GROWTH RATES, 1953–1963

	Annual Rate of Growth of GDP	Annual Rate of Growth of Manufacturing Production
Japan	9.6	13.6
Italy	5.6	8.2
West Germany	6.0	7.3
France	4.9	5.6
Netherlands	4.5	5.5
Belgium	3.6	5.1
Britain	3.6	3.2
United States	3.1	2.6

SOURCE: Nicholas Kaldor, *Causes of the Slow Rate of Economic Growth of the United Kingdom* (Cambridge: Cambridge University Press, 1966), 5.

Macmillan at times expressed his exasperation: "If we succeeded in losing two wars, wrote off all our debts, got rid of all our foreign obligations, and kept no force overseas, then we might be as rich as the Germans."[15] But the problem was not simply the effects of the war. The British did not adapt to the challenges of modernization. They did not train workers in new technologies, did not invest sufficiently in research and development, and faced a powerful labor movement that contributed to overmanning in some sectors. The result was slower growth in productivity than other leading economies demonstrated. In the period 1951–64, growth rates of output per worker employed increased on average by 2.3 percent per year. But in the United States, the figure was 2.5 percent, in France 4.3 percent, in Germany 5.1 percent, and in Japan a stunning 7.6 percent. Britain was falling alarmingly behind.[16]

Alongside these problems, Macmillan faced a serious choice on the question of Europe. Since 1950 and the formation of the European Coal and Steel Community, Britain had scorned continental blandishments to enter into a closer economic union. The British government felt a deep commitment to the Commonwealth trading bloc, to which most of its trade was directed. The British government expressed outright opposition to membership in common European political institutions such as the European Assembly and Court that might interfere with national sovereignty. And it just seemed un-English to join the EEC. By the late 1950s, however, as the EEC experiment aided economic expansion on the continent, the British grew distinctly uneasy that they might find themselves on the outside of a new trading bloc whose common tariff hurt their exports at a time when Britain's trade pattern was shifting increasingly away from the Commonwealth and toward the EEC Six. Britain had been able to rely on open markets in Commonwealth countries like Australia, New Zealand, South Africa, and Canada, which together took over a quarter of Britain's exports in 1950. But throughout the decade, trade with the continent grew in importance, and by 1965 the six states of the EEC had become the largest single market for British exports.

BRITISH EXPORTS TO SELECTED AREAS, 1946-1980
(PERCENT OF TOTAL EXPORTS)

	1946	1950	1955	1960	1965	1970	1975[3]	1980
EEC[1]	15.4	12.8	14.7	15.9	20.7	21.6	32	44
EFTA[2]	12.5	11	10.8	11.1	12.9	15.8	13.4	14.9
Australia, NZ, S. Africa, Canada	21	27.3	25.7	20.8	18.7	13.5	10.7	10.4
Africa (excl. North)	14.2	13.2	15.8	12.6	12	9.1	9	7.1
Asia	14.8	12.7	13	13	10.2	8.2	7	6.4
USA	4.4	5.8	6.9	9.6	10.9	11.5	9.1	9.9
India	8.7	4.5	4.5	4.2	2.4	.88	.84	1.1
Central and South America	6.1	7.2	4.2	5	3.4	3.5	3.5	2.2

SOURCE: Calculated from data in B. R. Mitchell, *British Historical Statistics* (Cambridge: Cambridge University Press, 1988).

1. Belgium, France, Germany, Italy, Luxembourg, Netherlands.

2. Austria, Britain, Denmark, Norway, Portugal, Sweden, Switzerland.

3. Britain, Ireland, and Denmark joined the EEC in 1973.

At first, Macmillan chose to face the challenge of the EEC by proposing an alternative: a free trade area for Western Europe that offered free trade with no political strings attached. Although the EEC Six conducted negotiations with the British and others on the issue of a free trade area, the idea was quashed by de Gaulle in December 1958, just six months after his return to power. Macmillan's government went on to sponsor a European Free Trade Area in 1959 with six other countries: Austria, Denmark, Norway, Portugal, Sweden, and Switzerland. The EFTA committed members to the gradual reduction of tariffs on industrial goods (though not, significantly, agricultural products). There was no common external tariff as there was with the EEC, nor were there to be any political institutions. As a rival to the EEC, however, the EFTA was a failure, for it had no political clout and the economies grouped within it, Britain aside, were small. In 1960, therefore, Macmillan began to think that it might be time to approach the EEC and ask for British membership.

This was not an easy decision. Though Macmillan thought of Britain as part of Europe, he also wished to maintain its world role as leader of the Commonwealth and as a partner of the United States in containing the Soviet Union. Yet Britain's global influence had been sharply curtailed since decolonization, its nuclear force was dependent upon American weapons, and it had become alienated from the booming continental union. "Shall we be caught," he wrote in his diary, "between a hostile (or at least less and less friendly) America and a boastful, powerful empire of Charlemagne?" Staying out of Europe could lead to economic ruin; entering it meant abandoning the Commonwealth and the EFTA, and hurting British farmers, who would have to compete with imports from Europe. "It's a grim choice," he concluded.[17] Macmillan felt he had to take the plunge nonetheless. His party was divided about this, Labour opposed, and the British public indifferent or hostile. Macmillan nonetheless believed that Britain must enter Europe. It was, his biographer has written, "the biggest single decision of his premiership."[18]

As Macmillan soon discovered, however, the choice was not his to make. Everything depended upon de Gaulle. The two men had known each other since 1942, when Macmillan had championed de Gaulle, over Roosevelt's objections, as a suitable leader for the Free French movement. Macmillan thought of him as a friend, insofar as de Gaulle was capable of friendship. Yet he also knew of de Gaulle's stubbornness and vanity. As he recalled in his memoirs, "among the many sobriquets or code-names for de Gaulle in common use at Allied Force Headquarters during the war, perhaps the most popular was 'Ramrod.' This nickname recalled the famous definition of a man who was alleged to have all the rigidity of a poker without its occasional warmth."[19]

Perhaps because of his wartime ties, Macmillan stubbornly refused to believe that de Gaulle would unilaterally block Britain's entry into the EEC. As Macmillan knew, de Gaulle did not like the supranational features of the EEC any more than he did. But Macmillan underestimated de Gaulle's determination to use Europe to promote French power; British entry could only dilute that. Macmillan felt that he did have one high card to play: nuclear weapons. Macmillan envisioned offering to France some kind of Anglo-French nuclear cooperation, using American technology to develop a European deterrent. This would place Britain and France on a separate political plane than the others in Europe. In exchange for the recognition of France's status as a great power, perhaps de Gaulle would open the EEC to Britain. Macmillan vaguely suggested something along these lines to de Gaulle in January 1961, at a meeting at Rambouillet, and thought the Frenchman "seemed genuinely attracted by my themes."[20] Unfortunately, Macmillan had great difficulty persuading the new US president, John Kennedy, to help France develop nuclear technology. And in any case, de Gaulle did not seek such assistance. In April 1961, the French tested yet another atomic bomb in the Sahara—their fourth—and started development of a ground-based ballistic missile. The French were building their own nuclear deterrent without Anglo-American help—an accomplishment that thrilled the French president.

These were discouraging developments, but Macmillan pressed ahead anyway, believing that de Gaulle would come under heavy pressure from the Germans and the Americans to allow Britain into Europe and avoid a division in Europe between the EEC and the rest. On 27 July 1961, the British cabinet agreed to apply for membership in the EEC. Macmillan, in the House of Commons, acknowledged that this decision was a departure from British tradition. But "in a changing world, if we are not to be left behind and to drop out of the main stream of the world's life, we must be prepared to change and adapt our methods."[21]

If Macmillan was willing to change, de Gaulle was not. For the next eighteen months, Macmillan worked tirelessly to secure agreement from de Gaulle to allow Britain into the EEC, and he also tried to enlist Kennedy and Adenauer to bring pressure to bear on the French president. In November 1961, Macmillan invited de Gaulle to his country home, Birch Grove, in Sussex. The visit, despite the intimacy of the setting, proved a severe disappointment. The French leader appeared "older, more isolated, more sententious, and far more royal. . . . He is well-informed, yet remote. His hatred of the 'Anglo-Americans' is as great as ever." Macmillan confided in his diary:

> The tragedy of it all is that we agree with de Gaulle on almost everything. We like the political Europe (*union des patries* or *union d'états*)

that de Gaulle likes. We are anti-federalists; so is he. We are pragma-
tists in our economic planning; so is he. . . . We agree; but his pride,
his inherited hatred of England (since Joan of Arc), his bitter memories of the last war; above all, his intense vanity for France—she must
dominate—make him half welcome, half repel us, with a strange
"love-hate" complex. Sometimes, when I am with him, I feel I have
overcome it. But he goes back to his distrust and dislike, like a dog to
his vomit.[22]

It is apparent here how deeply personal the problem had become for
Macmillan. He felt that de Gaulle owed him one; owed Britain anyway. De
Gaulle's refusal to bend left Macmillan feeling betrayed and deeply saddened.
In December 1962, the two men met again at Rambouillet. It was to be the last
time they would meet. Macmillan implored the Frenchman not to block
British entry. De Gaulle, now clearly determined to do just that, patronized
Macmillan and told him that in the EEC, "France could say 'no' even to the
Germans. . . . Once Britain and all the rest joined the organization, things
would be different." De Gaulle had been "brutally frank" and the discussions
were "about as bad as they could be."[23]

Indeed, a month later, with the negotiations still ongoing, President de
Gaulle announced that he intended to veto Britain's application to the EEC.
Why such hostility? In part because de Gaulle viewed Britain as an agent for
American interests; in part because he feared a possible Anglo-German alliance inside the EEC against France; and in part because of his genuine fears
that British entry would lead to the restructuring of the common agricultural
policy, which so handsomely subsidized French farmers.[24] As he said in his
press conference on 14 January 1963, "England is, in effect, insular, maritime,
linked through its trade, markets, and food supply to very diverse and often
very distant countries. . . . The nature, structure, and economic context of
England differ profoundly from those of the other states of the continent." De
Gaulle claimed that British entry would so change the character of the EEC
that it would soon become a meaningless conglomeration of members "under
American dependence and leadership." France, he said, rejected this model in
favor of "a strictly European construction." As Macmillan archly explained to
President Kennedy, de Gaulle "wants to be the cock on a small dunghill in-
stead of having two cocks on a larger one."[25]

The whole affair was a terrific blow to Macmillan. It embarrassed him politically and left Britain looking weak and rudderless. The former secretary of
state Dean Acheson had the previous month coined a phrase that now hung
on Macmillan's neck like a millstone: "Britain," he said, "has lost an empire

and has not yet found a role." Macmillan thought this unfair, for he knew that Britain's role was in Europe; it was de Gaulle who had rejected Britain. "All our policies at home and abroad are in ruins," he bitterly confided to his diary. "We have lost everything, except our courage and determination."[26] Later that year, his foreign policy in tatters, his cabinet torn by scandal, his health gone bad, Macmillan resigned.

DE GAULLE AND THE AMERICANS

Macmillan was the chief casualty of the EEC affair; was de Gaulle therefore the victor? If his goal was to derail the progress made by the federalists who had yearned since 1950 for a united Europe, de Gaulle certainly succeeded. De Gaulle's veto did a great deal of damage to the morale of the EEC member states. The clubby atmosphere that Monnet, Schuman, Adenauer, and Spaak had created in the early 1950s had disappeared, replaced by rancor and mistrust. The Frenchman's imperious veto of the British application, announced in a press conference in Paris rather than to the EEC negotiators in Brussels, outraged the other states. It also signaled the start of a sustained French effort to weaken the institutions of the EEC. To be sure, de Gaulle wished to keep the EEC intact, as a useful tool to help bolster French economic interests. But he also wanted to insure it gained no powers that could infringe on French sovereignty. The other five states, to varying degrees, sought to push ahead with the creation of stronger integrated institutions. In 1965, these competing ideas burst out into the open. The EEC Commission and its ambitious chairman, Walter Hallstein, began to press for wider powers for the European Parliament, greater authority for the Commission to raise its own revenue from import duties, and reforms to the common agricultural policy. De Gaulle saw these proposals as part of the creeping supranationalism that he opposed. He refused to consider them, and in fact withdrew his representative from the Council of Ministers altogether. Since the EEC operated on the principle of unanimity, the absence of the French meant that no work could be done. The "empty chair crisis" of 1965 brought progress within the EEC to a halt and cast a pall over the future of the European project. The following year, Hallstein's proposals were dropped, and the French once again rejoined the Council. The sense of dynamism of the 1950s, however, could not be revived. The EEC would not emerge in the 1960s as a nascent European government, as some of the ardent federalists had once hoped. In fact, well after de Gaulle's departure from office in 1969, the EEC remained little more than an intergovernmental conference devoted chiefly to economic questions and trade.

The advent of a true European Community would have to wait another twenty years.

De Gaulle demonstrated in the early 1960s that France did have the power to shape and to wreck the European project. Yet the French president was playing for higher stakes even than that. In the last five years of his presidency, he embarked on a sustained effort to challenge American global power, and by consequence to insert France into the dynamic of the bipolar world order. His effort failed, of course, though in the process de Gaulle did accomplish something important: he launched a wave of criticism at the United States that, while it befuddled France's American benefactors, found broad support in Europe. From 1945 to 1965, the United States had dominated Western Europe economically. It had promoted American tastes, habits of consumption, and industrial organization, and insisted on a high degree of conformity to American ideology. Though Europeans for the most part accepted this Pax Americana with eagerness, they also understood that the new Europe must soon find its own voice in world affairs or lose its identity. De Gaulle offered to speak for Europe, and though few Europeans liked de Gaulle, they applauded some of his more pointed words. In three areas in particular, de Gaulle broke all the old taboos: he criticized America's war in Vietnam; he decided to withdraw France from the integrated military command of NATO; and he launched a global campaign to dethrone the dollar as the world's leading currency.[27]

De Gaulle's criticism of the Vietnam War carried special irony: it had been President de Gaulle in 1945 who had directed French soldiers to return to Saigon and retake the French colony from the defeated Japanese. De Gaulle had been an ardent supporter of colonialism and the force needed to sustain it. He learned his lesson in Algeria, however, and now embraced decolonization with all the zeal of a convert. De Gaulle, forgetting France's own disastrous colonial experience there, now saw the Vietnam War as emblematic of American arrogance, overconfidence, and naïveté. Vietnam, he felt, should be allowed to unify, as the 1954 Geneva accords had foreseen. The Vietnamese Communists, in his view, were nationalists first, intent on winning national independence rather than spreading revolution throughout Asia. In taking this position, de Gaulle aligned himself with the public position of the Soviet Union, China, and the North Vietnamese themselves. De Gaulle worried that US adventurism in Asia could lead to a global conflict, and declared in June 1965 that "the US was the greatest danger in the world today to peace." His views were ignored: the next month, President Lyndon Johnson announced a major escalation of the American military commitment in Vietnam. Antiwar protests erupted in French cities in 1966 and 1967, and polls showed that the

French public strongly opposed US policy there. Soon, this combination of anti-Americanism, romantic support for the underdog Viet Cong, and fear of a wider conflagration in Asia would spark protest movements all across Europe.[28]

The Vietnam War called American leadership of the West into question, and de Gaulle was quick to exploit these doubts. In March 1966, he announced that France would withdraw from the military component of the NATO alliance. In a letter to President Johnson, de Gaulle declared that France, having recovered economically and having developed sufficient means to defend herself, now sought "to regain on her whole territory the full exercise of her sovereignty, at present diminished by the permanent presence of Allied military elements."[29] France would remain a member of the alliance, but NATO would have no control over French military forces. Nor could the alliance station foreign troops on French soil. NATO headquarters decamped to Brussels. The United States evacuated its thirty military bases in France and withdrew 26,000 military personnel. De Gaulle's decision, though hardly unexpected, infuriated the United States. Not only did it threaten to weaken NATO, but de Gaulle had acted with extreme ill grace in suggesting that the very forces that liberated France in 1945, and had then been invited by the French government to remain, somehow threatened French sovereignty. US secretary of state Dean Rusk, in an acid quip, asked the French leader if the United States should evacuate "the dead Americans in military cemeteries as well." This theme of French ingratitude was picked up by the French press. One cartoon depicted a homeward bound GI calling to de Gaulle: "If you ever need us again, remember our telephone number is 14–18 and 39–45," a pointed reference to US involvement in two world wars on France's behalf. But the public supported de Gaulle's move by a two-to-one margin. The French withdrawal from NATO typified de Gaulle's desire for greater latitude in world affairs. He tendered diplomatic recognition to Communist China in 1964, for example, traveled to Moscow in 1966, and sided with the Soviet Union in the United Nations during the Arab-Israeli War of 1967.[30]

Despite these gestures, France had little success in breaking down the Cold War order or challenging American leadership of the Western alliance. In one area at least, de Gaulle found he could inflict some real pain on the United States. Since the end of the war, the international monetary system had been underpinned by the dollar, which in turn was backed by gold. At the Bretton Woods meetings in 1944, the United States had agreed to exchange gold for dollars at the rate of $35 per ounce. Since at the time the United States held 80 percent of the world's gold, this seemed natural, and a good way to increase liquidity in a world economic system that had been shattered by war. In this system, dollars were literally as good as gold, and were used as the world's reserve currency. This system served the United States by allowing it to run large balance-of-payments deficits: rather than resorting to gold to settle international payments, the United States could simply print more dollars to settle its debts—a privilege no other country enjoyed. In the late 1950s, dollars flowed into Europe as American businesses began to invest in European companies at an astonishing rate. Large multinationals like IBM, Standard Oil, General Motors, Libby (food processing), and Chrysler soon joined the rush. Suddenly, European treasuries were bursting with US currency. In the mid-1960s, the Vietnam War began to hurt America's global reputation and raised doubts about the future of the US economy, so many nations began to change their dollars for gold. Washington persuaded West Germany, Japan, and Britain not to do so, but de Gaulle saw this situation as an opportunity to launch an attack on the dollar that would reveal America's weakness and Europe's newfound strength.[31]

In February 1965, in yet another patronizing press conference, de Gaulle called for an end to the dollar-centered monetary system. The current system, he claimed, allowed the United States an unfair advantage in the world market. The United States could invest overseas and swallow up European companies because it used a currency that had the same value as gold—even if in fact it was not backed up by gold in US banks. America was, de Gaulle claimed, exporting its own inflation. This forced other countries to bear the burden of US economic expansion.[32] De Gaulle followed through on this proposal by ordering the Bank of France to start cashing in its dollar holdings for gold, attempting to illustrate the fragility of the dollar-based monetary system. France's European partners, alarmed at the reckless plan to destabilize the US economy, refused to follow suit. The United States, however, had to acknowledge that it could no longer play the role assigned to it at Bretton Woods, and use the dollar as the world's official reserve currency. In 1971, in a defensive measure designed to protect the dollar from similar attacks, President Richard Nixon suspended the free convertibility of dollars into gold at a fixed rate of exchange. Though this action actually restored some flexibility to US monetary policy, it was perceived at the time as a sign of a weakening American power and prestige—just what de Gaulle had intended.

In taking the measure of Charles de Gaulle, one finds in this one figure many of the tensions and contradictions that characterized Europe in the late 1960s. He disliked the idea of a supranational Europe that eroded the power of the state, yet he made good use of the EEC to enhance French economic and agricultural growth. He claimed to despise the American way of life, with its homogeneity and mass production, yet he initiated an ambitious plan to reform French business and industry, and reveled in the greater power that a competitive, modernized economy brought to France. He claimed to have a vision of the future for France and Europe that transcended the Cold War, yet his rhetoric more often hearkened back to the eighteenth century, when France was great and America a distant outpost of European civilization. De Gaulle embodied all the anxieties of a Europe in transition.

In another way too he captured a central dynamic of Europe in the late 1960s. When he resigned in 1969, de Gaulle was almost eighty years old. He was the last of the titans who had fought in the Second World War and then shaped the cold peace that followed. Truman and Eisenhower; Churchill, Eden, and Macmillan; Adenauer; even Stalin and Khrushchev—all had been ushered off the stage. For these men, the war years had been the apex of their lives. They had seen Hitler's rise to power, the cowardice of appeasement, the early disasters of the war, then Stalingrad, Normandy, Berlin, Hiroshima. They saw postwar Europe through the lens of that war experience. By 1968, however, there were many millions of young Europeans who had no memory of those cataclysmic events and whose concerns could not be addressed in the language of the Cold War, or the rhetoric of patriotism, nationalism, and consumerism. De Gaulle's posturing and theatrics had masked the advent of a new European culture that would prove more powerful and more enduring than anything the old general could devise. The days of grandeur were about to give way to the days of rage.

PART THREE

REBELS

■

On 6 October 1973—the Jewish holiday of Yom Kippur—President Anwar el-Sadat of Egypt launched an invasion of Israel. Egyptian tanks stormed across the Suez Canal in an effort to retake the Sinai Peninsula, which Israel had seized during the 1967 Arab-Israeli War; at the same moment, Syrian troops attacked Israel from the north, in the Golan Heights. The Israelis struck back, and within a few weeks had regained lost ground. The combatants agreed to a cease-fire in November.

This short war in the Middle East had enormous consequences for Europe because it came at a time when the Arab world was seeking to exercise influence in world affairs by manipulating the price of oil. Through the Organization of Petroleum Exporting Countries (OPEC), Arab oil producers had already begun to increase oil prices on the eve of the 1973 war. When the Yom Kippur War broke out, OPEC imposed an embargo on those states that had aided Israel, and sharply increased oil prices. Oil that had cost $3 a barrel in October cost $11 dollars a barrel the following January. Although the embargo was lifted after five months, the oil price increases continued throughout the 1970s. By 1980, OPEC's oil cost $30 a barrel.

The sudden rise in energy prices created the "oil shock," a ripple effect that was felt across the industrialized world for the entire decade of the 1970s. It plunged the Europeans, who were dependent on oil imports to fuel their industrial sector, into a severe economic crisis. They had to pay much higher prices for energy, and passed those costs on to consumers, pushing inflation up to unprecedented levels. At the same time, their exports slumped and European countries experienced huge trade deficits. New investment slowed to a trickle, the energy-dependent heavy industry sector had to change its oil-guzzling ways, and industrial production slowed down markedly. After humming along at an average annual growth rate of 4.6 percent between 1950 and 1973, the European economy slowed down to a rate of 2 percent annual growth between 1973 and 1992. The boom years of the 1950s and 1960s were over.

ANNUAL GDP GROWTH, UNEMPLOYMENT, AND
INFLATION IN THE EUROPEAN COMMUNITY, 1973–1985

	1973	1974	1975	1976	1977	1978	1979	1980	1981	1982	1983	1984	1985
GDP	6.0	1.8	-0.9	4.9	2.4	3.1	3.2	1.0	-0.2	0.5	1.4	2.4	2.6
Unemployment	2.6	2.7	4.1	4.7	5.1	5.3	5.5	6.2	7.8	9.0	10.1	10	10.2
Rate of inflation	8.6	13.3	13.4	11.2	11.1	8.2	9.7	12.6	11.8	10.3	8.0	6.9	5.8

SOURCE: *OECD Economic Outlook*, 37–40 (1985) and 67–68 (2000).

Thirty years later, such rates of growth do not seem so bad. Annual growth of 2 percent is not robust, but has become the European norm: from 1990 to 1999, the European Community countries grew at an average annual rate of just 2 percent, with a high of 3 percent in 1990 and a low of minus 0.4 percent in 1993. But after the boom times of the 1950–73 period, expectations for prolonged, constant economic expansion had been internalized. The sudden falloff of growth rates and the rise of unemployment and inflation created an air of crisis and malaise in Europe that hung over the entire decade of the 1970s.

This sense of crisis was exacerbated by social and political problems that predated the oil shock. Most visible was the surge of student-led protest movements, which started as a response to poor university conditions but gained momentum as part of a broad rejection of the postwar consensus. The dutiful regimen of the 1950s—work, austerity, conformity, and Christian Democracy—had begun to break down during the 1960s as the baby boomers reached college age and began to question the social model created by their parents. These social protests were generated by more than the predictable alienation of college students: they expanded to become a massive protest against the foundations of a rigid postwar social hierarchy in which the voices of the young, the left, women, and workers were too often ignored. Most students made their case by marching in the streets, and occasionally bashing a few store windows. Some took the protest much further and declared war against the representatives of the social and political order. The result was a decade of terrorism that cast a pall across Europe throughout the 1970s.

The social and economic crisis generated a series of political responses. In Spain, Portugal, and Greece, the economic collapse of the early 1970s fell like a hammer blow on the anachronistic authoritarian regimes there, while stirring opposition forces to demand political liberalization. The result was the sudden and surprisingly bloodless transition to democratic rule.

In Germany, the resurgent left propelled Willy Brandt into power in 1969 as the first Social Democratic chancellor since 1930. He promptly broke with Adenauer's fearful shibboleths that prohibited contact with the Communist East, and initiated a diplomatic offensive toward the East—his *Ostpolitik*—that normalized relations between East and West Germany, eased the tension between the two blocs, and helped generate a broader détente between the superpowers.

In Eastern Europe, especially Czechoslovakia and Poland, the evident failure of the command economy to satisfy even the most basic consumer demands gave rise to various attempts at reform and liberalization, which encouraged workers and intellectuals to question the foundations of the Communist postwar order. The Poles and Czechs met stiff reprisals and felt the sting of increased repression in Prague in 1968 and in Warsaw in 1981. But they also signaled the growing intensity of resistance to Soviet hegemony in Eastern Europe.

In Britain, the old left looked dazed and confused in trying to control the combination of rising labor militancy, skyrocketing inflation, slumping productivity, and social protest. Labour's failure opened the way to a challenger from the far right of the political spectrum, Margaret Thatcher, whose ideas for dismantling the welfare state, imposing sharp government spending cuts, lowering taxes, and restoring Victorian values created a dynamic platform that placed the Conservatives back in power.

For all the rhetoric deployed in the 1970s by the partisans of change, this decade was not revolutionary. Neither the youngsters on the streets of Paris, nor the Poles in the gritty Gdansk shipyard, nor Brandt's diplomatic advisers, nor the Thatcherite monetarists, nor the Portuguese army captains—rebels all—triggered revolutions. They did, however, generate long-lasting political and social changes: they opened the political arena to young people, and women; they undermined the legitimacy of the Communist governments in Eastern Europe and laid the groundwork for the citizens' movements that would topple those regimes in 1989; they forced greater monetary responsibility upon profligate state treasuries; and they expanded the access of democracy to tens of millions of Southern Europeans. The decade was not revolutionary, but it belonged to the rebels nonetheless.

CHAPTER NINE

EUROPE AND ITS DISCONTENTS: 1968 AND AFTER

.

PARIS IN THE SPRINGTIME

OF ALL THE OUTBURSTS of student unrest in Europe in 1968, the most spectacular occurred in France; and though most major cities in the country were affected, Paris was hit hardest. This is not surprising. Paris possessed the nation's oldest, most venerable institutions of higher education and the largest student population. In the 1960s, those numbers had been rising. Longer secondary schooling, increased living standards, and greater demand for trained managers in the expanding economy had led to a great inrush of students into the university system, and by 1968 there were half a million students squeezed into universities that had not changed much since the nineteenth century. And 160,000 of them lived in Paris. The French Ministry of Education—which in typical French fashion controlled all decisions about higher education in the country—tried to relieve the overcrowding by building a ring of large campuses in the distant suburbs of the city. This cut students off from the dynamic city center, left them dependent upon infrequent train service into Paris, and forced them into ugly concrete-and-steel dormitories.

And these were not just any students. The generation of 1968 was fired up by a potent blend of Marxist radicalism, anti-Americanism, antiestablishment rhetoric, alienation from the values of their parents, and a yearning to challenge what they viewed as a static, consumer-centered postwar society. The Vietnam War conveniently encapsulated their entire worldview: on the one side, American militarism, imperialism, arrogance, and on the other, Vietnamese peasant radicalism, collectivism, and liberation. Their role models were the guerrillas who wanted to shatter the Cold War order and break down the hegemony of outdated ideologies: Castro, Mao, Che Guevara—a grab bag of revolutionaries at the disposition of a generation that had lost faith in its own culture.[1]

This mixture of student disaffection and radical idealism erupted on one of the suburban campuses outside Paris: the University of Nanterre, a series of drab blockhouses built in 1963 in the midst of a slum. On 22 March 1968, 150 students there, protesting the arrests of six anti–Vietnam War demonstrators, occupied the main administrative building. It was not the first time the students had marched. The previous year, sporadic demonstrations and student strikes had disrupted university life, as students called for better housing conditions and free access to dormitories of the opposite sex, which was still strictly forbidden. The leader of the Nanterre students was Daniel Cohn-Bendit, a young sociology student who in some ways was a perfect representation of the new Europe. He was born in 1945. His parents were German Jews who had fled to France to avoid persecution. He chose German nationality only to avoid the French military draft, but he pursued his schooling in France. His tousled mop of red hair, his disarming, boyish smile, and his quick wit obscured a deep conviction that the time for revolution was at hand.

Why did Cohn-Bendit seek revolution? The goals of the student movement in France, as elsewhere, are hard to define. Reforms in university life, certainly. As Cohn-Bendit put it, "the university has in fact become a sausage-machine which turns out people without any real culture, and incapable of thinking for themselves but trained to fit into the economic system of a highly industrialized society."[2] Yet that was not all. The university for them was merely a microcosm of a bourgeois, static, and authoritarian society. Professors, parents, government officials, and party leaders all were to be held accountable for the creation and perpetuation of a social system based on crass worship of wealth, on the rigid segregation of society along class and gender lines, and on a refusal to debate the profound philosophical questions about how society should be organized to bring about fairness and justice for every one of its members. Cohn-Bendit especially rejected the leadership of the Communist Party, which he regarded as old, ineffective, and beholden to the dictates of Soviet imperialism. There was also a considerable degree of humor and irony in the language of the protesters, as their graffiti revealed. "Be Realists: Demand the Impossible" and "Imagination Is Taking Power" were two slogans frequently scribbled on university walls. "Alcohol Kills; Take LSD." "Make Love—Then Start Over." There was a witty anti-Gaullist cry: "The General Will Against the Will of the General." And in a stairway: "Don't Take the Elevator; Take Power."[3]

How did this band of youthful rebels in a suburban university manage to bring about a near revolution in France? They had a good deal of help from the authorities, who responded in an unimaginative way to the protests at Nanterre. The dean of the university, facing total disruptions on his campus during the month of April, closed the school on 2 May. This had the effect of pushing the student movement into the city, where the Nanterre students occupied the courtyard of the Sorbonne, Paris's most illustrious university campus, right in the heart of the ancient Latin Quarter. Again, the authorities blundered, calling in the police to arrest the students. This merely inflamed the rest of the student body, which promptly rushed into the streets around the Sorbonne, launching bottles, bricks, and other projectiles at the riot police. They responded with tear gas and rubber truncheons. Now the urge to stop talking and start fighting seized the students, and in an instant the neighborhood around the university was in chaos. Iron gratings were ripped up and made into crude barricades; street signs, café chairs, and soon cars were piled up in the streets to slow down the movements of the police. By the end of the day, six hundred people had been arrested, hundreds wounded. The rector of the Sorbonne announced that his university would close its doors, effectively locking out the students. The student union responded with a call for a city-wide strike of all students in the Paris area against the behavior of the CRS— the Compagnie Républicaine de Sécurité, France's specially trained riot police. On Monday, 6 May, students chanting "CRS—SS"—a ghastly slogan likening the police to Hitler's henchmen—again clashed violently with the helmeted cops, who rushed the marchers. For the next week, students across the city marched, shouted, smashed, and burnt; they were met with ferocity by the police, who deployed tear gas, water cannons, mass arrests, and regular beatings. The violence reached a peak on the night of 10 May, when most city streets were blocked by flaming cars and police wagons. To the many news cameras and reporters present, it looked as if Paris was in the midst of a full-blown revolution.

The government, alarmed at the failure of the university officials to handle the crisis, now intervened. Prime Minister Georges Pompidou, who had been out of the country on a state visit to Afghanistan, managed to quell the worst of the rioting by offering concessions: on 11 May, he announced that the Sorbonne would be reopened and that the students arrested since 3 May would be released. But by now, the trade unions had sensed the weakness of the government when faced with the brazen challenge of the students. The student-worker alliance was purely a marriage of convenience. The union leadership had little use for the hyperintellectual, bourgeois students. Daniel

Cohn-Bendit called the Communist Party leaders "Stalinist filth" and they referred to him as "a German anarchist."[4] But they could see that de Gaulle's regime stood on the edge of a precipice. Another push and the government could be toppled. On 13 May, the unions called a general strike and staged a massive march of 200,000 workers through Paris. The student protest had become a social crisis.

The strikes that now paralyzed the country stemmed from causes very different from that which motivated the students. Ten years of Gaullist policies had pushed the unions into the background of public life; the Communist Party had been punished at the polls during de Gaulle's ascendancy; and the very nature of work itself, with its increased emphasis on mass production and hierarchy, stimulated resistance. Perhaps as many as 10 million workers went out on strike over the course of the next two weeks. This was shocking enough; but worse was the fact that the union leadership did not appear to have complete control of its rank and file. The Communist union, the CGT, wanted to use the riots to wrest from the government certain agreements on wage increases, a shorter work week, and pension plans. The government, in a series of meetings at the end of May, agreed. But the workers rejected the compromise, having been infected with the zeal of the students and sensing their power to overthrow the entire government. Leftist political leaders like François Mitterrand and Pierre Mendès-France began to speak of forming a national unity government and holding new elections for president. The Fifth Republic seemed on the brink of collapse.

Throughout all of this crisis, President Charles de Gaulle had maintained a studied silence. Uninterested in domestic affairs, he did not want to dignify the student riots with any expression of concern on his part. He delegated the whole affair to Pompidou, and at the height of the crisis he flew to Romania for a long-planned state visit. Upon his return on 18 May, he found that his lieutenants had failed to bring the situation under control. He briefly considered resigning. On 29 May, de Gaulle secretly flew to Baden-Baden, in Germany, to visit the commander of the French forces there, his old friend (and rival from Algerian days) Gen. Jacques Massu. According to Massu, de Gaulle was deeply shaken by the uprising in the city and had begun to think his regime might not survive. "For the first time in my life," he later told Pompidou, "my nerve failed me." Massu apparently revived the president's spirits and insisted that he return immediately to face down the strikers. On 30 May, he did so, delivering an address on the radio at 4:30 P.M. In a stern message that preyed upon many French people's fears of a Communist revolution in the country, he announced that he would dissolve the National Assembly and hold new elections. The country was "threatened with dictatorship, that of totalitarian communism." The people must come to the defense of the republic.[5]

It was an old tactic: use the Communists as the bogeyman and whip up support for a conservative reaction. And after a month of chaos in the streets of Paris, it worked to perfection. Within an hour of de Gaulle's address, crowds began to form on the place de la Concorde, the major intersection on the opposite side of the river Seine from the students' Latin Quarter. Perhaps as many as half a million people poured out of their homes into the streets, and marched up the Champs-Elysées behind the major political leaders of the Gaullist and right-wing parties, in an atmosphere of quiet, determined reproach to the students. From then on, the momentum switched to the forces of order. De Gaulle's elections, held on 23 and 30 June 1968, gave a huge majority to the Gaullist candidates. For the first time, de Gaulle's party had an overall majority in the National Assembly, winning 293 seats of 487. With their right-wing allies, the Gaullists now controlled three-quarters of the National Assembly. It was a stunning reversal. A country that a month earlier had seemed rudderless, on the brink of revolution, would now be governed by a parliament more conservative even than de Gaulle himself.[6]

ITALY

Unlike in France, where the events of 1968 burst out in a terrific display of fireworks in the spring and summer, the Italian protests burned longer and left a deeper mark. In Italy, the five years from 1968 to 1973 marked a period of intense, turbulent, and often violent protest: protest against institutions that appeared unresponsive to the interests of the people, protest against capitalism, protest against the sclerotic education system. In short, protest against the very foundations of postwar Italy.[7]

Students triggered the protest movement in Italy. This in part resulted from the reforms of education offered by the postwar state. In 1962, the government made secondary education up to age fourteen mandatory, with the result that the numbers of students in school doubled. The absence of sufficient schoolrooms, teaching materials, and trained teachers, however, aggravated this expectant new class of students, many of them from the increasingly ambitious middle classes. They took their grievances with them into the university system, which was also strained to the breaking point. By 1968, almost half a million students had enrolled in university, compared to 268,000 just eight years earlier. They found antiquated educational institutions with out-

dated curricula, poor facilities, and a disengaged faculty that spent precious
few hours actually teaching. For the privilege of attending this sort of shadow
university, students had to pay out of their own pocket: no state-sponsored
education grants yet existed.

The students had legitimate complaints; heavy doses of inflammable
Marxist rhetoric gave them greater force. The values of their parents, on which
the postwar Italian miracle had been based—materialism, free markets,
Catholicism, anti-Communism, party politics—offered little appeal to a
younger generation that sought intellectual, spiritual, and political fulfillment
outside the confines of the bourgeoisie and the Cold War. The Vietnam War
became the universal touchstone for the radical students, while Mao's agrarian, proletarian Cultural Revolution offered a model of a mass protest that
sought to initiate radical democratic socialism. (It is too easy to point out that
Mao at this time was waging ideological warfare against China's bourgeois intellectuals—the very sort of people at the forefront of the European student
movement.) Thus, Mao's *Little Red Book* and Che Guevara berets popped up
everywhere, the emblems of a challenge to the foundations of the modern
Italian state.

In the fall of 1967, well before the French students had launched their assault, the Italian universities exploded. The university in the northern city of
Trento, which had a strongly Catholic identity and had been founded in 1962
by Christian Democratic activists, was hit with a series of sit-ins and occupa-
tions of university buildings. There soon followed similar sit-ins at the
Catholic University in Milan, which had educated many of the Christian
Democrats' leading figures. The students were expelled by the police, a move
that only fanned the flames. Next came Turin, where students demanded cur-
riculum reform, interrupted professors' lectures, occupied buildings, and
brought university life to a halt. Similar protests erupted in Milan; and in
February 1968, in Rome, the protests took a violent turn. Police charged students who had tried to storm a university building. The students fought back,
hurled objects at the police, and set cars on fire. Forty-six policemen wound
up in the hospital; the tally of students injured is unknown.

Of course, students were motivated by more than unhappiness over university life. At its heart, the late-sixties clashes were driven by a desperate desire by young people to be heard. They had been given no role in the postwar
boom years. Their future had been spelled out for them, as technocrats, sales-
men, middle managers in the burgeoning service industry. It was assumed
that their loyalties would be those of their parents: they would vote the same
way, dress the same way, marry and have children the same way, and so on. But
no one had consulted them. In opposition to the nuclear family, the salaried

job, the paid vacations, and the joys of kitchen appliances, students proposed an alternative vision: of collectivism, loyalty to peers across class lines, personal fulfillment through participation in group movements, and direct democracy. Students also wanted to assert their freedom from their parents. Slogans like "I Want to Be an Orphan" could be seen scribbled on university walls. Recalled one young woman: "I knew that in my life I wanted to be everything except what my mother was. This was absolutely clear to me. And so I misbehaved quite a bit."[8] In rejecting parents, authorities, and leaders, the movement remained disorganized and did not cohere around a single institution that could realize its agenda. But what did that matter? The struggle came first; then one could discuss plans for the future.

This iconoclasm separated the student movement from the organized left, especially from the Communist Party and labor. Yet the students had put the state on the defensive in 1968, and the workers took full advantage of this temporary shift in the balance of power. Italian workers had been pressured by large waves of immigrants from the poor and rural south into the industrial north. Jobs became scarce and wages had stagnated. Mechanization too had taken its toll on skilled workers, while new techniques of mass production led to faster assembly lines. In the atmosphere of protest triggered by the students, trade unions in March 1968 went on strike, demanding higher pensions. The huge general strike in France in May bolstered the confidence of the Italian workers, and workers' committees sprang up in the large northern factories, calling for a radical rethinking of working-class politics and a total rejection of the postwar capitalist order. In the fall of 1969—a time that has ever since been known as the "hot autumn"—workers broke with the stodgy Italian Communist Party (whose reputation had suffered from the Soviet invasion of Czechoslovakia in August 1968). They called for a radical grassroots movement. Strikes, slowdowns, sit-ins, and demonstrations at factory gates all burst out across the industrial north and lent an air of insurrection to the country. In the fall of 1969, some 5.5 million workers went on strike, especially in the rubber, auto, and metalworking industries, and by the end of the year, trade unions won major new contracts for their workers, wage increases, a forty-hour workweek, and a right to organize inside the factories.[9]

Charged by these successes, other sectors soon agitated: in 1970 and 1971, railway workers and white-collar service workers went on strike. Union membership soared, and the struggle showed no signs of ending. In 1972, four and a half million workers went on strike. In 1973, the number reached 6.1 million. With the onset of the international economic crisis of the early 1970s, however, the workers' movement lost its edge. Wage increases were passed on to the consumers and prices rose significantly. Capital fled the country and investment slumped. In 1973, the government decided it could no longer defend the value of the lira and made it convertible. This effectively devalued the currency and made imports much more expensive, just at the time that the energy crisis made the cost of oil skyrocket. The economy lurched into recession. Though the workers had not caused the economic downturn, their militancy provided an easy target for the conservatives, who now saw the labor movement as an agent of subversion and instability. National elections held in May 1972 gave a slight edge to the parties of the center-right, which formed a government under Prime Minister Giulio Andreotti of the Christian Democrats. As in France, the events of 1968 had led to a consolidation of the forces of the center and right. Most notably, the neo-Fascist Italian Social Movement (MSI) had doubled its share of the vote, to almost 9 percent, suggesting a deepening divide between the right and left in Italy. It was a foreboding of what was to come.[10]

WEST GERMANY

The Germans, too, had their 1968; and as in France and Italy, it sprang chiefly from the universities. But there were a number of factors unique to the German case that reflected the growing pains of the young German democracy. The German students of 1968 protested not simply against a stuffy university hierarchy. In fact, the Free University of Berlin, where the student movement originated, prided itself on its innovation, openness to experiment, and intellectual freedom. The university was founded in 1948—with large financial grants from the Ford Foundation—as an explicit rebuke to the Humboldt University in the Soviet zone of Berlin and to the Communist regime. The Free University became a beacon to radical students, not least because West German military draft regulations did not apply in West Berlin.

German student activism in the mid-1960s stemmed chiefly from the anti–Vietnam War movement and the protests against nuclear weapons that started in the late 1950s. Yet it also reflected the sense among the young leftists that West German politics held no place for them and their radical vision. In 1956, West Germany banned the Communist Party, leaving leftists with just the Social Democratic Party (SPD) as a political home. But in 1959 the SPD jettisoned its revolutionary Marxist ideology, embraced the free market and private property, and accepted West Germany's role in the Western alliance. The SPD had not formed a government since 1930 and its support in the country never matched the conservative Christian Democrats'. In 1966, its electoral fortunes enhanced by its more moderate position, the SPD was invited to form a "grand coalition" government with the Christian Democrats under Chancellor Kurt Kiesinger. The SPD leader, Willy Brandt, became foreign minister. Yet to the left-wing socialists, this turn to the right by the party leadership was a betrayal. Worse, it created the appearance of a one-party state with virtually no opposition.

Generational conflict between parents and children drove the protest movement in all West European countries; in Germany, however, the tensions between young and old were inflected by the problem of Germany's past and the degree of participation in the Third Reich by the architects of Germany's "postwar miracle." In Germany, the usual student accusation that the forces of order were authoritarian carried special weight: Chancellor Kiesinger had joined the Nazi Party in 1933 and served during the Third Reich in the Propaganda Ministry; while Germany's then president, Heinrich Lübke, was rumored to have been a construction manager for a company that helped build concentration camps.[11] These awkward topics never received much attention in the Adenauer years. By the late 1950s, the ice began to break up and Germans started to examine the recent past more openly. In 1955, Anne Frank's diary was published and became the best-selling book in the country. In 1957, Alain Resnais's film *Night and Fog,* which brutally revealed the inner workings of the concentration camps, became a source of much comment. The trial of Adolf Eichmann in 1961 in an Israeli court laid bare the breadth and scope of the Nazi genocide machine, and in the early 1960s the central prosecutor's office in West Germany initiated proceedings against concentration camp guards and other perpetrators of genocide during the war. These efforts were laudable, but the sudden rise of the far right, neo-Nazi National Democratic Party, which won seats in local elections in 1966 and 1968, suggested that Germany had hardly overcome its past. In an atmosphere of youthful rebellion against the foundations of the postwar German state, the recent past served as a useful tool to goad the governing elites and to sustain the criticism of a state whose founders appeared too willing to forget their history.[12]

In response to the political and cultural stasis of the West German state, leftists formed an alternative political grouping, or "extraparliamentary opposition," that sought to group together the various dissenting strands in the country and launch a radical critique of the institutions of the postwar German state. Prominent in this opposition was the Sozialistischer Deutscher Studentenbund (Socialist German Students' Union, or SDS). It had originally been founded by the Social Democratic Party but forged its own more radical path as the party turned to the center. This group sought to place students and young people at the forefront of the revolutionary movement, arguing that the working class had been corrupted by materialism and prosperity and could no longer be counted on to engage in class struggle. Though the membership of the SDS remained small, it exerted wide influence on the student protests of 1968, largely because of the charisma of its leader, Rudi Dutschke. Born in 1940 of Lutheran parents, he grew up in Eastern Germany and fled to West Berlin in 1961, just before the Berlin Wall closed off the last hole in the Iron Curtain. A refugee from totalitarianism, he now claimed that West German "freedom" was a sham and must be rejected in favor of direct democracy and social equality. Germans, Dutschke urged, must liberate themselves from crass consumerism, American imperialism, and capitalist manipulation.

The spark for this tinderbox was provided by the authorities. On 2 June 1967, during a visit by the shah of Iran to West Berlin, a student named Benno Ohnesorg was killed by policemen in the wake of a violent demonstration. Dutschke and others declared this to be a political murder; 100,000 students all across the country marched in response to the killing. On 11 April 1968, the violence touched Dutschke himself: he was shot three times, grievously wounded by a Nazi sympathizer named Josef Bachman. Within hours, Berlin erupted as students attempted to seize the city hall, fought with police, and broke storefronts along the elegant Kurfürstendamm. Similar scenes played out in all the major cities, while the conservative tabloid press denounced the students as hooligans and criminals. Yet as in France and Italy, where student demonstrations prompted a rightist reaction, the Germans generally sided with the forces of order. Polls showed that 85 percent of adults disapproved of the student movement, perhaps having the collapse of the Weimar Republic all too fresh in their minds. Even the SPD showed how far toward the center it had moved when it agreed to support a measure introduced in the Bundestag by the Christian Democrats giving greater power to the government to rule by decree through emergency powers legislation if the country was in danger of civil unrest. The students pointed out that this was precisely the means Hitler had used to subvert democracy in Germany in 1933. To no avail. As violence raged in the streets, the measure passed on 30 May by an overwhelming vote of 384 to 100.

The summer of 1968 was the high-water mark for the student rebels in Western Europe. They learned that while they had the power to stage demonstrations, they had failed to rally the public, and especially the working class, to their call for revolution. Instead, the unrest had pushed the moderate left and the conservative parties closer together in common reaction to the challenge of the radicals. Yet there were those who were not willing to give up the fight. Rejecting political activism within the established framework, they would pursue their revolutionary goals not with speeches, marches, and pamphlets but with violence and terror.

THE RED AND THE BLACK

If the students could not change their countries through protest, what avenues remained open to them? In the early 1970s, the desire to keep the fight of '68 alive led a tiny number of radicals to deploy terror, murder, hostage taking, and armed violence, all in the name of revolution. It was fruitless effort, but remarkable in its intensity and in the degree to which some on the left who did not participate nonetheless sympathized with this new and alarming trend in West European politics.

In West Germany, perhaps the best known and most violent terror group was the Red Army Faction. Its leaders included Gudrun Ensslin, a philosophy student at the Free University, and Andreas Baader, a high school dropout, sometime artist, and petty thief. In April 1968, Ensslin and Baader were caught and imprisoned after setting fire to two Frankfurt department stores. In 1970, they were busted out of jail by a group of friends including Ulrike Meinhof, a thirty-five-year-old woman known for her incendiary column in a left-wing weekly. Baader, Meinhof, and Ensslin now founded the RAF and reached out to the Palestinian terrorist organization Al Fatah for training. They spent time in Jordan in 1970 before returning to Berlin to launch their struggle. They also received financial support from the East German regime. In 1970, they robbed three banks, amassing enough cash to pay for the weapons and supplies they needed, which were used to devastating effect. In 1972, they bombed US Army headquarters in Frankfurt, killing several US military personnel, and hit targets of the German federal and state government in Munich and Karlsruhe. On 1 June 1972, the police arrested Baader in Frankfurt, and captured Ensslin a week later in Hamburg. Meinhof was apprehended on 15 June.

This was hardly the end of the RAF. Devoted recruits carried on the violence, now motivated more by a desire to win the release of the captured leaders than to change German politics. Attacks on foreign embassies, US military installations, judges, business leaders, and the police continued. In 1975, RAF members took over the West German embassy in Stockholm, taking six hostages, and demanded the release of twenty-six fellow commandos. German chancellor Helmut Schmidt refused, and two hostages were killed before police stormed the building and captured the terrorists. In 1976, over 150 attacks in fifty German cities were carried out, and the violence reached a peak in 1977 with the assassination of the Federal Republic's attorney general, Siegfried Buback, and the murder of the head of the Dresdner Bank, Jürgen Ponto. In September 1977, RAF members abducted Hanns Martin Schleyer, president of the Federation of German Industry and one of Germany's most powerful business leaders. The terrorists demanded the release of eleven imprisoned comrades, including Baader and Ensslin; but the German government refused to budge. Schleyer was killed, and Baader and Ensslin committed suicide in their prison cells. (Ulrike Meinhof had already taken her own life in prison in 1976.) Overall, twenty-eight people were killed in terrorist acts in Germany; ten were policemen. The RAF and related groups carried out 247 bombings and arson attacks, sixty-nine bank robberies or serious thefts, and dozens of kidnappings. Although the violence continued throughout the 1980s, it did not reach the degree of intensity of the mid-1970s. Not until 1992 did the RAF announce a "cease-fire," having been deprived of its East German patron. In 1998, the group officially disbanded.[13]

The significance of these disturbing events is twofold. First, it reveals that some Germans, even if only a vocal minority, strongly dissented from the founding myths of the Federal Republic. Hard-core leftist activists were willing to carry on a violent struggle against the West German state because they believed it to be corrupt and authoritarian, a regime not much better than the Third Reich and indeed governed by many Nazi holdovers. And so they justified their campaign as part of a national resistance movement, with which some on the left openly sympathized. Radical critics of the West German establishment and of its emphasis on order, hierarchy, and prosperity could understand, if not support, the violence of the RAF. For example, Schleyer, the murdered industrialist, had been a Nazi Party member in 1933 and later a member of the SS. He received a state funeral. Why, some asked, did the government consider his murder so outrageous, while left-wing radicals were deemed enemies of the state? The lingering questions about Germany's recent past that Adenauer and his colleagues had so pointedly ignored continued to provoke ugly questions about the basic identity of the postwar German state.

Therein lies the second point of significance. For in handling the threat to democracy, the Bonn government pulled back the veil of the "normal" postwar Germany to reveal, if only briefly, the dark interior of the 1930s. Between 1974 and 1978, the Bundestag passed constitutional amendments designed to make prosecutions of troublemakers easier; offenses might include inciting others to violence, spreading propaganda harmful to the republic, and even rhetorical support for terrorist organizations. Limits were placed on the

February 1945. The ruins of Dresden. The German city was destroyed by US and British aircraft using incendiary bombs. Perhaps 50,000 people were killed. *(Getty Images)*

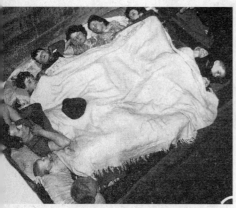

1940. Londoners seeking refuge in the Underground during the blitz. German bombing killed 60,000 people in Britain during World War II. *(Franklin D. Roosevelt Library)*

April 1945. Two men just liberated from the Nordhausen concentration camp. *(Franklin D. Roosevelt Library)*

1945. German civilians, under direction of US soldiers, walk past a group of thirty Jewish women starved to death by SS troops in a three-hundred-mile march across Czechoslovakia. *(Franklin D. Roosevelt Library)*

25 August 1944. US soldiers pause in front of the Eiffel Tower during the liberation of Paris. *(Franklin D. Roosevelt Library)*

Trummerfrau. A German "rubble woman" salvages bricks for reuse in a new building. *(US National Archives)*

14 April 1945. In Grenoble, France, soldiers of the Forces Françaises de l'Intérieur shoot collaborators. About 10,000 French people were summarily shot in the months after the liberation. *(Franklin D. Roosevelt Library)*

February 1945. Soviet leader Joseph Stalin talks to his foreign minister, Vyacheslav Molotov, in the Livadia Palace at Yalta, in the Crimea. *(Franklin D. Roosevelt Library)*

US secretary of state George C. Marshall.
(Library of Congress)

Clement Attlee, British prime minister and leader of the Labour Party. *(US National Archives)*

Ernest Bevin, British foreign minister.
(US National Archives)

Konrad Adenauer, leader of the German Christian Democrats and chancellor of Germany. *(US National Archives)*

Between July 1948 and May 1949, US and British aircraft delivered 2.3 million tons of food, coal, and other supplies into Berlin, which was blockaded by the Soviets. German children watch a US cargo plane approach Berlin's Tempelhof Airport. *(US National Archives)*

ABOVE A poster promoting the European Recovery Program: "Marshall Plan: New Life for Europe." *(Library of Congress)*

LEFT Poster for the Italian Christian Democratic Party from the elections of 1948: "For a life of liberty and peace!" *(Library of Congress)*

LEFT Naples, 1950. Nine-year-old Giuseppina Amato Antonelli washing her feet in a tub in a one-room apartment that she shared with eight other family members. *(US National Archives)*

MIDDLE East Berlin, 1951. Communist youth march with placards of Stalin, alongside a peace dove. *(US National Archives)*

BOTTOM East Berlin, 17 June 1953. Young protestors throw rocks into the peephole of a Soviet tank during the citywide uprising. *(US National Archives)*

January 1955. Three Jamaican immigrants in Birmingham, England. *(Getty Images)*

October 1956. The devastated center of Budapest after the Soviet invasion. *(Getty Images)*

2 June 1961. US president John F. Kennedy leaving the Elysée Palace with French president Charles de Gaulle. *(John F. Kennedy Library)*

3 June 1961. US president John F. Kennedy meets Soviet leader Nikita Khrushchev in the American embassy in Vienna. *(John F. Kennedy Library)*

TOP East Berlin, August 1961. Under the watchful eye of an East German police officer, a mason adds bricks to the new Berlin Wall. *(US National Archives)*

RIGHT West Berlin, August 1961. An elderly woman hangs from the window of her apartment building on the dividing line between East and West Berlin. East German police tried to pull her back into the apartment, but she managed to free herself and landed in a net held by West Berlin firemen. *(US National Archives)*

TOP 26 June 1963. US president John F. Kennedy speaking to a huge crowd in West Berlin. "Two thousand years ago," he said, "the proudest boast was *'Civis Romanus sum.'* Today, in the world of freedom, the proudest boast is *'Ich bin ein Berliner.'"* *(John F. Kennedy Library)*

ABOVE LEFT. 7 May 1968. Amidst clouds of tear gas, French students throw stones at the police on the rue Saint-Jacques in Paris. *(Getty Images)*

ABOVE RIGHT A poster that appeared on the streets of Paris during the riots of May 1968, drawing a crude parallel between Hitler and French president Charles de Gaulle.

7 December 1970. In Warsaw, Poland, German chancellor Willy Brandt kneels before the memorial to the Jewish victims of the Warsaw ghetto, an act of contrition that served his policy of improving relations with Eastern Europe, East Germany, and the USSR. *(Getty Images)*

March 1978. A photograph of the kidnapped Italian politician and former prime minister Aldo Moro, taken by his Red Brigade captors. He was later murdered. *(Getty Images)*

8 May 1979. A jubilant Margaret Thatcher, a few days after becoming prime minister of Britain, with her husband, Denis, and son Mark. *(Getty Images)*

RIGHT December 1981. Polish trade union leader Lech Walesa. *(Getty Images)*

LEFT 1982. Royal Marine commandos in the Falkland Islands. *(Imperial War Museum)*

19 November 1985. US president Ronald Reagan and Soviet leader Mikhail Gorbachev chat amiably about arms reductions in Geneva. *(Ronald Reagan Library)*

12 June 1987. US president Ronald Reagan at the Brandenburg Gate, in Berlin, with German chancellor Helmut Kohl on his left. Reagan declared: "Mr. Gorbachev, open this gate! Mr. Gorbachev, tear down this wall." *(Ronald Reagan Library)*

ABOVE 31 December 1989. New Year's Eve on the recently breached Berlin Wall. East Germans hold aloft a sign: "Good luck and peace for a new Germany." *(Getty Images)*

RIGHT 29 December 1989. Celebrating the election of Vaclav Havel as president of Czechoslovakia. *(Getty Images)*

24 February 1994. A cemetery in the Bosnian capital, Sarajevo. The field had been used for sports during the 1984 Winter Olympic Games. *(Getty Images)*

2 February 2001. Hopeful North African immigrants, picked up at sea by the Spanish coast guard while trying to cross the Strait of Gibraltar. *(Reuters via Getty Images)*

3 October 2001. A supporter of the far right German National Party during a march in Berlin. *(Sean Gallup/Getty Images)*

22 December 2001. A promotion for the advent of the common currency, the euro, which went into circulation on 1 January 2002. *(Carlo Allegri/Getty Images)*

amount of contact jailed terror suspects could have with the outside, and even access to defense counsel was curtailed. Telephone taps of lawyers for the defense were legalized. These measures were certainly an overreaction to what remained a small fringe movement in Germany. It seemed to show how quickly German governments—even a nominally socialist one, as Helmut Schmidt's was—could resort to repressive measures to ensure order.

Neither the actions of the far left nor the means used against it really jeopardized Germany's stability or the basic democratic foundations of the state. In Italy, by contrast, terrorist violence, committed both by the far right and the far left, led to a decade-long crisis that nearly destroyed the country. From 1969 until 1980, terrorism took the lives of 415 people and left over a thousand wounded. Assassinations, kidnappings, bomb attacks, and gunfights filled the pages of the newspapers almost every day during these *anni di piombo,* or years of lead. How had Italy, a Western country with a developed economy and democratic political institutions—one of the stars of the European "miracle"—come to such a tragic state of affairs?

The origins of the extreme left terrorism that struck Italy in the 1970s lie in the same fertile soil that nurtured the German radicals: a sense that the student movement of 1968–69 had failed to have an impact upon political structures and that the established left-wing parties, the Socialists and Communists, were themselves now part of the bourgeois establishment and did not seek revolution. In addition, the intense class conflict of the 1969–73 period in Italy radicalized some workers, who wished to keep up the pressure on the industrial elites through a network of autonomous workers' organizations. An important example of the new radicalism was the group Lotta Continua (Continuous Struggle), which rejected the leadership of the Communist Party and the unions and sought immediate revolution by the working class through violent struggle.

This highly volatile situation exploded in the summer of 1969, when Italy, already struggling with massive labor unrest, witnessed a concerted effort by far right terrorist groups to fight what they saw as a Communist threat to the authority of the state. Starting in 1969, Italy was a hair's breadth away from open civil war. Neo-Fascist formations calling themselves New Order and National Avant-Garde went on the offensive, hoping that by raising the level of violence they could trigger a military takeover of the country, which would then use extreme force to crush the Communists. Though the neo-Fascist groups operated underground, they had the tacit support and open sympathy of many leading officers in the armed forces. Indeed, Italian security forces had already prepared a detailed outline on how to seize power. In 1969, the far right groups staged about a hundred bombing attacks, culminating in a massive explosion in the National Agricultural Bank on the Piazza Fontana in Milan on 12 December 1969. Sixteen people were killed. Three other explosions occurred on the same day, wounding over a hundred civilians. Twenty-seven left-wing militants were arrested immediately, one of whom died in police custody. Although there was significant evidence linking far right groups to the bombings, law enforcement officials and police colluded to keep investigators from pursuing these leads.[14]

The attacks of the neo-Fascists seemed to confirm, for the left-wing radicals, that Italy was on the brink of a right-wing coup. In early 1970, two young student activists from Trento, Renato Curcio and Margherita Cagol, founded a revolutionary cell to engage in an all-out struggle with the forces of reaction: the Red Brigades. Drawing on the writings of Mao and adopting the revolutionary model of the Viet Cong, the Red Brigades sought to push the class conflict of 1969 into all-out revolutionary class warfare. In part, they saw themselves as carrying on a tradition of resistance against Facism that began during the Mussolini years, which they felt had been left unfinished in 1945. The Red Brigades ruthlessly targeted business executives, right-wing political figures, government officials, and judges. In 1974, they kidnapped Judge Mario Sossi, a magistrate known for his right-wing views. This was a sign that they could take their violence directly to agents of the state. Worse, the government was made to look incompetent, as thousands of police searched in vain for weeks for the hideout of the terrorists. The government at first refused to negotiate, then agreed to release eight prisoners in an exchange. But when Sossi was released, the government reneged and refused to release the prisoners. The state looked rudderless and confused.

This was just the start of a more radical phase in Red Brigade terrorism. Between 1975 and 1977, the violence surged, with attacks on Fiat plants, industrial leaders, and the murder of Genoa's attorney general, Francesco Coco. The Red Brigades profited from wide support among students and workers for their basic premise that the state was corrupt and antidemocratic. In 1977, student protests erupted across the country in yet another outburst, and when a young militant of Lotta Continua, Walter Rossi, was killed by neo-Fascists in September 1977, an enormous wave of violence broke upon Rome. The headquarters of the far-right Italian Social Movement were burned, gunfights erupted in the streets, cars were set alight, windows shattered. The Red Brigades could be excused for thinking that Italy was on the brink of revolution.

On 16 March 1978, the Red Brigades undertook their most audacious crime yet. They attacked a convoy of cars carrying the former prime minister and still leader of the Christian Democratic Party, Aldo Moro. It was 10 A.M. in downtown Rome, and Moro was on his way to church for his customary morning prayer. The terrorists wanted to take him alive, and they did, killing his entire retinue of bodyguards in the process in a brutally efficient kidnapping. The Red Brigades now held not just Moro hostage, but Italy as well. In periodic bulletins, the Red Brigades declared that Moro was the leader of the party that had kept Italy under the control of the capitalists since the end of World War II. Moro too wrote letters, probably coerced, in which he demanded that the government negotiate for his release. The government leaders were torn, especially as the pressure to win Moro's release by negotiation was intense. But the Christian Democratic government of Giulio Andreotti refused to be drawn into negotiations that could only weaken the confidence of the public in the political class still further. Moro was murdered on 9 May, his body stuffed into the back of a red Renault and left on a busy downtown Roman street for the police to discover.

The Moro murder proved a decisive turning point. After a decade of dithering, the Italian political class now closed ranks behind a strategy to defeat the terrorists. On 11 August 1978, the government agreed to give Gen. Carlo Alberto Dalla Chiesa unlimited powers to launch an antiterrorist campaign. Even the Socialist and Communist Parties did not object, for the Moro murder had made it clear that no Italian politician, judge, policeman, or businessman was safe from a similar fate. Slowly, Dalla Chiesa began to make headway, capturing Red Brigade militants and cracking open cells in the large cities. But for every police action, the terrorists responded with increased ferocity to demonstrate their continued effectiveness. In 1978, 2,379 attacks of various sorts were carried out, and in 1979, the number rose to 2,513. Judges, journalists, professors, policemen—dozens more victims of the terrorist assault on the agents of imperialism. But in February 1980, the police arrested Patrizio Peci, a Red Brigade leader who soon betrayed his fellow militants and gave the police a bonanza of information that led to raids on Brigade hideouts across the country. The terrorists were still dangerous, as they demonstrated in December 1981 by kidnapping a US military officer, Gen. James Lee Dozier. But Dozier was rescued by a team of commandos who had been tipped off to his whereabouts by an informer. The capture of the kidnappers was a huge blow to the Red Brigades and marked the decline in the group's effectiveness.[15]

These years of rebellion and terror in Italy, and in Western Europe as a whole, serve as a reminder that the postwar European miracle was never universally accepted by some segments of society. Young people who engaged in protests in 1968, leftist intellectuals who became embittered by the willingness of the Communist Party to settle down into a mature phase of political compromise and power sharing, ideologues who rejected modernization and prosperity as the ultimate goal of civilization—all of these people devoted themselves to a revolution that they believed could succeed. Their brief success was due in part to their zeal but also to the profound ambivalence of the states that they sought to overthrow. In Italy and Germany—two states that only twenty-five years earlier had been in the hands of totalitarian regimes—governments had to balance their postwar commitment to civil liberties and democracy against the obvious need for severe measures to contain the terrorist threat. It is an index of Europe's political maturation that throughout the "years of lead," this balance was maintained surprisingly well. By the end of the ugly 1970s, European democracy had survived, bloodied but intact, and perhaps the better for the struggle.

FEMINISM AND THE GREENS

There were other, far more constructive and enduring legacies of 1968 in Europe. The women's movement made enormous strides in the seventies, and it moved in parallel and often in conjunction with a new ecological campaign that by the early 1980s evolved into a political force of its own: the Greens. Yet these were ancillary results of the student protest, for initially neither women's issues nor the environment played any role at all in the political challenge of the student movement. The student leaders of '68 were almost all men, and their politics focused chiefly on Marxist analysis of class, labor, capital, and so on. The position of women in society simply did not emerge as a major issue for them. Many women who participated in the protests, erected barricades, distributed leaflets, ran the student cafeterias, and occupied factories found their political priorities neglected.

This is especially surprising in the French case: by 1963, 43 percent of all French university students were women, compared to 32 percent in Britain and 24 percent in Germany. But they did not receive proportionate attention during May 1968. When women's issues did arise, it was invariably in the context of sexual liberation. This reflected the growing preoccupation during the 1960s with sexuality and sex education, as popular magazines like *Elle* and *Marie-Claire* began to give more attention to such hitherto taboo subjects. Women's rights groups fought strenuously to change the abortion laws, and in 1967 the French parliament repealed a 1920 law that prohibited the sale of contraceptives. The students took up the theme of sexual liberation with gusto, for the idea seemed to undermine the normative values of family and marriage while also playing into the obvious desires of college students for more access to members of the opposite sex. (Integration of single-sex dormitories had been a leading demand at Nanterre.) Sex, freedom, and revolution were concepts that conveniently seemed to go together.

But sexual freedom reflected male desires more than women's. In practice, the student leaders tended to ignore women's political issues and indeed to ignore women altogether, a fact that led to numerous complaints. "I know about revolutions," wrote one disappointed radical after 1968. "First they say we're equal to men in everything, when it's about being sacrificed for the cause. Then they decide we're 'different' and send us back to the kitchen."[16] And when it came to women's political and social demands, these were markedly absent from the rhetoric of '68. Issues such as women's domestic work, child care, birth control, and abortion, which had been placed on the agenda by women's rights groups well before 1968, were not picked up by the student movement. To press these issues, women needed to step out from under the umbrella of the student rebellion and stake out their own territory.

In the wake of 1968, numerous women's groups appeared, determined to adapt the radical, antihierarchical stance of the student movement to the question of women's rights. Some were strongly separationist, like Féministes Révolutionnaires (founded in 1970), which rejected participation with men and with male-dominated political institutions and focused less on concrete political reform than on public protest and confrontation. In one such protest in 1970, women placed a wreath on the tomb of the unknown soldier in Paris but dedicated it to the unknown wife—a gesture that was considered an outrage to the hallowed memorial. The group Choisir, founded in 1971, concentrated on repealing the law banning abortion, a demand that won strong support from dozens of other splinter groups and from the organized political parties on the left. In 1971, the magazine *Nouvel Observateur* published a "Manifesto of 343 Sluts," a public acknowledgment by some of France's most prominent women of having had an abortion. In 1974, abortion was made legal on a trial basis, and in 1979 it was given permanent legal sanction. There were other successes: a 1972 law required equal pay for equal work, and a 1975 law allowed divorce by mutual consent. The 1970s also saw an explosion of feminist publications, journals, magazines, newspapers, and essays, much of which was highly theoretical and carried within it the persistent distrust of political institutions that had characterized the student movement of the 1960s. Even so, the French government in the 1980s, under the Socialist president François Mitterrand, took major steps to advance women's rights, with new regulations protecting women from discrimination in hiring, expanding access to contraception, and providing greater social services for women.[17]

In Italy, too, the class war of the late 1960s made little room for gender politics. Before the 1968–69 events, the women's movement in Italy had been split along political lines, with the Communist-funded Italian Women's Union and the Catholic-backed Italian Women's Center rivaling each other. Yet women had many grievances, especially as some Fascist-era laws banning women from certain careers and limiting their employment and educational opportunities were still on the books in the 1960s. Catholic strictures on abortion, contraception, and divorce made all the leading political parties unwilling to champion reform on these issues for fear of alienating Catholic voters and the Vatican. As a result, until 1967, adultery was a crime punishable only for women; until 1976, girls as young as twelve could be married; abortions were strictly prohibited, and only in 1971 was a ban on sales of contraceptives lifted. In the wake of the radicalism of the late sixties, numerous new women's groups such as Women's Liberation Movement and Feminist Struggle were founded to place women's issues on the political agenda.

The abortion issue dominated the women's movement in the 1970s. Abortion was still considered a crime and carried severe penalties. In 1973, a Socialist parliamentarian put forward legislation to amend the abortion law. It was denounced instantly by the Vatican and the Christian Democrats and was never debated. In December 1975, an enormous demonstration in Rome in favor of the right of women to abortions revealed a swing in public opinion, but the parliament refused until 1977 to consider taking up the issue. Only in 1978 did a less restrictive abortion law finally win passage. It mandated, however, that women must be over eighteen to have an abortion, that abortions would be restricted to the first ninety days of pregnancy, and that the doctor could refuse to perform an abortion on grounds of conscience. Even so, the new law marked a triumph for women's organizations against the power of the church. Other successes followed: in 1982, rape became a punishable offense; in 1984 a Commission for Equal Opportunities was established. By the 1990s, Italy had largely caught up with the rest of Europe in its provisions of social services for women, such as rape crisis centers, health and reproduction services. Yet Italy remained well behind Europe in the percentage of women in the workforce and in guaranteeing equal pay for women.[18]

The women's movement encountered still greater resistance in West Germany. The country had, of course, been ruled since its founding by the

Catholic Christian Democratic Party, whose chief goals had been to rebuild the country, restore its prosperity, and assure its citizens of stability. The unrest of 1967–68 was perceived by many Germans as a threat to the successes of the postwar state in achieving these aims. As a result, those forces that continued to challenge the system, especially women's groups, found little support from the established political parties. In the early 1970s, women's groups focused chiefly on abortion rights but were unable to make much headway. Only in 1977 did the Bundestag agree to a new law that would allow for abortion in a very few cases, such as rape or to protect the health of the mother. Beyond this the German political elite did not wish to move.

Even within the new left, women found it hard to gain a hearing. In 1968, at a meeting of the SDS, women speaking from the floor announced the formation of the Berlin Action Committee for Women's Liberation and were met with derision by the all-male panel. In response, a woman in the audience smashed a tomato in the face of one of the student leaders. The young revolutionaries saw women's issues primarily as a spin-off of economic and class issues: if capitalism could be eradicated first, then equality for all, including women, would be attained. This denied women a gender-specific political platform. West German feminism thus turned away from the established political channels. Women focused largely on the creation of a new network of social services, women's centers, feminist cultural groups, and periodical publications.[19]

The events of 1968 did place women in greater prominence in Western European cultural and social life. But did this prominence translate into political influence? Thirty years later, women still make up only a fraction of the representatives elected to national parliaments. The numbers have inched up over the years, and Germany especially has made notable strides in electing more women to national office. In Italy and France, however, some 90 percent of the deputies in the lower parliament are men—a figure that has changed little over the past half century. So embarrassed were the French authorities by these low numbers that in May 2000, the National Assembly passed a law requiring all political parties to field as many women as men in local, national, and European elections. By contrast, in elections to the European Parliament, held since 1979, women have fared well, and now hold about a third of the seats. This may reflect a perception among voters that women are well prepared to handle the tasks that European institutions face—for example, environmental protection, social welfare legislation, the expansion of rights and protections for the poor and sick, and human rights. Women appear to be having greater influence within the institutions of the new Europe than they ever enjoyed in the old.

WOMEN IN NATIONAL PARLIAMENTS IN EUROPE, 1989 AND 2001 (LOWER HOUSES ONLY)

	1989			2001		
	Number of Women	Total Members	Women as % of Total	Number of Women	Total Members	Women as % of Total
Denmark	55	179	30.7	67	175	38.3
Netherlands	32	150	21.3	52	150	34.7
Germany	83	519	16.0	211	669	31.5
Spain	27	345	7.8	97	350	27.7
Belgium	18	212	8.5	35	151	23.2
Portugal	25	250	10.0	46	230	20.0
UK	42	650	6.5	120	658	18.2
Luxembourg	7	64	10.9	10	60	16.7
Ireland	14	166	8.4	21	166	12.7
Italy	81	630	12.9	71	626	11.3
France	33	577	5.7	55	574	9.6
Greece	13	300	4.3	26	300	8.7

SOURCE: European Database: Women in Decision-Making (www.db-decision.de); *Women of Europe*, no. 30 (December 1989), 14.

WOMEN IN THE EUROPEAN PARLIAMENT SINCE 1979

Year of Election	Women/Total Seats	Percentage
1979	67/410	16.3
1984	75/434	17.3
1989	95/518	18.3
1994	168/626	26.8
1999	194/626	31.0

SOURCE: European Database: Women in Decision-Making (www.db-decision.de); *Women of Europe*, no. 27 (June 1988), 48.

Women also played a prominent role in the origins of the environmental movement. Whereas the '68ers had taken a Marxist stand against capitalism, decrying its inequalities, the fledgling Green movement took a still wider and deeper approach: capitalism, it claimed, had triggered an environmental crisis that would soon lead to the destruction of human life on earth. The Green movement adopted an anti-industrial, at times antimodern stance toward capitalism, but it captured the idealism of many people who had resisted the new forms of modernization so recently implanted in Europe and who wished for a slower, more humane way of life. It also appealed to the leftists who loathed the violence of the terrorist groups. Between the mid-1970s and the mid-1980s, almost every country in Western Europe saw the birth of a new Green party. Few had any electoral success, but the advent of the Greens marked a new development in European politics, which had been so predictably divided between the center-right and the center-left. Some of the high points for the Greens may be noted: in 1981, Belgium became the first country to elect Green candidates to national office when the party won 4.8 percent of the vote and four seats in the parliament. In 1989, the Belgian Greens won 13.9 percent of the vote in that country's European elections. In Britain in 1989, the Greens won 15 percent of the national vote in the elections to the European Parliament. The French Green party was able to win 10.6 percent of the vote in the European elections of 1989, and by 2001 had the largest Green delegation in the European Parliament, with nine seats. By 2001, there were thirty-one Green parties in Europe, and the European Federation of Green Parties could boast forty-six seats in the European Parliament, up from twenty-seven seats in the 1994–99 term.

The German Greens have been the most successful Green party in Europe in electoral terms. The early leadership was drawn from the student movement and from disaffected SPD activists.[20] At first, the movement focused strictly on local issues and had no national organization. In 1972 and 1974, protests against the building of nuclear power plants in the towns of Wyhl (in Baden-Württemberg) and Brokdorf (in Schleswig-Holstein) brought out thousands of marchers, who clashed with the police, occupied the building sites, and placed the antinuclear movement on the map of German politics. In 1978, the Greens won 5 percent of the vote in the local elections in Bremen, and then despite a poorly organized campaign won 3 percent of the vote in Germany's European Parliament elections. In 1983, the Greens had a national organization and won 5.3 percent of the national vote, breaking through Germany's 5 percent barrier and winning twenty-seven seats in the Bundestag. The Greens were now poised to surpass the Free Democrats, the small party that had always provided either the CDU or the SPD with the margin for a coalition. In 1987, the Greens won 8.3 percent of the vote; and though their electoral fortunes dimmed in the 1990s, in October 1998 they formed a coalition government with the SPD under Chancellor Gerhard Schroeder and entered into power. Joschka Fischer, an old street fighter from '68, became foreign minister of the most powerful state in Europe.[21]

Part of the Greens' success lay in the disaffection of the far left with the German SPD, which under Helmut Schmidt had become almost indistinguishable from the Christian Democrats. In particular, Schmidt's defense policies proved a godsend to the Greens. In 1979, Schmidt agreed to let the United States station a new generation of nuclear weapons on German soil—medium-range cruise and Pershing missiles. The FRG already had more nuclear weapons per square mile than any country in the world—controlled, of course, by the United States. Schmidt's hope was that the missiles could be used as a bargaining chip to win Soviet arms reductions. In the meantime, however, the missiles made it more likely that if war between the two blocs ever broke out, Germany would be the first target on the Soviets' list. The demonstrations against the missiles were the largest the FRG had ever seen: 300,000 people marched in Bonn in October 1981; in 1982 and 1983, marches held on Easter—the traditional protest day for the peace movement—drew well over half a million people across the country. When US president Ronald Reagan spoke to the Bundestag in the summer of 1982, 400,000 protesters marched in the streets outside. Similar protests were staged in Britain, where the conjunction between feminism and the peace movement was especially visible. In 1981, at an American military base at Greenham Common in Berkshire, women's groups staged protests against the cruise missiles to be deployed there. They chained themselves to fences, camped out, held marches, opened day care facilities, and settled down for the long haul. Incredibly, some women remained there for over ten years, until the last warheads were removed.[22]

The Greens have not emerged as a major political party in any European country. Many voters viewed their anti-American, anti-NATO, and left-wing social views as too extreme. But the willingness of the larger parties to adopt many of the proenvironment positions of the Greens as their own reveals the impact the Greens have had. This is evident in Germany especially, where in June 2001, the SPD-Green coalition government announced that Germany would phase out the use of all nuclear energy (despite the country's dependence on imports of foreign oil). More broadly, the entire political landscape has been altered since the Greens and women came to play an active role in it: sensitivity to the environment and to women's rights is now standard political practice for all the mainstream parties in Europe. Nineteen sixty-eight did not herald revolution. Instead, Europe witnessed an evolution of attitudes—slow, difficult, but certain—that could only barely be glimpsed by the young radicals in the streets in the spring of 1968.

SOUTHERN RENAISSANCE: THE TRANSITION TO DEMOCRACY IN SPAIN, PORTUGAL, AND GREECE

.

WHILE SOME WESTERN EUROPEANS in the late sixties and early seventies joined in a struggle against the democratic model that emerged after World War II, people in Southern Europe were just getting a taste of the fruits of democracy that had been denied them for many decades. In Spain and Portugal, two decaying authoritarian regimes collapsed in the early 1970s under the combined pressures of modernization, the mobilization of a democratic opposition, the failure to provide sufficient economic growth, the illegitimacy of the regimes, and in the case of Portugal, the impact of colonial war. In Greece, a military junta succumbed in 1974 to pressures from a burgeoning opposition movement and the humiliation of military defeat in Cyprus. These three states followed a strikingly similar trajectory. At the end of World War II, when many European countries were hammering out the political compromises that would bring to power moderate, centrist, democratic governments, democracy in Southern Europe was thwarted by authoritarian regimes whose power had, if anything, been enhanced during the war. In the case of Greece, the victory of the right-wing monarchist forces after a devastating four-year civil war divided the country and foreclosed any genuine democratic reconciliation of the kind visible in France and Germany. As a result, these three states remained locked in a time warp, largely absent during the European boom of the 1950s and 1960s and isolated from the ever-closer union of the democratic European states.

The transition to democracy, when it finally came in the mid-1970s, was remarkably free of bloodshed and violence. Indeed, it hearkened back to the swift consolidation of power by the French, Italian, and German Christian Democrats in the late 1940s, and presaged the largely bloodless revolutions of

1989–90 in Eastern Europe. Yet the advent of democracy was neither easy nor inevitable. As in the 1940s and in the late 1980s, the establishment of democratic rule required boldness and courage on the part of the forces of change, and required some degree of restraint and a spirit of national duty on the part of the old order whose days were coming to an end. In Spain, Portugal, and Greece, democracy sprang from compromise and reform, not revolution. That may explain why it has done so well there.

FRANCO'S REIGN IN SPAIN

That Spain has emerged as a stable, normal democratic country is remarkable, given this country's turbulent political history. Spain's brief experience with democracy between 1931 and 1936 polarized the people and alarmed the conservative elements of society, especially the army and the Catholic Church hierarchy. In 1936, when a coalition of left-wing parties formed a popular front government, the army launched a coup. Started by the overseas military forces in Morocco, the uprising spread to northern and central Spain. The working classes, who had welcomed the coming of the Republic, joined by elements of the police, fought fiercely to defend it, and the military suddenly faced the prospect of a civil war. The coup leaders turned for direction to the army's chief of staff, Gen. Francisco Franco, who at first was reluctant to join the rebels but in September 1936 accepted the role of commander in chief and leader of the Nationalist forces. For the next forty years, he ruled Spain as the Caudillo, or leader, at the head of an authoritarian regime.

Until the military uprising, Franco had been an exemplary soldier. Born into a devout middle class family in Galicia in 1892, Franco decided to pursue a military career at an early age and entered the Infantry Academy in Toledo at the age of fourteen. He served in Spain's colonial campaigns in Morocco, was recognized for his integrity and seriousness, and moved up the ranks swiftly, becoming the youngest captain in the army in 1915. After leading the Spanish Foreign Legion to victory over rebels in Spanish Morocco in 1926, he won national acclaim and was promoted to brigadier. He never adjusted well to the advent of the Republic, however; he was deeply dismayed by the dissolution of the monarchy in 1931. Yet he remained on active duty, and in May 1935 became chief of the general staff. Though not a politician, his instincts were conservative, monarchical, and religious. He became the perfect symbol for the reaction of the right-wing elites against the leftist Republic.[1]

The military uprising precipitated Spain into a three-year Civil War, from 1936 to 1939. On the side of the Republic were grouped a heterogeneous assortment of Communists, socialists, and workers, as well as untrained but zealous leftists who tramped into Spain from Europe to fight against the forces of Fascism. The Republicans, without an army or matériel, welcomed military aid from the Soviet Union, which allowed them to face Franco's forces with surprising effectiveness. Yet Franco had many more assets. The army was under his command and the right-wing political parties embraced him. Nazi Germany and Fascist Italy provided Franco with a steady supply of weapons. And the Catholic hierarchy gave Franco's campaign against the secular, Marxist "barbarians" its full support. The Nationalist cause was depicted as a just war to save the Spanish nation from an unholy alliance of Communists, foreigners, atheists, and anarchists. Unlike the divided Republicans, Franco in 1937 forged his supporters into a unified party called the Falange Española Tradicionalista (FET, or Traditionalist Spanish Phalanx). In March 1939, despite the determined resistance of Republican forces, Franco's army marched into Madrid. The Civil War, marked by atrocities, mass arrests, concentration camps, and periodic famine, cost at least 270,000 lives.[2]

Franco and his political allies immediately established the foundations of the dictatorship. First came the settling of scores: anyone who had supported the Republican cause was subject to arrest, imprisonment, and even death. Communists, leftists, labor activists, and peasants all now were punished for their Republican sympathies. Perhaps 400,000 people spent time in jail over the next four years, and at the very least 28,000 people were executed.[3] Franco worked swiftly to reward those who had supported his cause, returning lost property and wealth seized during the Republican period, giving the military a central place in the new state, and restoring the rights and privileges of the Catholic Church in Spain, including the right to maintain its own education system, the control of marriage, and a role as the arbiter of morality. The FET, Franco's political movement, was the institutional tool through which the state governed, but it was really an umbrella organization for various overlapping and competing interests, held together by loyalty to Franco. In economic matters, Franco faced great difficulties, since the war had destroyed the economy and Spain's trading partners in Europe and North America were by 1939 embroiled in World War II. The country suffered 200,000 deaths from malnutrition and disease in 1940–44 alone. During the war, Franco kept Spain neutral, though his sympathies clearly lay with the Fascist states.

By 1945, Franco's Spain faced enormous difficulties. The country was isolated and shunned in international affairs; it was kept out of the United Nations, the Marshall Plan, and NATO, despite Franco's ardent anti-Communism. The UN launched an economic boycott of the country between 1946 and 1953. Economically, the country was a basket case, and Franco's total ignorance of economic matters boded ill. His ideological principles dictated that Spain be renewed without recourse to outside aid or even economic interaction with the decadent capitalist states. Rather, Spain would pursue a policy of autarky, or self-sufficiency, and the state would take command of the economy. Franco's right-wing supporters rallied to these ideas because they meant that industrialization could move forward under the careful eye of the state, and the class conflict associated with economic growth and the free market would be avoided; strikes, political parties, and unions were banned. Predictably, these policies were disastrous for the economy. Import restrictions meant a dearth of raw materials, new machinery, fertilizers, and equipment; agriculture slumped; price controls inhibited output. Corruption, bribery, and the black market prevailed. Basic foodstuffs were in short supply until the early 1950s.

Such backward policies soon endangered the regime. So bad had conditions become for the laboring classes that strikes broke out in 1951, despite the risk of retribution. In July 1951, Franco brought in a new minister, Manuel Arburúa, to relax some aspects of autarky. He eased price controls, which brought more goods into the markets, and allowed wider access to desperately needed imports. In 1953, the United States finally embraced the dictatorship, and in return for access to military bases in Spain the US began to channel aid, providing $625 million between 1953 and 1957. These dollars allowed the regime to purchase goods abroad. But now, Spain's imports hugely exceeded exports, and the balance-of-payments deficit widened alarmingly. Acknowledging the failure of autarky, Franco in February 1957 brought in a new team of officials, who initiated a dramatic turnaround in Spain's economic policies.[4]

Many of the men Franco now turned to for economic advice had connections to a Catholic organization called Opus Dei, or God's Work. Composed of priests and laymen, Opus Dei was founded in Spain in 1928 and won the approval of the papacy in 1950. Its members, deeply devout and loyal to the church, pledged to seek a life of Christian perfection. The new ministers of commerce and finance were both members of this organization, and indeed Franco came to rely on Opus Dei members because of their reputation for integrity, their social conservatism, and their loyalty to him. The new cabinet members, trained in economics and finance, balanced the once preponderant role of the military in Franco's inner circle.

These new technocrats now instituted major changes in Spain's economic policies that over the next decade produced stunning results. In 1959, they persuaded Franco to adopt a Stabilization and Liberalization Plan that represented a total break with the policies of the past. The plan liberalized trade and investment, cut public spending, raised taxes, abolished import controls, actively courted foreign investment, and abandoned price and wage controls. These measures won the support of the World Bank and IMF, which now welcomed Spanish membership and opened up a line of credit. In the early 1960s, the government adopted a French-style plan for industrialization, granting tax breaks and incentives to companies that adhered to government-sponsored industrial targets. The results were impressive: after almost three decades of stagnation, Spain now enjoyed boom conditions. The GDP grew at 7.5 percent per year between 1960 and 1973. Franco, initially anxious about this liberal turn, reaped the benefits, as the regime could claim that it had delivered long-denied economic growth. But the good economic times came to a screeching halt in 1973. The sudden surge in energy prices and raw materials—the cost of Spain's energy imports tripled in 1974—hurt badly; the recession throughout the rest of Europe slowed foreign investment and tourism, on which the burgeoning service sector had become dependent; Spain's own exports slowed in part because of rising competition from cheap Asian textiles and clothing manufactures; and unemployment began to rise sharply.[5]

These problems would have presented any government with serious challenges, but Spain in the early 1970s was just entering an acute phase of political turmoil. Throughout Franco's reign, the question of what would happen after the death of the Caudillo hung over the political classes. Franco himself wished to restore the monarchy but thought the political instincts of the legitimate pretender, Don Juan, count of Barcelona, too liberal. Instead, Franco cultivated Don Juan's son Juan Carlos. Born in Rome in 1938, Juan Carlos was the grandson of Spain's last king, Alfonso XIII, and so had legitimacy without the baggage of his father. He was carefully nurtured by a watchful Franco: the young man received a military education in the army, navy, and air force academies, and completed studies at the University of Madrid. The young prince affected a mild, apolitical demeanor, living modestly with his wife, Princess Sophia of Greece, and avoiding controversy. He intended to gain the trust of Franco and reassure the hard-liners in Franco's entourage that he could be relied upon to maintain the regime in place after Franco's death. On 22 July 1969, Franco made it official: he presented to the Cortes, or parliament, a new law designating Juan Carlos as the future king of Spain and chief of state upon Franco's death. The prince swore loyalty to Franco's movement and its ideals; it now looked as if the regime would outlast its founder.

But what kind of Spain would Franco leave to the new king? Between 1969 and 1975, Franco's health slowly deteriorated and the leader delegated greater responsibilities to his close confidant and adviser Luis Carrero Blanco. This unswervingly loyal minister faced a wide range of problems. The working classes, tasting the fruits of the economic boom times, had become increasingly bold and launched a wave of strikes in the early 1970s, despite their being illegal. Whereas some 2 million working hours were lost to strikes in 1968, by 1974 this had soared to 18 million. The Basque nationalists, grouped in the Euzkadi Ta Azkatasuna (Basque Homeland and Liberty, or ETA), sensing the weakness of the regime, turned to violence to achieve an independent Basque state. In 1968 they began targeting police and officials for assassination, and despite ferocious reprisals, the regime could not quell the movement. Between 1968 and 1975, ETA killed forty-seven people. And most alarming to the regime, one of the most stalwart of Franco's supporters, the Catholic Church, had started to wobble. The liberalizing reforms of Vatican II marked the end of open support from Rome for authoritarian regimes, and freed Spain's clergy to join in the growing chorus of opposition to the government.

With the government unable to meet these challenges effectively, and Franco near death, a sense of crisis settled on the regime. This intensified when, on 20 December 1973, ETA terrorists blew up the car of Carrero Blanco, killing him and dealing a major blow to the regime itself. Franco appointed Interior Minister Carlos Arias Navarro as the new head of government. Although Arias had a reputation as a hard-liner, he attempted to put into place certain reforms designed to fix the ailing institutions of the state. He swept out the Opus Dei administrators, pushed most of the army officers out of the cabinet, eased restrictions on political and labor union activity, and tried to breathe life into the Francoist movement. His measures alarmed the hard-line Francoists while giving hope to the rapidly forming political opposition. When Franco finally died, on 20 November 1975, the survival of Francoism looked increasingly in doubt.[6]

Now the young king, sworn in as Franco's successor on 22 November 1975, showed his colors. It is rare that a monarch emerges as a champion of democracy, yet that is what happened in Spain. Evidently, Juan Carlos had been playing a shrewd game, waiting to be installed as king before revealing his liberal political instincts. Arias, unable to lead a reform movement from within the government, resigned in July 1976, and the king replaced him with the hitherto little-known director general of state television, Adolfo Suárez. This appointment proved shrewd, because Suárez was a product of the Franco regime as well as a centrist, apolitical man willing to pursue swift democratization. With remarkable finesse he steered through the Francoist Cortes a new electoral law that opened up the parliament to direct universal suffrage. He promised national elections within a year; he legalized political parties, offered a pardon to political prisoners, and removed the ban on the Spanish

Communist Party—all moves that embittered the army and the core of remaining hard-line Franco supporters.

Suárez was rewarded for his efforts by the voters: in the elections of 15 June 1977, the first free elections in forty-one years, his coalition of center-right parties, the UCD (Unión de Centro Democrático), won 34.3 percent of the vote, despite the presence in it of many conservatives who had served the Franco regime in one form or another. Suárez faced a resurgent and moderate Socialist Party opposition, which won 28 percent, but could take solace from the poor showing of both the far right party, Alianza Popular, with only 8.4 percent, and the far left Communists, who garnered 9.3 percent. The results closely mirrored the process of political transformation in Western Europe in the late 1940s, when coalitions of the moderate right, center, and moderate left emerged from the shadow of war to fend off challenges from the extremes. As in France in the early 1950s, when former Vichy ministers served alongside members of the resistance, so in Spain did the new government combine members of the old regime with the elements of the opposition. There was no settling of accounts, no retribution, no renewed civil war, and no revolution. After forty years of dictatorship, Spain was emerging as a normal European country.

There were still a number of obstacles on the road to normalcy: the country needed a constitution; the Basque terrorists stepped up their attacks; the army remained unreconciled to the new order; and Spain had to gain entry into the European Community. The first issue, the forging of a new constitution, forced the new legislators to hammer out agreements on many issues that surfaced once the authoritarian regime had been swept away. For example, the left had long been hostile to the cozy relationship between Franco and the Catholic Church, and the new constitution declared that there would be no state religion. But it also recognized a continuing relationship with the Catholic Church, and allowed some public funding of religious schools. Continuing influence of the church in politics resulted in a strict divorce law and a ban on abortions until 1985, after which the law allowed abortions only in cases of rape or fetal deformity, or when the health of the mother was in danger. The constitution also granted autonomy to seventeen regions within Spain in order to meet the demands of Catalan and Basque nationalists, among others. The constitution was adopted in October 1978.[7]

These constitutional debates moved forward against a backdrop of intensifying violence in Spain, most of it associated with the demands of Basque separatists for an independent state. The 850,000 Basque people—whose homeland lies in northern Spain, along the Bay of Biscay, and in southwestern France, in the foothills of the Pyrenees Mountains—had long demanded cultural and regional autonomy, which Franco denied them. With the new democratic regime still unstable, the ETA terrorists stepped up their campaign, hoping to catch the government at a moment of vulnerability. In 1976, ETA killed twenty-six people, and twenty-seven the following year; in 1978, eighty-five people died as a result of terrorist violence. The inevitable reprisals by police forces for the death of many of their colleagues only stoked the flames of nationalist resentment. The new government granted extensive regional powers to the Basques, allowing a Basque police force, recognizing the Basque language, establishing a television channel for Basque-language broadcasts, and granting autonomy in education. The new statute was accepted by the Basques in a referendum, but rejected by ETA since it fell short of total independence. ETA violence continued to plague Spain for the next two decades, claiming over seven hundred lives in attacks on police, politicians, and civil servants.[8]

Another problem for the new democracy came from the army, which had never adjusted to its loss of influence after the death of Franco. Shocked by the swift transformations that had occurred, feeling betrayed by the king, who had sworn allegiance to Franco's old order, and appalled at the failure of the new government to stamp out ETA violence, army officers began to prepare for a coup d'état. One plan, scheduled for 17 November 1978, was uncovered by the authorities, but the Suárez government was still so uncertain of its own power that it refused to take any measures against the plotters, which included some two hundred military officers. In an atmosphere of increasing Basque violence and political infighting in Suárez's cabinet—which led to his resignation on 29 January 1981—a group of army officers decided to try again. On 23 February 1981, Col. Antonio Tejero Molina, who had been involved in the previous plot, marched into the Cortes, pistol in hand, fired a few shots at the ceiling, and declared to the stunned legislators that they were all now under arrest. One of the highest-ranking generals in the army, Jaime Milans del Bosch, proclaimed martial law; tanks suddenly appeared in the streets of Madrid. The plotters hoped that the king would now come to their aid, or at least not stand in the way of a new government of "national salvation" that would restore the military and the political right to power. In fact, the king demonstrated determined opposition to the rebel officers. He moved swiftly to secure the loyalty of a number of leading military officers who did not support the coup. At one-fifteen in the morning on 24 February, King Juan Carlos appeared on television in his military uniform, denounced the plotters, and declared his full support for democracy and the rule of law. With no hope now of winning the monarch's support, the coup fizzled. By midday, the deputies in the Cortes were freed and Tejero arrested. The affair secured the reputation of the king as defender of democracy in Spain, but also showed how fragile that democracy still was in the early 1980s.[9]

In the wake of the coup attempt, Spain put its house in order with remarkable speed. In October 1982, the Socialist Party of Felipe González won a general election, and the transfer of power to this party of the left occurred without unrest. González, a young labor lawyer who had joined the Socialist Party when it was still illegal, went on to lead Spain as prime minister until 1996. He guided Spain's entry into the European Community in 1986 and pursued market-oriented policies that helped the Spanish economy grow at rapid rates for much of the 1980s. Spain's entry into NATO in 1982 also served notice to the army that it would now be expected to abide by the code of civil-military relations common among NATO's members and to refrain from political activity. Spain also emerged as a major player in Europe, since its size—a population of 40 million—gave it a large share of votes in the weighted voting system in the European Community. Moreover, development aid from Brussels helped boost Spanish modernization, while lowered tariffs boosted Spanish exports. By 2001, over 70 percent of Spain's exports went to other European Union members. Spain, historically one of Europe's poorest countries, improved markedly: GDP per capita in 1960 was only about half that of the European Community average; by 2001 it had reached 80 percent. In 1999, under the conservative government of José María Aznar, Spain fulfilled the stiff requirements for joining the common European currency. In less than a generation, Spain had moved from being a European anachronism governed by an aging autocrat to a stable, prosperous democracy.

PORTUGAL

No less remarkable has been the trajectory of Spain's neighbor Portugal. Long-lived though Franco's regime was, the Portuguese suffered under authoritarian rule even longer. In May 1926, the Portuguese military overthrew a troubled republic and established a military government. Portugal's brief experiment with democracy (1910–26) had led to political division and financial chaos. The army was determined to restore order and turned to an obscure lawyer and university professor named António Salazar, who promised to restore financial stability. In 1928, he was named finance minister and given complete budgetary control over the government. This deeply conservative Catholic established a power base, became prime minister in 1932, and dominated Portugal until 1968. His "new state," as he called it, was repressive and antidemocratic but not Fascist. Portugal under Salazar had more in common with Marshal Pétain's France than Mussolini's Italy. Salazar shunned the public and had no mass party or cult of personality. Static, cautious, isolated, steeped in Catholic doctrine, profoundly anti-Communist: these were the chief characteristics of Salazar's Portugal. A secret police rounded up the state's enemies, the government kept strict control over the media and crushed the trade unions, and the army was kept busy with Portugal's significant colonial empire.[10]

Salazar came to power on the strength of his self-generated reputation for brilliance in financial and economic matters. Yet in practice, his stewardship of the economy followed his ideological principles. He sharply restricted state spending on education, health, and welfare; he cut back the money supply and restored the gold standard; he kept the country closed to foreign investment, fearing outside interference in the economy; and he only selectively supported industrial development, by family-owned firms with personal ties to his regime. This allowed Portugal to ride out the storms of the depression years of the 1930s at the price of widespread poverty and unemployment. Rather than integrate Portugal into the world economy, Salazar chose to exploit Portugal's colonial territories. In 1930, Salazar demanded that cash crops be grown in large plantations for export, so as to build up Portugal's reserves. In Mozambique and Angola, peasants were enrolled in forced labor gangs and compelled to grow cotton and coffee. With subsistence farming curtailed, famine periodically afflicted Portugal's colonies.[11]

During the Second World War, Portugal remained neutral, though it was obliged by a previous treaty to allow British use of the Azores Islands. Salazar's anti-Communism made Portugal a candidate for Marshall aid and NATO membership, though the United Nations did not allow the country to join until 1955. With its closed economy and authoritarian regime, Portugal remained untouched by the rapid industrial boom of the 1950s. That suited Salazar perfectly. But the country could not avoid confronting another powerful current of the postwar years: colonial nationalism. In 1961, as British and French decolonization was entering its final stages, Angola broke out in rebellion against Portuguese rule, followed by Mozambique and Guinea-Bissau in 1962–63. With large white settler populations and an important role in Portugal's economy as providers of raw materials and purchasers of wine and textiles, the African colonies could not be let go. Salazar characterized the revolt as "the result of a terrorist action instigated and directed from the outside, with such violence and savagery that military means are forced upon us."[12] The army used extreme brutality to enforce colonial rule, but the rebellion was never extinguished. The doctrinaire Marxism of the guerrillas assured

Portugal of American military aid for its colonial war while also generating Chinese, Cuban, and Soviet support for the rebels. Portugal engaged in a long and costly war of attrition for thirteen years.

In order to pay for the war, Salazar had to open the economy to increased foreign investment. This created a small boom in the second half of the 1960s and served to generate increased support for the regime among the property-owning classes. But along with industrial growth came greater demands among the Portuguese middle classes for the sort of consumer goods that Western Europeans by now took for granted: high-quality foodstuffs, durable goods, automobiles, and so on. This sense of deprivation was accentuated by the advent of large-scale tourism, again encouraged so as to earn foreign currency. Yet the appearance of prosperous Europeans on sun-soaked Portuguese beaches only underscored how far Portugal had fallen behind its neighbors. Indeed, so poor was the country that hundreds of thousands of young men fled the country, in part to avoid military conscription but chiefly to earn a piece of the European miracle that had bypassed Portugal. In the decade of the 1960s, an estimated 1 million people—an eighth of the population—left the country in search of jobs in Europe.[13]

In August 1968, Salazar, seventy-eight years old and frail, fell and hit his head; a few weeks later he collapsed with a blood clot on his brain. He never recovered fully, and died in 1970. He was replaced as prime minister by Marcelo Caetano, Salazar's close associate and protégé since the 1930s. Caetano was quite prepared to continue Salazar's policies, especially his disastrous colonial wars. The army, however, had grown increasingly hostile to the brutal and unheroic colonial conflict. With the influx of new recruits into the military during the 1960s, many of them poor lads from the countryside, the army had gone through significant social change. The old-school aristocratic officers now faced large groups of uneducated troops who resented being thrown into a savage war of pacification with no end in sight. Some even found themselves drawn to the Marxist ideology of their purported enemies, for were they not also being exploited by a rich and repressive oligarchy? A chief prop of the regime was about to collapse. When Gen. Antonio Spínola, a former commander of Portuguese forces in Guinea, publicly called for an end to the colonial wars and autonomy for the colonies, junior army officers staged a coup in April 1974 and installed Spínola as president.

General Spínola, however, was no Juan Carlos, and the transition to democracy did not go smoothly. The new government, under the inspiration of radical army officers, freed up political life, restored the Communist Party and trade unions, expropriated farms from the landowners, nationalized industry, and granted immediate independence to Guinea, to be followed by

Mozambique and Angola the following year. This was far more drastic than anything the moderate and aristocratic Spínola had envisioned. He resigned in September 1974 and engineered a countercoup in March 1975. It failed and Spínola fled to Spain. In response, the radicals only tightened their hold on the regime, pressing ahead with seizure of the private holdings of wealthy families, nationalizing banking, insurance, oil refining, steel manufacturing, and so on. The prosperous classes took flight to Brazil, and the country teetered on the verge of chaos.

In April 1975, on the first anniversary of the revolution, the government held elections to a new constituent assembly. The Communists did poorly, the socialists and moderates considerably better. Though the leader of the socialists, Mario Soares, looked set to take control of a new government, the radical faction of the army refused to cooperate. Not until November 1975 did a moderate group of army officers stage yet another coup, oust the radicals, and restore some semblance of order. The putschists were led by a general named Antonio Eanes, who allowed fresh elections to be held. In April 1976, two years after the revolution, Eanes was elected president, and in July he appointed Soares prime minister. At last, Portugal could start down the long road to political normalcy.

It would not be easy. The colonial empire having been liquidated, a million settlers now flooded back to Portugal, creating a massive refugee problem in a country with no social services. The economy, already in shock from the political disruptions, also could not gain ground in the weak economic climate of the mid-1970s, with Europe's markets anemic due to the oil shock. One asset Soares possessed was American support. During the tumultuous two years of transition, US ambassador Frank Carlucci, with the support of the White House chief of staff, Donald Rumsfeld (both men would later become secretaries of defense), worked behind the scenes to bolster Soares' party and his position in Portugal rather than siding with the unpredictable right-wing alternatives. This allowed Soares to win prompt American economic support and an IMF loan, though at the cost of an austerity program that undermined his popularity.[14]

Soares looked to Europe for help as well and applied for full membership in the European Community in 1977. Entry to the EC was delayed for almost a decade, in large part because Greece was at the head of the line, and also because Portugal's application was paired with Spain's, which had gotten bogged down over its cheap agricultural products. Portugal, though smaller, faced the same problems: it had an inefficient agricultural sector, its average incomes were far behind Europe's, and its industries were puny. Nonetheless, freeing up all trade with Europe was vital for Portugal, since by the mid-1970s, 65.5 percent of its exports went to Europe.[15] Despite the difficulty Portugal faced in competing with the large advanced economies inside the EC, Portugal did benefit handsomely from membership, which came in 1986. Between 1989 and 1992, Portugal received $1 billion in grants from the European regional fund and $1.6 billion in loans from the European Investment Bank. In 1997, Portugal received a total of 2.8 billion ecus in aid from the EC; only Greece and Spain received more. Europe has not been a panacea, however: the country remains the EU's poorest, with a GDP per capita of about $15,800, or just 72 percent of the EU average in 1998.[16]

Of the three countries surveyed here, Greece has had the longest and most painful transition to democracy. While Spain and Portugal languished under authoritarian control, they at least were spared the ravages of World War II and its aftermath. Greece was not so fortunate. In 1940, Mussolini's troops invaded Greece, and though they were thrown back by a spirited Greek counterattack, the Duce's humiliation triggered Germany's invasion in April 1941, with far greater efficiency and ruthlessness. The king, George II, escaped to Crete and then to Cairo, and a collaborationist government under Gen. Georgios Tsolakoglou came to power. The country was then occupied by German, Italian, and Bulgarian forces and partitioned, with the Germans taking Athens and its hinterland. The Italians were granted control of much of the country, including the long Adriatic and Aegean coastline.

The war was a devastating experience for Greece. The Germans plundered the country, disrupted transportation and farming, and terrorized the people. The fragile Greek economy collapsed and Athens found itself in the grip of famine. Perhaps as many as 250,000 people starved to death in Greece in 1941–42 before the Red Cross was allowed to ship wheat into the country. In the face of such a ghastly occupation, many Greeks joined the resistance. In September 1941, the Communists established the National Liberation Front (EAM), with a military branch, the National People's Liberation Army (ELAS). Other, non-Communist resistance organizations also sprang up, and for the next three years they fought tenaciously against the Germans, despite appalling reprisals carried out by the Germans against the civilian population. They were supported to some degree by Britain, but Winston Churchill remained anxious about the Communist sympathies of many resistance leaders and about their antipathy toward the king, whom Churchill wished to see returned to the throne.[17]

Unlike wartime France, where diverse political factions were able to rally to the leadership of de Gaulle's government in exile, in Greece the resistance remained divided among itself and alienated from the British-backed monarchy. Yet it was enormously successful as a military and a political force. EAM/ELAS may have had half a million members at its height, and the strong backing of many non-Communist adherents. It could genuinely claim to speak for much of Greek society. Even so, Churchill's anti-Communism left him fearful of a Communist seizure of power in Greece and the consequent loss of British influence in the Mediterranean. In October 1944, as the Germans began withdrawing from Greece, Churchill famously bargained with Stalin, offering Soviet influence in Romania in exchange for British predominance in Greece. Stalin agreed, and the Communists, with prodding from Moscow, subsequently proved more amenable to a coalition with the government in exile. But this cooperation broke down quickly, as the war-toughened resistance refused to disarm. By December 1944, open conflict had broken out between ELAS soldiers and the British forces protecting the newly formed government. A large British force from Italy arrived and soon asserted control in Athens, but the damage was done: Britain appeared to be imposing a rightwing regime on a people radicalized by war and determined to wrest their independence from foreigners. The civil war had begun.[18]

The British-supported government held elections in March 1946, which the Communists boycotted. Predictably, the rightist parties won and claimed legitimacy and a popular mandate to restore order. In September, the government held a plebiscite on the monarchy, and 68 percent of the voting public favored the return of the king. Yet the Communists were still a major military force and controlled large swaths of the country. The Greek army was weak, its morale low, and its supplies poor. The guerrillas had considerable success against it, and in late 1947 the Communists declared a provisional democratic government. By now, however, the Greek civil war had become tangled up in the emerging US-Soviet conflict in Europe. In 1947, the British government informed the United States that it could no longer bear the financial burden of maintaining an army in Greece. The United States, anxious about reports that the guerrillas were being supplied by the Communist governments in Yugoslavia and Bulgaria, immediately seized on the Greek case as an example of Soviet-sponsored subversion of democratic governments in Europe. Having already been put on high alert by Soviet shenanigans in Turkey and Iran, the United States announced a new policy in March 1947—the Truman Doctrine—to provide military and economic aid to any government faced with internal or external threats to its liberty. Within a year, the United States had elbowed Britain aside as the chief benefactor of the Greek government.

For the United States, the stakes were high. Bordered in the north by Communist Albania, Yugoslavia, and Bulgaria, Greece was a western toehold on the Balkan Peninsula. One leading US official, in language typical of the time, declared the Greek civil war a test case, "which the peoples of the world are watching in order to ascertain whether the determination of the Western powers to resist aggression equals that of international Communism to acquire new territory and new bases for further aggression." The National Security Council agreed: "The defeat of Soviet efforts to destroy the political independence and territorial integrity of Greece is necessary in order to preserve the security of the whole eastern Mediterranean and Middle East, which is vital to the security of the United States."[19] With such alarmist counsel in mind, President Truman authorized economic and military aid to Greece, which by 1953 totaled over $2 billion.[20] The Communists could not compete against such largesse, and their fortunes worsened in mid-1948, when Tito, having been excommunicated by Stalin, closed Yugoslavia's border with Greece and cut off aid to the rebels. By 1949, the government could declare victory over the insurgency.

This decade of war left Greece a shambles. During the German occupation, half a million people died; the civil war took another 160,000 lives and created 700,000 refugees. A quarter of the country's homes had been destroyed. The country was yearning for peace and stability, and with the conclusion of the civil war, a right-wing government provided it, under the leadership of a former general, Alexandros Papagos. He promulgated a new constitution, reestablished basic democratic procedures—though the Communist Party was banned—brought Greece into NATO, and secured further US loans and credits. Upon the death of Papagos, in 1955, Konstantinos Karamanlis became premier and continued his predecessor's policies. Strongly anti-Communist, the government used forceful measures to deal with dissent and gave the police significant powers to monitor the left. Greece began to put its economic house in order and during the 1950s enjoyed its first period of sustained growth in decades, led mostly by a boom in construction to replace the housing stock lost in the war. Tourism and shipping emerged as the two leading industries for Greece, and by 1959, industrial production had doubled over its 1938 level. Greece was no industrial powerhouse, however: in 1960, still over half the labor force worked in agriculture, producing tobacco, olives, fruits, and cotton. The economy was also hobbled by rampant corruption and clientelism, through which political allies and business cronies dominated the banking, shipping, and construction sectors.

These were the ingredients for a long domination by the right of Greek political life. Even the centrist and moderately reform-minded government of Georgios Papandreou, which took office in February 1964, remained profoundly anti-Communist and oriented toward Europe and NATO.[21]

Greece's hard-won political stability began to fall apart in the early 1960s. In part, this was due to growing dissatisfaction with the domination of politics by parties of the right, but it also had to do with the emerging problem of Cyprus. This island, in the far eastern Mediterranean and just forty miles from the shores of Turkey, had been ceded to Britain in 1878 by the Ottoman Empire, and was formally made a British colony in 1925. Eighty percent of the island's population, however, was Greek, and called on Britain to allow union (enosis) with Greece. This the British steadfastly refused, as Cyprus formed a useful bulwark for British interests in the Near East. In the years following the Second World War, pressure to gain independence from Britain and enosis with Greece mounted. In 1955, an underground movement, the National Organization of Cypriot Struggle, began terrorist attacks on the British forces in Cyprus. In the context of the decolonization process under way in this decade, the British government knew that its days in Cyprus were numbered. Yet it did not wish to withdraw summarily, in part because Turkey, a NATO ally, rejected any union of the island with Greece and insisted that an independent Cyprus must possess specific safeguards for the Turkish minority there. In 1959, a compromise was crafted that gave Cyprus independence, ruled out enosis, and also assured the Turks on the island of 30 percent of parliamentary and government posts, and the power to veto legislation. The leading voice of the enosis movement, Cypriot primate Archbishop Makarios III, was elected president, and the island became independent in August 1960. The power-sharing deal between Greeks and Turks never worked, and by December 1963 the two communities were in open conflict across the island, with the Turks now calling for outright partition. Only a UN-sponsored peacekeeping force averted military intervention by Greece and Turkey.[22]

In this context of inflamed nationalist sentiment, the far right and the army grew increasingly anxious about the reformist program of the premier, Georgios Papandreou, which aimed at expanding social programs and cutting military expenditure. In particular, the radical notions of his son and economic adviser, the US-trained economist and leftist Andreas Papandreou, aroused mistrust on the right. Faced with growing hostility of the right and even the conservatives in his own coalition, Papandreou resigned in July 1965, leading to mass social protest. Two years of political chaos followed, as caretaker governments failed to bring any stability. On the eve of new elections in April 1967—elections expected to give a large victory to Papandreou's reformist party—a group of army officers led by Col. Georgios Papadopoulos staged a coup and seized control of the government. For the next seven years, Greece lay in the grip of a military dictatorship.

Although the junta claimed that its coup was justified by an imminent seizure of power by Communists, it never produced evidence to that effect, and instead prepared to transform Greece into a highly conservative, authoritarian regime, free from both the secular, liberal West and the Communist East. Papadopoulos instituted a new constitution, abolished political parties, made strikes illegal, and took personal control of most of the government ministries. In 1973 he abolished the monarchy and after a sham election proclaimed himself president. In addition, he relied on the KYP, the Greek Central Intelligence Service, to round up left-wing sympathizers and intern them. The KYP freely used torture to extract "confessions" from their prisoners. The European Commission of Human Rights investigated 213 cases of alleged torture carried out in 1967 and 1968, and found the predictably grisly evidence: beatings, electric shocks, mock executions, and so on. This was a regime of fear and terror. Even so, Greece's NATO partners did not make any moves to expel the country from the military alliance. Indeed, US aid continued to flow uninterrupted, and Vice President Spiro Agnew paid an official visit to the country in 1971.[23]

The brutality of the regime succeeded in quelling what little resistance emerged, though in 1973, university students occupied the Athens Polytechnic University and called for an end to the junta. The police attacked the demonstrators, killing at least thirty-four students and injuring hundreds. Hardliners in the regime now feared that Papadopoulos might lose his nerve in repressing dissent, and on 25 November 1973, the head of the military police, Gen. Dimitrios Ioannidis, deposed him. The new regime was universally loathed and had no chance of establishing any legitimacy. The final undoing of the regime came in Cyprus. Partly in order to bolster his nationalist credentials, Ioannidis was scheming to fulfil the long-held dream of *enosis* between Cyprus and Greece. But the Cypriot leader, Archbishop Makarios, who had once championed this idea, now proved hostile to it: he hated the junta and in any case had by now secured his own power base as president of an independent republic. In July 1974, the junta, conniving with Cypriot extremists, launched a coup against Makarios, who had to flee the island. Fearing that the regime in Athens would now seize full control of the island, Turkey launched an invasion on 20 July, exercising its rights to protect the Turkish minority and to block union with Greece. (After fierce fighting, the Turks seized 40 percent of the island.) Ioannidis called for the mobilization of the Greek army and an attack on Turkey, but the army refused this insane command. His authority now crumbled, and the army itself called for the return to civilian rule. On 24 July, the venerable politician Konstantinos Karamanlis, who had spent the previous eleven years in exile in France, agreed to return to Athens, take control of the government, and begin the process of restoring democratic rule.

This was no revolution. The junta had collapsed from within and was replaced by a conservative government that proceeded very cautiously to dismantle the worst aspects of the dictatorship without stirring fears of a witch-hunt against those that had supported the colonels. Karamanlis handled the task with great skill. He immediately freed political prisoners, amnestied certain political crimes, freed the media, and restored the rights of the banned political parties, including the Communist Party. He secured a cease-fire with Turkey over the conflict in Cyprus and asserted control over the military, while treating leniently most officers who had supported the military regime. Only the most egregious offenses such as the torture of prisoners and the shooting of the Athens students in 1973 were investigated. In November 1974, parliamentary elections were held that gave Karamanlis's party, New Democracy, an enormous victory, with 54 percent of the vote and 220 out of 300 parliamentary seats. Once again, Greece had a legitimate, albeit conservative, democratic government.[24]

Next to the restoration of democracy, the principal aim of the Karamanlis government was to secure entry into the European Community. In 1961, before the dictatorship, Karamanlis had successfully negotiated an association with the European Economic Community—the first country after the original six members to do so. Karamanlis hoped to gain access to Europe's markets for Greek agricultural exports, as well as secure Greek membership in "the West." The coup of 1967 put the Greek bid for full membership on hold, as the Europeans froze any further discussions with the military junta. Back in power in 1974, Karamanlis believed more than ever in the imperative of EC membership. It would secure Greece's role in Europe, dampen down neutralist sentiment, counterbalance the strong anti-American sentiment that had developed as a result of Washington's support for the junta, and legitimize Greece as a member of the democratic club. It might also serve to accentuate the differences between European Greece and Muslim Turkey. Thrilled at the return of democratic rule to Greece, the EC immediately began negotiations over Greek entry to the EC, and in 1979 signed an accession agreement. Greece became a full member of the European Community on 1 January 1981.[25]

Since then, Greece has had an unsettled relationship with its EC counterparts. In 1981, in a sign of Greece's growing democratization, a Socialist government under the leadership of Andreas Papandreou took office. Papandreou's party, the Panhellenic Socialist Movement (PASOK), had long been hostile to membership in the EC and NATO; it also promised the voters a series of economic reforms that would increase wages and socialize certain industries. In practice, Papandreou did not withdraw Greece from NATO or the EC, though he did launch frequent barbs at both for their procapitalist and anti-Communist views, which he thought excessive. More important, his stewardship of the economy was a disaster, as he pumped money into public-sector spending that boosted inflation and opened up a large budget deficit. For the entire decade of the 1980s, the Greek economy grew at a meager 1.5 percent per year, and consumer prices increased by about 20 percent a year in the same period. In these circumstances, the small Greek economy, with low investment, little technology, and outmoded infrastructure, faced serious obstacles to growth.

EC membership has brought certain hardships. It forced the country to dismantle its protectionist barriers, open up its inefficient state sector to external view, and align its often corrupt business practices with EC regulations. The only bright spot was that, as a member of the EC, Greece was available for significant development aid. Not until 1990 and the advent of a conservative government did Greece begin to grapple with serious reforms to the economy with the intention of bringing Greece in line with the European Monetary Union. When PASOK came back into power in 1993, it continued these policies, and though the economy continued to struggle, against all odds Greece did make it into the European Monetary Union in 2001.[26]

There has always been a tendency among the richer countries of Northern and Western Europe to look down at the newly democratic Southern European states. Poorer, less developed, and less important in the corridors of power, Greece, Portugal, and Spain often get grouped together as Europe's laggards. In fact, these three countries have achieved more than almost any other European country in so short a time. Consider that since the 1930s these three countries all experienced some combination of civil war, foreign occupation, authoritarian rule, colonial war, weak economic growth, and significant political turmoil. In a mere twenty-five years, these three countries, with almost no previous experience of democracy or market capitalism, have emerged as stable democracies and rather normal European countries. In the mid-1970s, when the rest of Europe was entering into the doldrums, Southern Europe had set sail for freedom.

CHAPTER ELEVEN

CRACKS IN THE WALL: EASTERN EUROPE, 1968–1981

•

PRAGUE SPRING

IN THAT EXTRAORDINARY YEAR 1968, Eastern Europe also experienced political turmoil. Yet in Czechoslovakia, where a sudden burst of liberalization was promptly repressed by a Warsaw Pact military invasion in August, the uprising was not motivated by youthful exuberance and alienation. It was part of the long-running, determined resistance to Soviet rule that periodically broke out in violence during the postwar years. The events of what became known as the Prague Spring fit a familiar pattern: a reform program undertaken by Communists that swiftly moved beyond the original intentions of the reformers to take on a life of its own. As in Hungary in 1956, so in Czechoslovakia in 1968, independent, autonomous Communists could not be allowed to challenge the integrity of the Soviet empire.[1]

By 1968, a series of pressures had begun to build that compelled the Czechoslovak leadership to undertake economic, social, and political reforms. Above all, the economy, robust by Eastern European standards during the 1950s, had stalled in 1962 and for most of the 1960s was in recession. Government economists declared that only greater liberalization of the economy, more efficient management, and more incentives for workers could improve the situation. At the same time, intellectuals—state sanctioned through the Czechoslovak Writers' Union—began to denounce the regime's control of cultural life. At the Fourth Writers' Congress of June 1967, thirty-one-year-old Vaclav Havel, along with Milan Kundera and other Czech writers, called for an end to censorship and greater intellectual freedom. Kundera suggested that the regime, "through bigotry, vandalism, uncivilized behavior, or close-mindedness," had stopped cultural progress and therefore "undermined the very existence of this nation."[2] And alongside this ferment came demands from the Slovaks for greater autonomy within the Czechoslovak state—promises that had been made in 1945 but never fulfilled. The leadership of the Slovak Communist Party complained about the persistent discrimination by the government against Slovak interests and the low rate of development in the Slovak lands.

By 1967, some members of the Central Committee of the Czechoslovak Communist Party began to pressure its first secretary, Antonin Novotny, to resign. Novotny was an old-school Stalinist who had succeeded Klement Gottwald in 1953 and strongly resisted the de-Stalinization policies initiated by Khrushchev. He had amassed great power, and occupied the position of first secretary of the party, supreme commander of the army, and president of the country. But his dictatorial style began to wear on his Communist Party colleagues. In October 1967, the leader of the Slovak Communist Party, Alexander Dubcek, obliquely challenged Novotny in the party plenum, using the failures of the government's Slovak policies as a wedge to criticize Novotny's rule. Even the Soviet leadership had begun to think Novotny was too inflexible to handle the problems inside the country. Soviet premier Leonid Brezhnev traveled to Prague in December 1967 to try to rally the Central Committee behind Novotny, but his effort was halfhearted and failed. On 5 January 1968, the Central Committee of the Czechoslovak Communist Party resolved that in order to address the country's problems, "there must be far greater encouragement of an open exchange of views." The plenum then announced that it had voted to replace Novotny with his principal nemesis, Alexander Dubcek.[3]

Dubcek, then forty-six, was an unassuming man with a résumé typical of a Communist official. A Slovak, he spent thirteen years of his youth in the Soviet Union because his father was an enthusiastic Communist who wanted to experience the birth of socialism up close; young Dubcek joined the Slovak Communist Party in 1938, and in 1944 joined in the Slovak national rising against the Germans. He worked his way up the party hierarchy, earning a reputation as a reformer. Yet he remained a party loyalist. Like Imre Nagy before him and Mikhail Gorbachev after, Dubcek believed deeply in the promise of socialism, and argued that if the party were properly democratized it would win popular legitimacy and so be better able to improve the country's fortunes. By no means did Dubcek intend to trigger a rupture in the Soviet bloc. As he told Brezhnev in Moscow in late January, "friendship and alliance with the Soviet Union are the cornerstone of all our activities."[4]

Dubcek quickly discovered that he could not reconcile his twin objectives of reforming the party through greater democratization and maintaining strong ties with the Soviet Union. In March, Dubcek ordered an end to censorship of the press and television, and purged most of Novotny's allies, including the heads of the internal security services and the military. Further, Dubcek's emphasis on openness within the party allowed Communist reformers to start a broad debate about the political direction of the country. Criticism of Novotny's reign erupted, and calls for radical changes became commonplace within the party. In Moscow, Brezhnev began to fret that "our earlier hopes for Dubcek have not been borne out." Polish leader Wladyslaw Gomulka and his East German counterpart, Walter Ulbricht, also had grown anxious about Dubcek because they feared that "antisocialist influences" might soon infect their countries. These were not idle concerns: in March, students in Warsaw protested for reform carrying posters of Dubcek.[5]

On 23 March, Dubcek was called to Dresden to meet with the leaders of the Soviet Union, East Germany, Poland, Hungary, and Bulgaria. They rebuked him sharply, with Brezhnev sternly declaring that the criticisms of Novotny's leadership had degenerated into "a denunciation of the actions of the entire party" over the previous twenty-five years. Worse, the criticisms had even been repeated in the press and on state television. "This is really an embarrassing story," he sputtered. He told Dubcek "to change the course of events and stop these very dangerous developments. . . . If you disagree, we cannot remain indifferent."[6]

Dubcek persisted in a course that he believed would revive public support for the flagging Communist Party. In April, his government released an action program that laid out the nature of the reforms it would initiate. This official document envisioned a Czechoslovak state based on popular legitimacy, a leadership accountable to a National Assembly, freedom of expression, transparency of government activities, and an independent foreign policy.[7] In the spirit of openness, the government formed a commission to investigate the purge trials of the early 1950s and rehabilitate the victims. Dubcek insisted that the Communist Party still exercise single-party control, and he frequently rebuked the press for its anti-Soviet and unsocialist attitude. Yet the freeing up of public debate led to an explosion of pent-up frustration directed at the party, the USSR, and the Soviet bloc. In theaters and coffeehouses, in street marches, in classrooms, and above all in the newly liberated press, once-heretical proposals for trade unions, free markets, multiparty democracy, and a revival of the Social Democratic Party were now heard. Writers, journalists, and students began to press for reforms that went way beyond what Dubcek had envisioned. On 27 June, writer Ludvik Vaculik published a manifesto, "Two Thousand Words," signed by over seventy prominent cultural figures, calling for a popular movement in defense of the reforms against internal and even external forces of reaction. It appeared that Dubcek was losing control of the reform process he had triggered.[8]

The crisis in Prague could not have come at a worse time for Leonid Brezhnev. In 1964 he was selected to replace Khrushchev as party leader. Unlike his unpredictable predecessor, Brezhnev evinced a willingness to rule by consensus, maintained a cautious view of reform, and had few ambitions beyond assuring the stability of the regime. Yet he faced a number of difficult foreign policy problems. He was already dealing with the serious split within the world Communist movement between his country and Mao's China. The Chinese leadership had come to believe that the Soviets were not sufficiently revolutionary. Khrushchev's de-Stalinization policies and his efforts at rapprochement with the United States angered Mao, as did the 1959 Soviet decision to halt nuclear sharing with the Chinese. In 1969, Sino-Soviet tensions would erupt into open military clashes along their shared border. Albania openly sided with the Chinese in the dispute, while Romania in the mid-1960s began to chart an economic policy independent of Soviet control. If Moscow wished to maintain the fragile unity of the Communist bloc, it would have to respond quickly and decisively to the Czechoslovak challenge.

On 4–5 May, the Soviets met with a Czechoslovak delegation to repeat their concerns about the direction of events in Prague. Dubcek insisted that his policy of openness had improved the standing of the party in the country. But N. V. Podgorny, one of Brezhnev's closest associates, expressed shock and disbelief about the freedom of the press. "One gets the impression nowadays," he said to Dubcek, "that anyone who wants to can be heard speaking about anything he pleases." Brezhnev followed suit. He declared that events in Prague were "no longer an internal matter." The "counterrevolutionary forces" threatened to undermine the socialist bloc. He was especially struck by reports of American flags appearing during demonstrations. The slander in the press and on television against the USSR outraged Brezhnev. "The truth is that drunken peasants at a country fair behave better than these journalists do," he fumed. Brezhnev made it clear that if Dubcek did not crack down, the other Warsaw Pact countries would have to do it for him. This conclusion was finally reached in mid-July, when Brezhnev, Gomulka, Ulbricht, Hungary's Janos Kadar, and Bulgaria's Todor Zhivkov gathered in Warsaw to assess the events in Prague. This time, Dubcek was not present. The condemnation was scathing. Gomulka declared that the "whole system of socialism was in danger" because of the events in Prague. Ulbricht stated that the entire affair was being orchestrated by Bonn and Washington as part of a global strategy to defeat socialism. Brezhnev, now determined to solve the crisis, agreed. "Czechoslovakia has become one of the focal points of the bitter ideological and political struggle between imperialism and socialism," he declared. The leaders issued an ultimatum stating that the Czechoslovak government must make "a decisive and bold stand against right-wing and anti-socialist forces" and "reassert control by the party over the mass media." Ominously, the letter asserted that "this is no longer your affair alone."[9]

The Soviets did not expect any results. Indeed, they now began massive preparations for a military invasion of Czechoslovakia by Warsaw Pact forces, and targeted late August as the time for an invasion unless things changed dramatically in Prague. They did not. The Czechoslovak Communist Party did not swerve from its political reforms, believing that it was building genuine socialism "with a human face." Dubcek found that having unleashed the forces of change, he was powerless to reverse course now. Despite repeated attempts by Dubcek to assure Brezhnev of his country's loyalty to the Warsaw Pact and to Communism, the Soviet leader remained unimpressed. He saw Dubcek as at best naïve, and at worst an accomplice in an act of subversion.

After a series of meetings by the Soviet Politburo and careful consultation with the other Warsaw Pact states, the Soviets decided to invade the country. Operation Danube took place on the night of August 20–21, 1968. Eighty thousand troops from Poland, Hungary, Bulgaria, and East Germany joined an enormous force of about 400,000 Soviet soldiers. It was an index of how much Dubcek and his colleagues wanted to avoid conflict with the Soviets that they ordered all military forces to remain in their barracks and to offer no resistance at all to the invaders. In a matter of a few hours, Soviet troops had seized the main administrative buildings and the radio and press offices. There was sporadic shooting across the country, but nothing like the 1956 Hungarian resistance. Some ninety civilians died in the fighting, and perhaps a thousand were seriously injured. But overall, the invasion unfolded methodically and with perfect precision. The Prague Spring was over.

The impact of the events in mid-1968 in Czechoslovakia rippled out across Europe for many years to come. In the short term, of course, the Soviet invasion meant the restoration of a pro-Soviet, hard-line regime in the country, under the control of Gustav Husak. Dubcek avoided the fate of Imre Nagy, though he was soon expelled from the Communist Party and forced to retire in rural isolation. Czechoslovakia became one of the most repressive countries in the Eastern bloc. Soviet troops remained in occupation for years, and the Czechoslovak people whom Dubcek had tried to rally to his brand of reform Communism now turned away from politics altogether. For Brezhnev, the invasion was used to demonstrate to the other members of the Eastern bloc, as well as to the United States and China, that the USSR would use force when necessary to protect its interests. In a speech given to Polish Communists in November 1968, he announced what came to be known as the Brezhnev Doctrine: "When external and internal forces hostile to socialism try to turn the development of a given socialist country in the direction of restoration of the capitalist system . . . [it] is the concern of all socialist countries." Here was a mirror image of the Truman Doctrine of 1947: the Soviets would use their power to advance their ideological interests and defend their allies from subversion.[10]

And yet, just as the construction of the Berlin Wall brought order to an unstable situation, so too did the invasion of 1968 send an important signal: the Soviet Union intended to stand fast against any current of internal liberalization within its own sphere of influence. Brezhnev presented the West with a clear choice. They could wring their hands, denounce Soviet imperialism, and refuse all contact with the East, or they could accept the reality of Soviet hegemony in Eastern Europe and attempt to improve relations with the East as part of a long-term strategy of engagement and dialogue. Due to a sudden reversal in the political situation in West Germany in 1969, the West chose to pursue dialogue. It was a choice of historic proportions.

WILLY BRANDT AND *OSTPOLITIK*

On 21 October 1969, Willy Brandt, the leader of the Social Democratic Party (SPD), became the chancellor of Germany. This event marked the first time since 1930 that a Social Democrat had led a German government. Since then, the left had been ruthlessly hounded by Hitler, and then kept at bay during the 1940s and 1950s by Konrad Adenauer's Christian Democratic Union (CDU). Not until 1966 did the Social Democrats enter into power, as the junior partner in a "grand coalition" with the Christian Democrats under Chancellor Kurt Kiesinger. Brandt then had served as foreign minister. But the elections of September 1969 showed the SPD's fortunes were climbing. It won 42.7 percent of the vote—less than the 46.1 percent garnered by the CDU, but enough to form a government with the small Free Democratic Party (FDP). It had been forty years, but the left was back in power.

Willy Brandt made this possible. Brandt was the most glamorous, appealing personality to emerge from postwar German politics, and also one of the most sincere and genuine politicians of recent European history. He combined socialist idealism with personal courage, sincere conviction, and a devotion to peace and reconciliation. His own past marked him as an unusual German: unlike Kiesinger, who had joined the Nazi Party in 1933, Brandt had been a member of the tiny German resistance to Hitler and Nazism. He was born out of wedlock in 1913 in the northern Baltic city of Lübeck. He never knew his father. Brandt's given name was Herbert Ernst Karl Frahm, and the boy was raised by his mother and his grandfather, Ludwig Frahm, whom he called Papa. Ludwig had been an agricultural laborer and a truck driver. Brandt's mother was a shopkeeper's assistant. Both were proud members of the Social Democratic Party and pushed their boy into the labor movement at an early age. Brandt came to maturity at a time when the Weimar Republic was nearing its collapse. In 1929, at the age of sixteen, he was already writing ardent essays for socialist newspapers. This brought him to the attention of the Nazis, who were just beginning their rapid ascent. After Hitler took power in January 1933, Nazi attacks on the Social Democrats intensified, and many of Brandt's colleagues were targeted for violence and even murder. In March 1933, he adopted the name Willy Brandt to avoid arrest. The following month, he fled to Norway, where he established contact with other socialist exiles and eventually joined the Norwegian resistance.[11]

After the war he moved to Berlin, where he climbed the ranks of the SPD and worked as aide to the influential mayor, Ernst Reuter. Living in close proximity to the Soviet zone, and witnessing the Berlin blockade and the 1953 East Berlin uprising, Brandt shed all illusions about the real nature of Soviet policy in East Germany. Though he remained a devoted socialist, he moved to the center of his party and rejected the anti-Western, neutralist position of many in the SPD. In 1957 he was named mayor of West Berlin, a position of enormous power, and one that gave him national prominence. When the East Germans built the Berlin Wall in 1961, Brandt won plaudits from Berliners for his staunch defense of Western rights in the whole of the city—a position for which he found little support from his Western allies.

As mayor of the Western half of this divided city, Brandt saw firsthand the pain that the wall had inflicted on Berlin families and other Germans who used Berlin as an access route to visit relatives on either side of the Iron Curtain. For him, the wall remained an obscenity and an egregious violation of the four-power agreements. Yet the wall was a fact that had to be dealt with. What stance should Germany adopt? Adenauer's position was unequivocal. His *Westpolitik* stipulated close association with the United States, membership in NATO, integration with Europe, and above all a refusal to recognize the legitimacy or sovereignty of East Germany. There was but one Germany for Adenauer, and part of it happened to be occupied by the Soviet Union and held captive against its will. Only reunification under democratic rule could solve the "German problem." This position led Adenauer to promulgate the Hallstein Doctrine (named after the secretary of state of the German foreign ministry, Walter Hallstein), which stipulated that West Germany would not maintain diplomatic relations with any nation that recognized the GDR.

But Brandt's instincts lay with the people, his Berliners, for whom the abstract idea of a divided Europe had become a cruel, bitter reality that had deprived them of their families, their city, and their freedom. As early as 1962, Brandt began to speak of the need to accept the fact of a divided Germany while also trying to develop a working relationship with East Germany so as to ease the plight of all the German people. The following year, his chief foreign policy adviser, Egon Bahr, gave this policy a name: *Wandel durch Annäherung,* an awkward term that implied a changing of the relationship with the East through accommodation and acceptance. These ideas were in the air. After Adenauer retired in October 1963, his own CDU successors began to move cautiously away from his harsh view toward the East. In 1963 and 1964, the FRG concluded economic agreements with Poland, Romania, Hungary, and Bulgaria. In 1966, Chancellor Kiesinger formed a coalition with the SPD and offered Brandt the post of foreign minister. In 1967, West Germany formally established diplomatic relations with Romania and opened a trade mission with Czechoslovakia; the following year Bonn established diplomatic ties with Yugoslavia. Yet Kiesinger remained beholden to a Christian Democratic party that would stray no further from the legacy of Adenauer.[12]

Given his work as foreign minister during the grand coalition, it was not surprising that as chancellor Brandt would take bolder steps than Kiesinger to improve relations with the East. Yet the speed with which he worked caught his countrymen by surprise. On 28 October 1969, Brandt gave his first address as chancellor to the Bundestag, and he laid out his *Ostpolitik,* or Eastern policy.[13] He announced that the Federal Republic would sign the Nonproliferation Treaty, thus renouncing nuclear weapons—a clear gesture of goodwill toward the Soviet Union. He declared his desire for a new modus vivendi with the GDR. While rejecting any formal offer of recognition, he did acknowledge that two states now existed in Germany. Brandt declared his willingness to negotiate a renunciation of the use or threat of force between the two states, and his hope for reaching a final settlement on the question of Berlin. He also launched an appeal to Poland and Czechoslovakia for talks, thus suggesting that West Germany was ready to recognize the postwar borders of the Eastern European states—a position well in advance of any of his predecessors. Brandt believed that if West Germany could show that it accepted the status quo of a divided Germany and Europe, it could begin to put into place practical improvements in East-West relations that would at least serve to stabilize relations and head off future conflicts like the Berlin crises.

Above all, he hoped to improve the lives of the German people, who each day faced the cruel reality of a divided homeland.

Even so, Brandt's ideas provoked deep anxieties among many Germans. In the West German parliament, the Christian Democrats claimed that Brandt was tampering with the very foundations of the Federal Republic, in particular the *Alleinvertretungsanspruch*—the claim that the FRG alone spoke for all Germans, both East and West. Moreover, argued some in the CDU, a weakened resolve to pursue German unity would condemn the country to permanent division. Brandt, claimed the CDU, was abandoning his fellow Germans in East Germany who yearned for reunification with the West.

The East German regime of Walter Ulbricht proved equally cool to Brandt's overtures. Ulbricht was perhaps the most hard-line leader in the Eastern bloc. He had championed the Soviet crackdown of 1953, had urged the Soviets to invade Hungary in 1956, pushed Khrushchev to agree to the construction of the Berlin Wall in 1961, and most recently, pressed for the invasion of Czechoslovakia in 1968. Ulbricht deeply distrusted the West German political class, whom he saw as neo-Fascist capitalist imperialists; for him, Brandt was a wolf in sheep's clothing, talking the language of peace while hoping to pry open the Berlin Wall. Therefore, Ulbricht took a totally inflexible attitude toward Brandt: if Brandt wanted to normalize relations with the GDR, he would first have to offer formal recognition of East Germany—the one thing no German chancellor could give since it was explicitly prohibited by the FRG's constitution. Although Ulbricht allowed his deputy Willi Stoph, chairman of the Council of Ministers, to meet with Brandt in Erfurt (in the GDR) in March 1970, and again in Kassel (in the FRG) in May, the East Germans proved unreceptive to Brandt's overtures.[14]

Brandt's policy received a boost, however, by the desire of the two superpowers to improve their relations. In 1969, newly elected US president Richard Nixon announced his intention to launch "an era of negotiation" with the Soviets. Nixon knew that the Russians now matched American missile strength; the task ahead was therefore to develop a balanced approach to world crises that avoided any US-Soviet conflict. Nixon also wanted to win Soviet aid in settling the war in Vietnam. Nixon's counterpart, Leonid Brezhnev, had his own reasons to pursue détente. The Soviets were deeply worried about China, an erstwhile ally that had veered away from Soviet control and by the late 1960s had developed its own nuclear arsenal. By 1969, the Soviets had placed twenty-five full-strength divisions on the border with China, and armed them with ballistic missiles. Facing trouble on its far eastern border, the Soviets wanted to increase stability in the west. Brezhnev also hoped that détente would open access to Western technology and trade, which the flagging Soviet economy badly needed. Finally, Brezhnev wanted to secure Western recognition of the permanence of the Soviet bloc in Europe; a settlement of the outstanding German problems, bringing with it a recognition of the legitimacy of East Germany, would be a major victory for the Soviet Union. These pressures led the two superpowers to begin the Strategic Arms Limitation Talks (SALT) in November 1969—the first in a decade-long series of US-Soviet meetings.

Brezhnev therefore accepted Brandt's offer to open negotiations. On 30 January 1970, Brandt's aide Egon Bahr flew to Moscow. After five months of arduous negotiations, Bahr produced a statement of principles on which the FRG and USSR could agree. Both states would agree that the borders of Europe were "inviolable," including the Oder-Neisse line—the border between Poland and East Germany, which the Russians had imposed in 1945 and which had sliced off Prussia and Silesia from Germany—and the FRG's border with East Germany. Both sides renounced the use of force and renounced any territorial claims against each other. West Germany managed to avoid giving formal recognition to East Germany, and Moscow agreed to accept a letter from the German government stating its ultimate desire to see Germany reunified. But the main achievement of what became the Moscow Treaty, signed on 12 August 1970, was that it committed both West Germany and the USSR to the political status quo. In light of the numerous crises of the previous twenty years, this simple agreement marked a new era in European diplomacy.

Brandt's *Ostpolitik* did not stop in Moscow. Since the treaty with the USSR implicated Poland, Brandt would have to work out a bilateral treaty with the government in Warsaw. The agreement, signed in December 1970, again offered West German recognition of Poland's borders, which set aside two decades of noisy West German claims, especially by the millions of expellees from the former German lands, for the return of its lost territories. In return for this and other agreements for greater trade, Poland agreed to expedite the emigration of the remaining ethnic Germans still living in Poland who wished to go to the FRG. The details of the treaty were overshadowed by Brandt's remarkable gesture of reconciliation and contrition when, upon paying a visit to the memorial for the slain Jews of the Warsaw ghetto, he fell to his knees. It was an unplanned gesture. He wrote later, "I simply did what people do when words fail them."[15] The image of a somber Brandt, kneeling in his raincoat, head bowed, hands clasped in front of him, revealed an essential truth about the man: Brandt knew Germany had to take responsibility for his country's past before it could hope for reconciliation with Germany's victims.

So far, Brandt had given the East a great deal and shown remarkable flexibility. In return, he wanted a settlement that would ease the tension in Berlin and improve the lives of Berliners. Since the construction of the wall in 1961, the East German authorities had made life very difficult in this isolated city. Since they controlled the access routes across East German territory into West Berlin, they could slow traffic to a crawl, demand payment of tolls, insist on careful searches, confiscate written material, and forbid West Berliners from visiting family in East Berlin. In reply, the West German government had made a brave show of establishing government offices in West Berlin and subsidizing the city's economy. But it was an exhausting struggle, and one that gave Berlin its air of tension and instability. Brandt now proposed to settle key issues about Berlin's status, and made it clear to the Soviets that the Moscow Treaty would not be ratified by the Bundestag unless he got an agreement. But because Berlin was a city still under four-power control, any deal would have to be settled by American, British, French, and Soviet negotiators. Brandt welcomed the participation of his Western allies, but Ulbricht refused to allow Moscow to settle any issues on Berlin without his explicit approval. East Berlin, after all, was Ulbricht's capital city. If Moscow negotiated with the West on Berlin and cut Ulbricht out, the GDR would be made to look weak. Ulbricht vehemently protested, but Brezhnev was determined not to let Ulbricht block his détente with the West. After back-channel contacts with Ulbricht's underlings, who had tired of this aging Stalinist, Brezhnev organized his ouster. In May 1971, Ulbricht was replaced by Erich Honecker, a man more willing to take Brezhnev's lead on dealing with the West.

Ulbricht's departure gave great impetus to the Berlin talks, and on 23 August 1971 the four powers agreed to a Quadripartite Pact on Berlin. It gave Brandt much of what he wanted. It assured unimpeded access to Berlin from the West. The Russians also acknowledged that while West Berlin was not a "constituent part" of the FRG—it had never been considered so—West Germany could represent West Berlin abroad and could maintain and develop political and economic ties to the city. The Soviets also agreed to allow West Berliners to visit East Berlin and the GDR, subject to the same restrictions applied to visitors from other countries. These agreements were hailed by Brandt as a means of improving the quality of life in West Berlin and offering the city a degree of stability not enjoyed since the end of the war. More important, the Soviets had proved willing to rein in an often recalcitrant, meddling, and unreliable East German ally. The West German Bundestag ratified the Moscow and Warsaw Treaties on 17 May 1972. The way now seemed open to a direct German-German agreement—the crowning piece of Brandt's *Ostpolitik.*

The last leg of the journey, however, proved arduous. Brandt's domestic political rivals, the Christian Democrats, who had become alarmed at the pace of his *Ostpolitik*, tried to unseat him. Brandt's parliamentary majority had always been razor thin, but in 1970–72, his diplomatic initiatives had alienated a handful of FDP deputies who thought Brandt was going too far, too fast. By April 1972, the CDU leader, Rainer Barzel, believed he had enough votes to oust Brandt in a vote of no confidence. But when this vote was held, on 27 April, it fell two votes short. It later emerged that at least one CDU deputy had been bribed to vote for Brandt. Brandt survived, but appeared weakened by the ordeal. He thus planned to take the offensive. Knowing that his *Ostpolitik* was popular in the country—whatever the CDU thought of it—he arranged on 20 September 1972 to have his own government fall, thereby triggering new elections. On 19 November, the SPD posted its best showing ever at the polls, winning 45.8 percent of the vote and outpacing the CDU for the first time. With his FDP allies, also bolstered by the vote, Brandt could easily control the Bundestag.

Brandt now moved swiftly to consolidate his gain by hammering out a Basic Treaty with the East Germans. Signed on 21 December 1972, the treaty stipulated that both states would renounce the use of force against each other and regard their respective borders as inviolable. Each agreed to respect the independence and sovereignty of the other Germany. While this still fell short of outright recognition for the GDR, it did mean that West Germany now accepted the existence of two German states. Both agreed not to claim the right to represent the other, which effectively ended Bonn's long claim to be the sole legitimate spokesman for the German people. And the travel rules set out for Berlin were now extended to the two Germanys as a whole, making penetration of the wall by Germans considerably easier.

What, then, was the lasting impact of *Ostpolitik* on Germany and Europe? Certainly, West Germany now looked like a major player in international affairs, and also one not beholden to its past. *Ostpolitik* did not fully solve the German question, but it pushed it to the side and allowed West Germany to behave like a normal state in the international community. Now that the Hallstein Doctrine was dead, the FRG could expand contacts into the Eastern bloc. In 1973, Brandt worked out a treaty with Czechoslovakia, again recognizing borders as inviolable and establishing diplomatic relations. Ties with Hungary and Bulgaria followed. In September 1973, both Germanys entered the United Nations—a move that cemented their status as separate states. The Soviet Union too profited: *Ostpolitik* opened up the FRG as a market for Soviet oil and gas, to be moved along pipelines supplied by the Germans. By 1977, trade between the USSR and West Germany quadrupled. Brandt's policy also helped German citizens: in 1973 alone, 2.3 million West Germans visited the GDR, and especially important for Brandt, the numbers of West

Berliners allowed to visit East Berlin went from a mere trickle to 3.8 million by the end of 1973. Negotiations now followed between the two Germanys on postal and telephone regulations, on joint sports events, and other border disputes. East Germany won handsome benefits too. Most countries now established diplomatic relations with East Germany, and the GDR was admitted to UNESCO, the World Health Organization, and the UN. The GDR's trade with the West also increased, and the FRG proved willing to give the East Germans billions of marks in low-interest loans. *Ostpolitik* seemed to work for everyone.[16]

Alas, the architect of the opening to the East, Willy Brandt, did not enjoy his triumph for long. In April 1974, the West German security service announced the arrest of Günter Guillaume, Brandt's personal aide. Guillaume confessed to being an agent of the East German *Staatssicherheitsdienst*—the notorious Stasi, or secret police. Brandt had known that Guillaume was under suspicion for over a year but refused to act on the knowledge. His failure to do so now cost him his job, and he resigned on 6 May 1974. He was replaced by Helmut Schmidt as chancellor. This sad tale is replete with irony. The East Germans, who had won so much from Brandt's *Ostpolitik*, were aghast at the damage they had caused. The GDR had come to believe that Brandt was the best thing to happen in West Germany since the end of the war. Indeed, the bribe that was given to CDU deputies and that saved Brandt's chancellorship in 1972 was arranged by Stasi agents. According to the East German spymaster Markus Wolf, Guillaume did far more harm than good for the GDR. His discovery, said Wolf in his memoir, "was the greatest defeat we suffered up to that time," not because of the loss of information but because it brought down the man who had engineered the international legitimation of the GDR. "We never desired, planned, nor welcomed his political demise," wrote Wolf, somewhat ruefully.[17]

Ostpolitik, of course, did not end the Cold War or even defuse superpower rivalry. Egon Bahr famously joked that instead of having no relations, the two Germanys now at least had bad ones. By the end of the 1970s, with the Soviet invasion of Afghanistan, US-Soviet tension flared once again and the successes of détente were forgotten. But for many individual Germans and Europeans, the agreements of the 1970s substantially changed the way they lived their lives. The Cold War had been subtly altered to become a cold peace. Tension between the two blocs eased, and the political settlement of 1945, which had once seemed arbitrary, unfair, and cruel, now became accepted as permanent. And here lay the deep irony of *Ostpolitik*: by normalizing the division of Europe, Brandt may have been the first European statesman to swing a pickax at the Iron Curtain.

FROM HELSINKI TO CHARTER 77

The effect of *Ostpolitik* was immediately apparent in the creation of the Conference on Security and Cooperation in Europe (CSCE) in 1973. The idea for a pan-European conference on enhancing security and stability on the continent had been a long-standing Soviet objective: since the United States was not a European country, the meeting would offer the Soviets a way of exerting influence into Western European affairs. For this reason, America's European allies rebuffed the Soviet proposal. But after *Ostpolitik*, the Soviets lifted their objection to US participation, and in fact welcomed it. Brezhnev believed that a broad conference on security that included the US would serve as a de facto peace settlement, and lend legitimacy and finality to the shape of postwar Europe, including tacit recognition of Soviet influence in Eastern Europe. The Europeans hoped that in exchange they could win Soviet commitments to ease the division of Europe, to open up trade and travel to the East, and to respect those basic human rights held dear in the West but routinely violated in the Soviet bloc.

The CSCE held its first meeting in July 1973 and met for two years, producing a series of agreements signed in Helsinki, Finland, called the Helsinki Final Acts. Over the course of the long negotiations, thirty-five countries (all European except Canada and the United States) hammered out statements in three central areas, or "baskets." Basket One outlined the political agreement sought by the Russians: recognition of the inviolability of the borders in Europe, which gave permanence to the division of Germany, the borders of Poland, and the Soviet absorption of the Baltic states. In Basket Two, the parties pledged to increase trade relations, giving the Soviets access to European technology and Europeans access to East European markets. In Basket Three, the thirty-five states made remarkable public commitments to "respect human rights and fundamental freedoms, including the freedom of thought, conscience, religion, or belief," and to "promote and encourage the effective exercise of civil, political, economic, social, cultural and other rights and freedoms all of which derive from the inherent dignity of the human person." The Russians thought they had won the better deal, and so did many shortsighted commentators in the Western press. In fact, the Soviets gave dissenters inside the Eastern bloc a powerful tool with which to upbraid their governments about their record on human rights. As one analyst noted, the USSR at Helsinki "received a better title to something it already had—control of its East European empire. But the West was given a means to facilitate the transformation of that Empire."[18]

It did not appear quite so revolutionary at the time. Repression, harassment, surveillance, jailings, and beatings remained the common tactics used
to enforce obedience and compliance throughout Eastern Europe. Even so, for
a small number of courageous activists, Helsinki offered a new method of
raising criticisms and pointing out injustice. In Czechoslovakia, Helsinki gave
inspiration to a small dissident movement called Charter 77. Founded in
January 1977, this group announced its existence in a declaration that was disarming in its simplicity and revolutionary in its implications. It simply stated
that the government was in violation of its own laws. Freedom of expression,
freedom from fear, a right to an education, the right to exchange information, freedom of religion, the right to establish trade unions, the right to pri-
vacy, the right to travel abroad—all rights duly enshrined in international
covenants to which the Czechoslovak state was a signatory—had been routinely violated. Charter 77 simply demanded that the regime obey its own
laws. The group avoided any political affiliation. It did not seek power, or an
overthrow of the government. It declared itself "an open community of people of different convictions, different faiths, and different professions united
by the will to strive . . . for the respect of civic and human rights in our own
country." The document announced that three men would serve as spokesmen: Dr. Jan Patocka, a philosophy professor; Jiri Hajek, once a high-ranking
Communist official who was disgraced by his support for the reforms of 1968;
and Vaclav Havel, a playwright.[19]

In eloquent public letters, appeals, and essays, the Charter 77 group kept
up constant pressure on the government, bringing to public attention abuses
large and small of civil rights guaranteed by law. It called for freedom of conscience, religion, expression, and the respect for basic human dignity. Havel's
eloquent essay "The Power of the Powerless" argued that simply by "living in
truth"—by pointing out the falsehood and the lies that perpetuated the political system in Czechoslovakia—one could restore some humanity to oneself
and one's neighbors.[20] Yet Charter 77 did not present any real threat to the
Czechoslovak state. Only 1,065 people ever publicly signed the document, and
the leaders were detained, interrogated, harassed, and frequently imprisoned.
In October 1977, four Charter members including Havel were put on trial on
charges of subversion. Of course, the defendants were found guilty, though
Havel received only a suspended sentence. In May 1979, the government arrested most of the leading members and again tried and convicted them on
grounds of belonging to an illegal and subversive organization. Havel received
four and a half years in jail. The arrests triggered a storm of protest abroad,
as the United States, Britain, France, West Germany, Sweden, Canada, and
the Vatican all denounced the proceedings. Even so, the regime stepped up

searches of homes, detentions, interrogations, and arrests of potential dissidents.

Through these repressive means, the Czechoslovak government managed to fend off the challenge of Charter 77. Yet the critique raised by the group left its mark. Charter 77 was a new kind of protest in Communist Eastern Europe. Unlike the events of 1956 in Hungary and Poland, or the Prague Spring of 1968, Charter 77 was not a reform movement launched by Communists from the top down. It was a grassroots movement that worked outside the established boundaries of politics. It called for a revival of the civic society in Czechoslovakia that the regime had stifled for so long. Havel and his friends were trying to breathe life into the strangled world of Eastern Europe.

POLAND AND SOLIDARITY

The most significant threat to the cohesion of the Soviet bloc did not come from Czechoslovakia but from Poland. This makes sense. Poland's prewar history was replete with nationalist, anti-Russian feeling and conflict with the expansionist tsarist and Soviet empires. Even under Communism, Poland had maintained a strong independent streak, as the return to power of the once-disgraced Wladyslaw Gomulka in 1956 had demonstrated. Sadly, Gomulka, once hailed for his ability to chart a Polish road to socialism, degenerated into a neo-Stalinist satrap of Soviet rule. In December 1970, after using the army to put down a strike in the shipbuilding port city of Gdansk—a clash that left forty-four strikers dead and over a thousand wounded—he was ousted and replaced by the more tolerant Edward Gierek. Gierek had been a coal miner for twenty years. In order to stop the strikes and restore order, he appealed to the workers on the basis of their shared experience. In a gesture remarkable for any Eastern bloc leader, he went in person to the Gdansk shipyard and promised to improve wages, pensions, and the availability of consumer goods, especially food supplies. Gierek won over the workers by lowering food prices and winning a large credit from the Soviets to buy meat abroad. The Soviets were eager to help Gierek consolidate his position and granted additional credits for imports of grain and oil, and also gave Poland permission to borrow on the international capital market. Western banks obliged, and Poland was soon running up a dangerously high amount of foreign debt.

Though the conditions in the country improved briefly with these measures, inflation began to pick up. In June 1976, Gierek was forced to raise food prices, and immediately the workers went on strike again. Though the strikes were swiftly put down by the police, Polish intellectuals were better prepared to respond to these abuses than in 1970. In September 1976, under the leadership of Adam Michnik and Jacek Kuron, a number of dissidents founded the Committee for Defense of Workers (KOR) to act as legal counsel to arrested strikers. With Gierek trying to improve Poland's reputation abroad so as to be able to continue borrowing from Western lenders, the government felt unable to crack down too fiercely on KOR. Within the next few years, KOR sponsored an avalanche of underground publications that called for working-class solidarity against the abuses of the state, the formation of free trade unions, and mobilization in defense of basic human rights. The language of Helsinki had resurfaced in Poland.[21]

Poland's economic crisis went from bad to worse. In 1971, Poland had a foreign debt of a mere $700 million; in 1975, this reached $6 billion. Gierek had gambled that by using foreign loans he could jump-start the economy, develop a stronger industrial base, promote exports, and also keep the population fed. The plan failed due to mismanagement, heavy bureaucracy, and deep worker dissatisfaction. The government, however, had no choice. In light of the 1970 and 1976 uprisings, it knew that a sharp cutback on foreign imports, especially of foodstuffs, would trigger a new round of unrest. So the regime continued to borrow: in 1979, the debt swelled to $18 billion; by 1981 it had reached $23 billion. Despite these foreign loans, the Polish economy stagnated, shrinking by 2 percent in 1979; industrial output declined by 5 percent.

On 1 July 1980, the government announced another rise in meat prices, and once again the workers took this as a cue to stage protest strikes across the country. Workers in Gdansk, Warsaw, Lublin, and Mielec put down their tools; by mid-July, over 150 factories had joined the strikes. The government feared another open clash with the workers and ordered local factory managers to concede wage increases, but the workers smelled the fear of the managers and demanded ever higher increases. KOR jumped into the fray by serving as a coordinating committee for the strikers across the country. Poland was on the verge of a nationwide general strike.

In the sprawling, grimy, rust-covered Lenin Shipyard in Gdansk, which had long been a hotbed of worker activism, disaffection with the government had reached a boiling point. In early August, the management there fired an elderly crane operator named Anna Walentynowicz, who was also a leading force behind the movement to establish a free trade union for workers. On 14 August, workers distributed 6,000 leaflets across the yard, demanding the reinstatement of their fired colleague. Within hours a large knot of workers had gathered to discuss the formation of a strike committee. The shipyard director scrambled up on top of a bulldozer and tried to persuade the workers to go back to work, assuring them that their complaints would be addressed. But as he spoke, a short, burly man with a handlebar mustache jumped up out of the crowd and pushed aside the manager. He was well known to the crowd. He had been an electrician in the yard for ten years but was fired for insolence in 1976. Since then, he had been causing trouble in Gdansk, trying to boost worker morale, distributing leaflets, and staying one step ahead of the police. His name was Lech Walesa.

Walesa was born in 1943 in Popowo, a small village in central Poland near the Vistula. At the time, his country was in the grip of German occupation and his father had been enrolled into a forced labor brigade by the Germans. The work killed him, and he died when Lech was eighteen months old. Lech grew up in rural poverty, working on a small farm, receiving an elementary education. At sixteen he enrolled in a state-run vocational school, where he learned his trade. But he was bored by rural life and in 1967 he hopped a train for Gdansk. He was hired in the shipyard as a naval electrician. The work and the life were hard. He found that the shipyard "lacked the most elementary accommodations for workers, such as proper lockers, changing rooms, or lavatories." Work began at 6 A.M. Workers could take only one short break, when sandwiches and coffee were brought to them on the site; there was no cafeteria. "When I arrived our shipyard looked like a factory filled with men in filthy rags, unable to wash themselves or urinate in toilets. . . . You can't imagine how humiliating these working conditions were." The housing was no better: workers lived in hostels provided by the shipyard. His room contained "a metal bedframe with a lumpy mattress, a floor and four gray walls, all in a filthy state and reeking of mildew, a rickety table and two chairs, each missing at least one leg." Each worker felt himself to be "a tiny cog in a vast machine. . . . We worked in an atmosphere of unrelieved tension and gloom. The men were dressed alike, in shabby attire, and we seemed to behave in vaguely military fashion, almost by reflex."[22]

Walesa played a leading role in the strikes in Gdansk in December 1970, which produced serious violence but at least led to the ouster of Gomulka and his replacement by Gierek. The new government raised expectations that it would improve the lives of workers in the country, but failed to do so. After the 1976 events, organizations like KOR and the Movement in Defense of Human and Citizen Rights emerged, and Walesa came into contact with the group of worker activists that published the *Coastal Worker,* an underground publication that called for free trade unions. Although he was repeatedly fired for his political activities, Walesa continued to spread the word through factories in the Gdansk region. "I set off every morning," he recalled, "with my toolbox bulging with underground literature."

By the time of the strikes of July–August 1980, Walesa was ready for a confrontation. When he climbed to the top of the bulldozer on 14 August, he rallied the workers to a series of modest demands: the reinstatement of the fired crane worker and a pay raise for the workers. But he and his associates knew that the government was on the defensive, that the whole country was mobilized and prepared for a major strike. This was the time to push for the one major demand that the workers had wanted for years: a trade union independent of Communist party control. On 23 August, the strike committee in the shipyards issued a statement of "Twenty-one Demands." Leading the list was the demand for a free trade union and a guarantee of the right to strike, freedom of expression, freedom to publish, and access to the media. In addition came demands that workers on strike be paid, that their salaries be increased, that prices of food be controlled, a lowering of the retirement age, better pensions, day care for working women, paid maternity leave, better housing, and a work-free Saturday.[23] The strikers were aiming very high indeed. But the government had no choice. By the end of the month, over seven hundred factories across the country were on strike, and then the coal miners joined in. The country was in a state of civil disobedience. After a week of negotiations, the government, on 31 August, agreed to virtually all of the demands. The workers were granted the right to organize a union. It would bear the name Solidarity.

Why did the Polish government not use force to crush the workers' movement in August 1980? Many factors militated against a violent confrontation with the strikers. Perhaps most important was that the government had no confidence that it could win. The spreading strike wave revealed that the entire country stood behind the workers. The loyalty of the army and police was wavering, and it was not clear that they would fire on Polish workers. Another factor was ideology. The Polish leaders believed that the use of force would be an acknowledgment of the failure of socialism, and for Gierek personally would mean the repudiation of his ten years of somewhat liberal rule. The Gdansk accords of 31 August did, after all, oblige the new union to recognize the leading role of the Communist party in the affairs of the state, and restricted the union from any overt oppositional activity. Gierek believed deeply that with the right methods—mobilization of the "healthy" forces inside Poland—Solidarity could be contained. Also, the international environment in 1980 was sharply different from that of 1956 or 1968: after Helsinki, détente, and the opening up of contacts between East and West, the Polish government stood to lose enormous legitimacy in the eyes of the world if it turned its army upon its working class. And of course, Solidarity was comprised of workers, not bourgeois intellectuals or foreign dissidents. Their grimy overalls, their callused hands, their thick working-class accents bespoke the truly proletarian nature of this challenge to the state. Could a socialist country founded to champion the interests of the workers now openly repudiate its basic principles?

Nor did the Soviets wish to intervene militarily. Brezhnev already had one military fiasco on his hands—Afghanistan, which the Red Army invaded in December 1979—and did not wish for another. He knew the historic animosity of Poles toward the Russians and had every reason to expect massive resistance to a Soviet invasion. Even if the invasion succeeded, the Soviets would then be faced with a prolonged occupation of a hostile country that was already an economic basket case. Nonetheless, the Soviet leadership and the other Warsaw Pact states were alarmed about events in Poland, and exerted enormous pressure upon the Poles to undertake a counteroffensive against Solidarity. The Soviets helped engineer the ouster of Gierek and his replacement by a man they hoped would take a stronger stand: Stanislaw Kania, a little-known apparatchik but one close to the defense minister, Wojciech Jaruzelski. The Soviet army prepared an invasion plan involving tank and infantry divisions from the USSR, the GDR, and Czechoslovakia. In August 1980, they called up 100,000 reservists, put some forces on full combat alert, and staged elaborate and visible war games throughout the fall of 1980. Recently released documents from the Soviet Politburo reveal Brezhnev's profound anxiety. During a meeting on 29 October 1980, Brezhnev declared that "there is in fact now a raging counterrevolution under way," and that it would soon be necessary "to impose martial law." His colleagues agreed. Foreign Minister Andrei Gromyko put it bluntly: "We simply cannot lose Poland."[24]

The problem was how to exert pressure on the Poles to crush Solidarity. In late October, Kania traveled to Moscow and met with Brezhnev. Kania said that Poland's economic situation was disastrous and that the country was totally dependent upon imports and loans from the West. If the government used force to crack down on Solidarity, the West would refuse further credits and "Poland will be brought to its knees." Of course, this dependence on the West was deeply embarrassing, and the Politburo agreed to "lend all possible economic assistance" to Poland. Though the Soviets had little to spare, they did cut back on oil exports to other Warsaw Pact countries in order to sell that oil on the world market and channel the hard currency to the Poles. Rather than threaten force, then, the Soviet leadership hoped to induce the Poles to take the repressive measures needed to crush Solidarity.[25]

But still, Kania refused to act. After a Soviet delegation visited Poland in January 1981, it reported back to the Politburo that the situation inside the country was disastrous. "The party has lost its creative ties with the people," the report stated, which was another way of saying that it had lost all credibil-

ity. Walesa "now has ten million people in Solidarity" and the union has become "essentially a political party" and "openly hostile" to the state.[26] With
other Eastern-bloc leaders complaining loudly to Moscow about the infection
from Poland, the Soviet leaders began to press very hard for the Poles to impose martial law. The head of the KGB, Yuri Andropov, insisted in the
Politburo that Kania and Jaruzelski must "adopt severe measures and not be
afraid of what might result, possibly even bloodshed." Brezhnev concurred:
"This means the introduction of martial law."[27]

Such a move on the part of the Polish authorities would not be easy.
During 1981, Solidarity became far more than a union; it began to take on the
trappings of a political party that could threaten to undermine the role of the
Communist party in Poland. Its membership swelled to 10 million people. Its
power was made apparent in March 1981 when, in the city of Bydgoszcz, police broke up a meeting of Solidarity activists and badly beat three participants. Lech Walesa called for a four-hour general strike in response and the
country came to a halt. The government agreed to investigate the beatings, but
the great majority of Solidarity members had become dissatisfied with the
gradualist, negotiated approach Walesa and the Solidarity leadership had
taken. Many began to press for a wider political challenge to the state. At the
first national congress of Solidarity in October 1981, the movement adopted
a platform that, in the eyes of the government, was truly incendiary. Its preamble made it clear that Solidarity now thought of itself as a revolutionary instrument. "Our union," it declared, "is the product of a revolt by Polish society
after three decades of political discrimination, economic exploitation, and the
violation of human and civil rights. It is a protest against the existing form of
power." The document went on to outline a series of demands for total social
and political change in the country, including pluralism in all branches of life.
The union was now openly challenging the control of the Communist party
in Poland.[28]

By the fall of 1981, the conflict between the union and the state had become acute. In response to the brazen challenge of Solidarity's October platform, the Polish Communists launched a wave of criticism at their own leader,
Kania, who promptly resigned. He was replaced by Gen. Wojciech Jaruzelski.
The general did not want the job, perhaps because he knew that the country
was headed toward a confrontation. The economy during 1981 had gone into
a tailspin, with production down by 12 percent and the national debt reaching $25 billion. The pressure from Moscow had become intense. In
September, before Kania's resignation, Brezhnev told him on the telephone
that Solidarity threatened other socialist countries with its subversive ideas
and was actively preparing to seize power. Worse, there was in Poland "a frenzy

of anti-Sovietism." The implications of Solidarity's threat had become enormous. "If Poland is ruled by Solidarity," Brezhnev said, the Warsaw Pact's security would be undermined. The whole structure of the Soviet sphere of influence could unravel overnight.[29]

The fate of the country now lay in the hands of a rigid, balding, fifty-eight-year-old general who, because of an eye ailment, always wore dark glasses. A son of a soldier who had fought the Russians in the Polish-Soviet War of 1920, Wojciech Jaruzelski was a devout Catholic and a Polish nationalist long before he became a Communist, just at the close of World War II. Caught up in the maelstrom of Poland's tragedy during the war, Jaruzelski joined a Polish exile army that was formed under Soviet control. He became enamored of the discipline, the hierarchy, and the certainty of success that the Communist party offered him, and he became both a loyal army officer and an ardent Communist. In 1968 he was named defense minister and had controlled the Polish army ever since. He knew better than anyone that the Polish army would not kill fellow Poles, and that if the Soviets intervened without explicit authorization, the army would probably turn its guns on the Russians. He made it his overriding aim to avoid a Soviet intervention in Poland. That meant, however, that he would have to solve the Solidarity crisis himself, and he chose to do so using the tool he knew best: force. With full Soviet approval and support, and promises of handsome economic rewards, Jaruzelski launched Operation X on December 12: the imposition of martial law in Poland.

The blow came swiftly and brutally. In the middle of the night, specially trained units of police—not the army—began arresting thousands of people across the country. The leaders of Solidarity were conveniently gathered in the Hotel Metropol in Gdansk for a meeting of the union's National Commission. The police went from room to room, handcuffing members and carrying them off in police vans. At 3 A.M., the police arrived at Walesa's apartment, woke the union's leader, and put him on a plane to Warsaw. He would spend the next year interned in a villa on the outskirts of the capital. Overall, perhaps 10,000 activists were arrested across the country; the union had been decapitated. At six in the morning, General Jaruzelski went on national television, bedecked in a full dress uniform. He declared that Poland "stands at the edge of an abyss." The economy and the governing institutions were collapsing, the country was wracked by conflict and hatred, and strikes had become endemic. "We have to say: that is enough." Jaruzelski announced that martial law would now be imposed under the rule of a Military Council of National Salvation.[30] Poland's new military dictatorship now suspended civil liberties, imposed strict censorship, and sealed the country's borders. Sporadic protest broke out, but there was no massive resistance, since all the leadership was behind bars. The army was prepared: it occupied factories, smashed strikes, and promptly jailed any troublemakers. Very quickly, after a year of freedom, the Polish people fell back into the old habits: fear once again ruled the streets.

Solidarity had been caught off guard. The formation of the union had been from the beginning a movement of protest against a regime that had assaulted the dignity of Poles for too long. Its power lay in its appeal to the conscience of the people. It could not match the state in a test of force, and in December 1981 the state struck back. Yet the story was hardly over. The imposition of martial law cost the Polish government a great deal: its legitimacy was ruined, its reputation shattered. The country was revealed to be little more than a massive internment camp, overseen by frightened guards. The regime could not survive long in these conditions. The cracks in the walls of the Communist bloc had started to widen.

CHAPTER TWELVE

RULE, BRITANNIA:
THE THATCHER ERA

THE BRITISH DISEASE

THE LABOUR GOVERNMENT of 1945–51 bequeathed to generations of Britons the great legacy of the welfare state. Born of wartime and prewar national experience, the welfare state committed the government to provide a better life for the people by using its power to counteract the harsh forces of market capitalism. The state after 1945 accepted the responsibilities of providing the public with a decent standard of living, education, housing, health care, jobs, and security in old age. To do so required wise leadership, efficient and far-seeing government, and a hardworking citizenry that would help increase the wealth of the country so that the government could judiciously distribute it. In the afterglow of wartime socialism and victory over tyranny, the British people believed they were up to the challenge. Such was the public support for the guiding principles behind the welfare state that during their thirteen-year tenure in power, from 1951 to 1964, the Conservatives embraced and indeed expanded it.

During the boom years of the 1950s, it proved quite easy for both Labour and Conservative leaders to adopt a consensus about the role of the government in the economic life of the nation. They committed themselves to provide a broad range of social services for the public, while also ensuring full employment. To accomplish these goals, the government had to make sure that the economy continued to grow, thereby creating jobs and producing revenue. The government used the tool of demand management—a concept championed by John Maynard Keynes—to adjust public spending, control the money supply, and promote expansion. In theory, the government could thus counteract a downward trend by increasing public spending and increasing the money supply, or conversely it could decrease spending and money supply so as to cool off an overheating, and inflationary, economy. Thus tinkering with the levers of monetary policy, the government could maintain strong and balanced economic growth.

However, sometime around the early 1960s, if not before, it became apparent that the British economy was not cooperating with the ideas of Lord Keynes. The economy simply would not grow fast enough to keep pace with the ever-increasing needs of the welfare state. Without strong economic growth, the government found it hard to maintain its obligations to provide salaries to a huge public sector workforce, to provide pensions to the elderly, health care to the sick, education to the young, homes for the homeless, and so on. Nor could the government maintain investment in new technologies or modernize the vast industrial sector that the nationalizations of the 1940s had brought under its control. Instead, British governments found themselves locked in a desperate downward spiral. In order to raise more revenue from a sluggish economy, the government would raise taxes, but that meant that wages had to be increased to counteract the loss of income for employees. This in turn tended to boost inflation upward, which led to greater demands for wage increases to keep up with rising prices. As inflation increased, British exports slowed because they became more expensive to foreign buyers, but slower exports meant less revenue for the government, and thus increased the need for higher taxes—which brought the cycle back to its starting point. If only the British economy would grow at the same vigorous rate as the continental European economies, the cost of the welfare state could be met. But it didn't, and it wasn't.

So what was wrong with the British economy? This debate has been raging since the 1960s without drawing any closer to a conclusion, though historians generally agree on at least five factors. First, the policies of demand management themselves, by which governments sped up and then slowed down the economy—the "stop-go" approach—may have actually worsened the problem of growth by deterring long-term investment and curtailing increases in productivity, the all-important measure of how efficiently an economy uses its resources. Second, many scholars now emphasize the role of long-term social and cultural factors in British economic development. The British, this argument runs, with their rigid class system and aristocratic political elite, tended to frown upon business, science, engineering, and manufacturing as suitable endeavors for gentlemen. The result was that moneymaking was left to the middle classes, while political power remained in the hands of a poorly trained though liberally educated governing class that

placed far too little emphasis on the sinews of economic power. In this explanation, the seeds of British industrial decline were sown in the nineteenth century, though it was the postwar generation that reaped this harvest of sorrow.

A third factor often pointed to is the problem of trade union militancy,
which certainly increased in the 1960s and 1970s and appeared to constrain
governments of both parties. There was an irony here: the great objective of
postwar British leaders had been to assure full employment, so as to banish
the dreaded memories of the 1930s, when millions went jobless. But full employment gave the unions the leverage to demand higher wages, which they
routinely won from governments determined not to break with the consensus
of the welfare state. The unions certainly made life difficult for British governments, but the unions were doing what unions do: seeking better terms for
workers. The government must take the blame for caving in repeatedly to
union demands.

Another problem faced by all British governments was its responsibility
to the Sterling Area—the grouping of nations, mostly former colonies, that
used the pound sterling as its reserve currency. The British felt that the
Sterling Area lent them prestige as the leader of a trading bloc and also provided ready markets for British goods. Unfortunately, it also required the
British to peg the value of the pound to the dollar at the predetermined rate
of $2.80 to the pound. This strong currency policy hurt British exports by
making them unnecessarily expensive. Yet any hint of devaluing the pound
relative to the dollar would lead all those holders of sterling to trade in their
pounds for some other currency, and thus wipe out British reserves. The
Sterling Area was thus a millstone around the neck of the British economy
that could not easily be removed. And finally, because of all these weaknesses,
Britain was especially vulnerable whenever an international economic crisis
erupted. The Suez crisis was one example; so too was the oil embargo of 1973,
which hit everyone hard but landed with particular force on an already reeling Britain.[1]

Because of these and other factors, the British economy grew more slowly
than any other industrialized country in the decades of the 1960s and 1970s.
And slow growth meant hard choices about how to meet the needs of the welfare state. The political history of Britain from the mid-1960s up to the 1979
election is thus dominated by the constant struggle of governments to improve the economic performance of the country. Sadly, the story is replete
with failure. The Labour government of Harold Wilson (1964–70), the
Conservative government of Edward Heath (1970–74), and the Labour governments of Wilson again (1974–76) and then James Callaghan (1976–79) all
faced the same problems, and they generally resorted to the same remedies,

without success. Harold Wilson's first government tried to deal with Britain's large trade deficit by raising taxes on imports, and also raised taxes on gasoline and corporations. But these measures failed and Wilson was forced to borrow 3 billion pounds from Western banks to cover the country's debts. In 1966, the National Union of Seamen went on strike, and British goods piled up on the docksides, unshipped. The trade deficit ballooned, and Wilson devalued the pound in November 1967, cut defense spending, and raised taxes still further. Worse, Wilson found his Labour government beset by disputes with the unions. Unable or unwilling to impose harsh measures to control union power, Wilson instead worked out a cooperative arrangement whereby unions would voluntarily restrain their wage demands in return for sympathetic policies from the government. This agreement gave the impression of a government beholden to the unions.

Labour was ousted in June 1970 by a Conservative government. The new prime minister, Edward Heath, had run on a right-wing program: he rejected state interference in the economy, he wished to liberate market forces, he pledged to cut taxes and trim the bloated public service budget. But within a year, Heath completely changed course—his infamous U-turn. Inflation was running at 20 percent in 1971, unions were demanding wage increases, and the engine manufacturer Rolls-Royce went bankrupt, requiring a massive government bailout. Heath tried to impose restrictions on trade union militancy, and the unions fought back ferociously. In January 1972, the coal miners went on strike. It was midwinter, and coal deliveries to the country's power plants were stopped dead. Heath had to impose a three-day workweek and wage and price controls. The police could do nothing to counter a well-organized, highly motivated union; the government caved in and granted a pay increase of 24 percent. The strike made the name of the young Yorkshire miner leader Arthur Scargill, who in the 1980s emerged as a sharp thorn in Margaret Thatcher's side. At just this moment, the Yom Kippur War of October 1973 triggered an oil embargo from Arab oil producers, and oil prices rose fourfold. Inflation skyrocketed; exports slumped. Heath called an election on the theme "Who rules Britain?"—an open challenge to the unions—and lost.

Harold Wilson got another chance, returning as prime minister in 1974. He squandered it. From 1973 to 1979, inflation averaged 15.6 percent, and hit the astonishing figure of 24 percent in 1975. Britain's GDP over the same period grew at the anemic rate of 1.3 percent, and actually shrank in 1974 and 1975. In 1976, James Callaghan (Wilson resigned in March 1976) agreed to a major loan from the IMF, though it was contingent on severe budget cuts and it made Britain look like an unstable, underdeveloped country—which in some respects it had become. Though the discovery and exploitation of North

Sea oil eased Britain's balance-of-payments problems, it did nothing to slow inflation or appease the unions. In early 1979, the country seemed to be coming unglued. Autoworkers went on strike and won a huge pay increase; firemen, bakers, and truck drivers soon followed suit, and as usual won raises. Public-sector workers then took their turn, as teachers, postmen, health care workers, garbagemen, and even grave diggers all went on strike. Refuse piled up in the streets, bodies went unburied. The government, exhausted and out of ideas, met the union demands. The press often invoked the words of Shakespeare's Richard III: "Now is the winter of our discontent. . . ." On 28 March 1979, in a final humiliation, Labour lost a vote of confidence in the House of Commons. It was the first time a government had been voted out by the Commons since 1924. Labour would remain out of power for the next eighteen years.[2]

IRON LADY

Margaret Thatcher, who became prime minister on 4 May 1979 after leading her party to victory in the general election, had no doubts about the causes of Britain's troubles. As she put it in her memoirs: "No theory of government was ever given a fairer test or a more prolonged experiment in a democratic country than democratic socialism received in Britain. Yet it was a miserable failure in every respect." British governments had adopted "a centralizing, managerial, bureaucratic, interventionist style of government" and "jammed a finger in every pie." The Labour Party, of course, was the principal exponent of this ideology. "It gloried in planning, regulation, controls and subsidies." But Thatcher reserved her sharpest barbs for her own fellow Conservatives, who in her view had done nothing to stop Labour and "merely pitched camp in the long march to the left." Her predecessor as leader of the Conservative Party, Edward Heath, came in for particular criticism: his imposition of price and wage controls and his caving in to unions "was the most radical form of socialism ever contemplated by an elected British government." The results of this unholy consensus between the parties were plain to see: inefficient industries, a bloated public sector, unions intoxicated by power, an intimidated government, and the replacement of old-fashioned values such as hard work and piety with "idleness and cheating."[3]

Humility was not one of Margaret Thatcher's personal qualities. "I know I can save this country and that no one else can," she said to herself upon taking up her new office.[4] This sentiment was not just bravado, the usual puffery of a newly elected leader. She possessed enormous confidence in herself and

in the righteousness of her cause. Yet in 1979, Margaret Thatcher was a political novice, having been the leader of the opposition for a mere four years and
having occupied no cabinet rank other than education minister under the
now-reviled Edward Heath. What made her think that she could single-
handedly reverse thirty years of British decline?

More than perhaps any other British leader, Margaret Thatcher made her
family background and upbringing a central part of her public persona as
prime minister. Hers was an ordinary life, and she made a virtue of its or-
dinariness. She was born in 1925 in the small middle English town of
Grantham, in Lincolnshire. Her father, Alfred Roberts, was an eminently re-
spectable and modestly successful shopkeeper who owned two grocery and
provisions shops in town. He was a Rotarian, led charity drives with great zeal,
and was elected alderman and later mayor. The family, she later wrote, was
"practical, serious, and intensely religious." They were devout Methodists. Her
father was a lay preacher, and young Margaret Roberts spent her Sundays either in Sunday school, in church, or playing hymns on the piano. The parents
ran the shop, always on call to meet customers' needs, which meant that there
were rarely any holidays. Her mother put her to work attending to chores,
ironing, cleaning, polishing, mending, cooking. On top of this came her
schoolwork, carefully supervised by her parents. She later made much of the
lessons she learned in Grantham: "The values instilled in church were faith-
fully reflected in my home. So was the emphasis on hard work. In my family
we were never idle—partly because idleness was a sin, partly because there was
so much work to be done, and partly no doubt because we were just that sort
of people."[5]

For the rest of her political career, she claimed that her formative years
spent in this world of middle-class, dutiful, earnest, upright citizens gave her
special insights into the concerns of ordinary English people. She may have
been right. But she did not, evidently, wish to stay in this world for ever. In
1943, she was offered a place at Somerville College, Oxford, to study chemistry, and she accepted it eagerly. She worked with predictable diligence and
also joined the Oxford University Conservative Association. In 1946, she became its president. This was a time when, under the social stresses of war and
shared sacrifice, the socialist ideals of the Labour Party were ascendant, and
the Tories looked old-fashioned and stodgy by comparison. Most young
Conservative aspirants advocated reform and a greater emphasis on social issues. That certainly seemed to be the lesson of 1945, and Margaret Roberts
joined a party that was moving toward the center, forging the consensus
around the welfare state that she would later try to dismantle.

After Oxford she worked as a research chemist, but politics remained her chief interest. In 1950, aged twenty-four, she ran for Parliament from a seat in Dartford, in Kent; she lost. The following year, in a general election that the Tories won, she ran and lost again, but in the meantime had become noted for her verve, her hard work, and her gender: there were few young women in the Conservative Party at the time. These were the years when she began to make political use of her familiarity with the travails of the housewife, who knew as most men did not how difficult it was to survive on ration cards in Attlee's Britain. For many, the Labour years of 1945–51 later became a shining moment when the idealism of a people shone through the dreary postwar gloom; for Margaret Roberts, this was when she came to loathe Labour's socialism. As she explained in her memoirs, "No one who lived through austerity, who can remember snoek, Spam, and utility clothing, could mistake the petty jealousies, minor tyrannies, ill-neighborliness, and sheer sourness of those years for idealism and equality."[6]

For all of her memories of thrift and privation in her youth, Margaret Roberts moved up the social and financial ladder quite quickly. She left chemistry behind and took up law; she duly passed the bar in 1953. In 1951, she married a self-effacing businessman named Denis Thatcher, who was the director of a medium-sized paint and chemical company in Kent. (The business grew, making Denis a wealthy man.) With Denis behind her, Mrs. Margaret Thatcher, as she was now, did not need to earn her own living, and could pursue a political career full-time. In 1959, she found a safe seat from which to run: Finchley, a prosperous London suburb. She entered the House of Commons at the age of thirty-two.

In the twilight of Macmillan's years in office, the Conservative Party remained centrist, moderate, and wedded to the basic principles of the postwar consensus. For a young radical like Thatcher, these were not promising times. Yet she was enormously ambitious and hardworking, and slowly made a name for herself in the party. After 1964, when the Tories went into opposition, she toiled away as a shadow junior minister, brought into the front ranks of the party by its new leader, Edward Heath. When Heath became prime minister in 1970, he brought Thatcher into the cabinet as education secretary—ironically, one of the fastest-growing departments, in which she fought for greater spending. Thatcher was delighted to have a ministerial portfolio but loathed Heath. She saw his willingness to impose price and wage controls in 1972 as a repudiation of his election promises and a continuation of the policies favored by the Labour Party. She believed that Heath's wobbliness spelled electoral disaster. Casting around for others who shared her views, she found them in isolated pockets within the party. She admired Enoch Powell, a pure conservative who ruined his career in 1968 by calling, in a speech with overtones of race war, for restrictions on immigration. More presentable was Sir Keith Joseph, a wealthy, intellectual MP, who like her had soured on Heath and wished to push the Conservative Party sharply to the right. Sir Keith became her real mentor, and together they established a think tank, the Center for Policy Studies, under the direction of another Conservative soul mate, the journalist Alfred Sherman. Here they laid out policy papers that proposed conservative approaches to Britain's problems. The ideas themselves were not new: free the private sector from government interference; cut back the welfare state; encourage self-reliance, innovation, and personal freedom. But Thatcher brought to these views greater intensity and conviction than any member of her party before her. She offered a coherent alternative not only to the Labour Party but to the wayward Conservative policies that she viewed as equally culpable for Britain's malaise.

In 1974, Heath did indeed lose an election to Labour, and it meant that Heath as party leader had lost three elections out of four (1964, 1966, and 1974) and would have to go. Yet Heath refused to resign, and refused to let his most able lieutenants run against him for the party leadership. This opened the way for Margaret Thatcher to challenge him. She was a bright, articulate, determined opponent who offered a break with the past. Heath was a loser tainted by electoral defeat and a dismal record as prime minister. In early February 1975, Thatcher defeated Heath on the first ballot, 130–119. After Heath dropped out, a few also-rans came in, and she thumped them all. The Conservative Party had a new leader.

Four years later, she was prime minister. How had she done it? A conviction politician, Mrs. Thatcher was pragmatic enough to gather around her a solid team of party regulars, all of whom had been prominent in the Heath government. Geoffrey Howe, later to become chancellor of the Exchequer; William Whitelaw, her deputy leader and later home secretary; Lord Carrington, later foreign secretary; and James Prior, later secretary of employment, all were very much insiders as Thatcher was not. That they were implicated in the failings of Heath's misrule did not bother the new leader, provided they now adopted her agenda as their own. She thus rallied the party behind her. She proved a skilled combatant in Parliament, able to match and even best Wilson and Callaghan in debate, and so allaying any doubts about her capacity for the job. She profited from the abysmal record of the Labour government, especially during the winter of 1978–79, when strikes virtually shut down the country. She pioneered the use of television and poster-board advertising, having hired the public relations firm Saatchi & Saatchi to firm up her reputation and denigrate her opponents ("Labour Isn't Working," said one sign, above a photograph of a dole queue). Above all, she offered a clear, comprehensible political platform. The Conservative manifesto of 1979 proposed to control inflation by reducing the money supply and limiting government borrowing; lower taxes; curb the unions; restore free markets; uphold the law (a clear jibe at Labour's inability to control the strikers); reduce welfare spending; and strengthen national defense. In the election of 3 May 1979, the Conservatives won 44 percent of the vote to Labour's 37. More embarrassing for Labour, many skilled workers and trade unionists abandoned the party for the Tories. Almost two decades of Conservative domination now commenced.[7]

These prospects seemed distant indeed during the first three years of Mrs. Thatcher's government. A change in the leadership of the country did nothing to alleviate the long-term, structural problems the country faced, and the remedies proposed by the new prime minister did a great deal to exacerbate them. Her economic proposals were spelled out in the budget presented by Chancellor of the Exchequer Geoffrey Howe in June 1979. Even for a public prepared for serious measures, the plan looked extreme. Thatcher's first priority was to stop inflation, and to this end she raised the minimum lending rate charged by banks from 2 percent to 14 percent; she also announced budget cuts of 1.4 billion pounds as a way to take more money out of the economy. In order to restore incentives to the private sector, she cut taxes on the wealthiest, lowering the top rate from 83 percent to 60 percent, and the basic income tax rate from 33 percent to 30 percent. This was offset by a dramatic increase in the value-added tax (VAT), which was levied on all purchases, from 8 to 15 percent. So the burden of taxation was switched from income earners to consumers. She also eased currency controls and abolished wage and price controls. The theory behind these measures was that by stopping inflation, there would be less pressure for pay increases. If wages and prices remained stable, the government could spend less on public-sector wages and could thus afford to cut taxes. By cutting taxes, the government would give employees more of their earned income and an incentive to work harder to create more wealth. Such a renewed competitive spirit would in turn lead to a new burst of economic activity. True, because of the high interest rates, some sectors would not have enough capital to invest and might have to shed jobs. It was expected that unemployment would increase in this scenario. But in Thatcher's view, British industry employed far too many underused workers; high interest rates should force industry to squeeze more out of fewer workers and thus become more efficient and more competitive. That was the theory.

In practice, the 1979 budget, followed by equally stringent policies in 1980 and 1981, administered a severe shock to a patient already gasping for breath.

Unemployment soared from 5.5 percent in 1979 to 13.3 percent in 1983—the highest rate in Europe. Three million people were out of work by 1983, a figure never before seen in Britain. Most of them were workers in the old, heavy industrial and manufacturing sectors. Yet despite the surge in unemployment, inflation perversely also continued to rise, from 10.3 percent in 1979 to 22 percent in 1980, before declining to single digits in 1982. In large part this was fueled by wage increases promised under the previous Labour government and honored by Thatcher. Nonetheless, it made a mockery of her economic policies. British GDP declined by 5 percent between 1979 and mid-1981. Some in her own party began to get weak knees, and argued for a more moderate course. Mrs. Thatcher, stubborn, determined, righteous, refused. At the Conservative Party Conference in Brighton in October 1980, she famously quipped, in a tag line that she gloried in years after: "To those waiting with bated breath for that favorite media catchphrase, the U-turn, I have only one thing to say. You turn if you want to. The lady's not for turning."[8]

This was brave talk. But the situation got worse, as Britain appeared to totter on the verge of social chaos. In the spring and summer of 1981, serious riots broke out in the impoverished inner cities of London, Liverpool, and Manchester. They were fueled by the usual causes: unemployment, a decaying urban environment, poverty, lack of education and prospects. There were disturbing racial overtones as well. Immigration from South Asia and Africa had brought communities of minorities to the poorer sections of large cities. Often targeted for harassment by local whites, especially young, unemployed whites, these immigrants also came in for special abuse from the police. In Brixton in South London, the spark for the April riots was the accusation of police racism and brutality toward minorities during an undercover anticrime sweep. In July, skinheads attacked South Asian communities in London, but the Asians fought back. Over a hundred police sent to intervene were injured. In the Toxteth district of Liverpool, minorities and police clashed over accusations of police strong-arm tactics against blacks. Rioters smashed storefronts and pelted police with stones; the police responded with tear gas and truncheons. In mid-July, copycat riots broke out in Birmingham, Blackburn, Leeds, Leicester, and elsewhere.

Naturally, the Thatcher government's stinging budget cuts and insensitivity to unemployment became the targets of heavy abuse from the Labour Party and some backbench Conservatives. A commission charged to investigate the riots found that unemployment and general despair were at the root cause, and deplored the racist outlook of the police. Mrs. Thatcher, true to her origins, thought it wrong to see the rioters as victims; "those poor shopkeepers," she declared when told of the looting in Toxteth. She elaborated in her memoirs: the problem was that the rioters had no "sense of respect for the law, for the neighborhood, and indeed for themselves." The old social constraints that once held "the high animal spirits" of young men in check had broken down. Instead, "welfare arrangements encouraged dependency and discouraged a sense of responsibility, and television undermined common moral values." Finally, the "decline of authority . . . in the home, school, the churches and the state" opened the way to such assaults on the social fabric. The answer to these disturbances was not more state aid but a revival of traditional moral and social values. If ever there was a good description of the Thatcherite social philosophy, this was it.[9]

By the fall of 1981, Margaret Thatcher was the most unpopular prime minister since Neville Chamberlain. Her approval rating had slumped to 25 percent. The economy had suffered its biggest one-year drop in output since 1931. The sharks in her own party were circling, ready to pounce and unseat her as leader.

WAR ON TWO FRONTS: THE FALKLANDS AND THE MINERS

Mrs. Thatcher's government, and her career, were rescued by a most improbable war that broke out in April 1982, on a tiny group of rocks in the South Atlantic called the Falkland Islands. Eight thousand miles from London, the Falklands were home to eighteen hundred British subjects, who scratched out a living by exporting wool. It was an odd accident of history that these islands should become the scene of a major international crisis, yet it was this accident that assured Thatcher of reelection despite an abysmal record on the home front, and helped cement the public persona of Mrs. Thatcher as an Iron Lady of strong will and decisive leadership.[10]

Since the eighteenth century, when Spain and England had each laid claim to them, the Falklands had been in dispute. English, French, and Spanish settlers had all made a go of settling the islands, but failed, though the English continued to claim ownership. When the Spanish Empire crumbled and Argentina emerged as an independent country in 1816, Argentina believed the Falklands to be part of its sovereign territory. England disagreed, and in 1833 invaded the islands to secure its claim. The Argentines considered this action illegal, but did nothing to oust the small enclave of English settlers there. And there things rested until the 1960s, when Argentina pressed for a negotiated settlement that would return the islands. British governments, both Labour and Conservative, were at first willing to compromise. The islands cost money and were worthless strategically, while Argentina was an important trading partner worth cultivating. But a zealous lobby of islanders managed to stoke up opposition to any plan for a dilution of Britain's role, and no government wanted to be smeared with the charge that it had sold out British citizens to foreign interests. This was made clear in 1980 when Nicholas Ridley, the junior minister asked to handle the Falklands portfolio, suggested handing over the islands to Argentina in return for a ninety-nine-year lease of the islands. He was denounced in the Commons and his plan scorned by other cabinet officers.

Without any plans for settlement, yet with no desire for conflict over the islands, the British government ignored the problem, hoping it would just go away. Yet for the Argentines, the issue loomed far larger. The country was in the hands of a military junta that had made a hash of the economy and faced massive unrest at home. The prospect of an easy victory against British imperialism might serve to legitimate the junta's leader, Gen. Leopoldo Galtieri, and win him popular acclaim. Moreover, the islands were so far from Britain that it would be all but impossible to retake them militarily; and besides, the Royal Navy had just withdrawn its only ship in the South Atlantic, the HMS *Endurance*, due to budget cuts. With the 150th anniversary of British rule looming, the junta decided to act. On 2 April, Argentine troops invaded the islands and after a brief struggle overwhelmed the small British detachment there.

The invasion shocked the British public, which immediately denounced it as unprovoked aggression against a sovereign British territory and its citizens. In the House of Commons, meeting on 3 April, members from both sides rose to express their indignation and their demand that the islands be restored to British control, by force if necessary. Even Michael Foot, leader of the Labour Party, spoke of Britain's moral duty to mount a vigorous response. For her part, Mrs. Thatcher, though she soon warmed to the role of war leader, feared the political consequences of this challenge to British power. The Argentines had caught the British off guard and unprepared; someone had to take responsibility for the lack of preparedness. The scapegoat was duly found in Lord Carrington, the foreign minister, who resigned on 5 April, leaving Mrs. Thatcher free from culpability. Meanwhile, the military chiefs told the prime minister that though it would be enormously difficult, they believed it possible to retake the islands by force. On 5 April, after merely a weekend to prepare, a task force sailed for the Falklands, with the aircraft carriers *Hermes* and *Invincible* joined by a fleet of smaller assault ships, destroyers, and supply craft. In all, forty-four ships were deployed, along with forty-five civilian ships, including the *Queen Elizabeth II*, which was pressed into use as a troop carrier. Twenty-eight thousand men were involved in the task force, of whom 10,000 were land forces. The putting of all this military hardware together in so short a time has been called "one of the most remarkable logistical feats of modern times."[11] The challenge ahead was an enormously difficult one: the objective was on the other side of the earth, in the midst of churning sea, with no place to resupply. The British had limited intelligence capability, and no satellites; and the Argentine military was outfitted with British- and French-built equipment, including 120 aircraft to the mere thirty-eight in the British task force. Finally, the Argentines had 10,000 troops on the islands in well-defended positions.

The possibility of failure, then, was very real. The last time the British had attempted such an operation, it had ended in disaster, and destroyed the career of a prime minister. But there were important differences between the Suez crisis of 1956 and the Falklands War. First, the British had the moral high ground in the Falklands and they never relinquished it. Whatever the legal status of Britain's claim to the islands, Argentina's invasion was widely denounced. The United Nations in a resolution of 3 April called for the withdrawal of Argentine troops, and even the usually dithering European Community imposed trade sanctions on Argentina on 10 April. Second, the United States did not block a military response as it had done in 1956. Instead, the American secretary of state, Alexander Haig, attempted mediation, but came up against total intransigence from the Argentines. The United States thereafter tilted toward Britain, and even shared satellite information with its ally. Finally, Margaret Thatcher was manifestly not Anthony Eden. Where Eden had huffed and puffed but then delayed the military invasion, only to lose his nerve once the invasion began, Thatcher proceeded methodically and with purpose toward the military confrontation she now expected and indeed perhaps even wished for. Failure in war might, of course, ruin her; but a failure to respond would be just as lethal to her political future. This central point had eluded Eden; Thatcher understood it instinctively.

The military campaign proceeded smoothly for the British, though mounting an amphibious landing in stormy South Atlantic seas 8,000 miles from home presented innumerable opportunities for disaster. On 25 April, the British scored a small but important preliminary victory in retaking South Georgia, an island seven hundred miles from the Falklands that the Argentines also claimed. Mrs. Thatcher had her first success of the war, and she relished it. After announcing the news to a press corps eager for additional details, she cut them short. "Rejoice," she told them. "Just rejoice." But the war took a nasty turn when a British submarine, *Conqueror*, torpedoed and sank the Argentine cruiser *General Belgrano*, with the loss of 368 Argentine lives. The action was taken on direct orders from the war cabinet in London and with Mrs. Thatcher's express approval. This was a major escalation and dashed any hopes for a peaceful settlement of the conflict, on which international mediators were at that moment working very hard. It later emerged that the *Belgrano* was moving away from the Falklands at the time it was sunk and was of little immediate threat to the task force. Some later claimed that the prime minister was looking for an excuse to avoid a peaceful settlement because she preferred to fight. She certainly got her wish. Two days later, a French-built Exocet missile fired from an Argentine fighter slammed into the HMS *Sheffield*, killing twenty British sailors. The war was for real. Over the next six weeks, the war went badly for the Argentines, as the superior British training and morale began to tell. On 20–21 May, after the arrival of the slower troop transports, the major land invasion was launched, and 5,000 troops established a beachhead. Though there were some sharp bursts of fighting, the British pushed quickly into the islands, and by the time they reached the capital, Stanley, the Argentine defenders had given up. The capital fell on 14 June. Overall, the war cost 236 British and 750 Argentine lives.

The importance of the Falklands War for Margaret Thatcher's career cannot be overstated. It transformed her from an embattled right-wing ideologue to a national leader with the qualities so many of her predecessors appeared to lack: decisiveness, confidence, and the ability to unite the country. Public opinion polls revealed this. In mid-April, 60 percent of the public thought the government had handled the crisis well; by the end of the month the figure was 76 percent, and topped out at 84 percent at the end of the conflict. This kind of national unity had not been seen in Britain since 1940. The British media encouraged this sentiment with heavy doses of jingoism, patently racist commentary on the backward "Argies," and thumping headlines praising British military successes. "Gotcha!" taunted a notorious headline in Rupert Murdoch's *Sun* after the sinking of the *Belgrano*. The bulldog phrase "Stick It Up Your Junta!"—from a *Sun* headline of 20 April—was later emblazoned on commemorative T-shirts sold by the newspaper.[12] Mrs. Thatcher saw such expressions as the natural pride of the people burning through the fog and darkness of postwar Britain. "We have ceased to be a nation in retreat," she boldly declared.[13] The electorate apparently agreed. When she called an election in June 1983, the Conservatives won handsomely. The Labour Party, hopelessly divided and led by the unelectable Michael Foot, could scarcely manage to win 27 percent of the vote. A third party, an alliance between the new Social Democratic Party and the Liberal Party, did almost as well as Labour in terms of percentage of the votes. The opposition thus divided, Mrs.

Thatcher cruised to victory with the largest Conservative majority since 1935. Overall, her party had a 144-seat edge in the House of Commons.

Yet as of 1983, Thatcherism had produced few concrete results. In fact, the economy suffered badly between 1979 and 1983. GDP had fallen by 4.2 percent in this period; industrial production was down 10.2 percent; manufacturing down 17.3 percent; unemployment had reached the figure of 3 million people. Overall, taxes had risen, and even public spending had increased. Only in the area of inflation, which fell to 4.6 percent in 1983, could she claim a success.[14] This was not a record to be proud of, and it reveals how much the Falklands War helped Mrs. Thatcher's political fortunes. Still, she was not deterred. In her new cabinet, she ousted some of her less enthusiastic colleagues and replaced them with loyalists. In particular, Nigel Lawson, a strict monetarist who wanted to cut spending and tighten the money supply, took over the Exchequer. With a strong majority in the Commons, she could press on with her economic experiment. She pledged a renewed campaign of privatization of state-run industry, tax reform, reform of local government, and less government expenditure. Naturally, she encountered some enemies along the path, none more determined and hostile than the leadership of the British trade unions.

Mrs. Thatcher considered the trade unions to be one of the chief causes of the "British disease." Not only had they used their power to extract huge pay increases from both the public and the private sector, but they had contributed in her view to the inefficiency of British industry by resisting technological improvements and modernization in order to protect jobs. As a Conservative, she remembered bitterly how the unions had destroyed the Heath government (1970–74) with their incessant strikes and demands for pay increases. The coal miners' unions in particular had made Heath look weak when during the 1972 strike they had brought the country to a standstill. Mrs. Thatcher in her first term introduced legislation to curb the rights of strikers to stage sympathy strikes, to limit the creation of closed (union-only) workplaces, and to compel unions to hold secret ballots to approve strike policy. These laws made it more difficult for union leaders to pressure workers to strike. Yet Mrs. Thatcher knew that a public confrontation with union power would be necessary before her economic policies could succeed. Though there were a number of disgruntled industries that might have taken on the government, the leading contender to engage in a trial of strength with Mrs. Thatcher was the National Union of Mineworkers (NUM).

The miners' strike of 1984–85 became a defining struggle for Mrs. Thatcher, a counterpart on the home front to the Falklands War. Indeed, Mrs.

Thatcher welcomed comparisons between the two campaigns, and saw the leader of the miners' union, Arthur Scargill, as another General Galtieri. In July 1984, she declared to a group of Conservative backbenchers: "We had to fight an enemy without in the Falklands. We always have to be aware of the enemy within, which is more difficult to fight and more dangerous to liberty."[15] Harsh words; yet she viewed the miners, or rather their leaders, as "revolutionaries who sought to impose a Marxist system on Britain whatever the means and whatever the cost."[16] To be sure, Arthur Scargill, the leader of the NUM, was a Marxist, and had been a member of a Communist youth organization. But the miners had genuine grievances. Their industry was dying. In 1923 there were 1.2 million workers employed in the coal industry. In 1947, when the industry was nationalized, coal still provided 90 percent of the nation's energy supply, though the number of workers had dropped to 700,000. Cheap oil and natural gas, and the advent of nuclear energy, cut demand for coal. By 1974, coal supplied only one-third of the nation's energy needs, and only three hundred mines remained open, from a high of a thousand at the end of the war. The use of mechanization in the mines dramatically reduced the need for manpower. By the time of the strike, there were only 200,000 workers left in the industry. Nationalization of coal in 1947 placed the government in the unenviable task of shrinking the industry as demand for coal declined. Coal mines closed, miners were laid off. Strikes were frequent, and the NUM won increased pay packages; but the industry was a black hole for government money. In 1984 alone, the mining industry cost the government 875 million pounds in losses.[17]

To restore the industry to solvency, the government hired Ian MacGregor, a Scottish businessman who had made a fortune in the United States as a steel manufacturer and financier, to run the National Coal Board. His brief was to consolidate the coal industry, make it more efficient, and where necessary shut down uneconomic pits and lay off the workers. Naturally, the government expected that this plan would lead to a miners' strike, and it did everything it could to prepare for it. Starting as far back as 1981, the government began stockpiling coal at power stations across the country to provide a constant supply should the mines be shut down. More power stations were switched to oil-fired generators, and nuclear generators were coming on line as well. The government also had learned the lessons from previous encounters with the miners: the police were better trained and equipped to confront the massed "flying pickets" that had halted coal deliveries in 1972.

The strike began in March 1984 when the Coal Board announced the closure of a small colliery in South Yorkshire called Cortonwood. The miners at

Cortonwood went on strike, and Scargill saw this as an opportunity to bring his whole union out in strike against the policy of closing mines that failed to make a profit. To his alarm, however, he discovered that a significant number of miners, worried about pit closures and unemployment, did not wish to strike. As a result, Scargill did not put the strike to a nationwide ballot of members. Instead, he got local branch leaders to use their clout to win a strike vote at the local level, where intimidation, pickets, and peer pressure could be so much more effective. This allowed the NUM to avoid putting the strike to a vote, a fact that Mrs. Thatcher never ceased to emphasize.

The strike, begun with great fanfare, went badly for Scargill. The usual solidarity of the miners broke down. In Nottinghamshire, a strike vote was held that showed 73 percent against the strike. Local ballots in the Midlands and the northwest and northeast coalfields also went against the strike. Moreover, workers in related industries such as steel, railways, electricity, and trucking refused to come out in support of the miners, so that when coal was mined in the nonstrike pits, it could still be delivered. Along with government stockpiles and other sources of energy, the government just managed to meet demand for energy; all the power stations were kept running throughout the strike. Frustrated miners resorted to increasingly violent attacks on police and nonstriking workers. But these clashes only turned the public, at first sympathetic, against the strikers. Worse still was the revelation that Scargill had solicited funds for the strike from the Libyan dictator, Col. Muammar Gaddafi. By January 1985, strikers began to drift back to work, and by February, more than half of the NUM members had returned to the mines. They had voted with their feet against Mr. Scargill. The following month, the strike was called off, a year after it started.

The strike cost over 3 billion pounds, and was the most expensive industrial action in the nation's history. But it cost the unions a great deal more than that. The NUM, which had brought down Edward Heath in 1974, had now been taken down by Mrs. Thatcher. Her victory over Arthur Scargill, coming so soon after the Falklands triumph, made her appear invincible. She had done what none of her predecessors had yet been able to do: engage in a long trial of strength with the unions and win. As she recognized, the contest was about more than coal. For her, Scargill was a tyrant who held the decent British worker hostage to an alien ideology. Now that Scargill was broken, workers were free "to defy the militants" in the union leadership.[18] Many did. Union membership dropped sharply in the 1980s in Britain, as did the number of strikes after 1984. In the year of the miners' strike, 27 million working days were lost to strike activity; in 1986, only 1.9 million days were lost—a postwar low. What the prime minister called "Mr. Scargill's insurrection" would prove to be the last hurrah for organized labor in twentieth-century Britain.

ASSESSING THATCHER

In 1987, Margaret Thatcher led her party to yet another victory in a general election. She stayed on in office until November 1990, when, after eleven and a half years as prime minister and leader of her party, she resigned. She did not go easily. Her last year in office had been a difficult one. The economy lurched into recession, a victim of the worldwide slowdown of the early 1990s. Interest rates were high, and by the fall of 1990, inflation returned, hitting 10.9 percent. She also became embroiled in a major controversy over local government taxation—a scheme called the "community charge." She had long believed that local city governments, often Labour controlled, spent too much money. In 1987, she proposed to limit their resources by abolishing the old property tax system and replacing it with a system in which taxpayers were assessed based on what their local governments spent: if their town councils were Labour spendthrifts, their taxes would accordingly be high. If more sober, restrained town leaders chose to spend less on local services, then the community charge would stay low. The system, derisively termed the "poll tax" because it used electoral registers to determine who should pay taxes, created a storm of protest. It was seen as a highly partisan attack on the power of local government, and unfair: it assessed taxes not on the grounds of ability to pay but on the budgetary priorities of local governments. In practice, this translated into a significant increase in taxes on those least able to pay, especially the urban working class. When the poll tax was introduced in England in early 1990, riots erupted in the streets around Trafalgar Square in London. Some taxpayers, egged on by Labour MPs, refused to pay. Many in the Conservative Party were uneasy about the tax, and when they saw the degree of hostility toward it, they turned on its chief proponent, the prime minister.

The grumbling against her mounted. In November, her longest-serving cabinet colleague, Geoffrey Howe, resigned as foreign minister over a disagreement about Britain's role in Europe. In his sharply worded resignation speech, he denounced the prime minister's dictatorial style and her intolerance for compromise or dissent. Suddenly, with the loss of even her staunchest allies, Mrs. Thatcher was isolated. The next day, Michael Heseltine, a former Thatcher minister but out of the cabinet since 1985, announced his intention to challenge Mrs. Thatcher for the party leadership. When the vote was held on 20 November 1990, Thatcher defeated Heseltine, but by so slim a margin that a second ballot was required by party rules. This she could not abide. Clearly, many in her party had lost confidence in her leadership. She chose to resign, though not before insuring that her personal favorite, the inexperienced chancellor of the Exchequer, John Major, would become her successor.

For over a decade, Margaret Thatcher dominated British political life. She came into office with great ambitions to reform Britain by liberating the creative powers of the free market and reducing the presence of government in the lives of the people. Did she succeed? Her own assessment was that her years in office had constituted a "revolution—of privatization, deregulation, tax-cutting, wider ownership, restoring self-reliance, building ladders out of poverty, strengthening our defenses, securing the Atlantic alliance, restoring the country's morale and standing." Can this claim for revolution be sustained?[19]

In the area that she placed greatest emphasis on, the economy, Thatcher could point to significant accomplishments. During the 1980s, the growth of GDP increased annually by 2.1 percent, not robust but just about the European average. By the late 1980s, growth had reached 4 percent. In 1988, GDP was 21 percent higher than in 1979. Inflation, the chief enemy of Thatcherism, had been contained though not vanquished. In 1986 it stood at 2.6 percent, the lowest in two decades, but reached double digits in 1990. Many people earned more. After 1983, real personal disposable income rose by about 3 percent a year. The later 1980s was a period of unprecedented prosperity for the country.

Mrs. Thatcher claimed that cutting taxes would be a chief priority of her government, and she did reduce income taxes, especially on the very rich, but she also increased the VAT, so that the overall tax burden increased during her tenure in office, from 34 percent of GDP to 38 percent in 1990. The other Thatcher bugbear, public spending, was reduced, though only after an increase in the early 1980s due to higher unemployment benefits. As a share of GDP, public spending was reduced from a high of 46 percent in 1983 to 39.5 percent in 1989—the lowest ratio since 1967. So the chief policy prescriptions of Thatcherism—cutting taxes and reducing spending—were only partially achieved.[20]

She also undertook a major program of privatization, that is, the selling off of the state-owned industries that had been nationalized by the Attlee government. This policy grew from Thatcher's belief that state-run industries were inefficient and that the state should remove itself from the economic life of the nation. British Aerospace, Cable and Wireless, British Petroleum, Jaguar, British Telecom, British Gas, British Airways, Rolls-Royce, and British

Steel, among others, were sold off, earning the government handsome returns. Though debate continues over the degree to which privatization has boosted efficiency and productivity, it did promote the buying of shares in the newly private companies, and so squared with the prime minister's efforts to change the public's attitude toward ownership. This motive also informed another major policy change of the Thatcher years: the sale of public housing (known as council housing). Unlike public housing in the United States, many homes financed and built by local government in Britain were attractive, desirable, and, most important, built in the much favored semidetached style—a single-family home nestled into a cluster of dwellings. The Thatcher government championed the idea of property ownership, and so allowed council tenants to buy their homes at a discount. Over a million did so.[21] If Mrs. Thatcher undid some aspects of Attlee's legacy, others survived intact. The welfare state, for example, remained popular in Britain, and efforts to weaken it were turned back. Indeed, spending on social security benefits, health services, and education increased in the Thatcher years—33 percent, 34 percent, and 9 percent, respectively, between 1979 and 1989. Although the government did privatize some service providers, which often gave the impression of an assault on the basic welfare system, Mrs. Thatcher went to great pains to assure the public that, for example, "the National Health Service is safe with us." The NHS continued to have its problems: long lines, little choice of doctors, less than stellar services. But it remained a popular institution that Mrs. Thatcher declined to challenge.

Though the welfare state survived the Thatcher years, the public tended to see Mrs. Thatcher as uncaring. In part, this was due to her personality: her righteousness, her high Protestant diction, the icy manner she cultivated. In part, it was due to her policies. Unemployment reached unprecedented heights during her reign. Divisions, both between rich and poor and north and south, were deepened. The rich got much richer, enjoying tax cuts that disproportionately benefited them. And the southern part of the country fared much better than the north: in East Anglia, the southwest, the southeast, and East Midlands, jobs grew substantially, but in Scotland, the north and the northwest of England, and Wales, jobs declined by almost 10 percent.[22] Nor did Mrs. Thatcher's own brand of Victorian values command wide support in Britain. One poll in 1988 asked respondents to describe aspects of the ideal society. Forty-nine percent thought socialism and a controlled economy should predominate, 55 percent thought public provision of welfare important, and 79 percent favored a society that valued caring more than wealth creation. By contrast, only 16 percent wanted a society in which the creation of wealth was highly valued. Another series of polls found that during the Thatcher years, the public actually moved away from Thatcherism on the question of taxes and public services. In 1979, only 37 percent thought the government should expand public services even at the cost of some increase in taxes. But by 1987, 66 percent agreed with this view, while only 11 percent wished to cut taxes at the expense of fewer public services.[23] Mrs. Thatcher's emphasis on self-reliance and individuality never found an enduring hold in British public opinion. Nor did she. Despite her electoral success, she herself was never a popular prime minister, leaving aside the brief Falklands period. From 1983 on, her average job approval rating showed that less than 40 percent of the public was satisfied with her performance—a significantly poorer rating than that enjoyed by Attlee, Churchill, Eden, Macmillan, and Wilson.

What, then, explains her astonishing electoral success? At least in part her victories must be attributed to the dismal performance of the Labour Party between 1979 and the mid-1990s. In fact, one of Mrs. Thatcher's greatest legacies was to force the Labour Party into a major overhaul of its political philosophy. In 1979, after losing to the Conservatives, Labour activists pushed the party further to the left by electing Michael Foot as leader. The Labour Party embraced a wide range of unpopular positions, including unilateral nuclear disarmament, withdrawal from the European Community, expanded state ownership of industry, more public spending, and higher taxes. Many disaffected Labour supporters switched allegiance to the new third party, an alliance of the Social Democrats and the Liberals. Even the working class itself ditched Labour. In the 1983 election, only 38 percent of manual laborers voted for Labour, down from a high of 69 percent in the 1966 election. Altogether, 62 percent of workers voted for parties other than Labour in 1983—a shocking repudiation. The task of reforming the party was delegated to Neil Kinnock, who became its leader, but Kinnock found stiff resistance from the hard left within his own party and from the unions. Kinnock wanted to soften Labour's stance on public ownership of industry and on Europe, but failed. In 1987 and again in 1992, he lost elections to the Tories. Even the modest, unexciting John Major, running as prime minister in 1992, had no trouble outpacing Labour.[24]

Not until Tony Blair became party leader in July 1994 did Labour really begin to reshape itself. Blair was young, unassociated with the trade union movement, university educated, and on the right of his party. After four successive election defeats, his own party rank and file were ready to join Blair in a major overhaul of Labour policy. He abandoned the party's commitment to public ownership of industry, and instead forced through a platform that embraced free enterprise, economic growth, and competition—principles central to the Thatcher era. He also pledged to control public spending, unlike all his party predecessors. Blair managed to break the hold of unions on the party by restricting their voting power. Yet he also used to great effect the appeal to values that remained strong in British life: community, social justice, fairness, and equal opportunities. Here were the key ingredients of New Labour. The work paid off: in May 1997, Tony Blair led his party to an enormous electoral victory, with Labour winning the largest parliamentary majority since 1935 (a margin of 179 seats). He would repeat this performance in the general election of 2001. Yet this was not a renunciation of Thatcher by any means. Labour had won its victory by adopting many of Thatcher's most effective policies—privatization, budgetary responsibility, low inflation, and a reliance on the market to sponsor growth—while avoiding her abrasive, hectoring style. Labour's renaissance was made possible by Margaret Thatcher. Despite her disdain for consensus politics, Mrs. Thatcher—that self-proclaimed revolutionary—had helped to build a new political consensus all the same.

THE TROUBLES

There was one area in which she could claim no victories or breakthroughs: the long-running problem of Northern Ireland. Of course, her predecessors in high office had all stubbed their toes on this difficult problem. Yet Mrs. Thatcher was particularly ill equipped to forge a new policy for Northern Ireland since her sympathies were quite clearly with the Protestants of Ulster and her loathing for the IRA, already intense, became even stronger in 1984. At 2:54 A.M. on Friday, 12 October of that year, a thirty-pound bomb exploded in the bathroom of Room 629 in the Grand Hotel in Brighton. At that very moment, on the first floor of the hotel, Thatcher was just completing a long day's work. She was putting the finishing touches on a speech she would deliver the next morning to the Conservative Party Conference. Along with her in the hotel were many members of her cabinet, her staff, and a large police escort. The prime minister escaped injury, though the bathroom to her suite was damaged and glass shards were strewn across the carpet of her room. But the hotel was shattered: the whole front of the building collapsed and a heavy chimney crashed through its twenty-eight floors. Five people died in the blast, including a member of parliament, Sir Anthony Berry. Her close adviser and secretary of state for employment, Norman Tebbit, was trapped under tons of rubble; badly injured, he survived. The bomb had been planted a month earlier by Patrick Magee, a thirty-three-year-old member of the Irish Republican Army. It was the closest the IRA has ever come to assassinating a British prime minister.

The Brighton bombing, though a profound shock to Mrs. Thatcher and to the country, was but one of thousands of murderous attacks, bombings, and assaults carried out by the participants in the long struggle over the province of Northern Ireland. Between 1966 and 1999, 3,636 people died as a result of the Northern Ireland conflict; the majority of these victims were innocent civilians. How is it that within one of Europe's wealthiest, most stable and democratic countries, such lethal violence persists?[25]

The contemporary passions that fuel the Northern Ireland conflict can only be understood in historical perspective. For five centuries at least, England has been a colonial power in Ireland: in 1541, Henry VIII of England was declared king of Ireland. Ever after, Protestant England looked to Catholic Ireland with grave suspicion, a likely staging point for popish plots against the kingdom. English monarchs sought to subdue Ireland by waging war there, which they did incessantly, and by seizing Catholic lands and giving them to transplanted Protestants from England and Scotland. The plantations proved most successful in the northern part of Ireland, where Protestants used their power and ties to England to maintain restrictions on Catholic political and economic rights. In 1801, in the Act of Union, Britain formally incorporated Ireland into what became known then as the United Kingdom of Great Britain and Ireland. For many centuries, Irish nationalists opposed English rule. During the late nineteenth century, when Liberals in England began to consider ways to devolve some political power to Ireland, the Protestant community there—known as Unionists or Loyalists—ferociously resisted, fearing that in an autonomous Ireland, Catholics would take for themselves the political prerogatives long held by the Protestant minority. They also feared that home rule would lead to outright independence and a loss of British citizenship for the Unionists. But even the promise of autonomy within the British Empire was not enough for Irish nationalists, or Republicans: they wanted an independent country. In 1916, as the First World War raged, Irish Republicans staged a military uprising against British rule, which was put down with great brutality by British troops.

But in December 1918, in elections to the House of Commons, the Irish voted overwhelmingly for candidates of Sinn Fein, the party that called for outright independence from Britain. The following month, Sinn Fein refused to take its seats in London and unilaterally established an Irish parliament, declaring the country independent. Two years of war ensued between the Irish Republican Army (IRA) and the British army, a struggle described by the English simply as "the Troubles." The British government, facing the prospect of a long war of attrition to hold on to an Ireland that was hugely in favor of autonomy, negotiated a compromise in 1921: southern Ireland, consisting of twenty-six of the country's thirty-two counties, in which Catholics were the overwhelming majority, would be granted self-government, but would remain part of the British Commonwealth. The six northern counties, where Protestants were in the majority—Antrim, Armagh, Down, Londonderry, Fermanagh, and Tyrone, collectively referred to as Ulster—would remain under British sovereignty, though they too would be granted limited powers of self-government. The country was partitioned.

This settlement emerged amidst bursts of fighting between Republicans, who felt that Britain had no right to slice off six counties of their new Irish Free State, and Protestants, who now saw Ulster as their rightful preserve. Yet the partition held: Ireland went on to sever all ties to Britain in 1949, becoming the Republic of Ireland; while Northern Ireland remained a Protestant-dominated rump state, part of the United Kingdom, electing representatives to the House of Commons. It also had its own assembly, which met at Stormont Castle outside Belfast. Protestants outnumbered Catholics in Ulster, 66 to 34 percent. Protestant ascendancy was held in place by gerrymandering to insure that Protestants would always hold the vast majority of seats in local government. The Royal Ulster Constabulary was created as Northern Ireland's police force, yet since it was controlled by Protestants, it was perceived by Catholics as an instrument of repression. The same was true of the many Protestant volunteer militias that sprouted up in Northern Ireland, ready to crack open a few heads if the RUC failed to enforce Protestant dominance with sufficient vigor.

In the 1960s, Catholics became more assertive in demanding reforms that would give them a greater say in the political and economic life of Ulster. In January 1967, the Northern Ireland Civil Rights Association (NICRA) was formed and called for changes in political institutions, an end to discrimination in public services, especially housing, and for limits on the powers of the police. Inspired by the student protest movements in France, Germany, and the United States, NICRA members staged marches, sit-ins, and demonstrations. The logic of Ulster, however, dictated that any challenge to Protestant power be met by force. On 5 October 1968, the RUC stopped a NICRA march in Londonderry by clubbing the demonstrators and turning water cannons on them. In reply, the demonstrators launched stones and Molotov cocktails at the police. Although the British government of Harold Wilson successfully pressured the Liberal prime minister of Northern Ireland, Terence O'Neill, to introduce reforms along the lines called for by NICRA, many Unionists feared that NICRA was the thin end of the wedge that would shatter Protestant dominance. The Reverend Ian Paisley, a fire-breathing, maniacally anti-Catholic preacher, stirred up fierce opposition to O'Neill. In 1969 and 1970, Protestant paramilitary groups such as Paisley's Ulster Protestant Volunteers and the Ulster Volunteer Force terrorized Catholic communities. Unable to control the extremists in his own camp, O'Neill resigned in April 1969.

The turbulence of 1968–69 opened the way for the radical Republicans to mobilize against Protestant violence. In 1969, a splinter group of the old IRA emerged under the name Provisional IRA and launched a campaign of violence against the RUC and the Protestant militias. (Among the group's leading members was a young bartender from Belfast named Gerry Adams.) That summer, during the traditional marches held each year to celebrate Protestant domination in Ulster, Catholics attacked with stones and bottles; Protestants responded in kind. The RUC was unable to contain the rioting, and in August 1969, 6,000 British army soldiers were deployed in Belfast and Londonderry to keep the peace. This move significantly radicalized the situation, for it laid bare the degree to which Protestant hegemony was dependent upon British support. It also gave the IRA an opportunity to escalate the violence. As the riots continued in 1969 and 1970, Catholic demonstrators clashed with British troops, who were sometimes lured into Catholic neighborhoods and then shot at. This in turn led to harsher measures from the British soldiers, and so the violence escalated. The IRA used the crisis to promote their claim as protectors of the Catholics against British imperialism and its Protestant lackeys. On 6 February 1971, the IRA killed its first British soldier. This was the start of three decades of war.

Catholic violence was used to justify harsh measures from the Northern Ireland government, which in August 1971 introduced internment without trial and began imprisoning suspected Catholic agitators. Some were tortured with the connivance of the British army. Such tactics only called forth an equally violent response, and the hold of the IRA over the Catholic population tightened. Hundreds of bombs went off across Ulster in 1971, killing and wounding hundreds of civilians; the IRA also killed forty-three British army regulars and eleven members of the RUC. Protestant militias responded in kind, and the cycle of violence ratcheted ever upward.

The year 1972 was the worst in Northern Ireland since the creation of the province. It started with a ghastly tragedy on 30 January—Bloody Sunday—when British army paratroopers, sent into the heavily Catholic Bogside neighborhood of Londonderry to contain a NICRA march, opened fire on the demonstrators. In thirty minutes of terror, British troops killed thirteen unarmed Catholics, including a seventeen-year-old boy. This event electrified the public in Ireland and Britain and revealed that the political situation in Ulster was out of control. Prime Minister Edward Heath announced the imposition of direct rule over the province from London and the dissolution of the

Stormont parliament. Catholic civilians actually welcomed this move, for it suggested that the British might contain the worst excesses of the Unionists. But there was no respite from violence. In fact, this boosted the confidence of the IRA, which now thought British rule was on its last legs. It also terrified the Unionists, who feared the end of their ascendancy. In the following six months, there were over 9,500 shooting incidents, and the deaths of 264 civilians and 108 soldiers. This year also saw the advent of that scourge of urban warfare, the car bomb. By the end of 1972, 467 people were dead, victims of both Unionist and Republican attacks.

There was a brief attempt at compromise in December 1973. In the English town of Sunningdale, the British government met with representatives of the political parties in Northern Ireland. These included the Ulster Unionist Party, the main Protestant party, which had dominated Northern Ireland since its creation; the small Alliance Party, a nonsectarian party, founded in 1970 as a rallying point for moderate Protestants and Catholics; and the Social Democratic and Labour Party, founded in 1970 by a French teacher named John Hume. The SDLP soon emerged as the chief voice of "constitutional nationalism"—that is, it favored union with Ireland but only through a peaceful and democratic process that incorporated respect for all traditions. At Sunningdale, the parties worked out a proposal for a Council of Ireland through which Northern Ireland and the Irish republic would address common economic and social policies. This was a major concession by the British and the Unionists, for it acknowledged that Ireland had a role to play in Ulster. In return, the Irish agreed to recognize the principle of majority rule in Ulster: any changes to the political structure of Northern Ireland would have to be acceptable to a majority of the people there. And the British offered to release some prisoners, stop internment without trial, and consider reforms of the RUC. This was the first exercise in power sharing in Ulster. It lasted five months. The Unionists finally rejected the scheme, and the Protestant militias who saw Sunningdale as a threat to their control of Ulster went on a rampage of violence against it. Until some moderate Protestant political force could be found to accept power sharing, there was little likelihood of peace in Northern Ireland.

And so Northern Ireland withered, like a damaged limb on a tree, starved for nourishment, ugly, weakened. The sectarian violence continued at a horrendous pace—250 killed in 1973, 216 killed in 1974, 247 killed in 1975, 297 killed in 1976—until falling to a grim harvest of about eighty deaths per year after that. The British now hunkered down in a kind of holding action—unwilling to withdraw but unable to create the basis for compromise. Unionists had no incentive to do so, for they believed that compromise meant an end to

Ulster. The IRA used Protestant intransigence as justification for its continued violence. And the ground under the feet of the moderates—a rare breed in any case—eroded. Northern Ireland took on the appearance of a war zone. Belfast was divided by barbed wire and army outposts. The city streets, subject to bombing and bullets, were deserted, lined by empty buildings and boarded-up shops. Unemployment soared, especially among Catholics: by 1984, 35 percent of Catholic males in the province were without work.[26]

Margaret Thatcher's arrival at 10 Downing Street did not offer much hope for a settlement. As opposition leader, by her account, she expressed "the greatest sympathy" for the Unionists. She declared in her memoirs that her "own instincts are profoundly Unionist" and she had "a good deal of respect for the old Stormont system," despite its association with discrimination against Catholics.[27] She nonetheless realized that there was no going back to the policies of permanent Protestant hegemony and that down the road some sort of political power-sharing scheme had to be created to protect and advance Catholic rights.

Northern Ireland dogged her first term as prime minister. On 30 March 1979, just as Parliament dissolved to prepare for the general election, she got her first personal taste of the tragedy: her close adviser and designate for the post of Northern Ireland secretary, Airey Neave, was killed by a bomb planted in his car while it was parked in the House of Commons parking garage. It was the work of the Irish National Liberation Army, a faction of the Republican movement. Five months later, on 27 August 1979, the IRA struck close to the royal family, killing Earl Mountbatten, the uncle of Queen Elizabeth's husband, the Duke of Edinburgh. He was killed by a bomb hidden on board his thirty-foot yacht. And in 1981 there began a long confrontation between IRA prisoners, incarcerated in the Long Kesh prison ("the Maze"), and the British government. This crisis stemmed from a British decision in 1976 to deny IRA prisoners political status and to treat them as common criminals, thereby forbidding them the right to wear their own clothing, have visitors and extra food packages, and meet freely with other prisoners. In protest, prisoners refused to wear prison clothes and draped themselves only in blankets. They also smeared their cells with excrement. On 1 March 1981, a twenty-seven-year-old IRA member, Bobby Sands, began a hunger strike, and was soon joined by other prisoners. The protest took an unusual turn when four days after Sands began his strike, he was nominated to run for a seat in a parliamentary by-election. On 9 April, he won the seat from his jail cell, giving his protest enormous publicity. Surely now the British government would have to relent. It did not. Mrs. Thatcher believed that the terrorists were waging "a psychological war" for public opinion; any concession to them once the strike

THE STRUGGLE FOR EUROPE

had begun would be an embarrassing defeat for the government. On 5 May, Bobby Sands died. One hundred thousand people attended his funeral in Belfast two days later. Overall, ten prisoners died during the hunger strikes before they were ended on 3 October.

Mrs. Thatcher declared the hunger strikes to have been "a significant defeat for the IRA."[28] But were they? The effect of the hunger strikes was to radicalize much of the Catholic population in Ulster and give credence to the IRA's accusations that the British government was a cruel, foreign occupying power that opposed basic human rights for Republicans. The political arm of the IRA, Sinn Fein, gained a significant boost in the wake of the strikes. In local elections, Sinn Fein began to rival the moderate SDLP, and in the general election of 1983 that saw Mrs. Thatcher's resounding victory, Sinn Fein's president, Gerry Adams, won a seat in the House of Commons (which he of course refused to take) as member for West Belfast. As Sinn Fein's electoral appeal increased, the moderate Catholic party, John Hume's SDLP, anxiously beseeched the British and Irish governments to restart negotiations toward a power-sharing scheme again so as to undercut the extremist IRA position. Hume, aware that the IRA was never going to defeat the British militarily, believed that the only solution to the Northern Ireland crisis was a broad settlement that included the participation of Ireland, Britain, and the parties inside the province. He envisioned a federal state in which Northern Ireland was joined to Ireland and to Britain both, and had institutions designed to protect and nurture the rights and traditions of both Protestants and Catholics. This vision would require enormous changes in the climate of relations between all the players.

Mrs. Thatcher did not support such a radical vision, but she did want to offer the SDLP some support, so as to help it fend off the electoral challenge of Sinn Fein. The result was the Anglo-Irish agreement of 15 November 1985. The agreement stated that the British and Irish governments would create an intergovernmental conference so that they could work together on certain problems, especially security and economic issues, relating to Northern Ireland. What this meant was that the British now recognized a major role for Ireland in the shaping of any future Northern Ireland settlement—a victory for Hume's constitutional nationalists. The Unionists were predictably hostile and staged massive protests against the agreement. Mrs. Thatcher had now managed to alienate both the Republicans and the Unionists in equal measure.

Hume and the SDLP had won a victory, but this was only the start of a very difficult process that would not see results until 1998. The first task that faced Hume, as the leading proponent of a negotiated compromise settlement, was to persuade his Republican coreligionists and rivals that the nationalist cause had more to gain from peace than from war. The IRA was not going to defeat the British. In fact, the British by the late 1980s had totally penetrated the IRA, was able to interdict most of its arms shipments, knew the membership and whereabouts of most IRA militants, and had effectively contained the terrorist threat. Starting in 1988, Hume therefore began a series of meetings with Sinn Fein's Gerry Adams, to persuade him to get the IRA to renounce violence altogether and join in the peace process. This was a tall order: violent struggle against Britain was the raison d'être of the IRA. To renounce violence was therefore to renounce the organization itself. Hume understood this, but argued that the British government had in the 1985 agreement made it clear that it would give up Northern Ireland if the majority there wanted it to do so. The job of the Nationalists was to persuade Unionists that an independent and united Ireland would be a place in which Protestants had a role and a future. Adams could see the logic of the argument but had trouble accepting that the British government would ever leave Northern Ireland by its own volition. For five more years, IRA violence continued, met tit for tat by violence from Protestants. But in 1993, after secret contacts between Sinn Fein and the British government, the British made it clear that if the IRA renounced violence, Sinn Fein would be invited to take part in negotiations for a new political settlement in Northern Ireland, one that was worked out in close accord with the Irish government. These intentions were announced in the Downing Street Declaration of 15 December 1993. These assurances finally persuaded the IRA to take a chance on peace. On 31 August 1994, the IRA declared a cease-fire: the violence, at least for a time, would end.

But building a peace process turned out to be harder than declaring a cease-fire. Unionists remained highly skeptical of the peace process. They believed the IRA would never agree to lay down arms, and insisted that total IRA disarmament precede any Unionist concessions on power sharing. The IRA, meanwhile, refused to consider disarming until after a settlement to their liking was finally implemented. The British government, now under John Major, also dragged its feet, reluctant to embrace Sinn Fein as a new political partner. The United States government played an important role in keeping the process moving. President Bill Clinton visited Northern Ireland in November 1995 and received a rapturous welcome from Catholics and Protestants alike. He appointed a mediator, former US senator George Mitchell, to head up a panel to examine the issue of decommissioning arms. When Mitchell's report emerged in January 1996, it suggested that decommissioning not be a precondition of negotiations. The British government rejected this proposal, and the IRA immediately broke its cease-fire. On 9 February 1996, it set off an enormous bomb in Canary Wharf, a recently redeveloped section of East London.

Another devastating bomb was set off in a Manchester shopping center a week later. The police hit back hard, arresting dozens of IRA members and seizing bomb-making materials. Further, the public in Northern Ireland was in agony over the return to violence, as their expectations had been raised so high since 1994. The IRA's bombings were a disaster from a strategic point of view.

In May 1997, the Labour Party returned to power after eighteen years out of office. The new prime minister, Tony Blair, immediately seized the initiative. He reached out to Sinn Fein and told them if the IRA renewed the cease-fire, Sinn Fein would be included in all-party talks. The issue of arms would be set aside for now. On 20 July 1997, the IRA announced another cease-fire. In September, Sinn Fein entered into peace talks alongside Unionists and members of the British government. The IRA had failed to achieve its aim of defeating the British and pushing them out of Ireland. But now a new track would be pursued: the path of negotiation. It proved far more promising. George Mitchell, installed as chairman of the talks, worked for eight months with the parties to hammer out a framework for a new government for Northern Ireland, the first since the Stormont system ended in 1972. The result was the best hope for peace in Northern Ireland in a generation: the Good Friday Agreement of 10 April 1998.[29]

The basic shape of the agreement was not new. Once again, the Irish and British governments agreed that any change in the political status of Northern Ireland would depend on the will of the majority of the province. But the agreement also outlined a new, 108-member Assembly in which Catholic and Protestant representatives would share power. Structures linking Ireland to the province were outlined. A British-Irish Council was created, designed to expand contacts between the two countries on economic and social matters. Wide-ranging human rights protocols were agreed to, a new investment strategy for economic aid to Northern Ireland was outlined, and most important, an International Independent Commission on Decommissioning was established to monitor the process of disarming all the paramilitary bodies. The British agreed to start scaling back their military presence, to reform the RUC so as to make it more open to Catholics, and to grant early release to many IRA prisoners, including those involved in some of the most notorious attacks.

The Good Friday agreement was not a peace settlement in itself. Rather, it created the institutions in which a peace settlement could be hammered out without resort to violence. It succeeded because of the many subtle changes that had taken place since 1968. First, the British had certainly moderated their views, moving away from the robust pro-Unionism of the early years to a more neutral and constructive role. Second, the IRA, under prodding from

Sinn Fein's Gerry Adams, had recognized that violence would never lead to a united Ireland. Of course, the IRA could still carry out lethal attacks and keep British troops pinned down in Ulster. But if it really wanted peace and a settlement, as John Hume had argued, it would have to move along a political track. Third, the Good Friday agreement also reflected the changed stance of the Unionists, who had sunk the 1973 Sunningdale agreement but now accepted power sharing, even if grudgingly. They could see that they had nowhere else to go. To reject power sharing would make them outcasts and court the risk of losing British support altogether. And finally, the Irish government in Dublin, historically hostile to British policy, had joined with the British government in a powerful partnership, ready to broker a deal between the warring parties.[30]

Despite the hopes raised by the Good Friday agreement, peace has not come to Northern Ireland. The parties inside the new Assembly found power sharing a difficult experience: the IRA remained deeply reluctant to disarm, while the Unionists have never really embraced the principle of power sharing with the Catholic minority. And splinter groups on both sides continued to resort to violence. On 15 August 1998, in the town of Omagh, a faction called the Real IRA set off a car bomb; it killed twenty-eight people in a busy marketplace. Protestant paramilitaries have also kept up sporadic attacks on Catholics. The Assembly has deadlocked numerous times, and almost collapsed in the fall of 2001. Only a last-minute agreement by the IRA on 23 October 2001 to disarm kept the fragile Good Friday framework alive. The ever-present risk of violence and the day-to-day reality of discrimination and sectarian hatred are sharp reminders, as if the Irish needed any, that beneath the veneer of political compromise and negotiation lies a broken, fragile country that has known nothing but war for most of the century—a country that may need a generation of healing before it can bear the burdens and responsibilities of peace.

PART FOUR

UNITY?

■

"It was the best of times, it was the worst of times." Dickens's memorable characterization of Europe in the revolutionary 1790s neatly captures the spirit of the continent two centuries later, in the revolutionary 1990s. And indeed, this was a revolutionary decade, certainly the most turbulent and complex since the end of World War II. The events of this decade will define Europe for at least the next half century.

First, the best of times. Between 1989 and 1991, a political revolution swept over Europe, one that few anticipated and that no one could have dreamed would progress with such a remarkable absence of violence. Communist ideology had long been a tattered, sorry spectacle, loathed by those forced to adhere to it, scorned and derided by those fortunate enough to have escaped it. But the brutal structures of power that supported the regimes in Eastern Europe remained sturdy, certainly strong enough to withstand the challenges presented by the growing dissident movements in Poland, Hungary, and Czechoslovakia.

It was not until the leader of the Communist bloc—the general secretary of the Soviet Union, Mikhail Gorbachev—signaled his own determination to reinvigorate the moribund Marxism that nominally bound his satellites together that Europeans began to get their courage up. Gorbachev, supremely confident, breathtakingly naïve, and humane to the end, dared to initiate a dramatic program of reform and restructuring in his own country, one he hoped the Eastern-bloc states would emulate. Gorbachev derided his predecessors for their unwillingness to repair the cracks in the leaky dam of socialism. No sooner had he gathered his tools, laid out his blueprints, and started to tap away at the soggy mortar than the whole edifice crumbled away, washing Gorbachev and the Communist satraps in Warsaw, Prague, and Budapest along in the flood. By the end of 1991, the Cold War was over, the Berlin Wall was destroyed, democratic governments had taken control in Eastern Europe, and even the mighty Soviet Union had ceased to exist. Revolutionary days, indeed.

Amid the euphoria that accompanied the collapse of Communism, there was much talk of the historic opportunity to unite Europe. The merger of the two Germanys that took place in 1990 seemed an appropriate metaphor for the larger task of building a new Europe that could house all the states of the continent. The twelve states of the European Community renamed themselves the European Union (EU) and began to move forward with plans for a stronger Europe, one that was more democratic, more forceful in international affairs, more courageous in addressing social and economic problems, and more united by common structures such as a European Central Bank and a common currency. In 1995, the EU admitted three more members, and the fifteen states began to consider whether and how to admit a dozen more. In 2002, in a gesture full of both symbolic and economic significance, the euro became the only legal currency in twelve EU states. Europe had never been richer, freer, or more stable than it was at the close of the twentieth century.

But with the best of times came some very bad times indeed. In 1991, Yugoslavia erupted into a grisly civil war between Croats, Serbs, and Bosnian Muslims, one that led to as many as 200,000 deaths. In certain ways, the war was really the first test of the European security architecture that had been put in place in the 1940s, and it failed miserably. For over three years, the EU, the UN, and the United States quibbled and dithered, and only in 1995, with the use of American air power, was a settlement finally imposed. And even then, the flames of war smoldered, only to spread to Kosovo in 1999, leading to yet another international military intervention. The war revealed that some Europeans had not given up the old language of nationalism, ethnic chauvinism, and race war, and also revealed that not all Europeans knew how to meet such threats when they surfaced. It left the EU humiliated and ashamed.

Nor could Europeans pretend that racism was something reserved to the Balkans. In the 1990s, as the walls dividing East and West came down, new barriers sprang up against millions of would-be immigrants from Asia, Africa, and Eastern Europe. Europeans began to engage in a shrill debate about the need to maintain traditional values, customs, and habits in the face of what was called a flood of immigrants from non-European, non-Christian lands. Across the continent, political parties pandered to this growing antagonism toward foreigners, and every country saw a sudden increase in far right groups blaring openly xenophobic slogans. Every day, immigrants suffered racial abuse, assaults, beatings, and murder in the streets of Europe's cities. Here was the dark underside to the shiny new Europe being built in Brussels.

Yet it would be wrong to suggest that the persistence of nationalism and racism and genocidal hatreds in some corners of Europe invalidates the European project. Europeans, for all the meanness and thuggery visible in soccer stadiums and depressed industrial towns, remain on the whole among the most tolerant, humane, and fair-minded peoples on earth, which should count for something. Among the killing fields of Bosnia and Kosovo, hundreds upon hundreds of European doctors, lawyers, human rights workers, electoral officials, engineers, teachers, and businesspeople are rebuilding these war-torn lands. In Afghanistan and Somalia, Congo and Haiti, the European-based Doctors Without Borders administers to the sick and poor. Europeans give more foreign aid, as a percentage of GDP, than any other countries in the world; and the EU provides half of the world's humanitarian assistance. The dozens of antidiscrimination groups, the hundreds of marches against racism, the thousands of politicians who refuse to launch electoral appeals based on racial differences all bear witness that Europe has made a sincere effort to act as a champion of human rights and human dignity. For a continent that only half a century ago lay in ruins under the dark clouds of Hitler's crematoria, that is progress indeed.

CHAPTER THIRTEEN

THE EUROPEAN REVOLUTIONS, 1989–1991

.

CAN THE EVENTS of 1989–91, when Europe's Communist regimes were overthrown, be considered revolutionary? The changes of government during that period were as much the result of reform and compromise as of violent confrontation. There were no beheadings, no regicide, little violence. Communism, it seemed, simply imploded like a house with fatal structural flaws.[1]

Yet it is wrong to rob the East Europeans of their place in history as authors of a genuine revolution. In 1989, thousands upon thousands of people in Poland, Hungary, East Germany, Czechoslovakia, and Romania, motivated by a simple yearning for personal freedom, pulled down the ramparts of the East European police state. Of course, they did not act alone. The political changes under way in the Soviet Union after 1986 stimulated gradual reforms in the Eastern bloc that in turn made revolution possible. Nonetheless, Soviet leader Mikhail Gorbachev did not desire revolution; Poles and Hungarians and East Germans did. They staged mass protests, mobilized millions of courageous citizens, rejected a despised ideology, forcibly took control of the reins of government, and sent the leaders of the old order into political exile (but not to the guillotine). Moreover, they did so in full consciousness of the international dimensions of their struggle. Poles inspired Hungarians, who in turn fired up East Germans, who in their turn passed the baton of freedom to Czechs and Romanians. What happened in 1989 fulfilled all the criteria for revolution, and more: for this was a European revolution, a shock wave that burst over the entire continent. Evermore, historians will look back on 1989 as the real starting point of the common, united Europe.

GORBACHEV

Revolutions are like earthquakes: the brief, intense upheaval is preceded by gradual, unseen shifts as the earth's tectonic plates grind inexorably against one another, creating instability and pressure. The events of 1989 too have their long-term antecedents. The East Berlin uprising of 1953, the Hungarian Revolution of 1956, the Prague Spring of 1968, the advent of Charter 77, the massive Polish workers' movement of 1980: these tremors signaled a future cataclysm. But one moment must stand out as the true start of the European revolution. On 11 March 1985, Mikhail Sergeyevitch Gorbachev was named general secretary of the Central Committee of the Communist Party of the Soviet Union. His name was put forward by the small group of top leaders, the Politburo, and unanimously approved by the full, three-hundred-member Central Committee. Little did they know that in a mere six years, Gorbachev would change the course of Soviet, European, and world history.

Gorbachev's relative youth—he was fifty-four years old—his charm and intelligence certainly struck Western observers as a marked change from previous Soviet leaders. Leonid Brezhnev, in his final years in power, had become a shell of his former active self; his waxen face and clouded eyes betrayed the gradual loss of his mental faculties. Upon his death, in November 1982, he was succeeded by Yuri Andropov, the veteran KGB chief. Andropov, aged sixty-eight, suffered from kidney failure and spent much of his time on a dialysis machine. He lasted a mere two years. His successor, Konstantin Chernenko, was if anything in worse physical shape: the seventy-three-year-old man suffered from lung disease and died after thirteen months in office. The Soviet leadership, like the country itself, looked old, infirm, and exhausted. Clearly, it was time for a change.

It was not at first obvious that Gorbachev would bring dramatic change to the Soviet Union. Though youthful and dynamic, Gorbachev was very much a product of a deeply conservative, authoritarian system, and his appointment as general secretary was preceded by a careful, dutiful march through the institutions of Soviet political life. He was, needless to say, a devout Communist Party member, a great admirer of Lenin, and an ardent believer in the transforming power of socialism. Nor did Gorbachev have any intention in 1985 of bringing about the end of the Cold War, the unification of Europe, or the collapse of the Soviet Union. Instead, he saw himself, and was recognized by his Politburo colleagues, as a reformer who could bring about much-needed structural change to a country desperately in need of it.

Gorbachev was born in 1931 in the village of Privolnoye, a small cluster of huts on the vast open plains north of the Caucasus Mountains, in southern Russia. It was not a propitious time to be born. Stalin's collectivization drive was raging, compelling farmers to pool their land and equipment into state-run collectives and imposing quotas on the farmers. Collectivization, and the terror that accompanied it, disrupted agricultural production. In the Ukraine, millions died of famine; in Gorbachev's home region, the suffering was almost as bad. According to Gorbachev, half of the population of his village died of hunger in 1933. "The half-ruined, ownerless huts would remain deserted for years," he recalled. Gorbachev's paternal grandfather was arrested in 1934 for failing to meet production targets; he was sent to a labor camp in Siberia. His mother's father, who was in fact the chairman of the local collective, also fell afoul of the authorities. In 1937 he was arrested on charges of being a member of a right-wing Trotskyist organization. He was tortured and imprisoned, but released. The family lived as outcasts, tainted simply by the shame of the accusation.[2]

In 1941 the Germans invaded the USSR, and Gorbachev, then ten, saw his father go off to the front. He recalled the brief German occupation of the northern Caucasus as a time of privation and fear, but his region was spared the terror imposed in other parts of the country. His formative years, then, were spent not fighting the Germans but in rebuilding Russia after the war. As a teenager he worked on his local collective with great zeal, attended the nearby secondary school, won excellent grades, and became the leader of his school's Young Communist League (Komsomol) chapter. In 1948, still working on the collective during the summer as a combine operator alongside his father, Gorbachev won an award—the Order of the Red Banner of Labor—when his team produced a record harvest. He was only seventeen, and this state award was a remarkable honor. It gave him the prestige to apply for, and receive, a position at Moscow State University, where he enrolled in 1950. Here, he met his future wife, Raisa, and earned a law degree in 1955.

Gorbachev now began his career as a politician. He moved up the ranks of the Komsomol and then the party apparatus. In 1966, at the age of thirty-five, he became head of the party in the city of Stavropol. Four years later he became Communist Party leader for the entire Stavropol region, a position of enormous power that brought with it a seat in the Central Committee. During the 1970s, Gorbachev made a name for himself as first secretary of the Stavropol region and developed close contact with Yuri Andropov, the KGB chief from 1967 to 1982 and himself a native of the Stavropol region. In 1978, with Andropov's backing, Gorbachev was made a secretary of the Central Committee with responsibility for agriculture. Two years later, in 1980, he was made a full member of the Politburo. At the age of forty-nine he had become one of the small handful of men who held the reins of power in the Soviet Union.[3]

When Andropov became general secretary in 1982, after eighteen years of Brezhnev's sclerotic rule, he embarked on a series of limited reforms in economic matters, and saw Gorbachev as an ally and a protégé. He cultivated Gorbachev by assigning him new portfolios, and as Andropov's health declined, he delegated many of his duties to the vigorous Gorbachev. Andropov's death deprived Gorbachev of his powerful patron, but by now he had established himself as one of the top members of the Politburo. Chernenko's brief interregnum only enhanced this power, for Gorbachev chaired meetings of the Politburo during Chernenko's frequent illnesses. His trip to Britain to meet with Margaret Thatcher in December 1984 clearly established him as the Kremlin's number two man. The British prime minister famously boosted his prestige by declaring that she "liked Mr. Gorbachev. We can do business together." That same month, Gorbachev evidently felt strong enough to give a daring speech that was seen as an open claim for the leadership. Delivered to a conference on ideological matters in Moscow, it broke many taboos and laid out a number of basic ideas that Gorbachev would later pursue. He declared that "profound transformations must be carried out in the economy" and a "higher standard of living must be ensured for the Soviet people." He called for a radical improvement in the economic life of the country through improved technology and higher productivity. The economy needed a total "restructuring," he said, using a word that would forever be associated with his name: "perestroika."[4]

Of course, the final decision to appoint Gorbachev as general secretary lay with the Politburo. Yet with the recent deaths of many of the top leaders—Andropov, Chernenko, and in December 1984 Defense Minister Dmitri Ustinov—there was no one left who could plausibly challenge Gorbachev. Upon Chernenko's death, on 10 March 1985, a brief effort was made by the Moscow party leader Viktor Grishin to win the top job; but his reputation as a corrupt member of the old guard made him unacceptable. When the senior statesman on the Politburo, Foreign Minister Andrei Gromyko, announced his support for Gorbachev, the others quickly jumped on the bandwagon. Mikhail Gorbachev would be the next general secretary of the Communist Party of the Soviet Union—and as it happened, the last.

STATE OF THE UNION

"On taking office as General Secretary," Gorbachev recounted in his memoirs, "I was immediately faced with an avalanche of problems."[5] This is to put it mildly. His country in the mid-1980s was in a state of rapid and terminal decline. The period of optimism of the early 1970s—when Soviet production in heavy industry seemed likely to overtake the West's, when détente had sanctioned Soviet control in Eastern Europe, when the United States was mired in Vietnam, and when Third World liberation movements in Asia and Africa looked to Moscow for inspiration—these days were gone. After two decades of Brezhnev's unimaginative, geriatric leadership, Gorbachev proposed to bring new energy and new ideas to reforming the country. But one need only consider the depth of the crisis the USSR faced to understand why Gorbachev failed.

The Soviet economy was slumping badly. Scholars still have difficulty penetrating the haze of official and therefore doctored statistics, but recent estimates suggest that Soviet growth rates, at best, stood at 4.9 percent per year in the 1965–70 period, then dropped from 3 percent for the 1970–75 period, to 1.9 percent for the 1975–80 period, and 1.8 percent for the 1980–85 period.[6] The causes of slow growth were numerous. The economy suffered from bureaucratic interference, an absence of incentives, overconcentration in heavy industry and too little production of consumer goods, low labor productivity, and far too little investment in high technology and robotics. Added to this was the complicating factor of energy. Soviet oil supplies, which had always been cheap and plentiful, became more expensive to produce—70 percent more, by some estimates—as newer oil fields in western Siberia required more elaborate and costly extraction methods. By the mid-1980s, the USSR was putting about 30 percent of its overall industrial investment into the energy sector alone. The Soviet Union had to run faster and faster just to stay in place.

The situation in agriculture was even worse than in industry. The USSR had once been one of the world's leading exporters of grain; by the 1970s it was importing 10 million tons of wheat and corn each year. This resulted despite, and perhaps because of, huge state subsidies and investment in this sector. During the 1970s, almost 30 percent of total state investment went into agriculture, and in addition the state subsidized food prices. The collectivization of agriculture remained a major obstacle to efficiency and higher productivity. Local ideas concerning appropriate crops, climate, and farming techniques were rejected in favor of the state-imposed plan. Farms that went into debt were simply bailed out by the state. Farming equipment and spare parts were in notoriously short supply; fertilizer was unavailable or unsuitable for local conditions; and farmers relied upon the black market to make a living, auctioning off state-owned goods and machinery. The results were predictable enough: during the entire decade of the 1970s, agricultural output increased by a mere 1.2 percent.

Darkening this already grim picture were social and demographic trends. The overall Soviet population grew during the 1970s, but the rate of growth was declining, from 1.8 percent in the 1950s to 0.8 percent in the early 1980s. Life expectancy fell during the 1970s from 69.3 years in 1969 to 67.7 years in 1979. Infant mortality increased from 22.6 deaths per thousand births to about 28 by the end of the decade. In large part this was due to poor nutrition and the awful condition of Soviet hospitals. In 1986, of the 3,900 district-level hospitals, only 35 percent had hot water; 17 percent had no water at all. The most basic medical supplies were in short supply. On top of this, the country was crippled by widespread alcoholism. By the mid-1980s, Soviet citizens consumed seventeen liters of alcohol a year for every person above fifteen years of age in the entire country—twice the European average. Perhaps as much as 8 to 9 percent of total national income was lost to the social costs of alcoholism.[7]

The news was no better in international affairs. In 1979, the Soviet Union invaded Afghanistan in order to prop up a pro-Soviet client government against Islamic rebels. Within a year, some 125,000 Soviet soldiers occupied the country. The United States saw this as part of a plan to threaten the Persian Gulf, and President Jimmy Carter declared the invasion "the most serious threat to peace since World War II." In response, the Americans increased arms shipments to Pakistan, which in turn channeled the weapons to the Afghan mujahedeen—or "soldiers of God"—that were fighting the Soviets. Carter's successor, Ronald Reagan, had a long history of anti-Communism and was ready to believe the worst about Soviet intentions. He expanded the covert arms program to Afghanistan and in March 1983, soon after labeling the Soviet Union "the focus of evil in the modern world," proposed to build a space-based missile shield to protect the United States from Soviet attack. Though highly improbable from a technological point of view, the Strategic Defense Initiative (SDI) appeared in Soviet eyes as a destabilizing measure that would upset the traditional nuclear balance. In any case, it triggered a frenzied boost in Soviet defense spending. By the start of the 1980s, the USSR was spending 12–13 percent of its GDP on its military budget—twice the proportion of US spending on defense. The tensions between the superpowers reached a highly dangerous point when, in September 1983, Soviet fighters shot down a civilian airliner, Korean Airlines 007, after the plane inadvertently strayed into Soviet airspace. Reagan declared the action a "crime against humanity." So bad had US-Soviet relations become that when NATO staged a large military exercise in November 1983, the Kremlin placed Soviet forces on high alert: they believed the exercise might be the preliminary to a nuclear attack.[8]

There seemed to be no end to the bad news. Just a year after becoming general secretary, Gorbachev faced a disaster that captured the essence of the Soviet crisis. On 26 April 1986, an explosion tore through one of the four reactors in the Chernobyl nuclear power plant in northern Ukraine. The explosion happened during an experiment on the reactor that required technicians to shut off the emergency water cooling system. The explosion blew off the lid of the reactor, ripped through the roof and walls of the plant, and ignited a huge fire. Thirty-one people died almost immediately. An enormous amount of radioactivity spewed up into the atmosphere—ten times the amount released by the atomic bomb on Hiroshima. Wind blew the radioactive cloud westward, across Europe as far as Ireland. It was the worst nuclear accident in history. The plant director, Viktor Bryukhanov, responded to the explosion in typical Soviet fashion: he reassured Moscow that despite the accident, radiation levels were normal; then he ordered all telephone lines to be cut. Thousands of people in the Kiev area went through the usual activities of a warm spring Saturday, unaware of the lethal radiation in the air. Two days after the explosion, Swedish monitors registered the high levels of radioactivity and concluded that a nuclear disaster had occurred. Only then did the Politburo release a statement acknowledging the accident. Yet while Western Europeans took active measures to protect themselves, Soviet citizens were left without information. Not until 5 May did the government begin an evacuation of over 100,000 residents within an eighteen-mile radius of the plant.[9]

The Chernobyl disaster had a profound effect on Gorbachev. The accident and the mishandling of the emergency response revealed the damaging effects of secrecy and compartmentalization within the Soviet bureaucracy. In early July, Gorbachev convened a conference of nuclear scientists and administrators and berated them for their false assurances and incompetence. "Throughout the entire system, there has reigned a spirit of servility, fawning, clannishness and persecution of independent thinkers," he declared. "For thirty years, you scientists, specialists, and ministers have been telling us that everything was safe. And you think that we will look on you as gods. But now we have ended up with a fiasco." Gorbachev realized that Chernobyl was more than a nuclear disaster: it was a vivid testament to the structural failures of the Soviet system. "As I pondered these matters," he wrote later, "I became ever more convinced that the problem could not be solved merely by administrative pressure, punishment, stringent measures, Party penalties and reprimands. We had to move perestroika forward."[10]

PERESTROIKA

What did that mean in practice? Gorbachev knew that perestroika would be judged on its ability to bring fundamental economic improvements. Yet he had no plan, and certainly no expertise in liberalizing a centrally planned economy. He began in typical old-school Soviet fashion, issuing directives from the top down. The five-year plan of 1986 spoke of doubling the national income by 2000, of boosting science and technology, of promoting the electronics and machine-tool sectors, of giving greater autonomy to the agricultural collectives, and of decentralizing decision making. By 1987, Gorbachev accepted the need to introduce incentives for workers, to reward those who worked best, and to allow for individual enterprise. The law on state enterprise of 1987 tried to impose basic accounting procedures on industry, making them accountable for their losses. In 1988, the state passed new laws allowing for small and medium-sized businesses to operate outside of state control and to fix their own prices.

Bold moves, certainly. But for all of Gorbachev's enthusiasm, the Soviet economy went from bad to worse. To be sure, Gorbachev had his share of bad luck. The Chernobyl accident, followed by the devastating Armenian earthquake in 1988, cost the state huge sums of money, just at a time when the drop in world oil prices deprived the state of oil revenues. On political grounds, Gorbachev's efforts to reform management practices and to break the control of the ministries over the command economy encountered massive resistance from the bureaucracy and the Soviet leadership. So while Gorbachev issued orders, industrial production slumped from 4 percent growth in 1988 to 1.7 percent in 1989, and then shrank by 7.8 percent in 1991. The piecemeal efforts to free up production led many small enterprises to concentrate on profitable goods for those who could pay for them. Basic goods like soap, salt, toothpaste, sugar, even bread and meat became scarce. For many consumers, perestroika meant nothing more than long lines and shortages.[11]

In the political arena, Gorbachev proceeded with great zeal. He decided to mobilize the intellectuals and the public by loosening the control of the media and encouraging freedom of expression—the policy of glasnost, or openness. Progressive editors were appointed to the major newspapers and journals, and soon a new cultural awakening was visible in the arts, culture, television, and the press. In December 1986, Gorbachev freed the Soviet Union's most famous dissident, the physicist Andrei Sakharov, from internal exile in Gorky and began proceedings to release many more political prisoners. In January 1987, he lectured the Central Committee about its recalcitrance to embrace perestroika and insisted on more radical democratization. "We must not retreat" from perestroika, he said. "We have nowhere to retreat to."[12]

But Gorbachev was walking a very fine line. His talk of democratization alarmed many conservatives in the Central Committee, while emboldening the liberals. In late October 1987, during a plenum of the Central Committee, Boris Yeltsin, then a junior member of the Politburo and chief of the Moscow Communist Party, launched a blistering attack on Gorbachev, asking why perestroika had been so slow to produce any concrete results and denouncing what he called the emergence of a personality cult around Gorbachev. Though Yeltsin was summarily denounced for his outburst, and soon lost his job as Moscow party boss, his remarks revealed new fissures in the political landscape. Meanwhile, just a few months later, the conservatives struck. In March 1988, a letter appeared in the daily newspaper *Sovetskaya Rossiya*, written by a Leningrad chemist named Nina Andreeva. It was a full-scale attack on perestroika, especially on the denigration of Stalin and his legacy. Andreeva depicted perestroika as the work of pro-Western liberals and Jews who were basically hostile to the Soviet Union. The letter appeared just as Gorbachev was leaving the country for a visit to Yugoslavia, and was immediately embraced and praised by Gorbachev's deputy Yegor Ligachev, who insisted that it be reprinted in all the country's newspapers. It soon became clear that Ligachev was mobilizing the conservatives in the Politburo for a counterattack on perestroika, and planned to use the letter as a rallying cry. Gorbachev dithered but then revoked Ligachev's responsibility for ideological matters. But conservatives, no less than liberals, were marshaling their forces against the general secretary.[13]

This may explain why Gorbachev moved so quickly to impose dramatic constitutional changes in 1988. Gorbachev had concluded that the party could not, after all, be relied upon to reform itself. It would do so only under the pressure of public opinion and the prospect of losing its leading role in society. Such a threat could be made real through genuine, contested elections. At the critically important nineteenth All-Union Conference of the Communist Party in June 1988, Gorbachev pushed through resolutions on accelerating perestroika and, most notably, the democratization of Soviet society.[14] By this, Gorbachev meant the introduction of contested elections for a new legislature. It was to be called the Congress of People's Deputies; it in turn would elect the members of the Supreme Soviet, who would carry out the day-to-day work of legislating. It was cumbersome, since the congress was to have 2,250 members. It was not fully democratic, as 750 seats were to be reserved for deputies named by state-sanctioned institutions (the party itself was allocated a hundred seats). In local constituencies, nominees were put forward by committees comprised of party members. The great majority of candidates in the election of March 1988 were therefore Communists. Overall, 2,884 candidates contested the 1,500 open seats, giving Soviet voters a real choice: the first time this had happened since 1917. The new congress, when it convened in May, contained many party leaders, to be sure, but also scientific and cultural figures (Andrei Sakharov was elected by the Academy of Sciences), writers, scholars, and even religious leaders. Despite opposition from party officials, Boris Yeltsin was elected by an overwhelming vote from his Moscow constituency. In the first meetings of the new congress, aired on live television, deputies engaged in open discussions, made pointed criticism about the slow pace of reform, condemned the KGB, and delivered speeches filled with complaints about the economy and the environment, among other topics. Andrei Sakharov called for the Communist Party to be disbanded.[15]

Gorbachev could be well pleased by his political reforms, but it was in the arena of foreign policy that he made his boldest moves. Gorbachev did not enter office determined to end the Cold War. But he did believe that his plan for domestic reform could only succeed alongside a corresponding transformation in the international system. The expense of the nuclear arms race, the constant drain of subsidizing socialist-bloc countries, the huge expense of the military infrastructure in occupied Eastern Europe—all of this impeded economic growth and political liberalization. If the nuclear arms race and the international tension it created could be reversed, then perestroika had a chance.[16]

In November 1985, just eight months after becoming general secretary, Gorbachev made his desire for radical change in US-Soviet relations dramatically clear. In Geneva, he met US president Ronald Reagan in a summit that marked the beginning of the end of the Cold War. It was the first such meeting of American and Soviet leaders in over six years. Reagan had a reputation as a vehement anti-Communist who in his early years as president frequently relied on anti-Soviet rhetoric to placate his conservative supporters. But by the end of his first term in office, Reagan had moderated his views slightly. After his massive reelection victory in November 1984, he set out to restart US-Soviet arms control talks in the hope of restraining the arms race that he had done much to intensify. Progress was painfully slow, but during 1985, negotiators laid out the lines of debate. The Americans wanted to talk about reducing the massive numbers of nuclear missiles each superpower possessed. The Soviets, by contrast, wanted the Americans to limit production of the space-based missile shield—the SDI program. When the two leaders met in Geneva in the fall of 1985, Gorbachev showed unprecedented willingness to agree to massive nuclear arms cuts, but asked that in return SDI, which he saw as destabilizing and a violation of the 1972 Anti-Ballistic Missile Treaty, be shelved. Reagan refused. SDI, he believed, was a separate issue, since SDI was not an offensive weapon but a protection against nuclear attack.

Despite the failure to secure any arms agreement, Geneva created a new dynamic in US-Soviet relations. Gorbachev and Reagan spoke to each other in sincere, unscripted words, meeting in small, informal sessions, probing each other's assumptions, and engaging in genuine dialogue. Though polar opposites ideologically, both men had a romantic, theatrical streak, and both were eager for a breakthrough deal that might secure their places in history. Gorbachev believed that a major agreement was tantalizingly close. He was willing to reduce Soviet nuclear weapons, and even eliminate them altogether, if only the Americans would give up on the unproven, expensive, and in any case unnecessary plan for SDI. In January 1986, Gorbachev proposed that the two superpowers eliminate all nuclear weapons by the year 2000. Reagan was intrigued, but refused to accept the quid pro quo of giving up SDI. In October 1986, at a summit meeting between the two leaders in Reykjavik, Iceland, Gorbachev tried again. He made dramatic proposals, offering to halve Soviet long-range strategic missiles and eliminate intermediate-range missiles in Europe. Reagan was amazed by these concessions, and casually introduced the idea of eliminating all nuclear weapons over a ten-year period. Gorbachev accepted. But the whole deal still depended on US agreement to the Soviet demand that SDI be restricted to the laboratory, as the ABM Treaty required. Reagan held fast, refusing to restrict development of SDI. Once again, the leaders failed to reach what would have been a stunning, unprecedented agreement.

This was a serious disappointment for both leaders. Gorbachev had to face a disgruntled public that had expected swift changes in policy. Reagan returned to Washington to face a scandal about his administration's policy of trading arms to Iran in return for US hostages held in Lebanon. It took another year to pick up the pieces after Reykjavik. But Gorbachev was as determined as ever to win some agreement on nuclear arms: perestroika required it. Yeltsin's criticisms came in October 1987, and Ligachev had already begun jockeying for a conservative reaction against Gorbachev. Something had to be accomplished. In December 1987, Gorbachev traveled to Washington to sign an agreement eliminating Soviet SS-20 missiles and US Pershing and cruise missiles—the short- and intermediate-range missiles that had provoked so much protest and anxiety in Europe. He had quietly given up his insistence on linking the agreement to restrictions on SDI, and the deal outlined the destruction of 1,800 Soviet missiles in exchange for only 846 US weapons. Still, the 1987 Intermediate-Range Nuclear Forces (INF) Treaty marked the first time since the start of the nuclear age that the superpowers had agreed not simply to limit production of weapons but to begin destroying them.[17]

During 1988, just as Gorbachev's reforms at home had reached a fever pitch, the general secretary took two additional steps of enormous importance in international affairs. In April 1988, he agreed to begin withdrawing Soviet troops from Afghanistan, and in December 1988, he went to the United Nations to deliver an address to the General Assembly. The last Soviet leader to address the UN was Nikita Khrushchev, in 1960; he demonstrated his contempt for the world body by haranguing the delegates and banging his shoe on the podium. Gorbachev, far more sophisticated than his earthy Ukrainian predecessor, received a warm welcome upon his arrival in the United States, meeting with Ronald Reagan and the president-elect, George Bush. Speaking to the UN, Gorbachev reviewed the progress his own country had made in embracing human rights and the rule of law and easing emigration rules. In language unprecedented for a Soviet leader, he declared that the time had come for great powers to free themselves from ideological struggle and to advance "the common interests of the whole of humankind." All states, especially the strongest, should "renounce the use of force in the international arena." In words that reverberated across Europe, he told his audience that "freedom of choice is a universal principle. It knows no exceptions." In that spirit, he announced that the USSR would reduce its standing army by half a million men, cut its conventional weapons, and—most surprising—reduce the numbers of Soviet troops in East Germany, Czechoslovakia, and Hungary.[18]

Gorbachev's UN address was probably the most important ever delivered to that body. He hoped that the speech would become "the exact opposite of Winston Churchill's famous Fulton speech"—when the British leader spoke of an Iron Curtain dividing Europe.[19] Certainly, after December 1988, there could be no going back to the "old" Cold War. Gorbachev had transformed the political structure of his country, eased censorship, significantly improved relations with the United States, ended the war in Afghanistan, and at the close of 1988, virtually declared unilateral Soviet withdrawal from the Cold War. It now remained for the Eastern Europeans to put Gorbachev's words to the test.

BREAKING THE SHACKLES IN
HUNGARY AND POLAND

During the year 1989, the institutional structures of Communist rule in Eastern Europe collapsed. Their demise was unforeseen, and for a time appeared almost miraculous. With the benefit of hindsight, it has become possible to examine more carefully the revolutionary process of that remarkable year. Certainly, the role of Gorbachev was decisive. Soviet power held Communist rule in place in Eastern Europe for forty-five years; when the power of coercion was removed, Eastern Europeans rushed to seize hold of their political destinies. Yet the Soviet leader did not want revolution. Gorbachev, for all his courage and reformist zeal, remained a man of the Soviet era, a believer in the power of socialism to improve the welfare of mankind. He never understood how completely Communism had been discredited in Eastern Europe. He hoped that perestroika might spark internal reform in the neighboring Communist states, and that perhaps a number of like-minded leaders, second Gorbachevs, would come forward to take up the cause of socialist renewal. This astonishing naïveté marks the later Gorbachev years. For rather than promote reform, his own policies gave renewed life to long-standing opposition in Eastern Europe to Soviet-backed regimes. The events of 1989 must be seen as the final breakthrough, after four decades of struggle, of a citizens' movement with a history that predated Gorbachev and in fact reached back to the 1940s. Gorbachev did not give Eastern Europeans their freedom in 1989. They took it.

Hungary offers a good example of the way in which the revolutions of 1989 emerged from the interconnected and reinforcing dynamic of Soviet perestroika and internal political transformation. Since 1956, Janos Kadar had ruled Hungary with a firm hand. His regime combined stern political repression and Communist control with a surprisingly liberal economy. Kadar's New Economic Mechanism, started in 1968, presaged perestroika by two decades. It allowed for autonomous control of collective farms, the legalization of private production, access to world markets—in short, a mixed economy. In 1982, Hungary joined the International Monetary Fund and the World Bank. Hungary's economic progress made it easier to maintain political control. When the economy began to falter in the mid-1980s, not least as a result of the economic troubles in the USSR, on which Hungary relied for raw materials, Kadar's claim to legitimacy was put in jeopardy. Some members of the Communist leadership argued that economic reforms would have to continue if the country was to be kept happy and politically docile. In June

1985, the regime allowed contested elections to be held, and though the candidates were mostly nominees of the Communist apparatus, a number of prominent independents were elected to the parliament. Hungarian Communist leaders began an internal debate about the need to accept further political reforms as a means of boosting the economy. The leading voice for reform within the party was Imre Pozsgay, a former culture minister, who in late 1986 launched an appeal for market reforms and political overhaul. The turmoil of the Communist leaders prompted further demands from Hungary's small but growing dissident movement, and in 1987 the leading underground journal published a call for a pluralist society and withdrawal from the Warsaw Pact. In May 1988, the Hungarian Politburo ousted Kadar and replaced him with Karoly Grosz, a cautious reformer who eased censorship and allowed the formation of independent trade unions and political organizations outside Communist control.

Naturally, the signals from Moscow were vital to this process of reform. Hungarian leaders watched Gorbachev's June 1988 party conference very closely, and when his proposals on political reform and constitutional changes were adopted, the Hungarians assumed that there would be no repeat of 1956. Indeed, the shadow of 1956 hung over the country in this final stage of Communist rule. The reformers within the party wished to identify with Imre Nagy, the last Communist leader that had embraced a policy of reform and independence for Hungary. They therefore undertook a historical inquiry into the events of 1956, and released a report that rehabilitated Nagy and depicted the 1956 revolution as a heroic challenge to a decrepit political order. On 16 June 1989, a massive state funeral was held in Budapest during which Nagy's remains were reburied. Two hundred thousand Hungarians turned out in the streets. The event marked Hungary's declaration of independence from the Soviet bloc, and was followed by concrete manifestations of this new spirit: in the summer of 1989, the regime entered into dialogue with opposition groups and laid the groundwork for multiparty elections that would take place in the spring of 1990 (and lead to the end of Communist rule). In October 1989, a month before the fall of the Berlin Wall, the Communist party renamed itself the Socialist Party and the Hungarian People's Republic was renamed the Republic of Hungary—the final death knell for Communism in Hungary.[20]

Still more remarkable than Hungary's quiet dismantling of the one-party state were the events in Poland in the late 1980s. General Jaruzelski, since imposing martial law in 1981, had tried to follow a course not unlike Kadar's in Hungary: repression, followed by a gradual thaw and economic liberalism. Jaruzelski purged the media and press, banned Solidarity, imprisoned activists, and placed the trade union leaders on trial. Lech Walesa himself was in-carcerated for a year. Those Solidarity activists not in prison went under-ground, where they continued to publish newspapers and journals and kept alive a vibrant dissident culture. Significant police repression, and a general desire to resolve the crisis atmosphere of the 1980–81 period, compelled many Poles to head back to work and to accept the Jaruzelski regime. The general tried to exploit this desire for normalcy by introducing gradual reforms. In July 1983, he announced the end of martial law and eased censorship restric-tions. The state sponsored new trade unions, which, despite Solidarity's ap-peals, attracted millions of workers. Solidarity took comfort from the June 1983 visit to Poland of Pope John Paul II, and noted the pontiff's references to human and civil rights. In October 1983, Lech Walesa won the Nobel Peace Prize. But the euphoria of 1980 was gone. Instead, Jaruzelski sought to win le-gitimacy by introducing political reforms, allowing contested elections to the parliament, and granting broad freedoms to writers and journalists. In 1986, Poland joined the IMF, and in September of that year, Jaruzelski issued an amnesty to all those interned under martial law.

He did not, however, solve Poland's economic problems—its huge debt soared out of control, inflation rendered the currency worthless, and Polish exports, over a third of which were sent to the Soviet Union, slumped. The government announced a rise in the prices of basic goods, many of which were already in short supply, and just as in 1980, this triggered massive social protest. In April, and again in August, nationwide strikes broke out. These were not organized by Solidarity but in many cases were wildcat strikes de-clared by younger activists who wanted a trial of strength with the govern-ment. Jaruzelski, realizing that his efforts had done little to legitimize his own regime, announced in August 1988 that he would enter into negotiations with Solidarity representatives to discuss political reform.

In February 1989, the government convened a conference of Solidarity activists, church leaders, intellectuals, and political figures to discuss a grand political compromise. Solidarity was to be legalized. In return, Solidarity would participate in a nationwide election to two legislative bodies: the Sejm, or lower house, and a Senate. The catch: 65 percent of the seats in the Sejm were to be reserved for government representatives; only 35 percent of the seats were to be openly contested. However, all one hundred seats in the Sen-ate would be freely contested. This arrangement mirrored the compromise that Gorbachev had engineered for his Congress of People's Deputies. It de-manded that Solidarity agree to lend its moral authority to an electoral pro-cess that was designed to allow the Communists to remain in power and that would insure Jaruzelski's election as president. Walesa lamented that the elections were "the terrible, terrible price we have to pay to get our union back."[21] But the results of the election, held in June 1989, humiliated Jaruzelski and the Communists. Solidarity candidates won all of the 161 seats they were allowed to contest in the Sejm, and all but one of the hundred Senate seats. Although, technically, party members still controlled two-thirds of the Sejm, and duly elected Jaruzelski president in July, the vote was a massive rejection of the Communists. Jaruzelski's gamble, his search for some kind of transitional arrangement, had failed. Given the rejection at the polls, Jaruzelski could not possibly impose a Communist prime minister on the Sejm and the nation. On 18 August 1989, he asked Tadeusz Mazowiecki, a devout Catholic journalist and lawyer and long-time Solidarity supporter, to form a government. On 24 August, he became the first non-Communist premier in Eastern Europe for over forty years.

BREACHING THE WALL

The elections in the Soviet Union, Hungary, and Poland marked the 1988–89 period as one of stunning political transformation in Europe. Yet few observers believed that the Communist bloc was in danger of collapse. Perestroika and its Polish and Hungarian variants were seen as adaptations, the necessary compromises made by old and tired regimes trying to survive. No one spoke of revolution. Hungarian dissidents writing in January 1987 believed that "the country's present political situation . . . will probably not change significantly for a long time to come."[22] Gorbachev himself, in July 1987, told German president Richard von Weizsäcker that German unity might occur in a hundred, or at best fifty, years.[23] The *New York Times* correspondent in Warsaw reported that the June 1989 election in Poland "poses no immediate threat to the Communist Party's monopoly on power."[24] And in China, where thousands of students had been staging prodemocracy demonstrations since April 1989, the world was given vivid evidence of the determination of some Communist regimes to fight back against the rising tide of political liberalization. On 4 June, the Chinese government sent tanks and infantry to crush the demonstrators in central Beijing, killing hundreds. As the momentum for change gathered force, the Communist governments in Czechoslovakia, East Germany, and Romania seemed to gird themselves for a confrontation. Indeed, Egon Krenz, a leading East German Politburo member, declared his government's support for the Chinese crackdown. Throughout the summer of 1989, there loomed over the demonstrations and protests the possibility of a violent confrontation between the reeling Communist regimes and their increasingly bold citizens.

This fact renders the East German protests of the fall of 1989 among the most courageous gestures in a year already filled with heroism.[25] Unlike Hungary and Poland, the German Democratic Republic had not witnessed any serious political challenge since 1953. The leaders of the Socialist Unity Party (SED) that dominated the country prided themselves on the stability of the regime, founded on the twin pillars of economic prosperity (by Eastern European standards) and strict repression. By the start of the 1980s, the GDR was the tenth largest economy in the world. Its citizens possessed more consumer goods than their Soviet bloc neighbors; by 1985, half of all East German households owned a car, and almost all possessed durable goods such as television sets, refrigerators, and washing machines. After the 1972 agreements normalizing relations with West Germany, East Germans enjoyed some contact with the West. Many millions of West Germans visited family and friends in East Germany, bringing with them valuable deutsche marks.[26]

Alongside these carrots, the regime deployed sticks, especially the notorious state security apparatus, the *Staatssicherheitsdienst,* or Stasi. By 1989, the Stasi employed over 100,000 full-time employees, one for every 165 people in the GDR. In addition, there were hundreds of thousands of *inoffizielle Mitarbeiter*—unofficial colleagues—who collaborated with the regime by reporting on neighbors, friends, and in some cases spouses. The Stasi monitored all aspects of life in the GDR, from postal and telephone communications to education, the professions, the churches, the writers. In this environment, dissidence was easily unmasked and crushed. Over this power structure ruled the seventy-seven-year-old Erich Honecker, GDR leader since 1971. Honecker had been a Communist since the age of ten. He was a veteran of Nazi prisons and a member of the East German Politburo since 1950. It was Honecker himself who had overseen the construction of the Berlin Wall in 1961. He was not a likely candidate for the role of East Germany's Gorbachev.[27]

In 1989, however, the instruments of coercion were blunted by Soviet perestroika and the political liberalization in Poland and Hungary. In May 1989, Hungary struck perhaps the most important symbolic blow by removing its barbed wire border with Austria, thus tearing a hole in the Iron Curtain. Though the Hungarians maintained travel restrictions and border controls, thousands of East Germans in the early summer traveled to Hungary to try their luck at crossing into the West. Some managed to do so by walking through unguarded forests and fields; others simply went to the West German embassy in Budapest to seek visas. What motivated these East Germans to try to leave the country? The Stasi itself knew all too well. A report of 9 September described the emigrants as dispirited by the lack of consumer goods, inadequate services, poor medical care, harsh working conditions, and oppressive bureaucracy. East Germans wanted out of Honecker's GDR.[28]

On 10 September, the Hungarian government, reluctant to act as jailer for the GDR, announced that it would cease to patrol its border with Austria altogether; GDR citizens were free to cross. The alarmed East German leadership called on the Czech government to plug the hole in the Iron Curtain by stopping East Germans from traveling into Hungary from Czechoslovakia. This only trapped thousands of would-be emigrants in Prague, where they stormed the West German embassy, seeking entrance visas. Camping out in filthy conditions on the embassy grounds, the refugees were a painful embarrassment for the GDR regime. Its citizens seemed willing to endure anything for a chance to flee to the West. Honecker responded in the way he knew best: on 3 October, he suspended travel to Czechoslovakia. East Germans could not even visit "fraternal socialist" countries. Never had the prisonlike quality of the GDR been more evident.

Just as the refugee crisis began to gather momentum, a fledgling East German opposition emerged. On 9 September, a group called Neues Forum—New Forum—announced its creation, and in a manifesto signed by thirty intellectuals, doctors, physicists, and clergymen, proposed to open a dialogue on political reform. The tone was cautious. The New Forum stated its desire to maintain those aspects of socialism that enhanced fairness and equality while correcting the abuses of the system. In Honecker's Germany, even these notions were treasonous. Yet they spurred a sudden rush of opposition movements. Three days later, another group announced the formation of a new Social Democratic Party and called for pluralism, free trade unions, and a market economy. Bolder still were the claims of another opposition group, Democracy Now, which spoke of the "political, economic, and ecological signs of the crisis of state socialism."[29]

These political manifestos appeared amidst a growing protest movement in the streets of Dresden, Berlin, and especially Leipzig. The Nikolaikirche in Leipzig, long a haven for weekly prayer vigils and peace activists who had won the support of some of the Protestant clergy, became the focal point of ever larger demonstrations. On 4 September, a small band of protesters gathered at the church, holding banners that called for freedom and open borders. They were met by Stasi agents who broke up the rally. But the usual tactics were losing their effect. On 18 September, another, larger gathering at the church formed, this time staging a candlelight vigil. Then on 25 September, 5,000 people converged on the church, this time shouting a new slogan, "We're staying here," suggesting that East Germans now aimed to change their country, not flee it. Significantly, cries of "Gorbi, Gorbi" could also be heard. A sign of the times: revolutionaries drawing inspiration from a Soviet leader! The next week, on 2 October, the pattern repeated, though the crowds were larger—now 20,000—and the Stasi agents less confident.

There now intervened one of those astonishing historical coincidences that often define great turning points. On 7 October, the GDR celebrated its fortieth anniversary. Naturally, to mark this triumphant date for the socialist world, the leader of the Soviet Union would be the guest of honor. And so on 6 October, Mikhail Gorbachev arrived in Berlin. Gorbachev had met Honecker on numerous occasions since 1985, and he had periodically urged the GDR leader to adopt a reform program. "It was as if I had been speaking to a brick wall," he later observed. Indeed, Gorbachev was anxious about his visit to Berlin in October, knowing full well that his presence there might cause some embarrassment to Honecker. But no one was prepared for what transpired. After giving a speech that lauded his own policy of perestroika, Gorbachev joined Honecker and other Eastern bloc leaders on a reviewing stand to observe an official mass parade in honor of the anniversary. It was a torchlight procession down Unter den Linden, the central avenue that ran up to the Brandenburg Gate and the wall. Gorbachev described the scene: "The spectacle was impressive, I must say. Orchestras playing, drums banging, searchlights, torches gleaming, and most of all—tens of thousands of young faces. Participants in the march, I was told, had been hand-picked in advance." This fact made it all the more stunning when, from out of this sea of party youth, came the shouts of "Perestroika! Gorbachev! Help us!" The Polish prime minister, Mieczyslaw Rakowski, standing next to Gorbachev on the stand, seethed. "These are party activists!" he sputtered. "This is the end."[30]

Not quite. Once Gorbachev was safely out of the country, the police struck back with great ferocity on 8 October. In East Berlin, Dresden, and Leipzig—where demonstrators were still massing with chants of "Gorbi!"—the police deployed nightsticks and water cannons and dragged thousands off to jail. Protesters received the usual punishment: beatings, interrogations, forced confessions. It didn't work. The next night, 9 October, the prayer vigil outside Nikolaikirche swelled to 70,000 protesters. The regime would have to use overwhelming force to turn back the tide. Honecker tried to issue an order to the Stasi to crush the protests, but his Politburo rebelled. Egon Krenz, the Politburo member with responsibility for internal security, countermanded the order. Instead, Krenz flew to Leipzig and met with city officials and local party leaders to insure that the protests remained peaceful.[31] Krenz now presented himself as a moderate figure who could replace Honecker and save the regime. On 18 October, the Politburo duly ousted Honecker and installed Krenz. The new leader, at fifty-two the youngest member of the East German Politburo, immediately spoke of the need to open "dialogue with the citizens." As Honecker's right-hand man, however, he had no credibility with the public.[32]

The East German regime, its leadership in disarray and its Soviet patron openly urging democratization, swiftly crumbled. Gorbachev, speaking in Helsinki, Finland, on 25 October, stated openly that the Soviet Union had no moral or political right to interfere in the affairs of its neighbors, and his spokesman told reporters, "I think the Brezhnev doctrine is dead."[33] These statements provoked an enormous outpouring of relief among East Germans, whose memories of Beijing were still fresh. Now the citizens swarmed into the streets in massive marches: in Leipzig, 100,000 people gathered on 16 October; the numbers rose to 225,000 on 23 October and 350,000 on 30 October. In East Berlin on 4 November, half a million people flooded the streets, bearing banners, shouting slogans: "Gorbi!"—"The Wall Must Go!"—"*Deutschland, Vaterland!*"

Krenz tried to create support for his new government through piecemeal concessions: he called off the police, allowed the marches to continue, opened up the press and television, purged the hard-liners from the Politburo, and eased travel regulations for those wishing to go abroad. The new rules stipulated that any GDR citizen with a passport could apply for travel visas to any country. The government envisioned an orderly process of applications and the usual bureaucratic review. But on the evening of 9 November, the government spokesman and East Berlin SED chief Günter Schabowski announced haphazardly to a press conference that a new law would grant free travel to those who wished to go to West Germany. Poorly informed about the details, he suggested that visas would be available at the border. When would the new rules go into effect? asked the puzzled journalists. Searching nervously through his papers, Schabowski stalled, then said, "Immediately." By 11 P.M. that night, thousands of East Berliners rushed to the checkpoints along the Berlin Wall, demanding to be let through. Stunned border guards, taken completely by surprise, tried to hold back the crowds. When told about the new laws, they relented and opened the gates. The Berlin Wall, once the most fearsome and heavily guarded border in the world, became nothing more than a mass of spray-painted concrete. Within hours, Berliners from both sides of the city attacked it with hammers and chisels. The next day, the heavy bulldozers arrived and began dismantling the most enduring symbol of the Cold War.[34]

UNIFICATION

Events now began to move with startling rapidity. In Prague, enormous street demonstrations in mid-November undermined the stability of the hard-line regime of Gustav Husak. Vaclav Havel, the longtime dissident and principal agent behind Charter 77, formed an opposition group called Civic Forum, and called for a general strike on 27 November. That strike shut the country down, revealing the total unity not only between workers and intellectuals but between Czechs and Slovaks in opposition to Husak. Faced with the complete breakdown of Communist Party control, Husak resigned on 10 December. On 29 December, Havel was elected president of the country by the Federal Assembly—a body made up of erstwhile Communists.[35]

Next to the Velvet Revolution in Czechoslovakia, revolutionary events in Romania were far more sinister and bloody. There, the deranged dictator, Nicolae Ceaușescu, by now the lone remaining hard-liner in power in Eastern Europe, prepared for a confrontation with his people. On 17 December, Ceaușescu ordered his secret police to fire upon demonstrators in the provincial city of Timisoara, which they did. But the killing there only stimulated greater opposition, which now surfaced in Bucharest itself. On 21 December, Ceaușescu staged a huge rally in the main plaza in front of his gargantuan government palace. Expecting the usually obedient crowd to applaud his denunciations of foreign infiltrators, Fascists, and conspirators, Ceaușescu instead encountered a restless, angry crowd that heckled the leader, despite the presence of police. Shocked, Ceaușescu and his wife, Elena, attempted to flee the capital, but were caught and on 25 December, after a summary trial, shot to death. Rather than the usual coalition of dissidents and reformers acceding to power, there now emerged a shadowy band of former Communist officials calling themselves the National Salvation Front, who took power and reasserted state control. Romania didn't get its revolution, only a coup d'état, an ill omen for the next decade of political transition to democracy.

The wave of revolutionary change struck Bulgaria as well, where Todor Zhivkov had dominated political life since 1954. Already facing internal unrest in the wake of Gorbachev's reforms, Zhivkov's regime could not withstand the collapse of the GDR. The day after the fall of the Berlin Wall, on 10 November 1989, Zhivkov was ousted by his colleagues on the Politburo and placed under arrest. His successors moved quickly to show their support for the reform movement, and in early 1990, the Bulgarian Communist Party changed its name to the Socialist Party and allowed the formation of opposition groups. In June 1990, Bulgaria held free national elections for a new parliamentary assembly. Even Albania, which under the leadership of a neurotic, xenophobic Communist regime had virtually cut itself off from the outside world, now felt the impact of events in Germany and the region. In December 1990, the government of Ramiz Alia allowed for the formation of independent political parties. Though slower than elsewhere in Eastern Europe, reforms to the political structure allowed for national elections in March 1992, when Sali Berisha became the first democratically elected president of Albania since 1924.

These events, though startling, were only the backdrop to the drama in Germany, which occupied center stage in Europe from November 1989 to October 1990. In a remarkably short time, the two German states agreed to merge, on terms almost entirely dictated by the West. The fall of the wall had been a symbolic breakthrough, but German unification in 1990 marked the end of the Cold War and its principal legacy, the division of Europe into two competing blocs.

German unification was peaceful, and it was swift. Yet this happy outcome was by no means inevitable. There were powerful forces arrayed against it. When the East German regime opened the wall on 9 November, it believed it could win legitimacy through a process of reform and democratization. The Krenz government had no intention of surrendering itself to the West. In this, it had the support of the East German dissident groups that also wished to see East Germany changed from within rather than merged with the capitalist West. Nor did Gorbachev want to see his East German client swallowed by the Federal Republic. Rather, he hoped the East Germans would follow his own brand of perestroika and show that socialism still had a place in Europe. Other Europeans expressed some dismay at the prospect of a unified Germany: France's president, François Mitterrand, worried that a unified Germany might not support continued integration in Europe, while Prime Minister Margaret Thatcher was quite firmly opposed to unification, which she thought would enhance German power and disrupt NATO. How is it that despite these obstacles, unification came so quickly?

The answer lies in the actions taken by German chancellor Helmut Kohl and by US president George Bush. These men and their advisers seized upon the historic opportunity offered by the collapse of the wall to press for a swift unification of the two Germanys. In this, they had a powerful ally: the German people, East and West, who came to support Kohl's vision of unification. They also profited from the realism and sense of moderation shown by Mikhail Gorbachev. The Soviet leader did not like the idea of German unification, but once he saw that it would come anyway, he decided to stand aside with dignity and to exchange his assent for important concessions to Soviet interests.

Although brief, the process of uniting the two Germanys was immensely complex, involving dozens of players, hundreds of ministerial meetings, thousands of hours of negotiations.[36] For the sake of simplicity, we can arrange the process into four stages. In the first stage (November–December 1989), Helmut Kohl took the initiative at a time of immense confusion and fluidity and set the agenda for unification. In the second stage (December 1989–February 1990), Kohl, backed strongly by George Bush, persuaded Gorbachev to support unification and also turned back various East German and Soviet rival ideas for a confederal and neutral Germany. In the third stage, the East German people gave Kohl's policy an enormous boost: in March 1990, in their first free elections, they overwhelmingly supported candidates that backed unification with the FRG. That led to the final stage, running from May to September 1990, in which the four occupying powers—USSR, USA, Britain, and France—joined with West German and East German negotiators to hammer out the precise terms for unification. The final treaty of unification was signed on 12 September 1990, and the two Germanys were formally united on 3 October 1990.

None of this would have happened without Helmut Kohl. In 1989, he had been German chancellor for seven years, yet he was unloved. His Christian Democratic government came to power in October 1982 when the Bundestag ejected Helmut Schmidt in a vote of no confidence. Kohl had been state president of the Rhineland Palatinate, in southern Germany, and had run an unsuccessful campaign for the chancellorship in 1976. He was a plodding speaker, had little charisma, and after the sly, elegant Schmidt, Kohl, with his thick Bavarian accent, his country manner, and his enormous girth, seemed somewhat out of place in the chancellor's office. Kohl, however, had deep convictions. As a Catholic Rhinelander he had long admired Konrad Adenauer, and for years had defended Adenauer's stance toward the East. For Kohl as for Adenauer, the GDR was illegitimate. Unity, should it come, must be on terms that protected West Germany's democratic institutions and market economy. Like many in the CDU, he was uncomfortable with Brandt's *Ostpolitik,* which had placed coexistence and stability above the long-term goal of unification.

Kohl therefore knew where he stood as the events of 1989 unfolded. Indeed, on the very day before the fall of the wall, as the crowds in East Berlin and Leipzig swelled into mass demonstrations, Kohl delivered an address that made clear his support for the protesters and their demands for an end to the GDR. "The division of our Fatherland is unnatural," he said. "Walls and barbed wire cannot last for long." Bidding farewell to *Ostpolitik,* he said "We have less reason than ever for resignation or permanent acceptance of the two German states." What was needed now was for the SED to surrender its monopoly of power and allow free elections, which, Kohl had no doubt, would promptly lead to a united Germany.[37] This speech made clear that Kohl would not help stabilize the GDR until Krenz allowed free elections. Mikhail Gorbachev denounced these words as "political extremism" and in a letter to the Western leaders argued that Kohl threatened to destabilize the European order. Not for the last time, Kohl and US president George Bush defied Gorbachev. Though Bush kept a low profile publicly—he refused to "dance on the wall," as he put it—he privately reassured Kohl that the United States trusted the West Germans to handle the issue of unification while not endangering the Western alliance or harming the institutions of the European community.

American support allowed Kohl to press ahead with his plan for a unified Germany. On 28 November, Chancellor Kohl announced a ten-point plan for German unification. He caught the public and the East Germans by surprise. Less than three weeks after the fall of the wall, few were openly prepared to advocate unification. The plan was an artful attempt to present a gradual program for unification, when in fact it implied the rapid eradication of the GDR and its absorption by West Germany. Kohl called for free elections in the GDR, after which the two Germanys could develop joint political structures and the FRG would provide economic aid to the GDR. Kohl made clear that "national unity remains the political goal of the federal government." He didn't have to spell out that this implied the end of the GDR. Although Kohl did not address the difficult questions of Germany's future alliance status—would East Germany be swallowed up by NATO?—privately he reassured President Bush that this was precisely what he had in mind.[38] Within a week, at the summit of NATO member states in Brussels on 4 December, President Bush demonstrated his support for German unification based upon the self-determination of all the German people and—a critical point—continued German membership in NATO and the European Community. Kohl and Bush had now jumped aboard the fast train toward unification.

The second stage of the process now began. Over the next eight weeks or so, Bush and Kohl had to persuade Mikhail Gorbachev that he had nothing to fear from German unification, and in any case could not stop it. Gorbachev was worried. The loss of the GDR, alongside the erosion of Communist control in Eastern Europe, might embolden conservatives in the USSR to unseat him. He reportedly told the French president François Mitterrand that if Germany was united, "a Soviet marshal will be sitting in my chair."[39] Gorbachev began to work in coordination with the new East German leadership. Egon Krenz, much despised for his close ties to Honecker, resigned on 6 December and was replaced by the more credible Hans Modrow, a reform-minded Communist party leader from Dresden. With Modrow, Gorbachev countered the West's proposals with an idea for a "confederal" Germany—one that was united in some economic respects but maintained a separate East German identity. Indeed, he insisted in a speech to the Central Committee that "no harm will come to the GDR."

This was wishful thinking. Gorbachev had no clear or viable alternative to unification, and certainly anything he and Modrow proposed would have to be forced on an unwilling German population. True, the East German dissident community that had unseated Honecker supported the confederal model. Their numbers included many of the GDR's most prominent intellectuals, who wished to see some sort of third way between capitalism and state-imposed Communism.[40] But the people in East Germany wanted more. Throughout November and December, hundreds of thousands of East Germans continued to leave the GDR. By January, 2,000 East Germans a day were leaving the country. On 19 December, when Kohl went to Dresden to meet with Modrow, hundreds of thousands of ecstatic East Germans came to hear him deliver a public address. Banners and cheers calling for prompt German unity made clear that the neutralist model favored by the East German leadership and by Gorbachev would never be accepted by the people.

Further, Gorbachev's hope for a viable East Germany led by a reform-minded government was little more than illusion. The GDR was falling to pieces. The economy was in a free fall, in part due to the massive exodus still under way. East Germany had a huge foreign debt, and no banks would lend to the collapsing government. The GDR needed immediate economic aid from Kohl if it was going to survive. This gave Kohl enormous leverage to dictate the pace of unification. The East Germans helped him too. On 15 January, in a defiant act against the legitimacy of the GDR, a huge crowd stormed the headquarters of the Stasi and ransacked the building. Meanwhile Modrow's government was losing all credibility and was forced to restructure itself as a "government of national responsibility" by bringing dissident groups into a power-sharing cabinet. The single-party SED regime was gone forever. Modrow himself told Gorbachev on 30 January that "it has become impossible to preserve the republic."[41]

The impending collapse of the GDR called for a prompt solution to the crisis. US secretary of state James Baker met with his Soviet counterpart, Eduard Shevardnadze, in Moscow in early February. He made it clear that the United States opposed Modrow's idea for a neutral Germany. Germany would stay in NATO. But Baker said the United States wanted Soviet help to frame the terms of unification. Baker proposed the two-plus-four framework: a negotiation between the four occupying powers and the two Germanys. A few days later, on 10 February, Helmut Kohl met with Gorbachev and delivered the same message. But he sweetened the pill by stressing the economic advantages to the USSR of allowing German unification. Instead of being tied to a failing GDR, the Soviets would win access to and credits from the robust West German state. Gorbachev was resigned. He could see that unification was a fait accompli. He might as well try to win something in return for his cooperation. He accepted the two-plus-four framework. Talks for unifying Germany would begin after the East German elections, scheduled for 18 March.

All eyes now turned to the elections. Though the people were voting for a new government, in fact the election was a referendum on unification. A vote for the newly renamed Communists (Party of Democratic Socialism, or PDS) or for the Social Democrats would be a vote for maintaining an East German identity separate from the West. A vote for the East German Christian Democratic Party would signal support for unification. The stakes were thus very high. Conventional wisdom held that the left would do well. The PDS still controlled the media and had a mass membership. The Social Democrats were heavily supported by their Western counterparts, and Willy Brandt came to East Germany to campaign for them. They were well organized and believed that their opposition to a swift, complete absorption by the West would lead them to victory at the polls. The small civic groups that had been so important in October 1989 merged into Bundnis 90 and adopted a neutralist position, hoping to stave off a capitalist takeover of the GDR. The East German Christian Democrats, though starting slowly and without any organization, had an ace in the hole: Helmut Kohl. They campaigned on simple slogans like "Freedom and Unity" and "Prosperity for All." The CDU turned the election into a popularity contest between the old Communist regime and Kohl's West Germany. Kohl himself gave six speeches at huge rallies. He made clear what unification would mean for East Germans: "freedom, affluence, social security, and a peaceful and secure future."[42] No wonder the leftist parties warned against "Kohlonization."

The results were a triumph for the CDU, for Kohl, and for unification. With a 93 percent turnout, the East German voters made clear their wishes: 48 percent supported the CDU and its allies; 22 percent supported the Social Democrats. The former SED won but 16 percent, and the civic movement barely 3 percent. The head of the East German CDU, Lothar de Maizière, became prime minister of the first and only democratically elected East German government. He invited the Social Democrats to share power in a coalition, which they did. But the path to unity was now clear.[43] Almost immediately the two German governments began negotiations for an economic union of their two states. By giving the East Germans the deutsche mark—the symbol of

West Germany's prosperity and stability—Kohl was rewarding them for their support of his plan for unity. On 2 May, the two governments laid out their plan, and it amounted to an extremely generous offer to the East Germans. Salaries, wages, scholarships, rents, leases, and pensions in East Germany would be converted to the deutsche mark at a one-to-one ratio. Savings accounts and other assets were to be given varying ratios, but on average, the GDR paid 1.5 East German marks for every deutsche mark it received in exchange—a huge windfall considering that the unofficial rate before the fall of the wall was about ten to one. The treaty on monetary union was signed on 18 May and went into effect on 1 July 1990: the two Germanys were now fused together with the powerful deutsche mark as an adhesive.[44]

Though economically united, Germany was not yet sovereign. Not until the four occupying powers gave their assent could Germany declare its unity and freedom. From May to July, the four powers hammered out the final details. It was not all smooth sailing. The French president demanded assurances from Helmut Kohl that a united Germany would not slacken its support for European integration. For France, the European Community was a crucial political bargain: the French acknowledged German economic predominance in Europe, and in return, the Germans deferred to French political leadership on European matters. Kohl assured Mitterrand that a united Germany would remain as committed as ever to the European project. In Britain, Prime Minister Thatcher's concerns focused less on the European Community, for which she had little respect, than on the simple issue of German power. Would a united Germany once again threaten European stability, as it had done twice before in the twentieth century? Evidently, her anxieties about a future German menace lay close to the surface. In a seminar she convened with various scholars of Germany and many of her cabinet members, the minutes of which were later leaked to the press, she expressed her concerns that certain "German characteristics" might soon reappear: "angst, aggressiveness, assertiveness, bullying, egotism, inferiority complex, and sentimentality." Mrs. Thatcher denounced recent "triumphalism in German thinking and attitudes," bemoaned the "strong pacifist, neutralist, anti-nuclear constituency in East Germany," and wondered if a united Germany might break apart NATO. Though Mrs. Thatcher was roundly criticized for lending her support to such hostile views, they were, after all, legitimate fears. How would this new German colossus affect the future of Europe? Could NATO and the European Community continue to anchor Germany in place?[45]

Mikhail Gorbachev had his own concerns. When the two-plus-four negotiations began in earnest in May, Gorbachev and his foreign minister, Shevardnadze, insisted that a united Germany remain neutral, outside of the

NATO alliance. To allow West Germany to swallow the GDR was one thing; but to surrender the former GDR to NATO was a humiliation for the Soviet Union. Kohl and Bush were adamant: Germany would stay in NATO. But they recognized that they had to help Gorbachev swallow this bitter pill. Two incentives were proposed: the Germans would offer economic credits of 5 billion deutsche marks to the Soviet Union, and NATO would alter its posture in Europe to reflect the new relationship with the USSR. In particular, NATO troops would stay out of the former GDR for a specified period of time; Soviet troops would have four years to withdraw; the size of the German army would be limited; and NATO would reduce its conventional and nuclear forces.

Gorbachev, desperate for foreign aid and fearful of a rift in US-Soviet relations, relented. After all, by the summer of 1990, Gorbachev had better relations with Bush and Kohl than he did with many members of his own government. He needed strong, reliable, honest partners in international affairs so that he could turn his attention to shoring up his domestic reform program. If Gorbachev had fought Bush and Kohl to the bitter end, he might have triggered an international crisis, giving his enemies at home more ammunition to use against him. In early July, Gorbachev faced serious criticisms during the Twenty-eighth Party Congress of the Communist Party of the Soviet Union. Though he beat them back and was reelected general secretary by a three-to-one margin of the party delegates, the congress showed that many party leaders were fearful and angry about the state of the country. Gorbachev clearly had much work to do to advance his reforms, and in this environment, he decided to settle the German question quickly.[46]

Gorbachev invited Kohl to come to Moscow, and then go for a visit to the Caucasus, Gorbachev's homeland. On 15 July, the two leaders met in Moscow. Within a matter of hours, much to Kohl's amazement, Gorbachev indicated his willingness to allow German membership in NATO and to terminate all Soviet rights in Germany, provided that the two countries could agree to a bilateral treaty regulating Soviet troop withdrawal and that Germany would limit its armed forces to 370,000 men. The next day, the leaders flew to Stavropol, and Gorbachev took Kohl on a tour of his hometown. They swapped stories, ate bread and salt together, and hiked in the nearby hills. Although the precise details still had to be ironed out, Gorbachev had brought the USSR into line with Western thinking on Germany. Germany would be united, sovereign, and part of NATO.[47]

With Soviet agreement secured, Kohl and the East German premier, Lothar de Maizière, now moved quickly to settle the remaining issues for the complete political absorption of the GDR into the Federal Republic. The treaty spelling out the mechanics of German unity was signed on 31 August and ratified by the parliaments of both Germanys. Just two weeks later, on 12 September, representatives of the four occupying powers met in Moscow to sign the treaty that would end their rights in Germany. On 3 October 1990, the GDR ceased to exist, and a united Germany became fully free and sovereign.

Germans had won the great prize that had eluded them since 1945: unity and sovereignty. East Germans now experienced freedom, something they had not enjoyed since Hitler came to power in 1933. The new Germany faced many problems. The cost of unification was immense, perhaps 1 trillion deutsche marks, saddling the German government with budget deficits and higher taxes for most of the 1990s. The government established a privatization agency, the Treuhandanstalt, to sell off the massive state monopolies of the GDR. But in the process it closed down thousands of inefficient businesses and firms, throwing millions of East Germans into unemployment. The GDR had to be completely rebuilt with Western technology; the workforce had to be retrained; the social welfare packages that cost so much now had to be extended to 16 million new citizens. And of course, these two foreign cultures, one shaped by forty years of extraordinary prosperity, the other by forty years of repression, had to rediscover each other. They were like twins separated at birth and reunited as adults: they looked alike, spoke the same language, and sensed an intuitive bond, but they still had to learn to live together. Unlike unification, that would take time.

THE END OF THE SOVIET UNION

Just as Germany was overcoming its divisions, the Soviet Union was splitting apart. The two events were, of course, closely related, for as the USSR gave up control of its satellites in Eastern Europe, so too did it face challenges from the constituent republics that had been fused into the Soviet empire in the 1920s and kept there by terror and repression. Gorbachev's internal democratization and his foreign policy toward Eastern Europe allowed the nationalities of the USSR to express a desire for a new form of union, one that delegated far more control to the republics. In some cases, indeed, the republics wished to secede altogether.

This was true in those areas most recently incorporated: the Baltic states, which had been grabbed by Stalin in 1940 as part of his pact with Hitler. In November 1988—a year before the fall of the Berlin Wall—the Estonian Supreme Soviet declared its right to veto laws passed in Moscow. In January 1989, Lithuanian nationalists protested against the presence of Soviet troops. In May and July, Lithuania and Latvia too declared their legal and political sovereignty within the union. And on 23 August 1989, a million Balts joined hands to create a human chain stretching from Tallinn to Riga to Vilnius: a powerful protest on the fiftieth anniversary of the Nazi-Soviet pact. In light of the rapid collapse of the Eastern European Communist regimes in November–December 1989, it now became possible for Soviet nationalities to declare independence as well: on 11 March 1990, Lithuania did so. This presented Gorbachev with an agonizing decision. He could allow the Germans and Poles to secede from the Eastern bloc, but if the Baltic states broke away, the Soviet Union itself, which he was striving to renew and reform, might soon disintegrate. He thus ordered tanks into Vilnius, Lithuania, but did not have the nerve to order naked repression. Gorbachev was anxious to avoid a bloody confrontation with the Soviet Union's many nationalist groups. He had already suffered a major blow to his prestige when, in Tbilisi in April 1989, Georgian demonstrators were attacked by Russian troops. Nineteen civilians, many of them women, were killed. So the Baltic states defied Gorbachev, and his power weakened.

Unable to handle the Baltic crisis, Gorbachev became more vulnerable in domestic politics. Using the tools of democratization granted by Gorbachev, the republics elected national assemblies that pressed their own claims to sovereignty, none more vigorously than the Russian Republic. In March 1990, Boris Yeltsin, who had made a name for himself as a populist Moscow party chief and then critic of the slow pace of Gorbachev's reforms, was elected to the Russian Congress of People's Deputies. He soon became chairman of the Russian Supreme Soviet. He declared Russia's sovereignty within the USSR in June 1990, which encouraged Belarus and Ukraine to follow suit in July. The Central Asian republics did so in September and October. These actions threw into question the extent of Gorbachev's power: if Gorbachev did not govern the republics, what purpose did he serve at all? Gorbachev, still president of the USSR and chief of the Communist Party, now proposed to create a new federal union, over which he would preside. And in order to counter the growing boldness of the republics, Gorbachev in December 1990 appointed a new cabinet, made up of hard-liners who were determined to maintain party control in the state and who strongly opposed Yeltsin's plans for breaking up the Soviet Union. It was a move Gorbachev would later regret. Gennadi Yanaev became vice president of the USSR, Boris Pugo became minister of internal affairs, Valentin Pavlov prime minister. All were opponents of reform. At the same moment, his liberal supporters deserted him, including Foreign Minister Eduard Shevardnadze. Gorbachev had turned to the right. This was made clear in January 1991, when Soviet troops attempted an armed suppression of the breakaway republics of Lithuania and Latvia. In Vilnius, fourteen civilians were killed; Gorbachev's credibility as a reformer lay in tatters.

And yet, perhaps Gorbachev had hoped to disarm the far right by bringing them into his embrace. For in April 1991, Gorbachev proceeded to engage in negotiations with the leaders of the Soviet republics to draw up a new union treaty that would grant significant powers to them. The draft was concluded on 23 July, and scheduled to be signed on 20 August. It looked as if Gorbachev had come to terms with Yeltsin, who himself was elected president of Russia on 12 June 1991. Certainly, the right wing saw Gorbachev's new union treaty as a betrayal. In a matter of months, Gorbachev had alienated both the left and the right. And as the economy worsened, as lines in the shops lengthened, as Communism as an ideology was pilloried across Europe, Gorbachev's standing in the Soviet Union dropped to an all-time low. On 4 August, he left Moscow, eagerly looking forward to a vacation at his dacha in the Black Sea village of Foros, in the Crimea.

At 5 P.M. on 18 August, his peaceful vacation was rudely interrupted by a delegation of government officials who arrived unexpectedly at his dacha. They included Oleg Baklanov, deputy chairman of the Defense Council; the party secretary, Oleg Shenin; deputy defense minister Gen. Valentin Varennikov; and even Gorbachev's chief of staff, Valery Boldin. Baklanov told Gorbachev that an emergency committee had been created in Moscow to take control of the government, and asked Gorbachev to sign a decree handing over authority to Vice President Yanaev. Baklanov said the committee planned to restore order in the country; Gorbachev could remain president if he sided with the plotters now and legitimized the coup. Gorbachev showed considerable courage, especially since it soon became clear that the dacha was surrounded by security forces controlled by the plotters. He refused to join their conspiracy and gave them a sharp dressing down. Gorbachev tried calling Moscow to find out what was going on, only to discover the lines had been cut. He did, however, have a radio, which allowed him and his wife to follow developments.

It soon became clear that almost all of Gorbachev's cabinet was involved. KGB chairman Kryuchkov and Interior Minister Pugo, along with Prime Minister Pavlov and Defense Minister Yazov, formed the leadership of the coup. They declared Yanaev acting president. But they were ill prepared. On 19 August, at a press conference held to announce the imposition of emergency rule, Yanaev's hands shook uncontrollably. Pavlov had turned to vodka for courage and was too drunk to attend. The media were not shut down, telephone lines remained open, and crowds began to gather at the Russian parliament building. There, a defiant Boris Yeltsin made a courageous stand against the plotters, called for the immediate release of Gorbachev, and clambered up on a tank to declare his contempt for the coup. During the next forty-eight hours, there was a stand-off at the parliament. Thousands of Muscovites rallied at the parliament building to show their support for Yeltsin. In these circumstances, the military lost its taste for confrontation and refused orders to storm the parliament building. At midday on 21 August, the plotters decided their coup had failed. Yeltsin sent a plane to retrieve Gorbachev from the Crimea; he returned to Moscow at midnight on 22 August.[48]

The coup failed, but Gorbachev had been undone nonetheless. The Soviet leader had looked weak and vulnerable; his rival, Yeltsin, robustly defended democracy and defied the plotters. The coup was the last gasp of the old Communist Party bosses trying to turn back the clock, to use force and state control to resist change. Since Gorbachev had appointed these men in the first place, he too bore much blame for the coup, even though he was its chief victim. The way was now open for Yeltsin to implement his more radical vision for Soviet reform. The day after the coup, he suspended the operations of the Communist Party in Russia. Gorbachev himself resigned as general secretary of the party. On 6 November, the Communist Party was banned altogether. After the coup, the republics, already sovereign within the union, now declared their complete independence. The Soviet Union effectively ceased to exist in late August. The only question was what would replace it. In a treaty of 1 October, twelve republics joined in an economic union. But there would be, thanks in large measure to Yeltsin, only the merest vestige of a political union, to be called the Commonwealth of Independent States. There would be no role for a Soviet-era president in this new confederation; Gorbachev would have to go. On 25 December 1991, the red flag came down from the Kremlin and was replaced by the Russian tricolor. The USSR ceased to exist.

In the states of the former Soviet Union, Mikhail Gorbachev today is widely reviled. He failed in his objectives to reform the Communist Party and to renew the Soviet Union. Instead, he allowed the dismantling of the Soviet sphere of influence in Europe, presided over the collapse of the Soviet economy, allowed the unification of Germany to proceed with almost no quid pro quo, and failed to create strong, stable political institutions to handle the political transition to democracy. Yet history is likely to be much kinder to Gorbachev. In a matter of six years he reshaped the destiny of his country and affected the lives of millions of Europeans, and indeed millions of Americans as well. Almost single-handedly, he ended the Cold War, withdrew the repressive hand of Soviet power from Eastern Europe, and granted his own people the tools to shape their political future. Not only did he liberate his own people, but he opened up the prospect of freedom for Eastern Europeans, who since the early 1930s had lived in the shadow of terror and war. That he did not intend to accomplish these objectives is beside the point. Things could have worked out much differently, and the option of using violence to crush the momentum of change was always there. Yet Gorbachev refrained. Here, he made common cause with the reformers and the moderates who have defined European politics for most of the postwar era. In allowing an organic process of political change to go forward while keeping chaos and war at bay, Gorbachev showed that even after the torments of the twentieth century, Russia belonged in the "common European home" after all.

CHAPTER FOURTEEN

THE BONES OF BOSNIA

·

THE GRIM STORY of Yugoslavia's demise in the 1990s presents the historian with many complexities. It is a narrative replete with half a dozen rival national traditions, intractable territorial disputes, profound religious and ethnic divides, and above all, grisly atrocities. There are innumerable villains, few heroes. This story also obliges us to confront an unwelcome paradox: Yugoslavia's self-destruction was contemporaneous with the stunningly successful revolutions of the 1989–91 period elsewhere in Eastern Europe. How can we square the presence of concentration camps, mass murder, ethnic cleansing, and petty tyrannical dictators with the sudden burst of humanity, reasonableness, and transparency that took hold of the rest of Europe in 1989–91? It is no easy task.

The approach taken here is to suggest, first, that the Yugoslav wars of the 1990s sprang from a unique set of circumstances, and certainly a uniquely evil cast of characters, that thankfully did not combine together elsewhere in Europe in the fluid moments of 1989–91. But second, some of the same characteristics that drove the crisis in Yugoslavia have existed and exist still in many places in Europe, and the story of Yugoslavia offers a cautionary tale. There is no reason to believe that, given the opportunity, forces of nationalism, totalitarianism, racism, xenophobia, religious chauvinism, and pure old-fashioned thuggery cannot strike elsewhere, with equally appalling results. The Yugoslav case was unique; it is Europe's task to keep it that way.

TITO'S COUNTRY

This beautiful, unforgiving land of the south Slavs first emerged as a political unit after the collapse of the Austro-Hungarian Empire in the wake of World War I. Established in 1918, the Kingdom of the Serbs, Croats, and Slovenes was a constitutional monarchy that grouped together Slavs and Muslims once under Habsburg rule with the independent kingdoms of Serbia and Montenegro. This was not a promising land from which to craft a nation-state. Within the new kingdom there were Serbs, Croats, and Slovenes, but also Germans, Magyars, Albanians, Romanians, Turks, Czechs, Slovaks, Ruthenes, Bulgars, and Greeks. About 47 percent of this diverse population adhered to Orthodox Christianity, about 40 percent to Roman Catholicism, and about 11 percent to Islam. At the time of its creation, this new kingdom had five currencies, four railway networks, four legal systems, three banking systems. The country was more developed in the north, especially Slovenia, which had long been under Habsburg rule, and undeveloped in the south, where the Ottoman Empire had ruled until the early twentieth century. Seventy-nine percent of the country depended upon agriculture for its livelihood in 1921; half the population was illiterate.[1]

In these divided circumstances, it proved hard for parliamentary democracy to take hold. Claims of unity and nationhood only fostered fear of Serbian hegemony among the country's many minorities, and so the new democratic political institutions were torn asunder by distrust and rivalry. The brief experiment was killed off in 1929, when King Alexander (of the Serbian Karadjordjevic dynasty) imposed a royal dictatorship on the country he now renamed the kingdom of Yugoslavia. Alexander, however, was assassinated in 1934 during a visit to France. (His murderer was under orders from the Croatian nationalist leader Ante Pavelic.) For the next seven years, the king's cousin Prince Paul acted as regent and head of state. In April 1941, the German invasion put an end to this period of Yugoslavia's existence.

There now opened up the darkest chapter in Yugoslavia's history: the foreign occupation and civil war during World War II. Since most of the nationalist leaders of the 1990s used the events of World War II to contextualize their actions and beliefs, we must treat this period in some detail. Many Serbs, including the regent, were in favor of the Western allies in the war, with whom they had fought in World War I. The country's second largest national group, the Croatians, disliked the Yugoslav state and its Serb monarchy and saw alliance with the Germans and Italians as the means to Croatian independence. Hitler's ideas of national and racial hierarchy aided in destroying the Yugoslav state. The Slovenes, in the north, were declared suitable for Germanization and so incorporated into the Reich. The Catholic Croats were given a much-enlarged independent state of Croatia, explicitly aligned with Germany and Italy; the Slav *Untermenschen* were to be consigned to history's ash heap. Serbia was placed under direct military occupation, Macedonia sliced off and given to Bulgaria, and Kosovo and portions of the Dalmatian coast assigned to Italy.

Hitler's anti-Slav mania freed the Croatian nationalists to dispense with the 2 million Serbs in their new puppet state as they wished. The result was genocide, carried out under the direction of the Croatian nationalist Ante Pavelic and his Ustase (Insurrectionary) Movement. Not popular before the war, Pavelic had been fomenting a radical nationalist and Fascist program in exile for many years; he now willingly served as a tool of the Nazis and governed with extreme brutality in his new domain. The Ustase was a militia, akin to the SS, devoted to Pavelic and his Fascist regime. The Serbs in the new Croatian state became immediate targets for conversion to Catholicism, deportation, or liquidation. The Croatian thugs destroyed villages, burned Serbs alive in churches, deported clergy to concentration camps, and wrought untold havoc in the territory they ruled. Perhaps half a million Serbs died at the hands of the Ustase regime; 100,000 were killed in the Croatian concentration camp at Jasenovac, some sixty miles from Zagreb. Even the Germans were shocked and pleaded for the Pavelic regime to restrain itself.

The Germans had good cause to fear Ustase atrocities: they fueled the resistance to the German and Italian occupation. But like everything else in Yugoslavia, this resistance was divided along political and ethnic lines. Many Serbs turned to the *cetnik,* or guerrilla, movement established by members of the Royal Serbian Army and now led by a Serb nationalist named Draza Mihailovic. At first, Mihailovic was the darling of the British, who approved of his anti-Communism almost as much as his anti-Axis views. Yet he was a poor leader, too cautious in fighting the Germans, too fearful of the Communist-inspired resistance. He was soon overshadowed by Josip Broz, the partisan leader and lifelong Communist, who adopted the nom de guerre Tito.

Tito was born in 1892, the son of a Croatian father and Slovene mother. He trained as a locksmith and from an early age showed an interest in politics, joining a metal workers' union. He fought in the First World War in the Austro-Hungarian army but was captured by the Russians and spent much of the war in a POW camp in the Ural Mountains. He escaped in early 1917 and found himself in Saint Petersburg at the time of the overthrow of the tsar. The Bolshevik revolutionaries thrilled him and he joined the Red Guards to fight on their behalf. When he returned to Yugoslavia in 1920, he immediately joined its tiny Communist Party. For the next twenty years he worked his way up the party hierarchy, spending time in jail for his party activities, solidifying his support in Moscow. In 1937 he was made the party's general secretary, and his drive, charisma, and ruthlessness proved vital in building this still illegal organization into a powerful underground force. When the USSR and Germany went to war in June 1941, Tito's armed revolutionary bands were ready to fight not just against the Germans but for a socialist Yugoslavia. This they did with great effectiveness. Not only was their ideology capable of rallying support across ethnic dividing lines, but Tito was an effective guerrilla leader, outmaneuvering the Germans, Italians, Croatian Ustase, and even Mihailovic's *cetniks*. Their numbers grew, in large part thanks to the barbaric reprisals of the Germans, who often rounded up and killed a hundred civilians for every German soldier killed by partisans. By late 1943, Tito's movement was strong enough to declare a provisional government. It won the support of the Allies, who needed Tito to harass the Germans, while Stalin saw Tito as a likely ally in the future conquest of Eastern Europe. In November 1944, Tito's army, with some Red Army support, took the city of Belgrade from the retreating Germans. Tito now held the reins of power in the liberated country.[2]

Perhaps 1.7 million people died in Yugoslavia during the war; about 1 million of them were killed by other Yugoslavs. There were, then, two competing legacies to emerge from the war. One was ethnic hatred, the product of the barbaric Croatian-Serb civil war and the partisan-*cetnik* rivalry. The other legacy was that of Communist "brotherhood and unity," the product of the people's struggle to drive out the foreign occupation. Naturally, Tito founded his new state on the latter ideal, but the former remained a very large part of the subtext of postwar Yugoslavia. There were grievances that even thirty-five years of Tito's rule could not settle.

Even so, Tito made a bold attempt to overcome Yugoslavia's historical ethnic, national, and religious divisions. The 1946 constitution established a federation of six republics: Slovenia, Croatia, Bosnia-Herzegovina, Serbia, Montenegro, and Macedonia. Each was given equal status. In order to ensure a balance of power between the more numerous Serbs and the rest of the country, Serbia lost two chunks of territory: Vojvodina in the north, which had a large Hungarian minority, and Kosovo in the south, which had an Albanian majority. These two provinces were made autonomous, but remained technically a part of the Serbian republic. Bosnia was the most ethnically complex of the republics, containing Croatians, Serbs, and Muslims (most of whom spoke Serbo-Croatian but were recognized as a distinct national group). This settlement was, of course, a compromise, but prompted much distress among Serbs, who believed that their historically dominant role had been taken away from them. The impression of anti-Serb bias in the new state was encouraged by the arrest, trial, and execution of numerous members of the Serb *cetniks,* including in 1946 Draza Mihailovic himself.

Tito made enormous strides in uniting this country, encouraging economic development, and pursuing his own path of socialist unity. The split with Stalin in 1948 forced Yugoslavs to devise an alternative model of socialist rule from the one on offer in Moscow. Tito's theorists outlined the idea of "workers' self-management," through which workers were granted active participation in the organization and operation of factories and enterprises. Tito hailed the model as genuine workplace democracy, though the League of Communists of Yugoslavia (LCY), as the Communist party was now known, remained the only political party in the country and Tito himself ruled with an iron hand. The economy made impressive strides in the 1950s, with industrial production increasing by an astonishing 70 percent between 1957 and 1961. Yugoslavia developed a lucrative tourist industry, opening its pristine beaches along the Adriatic to sun-starved Northern Europeans. Tito also hewed closely to his own independent instincts by refusing to join the Soviet bloc even after Khrushchev denounced Stalin. Instead he fostered connections with the newly liberated Third World nations, and in 1961 the founding conference of the Non-Aligned Movement was held in Belgrade. By the mid-1960s, Yugoslavia had become a rare bird in Europe: Communist, yet moderately tolerant, open to trade with the West, and politically independent of both Cold War blocs.

Yet all was not well within Tito's land of "Brotherhood and Unity"—the national slogan. The republics, already granted wide powers within the federation, sought greater independence, and in Croatia, nationalist intellectuals called for more cultural autonomy. During the 1960s, Tito devolved even more powers upon the republics in the hopes of nipping these nationalist forces in the bud. In late 1971, students led demonstrations in Zagreb against perceived injustices toward Croatia by the federal government. Tito sent in police and the army, arrested the student leaders, banned Croatian nationalist organizations, and purged the Croatian Communist Party. Tito also cracked down on dissent in general, waging a stern campaign against liberals and reformers. Anyone suspected of harboring national sentiments detrimental to the integrity of Yugoslavia was quickly arrested and interned.

In 1974, Tito began to think about the long-term stability of the country after his death. How would such a gang of squabblers keep the country together? His solution was the collective presidency, a cumbersome federal institution whereby each republic and province named a delegate to the presidency; the delegates in turn elected a president for a one-year term along a rotating list, so that each republic had a chance at the top office. This way, no one entity could dominate the federal government. Along with the army and the LCY, the federal government would be able to hold the republics in check. The theory was soon put to the test: on 4 May 1980, Tito died.

Almost immediately, the country began to revert to nationalist divisions. First to erupt was the autonomous province of Kosovo, the overwhelmingly Albanian region under nominal Serb control. Here Serbs constituted a small minority, of about 13 percent, in 1981, but they dominated the province, held the most influential positions, had the best housing, and had access to the best professional opportunities. Tensions between the Albanian-speaking Kosovars and the Serbs had been long in the making, especially since the late 1960s, when the University of Pristina became a hotbed for Albanian nationalism. In March and April 1981, Kosovars rioted in favor of full republican status for Kosovo and for an end to dominance by the Serb minority. The army had to be called in and martial law imposed. Nationalist leaders were arrested and imprisoned. The Kosovo riots only raised the question in all the republics: how should Yugoslavia deal with its national divisions? Was greater autonomy needed, or stronger federal control? During the mid-1980s, the federal government was able to assert control. The army and the LCY remained loyal to Tito's Yugoslav ideal. But what would happen if even those institutions were split apart by rival national claims? Then the country itself would soon collapse.

TOWARD WAR, 1988–1992

What made the nationalist problems facing Yugoslavia in the mid-1980s so difficult was that they emerged in tandem with other centripetal forces that weakened the federal government. During the 1980s, the Yugoslav economy was mired in a deep slump that only worsened as the decade wore on. Foreign loans had ballooned to unmanageable proportions, the controlled heavy industries were inefficient and corrupt, national production dropped, and the currency became worthless. The economic crisis erupted at a time when Yugoslavia's ideological moorings were coming loose because of the collapse of Communist regimes across Eastern Europe. Communism, Tito-style, had offered Yugoslavs an antidote to nationalism. With it gone, the old ghosts quickly reappeared. This became evident in Serbia especially. Leading Serb nationalists, who had long felt unjustly fettered by the Yugoslav constitution, began to call for a reconfigured Yugoslavia that allowed Serbs to play a dominant role, especially given that there were large Serb communities in all the republics except Slovenia. In 1986, the Serbian Academy of Sciences published a much-heralded document declaring that postwar Yugoslavia had unfairly discriminated against Serbs, that Tito had conspired to keep them in check and robbed them of their ancestral lands of Vojvodina and Kosovo.

The increased stridency of Serb nationalist rhetoric flared up most visibly in Kosovo itself. This province, though heavily Albanian in population, held special significance for Serb national mythology. Kosovo had lain at the heart of the medieval Serb kingdom, and it was at Kosovo Polje—the Field of Blackbirds—that on 28 June 1389, the Serb king Lazar faced off against the invading Turks. The Serbs lost the battle and Lazar lost his head; yet ever after, the Serbs used the Battle of Kosovo as a symbol of their willingness to die in defense of their own civilization against the infidel. The twenty-eighth of June is a national holiday for Serbs. Moreover, many Serb monasteries are in Kosovo, as is the patriarchate of the Serbian Orthodox Church. The result of Tito's decentralizing constitution was to allow the Albanians to gain greater control of the province, thus threatening the dwindling Serb minority in Kosovo. Serbs started to emigrate from Kosovo; by 1991, they constituted just 10.9 percent of the Kosovo population. Kosovo would soon be denuded of Serbs. This Serbia could not accept, and it became a central component of Serb nationalist rhetoric to rescue Kosovo once again from domination by the Albanian—and heavily Muslim—population.[3]

By the mid-1980s, Kosovo had become a tinderbox, one whose explosive power might be harnessed by the right sort of political leader. Unfortunately, one was waiting in the wings: Slobodan Milosevic, a former bank president, an admirer of Tito, a lifelong Communist apparatchik, and oddly enough, a man with a strongly pro-Yugoslav, antinationalist record. A protégé of the Serb Communist Party leader Ivan Stambolic, Milosevic moved up the ranks quickly, becoming Belgrade party chief in 1984. In 1986, when Stambolic became Serbian president, Milosevic was named Serbian Communist Party leader. In this capacity, Milosevic was deployed by Stambolic to Kosovo, to listen to the grievances of local Serbs and assure them of Belgrade's support. On 24 April 1987, he did so, but his visit was carefully disrupted by Serb nationalists, who purposely attacked the Kosovo police with stones so as to provoke retaliation. When Milosevic saw Albanian police battling with Serbs, he declared—within range of the video cameras—"No one should dare to beat you!" This scene, with Milosevic angrily defending the rights of Serbs, and then going on to assert Serbia's historic claim to Kosovo, assured his reputation as the emerging leader of the Serbs.[4]

Milosevic now devised a cynical and ambitious plan not simply to restore

Serbian rights over Kosovo but to win support among Serbs for the restoration of their natural domination within Yugoslavia. Milosevic claimed
throughout the crises of the 1990s that he was a supporter of maintaining a
strong Yugoslavia; he was not a secessionist. True enough. The reason for this
was that he set out to transform Tito's carefully balanced Yugoslavia into a
Serb-dominated state with only nominal autonomy for its republics: a
Serboslavia, as its detractors claimed. In creating a Serbian-controlled state, he
would also assure a dominant role in Yugoslavia for Serbia's leader—himself.
The plot worked smoothly. He first turned his sights on Vojvodina and
Montenegro, where Serb demonstrators, carefully coordinated by Milosevic
allies, pressured the governments to resign in October 1988. They were replaced by handpicked Milosevic men. In November, Milosevic demanded a
constitutional amendment to strip Kosovo of its autonomous status. He
rammed it through the Kosovo parliament, which at the time was ringed with
Yugoslav army tanks. Suddenly Milosevic had in his personal control the votes
of four states in the federal Yugoslav presidency: Serbia, Kosovo, Vojvodina,
and Montenegro. In December 1988 he ousted his longtime mentor, Stambolic, and the following May replaced him as president of Serbia. His plans for
a Serb-dominated Yugoslavia seemed to be moving ahead flawlessly.

Milosevic befuddles historians. He does not appear to have been a Serb
nationalist at heart, though he certainly was willing to use nationalism to create support for his vision of a Serb-dominated Yugoslavia. According to a
leading historian of the region, Milosevic's ideology combined various strains
that have been present in Yugoslav politics for decades: Milosevic was antidemocratic, the result of his longtime adherence to Communism. He was
anti-Western and antiliberal, also the result of the Communist period but also
a view shared by Pan-Slavic agitators since the nineteenth century. His ideology was anti-Catholic, seeing the Vatican as a historic enemy to Slavic,
Orthodox Serbia. And most sinister were the elements drawn from the Fascist
and totalitarian period. Milosevic supported an anticonservative, dynamic approach to settling the Yugoslav question. He would uproot the old order and
replace it with one that reflected Serb hegemony, even if this meant the physical regrouping and transfer of peoples. Serbs must live in and be protected by
a greater Serbia. This stance opened the door to the policy of ethnic cleansing
that would soon typify the Yugoslav wars. Combining these many strands together, Milosevic offered a powerful, irresistible ideological framework to
Serbs everywhere in Yugoslavia.[5]

Precisely for this reason, Milosevic deeply alarmed the other republics in
Yugoslavia, especially Slovenia and Croatia. In Slovenia, Yugoslav's wealthiest,
most developed republic, the Communist leadership had been following a

program of gradual thaw, much like the Hungarians, since the late 1980s. They wished to open up the republic to wider democratic participation and embrace a closer relationship with its West European neighbors to the north, especially Germany, Austria, and Italy. Milosevic's assault on the independence of Kosovo horrified the Slovenes, who feared that he might try to strip other republics of their constitutional rights in the federal state. In September 1989, the Slovene leadership confronted Milosevic by demanding new constitutional guarantees that would allow Slovenia to secede from Yugoslavia if its rights were not protected. Slovenia was following Milosevic's lead, of course: it was he who had redrawn the constitution to swallow Kosovo. Nonetheless, the Serb leader took this as an affront to the integrity of Yugoslavia, which it was. On 1 December 1989, he announced an economic boycott of Slovenia. The wedge was driven further still when in January, the federal Communist party, the League of Communists, met for its party congress. The six republics were all represented, but Milosevic ganged up with his Montenegrin and Macedonian allies to humiliate the Slovenes and reject all their proposals. The Slovenes walked out of the congress, and the Yugoslav Communist party—one of the key institutions holding the country together—shattered.

Slovenia was not alone in challenging Milosevic. Croatia too rejected Milosevic's vision of a Serb-dominated Yugoslavia. Croatia lent support to Slovenia's claims, and the two republics, in defiance of Belgrade, held multi-party elections in the spring of 1990. In Slovenia, a coalition of prodemocratic, pro-European groups won. In Croatia, however, the public registered its ardent nationalist sentiment, and its disgust with Milosevic, by giving overwhelming support to the Croatian Democratic Union—the nationalist party led by the former general Franjo Tudjman. A partisan during the war, Tudjman was nonetheless a longtime nationalist agitator who had been imprisoned frequently by Tito for his anti-Yugoslav activities. During the election campaign, his nationalist rhetoric inflamed passions among both Croatians and Serbs, of whom there were 580,000 living in Croatia. Tudjman promised to create a new Croatian state, one that grouped together the Croatian people wherever they might be—even in Serbia or, most especially, Bosnia-Herzegovina. Tudjman's own willingness to defend the actions of the Ustase regime in World War II, and his embrace of the Croatian red-and-white checkerboard flag that the Ustase had used, seemed designed to provoke a hostile reaction from Serbs. His inauguration as Croatia's president, no less than the rise of Milosevic to power, spelled doom for the Yugoslav state.

No sooner had Tudjman taken office than Croatia's Serbs began to plan for secession from the Croatian republic. Operating in the town of Knin in the Krajina region—in the southwestern part of Croatia, inland from the Adriatic coast—Croatian Serbs challenged the right of the Croatian police to enforce order in the Krajina and demanded autonomy for Serbs in the region. This explicit rebuke to Tudjman's authority could not go unanswered, and on 17 August 1990, Croatian Interior Ministry helicopters were flown toward Knin to drop troops in and restore order. They were intercepted, on orders from Milosevic, by Yugoslav army jets and forced to return to Zagreb. The war had in effect begun: Serbia was going to use the force of the Yugoslav army to defend Serb rights anywhere in Yugoslavia. The Krajina Serbs now enforced their own mini state inside Croatia, blockaded themselves in with arms supplied by Serbia, and prepared to do battle to hold on to their land. Croatia could not face down the Belgrade-backed Serbs because it had no army: Milosevic controlled the Yugoslav People's Army (JNA), 70 percent of whose officers were Serbs. So during the fall and winter of 1990, the Croatians began to purchase arms from Hungary in order to transform their police into a regular army.

In the early spring of 1991, the Croatians began a military operation to break the defiant Serbs in the Krajina and also in Eastern Slavonia, a region in eastern Croatia that borders heavily Serb Vojvodina. In February and March, Croatian police forces succeeded in retaking control of a number of towns in these areas that had been held by rebel Serbs. But on 2 May, a busload of Croatian police were ambushed by Serbs in the village of Borovo Selo, near Vukovar in Eastern Slavonia; 12 Croat policemen were killed. The encounter electrified Croatia and played into Tudjman's hands by confirming in the public's mind the image of Serbs as bloodthirsty terrorists, bent on the breakup of Croatia. On 19 May, in a referendum, Croatians voted overwhelmingly to secede from Yugoslavia. On 25 June 1991, both Slovenia and Croatia declared their independence. Tito's Yugoslavia was officially dead.

Slobodan Milosevic, Serbia's leader and de facto Yugoslav strongman, depicted the war that followed as a conflict between Slovene and Croatian secessionists and those who wished to defend Yugoslavia. It was nothing of the sort. Milosevic and his Serb allies engaged in war not to defend Yugoslavia but to wrest control of Serb-populated areas in Croatia (and later Bosnia) away from the secessionist republics. This war was a territorial land grab. This fact explains why the conflict between Slovenia and the Yugoslav army was brief and desultory: there were no Serbs in Slovenia. When on 26 June the JNA mobilized to seize key locations in Slovenia—the airport in Ljubljana, railheads, the border crossings—the Slovene militia erected barricades, surrounded JNA troops in their barracks, cut off electricity and water, and even fired on a JNA helicopter attempting to resupply the troops. The JNA was a modern, well-equipped, and well-trained army. Had it wished to do so, it could have begun a major land invasion of Slovenia. But Milosevic did not care about Slovenia.

Within three days of the fighting, to the astonishment of the JNA generals, the Yugoslav federal presidency ordered the withdrawal of JNA troops from Slovenia. On 8 July, at a summit on the Adriatic island of Brioni, the Yugoslav government and the Slovenes, under the auspices of a European Community negotiator, agreed to Slovenia's independence.

Croatia suffered a far different fate. Serb nationalists, backed by Milosevic, planned to carve out Serb-populated parts of Croatia and link them up to a greater Serbia. This required the ethnic cleansing of Serb areas in the Krajina and Slavonia: the non-Serbs would have to be removed. Starting in August 1991, the Serbs—including Yugoslav army units, militia units from Serbia and Montenegro, Serbian Interior Ministry troops, and paramilitary groups—began deporting Croatians out of the Krajina and Slavonia. The Serbs engaged in the murder of thousands of non-Serb civilians in these areas, including women, children, and the elderly. The Serbs deported 170,000 non-Serbs from these areas, and hundreds of thousands fled on their own accord. In late August, Serb forces in Eastern Slavonia laid siege to Vukovar, a town of 84,000 people, 37 percent of whom were Serbs. After three months of shelling, Vukovar fell to the Serbs. Those inhabitants who had not fled were deported, or simply murdered. One grisly example illustrates the Serb methods. On 20 November 1991, Serb forces seized the Vukovar hospital and transported about 260 Croats and non-Serbs who had taken refuge there to a Yugoslav army barracks south of the town. After hours of beatings and torture, the victims were shot and buried in a mass grave.[6]

In the late fall of 1991, most of the Serb territorial objectives in Croatia had been achieved. One-third of the republic was in Serb hands. Half a million Croats were refugees (and 230,000 Serbs fled Croatia at the same time). Milosevic could now accept a UN-sponsored plan for a cease-fire, which until this point he had rejected. In January 1992, the UN deployed 14,000 peacekeeping troops across Croatia, but they enforced cease-fire lines that were the result of Serb military gains. Nor did the UN presence stop the ethnic cleansing in Serb-held areas of Croatia, which continued until June 1992. The only consolation for Croatia was that in January 1992, the European Community, under heavy pressure from German foreign minister Hans-Dietrich Genscher, granted diplomatic recognition to Slovenia and Croatia. Genscher believed that a recognition of independence would shore up Croatia's legitimacy and deter the Serbs from making any further inroads into Croatia. But the action also served to legitimize the policy of secession, and presented a stark choice to Yugoslavia's only remaining non-Serb republic, Bosnia-Herzegovina. Bosnia could remain in a rump Yugoslavia dominated by Serbs, or follow Slovenia and Croatia down the path of independence—and war.

GENOCIDE IN BOSNIA

In November 1990, six months after the Slovenes and Croats held their first free elections, the republic of Bosnia-Herzegovina followed suit. Bosnia was Yugoslavia's most ethnically balanced republic: of its 4.4 million people, 44 percent were Muslim, 31 percent were Serb, and 17 percent were Croat. Bosnia had a long history of ethnic diversity and integration, as well as a rich culture that reflected its history as a point of contact and conflict between Christianity and Islam. Its capital city, Sarajevo, had flourished as a multiethnic city of half a million educated, urbane inhabitants. About half the city's residents were Muslims, though only a fraction observed Muslim religious practices; a third were Serbs. But in the fall of 1990, as the Yugoslav state broke apart into ethnonational groupings of Slovenes, Croats, and Serbs, Bosnia too began to split apart, pulled in opposite directions like a man being drawn and quartered. Some of Bosnia's Croats looked to Zagreb and the prospect of an independent Croatia. Some of Bosnia's Serbs looked to Belgrade and yearned to be included in a greater Serbia; and between them were grouped the Bosnians—many of them Muslim, but not all—who wished simply to maintain the republic intact and preserve its multiethnic heritage, free from Croatian and Serb meddling.[7]

The elections of November 1990 revealed the deepening divisions. The main Muslim party, which called for the autonomy and unity of Bosnia, won eighty-six seats in the assembly. The Bosnian Serb party, led by a Sarajevo psychiatrist named Radovan Karadzic, won seventy-two seats; while Bosnia's Croatian party won forty-four seats. The Muslim leader, Alija Izetbegovic, duly became president and attempted to create a government of national unity by including Croats and Serbs in his cabinet. But such tolerance had to face the counterpressures created by the rapidly deteriorating situation in the country as a whole. When war broke out between Serbia and Croatia in the summer of 1991, the Bosnian government tried to stay neutral. Yet Bosnia's Serb leadership was anything but. In July, it began receiving arms deliveries from the Serbian Interior Ministry. In September, the Bosnian Serbs—following the path blazed by the Serbs of Croatia—declared various parts of Bosnia to be "Serb autonomous regions" and invited the Yugoslav army to give them military protection, which it did. On 14 October 1991, the Bosnian Serb delegation walked out of the Bosnian assembly, using as a pretext the Bosnian government's demand for autonomy within the remaining Yugoslav state. Karadzic, the Bosnian Serb leader, openly threatened the Bosnian government and President Izetbegovic: "The Muslims cannot defend themselves if there is war," he shouted. "How will you prevent everyone from being killed in Bosnia-Herzegovina?" Izetbegovic later recalled this as Karadzic's "death sentence to the Muslim people."[8] Ten days later, the Bosnian Serbs declared their own parliament and government, and in effect announced their secession from Bosnia. Karadzic then prepared for war by using Yugoslav troops to build artillery positions around Bosnia's major towns and cities, and receiving the Serbian militia groups that had been active in Croatia. In January 1992, Milosevic transferred Yugoslav army officers of Bosnian Serb nationality to Bosnia, allowing them to fight for the new Bosnian Serb state. There could be no question that the coming war in Bosnia was planned and executed with the full knowledge and support of the Serbian government and the Yugoslav army.

By the spring of 1992, it was clear that war would soon break out in Bosnia. President Izetbegovic faced a breakaway insurrection by Bosnia's Serbs backed by Belgrade. To save his country he had to respond to the challenge. As preparation, he would seek to win the battle of international public opinion by demonstrating that a majority of Bosnia's citizens wished to secede from Yugoslavia and defend Bosnian sovereignty, thus putting the onus of the war on the Serbs. On 28 February 1992, the Bosnian government held a referendum on independence. The Serbs boycotted it, but 63 percent of the electorate voted and they overwhelmingly favored independence. On 27 March, the Serbs declared their territory to be the Serbian Republic of Bosnia-Herzegovina. A week later, on 5 April, war broke out between the Bosnian government, fighting for its independence and survival, and the breakaway Bosnian Serbs, fighting for a Serb entity in Bosnia that would comprise a part of the greater Serbian state. The war would last three and a half years, and lead to the deaths of perhaps 200,000 people.[9]

It is easy enough to construct a narrative of the war in Bosnia. It is much more difficult to explain its ferocity. During this war, Serb troops engaged in the most horrific acts of organized violence in Europe since 1945. They pursued a policy of forced expulsion, mass incarceration of civilians, the torture of prisoners, the rape of some 20,000 Muslim women, and the mass murder of thousands of civilians. By the standards of the United Nations, these acts constituted genocide and crimes against humanity.[10] Why did they do it? Any reasoned explanation falls short, somehow. Certainly, the Serb troops were goaded on by a barrage of propaganda organized by Belgrade television, which for years had portrayed Croats as Fascist Ustase and Muslims as fundamentalists bent on the destruction of the Serb people. As the Balkan analyst Noel Malcolm has written, "It was as if all television in the USA had been taken over by the Ku Klux Klan."[11] Serbs labeled Muslims mujahedeen, Turks, or janissaries. Serb nationalists declared that their people faced extermination if they did not defend themselves from the Muslim hordes. The war in Bosnia became another Serb war of survival against the anti-Serb conspiracy that had permeated Yugoslav history. Added to this was the fact that the war itself radicalized the Serbs still further. As they committed atrocities, they created a brotherhood of terror that implicated them all. Increasingly isolated in world opinion, and in some cases the targets of Muslim and Croat reprisals, Serbs grew even more firmly convinced of their victimization at the hands of their enemies. Here we have the twisted inversion of truth that characterized Hitler's race war on the Jews: since the Jews "threatened" the survival of the German *Volk,* they must be eradicated. Milosevic and Karadzic were following a familiar script.

Within days of the Bosnian Serb declaration of independence, Serb forces began in earnest to secure territory they claimed lay within the Bosnian Serb republic. In just a few weeks, the Bosnian Serbs, backed by the Yugoslav army and led by a JNA general named Ratko Mladic, seized control of about 60 percent of Bosnia.[12] Their swath of territory looked on a map like a fat horseshoe, running from the Croatian border and the Krajina across most of northern Bosnia to Slavonia, then south along the Serb and Montenegrin borders. Naturally, within these "Serb" areas there were hundreds of thousands of Muslims. The Bosnian government, badly outgunned and with no army to speak of, could hold only a narrow peninsula of territory in central Bosnia, running from the southwest to the northeast. The war settled down into a standoff. The Serbs used heavy artillery to pound at Bosnian government positions, especially Sarajevo, which they besieged. For the next forty-four months, Serb forces shelled the city and aimed sniper fire at its civilians. They also cut off gas, water, and electricity in the city. The city's historic mosques and its sixteenth-century library were soon in ruins.

While the fighting along the front lines settled into a grim standoff, the Bosnian Serbs were free to carry out the ethnic cleansing of the territory under their control. Reports gathered by journalists, by Human Rights Watch investigators, and by the prosecutors of the International Criminal Tribunal at the Hague make it clear that Serb forces used extreme brutality to terrorize the Muslim population. Beatings, torture, forced labor, rape, and murder of Muslims became routine all across Serb-held territory. As early as May 1992, Serb forces began to segregate Muslims and Croats in northwestern Bosnia and intern them in camps. The most notorious was established in an abandoned mining complex at Omarska, near the town of Prijedor and not far from the Serb stronghold of Banja Luka. Non-Serb civilians around Prijedor were marched in columns to Omarska; women, children, and the elderly were sent to a camp at Trnopolje. A third camp, Keraterm, was established just out-side Prijedor. At Omarska, prisoners were beaten, deprived of food and water, housed in unspeakable filth, sexually assaulted, tortured, and after interroga-tions, shot to death. At Trnopolje, the women and girl prisoners were rou-tinely and repeatedly raped by police and military personnel. Most likely to be targeted for killing were the educated civic and political leaders, intellectuals, the wealthy, and any non-Serb who had resisted Serb rule. Other civilians in the region were placed on sealed railway cars and deported to Bosnian gov-ernment territory. Similar scenes were repeated across Serb-held Bosnia.[13] These actions resulted in the mass exodus of Muslims from Serb-controlled territory. Of the 550,000 Muslim and Croat residents of northwest Bosnia, fewer than 50,000 remained by June 1994; and by 1996, this number was re-duced to 22,000.[14] The area had been "cleansed."

Eastern Bosnia fared no better. Some of the most gruesome tales of the war emerged from the town of Foca, southeast of Sarajevo near the Monte-negrin border. In mid-April 1992, Serbs seized control of the town, half of whose residents were Muslim. Thousands of Muslims from the town and the surrounding area were arrested and jailed in the Foca prison, one of Yugosla-via's largest. Women were usually separated from men and taken to the Foca high school, to the Partizan Sports Hall, or nearby motels. Here, according to the International Criminal Tribunal, imprisoned women and girls, some as young as fifteen years of age, were beaten, tortured, and savagely raped by hundreds of Serb soldiers over a period of months. One Serb paramilitary commander imprisoned nine women in his home in Foca, which he trans-formed into a brothel for his troops. "The physical and psychological health of many female detainees," reads the war crimes indictment, "seriously deteri-orated as a result of these sexual assaults. Some of the women endured com-plete exhaustion, vaginal discharges, bladder problems, and irregular menstrual bleedings. The detainees lived in constant fear. Some of the sexually abused women became suicidal." Two courageous women attempted to report these horrific events to Foca's chief of police, a man named Dragan Gagovic. He promptly drew his pistol and raped one of the women. Often the Serb soldiers, after raping their victims, declared that the women would "now give birth to Serb babies."[15]

The consequences of this brutality were predictable: Bosnian Muslims fled Serb-held territory in huge numbers. By November 1992, 1.4 million Bosnians had become refugees inside the former Yugoslavia; another 220,000 were taken in by Germany, 65,000 by Austria, 54,000 by Hungary, 70,000 by Switzerland, 67,500 by Sweden. These numbers grew as the war dragged on. The Serbs had triggered Europe's worst refugee crisis since World War II.

Those Muslims who remained in Bosnia tried desperately to make it into government-controlled territory, either in central Bosnia or in a few cities in eastern Bosnia that had managed to fend off the Serb onslaught. These cities—Srebrenica, Gorazde, Zepa, and Sarajevo itself—now swollen by the flood of refugees and ringed by Serb troops, became Muslim ghettoes deep inside Serb territory. By late 1992, then, the Serbs had effectively achieved their war aims: they had seized two-thirds of the country, expelled or killed most of the Muslim inhabitants, and could leisurely, murderously, consolidate their control in the Bosnian Serb Republic.

THE INTERNATIONAL RESPONSE

The world reaction to the events in Bosnia was one of horror and shock. Once word of the concentration camp at Omarska made it into the Western press, by July 1992, international opinion unanimously denounced the Serb rampage. Yet to the enduring shame of the leading states of Europe and the United States, nothing concrete was done to stop the genocide in Bosnia. Indeed, many decisions taken by the Western states seemed only to reward the aggressive acts of the Serbs or to prolong the conflict by engaging in fruitless negotiations. Why, after fifty years of education about the evils of the Holocaust, after so many earnest cries of "Never again," did Europeans and Americans sit idly by for over three years, weak-kneed witnesses to genocide?

To be sure, the Bosnian Serbs had effected a fait accompli, and the genocidal aspects of their campaign unfolded very swiftly and early on in the war, before a Western response could be orchestrated. The Bosnian Serbs held most of the country under military occupation; stopping the genocide would require military intervention in Bosnia against the Serbs. Even so, it took three years of dithering before this inescapable conclusion finally registered in the West. This long period of delay and denial has burdened the Western governments with the charge of complicity in the Serb genocide.

Their inaction can be explained, though not justified. For the Americans, the war in Bosnia occupied a low rank on a long list of international commitments. In 1991, the United States fought and won a war in Kuwait and Iraq, sending half a million troops to the Persian Gulf in order to protect pro-Western Arab states and secure the West's access to Arab oil. That year, US diplomacy was also focused on the demise of the Soviet Union. By 1992, the US economy was in recession and the president, George Bush, faced a difficult reelection campaign. The US simply did not want to get involved. US policy makers knew all about the nature of the Serb campaign, but misunderstood its origins and its purpose. For most Americans, Bosnia's Muslims, Croats, and Serbs were all equally bloodthirsty, equally guilty in starting the war, and equally determined to carry out their own ethnic agenda. When Lawrence Eagleburger, a former ambassador to Yugoslavia, succeeded James Baker as secretary of state in late 1992, he made this view official policy: "Until the Bosnians, Serbs, and Croats decide to stop killing each other," he said, "there is nothing the outside world can do about it."[16]

American inaction left the problem on Europe's doorstep. Europe publicly welcomed the challenge of attempting to bring peace to Yugoslavia. "The hour of Europe has dawned," declared the foreign minister of Luxembourg, Jacques Poos, in June 1991, when his country held the rotating presidency of the EC. After all, if Europe could manage the overthrow of Communism and the unification of Germany without resort to violence, surely it could bring its brand of civilized discourse to Bosnia. But there was a problem. The Europeans, like the Americans, refused to see the Bosnia war as one of aggression and genocide by one people against another. Rather, Europeans viewed the conflict as part of a long-term ethnic contest that had been under way for many centuries and whose real origins lay in the murky Balkan past. Since all sides were equally guilty, the argument went, the only solution was to mediate and compromise over territorial issues. Therefore, the Europeans staked their entire effort not on punishing Serb aggression but on securing a cease-fire and administering humanitarian aid to the displaced refugees. Noble aims, perhaps, but rather like offering a Band-Aid to a man being attacked by wolves.

The institution chosen to provide succor to the Bosnians was the United Nations. This body was perfectly designed to carry out the nonpolicy of the West: it provided a superb soapbox from which to denounce the atrocities but had no resources of its own with which to intervene in the conflict. Only when the member states decided to commit resources could it act; and even then, its personnel steadfastly refused to take sides in the war, seeing their role as strictly humanitarian. In September 1992, the UN Security Council agreed to deploy troops—mostly French and British—as a UN Protection Force (UN-PROFOR), with a mandate to monitor troop movements in Bosnia and protect humanitarian aid convoys. The troops had no authority to use military force. In November, 6,000 soldiers under UN command arrived in Bosnia. At the same time, peace talks spearheaded by the EC negotiators, David Owen and Cyrus Vance, proposed the division of Bosnia into ten "cantons" of ethnic communities. By subscribing to the Vance-Owen plan, the EC accepted in principle that Bosnia would become ethnically divided and its people physically separated. However, the Bosnian Serbs rejected the plan because it required them to give up territory they had already seized and cleansed of

Muslims. So the pattern continued: the earnest search for a peace settlement acceptable to all sides, the delivery of humanitarian aid, and a long, slow strangulation of the Bosnian Muslims.[17]

The Serbs demonstrated an uncanny ability to humiliate UNPROFOR and its international backers. The UN consistently overestimated its own prestige and assumed that the presence of blue-helmeted soldiers, however few, would restrain the Serbs. The Serbs simply ignored them, and the UN found that it did not have the power to back up its own war of words. The Serbs concentrated on taking the government-held eastern enclaves (Srebrenica, Gorazde, Zepa, and Sarajevo itself) that Karadzic and Mladic needed to complete their carve-up of Bosnia. In April and May 1993, the UN declared these cities, ringed with Serb troops and subject to constant artillery barrages, to be "safe areas."[18] They would hereafter be protected by the will of the international community, along with a few hundred peacekeepers. This declaration was worthy of King Canute, since the UN had no power to make the cities safe. The Serbs besieged the eastern enclaves, slowed UN relief supplies to a trickle, and terrorized the inhabitants with artillery and sniper fire. Why did the UN not act more forcefully in responding to Serb aggression? First, the UN troops on the ground were far too weak to oppose Serb troops by force, and in any case their mandate required them to maintain peace between the "warring parties" rather than taking sides. As the British commander of UN troops in Bosnia declared, "You cannot fight a war from white-painted vehicles." Second, the UN negotiators placed all their hopes on a negotiated settlement of the war. The UN became a hostage of its own obsession with peace talks. The UN special envoy in Bosnia, Yasushi Akashi, wanted to take no steps that might result in the UN's loss of impartiality and lead the Bosnian Serbs to break off talks. So he was extremely reluctant to use force against the Bosnian Serbs even when they shelled safe areas and murdered civilians. Here lay the cruel irony at work in Bosnia: as long as the UN insisted on a peaceful settlement to the war, the war would go on.

Only in mid-1994 did the picture begin to change. First, in March 1994, the United States managed to broker an alliance between the Bosnian government and Croatia, which until this time had been trying to effect its own land grab of northern Bosnia. And second, the US and Europeans began to try to divide the Bosnian Serbs from their master in Belgrade, Slobodan Milosevic. They offered him economic inducements, agreeing to lift sanctions against Yugoslavia if he helped get his Bosnian Serb partners to agree to a peace settlement. If he refused, the US would take sides and ship arms to the Bosnian Muslims. Milosevic, tired of the war and fearful that his fanatical Bosnian Serb counterparts might trigger a war with the United States, was willing to make a deal. But when the Western powers proposed a peace plan that gave the Bosnian Serbs only 49 percent of Bosnia, at a time when they held 70 percent of the entire republic, their leader, Radovan Karadzic, defied them. In doing so, he angered Milosevic, who in August 1994 imposed an embargo on the Bosnian Serbs, cutting off all supplies to Karadzic. Milosevic, in a stunningly duplicitous move, then denounced the Bosnian Serb regime as courting disaster for all the Serb people. Suddenly, the Bosnian Serbs were totally alone.

Cornered like a rabid dog, the Bosnian Serb regime struck out with great ferocity. In October and November 1994, Mladic's forces assaulted the "safe area" of Bihac in northwestern Bosnia and intensified the shelling of Sarajevo. The UN finally agreed to permit retaliatory air strikes by NATO aircraft, but these were merely pinpricks—a few bombs dropped on a Serb airfield. In response, however, the Serbs seized UN peacekeepers as hostages—a tactic that enraged the Western powers but also temporarily panicked them. In the winter of 1994–95, the Europeans debated withdrawing their troops altogether from Bosnia. In May 1995, after another brief and minor NATO air strike on Bosnian Serb positions around Sarajevo, the Serbs seized 350 UN peacekeepers and chained them to telephone poles at military installations as human shields. It was a grotesque act of defiance against the West. Yet the Bosnian Serbs knew that they had entered the endgame of the war. These actions formed a part of a broader strategy: to deter the Western powers from taking military action just long enough to allow the Serb forces to seize the final pieces of its territorial puzzle. They wanted the eastern enclaves, and the first target on the list was Srebrenica.

FROM SREBRENICA TO DAYTON

In July 1995, the Bosnian Serb forces carried out the war's most efficient act of genocidal ethnic cleansing in the town of Srebrenica. This small town—with only 8,000 residents before the war—had been declared a safe area by the UN in 1993, and as a result many thousands of Muslims sought refuge there. By 1995, some 40,000 people were encamped there, living off food shipped in by occasional UN convoys. A few thousand Bosnian government troops manned the city's defenses. In addition, a battalion of four hundred Dutch peacekeepers had been stationed on the outskirts of town to protect it. In the first week of July, 5,000 Bosnian Serb forces converged on the town, bringing with them artillery, armored personnel carriers, and tanks. This force attacked the town on 6–7 July with a huge artillery barrage. The Serbs stormed some of the UN outposts on the edge of town and seized fifty-five Dutch troops. Although NATO was prepared to undertake air strikes against the Serb forces, the Serbs threatened to kill the Dutch hostages in retaliation. The Dutch Defense Ministry promptly vetoed the use of air strikes against Serb forces, and the city was engulfed by Serb forces on 11 July.[19]

There now followed a chaotic exodus of people out of the city. About 25,000 Bosnian Muslims—most of them women and children—fled northward toward Potocari, where the Dutch had a military compound. It was a steaming hot summer day, and there were no facilities at all in Potocari: no water, no food, no toilets, no doctors. The small battalion of Dutch troops were totally overwhelmed, and their commander appealed to the Bosnian Serbs for a cease-fire so that the refugees could be transported out of the area. This squared precisely with what the Serbs wanted. But General Mladic, who personally directed the entire operation, upped the ante: he insisted that the refugees be divided into groups, with the wounded, women, and the elderly separated from the men. At about noon on 12 July, buses began to arrive in Potocari to transport the refugees. The women were bused to Kladanj in Bosnian government territory. But the men were taken north to a camp at Bratunac. By 13 July, the Potocari compound was empty.

Meanwhile, about 15,000 men in Srebrenica, expecting Serb atrocities, tried to flee by infiltrating across Serb lines into Bosnian government territory, some thirty miles away. There were armed soldiers among them, but most in the group were civilians. The Bosnian Serbs were prepared for this, and they trapped many of the fleeing Muslim men at bridges, rivers, and crossroads. Many of those who surrendered were shot on the spot. Others were placed on buses and transported to Bratunac, some to a soccer stadium in Novo Kasaba, northwest of Srebrenica. In Novo Kasaba, perhaps a thousand men were shot to death at the soccer field and buried in a mass grave on 13–14 July. Other Muslim prisoners were bused to Bratunac, and then on to the village of Karakaj. Here, many thousands of Muslims were herded together in a school building. Over the course of two days, the Serbs placed groups of Muslim men onto buses, took them to nearby fields, shot them, and buried them in mass graves. Remarkably, a few men survived the ordeal. "We were driven about two kilometers" out of Karakaj, remembered one.

> When the truck stopped, they told us to get off in groups of five. We immediately heard shooting next to the trucks. . . . About ten Chetniks [Serbs] with automatic rifles told us to lie down on the ground face first. As we were getting down, they started to shoot, and

I fell into a pile of corpses. I felt hot liquid running down my face. I realized that I was only grazed. As they continued to shoot more groups, I kept on squeezing myself in between dead bodies.[20]

The testimony gathered by Human Rights Watch, both from men who survived and from the many women who witnessed the murder of their menfolk on 11–14 July 1995, make it clear that the plan to massacre the inhabitants of Srebrenica was worked out well in advance, and was overseen by General Mladic, who was present in various locations during this three-day period. To this day, an exact number of the dead has not been determined, but the Red Cross and the International Criminal Tribunal believe that between 7,000 and 7,500 men and boys were murdered.

United States and European officials knew perfectly well what happened at Srebrenica: they had satellite images that clearly showed both the prisoners in the Novo Kasaba soccer field and also the mass graves in which they were subsequently buried. But it was not these massacres alone that finally forced Western intervention. The Bosnian Serbs also attacked the safe areas of Gorazde, Zepa, Bihac, and Sarajevo with great intensity in July. And they probably would have succeeded in taking these towns had it not been for the sudden, lightning offensive undertaken by the Croatian army in August 1995. The Croatians had suffered Serb occupation of a large swath of their country since 1992, and in the summer of 1995 launched a military campaign to take back the lost ground. With explicit American support and military training, the Croatians did more than that: they pushed the Serbs not only out of Croatia but out of northwestern Bosnia as well. These were the first military reversals the Serbs had ever suffered in the war. It gave the Western powers hope and determination to strike while the Serbs were on the run. After a Serb mortar shell landed in the Sarajevo marketplace on 28 August, killing thirty-eight civilians, the NATO powers finally agreed to a major air strike against Bosnian Serb military positions around Sarajevo. On 30–31 August 1995, NATO carried out what was up to that point the largest military operation in its forty-five-year history. Within days, the air campaign was expanded to include military targets across Bosnia. Seizing the opportunity presented by these air strikes, the Croatian and Bosnian government armies attacked the Serbs on the ground. By mid-September, the Serbs, who for three years had controlled 70 percent of Bosnia, held only half the country.

With the enormous firepower of NATO finally engaged in the war, and their military position crumbling, the Serbs sued for peace. Slobodan Milosevic, who had done more than any single man to start the war, graciously offered to broker the deal, speaking for his Bosnian Serb counterparts, Karadzic and Mladic. Under the threat of continued bombing, the Serbs agreed to a cease-fire on 5 October and the convening of an international peace conference to finalize a settlement for Bosnia. At last, the Serbs had been spoken to in a language they understood: force.

The conference took place in November 1995 at an American air force base in Dayton, Ohio. In an intense three-week period, the presidents of Bosnia, Serbia, and Croatia hammered out a deal that was supervised by representatives of the United States, Britain, France, Russia, and Germany. (Though the EU was represented at the talks, the UN had been quietly but deliberately left out.) The most important aspect of the plan, on which the Americans insisted, was that Bosnia remain a single, united republic. Yet obviously, Bosnia had already been partitioned. The solution to this contradiction was to give Bosnia a "dual government." The Bosnian Serbs would be allowed their own state—the Republika Srpska. The Muslims and Croats joined together in a Federation of Bosnia and Herzegovina. But both entities coexisted inside a single state: the Republic of Bosnia and Herzegovina. Each entity had its own government, but each also would share power in the new institutions of the Bosnian government, such as a joint presidency and a shared constitutional court. The agreement also demanded that anyone under indictment by the International Criminal Tribunal would be ineligible to hold office in Bosnia—so Karadzic was finished as a politician. The Dayton accord also granted the right to all displaced persons the right to return to their homes—a stipulation that, in the end, proved impossible to implement. The most important element of the agreement, however, was that the United States and Europeans agreed to place 60,000 heavily armed soldiers, under NATO command, on the ground in Bosnia to enforce it. Significantly, 20,000 of these soldiers were American. The international community appeared willing at last to back up its words with force. On 12 December 1995, this Implementation Force (IFOR) began deploying in Bosnia.[21]

The lessons of Bosnia depended on who was doing the learning. For Europe, the lessons were unpleasant ones: genocide could still happen in Europe, and Europeans alone could do little to stop it. Only when the United States became fully engaged in the war did the Bosnian Serbs back down. The Europe whose future had looked so rosy in 1991 was humiliated by a band of bloodthirsty thugs. The United States learned a hard lesson too. There would be no easy retreat across the Atlantic in the wake of the Cold War, a heroic return after a half century of containment. The United States was Europe's sole great power. Only the United States had the power—and the military hardware—to wage war and broker peace. Without strong US leadership in Europe, there would be more Srebrenicas.

But others learned lessons too. Slobodan Milosevic learned that the West was extremely reluctant to use force, even to stop genocide. The West could be manipulated and deceived. Aggression paid: Dayton effectively recognized the partition of Bosnia and protected Serb claims to autonomy there. Meanwhile, Bosnia's Muslims—the one community dedicated to preserving Bosnia's multi-ethnic identity—drew the lesson that the West spoke loudly and carried a small stick. The only thing that mattered was force. So as Bosnia emerged from war, the Muslims retained no faith in the tolerant ideal they once cherished, and instead sullenly nursed ideas of revenge. And for the Bosnian Serbs, the war experience served only to enhance their sense of victimhood and tragedy. Cut off even by Belgrade, they clung to their statelet like a tin trophy, a worthless symbol of their victory in the field. Their Republika Srpska became a haven for war criminals, drug traffickers, and thugs. In dingy cafés, Bosnian Serb veterans sipped cheap plum brandy and told stories of the good old days, when one could rape and pillage with impunity. So there were many lessons in Bosnia; indeed, no end of a lesson.

NEMESIS: MILOSEVIC FROM KOSOVO TO THE HAGUE

During the 1990s, while Croatia and Bosnia languished in war and a painfully slow reconstruction, Kosovo—the cradle of Serb nationalism and the stage on which Slobodan Milosevic made his debut in 1987—had largely been forgotten. But it was not quiescent. After Milosevic stripped Kosovo of its autonomy in 1989, the Yugoslav government passed a series of measures designed to secure Serb control of Kosovo. The public sector, the hospitals, the schools, the administration were purged of Albanians, as was the police force. Workers had to swear loyalty oaths to Yugoslavia. Television and radio were taken over by Serb propagandists. The province was being Serbianized. These actions pushed Kosovo Albanians to develop an underground resistance network and a kind of parallel government. In 1991, a Kosovo parliament declared the independence of the province, though it could not as yet do anything to ensure its sovereignty. A pacifist professor of literature, Ibrahim Rugova, was elected president in an unofficial, underground ballot in May 1992. This was just when the war in Bosnia was getting under way, and the Serb authorities chose to look the other way. But the Kosovars began to establish a rudimentary underground state, complete with political institutions, an Albanian press, health

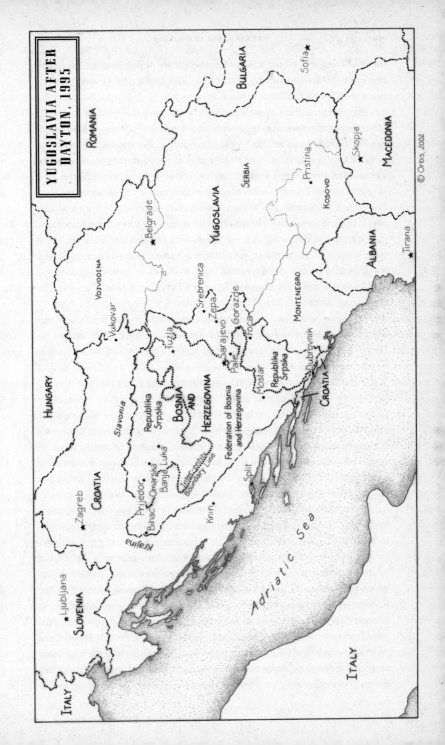

YUGOSLAVIA AFTER
DAYTON, 1995

© Orbis, 2002

care facilities, and schools. Naturally, there were widespread human rights abuses by the Serb authorities, but before 1995, neither the Kosovars nor the Serbs sought a violent confrontation.[22]

Yet alongside the underground state in Kosovo there did arise a small group of young nationalists who advocated a military response to Serb rule in Kosovo. Founded in December 1993, the Kosovo Liberation Army (KLA) remained very small: by 1997, it had only 150 active members. Initially, the Kosovo leadership hoped to avoid military confrontation with the Serbs. After all, they reasoned, look at what the Serbs had done to the Bosnian Muslims. But the Dayton accords of 1995 left the Kosovars feeling abandoned and anxious. They had settled the war, thus freeing up the Serb army. More important, they legitimated Miloscvic and made him into a partner of the West. In return, Milosevic was rewarded: the sanctions against Yugoslavia were lifted, and the Federal Republic of Yugoslavia (FRY)—including Serbia, Montenegro, and Kosovo—was given recognition by the European Union. The Kosovars were being left to their fate.

Armed with weapons trekked into Kosovo from neighboring Albania, the KLA began to mobilize for a direct confrontation with the Yugoslav government. In 1996, the KLA began attacking Serb policemen and civilians across Kosovo and issuing communiqués outlining their military campaign against Serb "colonists." The international community condemned the "terrorist" attacks of the KLA; Milosevic read that as approval for a sharp military response. In early 1998, the Serbs escalated their attacks, using helicopters and armored personnel carriers against a wide range of civilian targets, destroying homes, villages, crops, and cattle. These actions, which rarely netted any KLA members, only served to radicalize the Kosovars. The KLA was flooded with volunteers, which in turn prompted even harsher Serb reprisals. By August 1998, 200,000 Kosovars had been displaced by Serb persecutions.

The international community did not want to take sides in this conflict. Kosovo was, after all, a part of Yugoslavia, and the KLA was carrying out attacks on police and Serb civilians. But the humanitarian crisis that Serb actions created—a pattern all too familiar after Bosnia—prompted a stern and relatively swift condemnation from the United States and Europe. Brandishing the threat of NATO bombing, the Western powers compelled the Kosovar and Yugoslav leaders to convene at Rambouillet, outside Paris, in February 1999. The goal was to work out a settlement for the province that would protect the Kosovo people from Serb attacks while also keeping the province within the FRY. As leverage, the Western powers told the KLA leaders that if they did not agree to restrain their demands for independence, they would be abandoned by the West. To the Serbs (Milosevic himself refused to attend the conference) they declared their intention to use massive air strikes to crush the Yugoslav army in Kosovo and in the FRY proper. After weeks of tense negotiations, the KLA leaders agreed to a plan that would have brought NATO peacekeepers into Kosovo, would have obliged the FRY troops to withdraw, and would have left Kosovo as an autonomous province in the FRY. But the Serbs refused to sign. Milosevic was willing to risk NATO bombing instead of capitulating to what he saw as a Western ultimatum over Kosovo. He got his wish: on 24 March 1999, NATO aircraft began to bomb military targets all across the FRY, including Kosovo.

Why did Milosevic court war? He believed that Rambouillet would bring nothing but humiliation for himself and Serbia, and a loss of Kosovo to the Albanians. By contrast, he felt his odds in a war with NATO were pretty good. First, he knew that NATO had no stomach for a long war. The alliance was riven by internal debate, and any one of its nineteen members could derail a NATO campaign. Milosevic placed his hopes on Greece, which publicly opposed the use of force against the FRY. He also thought the Russians would pressure the West to stop the bombing. So Milosevic expected a short bombing campaign, which his forces could withstand. Second, Milosevic believed he had right on his side. Kosovo was Serb land, he reasoned. What better cause to rally public opinion? Third, and most important, Milosevic believed that he could use the bombing campaign to undertake a massive program of ethnic cleansing in Kosovo. By the time the bombing stopped and a peace settlement was negotiated, Kosovo would be denuded of Albanians. Kosovo would be Serb land again, at last.

The proof for this lies in the existence of Operation Horseshoe, a sinister scheme to use 40,000 FRY soldiers to evict the entire Albanian population of Kosovo. The operation began even as Milosevic's men were still holding talks at Rambouillet. The troops used terror, beatings, rape, executions, and the burning of villages to force hundreds of thousands of Kosovo Albanians to run for their lives. Village by village, the Serb forces uprooted and expelled Kosovars, robbing them in the process and confiscating identity papers to make their return to Kosovo impossible. Once the NATO bombing campaign began, the expulsions picked up speed. Not since the days of the ethnic German expellees had Europe witnessed such a swift and massive dispersal of a people. The Organization for Security and Cooperation in Europe (OSCE), in a chilling report, recounted how this plan was carried out:

> Typically, Serbian forces would shell a village for some hours, with the result that Kosovo Albanians hid in basements or fled to the hills. Then, when the shelling stopped, Serb forces . . . would enter the vil-

lage, shooting in the air. They would break down doors to enter Kosovo Albanian houses, threaten everyone who had not already fled and order them to leave. . . . Frequently a Kosovo Albanian would be intimidated, injured or killed in full public view to enforce the departure of other villagers. Houses were also looted and set alight. Those who refused to leave were often killed.[23]

By the end of March 1999, 180,000 people had crossed over into Albania, Montenegro, Bosnia, or Macedonia. By 11 April, this number had soared to 500,000. A month later, the total reached 781,000. And by 10 June, when the NATO bombing finally ceased, 863,000 Kosovars had fled the province. Within three months, approximately half the Albanian population of Kosovo had been forcibly expelled from the country; the rest were on the run, living in tents in the hills and woods. Perhaps as many as 10,000 Kosovar Albanians were killed by Serb forces.[24]

The NATO bombing campaign, begun with much fanfare as the answer to the humanitarian crisis, seemed only to have aggravated it. Yet as Milosevic increased his campaign of terror against the Kosovo Albanians, he also insured that NATO would remain united and determined in the face of what all agreed was a genocidal war against civilians. The egregious defiance of NATO power by the Serbs meant that NATO had to win, or lose all credibility. After the first week of bombing, NATO was no longer fighting for Kosovo, but for itself. After seventy-eight days of bombing, during which hundreds of civilians were killed, electricity and telecommunications knocked out across the FRY, factories and bridges destroyed, Milosevic decided to give up. It was not an easy call. His army in Kosovo was holding up rather well and could have been dislodged only by ground troops, which NATO was profoundly reluctant to deploy. On the other hand, NATO had not broken up, as he expected, nor had the Russians been able to stop the bombing. Daily life inside Serbia had come to a halt. Milosevic's own house had been hit by a bomb, and there was no prospect of an end in sight. Thus, on 10 June 1999, Milosevic agreed to withdraw his troops from Kosovo in return for a cessation of the bombing. In addition, he agreed to abide by UN Resolution 1244, passed on the same day. This demanded the return of all refugees to Kosovo and the withdrawal of FRY troops. The KLA was to be demilitarized, and the UN would establish an interim political administration to ensure civil order. A NATO force would keep the peace. And the UN insisted that Kosovo be granted "substantial autonomy and self-government" even while remaining a part of Yugoslavia.

The war was over, but the postwar had just begun. Virtually all the Kosovo Albanian refugees returned by the end of June to find their homes and villages destroyed. In response, they vented their rage on the Kosovo Serbs, whom they not unreasonably held responsible for their misfortune. Now came a grim role reversal: Albanians beat up, terrorized, killed, or expelled Kosovo's Serbs. By October, according to the OSCE, 186,000 Serbs had fled the province.[25] In the meantime, the UN Mission in Kosovo (UNMIK) faced the immense task of restoring order to the devastated province. Once the humanitarian crisis was eased, the UN began a huge state-building project, creating from scratch a civil administration, a justice system, and basic democratic structures to allow for voting. In addition, the European Union led international reconstruction efforts to pay for the rebuilding of the infrastructure of the province. Alongside these civilian efforts, some 40,000 NATO troops were sent to Kosovo to assure order and stability, to disarm the KLA, to undertake demining efforts, to provide basic medical facilities, and to help repair roads, bridges, and transportation networks. These noble efforts only underscored that Kosovo, far from enjoying a newfound independence, had become a protectorate of the UN and NATO. Nor was there any hope of ethnic reconciliation: the Albanian Kosovars remained overwhelmingly committed to independence, while the few Serbs that remained gathered nervously in ghettoes under heavy NATO guard.

Whatever Kosovo's fate, it will be decided by the Kosovo Albanians and the international community that is painstakingly building its civil society. Serbia will have little say there. This is because in the fall of 2000, the Serbs at long last rid themselves of their impresario of violence. On 24 September, Slobodan Milosevic was defeated in his bid for reelection to the presidency of the Federal Republic of Yugoslavia. His opponent was a bland constitutional lawyer named Vojislav Kostunica, the consensus candidate of the perennially divided Serbian opposition. True to character, Milosevic tried to falsify the results. But for the first time in his ten-year reign of terror, Milosevic found that his allies had deserted him. The army, the secret police, the politicians, and the workers had had enough of him and were ready to make their peace with Kostunica, a moderate nationalist who sought reconstruction and peace. On 5 October, with Milosevic still clinging to power, an enormous crowd massed in Belgrade, and a group of toughs—many of them soccer hooligans—stormed the parliament building and set it on fire. There was only token resistance from the police, and the army kept its troops in their barracks. The next day, Milosevic went on TV and congratulated Kostunica on his victory, as if it were the most normal thing in the world.[26]

Serbia had its revolution after all: the last of the Communist-bloc states had fallen. Unlike the other changes of government, though, Yugoslavia's revolution was hardly peaceful. Over 200,000 people paid for it with their lives.

For Serbia, Milosevic's departure marked the beginning of a path back toward Europe. Kostunica worked closely with the international community in its efforts to restore stability in Bosnia and Kosovo, and received extensive financial aid in return. The IMF offered loans to rebuild bridges over the Danube that NATO had destroyed a year earlier. Few mourned Milosevic. Thanks to him, Yugoslavia was in tatters, the country isolated and despised, its people's name forever linked with genocide. Nor did the nationalists regret his fall: greater Serbia had shrunk, not grown, and NATO had taken up permanent residence on Serbia's borders. Everything he had touched had turned to ashes. Milosevic may yet answer for his crimes. On 28 June 2001, the Serbian government turned him over to the International Criminal Tribunal in the Hague, to be tried for war crimes committed in Kosovo, Bosnia, and Croatia. He will likely spend the rest of his life in a Dutch prison.

The war in Yugoslavia is over. But Serbs, Kosovars, Bosnians, and Croatians are all still living in the uneasy *après-guerre*. The United States and Europe, after so much indifference in the early 1990s, are now heavily engaged in Bosnia and Kosovo. They created the powerful Office of the High Representative (OHR) to implement the Dayton agreement. Over 30,000 NATO soldiers remain in Bosnia in 2002. There are over thirty international organizations operating in Bosnia today. They have spent over $5 billion to rebuild schools, roads, sewers, and transport networks, and they hold earnest workshops on reconciliation and consensus building. In Kosovo, the presence of aid organizations and NATO troops is even greater. Yet there are troubling signs. There is little reason to think that Serbia will reconcile itself to the loss of Kosovo forever, or that Kosovo Albanians will resist the pull of independence. In Bosnia, Muslims and Serbs do not wish to live together, though they are cooped up in a jury-rigged dual state held together solely by NATO troops. All the elections held in Bosnia since 1995 have been won by parties that seek greater separation between Muslim and Serb. Eight hundred thousand refugees cannot return to their homes for fear of reprisals. Elected public officials are frequently removed from office by the OHR because they try to obstruct the provisions of Dayton. The radio networks have had to be seized by the OHR to stop the flood of racist propaganda. In Kosovo, crime is endemic, arms smuggling is rife, dreams of a greater Albanian state flourish. The few Serbs left there have boycotted all elections. Bosnia and Kosovo are NATO protectorates, troubled outposts on the margins of Europe.[27]

Plenty of bad news, then. Yet also signs of hope. Thousands of Europeans and North Americans are trying to bring peace, security, and dignity to a land that has had precious little of these commodities. It will be a long effort. It may not work. "If you're going to change civilization," George Kennan once said, "it can be done only as the gardener does it, not as the engineer does it. That is, it's got to be done in harmony with the rules of nature."[28] Building roads and bridges won't be enough. Europe and America will have to nurture the tender plant of Balkan democracy for many decades to come, while attacking the invasive weeds of nationalism, ethnic chauvinism, and war. But if this garden grows, will not the harvest be the more bountiful for all the blood that has watered the soil?

CHAPTER FIFTEEN

WHO IS EUROPEAN?
RACE, IMMIGRATION, AND THE POLITICS OF DIVISION

•

FOREIGNERS OUT!

EARLY ON THE MORNING of 23 November 1992, in the town of Mölln, north of Hamburg, Germany, Michael Peters, twenty-five, and Lars Christiansen, nineteen, threw a gasoline bomb into the home of a Turkish family. Peters then anonymously called the police, reported the attack, and screamed "Heil Hitler" into the phone. In the ensuing blaze, fifty-one-year-old Bahdie Arslan, her ten-year-old granddaughter, Yeliz, and a fourteen-year-old relative were killed. Six months later, a strikingly similar incident occurred, this time in Solingen, an industrial city in northwest Germany, near Düsseldorf. At 1:30 A.M. on 29 May 1993, a gang of neo-Nazi skinheads, aged sixteen to twenty-four, firebombed the home of Durmus Genc. Nineteen people were asleep inside. Within minutes, the house was engulfed by fire. Four girls, aged four, nine, twelve, and eighteen, died in the flames. A twenty-seven-year-old woman died later of injuries suffered when she jumped from a window. Ten others were injured. The press depicted these victims as Turks, though in both attacks, the dead women either were long-term residents of Germany or had been born there. In the ensuing riots that broke out in protest against these and other racially motivated attacks, Turkish residents demanded equal rights and legal protection. In Solingen, a banner read "Born Here, Burned Here."[1]

In the summer of 2001, race riots in the north of England revealed how little had changed during the 1990s. In the depressed industrial towns of Oldham, Burnley, and Bradford—former mill towns in the greater Manchester area—running battles between police and Asian youths left parts of the towns burned out, shops shuttered, the residents fearful. It had started on

26 May 2001, when a gang of white toughs tossed a brick through the window of an Asian family in Oldham, injuring a pregnant woman, and broke windows of Asian-owned storefronts. Within minutes, a large gang of Asian youths appeared on the scene and attacked the white-owned Live and Let Live pub with rocks and gasoline bombs. Assaults on the police followed, and for three days the town was a battle zone. The conflict spread to nearby towns, presenting Britain with its worst race riots since 1981. Again, the press depicted the rioters as Asians, though many of them had been born and raised in Britain. "When our parents came over," explained a cabdriver in Oldham, "they accepted being second-class citizens. Now youngsters who are educated here see themselves as on the same level as others. We are standing up for our rights. And that is what the police don't like."[2]

In the 1990s, there was much talk of the unification of Europe. But Europe was still deeply divided, not least along lines of race. No sooner had the Berlin Wall come down than the numbers of racially motivated assaults soared, as did the fortunes of far right parties calling for stiff restrictions on immigration and the rights of foreigners. In part, this reflected the sudden increase in the numbers of immigrants and asylum seekers in Europe in the early 1990s, many of them now able to reach Europe precisely because of the end of the Cold War. But the burst of xenophobia was part of a larger process. During the past fifty years, Europe has gradually become—despite itself—a multicultural society. The historic process of European emigration was reversed in the wake of the Second World War, as Europe sucked in laborers from across the globe to fuel the booming economy. During the process of decolonization, more former colonial subjects came; and many refugees from the Communist bloc and war-torn regions of the Third World joined their ranks. They brought with them their religious customs, their languages, their social and political values. And while many immigrants conformed to European norms, some did not. How would Europe respond to this sudden transformation of its cultural identity?

Not well, if recent reports are any indication. It is all too common to find in European newspapers of the past decade the reports of abuse, discrimination, and physical attacks on minorities, refugees, immigrants, Gypsies, and others. Often, these attacks are the work of soccer hooligans, unemployed thugs, and neo-Nazi skinheads; but there are numerous accounts of police brutality against minorities and immigrants as well. Though most states in the EU maintain some sort of database, racially motivated attacks are often underreported. Even so, the numbers that do get reported are alarming. Consider the figures compiled by the European Union Monitoring Centre on Racism and Xenophobia for the year 1999. In Belgium, 919 complaints of racial harassment and assault were reported, and 101 of these identified the police as the assailants. In Germany, criminal offenses with racist motives totaled 10,037; violent attacks rose 5.4 percent over 1998. Forty-seven Jewish cemeteries were desecrated in Germany in 1999. In Greece, the police have come in for serious criticism from international organizations for the ill treatment of Gypsies and Albanians, especially. In Spain, anti-Muslim riots broke out in towns in Catalonia in July 1999, with crowds shouting, "*Moros fuera!*"—Muslims out! In France, a 1996 poll revealed that two-thirds of French people felt that there were "too many Arabs" in the country. And France's half a million Jews have suffered a rise in anti-Semitic assaults: between September 2000 and November 2001, according to the Anti-Defamation League, 330 anti-Semitic incidents occurred in the greater Paris region alone: almost one per day. In the Netherlands, watchdog groups report some 3,000 racially motivated assaults per year since 1997. In Austria, the 378 reported incidents included desecration of Jewish gravestones; nine police officers were suspended in 1999 for racially motivated attacks. In Sweden, 2,363 crimes with racial motives were recorded, including 281 assaults. Between 1997 and 1999, the numbers of crimes committed by neo-Nazi organizations in Sweden have doubled. In Britain in 1997–98, 13,878 racial incidents were reported to the police; 21 percent of these involved physical assaults.[3]

The statistics are only partial, but combined with the public opinion surveys carried out by the EU, the overall impression is of a continent that has a serious problem with race. For example, in a survey carried out in 1997, which questioned over a thousand people in each of the EU states, 33 percent of the respondents stated that they were "quite racist" or "very racist"; 41 percent said that ethnic minorities and foreigners were too numerous in their countries. One person in ten said that they approved of racist movements or the position of racist organizations toward foreign immigrants. In every category, the percentage of those with antagonistic views toward foreigners and minorities was higher than in a similar survey conducted in 1989.[4] A survey taken in 2000 showed that most Europeans think that minorities have worsened their quality of life. For example, 52 percent of Europeans believe that the quality of education declines in schools with too many minority children. (In Denmark, Sweden, and the Netherlands, this fear is highest.) Fifty-two percent of Europeans believe minorities abuse the social welfare system; in France, 66 percent support this view. Fifty-one percent of EU citizens believe that immigrants increase unemployment. (Germans, at 61 percent, hold this view strongly.) In light of these findings, it is not surprising that 39 percent of EU citizens believe that legally established immigrants from outside the EU should be sent back to their country of origin. In all of these categories, the figures demonstrating antagonism toward minorities, immigrants, and foreigners had increased since 1997.[5]

The good news is that the majority of Europeans are tolerant of ethnic, cultural, and religious diversity. The bad news is that the number of those who are intolerant is large, and growing. Even though foreign residents remain a small fraction—about 4 percent—of the European Union's population, the actions of the racist minority have created an atmosphere of tension and crisis, with public opinion calling on governments to do something about the "race problem." The results are visible in at least three areas: first, in the more restrictive policies pursued by national governments concerning immigration; second, in the legitimization of the anti-immigrant rhetoric espoused by the far-right-wing parties and political movements that are active in every European country; and third, in the policies of the European Union, which has developed a battery of international control mechanisms to keep foreigners—especially poor, dark-skinned foreigners—out, creating what critics have called a "Fortress Europe." This issue comprises far more than a debate about immigration policy, however. At the heart of the debate is the awkward question, who is European? Or, to put it another way, who is to be welcomed into the European family, with all it promises—equality, prosperity, dignity, freedom, tolerance—and who is to be excluded? And why?

LEGACIES OF EMPIRE: IMMIGRATION IN BRITAIN AND FRANCE

In Britain, the debate about immigration emerged in tandem with the withdrawal from the colonial Empire during the 1950s. In that decade, most immigrants came to Britain from the West Indies, India, and Pakistan. They happily took advantage of Britain's historically open immigration policies, which the British had encouraged as part of an imperial credo: the British Commonwealth was a family of nations, and its inhabitants should be free to move about within it. This tolerant view was reinforced by the 1948 Nationality Act. Even so, during the 1950s, British leaders grew anxious about the prospect of unlimited immigration. In 1955, Lord Swinton, secretary of state for commonwealth relations, expressed alarm at the growing number of "working-class Indians coming here. This is a new development and unless it is checked, it could become a menace." The British cabinet, though loath to introduce explicitly racial immigration controls, did agree that "if immigration from the Colonies and, for that matter, from India and Pakistan, were allowed to continue unchecked, there was a real danger that over the years there would be a significant change in the racial character of the English people." Lord Salisbury, a veteran Conservative Party leader deeply involved in colonial policy during the 1950s, argued that something had to be done. "The main cause of this sudden increase of the inflow of Blacks," he wrote to his friend Lord Swinton, "is of course the Welfare State. So long as the antiquated rule obtains that any British subject can come into this country without any limitation at all, these people will pour in to take advantage of our social services, and we shall have no protection at all."[6]

ESTIMATED NET IMMIGRATION INTO BRITAIN FROM THE NEW COMMONWEALTH, 1953–1962

	West Indies	India	Pakistan	Others	Total
1955	27,500	5,800	1,850	7,500	42,650
1956	29,800	5,600	2,050	9,350	46,800
1957	23,000	6,600	5,200	7,600	42,400
1958	15,000	6,200	4,700	3,950	29,850
1959	16,400	2,950	850	1,400	21,600
1960	49,650	5,900	2,500	–350	57,700
1961	66,300	23,750	25,100	21,250	136,400

SOURCE: Zig Layton-Henry, "Britain," in Tomas Hammar, ed., *European Immigration Policy: A Comparative Study* (Cambridge: Cambridge University Press, 1985), 93.

The issue became increasingly potent in British politics. As immigrants settled in inner cities, placing demands on social services and competing for jobs with working-class whites, racial tensions began to mount. Clashes between West Indians and whites in Nottingham and London in August 1958 prompted calls for a halt to immigration. In 1962, the first Commonwealth Immigrants Act introduced a system of employment vouchers that required immigrants from Commonwealth countries to demonstrate either specific employment plans or recognized skills and qualifications.[7] In 1967 the National Front was founded, which was an umbrella group for all manner of anti-immigrant (and anti-Semitic) organizations that appealed to some disaffected whites. Outbreaks of racial violence in the larger cities became frequent as gangs of young toughs engaged in open persecution of Asian immigrants. Even national political leaders fanned the flames. In April 1968, a Conservative MP and former minister of health, Enoch Powell, gave a notorious speech in Birmingham in which he declared that immigration had led to a "total transformation to which there is no parallel in a thousand years of English history." He painted a desolate portrait of a Britain in which working-class inner-city whites now "found themselves strangers in their own country. They found their wives unable to obtain hospital beds in childbirth, their children unable to obtain school places, their homes and neighborhoods changed beyond recognition, their plans and prospects for the future defeated. . . . They began to hear, as time went by, more and more voices which told them that they were now the unwanted." He called on the government to adopt "a simple and rational" solution: halt immigration and expel immigrants. To allow uncontrolled immigration, he declared, "was like watching a nation busily engaged in heaping up its own funeral pyre." He concluded with a notorious flourish that drew on a passage from Virgil and seemed to predict race war in Britain: "As I look ahead, I am filled with foreboding: like the Roman, I seem to see 'the river Tiber foaming with much blood.' "[8] The speech led to an uproar and Powell was promptly disowned by the leader of his own party, Edward Heath. But thousands marched on his behalf, especially in the working-class districts of London, where they held aloft signs saying "Don't Knock Enoch."

Though denouncing Powell, both parties vied to embrace his cause of immigration restriction. The Tories, out of power in the sixties, insinuated that Labour was soft on immigration, and in the 1964 and 1968 elections (both won by Labour) the Tories whispered the electoral slogan "If you want a nigger as a neighbor, vote Labour."[9] Not to be outdone, the Labour government slammed the door on the British-passport-holding Asians who had lived in Kenya and were being expelled by Africanization policies. The 1968 Commonwealth Immigrants Act restricted immigration of nonwhites while leaving open a loophole for white Commonwealth citizens. The 1971 Immigration Act divided British colonial subjects into "patrials"—those with a British parent or grandparent—and "nonpatrials," who happened mostly to be nonwhite. Patrials, as British subjects in the colonies, had rights to immigration, while nonpatrials now required work permits to enter Britain. This looked like, and was, a capitulation to the race-baiting calls launched by Powell and his supporters. Indeed, anti-immigrant sentiment, which according to opinion polls was widespread in Britain, seeped into the public discourse of both parties. In 1978, Margaret Thatcher would deploy the bogey of Britain being "swamped" by immigrants as part of her successful bid for power a year later. In 1981, Mrs. Thatcher's home secretary, William Whitelaw, announced new restrictions on immigration, seeking "to dispose of the lingering notion that Britain is somehow a haven for all those whose countries we used to rule."[10] Despite such sentiments, Britain had become a multicultural society. By the start of the 1990s, there were about 2 million British residents with racial and ethnic origins in India (840,000), Pakistan (475,000), the Caribbean (500,000), and Bangladesh (160,000).[11]

British immigration policy has been marked by a high degree of consensus between the parties, which support strict restrictions on immigration. During the 1990s, immigration numbers stabilized and entry into the UK became possible only for those with work permits or family members already in Britain. Most immigrants came from Europe or North America.[12] The British government deployed a wide array of new policing techniques and new technology to crack down on illegal immigration.[13] But starting in the late 1980s, Britain—along with the rest of Europe—faced a new problem: the application by thousands of refugees for asylum. In 1989, only 17,000 people sought asylum in Britain; this figure more than doubled the next year. In 1999, the number reached 70,000, and in 2000, topped out at 76,000. The early 1990s saw a sharp increase in applicants from the former Yugoslavia, but for most of the decade, asylum seekers have come from a diverse array of conflict-torn nations. The top ten countries of origin for UK asylum seekers in 2000 were Iraq, Sri Lanka, Yugoslavia, Afghanistan, Iran, Somalia, the former USSR, Turkey, China, and Pakistan.

ASYLUM APPLICATIONS (THOUSANDS)

	1989	1990	1991	1992	1993	1994	1995	1996	1997	1998	1999
EU	292	397	511	672	517	300	264	227	241	289	342
Germany	121	193	256	438	323	127	128	116	104	99	95
France	61	55	47	29	28	26	20	17	21	22	30
Neth.	14	21	22	20	35	53	29	23	34	45	39
UK	17	38	73	32	29	33	44	30	33	46	71

SOURCE: *Eurostat Yearbook, 1989–1999* (2001).

The 1951 United Nations Convention Relating to Refugees directs signatories to offer support and refuge to those people who find themselves outside of their country of residence and who, because of "a well-founded fear of being persecuted for reasons of race, religion, nationality, membership of a particular group or political opinion," cannot or will not return. It is left up to individual governments, however, to evaluate the requests of refugees for asylum. Although Britain was by no means the largest recipient of asylum seekers in Europe, the domestic political climate in the UK was highly charged on this issue, and asylum seekers became targets of a vituperative media campaign. It became standard practice for British tabloids to refer to asylum seekers as "scroungers, beggars, and crooks," part of a "tide of illegal immigrants," and likely to bring "terror and violence to the streets of many English towns."[14]

The British Home Office argued that most asylum seekers were not victims of persecution but were in fact "economic migrants," that is, people hoping to find a better life in Britain. As a consequence, according to the Home Office, "many claims [for refugee status] are simply a tissue of lies."[15] Few applicants passed muster. In 1997, only 19 percent of the applicants were allowed to remain in the UK. In 2000, 31 percent—21,550 applicants—were accepted.[16] Though bound by law to consider refugee applications, the government made life hard for asylum seekers. They were herded into disused public housing in squalid sections of British cities, or dispersed across the country in order to ease the tension in London and the southeast of the country. They were given vouchers rather than cash with which to buy food, which many considered demeaning. Although the small benefits they received kept them well below the poverty line, they were not allowed to find jobs during their first six months in Britain. The result was predictable enough: the public face of the asylum seeker usually belonged to a young, unemployed, poor Asian male, only reinforcing the popular perception that asylum seekers had no place in Britain.

In France, immigration policy was deeply informed by a republican tradition that sought to forge the people into one united, homogenous, and patriotic nation. As such, the French government rejects the classification of citizens into racial or ethnic categories. Multiculturalism is anathema to the French state because it stresses ethnic, religious, or cultural difference in a society that has long prided itself on the universal, enduring appeal of French ideals. The French claim that this view is far more progressive than the Anglo-American emphasis on minority rights and privileges, which are discriminatory and in any case weaken the fabric of national unity. This ideology of nationhood was reflected in long-standing immigration and nationality policy. Immigrants and their children born in France could easily acquire French citizenship, provided that they accepted its obligations: loyalty to the French nation, language, and social norms. Before the 1960s, this approach to immigration policy aroused little debate. The great majority of immigrants came from other European countries, notably Belgium, Italy, Spain, Poland, Russia and, later, Portugal. White, Christian, and European, these immigrants—though mostly poor—assimilated fairly easily into French society. (The 135,000 foreign-born Jews in France on the eve of World War II, however, remained vulnerable to official persecution, and the Vichy government conspired with Nazi Germany to expel and exterminate them.)[17]

During and after the period of decolonization, the issue of immigration developed into a major political and social problem for the French govern-ment. The brutal war in Algeria left the French people angry and vengeful: having been expelled from Algeria, it was only natural that the French might resist large-scale immigration by North Africans into France. The French set-tlers who fled Algeria in 1962 settled in France's southern cities and became a reliable source of hostility toward Algerian immigrants. Yet by the terms of the Evian agreements that ended the war, Algerians born before 1962 were enti-tled to keep their French citizenship if they chose. Many came to France in the 1960s in search of better economic opportunities. They were joined by Moroccans, Tunisians, Vietnamese, Africans, and other members of the for-mer French imperial community.

Initially, the French government did little to regulate immigration, seeing in it a solution to the labor shortage in the country. But once the recession of the early 1970s hit Western Europe in the wake of the 1973 oil shock, the gov-ernment declared a moratorium on immigration and initiated repatriation policies. These failed, though they created a great deal of tension as the gov-ernment used the flimsiest of excuses to expel troublemakers, labor activists, and the unemployed from the country. By 1990, there were 615,000 Algerians living in France, 573,000 Moroccans, and 206,000 Tunisians. These North Africans constituted about 40 percent of France's immigrant residents. In ad-dition to North Africans, workers from sub-Saharan Africa began to come to France in the 1960s, mostly from Senegal and Mali. Their numbers reached 100,000 by the start of the 1990s.[18]

The impact of immigration upon France was felt in many ways. One area was in the urban landscape. Postwar France had an acute shortage of housing, the result of four years of German occupation, war damage, and the economic crisis of the 1930s, which had hampered building. Postwar immigrants faced an already extremely tight housing market and were forced to rent homes and apartments in the poorest districts. In the 1950s, *bidonvilles*—shantytowns—sprang up on the outskirts of the major cities as immigrants fashioned crude shacks with roofs of corrugated tin *(bidon)*. These slums were destroyed in the late 1960s and replaced by public housing projects—the much-derided HLM *(habitation à loyer modéré)*, which began to appear in working-class areas and in the distant suburbs. Here, large immigrant families, mostly Muslim, began to converge, separated by religion, class, customs, and appearance from their French hosts.

Another impact has been the heightened role of Islam in French public life. There were at least 4 million Muslims in France by the end of the 1990s, making France the home of Europe's largest Islamic community. In 1976, there were 131 Muslim places of worship in France; by 1998, the number had passed a thousand. Although only 15 percent of France's Muslims worship regularly, the state has made life difficult for those who wish to follow Islamic traditions. In October 1989, three fourteen-to-fifteen-year-old girls appeared at their local school in the town of Creil (Oise) for the first day of classes dressed in the religious head scarf often worn by observant Muslim women. The headmaster refused the girls permission to attend classes, declaring that the head scarf was a religious symbol and as such inappropriate in a state-run secular school. The affair aroused a storm of debate between those who championed the right to freedom of expression and religion and those who insisted on the principle of a secular state. After two months, the French Conseil d'Etat ruled that religious symbols are "not incompatible" with secular schooling, except where they are provocative, or where they infringe on the right to freedom or dignity. This ambivalent position allowed local administrators to make their own judgments about the scarf, and so the issue festered. In 1994, François Bayrou, France's education minister, prohibited Muslim students from wearing the head scarf, calling it an "ostentatious" symbol.[19]

MUSLIMS AS A PERCENTAGE OF TOTAL POPULATION

France	7.5
Netherlands	4.4
Germany	3.9
Britain	3.3
Spain	1.8
Denmark, Norway, Sweden	1.4
Italy	1.2

SOURCE: *Economist*, 20 October 2001, 52.

Above all, the increase in immigration, especially of Muslims, into France created a groundswell of support for the introduction of new restrictions on immigration and asylum. As unemployment in France surged in the early 1990s to 13 percent, conservative parties used anti-immigrant sentiment to their advantage in the parliamentary elections in 1993. They won in a landslide. Prime Minister Edouard Balladur's government then adopted a muscular position on immigration, restricting rights of immigrants to welfare benefits, curtailing civil rights of immigrants, and increasing the powers of the police to detain and deport unwanted immigrants. In 1994, an adviser to then interior minister, Charles Pasqua, declared that "Muslim extremists have begun arriving in France as colonizers, with gods and weapons in their baggage."[20] After the Gaullist leader Jacques Chirac won the presidency in 1995, his government began a vigorous policy of repatriating illegal immigrants. This led to some ugly incidents. In the summer of 1996, French police stormed a church in Paris where 220 Africans had started a hunger strike to demand asylum. They were put on a plane and sent home. President Chirac declared: "France cannot accept all the wretched of the earth."[21]

THE GERMAN DILEMMA

No European country has been more affected by recent immigration trends than Germany. Its geographic location at the center of the continent, as well as the size of its economy and its large foreign population—the largest in Europe—have made Germany a magnet for immigrants. The tumultuous political changes of the late 1980s exacerbated the problem: between 1988 and 1992, almost 4 million new immigrants settled in Germany. Yet the paradox is that Germany traditionally has maintained one of Europe's most restrictive citizenship laws, and is officially *kein Einwanderungsland*—not a country of immigration. "Germany's capacity to cope with immigration is exceeded," said Social Democratic interior minister Otto Schily in 1998.[22] It had long been common for the conservatives to claim that "the boat is full," but now the left has joined in. The result has been a twofold progression in German immigration policy in the 1990s. On the one hand, the government has tightened border security, cracked down on illegal immigration, and taken in fewer asylum seekers. On the other, it has reluctantly accepted the need to integrate the long-term foreign resident population more fully into German public life. Both developments present a marked change from Germany's historical attitudes.[23]

Unlike the British or French, the Germans faced a major immigration crisis in the immediate postwar period. Between 1945 and 1949, some 12 million ethnic Germans from Eastern Europe fled or were expelled to Germany. About 8 million reached West Germany, where they represented 16 percent of its population. Because these Germans were victims and refugees, the West German government felt morally obliged to receive them. It became an axiom of postwar Germany that any German from the East who could make it to the Federal Republic was welcome. Article 116 of the Basic Law (Germany's constitution of 1949) guaranteed these *Heimatvertrieben* (expellees) citizenship and social benefits in the FRG.

Not all ethnic Germans made it to the West. About 4 million remained in the East during the Cold War and could not flee. Despite periodic efforts to secure their release, especially during the *Ostpolitik* period, many remained under Communist rule in Poland, Romania, and the USSR. In the late 1980s, Gorbachev allowed many more ethnic Germans to emigrate to West Germany. But after 1989, as Eastern Europe opened up and as Germany re-unified, many more began to come into Germany: almost 400,000 came in 1990 alone. Most came from Poland and the former USSR. In the context of a worsening economic picture in Germany, public opinion began to turn against the open-door policy. Many ethnic Germans spoke no German and af-ter five decades of Communist rule had totally different cultural backgrounds than their prosperous, democratic German cousins. Moreover, as Eastern Europe democratized, they could not claim that they were fleeing totalitarian governments. It looked as if ethnic Germans were abusing their status to re-ceive generous handouts from the FRG. In July 1990, the government stipu-lated that ethnic Germans had to apply for entry from their home country before arriving, and must also demonstrate command of the German lan-guage. In 1991, the government placed an annual limit of 200,000 on new ar-rivals of ethnic Germans. The German government also began to spend money on improving the lives of ethnic Germans in their own countries, in the hopes of getting them to stay there. The result was a gradual slowdown of the numbers of new arrivals: between 1998 and 2000, about 100,000 ethnic Germans per year were admitted to Germany.[24]

IMMIGRATION OF ETHNIC GERMANS TO GERMANY, 1950-1998

Areas of Origin	
Former USSR	1,781,743
Poland	1,441,957
Romania	427,811
Former Czechoslovakia	105,024
Former Yugoslavia	90,322
Other areas	55,704
Total	3,902,561

SOURCE: Barbara Marshall, *The New Germany and Migration in Europe* (Manchester: Man-chester University Press, 2000), 55.

Before 1990, an ethnic German who spoke no German and had lived his whole life in the Ukraine could become a German citizen; but a person born in Germany of Turkish parents, speaking perfect native German, could gain German citizenship only with great difficulty. What accounted for this pecu-liar state of affairs?

In the booming 1950s, Germany had a labor shortage. Between 1955 and

1968, the West German government signed agreements with Italy, Spain, Greece, Turkey, Portugal, Tunisia, Morocco, and Yugoslavia to recruit workers. These workers were brought in for a set period of time, and there was no discussion of their being allowed to stay in Germany or become integrated into German social life. By 1973, there were 3.9 million foreigners in Germany. With the economic slowdown after 1973, these work arrangements were ended. Yet many workers, rather than return home, stayed on in Germany. They brought their wives, had children, and set down roots. As a result, the foreign population of Germany continued to grow, reaching 4.8 million in 1989, 6.8 million in 1993, and 7.3 million by 1996 (where it has since stabilized). A large number, certainly, but by the late 1980s, 60 percent of these "foreigners" had been born in Germany. They had few civil rights and German law made it difficult for them to become naturalized citizens. As they constituted a large body of low-paid workers, they were housed in cheap public accommodations, usually in undesirable parts of the larger cities. The result was that they stood on the margins of German society, unrecognized and stigmatized. About a third of these people were Turks, a people that many Germans considered alien to their customs and traditions, and who became the favored target of German xenophobes.

In German nationality law, one's place of birth did not matter; only one's parentage, or blood, did. Germany's reliance on this *jus sanguinis*—or law of blood—reflects Germany's unique history. A distinct German culture, language, and identity predated by many centuries the formation of the modern German state, which emerged only in 1866. The German nation was, therefore, defined not by a contiguous territory but by ethnicity: Germanness. When the German state did finally codify its citizenship laws in 1913, it insisted on a cultural, linguistic, and hereditary definition of the German nation. Those who spoke German and valued German *Kultur*—wherever they might live—had rights to citizenship. But those who were not German, for example, Poles, Jews, and later, Turks—those whose cultural identity lay outside the German community—could never be German. This definition of a German citizenry that transcended national borders was, of course, manipulated by Hitler to justify his territorial claims to "German" lands in Austria, Czechoslovakia, and Poland. But it also served as a magnet during the Cold War to refugees from the Communist bloc, who risked life and limb fleeing East Germany because they knew they had rights in the Federal Republic. Still, the emphasis on *jus sanguinis* instead of *jus soli*—the law of soil—denied citizenship to millions of people born in Germany simply because of their parents' origins. It created a class of Germans who, despite their long presence in Germany, remained on the margins of German public life.[25]

The end of the Cold War brought about a gradual, but piecemeal, change in German citizenship laws. Before 1990, a foreigner could become a German citizen only after demonstrating his immersion in and admiration for German culture and language, a minimum of ten years' residence in Germany, and only if he had a permanent home, a job, and no criminal record. Activities in foreign political organizations were discouraged, and dual citizenship disqualified the candidate. In 1990, the state slightly eased the residence requirement, but the CDU, which had long championed *jus sanguinis* as the basis for citizenship, firmly opposed the granting of dual citizenship to German residents on the grounds that it violated the sense of loyalty and national community that membership in the German nation historically implied. It also might encourage more immigration. After the sudden upsurge in right-wing, antiforeign violence in 1993, the government of Helmut Kohl, under heavy pressure from the Social Democrats and Greens, agreed to ease access to citizenship for longtime permanent residents, regardless of their ethnic identity. The government was keen to show that it would not use culture as basis for discrimination; yet it refused to recognize the principle of *jus soli* or to allow dual citizenship.[26]

Not until May 1999, under the leadership of a Social Democratic–Green coalition government, was the law revised. Children born in Germany would obtain German citizenship if one parent had also been born in Germany; if both parents were foreigners, then the child would receive dual citizenship but be required to choose German or foreign citizenship before his or her twenty-third birthday. Failure to do so results in the loss of German citizenship. The law significantly scaled back the principle of *jus sanguinis* but did not fully repudiate it. At the same time, the residency requirement was reduced to eight years. Even so, would-be citizens still had to demonstrate command of the German language, a steady job, and no criminal record. For many of the poorest, least educated, and unemployed foreigners in Germany, these rules provided effective barriers to citizenship.

If Germany has eased access to citizenship for those people who arrived in Germany many years ago and their offspring, it has presented new arrivals—especially asylum seekers—with a formidable series of obstacles. This tightening of asylum laws marks a change from Germany's historically open embrace of those whom the state recognized as politically persecuted. When the Basic Law was written in the late 1940s, the new West German government wished to demonstrate its willingness to offer asylum to the persecuted peoples of the world, as a measure of recompense for the murderous persecutions inflicted by the Nazi regime. Not until the late 1970s did more than a few thousand people a year take advantage of Germany's open asylum provision.

But in 1980, the numbers of asylum seekers topped 100,000. The German government, constitutionally bound to accept asylum seekers, tried to deter them anyway by allowing the German states *(Länder)* wide latitude in implementing harsh rules restricting benefits, employment, and housing. Though this made the life of asylum seekers miserable, it did not stop them. In 1990, just when large numbers of ethnic Germans were arriving, Germany faced a huge surge of asylum seekers, mostly from Romania, Turkey, and Yugoslavia. By 1992, these numbers reached unmanageable proportions: some 439,000 asylum seekers entered Germany that year, mostly from within Europe; 156,000 of them were from Yugoslavia, but they were joined by 100,000 Romanians.

Overwhelmed by the numbers of asylum seekers, fearful about their adverse impact on the economy during the slowdown of the early 1990s, and heavily pressured by public opinion to assert control over the problem, the German parliament passed a law in June 1993 that amended the constitution. While the basic right to asylum remained intact, this right was circumscribed significantly. Individuals who arrived at the German border from a "safe third country" would be denied entry on the grounds that the applicant should seek asylum in that country instead of Germany. Since Germany is surrounded by safe, democratic countries, any asylum seeker arriving overland could be rejected. Moreover, the new law excluded from the German right to asylum anyone who came from a "safe country of origin"—a judgment reserved to the German authorities. The only legal way to be considered for asylum, then, was either to arrive at a German airport (and face detention there) or—ironically—enter the country illegally and destroy one's travel documents so as to cover traces of having traveled through a safe third country. In any case, the numbers of asylum seekers dropped considerably, and with stepped-up efforts to reject their cases and expel failed applicants from the country, the actual numbers of successful asylum candidates has dropped to an all-time low. In 2000, only 3,128 applicants—just 4 percent of all those who applied—received legal asylum. Germany is no longer a safe haven for the politically persecuted.[27]

IN HITLER'S SHADOW

The growing sense of alarm in Europe over immigration, racial conflict, and multiculturalism had a major impact in the arena of electoral politics. Far right nationalist and populist parties expanded their reach in almost every European country in the 1990s, and in some cases—Austria and Italy, most notably—became part of governing coalitions. While skinheads and hooligans tended to attract media attention, the organized parties of the far right began to attract something far more valuable: votes.

Perhaps the godfather of the European far right is Jean-Marie Le Pen, France's irrepressible leader of the Front National (FN). Le Pen's career is intimately bound up with the history of decolonization. Born in 1928, he was too young to play an active role in the Second World War (though he falsely claimed to have participated in the resistance). Instead, he took up the cause of the French empire, joining in demonstrations in the early 1950s in favor of keeping French control of Vietnam. At the age of twenty-five he volunteered to join the French army in Indochina. In 1956, he became a right-wing deputy in the National Assembly, where he made a name for himself as one of the staunchest defenders of French Algeria. So ardent was he on behalf of this cause that he resigned his parliamentary seat and reenlisted in the army, and he was sent first to Suez and then to Algeria. He joined up with the Tenth Airborne Division, the force that would prove so effective and ruthless in controlling Algiers. Le Pen himself was alleged to have participated in the torture of Algerians.

In 1960, once again a deputy in Paris, Le Pen fiercely opposed President de Gaulle's policy in Algeria. He became the hero of the returning French Algerians, as well as the military men who felt that their colonial wars had earned them nothing but the condemnation of their countrymen. Here was the basis of his political movement. In 1965, he directed the presidential campaign of Jean-Louis Tixier-Vignancourt, a lawyer who had been a minister in the Vichy government during World War II; he also opened up a record company that issued recordings of Nazi marching songs. In 1972, he helped establish the Front National. Though his presidential bid in 1974 did not win even 1 percent of the vote, his stance on immigration, and his general platform of "France for the French," started to attract attention in the 1970s and early 1980s. He depicted immigration as a biological-epidemiological threat to French purity, and immigrants as responsible for unemployment, overcrowded schools and public housing, crime, AIDS, and so on. He also rolled his xenophobia into a broad attack on the welfare state and on the movement of European integration, which he saw as unpatriotic and subversive of true French national interests. The appeal of these ideas in French political life led to an improvement in Le Pen's political fortunes. In 1984, he was elected to the European Parliament, and in 1986 his party won almost 10 percent in national parliamentary elections. In 1988, his presidential bid won 14.4 percent of the vote; in 1995, he pulled in 15 percent. The FN went on to win more than 30 percent of the vote in municipal elections in fourteen large towns, and won outright control of city governments in Orange, Marignane, and Toulon, all in the southeast. "At last," said a supporter, "we can say what we really think, and at last, we have somebody who says it for us."[28]

Le Pen's greatest success came in the presidential elections in April and May 2002. In a result that shocked the French political establishment, the right-winger won 4.8 million votes in the first round of the election, or 16.8 percent of the vote, thus edging out the Socialist prime minister, Lionel Jospin. Le Pen thus earned the chance to face the incumbent president, Jacques Chirac, in the second round. Le Pen was helped by a large field of candidates who stripped votes away from Jospin, and by a low voter turnout. In the days following Le Pen's first-round success, hundreds of thousands of French people took to the streets to denounce the National Front and its racist message. For two weeks, the country writhed, ashamed that a man of Le Pen's views could have emerged as a legitimate candidate for president. Le Pen's supporters, by contrast, declared the poll results to be evidence of the persistent antagonism in France toward an ossified political establishment, rising crime rates, lax immigration laws, and an expanding European bureaucracy that had robbed France of its national sovereignty. In the final round, Chirac trounced Le Pen, 82 percent to 18 percent. Still, 5.5 million French people voted for Le Pen. Le Pen's anti-European, anti-immigrant, and anti-crime message clearly had an appeal far greater than the mainstream political parties ever cared to admit.[29]

In Britain, by contrast, the far right has never enjoyed electoral success. Even in the 1930s, when millions of Europeans willingly supported Fascist parties, Britain's Sir Oswald Mosley, the founder of the British Union of Fascists, failed to win popular support. In the mid-1960s, the National Front was founded as a rallying point for various right-wing groups. By the mid-1970s, the group had about 17,000 members and received support from a hodgepodge of racist, anti-Semitic, neo-Nazi advocates, as well as the Libyan government. But after 1975, the new Conservative leader, Margaret Thatcher, adopted anti-immigration policies as part of her platform and so stole the far right's thunder. During the 1980s, the neatly dressed, well-scrubbed, Cambridge-educated Nick Griffin emerged from a divided and fractious movement to head up the British National Party. It remained tiny: in 1997, the BNP put up only fifty-seven candidates, and in 2001 it had only thirty-three—out of 659 constituencies. It ran on a violently anti-immigration and anti-Muslim platform, calling for a halt to all immigration and the expulsion of foreigners. "We think that reducing the number of non-whites," a BNP flyer claimed, "is the only way to restore peace and racial harmony." It also opposed further ties to Europe, called for a crackdown on crime, an end to multicultural "brainwashing" in the schools, and support for a strong British presence in Northern Ireland. In 2001, the BNP won on average 3.9 percent of the vote in the seats it contested. Its most conspicuous success came in the same greater Manchester constituencies that had been the scene of the race riots the previous month. In Oldham West, Nick Griffin won 16.4 percent of the vote, and in Oldham East, the BNP candidate won 11.2 percent. Overall, the BNP candidates won over 5 percent of the vote in seven constituencies. A shock to the establishment, yes; but in a first-past-the-post electoral system, the BNP has little hope of ever gaining a seat in the House of Commons.[30]

In Germany, the far right cannot be dismissed so lightly. Though the various far right parties have had minimal success at the polls, such is the burden of history that even the slightest rise in support for the German parties that espouse racist, nationalist, and xenophobic views provokes soul-searching and angst. The German Basic Law gave the government considerable powers to ban parties whose platform was inconsistent with German democracy. In 1952, the federal government banned the Socialist Party of the Reich (SRP), a party made up mostly of former Nazis. Its successor, the German Reich Party (DRP), barely managed to win 1 percent of the vote in federal elections of 1953, 1957, and 1961. In 1964, the DRP dissolved itself and made way for the National Democratic Party of Germany (NPD); among its founders were various former Nazi party members. The party was fiercely nationalist and anti-Semitic. The NPD did better than its predecessors, winning 2 percent of the national vote in 1965 and 4.3 percent in 1965. It did not win seats in the Bundestag, but did gain seats in state elections between 1966 and 1968. Its membership peaked at about 38,000 in 1967, but thereafter slumped to a few thousand. In the 1980s, the NPD failed at the ballot box, but started to attract support from young skinheads and rabble-rousers, who thrilled to its anti-Semitic and xenophobic discourse. The party leader in 2001 was Udo Voigt, an anti-Semitic former West German military officer who depicted himself as the advocate of "the ordinary German under siege by foreigners." This party's inflammatory rhetoric aroused deep concern among the federal government, and in January 2001 the interior minister, Otto Schily, asked the constitutional court to ban the party altogether.[31]

In the 1990s, Germany's best known far right party was the Republikaner (the Republicans). Founded in 1983 by Franz Schönhuber, a former member of the Waffen-SS and sometime journalist, the party's first breakthrough came on 29 January 1989, when it won 7.5 percent of the vote in West Berlin's state elections, and thus garnered eleven seats (out of 138) in the Berlin parliament. Though he rejected Nazism, Schönhuber refused to express any regret about his wartime service, and dismissed Nazi atrocities as the work of a "few rotten apples" in an otherwise honorable regime.[32] The party's platform was strongly nationalist, anti-Europe, opposed to Germany's close alliance ties to the West, and above all hostile to the presence of foreigners in Germany. In Berlin, this issue scored well among voters; at the time, foreigners made up over 10 percent of the city's population, the city had a serious housing shortage, and unemployment was high. Building on its success in Berlin, the Republicans won 7.1 percent of the vote, and six seats, in Germany's elections to the European Parliament in June 1989; in Bavaria, Schönhuber's home region, they won 14.6 percent of the vote. In 1992, as the postunification euphoria turned to anxiety and tension over high unemployment, slow economic growth, and the surge of asylum seekers, the Republicans pulled in 10.9 percent of the vote in state elections in Baden-Württemberg in April, and 10 percent in May in Berlin's elections. In March 1993, the Republicans won over 8 percent of the vote in state elections in Hesse, a prosperous region that includes Germany's financial capital, Frankfurt. The main election slogans were simple, but effective: "The boat is full" and "Germany for the Germans."[33] After these early gains, the Republicans had only modest success in local elections, winning 9 percent in elections in Baden-Württemberg in March 1996; the party failed to make a breakthrough at the federal level. In 1994 and 1998, the party did not come close to the 5 percent hurdle necessary to win seats in the Bundestag.

While the fortunes of the NPD and the Republikaner had worsened by the late 1990s, a new force emerged on the far right: the German People's Union (DVU), founded in 1987 by the right-wing newspaper tycoon Gerhard Frey. Though the DVU performed miserably in nationwide elections, it did better in state elections. In 1998, after campaigning on a violently xenophobic platform that blamed unemployment on recent immigrants, the party scored its biggest success, winning 12.9 percent of the vote in elections in Eastern Germany's state of Saxony-Anhalt. It was the highest percentage of votes won by a far right party in any postwar German election. The DVU profited from the failure of the mainstream parties to improve the economic fortunes of the former Communist lands: in Saxony, the unemployment rate stood at 24 percent in 1998.[34]

Economic hard times clearly aided the far right in Germany. But what explains the sudden surge of the far right in Austria, Switzerland, and northern Italy in the late 1990s—three countries that are among the richest on earth? The most successful far right politician in Europe in the 1990s was Austria's Jörg Haider, the leader of the Austrian Freedom Party. In October 1999, at a time when Austria had a mere 4 percent unemployment, low crime rates, and low inflation, Haider's party won 27 percent of the vote in national elections. He outpolled the conservative People's Party and came close to matching the

Social Democrats. In February 2000, to jeers from the rest of Europe, the Freedom Party and the People's Party formed a coalition government.

Haider, a lawyer and provincial governor, had been in politics since 1979. Youthful and telegenic, Haider was elected as the Freedom Party's leader in 1986. In 1994, the Freedom Party became a major player in Austria, winning 22 percent of the national vote, and in 1997 his party won 28 percent in elections to the European Parliament. Haider developed a reputation as a Nazi sympathizer. His father had been in the Hitler Youth and the Nazi SA; his mother had been devoted to the Nazi cause; and Haider often made damaging public statements that appeared to offer support for the economic policies of the Third Reich. In 1995, he spoke at a reunion of Waffen-SS veterans and praised their courage for staying "true to their convictions." But it is not his evident nostalgia for the Nazi past that has boosted Haider's party, but his anti-immigrant rhetoric and his anti-European views. He insisted that immigrants take away jobs from Austrians, bring crime and drugs to Austrian towns, and so should be removed from the country. He also tapped into serious concerns among Austrians about the process of European integration. Both the major parties in Austria had been supportive of close ties with the European Union. But in 2000, only 38 percent of the Austrian public thought membership in the European Union was a good thing. Only 32 percent supported the enlargement of the union to the East.[35] Perhaps most important, Haider offered a clear alternative to the dominant two parties that had governed in a cozy coalition since 1986. In Switzerland, the far right Swiss People's Party followed a similar line: opposition to immigration and to joining the European Union. The result: the far right emerged in 1999 as Switzerland's second-largest party, winning 23 percent of the votes.[36]

Regrettably, the story is the same in almost every country in Europe. In Belgium, it is the Flemish Bloc (Vlaams Blok) that demands the expulsion of immigrants; in Denmark, that is the position of the Danish People's Party; Norway has the Progress Party, which deploys anti-Muslim rhetoric and pro-Christian sentiments. Is Europe, then, on the threshold of a neo-Nazi seizure of power? Hardly. The rise of the far right in most countries was fueled by a combination of factors that had little to do with admiration for Hitler. Weak employment prospects, a sudden influx of foreigners, the weakening of national sovereignty, and an understandable reflex to praise traditional values in times of enormous political change: all these issues played a role.[37] There was also the protest factor: since 1990 and the collapse of Communism as a viable ideology, there has been no real protest vote for those fed up with the large established political parties. And since these large parties have converged over most of the big political issues—they all tend to favor the welfare state, high taxes, and European integration—dissenters must look either to the far right or to the far left for parties that are willing to break with the old shibboleths. It is no coincidence that the decade of the 1990s saw significant increases for Green parties in Europe at the same time as the far right surged. The rise of the extreme right, then, reflected the persistent reluctance on the part of—at most—10–20 percent of the voting public in Western Europe to embrace the consensus politics that have defined the postwar era. That is too high a number. Still, 80 percent of European voters—four out of every five—reject the appeal of the far right. Perhaps there is some small comfort in that.

GETTING THE BOOT: IMMIGRATION AND THE RIGHT IN ITALY

Between 1876 and 1965, some 25 million Italians emigrated from their homeland. Only in the mid-1970s was this historic outflow reversed; Italy is today a country of immigration. This is just as well: Italy's birth rate is so low that it will need immigrants to maintain its labor force. Despite the need for immigrants, however, and despite the familiarity of many Italians with the humiliating immigration restrictions their families have experienced in foreign countries, the Italian government has not been eager to lay out the welcome mat to foreigners.

Until the 1980s, Italy's borders were very porous. Although a number of laws on the books, dating from the 1940s, restricted the entry and movement of nonnationals and allowed authorities to expel foreigners who had no resources or employment, these laws were rarely enforced. Illegal immigrants, willing to work for low wages and live in slums, were not unduly harassed if they kept quiet. In 1986, just two years after the electoral breakthrough of the far right in France, the Italian parliament passed a law defining a new immigration policy. It assured the rights of foreign workers; it instituted hiring procedures for immigrants; and offered an amnesty to undocumented workers. It did not address the issue of refugees or asylum seekers. Nor did it affect the policing of illegal immigration, which remained a serious problem. Pressure from Italy's own far right parties, as well as members of the EC, pushed Italy to adopt more comprehensive legislation. In 1990, the Martelli Law (it was championed by the Socialist vice premier, Claudio Martelli) again offered an amnesty to illegal workers, but also stepped up border controls, required visas for visitors from North Africa and South America, and required would-be immigrants to apply for work permits. The main goal: to stop illegal immigration and assure employment and integration of immigrants already in the country. As for refugees, the law adopted the safe-third-country principle: refugees that passed through a safe country en route to Italy would be turned away.[38]

In 1991, the new law was put to a severe test. In the spring and summer of 1991, thousands of Albanians, fleeing the chaotic collapse of the hard-line Communist regime in their country, crossed the Adriatic and landed on Italy's shores. They made the fifty-mile voyage in leaky fishing boats, some powered only by oars; 20,000 arrived in the first ten days of March. The government was totally unprepared for this sudden influx. The Albanians were set up in sprawling camps and soccer stadiums with few amenities; in June refugees clashed with Italian police during protests over poor conditions. In August, the government set up a blockade of Italian ports to turn away Albanian vessels and resolved to repatriate the Albanians, even though they would appear to have qualified for asylum status. Using military aircraft and requisitioned ferries, the Italian authorities returned most of the immigrants to Tirana. In 1992, the government passed new legislation giving the police wider authority to expel undocumented aliens.

Just as Italy was facing up to the difficult problems of immigration control, the country's political structure went through massive changes. The old parties of the postwar era, the Christian Democrats, the Socialists, and the Communists, all imploded, their supporters fed up with the cronyism and corruption that had permeated the political establishment. This political shake-up opened the way for a surge of new parties to take the field in national elections in 1994. The Communists reformed themselves into the Democratic Party of the Left (PDS) and shed some of their most radical ideology. But the Christian Democrats and traditional parties of the right were pushed off the electoral landscape by the dramatic entrance into politics of Silvio Berlusconi, a media, publishing, and real estate tycoon. The fifty-seven-year-old Berlusconi also owned AC Milan, Italy's most successful soccer team. When he founded his new political party, he called it Forza Italia (Come on, Italy!), a name drawn from the popular chant for Italy's national soccer team. Amidst ongoing bribery and kickback scandals that had shaken the old parties, Berlusconi rapidly won new adherents. He promised efficiency and a restoration of Italy's prestige; he also made anti-Communism part of his campaign. He took Italy by storm in the spring of 1994, using his own media empire— he owned three of Italy's six television stations—to run political advertisements on his behalf. When elections were held in March 1994, Forza Italia became Italy's largest political party, winning 8 million votes. The Christian Democrats, who had been in every postwar Italian government, were decimated, while the Socialists failed to win a single seat. The reformed Communists, however, pulled in 7 million votes and emerged as Italy's second largest party. The country, it seemed, had split between two extremes.

What alarmed many Italians and Europeans about Berlusconi's success was his choice of friends. Riding his coattails were two parties of the far right, the Italian Social Movement (MSI) and the Northern League. Both parties had been fringe movements until Berlusconi legitimized their right-wing platform and formed a coalition with them called the Freedom Alliance. The Northern League was a single-issue party, and called for the breakup of Italy into three autonomous regions, thereby freeing the wealthy north from subsidizing southern Italy's poorer regions. It maintained an implicitly racist attitude toward immigrants and southerners alike. The MSI was the direct descendant of Mussolini's Fascist Party. Led by Gianfranco Fini, the party embraced the mantle of Fascism and staged street demonstrations with militants giving the stiff-armed Fascist salute. The MSI had been around since the 1940s and had a small but loyal following. Since the early 1970s, the party tended to win between 5 and 8 percent of the vote in national elections. It did well in the poorer, rural south, where resentment against the large parties was strongest, and tried to draw on anxiety about the far left's role in the terror attacks of the 1970s and 1980s. In the early 1990s, as the old order in Italy was collapsing, the MSI's message of anti-Communism, order, security, and anti-immigration struck a chord. In the elections in March 1994, the MSI, now under the name National Alliance, won 5 million votes, or 13 percent of the vote; two years later, it won 15.7 percent of the vote. In 1994, the neo-Fascists entered Berlusconi's coalition government.[39]

Anti-immigrant sentiment was not the dominant factor in the success of the far right parties or of Berlusconi. The corruption of the old parties and fear of the reformed Communists provided the right with plenty of ammunition to wage a successful campaign. But in the 1990s, the Italian government, whether led by Berlusconi or by parties of the center-left that returned to power in 1996, sharply tightened immigration laws. In large part, however, the changes to Italy's laws were the result of pressure from Italy's neighbors, especially Germany, Austria, and France. The Italian law on refugees allowed failed applicants for entry a grace period of two weeks before they had to leave the country. During this time, many of them fled north to Germany. In late 1997, when a sudden upsurge of Kurds from Turkey and Iraq arrived on Italy's shores, the German government protested that the Kurds were simply passing through Italy en route to Germany. Both French and German border guards were beefed up to keep them out. In February 1998, the Italian government responded by tightening its laws against illegal immigrants and revoked the fifteen-day grace period.[40] The result was a sharp increase in the numbers of expulsions, from about 5,000 a year in the early 1990s to 54,000 in 1998, 65,000 in 1999, and 66,000 in 2000.

FORTRESS EUROPE

The pressure on Italy to tighten its border controls reveals that immigration policy transcends national boundaries and has been caught up in the process of European integration. As Europe has worked to free up its internal borders to make travel and trade easier within the EU, it has also tried to enforce a unitary immigration system to make its external border more secure. The process began in the mid-1980s, when France, Germany, and the Benelux countries agreed to remove their common border controls so as to allow easier transit for goods, services, and labor. In 1985, these states signed an agreement in the Luxembourg town of Schengen that marked the start of a common border control policy in Europe. But with the sudden upsurge of immigration in the late 1980s, European states grew anxious that immigrants, once having arrived in a country with porous borders—like, say, Italy or Spain—could then easily make their way to the large cities of Northwestern Europe. Some European states resisted the Schengen agreement as a result, and it was not until 1990 that it was actually put in place; even so, Britain, Denmark, and Ireland refused to join the regime, while Austria, Italy, and Greece were told that their own border controls were so lax that they would not be included in the Schengen community. The result of this, as was clear in Italy in 1998, was a swift imposition of stiffer external border controls so that the internal barriers to trade and movement could be removed. In addition, the Schengen states established new common policing measures and a database called the Schengen Information System, which is designed to provide border police with immediate information on the backgrounds and police records of potential entrants.[41]

For some, these measures are merely good police work, a commonsense effort to crack down on illegal immigration and the crime that often accompanies it. For others, these measures represent a crude effort to keep out the poor, the weak, the homeless, the persecuted, who naturally yearn for a taste of Europe's riches. In either case, the perception created by these measures is that Europeans do not want to share their prosperous continent with any more migrants, especially those from the poorer parts of the world. It is hard to escape the conclusion that Europeans have grown less and less tolerant of outsiders even as they take pride in pressing ahead with ever-wider forms of political and economic integration with their neighbors. In 1968, the British politician Enoch Powell destroyed his promising career by calling for a halt to immigration and the repatriation of immigrants. Today, such views are routinely aired by government ministers and members of parliament in Austria, Belgium, Denmark, France, Norway, Italy, and Switzerland.

Ironically, despite the sort of foaming nationalist rhetoric deployed by some politicians in Europe today, the continent does not in fact have the luxury of ending immigration. With its own population growth slowing—the working population of the EU will shrink by 5 percent in the next twenty-five years—Europe will have to import millions of workers in the next three or four decades to keep its economy growing. Some countries are revisiting the labor schemes of the 1950s, with Spain hiring tomato pickers from Morocco, Germany and Britain bringing in Poles to harvest vegetables, and so on; but this time, the workers are seasonal only and must be sent back when the harvest is over. For all the talk of keeping immigrants out, most governments are now facing such a shortfall in workers that they soon will be forced to let them in.[42]

And so they keep coming. Despite the risks, despite the hardships, hundreds of thousands of illegal immigrants—perhaps half a million each year—make their way to Europe's borders. And why not? Will a young male Somali, whose country is wracked by civil war and famine, whose country's population is increasing rapidly, and where his annual income might, if he has employment at all, total $600, be deterred by European border police? Will he not look longingly to Western Europe, where the average per capita income is forty times his own? Every day, by the thousands, hopeful migrants jam their bodies into cars, trucks, buses, ferries, and barges, hand over a life's savings to unscrupulous brokers, and hope that they do not suffocate or drown in transit. One Turkish migrant who failed to penetrate Europe's walls described his harrowing odyssey, which included travel through Bulgaria, Romania, Ukraine, and Poland, where he was arrested and turned over to the Ukrainian police. There he spent a month in jail, suffering beatings and surviving on starvation rations. Once released, he made his way back to Istanbul where, despite his ordeal, he still dreamt of Europe. "Europe," he said, "is life, humanity, everything. You feel you are a human being in Europe." He declared his determination to try again, whatever the risk, to get into Europe. For him, Europe is a fortress, but within its walls lies the promised land.[43]

CHAPTER SIXTEEN

THE ELUSIVE EUROPEAN UNION

∎

WHAT IS "EUROPE"?

ONE OF THE MOST PUZZLING, and perhaps alarming, things about the European Union is that few people can easily define it. The *Economist*, which can usually be counted on to avoid jargon, offers a helpful starting point: it is "a union of democratic states, whose members must meet agreed-upon standards of political decency as well as economic competence. It is a cooperative venture, in which states accept a measure of mutual interference in specific areas. And it is a work in progress, which must constantly debate its direction, its speed, and its geometry."[1] True enough. If the union were merely a friendly club of fifteen nation-states, the debates among its members about the purpose and powers of the union would not be so sharp and sustained. It is precisely because the European Union is a constantly evolving set of institutions with far-reaching powers that the rows among its members have been so fierce.

Today, the European Union is the world's largest trading bloc, incorporating fifteen states and 370 million people, and possessing a single currency that is used by twelve of its members. It promulgates and enforces laws that touch almost every aspect of life in Europe, from business, trade, farming, and finance to work, health, and the environment. It even has a Parliament, a flag, an anthem, and a 60,000-soldier army. Yet it is not a state, or a federal government, or a confederation. Perhaps the best way to think of it is as a web of overlapping institutions designed to allow its members to achieve together certain objectives—security, stability, prosperity—that they could not attain alone.

It has not been easy to build. Many of the early enthusiasts for European integration, especially Jean Monnet, liked to portray the process of an ever-closer union of Europe's states as natural, sensible, even inevitable. But there has been nothing inevitable about it. In fact, the history of European integration is replete with rivalry and conflict, as well as compromise and progress. To focus on the latter without sufficient attention to the former is to miss the essential nature of the enterprise, and indeed its very novelty: for the first time in their long history, Europeans have discovered a way to settle national differences without resort to war. Integration is a process that can only be called revolutionary. How and why has it occurred?

STUMBLING TOWARD EUROPE, 1969–1989

The European Economic Community, which came into operation in 1958, owed as much to the geopolitical aim of securing West Germany into Western Europe as it did to economic objectives. In both respects, it worked spectacularly. Not only did Germany become a stalwart of the Western alliance, but during the 1960s, the EEC contributed to a massive surge in intra-European trade and amply justified the small concessions of sovereignty each of the six member states had made when they joined it. Yet the EEC remained unable to progress beyond its humble beginnings, in large part because the French president, Charles de Gaulle, refused to tolerate any further dilution of French sovereignty and because he refused to accept British membership in the community. With de Gaulle's resignation in 1969, the prospects for the deepening of European integration improved.

De Gaulle was succeeded by his longtime prime minister and protégé, Georges Pompidou. Pompidou, though a convinced Gaullist, nonetheless proved far more amenable to the European Community (as it became known in 1967) than his predecessor. In large part this was because Pompidou did not have the robust national economy that de Gaulle had enjoyed in the 1960s. France's economic picture had worsened in 1968–69, and Pompidou faced a trade deficit, rapid inflation, and a collapse in the value of the franc. Also, the dynamic leadership in international affairs by German chancellor Willy Brandt left France looking feeble. *Ostpolitik* had boosted Brandt's prestige, and the West German economy was booming. France could not afford to be left behind by a resurgent Germany. One way to boost France's role and offset Germany's growing preponderance was to champion an expansion of the EC: to do just what his mentor had fought against, and bring Britain into the community. At the Hague Summit of December 1969, Pompidou laid out a plan for giving new force to the European project. Although Pompidou demanded his pound of flesh in return—a stronger European voice in foreign affairs, greater monetary coordination to protect the franc from wide currency fluctuations, and a clear financing arrangement for the common agricultural policy—he was nonetheless willing to open the way to Britain's entry.

In 1970, the Conservative party leader Edward Heath became Britain's prime minister. Like Macmillan before him, he believed that membership in the community was vital to Britain's economic health. And like Macmillan, Heath faced a great deal of skepticism from within his own party. The issue also split the Labour Party, whose leader, Harold Wilson, had once favored entry and now opposed it. A small group of Labour MPs, led by Roy Jenkins, supported entry and gave Heath's government the majority it needed to secure it. In 1972, referendums in Ireland and Denmark gave strong support for entry into the EC, though the public in Norway voted against it. On 1 January 1973, the EC welcomed in Britain, Ireland, and Denmark, and now counted a total of nine members.

Almost immediately the larger community faced an avalanche of problems, mostly triggered by the international financial crisis of the early 1970s and the Arab oil embargo. Rising inflation, higher unemployment, and large trade deficits bedeviled the EC members, just at the moment when the United States had ended the Bretton Woods system and suspended the convertibility of the dollar. The members found that the political and economic crisis divided them from the United States and from one another. The hopeful plans for a widening of political and economic cooperation launched in 1969 were shattered.

The spring of 1974 brought a sudden shift of political leadership in Britain, France, and Germany. In February, Labour's Harold Wilson ousted Heath and announced that he would seek to renegotiate the terms of Britain's membership in the EC. In April, Pompidou died and Valéry Giscard d'Estaing became president of France; and in May, Helmut Schmidt took over as German chancellor following Brandt's resignation. Schmidt and Giscard, two cosmopolitan, intelligent men with a highly nuanced understanding of economic matters, soon became fast friends, and worked hard to keep the community together during the turbulent 1970s.

Their British friends made things as difficult as possible. Wilson carried out his campaign promise to renegotiate the terms of British entry. Wilson's principal concern was that Britain paid too much to the community and got too little in return. In this he had a point. As a major importer of food and industrial goods, Britain had to levy import duties on these goods and turn them over to the community as part of the common agricultural policy. But in return, Britain's efficient farming sector received less in development aid and subsidies from the community. Wilson demanded that this be rectified by trimming the size of Britain's contribution. The deal reached offered Britain a rebate, but did not permanently solve the issue. And the arduous, exhausting negotiations left the member states embittered and resentful toward Britain. Though the British public approved the new terms in a referendum in June 1975 by a 67–33 percent margin, the atmosphere in the community following the negotiations was distinctly pessimistic.

With Britain on the margins, the Franco-German relationship deepened. This had its positive aspect. Despite the economic downturn of the early 1970s, France and Germany resisted the natural inclination of states to fall back on national remedies to protect their home economies. Instead, the two countries maintained a high degree of cooperation and kept the spirit of Europe alive. Yet the Franco-German duopoly also alienated the smaller states and showed how weak the supranational institutions of Europe, especially the Commission and Parliament, really were. Indeed, Giscard worked to weaken the Commission still further so as to reserve greater power for France in running the affairs of the community. In 1974, he and Schmidt urged the creation of a new European Council, made up only of heads of state and obliged to meet at least twice a year. This signaled a reduced role for the Commission and its team of bureaucrats, and heightened the perception that the European Community was simply a forum for debating and resolving transnational economic and political issues. The hope that the EC represented the start of a genuinely federal Europe was dead by the end of the 1970s. The community still lived, but its pulse had slowed to an alarmingly low rate.[2]

There were a few significant breakthroughs in the late 1970s that foreshadowed a possible revival of ambition. In 1979, the European Parliament held its first direct elections, expanding the democratic character of the EC. In 1981, Greece entered the EC, and discussions with Portugal and Spain got under way. But the most significant development came in economic matters. In the midst of the international economic chaos that had been triggered by the dual hammer blows of the collapse of the Bretton Woods system and the oil crisis, Germany and France began to discuss ways to create a zone of currency stability in Europe, to protect the European currencies from rapid fluctuations against one another and against the dollar. For the Germans, this made sense: the powerful deutsche mark was overvalued, which hurt exports. Rather than devalue the mark, Schmidt wanted to appreciate other European currencies and even out the burden of a strong currency across the EC. For the French, a stable and stronger currency would raise business confidence and help lower inflation. The scheme was advanced under the creative leadership of Roy

Jenkins (the president of the European Commission from 1977 to 1981) and given a name: European Monetary System (EMS). The idea involved some clever legerdemain. Jenkins envisaged the creation of a European currency unit, the ecu, which would be given a value based on a basket of European currencies. Members would then peg their currencies to the ecu, within a narrow range of fluctuation. The goal was to stabilize currencies, reduce inflation, and promote intra-European trade. The EMS came into operation in March 1979 and helped bring about monetary convergence of the EC members. Although some countries, notably Britain, did not immediately join the system, the EMS revealed that the sense of common purpose within Europe was not dead, and had in fact been sustained by the French and German governments in the late 1970s.[3]

The progress on monetary coordination, however, was largely overshadowed by a long-running feud between Britain and the EC over the perennial problem of the British contribution to the community. This issue had been papered over by Harold Wilson in 1974, but not finally resolved. Each year, the British sent far more to the EC than they received. Britain's net payments soared in the 1970s, from 60 million pounds in 1973 to 947 million in 1979. The privilege of membership in the EC cost Britain almost a billion pounds a year. The new British prime minister, Margaret Thatcher, decided to settle the issue once and for all. Another prime minister might have quietly cajoled the EC to adjust the size of Britain's contribution. After all, Britain was simply asking to set right an obvious imbalance. Yet Mrs. Thatcher decided to use the issue not simply to correct the size of Britain's contribution but to generate domestic political support for the Conservative Party. She castigated the Brussels bureaucrats, claimed that she was waging war with them in Britain's best interests, antagonized all the member states, and promoted strongly anti-European views in Britain. "The situation is demonstrably unjust," she declared in October 1979. "I cannot play Sister Bountiful to the Community while my own electorate are being asked to forego improvements in the fields of health, education, welfare and the rest."[4] This helped her politically at home, but turned what should have been a simple issue into a long, ugly quarrel.

She did succeed in winning a reduction of Britain's contribution. In the end, the EC had no choice. In the early 1980s, the cost of subsidizing farming in Europe had skyrocketed, and the EC began to contemplate raising more money by increasing the national contributions to the EC drawn from value-added tax (VAT) revenues. Mrs. Thatcher would not agree to any such increase without an agreement on the British contribution. Not until an EC summit at the Fontainebleau château in June 1984 was a deal reached that promised to

rebate to Britain 66 percent of its annual VAT contribution. But there had
been significant damage done. Not only did the fight leave EC members bitter, but Thatcher's own Conservative Party grew increasingly hostile to the entire European project. Mrs. Thatcher's language seethed with contempt for her
European partners: she thought them unfair, shameless, power hungry, unaccountable, cynical, indifferent to Britain's concerns. And their greatest fault,
their unpardonable sin, was that they were "quintessentially un-English."[5]
Mrs. Thatcher's crude brand of nationalism may have won her some political
points at home, but it hurt her party in the long run. The bold stance taken by
Winston Churchill, Harold Macmillan, and later Edward Heath in making the
Conservatives the party of Europe was abandoned. It now became fashionable
to heap scorn on the institutions of Europe and to hold the line against any
further widening of EC powers. It is a legacy that led the Conservative Party
down the path of electoral defeat in 1997 and has kept it divided and fractious
ever since.

The resolution of the British budget dispute cleared the way for another
round of enlargement, this time southward. Portugal and Spain had consolidated their transition to democracy by the early 1980s, and both ardently
wished to join the EC. In principle, the EC wanted to reward these fledgling
democracies with the benefits of community membership. In practice, however, the negotiations were long and difficult. Both Spain and Portugal were
poor countries whose economies could not bear a sudden inrush of competition with their advanced neighbors. This militated in favor of a continued
regime of protection for certain sectors, and it also meant that both countries
would need significant EC aid to modernize their economies. Further, Spain
and Portugal produced large amounts of agricultural goods that were already
in surplus in the EC, such as wine, olive oil, fruits, and vegetables. France,
Europe's largest agricultural producer, feared the competition from the south
and wanted assurances that its own farming sector would not be harmed. In
short, Spanish and Portuguese entry would cost the EC a great deal of money,
both in development aid and in additional subsidies to farmers and fishermen
to offset the influx of cheap southern produce into the community. Not until
the budget issue was settled could an arrangement be worked out, and in 1986
both Portugal and Spain became EC members.

The early 1980s had been a difficult period for the European Community:
the budget dispute and the prolonged enlargement negotiations had soured
relations between the member states. The EC had also wasted a great deal of
precious time, during which the United States, Japan, and the newly industrialized Asian economies had expanded rapidly, especially in the production of
automobiles, electronics, and durable goods. Europe was being left behind.

Under increasing pressure to produce concrete economic results rather than merely bloated farming subsidies, the leading states, along with a new and highly capable European Commission president named Jacques Delors, began to consider ways to boost European trade and competitiveness in the world market. The result was the Single Europe Act (SEA) of 1986, an initiative that outlined the way toward a truly open internal market in the EC by 1992, and also introduced important institutional reforms to the community itself. The SEA proved to be the most successful measure in EC affairs since the Treaty of Rome of 1957 and marked a dramatic improvement in the fortunes of the community.

What explains the sudden success of a new project of market liberalization after three decades of paltry accomplishments by the EC? The most important reason is that all the major states had concluded by the mid-1980s that the only way to keep Europe competitive was to establish a single internal market. The dirty secret of the EC was that for all its talk about unity and integration, EC members deployed various forms of nontariff barriers (tariffs having been eliminated in stages since 1958) to protect their economies from competition. For example, the members maintained divergent national regulations on consumer protection and safety over a very wide array of products, including cars, manufactures, appliances, even insurance and banking. Regulations were not standardized, and so goods and services from one EC country often could be excluded from another on regulatory grounds. Opening up more trade on the continent required harmonization of such regulations. Another barrier to trade was the sharply varied value-added-tax rates imposed by member states on goods and services, and excise taxes on alcohol and tobacco products. Divergent rates of taxation distorted trade and led to increased border controls to stop cross-border smuggling, which tended to inhibit a free flow of goods. And finally, customs and immigration controls slowed transport and delivery of goods across national borders, thereby raising the cost of doing business in Europe and making Europe less competitive than Japan or the United States. The single market program, laid out in 1985, made 279 proposals for increased trade liberalization in order to rid Europe of its internal barriers to the movement of people, goods, services, and capital. The EC also provided a strict timetable, and envisioned a single market by December 1992.[6]

This far-reaching program could never have advanced without strong support from the largest economies. This was forthcoming, especially from Britain. Margaret Thatcher did not like federalism and bureaucracy, but she embraced the cause of trade liberalization as consistent with her own struggles against regulation and nationalization in Britain. The Germans welcomed liberalization too, since about half of Germany's exports went to other EC members and Germany would profit from easier access to those markets. Even France, traditionally protectionist, came around. In 1981, the socialist government of François Mitterrand embarked on a dramatic series of statist economic measures designed to promote socialism and jump-start the flagging French economy: nationalization of industry, heavy state subsidies, full employment. The plan failed miserably, and in 1983 Mitterrand made a sharp U-turn, embracing liberalization, deregulation, and a strong franc pegged to the deutsche mark. By 1985, Mitterrand accepted the Single Europe Act as the next logical step for the French economy.

The other major factor in the success of the SEA was the role of Jacques Delors. A former French finance minister, a crafty politician with a terrific capacity for hard work, Delors was also a devoted European federalist. His ultimate goal was the genuine monetary union of Europe and a wider array of decision-making powers for the community institutions. Yet Delors deserves credit for developing a long-term strategy. He played down his own ambitions so as not to antagonize Britain and to develop the internal market. Once that was achieved, he reasoned, the momentum for monetary union would be overwhelming, indeed irreversible. Delors did not come out of the SEA process empty-handed: he got the EC to agree to accept qualified majority voting instead of unanimity in the Council of Ministers as they faced the implementation of the single market program. This would increase efficiency and avoid the prospect of the EC being held hostage by one recalcitrant member. And he managed to win a small increase in the role of the European Parliament in developing EC policy. Far more important, the SEA gave Europe a sense of purpose and achievement that it had not had since the 1950s. It came into force on 1 July 1987.

FROM COMMUNITY TO UNION, 1989–2002

Jacques Delors's gamble that a single market would create greater momentum for full monetary union paid off. In June 1988, with European business and industry leaders calling for the complete abolition of national exchange controls and the permanent fixing of exchange rates, the European Council instructed Delors to prepare a report on monetary union. He presented a report that called for the progressive monetary union of all member states, the creation of a European Central Bank, and the establishment of a common currency. The argument in favor of monetary union was simply an extension of the Single Europe Act: if there was to be a genuinely open internal market in

Europe whose aim was the free flow of capital, goods, and services across national boundaries, then member states would have to coordinate their monetary policies with one another very closely to achieve the full benefits of the single market. Indeed, the best way to harness the potential of a single market was to abolish all national currencies and replace them with a single currency. This way, there would be no need to worry about currencies competing against one another, and trade between member states would not be hampered by the need to denominate all business transactions in twelve currency units. This was a bold idea that raised many complex issues. A single European currency that replaced the franc, the deutsche mark, and the lira required a single European bank to control it. It also would mean the loss of national control over monetary policy. A nation's currency is the very symbol of its sovereignty, and macroeconomic policy is a field jealously guarded by states. At times of economic slowdown, for example, central banks can lower interest rates to provide a boost in the economy; or if inflation is running high, central banks might tighten their lending policies. All these decisions would now be transferred to a genuinely European institution.

Why did the states of the EC support such a dramatic transfer of national sovereignty to a European institution? As ever, they believed it in their economic interests to do so. For Germany, the experience with the European Monetary System had been a success, helping to ease the value of the mark and contribute to large trade surpluses. German business groups saw that a deepening of monetary union, by removing obstacles to capital movement, would be good for the German economy. The chief concern of German business and bankers was the risk that monetary union would import inflation from other, weak-currency countries in the EC, and for this reason the Germans insisted on a European Central Bank that had as its chief objective low inflation. If the Germans were going to give up their beloved and rock-solid deutsche mark, they wanted to replace it with a currency every bit as strong. France was the strongest advocate of monetary union. Both the French Socialists and the Gaullists supported increased trade liberalization and monetary convergence in Europe. With its currency linked to the mark, France had lowered its inflation and significantly improved its international competitiveness. However, the French chafed at the domineering role of the German Bundesbank and wished to see it replaced with a European Central Bank in which France would have greater influence. As usual, France's economic interests also reflected a concern for counterbalancing Germany's greater power in Europe. As for Britain, Mrs. Thatcher predictably and unwisely rejected monetary union as far too great an intrusion on Britain's national economic policy. Only after her departure from office in November 1990 could her successor, John Major, adopt a more nuanced stance that kept the pound in the EMS but opted out of the common currency.[7]

These strong economic arguments in favor of monetary union predated the fall of the Berlin Wall. However, with the collapse of Communism, the argument for union took on greater urgency in both France and Germany. As Helmut Kohl embraced swift unification between East and West Germany, France faced the unenviable prospect of an increase in Germany's economy, its population, and its relative power inside the EC. Mitterrand saw a deepening of European integration as a way to insure the continued containment of German power—the perennial goal of all postwar French leaders. Fortunately, Helmut Kohl believed that movement on European integration would dissipate any anxieties about Germany's preponderance in Europe. Indeed, Kohl wanted not only monetary union but widened powers for the EC, a stronger European executive, more authority for the European Parliament, and greater involvement in foreign affairs. As Kohl was fond of saying, his goal was not a German Europe but a European Germany.

With these two powerful states so strongly committed to monetary union, progress moved remarkably fast. But monetary union also required major institutional changes to the EC, and so the community members agreed to set up two parallel intergovernmental conferences, to deal, on the one hand, with expanding the political and institutional aspects of the EC, and on the other, to outline a plan for full monetary union. The work of these two conferences was brought together in the Treaty on European Union, agreed to in December 1991 and signed in the Dutch town of Maastricht in February 1992. The Maastricht Treaty's most concrete achievement was its plan for monetary union. It set out a specific timetable for achieving this by 1 January 1999, at which time those countries who had met certain "convergence criteria" would irrevocably fix their exchange rates and join in a common currency. Those states that did not meet the criteria by 1999 would be left out. The criteria reflected Germany's insistence that the new currency be a sound one. To qualify for the membership in the monetary union, states had to have low inflation, low long-term interest rates, stable exchange rates, budget deficits no more than 3 percent of GDP, and government debt less than 60 percent of GDP. A European Central Bank would control the monetary policy of the member states. On the political front, the Maastricht Treaty somewhat breezily introduced a common foreign and security policy (CFSP) for its member states, European citizenship, expanded powers for European agencies in social and justice affairs, and a modest increase in the powers of the European Parliament. Finally, the EC was renamed the European Union. Overall, the treaty represented an enormous leap toward a genuinely united Europe.[8]

Perhaps it was a leap too far. Over the next three years, the EU faced a series of crises that turned the sense of optimism on display at Maastricht to despair. A combination of factors, political, economic, and international, played havoc with the newborn institutions of the EU and humbled its members. First came the ratification crisis. All the states were obliged to ratify the Maastricht Treaty before it could come into force. But only two, Ireland and Denmark, were constitutionally bound to place the treaty before a referendum. In Ireland the treaty passed comfortably, with 69 percent in favor; but Denmark shocked its EU partners by rejecting the treaty on 2 June 1992. Although the margin was a mere 30,000 votes—50.7 percent against to 49.3 in favor—the Danish "no" provoked a serious crisis. For the first time, the momentum toward integration had been halted by the voters.

In the aftermath, many Euroskeptics praised the courage of the plucky Danes to stand up against an overweening European bureaucracy that had not listened to the concerns of the public. The Danish complaints, it appeared, were widely shared: too much power for European institutions, a loss of national sovereignty, discomfort with the idea of a common currency, the stiff criteria for monetary convergence, fears of mass migration across Europe as national borders disappeared. The Danish vote revealed how poor a job the EU had done in explaining to the public the relative merits of Maastricht. The sense of crisis was only enhanced by French president François Mitterrand's decision to hold a referendum on Maastricht in France, though it was not constitutionally required. The referendum allowed anti-Europe parties to air their grievances, and revealed once again how muddled the pro-Europe forces were in explaining their case. On 20 September 1992, the French approved the treaty, but only by a tiny majority: 51 percent in favor, 49 percent opposed. Hardly a resounding success for the "new Europe." And when in October 1992 Denmark negotiated special "opt-outs" from Maastricht, which would keep it out of the common currency and the common foreign policy of the EU, the public sensed that the wind was slipping out of Europe's sails.

The growing antagonism toward European integration intensified in 1992–93 as the continent lurched into its worst economic slowdown in two decades. In large part, this was a knock-on effect from the costly process of German unification. As Germany borrowed huge sums of money to rebuild the decrepit Eastern part of the newly united Germany, interest rates soared. These high interest rates were passed on to other economies through the European Monetary System. This slowed growth just at a time when EU states were trying to institute greater fiscal discipline so as to meet the convergence criteria for the common currency. The result was a sharp slowdown in economic growth and a surge in Europe's already high rates of unemployment.

By the middle of 1993, unemployment across the EU had reached 11 percent. As growth slowed, revenues sagged; as unemployment grew, so did unemployment benefits. The burden was too much, and government budget deficits began to widen. The only way out of the crisis, argued Jacques Delors, was to improve Europe's growth by cutting its costs and making it more efficient. This required trimming Europe's massive welfare benefits and its wage rates, which were the highest in the world. Such talk only stimulated dislike of the EU and enhanced the perception that somehow the community and the Maastricht criteria were responsible for Europe's malaise. On top of these woes, Europe's alleged common foreign policy failed miserably to bring stability in Yugoslavia, despite the repeated efforts of well-intentioned EU representatives.[9]

Yet the European project survived. For all the alarmist talk of Europe coming unglued in the early 1990s, the progress toward European integration continued. There are several reasons. Above all, Europe slowly pulled out of recession by 1994, in part aided by a booming US economy. In 1994, the GDP of the EU grew at almost 3 percent, and remained steady at about 2.5 percent for the rest of the decade.[10] Another boost to the economy came from the conclusion of the tempestuous world trade agreements (the GATT) in December 1993. The talks had been arduous largely because they focused on cutting agricultural tariffs. In the end the EU and the United States agreed to reduce their tariffs on each other's goods almost in half, enhancing the prospect of an expansion of world trade.[11] The Maastricht Treaty itself was rescued by a second, and favorable, Danish referendum in May 1993, and Britain followed suit, approving the treaty but deciding, like Denmark, to opt out of the common currency. This flexibility proved to be vital in keeping the EU project moving forward. In 1995, the war in Bosnia was ended, putting an end to the squabbles and finger-pointing over Europe's role there. Three new members joined the EU in 1995: Austria, Sweden, and Finland. And perhaps most important, the EU's member states remained committed to the principle of monetary union. Indeed, the recession of 1992–93 only underscored the need for a more united, efficient, and productive Europe. Monetary union steamed ahead. In December 1995, the EU settled on a name for the new currency: the euro. And much to the surprise of the many naysayers, Europe's national economies made great progress in meeting the tough convergence criteria. In May 1998, the EU declared that eleven of its members had successfully met the criteria for monetary union. (Greece failed to do so, while Denmark, Britain, and Sweden opted out of the common currency.) On 1 June 1998, the European Central Bank came into operation, and on 1 January 1999, the exchange rates of the eleven qualifying currencies were irrevocably fixed. Greece joined the group at the start of 2001. On 1 January 2002, as 14 billion new banknotes and 50 billion new coins went into circulation, the euro became the sole currency of twelve EU states.

THE EUROPEAN UNION TODAY

With this historical background in mind, we can now lay out the full shape and scope of the European Union. The EU is made up of five institutions: the Commission, the Council of Ministers, the European Parliament, the Court of Justice, and the Court of Auditors. The **Commission** is the executive of the EU. Its twenty members are appointed by national governments for a five-year term, though they are not beholden to their governments. The Commission is led by a president, also appointed by mutual arrangement between the national governments. The Commission initiates legislation and places it before the Council; once legislation is approved, the Council has the power to implement and enforce it. The main check to the power of the Commission is the **Council of Ministers,** which is made up of national representatives from each member state. The Council has a rotating presidency, with each state taking the chair for a six-month period. The Council acts on all legislation sent to it by the Commission. In most cases, the representatives strive to agree on legislation unanimously. In some areas, the principle of qualified majority voting applies, and here, each state is given a weighted vote, with the larger states having more votes. The Council must also approve the EU budget. In the past, certain especially dynamic EU commissioners, such as Walter Hallstein and Jacques Delors, have been able to dominate EU politics. Recently, however, the Council of Ministers has evolved as the union's most powerful body, combining features of both a legislative and an executive body.

In theory, the **European Parliament,** located in Strasbourg, represents the citizens of the union and inserts some public accountability into the union's proceedings. In fact, its powers are limited. Originally called the European Assembly, it held its first direct elections in 1979, and today has 626 members. Each member state elects its own slate of representatives for a five-year term, but once in parliament, the MEPs sit in political groupings (Christian Democratic, Socialist, Green, and so forth) rather than national blocs. The principal role of the Parliament is to provide a balance of legislative power with the Council of Ministers. Since the 1992 Maastricht Treaty and the 1997 Amsterdam Treaty, the powers of the Parliament have been somewhat expanded. The Parliament has the power to approve and propose legislation in conjunction with the Council, but on some important areas of policy—for example, taxation and farm subsidies—the Parliament has no binding power and can only give an opinion. The Parliament does not control the EU budget but must approve it, and so has the power to reject a budget it does not like. The Parliament also has the right to call hearings on a variety of topics and must approve the appointment of commissioners to the European Commission. The Parliament has the power to censure the Commission (by a two-thirds majority vote) and force it to resign, though no motion of censure has ever been adopted by the Parliament.

The **European Court of Justice,** made up of fifteen judges (one from each member state), ensures that law is applied throughout the union. It considers disputes between member states, between the union and member states, between union institutions themselves, and between individuals and the union. Although it cannot interpret national laws, the judgments of the Court are binding on all member states and supercede national laws. Finally, the **Court of Auditors** oversees the finances of the union and ensures proper and legal management.

Perhaps the union's most important body is not formally a part of the union structure: the **European Council,** which convenes heads of state and government at least twice a year in session with the president of the Commission. The meetings are usually informal, but as the union takes on larger and more important issues, the European Council has grown in importance, since major issues such as monetary union and a common foreign policy can be approved only by heads of state. The European Council serves as a constant reminder that the union is the servant of the national interests of the member states, and brings the heads of state into direct contact to sort out major European policy decisions.[12]

The powers of the EU are wide-ranging; consider just a few major categories. The chief objective of the Treaty of Rome of 1957 was to create a **common market** among the six founding states of the European Economic Community. The goal was to boost trade and productivity among the six by reducing barriers to one another's goods and setting a common external tariff. This was achieved in stages between 1958 and 1969. Since then, the EU has taken various steps to continue the process of breaking down barriers to the movement of goods, services, and capital across the borders of the member states. These policies have led to the creation of a single market, and the adoption of the **euro,** which is controlled by a **European Central Bank.**

The Treaty of Rome also envisioned the elimination of barriers to agricultural produce within the community. At the same time, however, the treaty insisted that the member states endeavor to improve productivity, ensure a fair standard of living for farmers, stabilize prices, guarantee supply, and provide consumers with reasonable prices. These were ambitious goals, especially since most states had in place elaborate subsidies, price supports, and protection for their farmers. The states therefore worked out a **common agricultural policy** (CAP) which imposed a community-wide system of farm supports. Members agreed that prices would have to be fixed across the community so as to protect the farmers. Furthermore, levies were raised against cheaper imports from outside the community. The money raised by levies were then used by the community to provide subsidies to farmers, allowing them to sell their goods on the world market despite higher European prices. The problem of this policy was that it generated massive overproduction, since advances in technology and guaranteed prices made it possible and profitable for farmers to increase their yields. The CAP had to pay farmers for those surpluses and as a result the CAP has become the most expensive component of the EU's budget. In 1992, the EU adopted proposals for cutting farm prices and export subsidies in an effort to bring the CAP under control. But it still costs an enormous amount of money. In 1980, the community spent 11 billion euros on the CAP; in 1990, this had risen to 26 billion; in 2000, it reached 41 billion, or 44 percent of the union's budget.

The other major component of the EU's budget pays for the **cohesion policies.** These aim to provide development aid to the EU's poorest regions, whether in rural areas (Portugal, Greece, southern Spain, southern Italy, Ireland) or in declining industrial zones (in the UK, France, and Belgium). Through the European Regional Development Fund, the EU provides job training, education, and modernization aid. In 2000, these and other social policies consumed 33 billion euros, or 35 percent of the overall budget. The high cost of these policies raises the question of **financing:** where does the EU's money come from? There are three sources: customs duties and agricultural levies against imports from outside the union (14 percent); a contribution by member states raised from value-added taxes (35 percent); and a proportional contribution from member states based on the size of their gross domestic product. Under these rules, the larger, richer countries pay the most, with Germany, which provides about a quarter of the EU budget, making the largest contribution.[13]

The European Union is active in many other areas that relate to the economic, social, and legal life of the member states. The EU, which represents its members in matters of external **trade,** is the world's largest trading bloc, with 17.5 percent of total world exports (compared to 15.6 percent for the United States).[14] The Commission has the power to enforce fair **competition** between its member states, and since most large companies are multinational, this gives the Commission enormous influence in global business. An example of this came in July 2001, when EU competition commissioner Mario Monti blocked a $42 billion merger between two US corporate giants, General Electric and Honeywell International. The large European operations of these two companies gave the EU the right to investigate—and in this case block—the merger, on the grounds that the merger would drive competitors out of the aerospace engine market. The EU has started various projects to encourage **research and development** in information technology, biotechnology, telecommunications, aerospace, and other areas in which Europe had lagged behind the United States. The EU works with member states in formulating an **employment** policy, and given the stubbornly high unemployment rates, especially among the young, EU activity has increased in this area. The EU also adopted a Charter of Fundamental Social Rights of Workers, which defines **workers' rights.** The EU oversees many of Europe's large **industrial sectors,** such as steel, energy, transport, and fishing. It shapes and applies consumer protection legislation, health regulations, and environmental standards.

The EU has had far more difficulty in defining a **common foreign and security policy.** Countries with a larger international profile, especially Britain and France, have been reluctant to allow the EU to speak for them in matters of defense and security. Also, the United States has not championed the idea of an independent EU foreign policy since it might conflict with NATO, which the United States indisputably leads. The EU foreign ministers meet regularly, and the European Council treats foreign affairs, but a coherent uniform policy has been lacking. The EU was humiliated by its inability to play a serious military role in the conflict in Yugoslavia during the 1990s, and resolved to create a more coherent security structure. The Amsterdam Treaty, which came into force on 1 May 1999, created a high representative for the common foreign policy. It also worked out arrangements for the creation of a 60,000-soldier rapid-reaction force, designed principally for humanitarian, rescue, and peacekeeping tasks. This agenda reflects the broad priority of the EU to become a force for conflict resolution and peace rather than warmaking. In this respect, the EU provides over 50 percent of the world's humanitarian aid, a third of world aid to the Middle East, 60 percent of world aid to the former Soviet Union, and 40 percent of reconstruction aid to Bosnia.[15]

The EU is a remarkable institution, certainly more powerful than most of its founders could possibly have imagined. But problems remain in the EU, not the least of which is that the 370 million people it now incorporates are often indifferent to it, ignorant of it, confused by it, and occasionally hostile toward it. The Danish and French referendums on Maastricht revealed that when given an opportunity—in itself rare enough—to vote on the policies of the EU, Europeans are deeply divided. These doubts, and the general failure of the EU member governments to assuage them, remain one of the most notable features of the EU at the start of the twenty-first century. Scholars call this the "democratic deficit," which means that the institutions of the EU are insufficiently subject to the dictates of the voters. True, citizens vote for their national leaders, who then carry out European policies; but given the wide powers now in the hands of, for example, the director of the ECB, the president of the European Commission, and the newly created high representative for the common foreign and security policy, many citizens perceive the EU as a powerful but unaccountable superstate.

Certainly the many polls carried out by the EU's Eurobarometer reveal this. In 1991, 71 percent of EU citizens expressed support for their country's membership in the union. But this support had slumped to 46 percent in the spring of 1997. Since then, support for the EU has hovered at about the 50 percent mark. In 1999, 41 percent of EU citizens declared themselves dissatisfied with the way democracy works in the European Union, while only 40 percent were satisfied. Nor do Europeans know much about the EU. On a scale of one to ten, with ten meaning high knowledge of the EU, Europeans rated themselves a four. Forty percent of Europeans do not trust EU institutions, while only 39 percent do. In 2000, 55 percent of Europeans supported the common currency, but 37 percent opposed it. Finally, Europeans do not themselves feel very "European": 42 percent think of themselves as combining a European and a national identity, but 45 percent reject any European identity at all, and simply think of themselves in national terms. The ideal of a European citizen, then, is not widely shared.[16]

For skeptics, these figures suggest a high degree of resistance to the European integration project. Certainly, they suggest that Europeans still pride themselves on their unique cultural, linguistic, and geographical characteristics and want to maintain them. That is as it should be. Indeed, what makes the EU so successful is that it has promoted a single market and a common currency while allowing Europe's diversity to flourish. The EU has accomplished its goals by providing the nations of Europe with certain tools to achieve the economic prosperity and continued growth that each nation, left to itself, could never have attained. In the process, it has created shared institutions in which national differences can be worked out, and where the burdens of adapting to a dynamic, global economy can be more evenly shared across the fifteen members. In Europe's all too recent past, national rivalries were usually solved by war. Today they are solved by technical experts drinking bottled water and sipping espresso. Less dramatic, perhaps—but who would wish to go back in time?

LOOKING EAST

In the 1990s, the EU met the daunting challenge of monetary union. Its next act: opening up the EU club to a dozen new members in Eastern and Southeastern Europe. This will prove a defining moment in European history and will mark the date at which one can finally speak of a united Europe. Yet it will be difficult, and will certainly change the character of the EU itself. Between 1950 and 1973, "Europe" remained a club of six states; over the next twenty years it added nine more. Can the EU really take in still another dozen, and do so all at once, without substantially weakening the basic mechanisms of shared governance that have been so painstakingly crafted over the past five decades?

In forming an answer to that question, the EU must first settle a few preliminary issues. First: why expand at all? There is no good economic reason to expand the EU. True, EU trade with Eastern Europe has expanded a great deal in the past ten years, and the thirteen candidate countries now take 16 percent of the EU's exports and provide 11 percent of its imports. The problem is that the weaker, less developed, politically fragile Eastern democracies will be a massive drain on the EU coffers, requiring significant development aid and subsidies. So the logic for expansion is largely political: Eastern Europeans, having suffered under totalitarian rule for half a century and having at long last liberated themselves, surely earned the right to share in the construction of Europe. Furthermore, membership in the EU should, in theory, promote stability and extend the bloc of market democracies all the way from Ireland to the Russian border.

That settled, a second issue arises: who comes in and who stays out? Simply settling on the list of new members is a delicate task. Some are stronger candidates—Poland, Hungary, the Czech Republic, Slovenia, Estonia, Cyprus—than others: Lithuania, Latvia, Romania, Bulgaria, Malta, Slovakia. A few are not to be contemplated—Russia, Ukraine, Belarus, and the other former Soviet republics. Turkey, an official candidate, has been given the cold shoulder since it applied in 1987. But who makes these decisions, and on what grounds? Assuming that a list of new members has been drawn up, the next question is: on what terms do they enter? Will they share the common currency and monetary union from the start? Will they be eligible for the massive farming subsidies that Western European farmers enjoy? And development aid? If so, who will pay? Finally, what about the excluded states? Is it possible that a much expanded EU will simply be erecting new dividing lines in Europe by keeping out some of Europe's largest, most populous, though admittedly troublesome nations?

KEY DATA ON THE THIRTEEN CANDIDATE COUNTRIES, 2000

	GDP Per Head, PPS (Euro)	Unemployment	GDP Growth, 1995–99
Bulgaria	5400	16.2	–1.8
Cyprus	18500	4.9	4.0
Czech Republic	13500	8.8	1.5
Estonia	8500	13.2	4.6
Hungary	11700	6.6	3.3
Latvia	6600	14.2	3.2
Lithuania	6600	15.6	3.2
Malta	11900	6.5	4.5
Poland	8700	16.3	5.7
Romania	6000	7.0	–0.6
Slovakia	10800	19.1	5.0
Slovenia	16100	6.9	4.2
Turkey	6400	6.6	3.9
EU-15	22530	8.2	2.4

SOURCE: Eurostat, News Release No. 129/2001 (December 2001).

These are difficult questions, and the EU has been working on them since the early 1990s. In 1993, at the Copenhagen European Council, the member states set out quite explicit criteria that each candidate for membership would have to meet. The first criteria were political: new members must have stable, democratic political institutions that can guarantee the rule of law, respect for human rights, and protection for minorities. The second criteria were economic: each candidate must have a functioning market economy and be able to withstand the pressure of competition and market forces inside the union. The third criteria were legal: each candidate must be able to accept and enforce the full range of all existing EU laws and treaties, including obligations of all members in the economic and political sphere. This meant that each member must abide by the rules governing trade, farming subsidies, monetary union, the environment, health and safety regulations, energy, transport, justice affairs, and so on. It will not be easy for most of the applicant countries to meet these criteria, and that, of course, is why they were established. As in the experience of setting the Maastricht criteria for monetary convergence, the criteria for enlargement were deliberately made difficult to achieve so that when enlargement happens, the entering states will not create too much chaos inside the union.

In March 1998, accession negotiations were formally opened with six countries: Poland, the Czech Republic, Hungary, Slovenia, Estonia, and Cyprus. Why did these six appear the early leaders? The first four were the easy ones. They are geographically part of Central Europe and share borders with Germany, Austria, or Italy. They fall within an informal German sphere of influence, as Germany is by far the largest trading partner for each. In 1997, the Czech Republic, Poland, and Hungary were invited to join NATO. And as Eastern Europe's most developed economies, with stable political institutions, they can fulfill the Copenhagen criteria. That doesn't mean it has been smooth sailing.

Poland, by far the most populous of the Eastern European candidate countries, also has the region's largest economy, with a GDP of about $327 billion in 2000. The economy has expanded robustly and the government has pursued a vigorous privatization program. But Poland has a huge agricultural sector that is burdened by surplus labor and a lack of modernization. Over 27 percent of the labor force works in agriculture, as compared to just 5 percent in the EU. Entry into the EU will certainly force the farming sector into difficult reforms, and the Polish government can look forward to obstreperous demands from farmers for continued protection and subsidies. Another problem is the free movement of labor. Germany fears a sudden inrush of Polish workers looking for high-wage jobs, and may impose a transition period before the border controls are completely dismantled. Finally, Poland's high rate of inflation—10 percent in 2000—and its mounting deficits raise the prospect that it may fail to hold itself in line with convergence criteria.

The Czech Republic is among Eastern Europe's most prosperous states, with the second highest GDP per capita (after Slovenia) in the region, and politically it is stable. The economy has been sluggish, but it emerged from a prolonged recession to grow at about 2.5 percent in 2000. It is one of the few applicants that easily meets the criteria for monetary convergence, though budget deficits and inflation have been rising in the past few years. The obstacles to EU entry are chiefly legal. Its public administration and the judiciary have not been sufficiently reformed; corruption remains a problem, and the Czechs have not sufficiently improved their record in the treatment of minorities, especially the Roma (Gypsy) community. The EU has also chided the Czechs about lax border controls. Hungary can make a strong case for EU entry. Its political and legal institutions have been sufficiently reformed, and its economy has been growing at about 4.5 percent a year since 1997. One problem Hungary faces is aligning its environmental standards, especially on air, soil, and water pollution, with much stricter EU regulations. Also, inflation has been running at 10 percent a year, and both the government budget deficit and the debt exceed the criteria for monetary convergence. Only Slovenia, with a tiny population, a strong economy, good fiscal management, and a stable political system, would be a shoo-in for EU membership.

After these four, things become tricky. Estonia's case has been advanced by Sweden and Finland. True, its economy is in good shape, and its political and legal systems seem fairly well adapted for EU entry. (It does face massive environmental problems from oil-shale-burning power plants and widespread contamination of soil and groundwater.) But once Estonia comes in, it would be ludicrous to deny entry to its two much poorer neighbors, Latvia and Lithuania. Cyprus is being pushed by Greece, which has threatened to veto the entire enlargement process if Cyprus is not included. This poses awkward problems, since Cyprus is a divided island and Turkey, which controls 40 percent of the island, is not a member of the EU.

If these six states, judged to be the leading contenders for entry to the EU, have so far to go before meeting the stiff Copenhagen criteria, what of the laggards? In February 2000, the EU started accession negotiations with six additional countries: Bulgaria, Romania, the Slovak Republic, Latvia, Lithuania, and Malta. Most of these countries are far from meeting the criteria for membership. Bulgaria and Romania, for example, despite basic democratic institutions, have weak judicial systems that could not enforce EU laws, widespread corruption, and a poor record on minority rights, and neither state has a fully functioning market economy that could handle the pressure of competition from the EU. Romania is especially ill prepared for EU membership on economic grounds. Its large agricultural sector, which accounts for 18 percent of its GDP, needs a major overhaul, but the relevant ministries have made little headway. Romania's economy has been shrinking, and its inflation rate has soared to 60 percent. Slovakia's democratic institutions suffered during the 1990s as the nationalist prime minister, Vladimir Meciar, dominated the government. (He was voted out in 1998, and arrested in April 2000 on corruption charges.) The transition to a market economy has been slow, and the country suffers from large budget and current account deficits, fast-growing external debt, and corruption. Unemployment has neared 20 percent. The EU is especially concerned about Slovakia's poor treatment of its Roma population. Lithuania and Latvia, though politically stable, are among the poorest of the candidate countries—per capita GDP is less than a third the EU average.[17]

The EU faces a difficult choice: it wants to allow the richer states in but does not wish to alienate the weaker, poorer ones by leaving them out. So the most likely scenario: they will all have to wait until the slowest among them are better prepared for EU membership. That means a long process of economic and political restructuring, and a frank recognition that even when the candidate countries have met the criteria for membership, they will still stand somewhat apart from the more developed members. For this reason, the new members will not in all likelihood adopt the euro as their currency until well after they have joined the union. And there will need to be transition periods for the gradual removal of tariffs, especially in agriculture. In the meantime, the effort to win membership has already imposed much-needed fiscal discipline and market reforms in these countries, and also opened their political, judicial, and financial institutions to scrutiny from the EU. By the fiftieth anniversary of the Treaty of Rome, in 2007, it seems reasonable to assume that the EU will have welcomed at least ten new members.

Alas, a few countries will not be invited to the party. Croatia would like to join, but the far less stable and poorer former Yugoslav republics, Bosnia, Serbia, and Macedonia, have a long way to go before they meet the criteria. Strife-torn Albania and Kosovo have no hope, though they are so dependent on the EU for their survival that they are already in essence EU protectorates. Turkey is a more difficult case. It is a stable country, though with the army exercising enormous influence it cannot be said to be fully democratic. It has long been a NATO ally. It has the largest GDP and population of all the candidate countries, though its economy is troubled, its people poor, and its human rights record spotty, to say the least. The real—and unspoken—obstacle to EU entry, however, is that Turks are Muslims. Already anxious about the 13 million Muslims in Western Europe, Europeans are loath to welcome 63 million more. As for the former Soviet republics, they are still seen as outside the orbit of Europe, politically unstable, economically hobbled by heavy state interference in the economy, and too corrupt. On the other hand, Europe cannot dismiss Russia lightly. EU enlargement will extend the bloc of market democracies right up to the borders of the old Soviet Union, and the long-term success of a much larger EU will be secure only when Russia itself is stable. For most of the 1990s, that prospect seemed distant indeed.

In August 1991, Russian president Boris Yeltsin helped fend off a right-wing coup attempt against Mikhail Gorbachev and saved the Russian reform process. But as a leader, Yeltsin proved a monumental failure: an unimaginative, dim-witted political bully who refused to bring serious reform to the country during the first decade of its transition. He did little to consolidate democracy and soon fell to quarreling with the Congress of People's Deputies, which tried to oust him in September 1993. Yeltsin responded by turning Russian army tanks on the Congress. While the countries of the former Eastern bloc made steady progress toward economic reform and political stability, Russia stagnated. Between 1990 and 1999, its economy shrank by four-fifths, from a GDP of $1.1 trillion to $193.2 billion. During the decade of the 1990s, industrial production declined by an average of 7.6 percent per year. Inflation soared to 300 percent by 1994; the government could not pay public sector employees like teachers, doctors, or the army; and the basic mechanism of exchange in the economy was barter. By 1996, most businesses didn't even bother to pay their taxes, and the government was broke. Yeltsin's privatization schemes gave away the hugely valuable national assets at fire-sale prices, enriching a small handful of often corrupt wheeler-dealers. On top of this, in 1994 Yeltsin led the country into war against the breakaway province of Chechnya, and two years later the Russian army was defeated by the ferocious Chechen rebels. Russia's humiliation was complete.

Despite this dismal catalogue of failures, Yeltsin's allies in the business sector, having been enriched by his policies, supported him in his reelection bid in June 1996. He won, despite serious competition from a ghoulish array of Communists, nationalists, and populists, all of whom promised to stop the reforms and restore order with a firm hand. Alexander Lebed, a gruff army general with little tolerance for democracy, won 15 percent of the vote, while Vladimir Zhirinovsky, a foaming xenophobe and anti-Semite, attracted 4 million votes. (Zhirinovsky would be comical if he were not so dangerous. For example, he called for gigantic fans to be built that could blow nuclear waste into the separatist Baltic states, and for the seizure of Alaska from the United States.) The leader of the Communist Party, Gennady Zyuganov, ran Yeltsin a close second and faced him again in a run-off election in July 1996. Yeltsin's reelection solved nothing. In August 1998, in the midst of a long-running financial crisis, Russia defaulted on its international debt and the ruble collapsed. On 31 December 1999, Yeltsin, suffering from advanced heart disease, resigned. He was succeeded by an unknown former KGB colonel named Vladimir Putin, who was elected president on 26 March 2000.[18]

Putin's background made it seem plausible that he would reverse course and rule with a firm hand. Instead, Russia's fortunes have improved under the new president. The economy has made a significant turnaround, growing at 5.4 percent in 1999 and about 6 percent in 2000. The weak ruble helped exports, and Russian oil sales, at a time of rising world prices, gave the country a bulging trade surplus. Politically, Putin brought much-needed stability to the presidency, unlike the mercurial Yeltsin, who hired and fired dozens of ministers. Putin, who speaks perfect German from his days as a spy in East Germany, has improved relations with Europe and the United States.

But Russia is far from happy. The military conflict in Chechnya continues to smolder. Putin has moved cautiously in handling the bureaucracy, and seems reluctant to break the control of the oligarchy over large sectors of the economy. Organized crime has been brought under control, but the perception remains that Russia is a hugely corrupt place to do business, and that hampers foreign investment. The infrastructure of the country is in an advanced state of decline, and the economy is heavily dependent on exports of commodities, especially oil, natural gas, metals, and timber, whose prices are notoriously unstable. Above all, the majority of Russians still exist in desperate economic circumstances. Basic health care is unavailable to most citizens, and life expectancy—now about sixty-one years for males—has plunged to the levels normally reached only by developing nations. GDP per capita is about $7,700 (purchasing power parity)—about half that of Portugal, the poorest EU nation. Some estimates suggest that 40 percent of the population lives below the poverty line. The United Nations Human Development Index, which measures well-being in countries based on GDP, literacy, and life expectancy, places Russia alongside Lebanon, Romania, and Mauritius. Perhaps the greatest challenge for the EU in the next few decades will not be incorporating the relatively well-off Eastern European states but in helping to bring this giant, humbled, unpredictable nation into the fold of developed, stable market democracies.[19]

THE CONTINUING STRUGGLE

The advent of the euro in 2002 as the single currency for twelve EU member states naturally stimulated a certain degree of optimism about the future of Europe. Twelve years after the fall of the Berlin Wall, it began to look as if Europe might really emerge as a continent of peaceful, prosperous, democratic states that share—and are willing to defend—a common set of political values. In early 2002, Romano Prodi, the European Commission president, hopefully predicted that Europe will be "the new protagonist of the new century."[20] It is an appealing vision, especially when one thinks of what Europe brought the world in the last century: two world wars, genocide, Fascism, Nazism, Communism, and Cold War.

But if the past fifty years teach us anything, it is that Europe has a frustrating habit of dashing the hopes of its many citizens who keep waiting for the new Europe to arrive. The shining moment of political transformation of the early 1990s was swiftly darkened by the cloud of the Bosnian genocide. The democratic values Europeans rightly champion have also opened the way to demagogues and crude populists. European unity has shed light on Europe's divisions between the rich states and the poor, between the West and the East, between the nationalists and the federalists, and so on.

And so the struggle for Europe continues. In particular, the European Union itself, the continent's most visible success, remains embattled. Despite the strong arguments on behalf of a united Europe, there remains a vocal minority of Europeans who oppose the European Union, or at least who wish to see the movement toward integration and political union slowed and even stopped altogether. This is not new: as early as 1950, when Robert Schuman and Jean Monnet first outlined the plans for the European Coal and Steel Community, many people have expressed concern about placing too much power in the hands of a few unelected technocrats who seem determined to erode national sovereignty and who denounce as atavistic the old enduring appeal of national pride. These criticisms of Europe were given an enormous boost in the 1960s by Charles de Gaulle, who would countenance a united Europe only if it was led by France. The economic crisis of the 1970s and the political tumult of the late 1980s offered proponents of European integration an opening to argue that a closer union would promote economic growth and provide a framework for the reintegration of Eastern Europe into the western fold. Now, at the start of the twenty-first century, with the Cold War a receding memory, what will become of the European integration project? Can Europeans be mobilized on behalf of a stronger and better union, one that can integrate new members, expand economic growth, assure social justice and economic equality, and expunge the residue of racism and xenophobia from the body politic? If so, who will come forward to make these arguments? Who will continue to fight for Europe?

The sad tale of the Treaty of Nice might be taken as emblematic of Europe's travails. In December 2000, the fifteen EU states convened for a summit in the southern French city of Nice. Their task: to settle on institutional reforms so as to prepare for the arrival of a dozen or so new members. It sounds innocuous, but in fact the member states had to agree on which states would have the most power in the new, expanded union. Assuming that the new EU will have as many as twenty-seven members in all, how will such a huge operation maintain any sort of efficiency? Votes in the Council of Ministers—the all-important decision-making body that approves or rejects legislation sent to it by the commission—have always been weighted by population, thus ensuring that Germany (83 million people), Britain (59 million), France (59 million), and Italy (58 million) wield greater influence than small states. Naturally, they wish to maintain such a system in the expanded union. But Poland and Romania, poor newcomers, have populations (39 million and 22 million respectively) that would give them greater weight than some of the

EU's founding members such as the Netherlands and Belgium. They might be tempted to band together with other Eastern European states on issues dear to them, such as regional aid and agricultural protection.

To resolve this puzzle, the leaders in Nice devised a numbingly complex system of voting in the expanded Council of Ministers. They proposed that any decision in the council would have to win approval on three criteria: it would have to have a simple majority of member states; it would have to have a majority of the weighted votes given to each state; and it would have to have the support of 62 percent of the EU population, as calculated by the populations of each member state. This latter component was crucial, because it meant that Germany, which has about 22 percent of the EU's population, could team up with Britain, France, or Italy and block any legislation. This system was designed to keep more power in the hands of the large countries and ensure that small states could not defy the bigger ones. The treaty also set a ceiling of twenty-seven members on the European Commission, and stipulated that majority voting, instead of unanimity, would be applied to a wider array of topics, so that one state could not easily block a consensus among the other twenty-six.

Byzantine seemed a good word for it. To make matters worse, the treaty emerged only after a marathon summit at which barely disguised national rivalries kept disrupting progress. Britain insisted on defending its veto right over certain EU proposals on taxes and social security. France demanded a voting system that gave it parity with Germany despite Germany's larger population. The smaller countries like Belgium, Greece, Portugal, and Ireland claimed that the system set up a directorate of great powers, and almost walked out of the summit in protest. Spain, which receives large subsidies from the EU's structural funds, lobbied to delay for over a decade the spending of these monies on the poorer new members from the East. And so it went.

Lost in all this backroom dealing was the common European citizen. How would the EU explain this morass to the voters? The EU failed to do so, knowing that in most countries, the Treaty of Nice would not be put to a vote. They forgot about Ireland. The Irish government, constitutionally bound to place the treaty before a national referendum, assumed that the voting public would support the Treaty of Nice. Ireland, after all, had passed the Maastricht Treaty in 1992, and was a country that strongly supported the European Union—mainly because it had profited so handsomely (over $15 billion since the late 1980s) from EU development aid. But on 8 June 2001, the Irish defeated the referendum, 54 to 46 percent, thus halting progress on EU enlargement. What happened?

The Irish referendum is a case study in the problems the EU is likely to

face over the next decade. Turnout was abysmal, at 35 percent of eligible voters. Such apathy among the electorate was a glaring sign that the EU failed to
mobilize the public and explain the high stakes involved in this election. A
week before, more than 50 percent of the Irish voters said they did not understand the treaty. Small turnout opened the way for a broad coalition of opponents who generated an impassioned grassroots campaign on a series of
issues. For example, the treaty had a clause that stipulated a heightened foreign military presence for the EU, and some voters opposed the treaty on the
grounds that it might compromise Ireland's neutrality. Sinn Fein, the nationalist Republican movement, opposed it; the far left opposed it, the Greens and
pacifists opposed it, as did assorted voters who believed that Nice would spell
an end to handouts from Europe and the start of a binge of spending on
Eastern Europe. And some argued that Nice was unfair to small states. The
opposition had a simple slogan: "You will lose power, money, and freedom." Although the main political parties supported the treaty, they could not
find the words to explain why they did so. After the vote, a chastened Bertie
Ahern, the Irish prime minister, conceded that "there is, unfortunately, a widespread sense of disconnection between the institutions of the union and its
citizens."[21]

The Irish vote looms so large by reason of its singularity: Ireland was the
only country to hold a referendum on the treaty. But it is evident that, had
more referendums been held on Nice, or indeed on the existence of the
European Union itself, the European electorate would show itself to be deeply
divided on the subject. In the fall of 2001, 54 percent of Europeans agreed that
membership in the EU was "a good thing." Not bad, but hardly a resounding
consensus. In some of the largest states, the numbers are dangerously low: in
France, 50 percent call membership a good thing and in Britain only 33 percent do so. Even in Germany, on whom the whole edifice of the EU depends,
only 55 percent see membership as a good thing and a mere 44 percent believe
Germany has benefited from EU membership. And in a sign of coming difficulties, support for enlargement of the union remains quite weak, especially
in Germany, France, Britain, and Austria.[22] These numbers suggest that support for the EU is soft and that a determined and mobilized minority may be
able, as in Ireland, to block further advances.

Why is support for the European Union less than overwhelming, especially when European integration has been the principal engine of prosperity
and stability on the continent over the past half-century? Perhaps the easiest
explanation is the EU—or Brussels, as European analysts refer to the complex
of institutions located in the Belgian capital—has become a scapegoat for
many of Europe's economic and social ills. As the EU increases its power over

European life, so does the resentment toward it grow. During the Cold War, Europeans both East and West reserved their ire for the domineering super-powers who used to lay down the law on matters economic and military. Nowadays, some of this anger has been turned against the European Union.

And there have been plenty of ills to complain about. The economy, for one, has remained anemic for most of the past decade. Between 1990 and 1998, British GDP grew on average 2.2 percent per year, while France and Germany came in at 1.5 percent, Italy at 1.2 percent. Slow growth meant weak employment prospects: unemployment in the EU averaged about 10 percent in the 1990s, and in 1998 spiked to 11.8 percent in France, 12.8 in Italy, and 9.7 percent in Germany. These figures improved briefly between 1997 and 2000, but a global economic slowdown after 2000 nipped a strong recovery in the bud. In the spring of 2002, economic growth was at a standstill and un-employment stood above 9 percent in France, Germany, and Italy, at 10.8 per-cent in Belgium, and almost 13 percent in Spain. Naturally, the EU alone is not to blame for these figures. But some argue that the EU has made a recovery more difficult by forcing its members to adhere to strict rules about balanced budgets and thus making it harder for a government to increase spending or meet the social security demands of the unemployed.[23]

On a more emotional level, some European voters see Brussels as respon-sible for the rapid and at times unwanted social changes of the past few decades. The sharp decline in rural livelihoods, the exodus from small villages to the cities, and the sense that modernization has snuffed out the once-vibrant traditions of the countryside are often bemoaned. The EU is seen as a willing agent of these disorienting social changes because it has forced mod-ernization, competition, and standardization onto a continent that—even af-ter fifty years of change—strongly identifies with pastoral values, the charms of village life, and age-old habits of life and labor.[24] Others claim to see the EU as a Trojan horse for American commercialization of Europe, bringing in Hollywood films, Euro Disney, baseball caps, T-shirts, skateboards, music, and fast food into a Europe that thought of itself as disdaining such emblems of bad taste. The issue of sovereignty is also raised by critics: the EU has de-manded open internal borders for easier trade but failed to control the union's common external border, resulting in a wave of illegal immigration that, the argument runs, only worsens employment prospects and threatens European cultural identity still further. Thus, when a young, unemployed Tunisian com-mits a crime in a run-down Paris district, some see Brussels at fault. And these resentments exist even in countries that are not yet in the EU. In Poland, the League of Polish Families—a small far right party with 8 percent of the seats in the lower parliamentary house—has denounced the European Union as a vehicle for the German takeover of Polish lands, and says the EU will force the small Polish farmers out of business. The Polish farmers' union Self-Defense has declared that EU membership will amount to Poland's enslavement to wealthy westerners.

Of course, these problems were not created by the European Union, but the perception is alive and well that the EU has failed to solve them while weakening the powers of national governments to do so. As the political analyst Dominique Moïsi recently pointed out, some Europeans think of Brussels as having power and yet no legitimacy, and see their legitimate national governments as increasingly powerless.[25] Plenty of politicians are willing to exploit this perception for their own gain. French rightist Jean-Marie Le Pen raged against the "dictatorship" of Brussels in his 2002 presidential bid. Silvio Berlusconi, Italy's maverick prime minister, has used the EU as a whipping boy to rally his right-wing coalition members, who also see the EU as interfering and hegemonic. The entire political debate in Britain is deeply infused with Euro-skepticism, and even the powerful and popular prime minister, Tony Blair, fears wagering his political capital on a referendum on adopting the euro as the national currency because he knows it would probably fail. The far right Freedom Party in Austria, which shares power in a coalition government, opposes enlargement of the EU and uses fear of uncontrolled immigration to generate support for its position. In Denmark, which rejected adopting the euro, the far right People's Party espouses anti-immigrant and anti-EU views and now helps prop up a center right government. In the German elections of September 2002, both the incumbent chancellor, Gerhard Schroeder, and the challenger, Bavarian premier Edmund Stoiber, ran against Brussels: Stoiber denounced the erosion of national powers by the EU while Schroeder criticized Brussels for its pressure on economic liberalization.

Is the European Union, then, likely to come unglued? Might Europe return to the old ways of rivalry, conflict, and war? Europe's history is too full of violence to allow for any confident assertions that war has been banished from Europe forever. Yet the progress made since those horrific years of the mid-1940s is so great that no one wishes to go back and revive the old ghosts of national antagonism, totalitarian ideologies, and war. With all its faults, the European Union remains the greatest achievement of twentieth-century Europe, a political and economic experiment of enormous proportions that Europeans must embrace and indeed defend.

They will do so only on two conditions. First, the European Union must open itself to greater public scrutiny—incredibly, the deliberations of the Council of Ministers and the commission have always been shielded from public view. The EU must also develop a people's parliament that has real and not just supervisory powers to check and balance the commission and the Council of Ministers. One of the unfortunate hallmarks of the EU has been its inherent fear of the people: that less educated, parochial citizens might undo the patient work of decades by using the ballot box to express their anxieties about a too-swift erosion of national sovereignty. It is a risk, but one that the EU must take in order to thrive. For by placing the very existence of the EU before the public in regular, meaningful elections, and by creating genuinely democratic institutions that can express the will of the people, the EU will give the citizens of this great continent a stake in its success. Without such participation, the EU will always remain a distant, unaccountable behemoth, a Leviathan beyond the control of the citizens, and a focus of anger and resentment.[26]

Yet institutions alone do not make a democracy. People do. And those people, if they believe in the enterprise, must be willing to fight for it. Citizens have rights, of course, but also responsibilities. Europeans must come to see that while they have a right to expect certain benefits from the union, they also owe it certain duties and obligations: that is the meaning of citizenship. And so the task of the next few decades lies less in the narrow science of calibrating power and votes within the EU structures. Rather, Europe must find a better way of mobilizing its people and generating the open, proud, and sincere support that any truly united community requires. Is Europe, after a century filled with war, genocide, and fascism, prepared now to advance the ideals of democracy, tolerance, equality, and unity? If so, then the people of this continent must be willing to fight for them, and engage themselves in this continuing struggle for Europe.

Europe and America After September 11

.

"HAS YOUR COUNTRY gone completely mad?"

This was the text of an anguished e-mail from a dear European friend in the summer of 2002. He was a man who had fought in World War II alongside Americans, had traveled and worked in America, and was fully conscious of the steadfast support America had given Europe throughout the long, tense years of the Cold War. Yet by mid-2002, even America's oldest friends had begun to wonder: what happened to the America we used to know, to which we could look for global leadership, and whose people and culture we could genuinely admire?

What happened, of course, is known by the simple numerical designation 9/11. At 8:45 A.M. on September 11, 2001, a hijacked American Airlines passenger jet, flying at about 500 knots, slammed into the north tower of the World Trade Center in New York City. Eighteen minutes later, a United Airlines plane struck the other tower. Indelible features of New York's skyline and the global nexus of finance, trade, and media, the twin towers were now burning, with huge plumes of black smoke belching from the gaping holes in their steel skins. Forty minutes later, a third aircraft crashed into the Pentagon, the Washington, D.C., headquarters of the American military. A fourth plane plummeted into an open field in Pennsylvania, after a valiant struggle by the passengers and crew to retake control of the plane. At five minutes after ten o'clock, the south tower of the World Trade Center collapsed; about twenty minutes later, the north tower imploded. The silver towers had once stood one hundred and ten stories high; they were now reduced to a hellish mountain of red-hot steel and concrete. In less than two hours, some 3,000 people had been killed.

From this appalling carnage could have—should have—emerged a renewed US-European partnership in the face of global terror. Instead, the events that followed 9/11 split the Atlantic alliance, spurred a huge wave of anti-Americanism in Europe—and anti-Europeanism in America—and left analysts writing obituaries of the West. What had gone wrong? As this book has shown, there have always been tensions between Europe and the United States during the postwar era. During much of the Cold War, the European public played down the threat of Communism, was lukewarm about the formation of the NATO alliance in 1949, often criticized the American dominance of the global economy and derided (while copying) American fashions and habits of life. The 1956 Suez crisis, de Gaulle's withdrawal from NATO in 1966, the sharp debate over the deployment of US Pershing missiles in Europe in the 1980s—these are just a few of the sore points in this transatlantic relationship. But again and again, Europeans and Americans were drawn back to one another, joined in an enduring bond of common values. They shared a commitment to democracy, liberty, economic growth, to the strategic doctrine of containment, and finally in 1989 they tasted the fruits of their long labor as the Berlin Wall was torn down. After all these years of common endeavor, it was especially saddening to watch as the acute international crisis triggered by the 9/11 attacks divided rather than united this venerable alliance.

Perhaps Europeans never fully understood the impact of 9/11 on the American psyche. The country was shocked and appalled by the scale of devastation to lower Manhattan, fearful that additional attacks might soon follow, and quickly roused to passionate fury toward the perpetrators. The hijackings were carried out by a band of nineteen Islamic radicals, mostly Egyptian and Saudi nationals. They were bankrolled by a Saudi millionaire and self-proclaimed holy warrior named Osama bin Laden, whose al-Qaeda terrorist network had found refuge and support from the Islamic government of Afghanistan. In the wake of the events of that awful day, it was perhaps natural that America's entire political discourse would be focused on how to exact revenge and ensure that terrorist attacks not happen again. September 11 marked the start of a new period in America's military history that the American president, George W. Bush, termed "the war on terror."

For Europe, the effect of the attacks was less direct, less personal. Naturally, from across the continent came expressions of horror and a desire to reach out and help an old friend. The editor of the influential French daily *Le Monde* caught the spirit of the moment in an editorial the day after the attack:

At a moment like this, when words fail so lamentably to express one's feelings of shock, the first thought that comes to mind is that we are all Americans, all New Yorkers, just as inevitably as President John Kennedy pronounced himself to be a Berliner in his famous 1962 speech in what has since become the German capital. As during the darkest hours of French history, there is absolutely no question of not showing solidarity with the United States and its people, who are so close to us, and to whom we owe our freedom.[1]

German Chancellor Gerhard Schroeder called the attacks a declaration of "war against the civilized world," and church services and candlelight vigils were held across Germany. "I have assured the American president of our unlimited solidarity, and I stress unlimited," Schroeder told the Bundestag. British Prime Minister Tony Blair, whose country lost sixty-seven citizens in the inferno, emphatically declared that his country "stands shoulder to shoulder with our American friends in this hour of tragedy and we, like them, will not rest until this evil is driven from our world."[2] On September 12, NATO, for the first time ever, invoked Article V of its collective security treaty and declared the terror strikes to be an attack on all nineteen members of the alliance. On September 14, all the EU member states held memorial ceremonies. Four hundred million Europeans joined in shared grief with America.

It didn't last. Lamentably, divisions between America and Europe over the meaning of 9/11 became apparent even as the smoke was still billowing from the ruined streets of downtown Manhattan. Europeans, though genuinely grieved by the attacks, were uneasy with the quite justifiable anger that Americans now directed at their attackers. In part it was a matter of style. Americans mourned, but they also indulged in an orgy of patriotic songs, lachrymose ceremonies, and frantic flag-waving. President Bush delivered a series of terse addresses in the days after the attack that sounded like a Wild West script: Osama bin Laden, he declared, was "wanted, dead or alive." His words left no doubt that America would unleash its formidable power upon any country it deemed a threat to its security. "Whether we bring our enemies to justice, or bring justice to our enemies, justice will be done." EU foreign ministers, meeting on September 12, offered support to the United States, but some sounded a note of caution: the Norwegian Thorbjorn Jagland said, "It's not easy to warn the United States in such a situation, but we must hope that there will not be an irrational revenge." Alain Richard, French defense minister, suggested that if "an act of retaliation leads to a new destabilization, you haven't won anything at all." The German defense minister contradicted President Bush, claiming, "We do not face a war." Instead, he called for stepped-up international police measures against terrorism.[3]

But something more than style and rhetoric was splitting Europeans and

Americans apart. Even before 9/11, many in Europe had expressed hostility toward President Bush and his policies.[4] In the first year of his administration, Bush took a series of actions that Europeans saw as unilateralist, selfish, and destabilizing. He had withdrawn the United States from the Kyoto Protocol on global warming, turned up his nose at the Rio Pact on biodiversity, declared the antiballistic treaty with Russia to be outdated and defunct and pursued an American ballistic missile shield, opposed a ban on land mines, and denounced the new International Criminal Court. Bush, it seemed, had nothing but contempt for America's allies and the international institutions they championed. With such actions in mind, some Europeans suggested that the September attacks, while not justified, were in part a consequence of America's ham-fisted, self-centered behavior on the world stage.[5]

Therefore, while European states and NATO partners lent support to the invasion of Afghanistan by the US military in early October—an invasion designed to destroy bin Laden and the extremist Afghan regime that had sheltered him—most European citizens refused to sanction a wider military campaign against other states that might harbor hostile intentions toward America.[6] While Bush felt 9/11 gave him carte blanche to use American power to crush his enemies, Europeans called for precisely the opposite: a calm analysis of the roots of Islamic terror, the development of global solutions to problems such as poverty and ethnic warfare that seemed to fuel anti-Western sentiment, and a renewed effort to resolve the Israeli-Palestinian conflict, which had so radicalized millions in the Islamic world.[7]

This counsel of restraint was not heeded in Washington. With operations in Afghanistan still under way, President Bush announced in his January 2002 State of the Union address that America faced an "axis of evil" comprised of three states—Iraq, Iran, and North Korea. These countries had not been implicated in the 9/11 attacks, but, the president claimed, they sought to do harm to America and its friends around the world and must be called to account. For Bush, it made perfect sense to push the war on terrorism beyond Afghanistan, to those states that had the capacity, either through unconventional weapons, religious ideology, or both, to harm the United States. Iraq, it seemed, was one of these, and it would now feel America's wrath.

Though most of the European public grew ever more agitated by President Bush's bellicosity, British Prime Minister Tony Blair warmed to it. Unlike Chancellor Schroeder, who had declared his solidarity only to withdraw it once he saw how far Bush planned to go, Blair was true to his word: he doggedly, tirelessly supported American policy. Although the British press mercilessly depicted Blair as "Bush's poodle," there was a certain logic to Blair's position. Since the end of the Gulf War in 1991, British aircraft had shared the chore of patrolling Iraq's airspace, enforcing a UN-mandated restriction on Iraqi flights in northern and southern zones of the country. This had created a sense of solidarity between the United States and Britain over how Iraq was to be handled. Blair's intelligence services, like Bush's, told him that despite the intensive inspections undertaken by UN monitors, Iraq maintained the capacity to produce and deploy chemical and biological weapons and perhaps even to proliferate these weapons to terrorists. Blair also believed that he could use his influence in Washington to urge the United States to work through the UN to create a broad coalition and a mandate to invade Iraq rather than act by itself. It may also have occurred to Blair that by supporting Bush, Britain was demonstrating its position as the only state in Europe with a global military reach.

So in late February 2002, as European criticism of Bush was gaining momentum, Blair praised the American leader, saying he had "shown tremendous leadership since September 11." As for supporting a US-led invasion of Iraq, Blair was clearly moving in that direction. "Saddam Hussein's regime is a regime that is deeply repressive to its people and is a real danger to the region." In his view, "The accumulation of weapons of mass destruction by Iraq poses a threat, a threat not just to the region but to the wider world." Visiting the president's ranch in Texas in early April, Blair declared, "We must be prepared to act where terrorism or weapons of mass destruction threaten us. If necessary the action should be military, and again if necessary and justified it should involve regime change." The special relationship seemed stronger than ever, though Blair's position cost him at home: over 100 Labour backbenchers announced their opposition to any war with Iraq, and the party threatened to split over the issue. But Blair, no less than Bush, believed in the moral rectitude of the issue: that prosperous, powerful nations should do what they can to squelch the rule of tyrants.[8]

The US-Europe rift grew significantly wider in September 2002. President Bush, visiting New York for the one-year anniversary of the 9/11 attacks, delivered a somber and threatening speech to the UN General Assembly. He alleged that Iraq represented a major threat to the Middle East and the world because of its covert and illegal weapons program, and he called on the UN to marshal its forces against this rogue state. To Europeans, however, this seemed a brazen bid to win UN approval of a unilateral and preemptive attack on Iraq. It didn't sell well in Germany, where at just the same moment, nationwide parliamentary elections began. Facing a tough reelection battle in troubled economic times, Chancellor Schroeder played the antiwar card and warned Bush "against playing games with war and military intervention." Immediately, his poll numbers began to improve. In the German election, it became acceptable to say almost anything derogatory about Bush. On the eve of the vote, one of Schroeder's cabinet colleagues, Justice Minister Herta Daeubler-Gmelin, drew a loose comparison between George Bush's Iraq policy and Adolf Hitler's conjuring of foreign enemies to draw attention away from domestic crises. In response, Bush's national security adviser, Condoleezza Rice, said US-German relations had been "poisoned." She added, "There have clearly been some things said that are way beyond the pale. The reported statements . . . are simply unacceptable." Most awkward of all for Washington: Schroeder won the election.[9]

The gloves now came off. As Europeans, especially the French and Germans, voiced sharp criticism of Bush's saber-rattling, American pundits launched an unprecedented tirade of bilious anti-European commentary. Editorialists for the nations' papers expressed shock at the ingratitude of those Europeans who had forgotten all the sacrifices America made on their behalf. The American press seemed to enjoy targeting the French in particular, who, it was now declared, were habitual appeasers, cynical backstabbers, anti-Semitic and pro-Arab, envious of American power, and determined to sabotage America's effort to liberate the Middle East from tyranny. Merchants threatened to boycott French wines; the restaurant of the US House of Representatives refused to serve French Fries and offered Freedom Fries instead. Even the moderate and influential columnist for the *New York Times*, Thomas Friedman, called for France's permanent seat on the United Nations Security Council to be revoked.[10]

Bush was, if anything, emboldened by European criticism. It freed him from the painstaking work of coalition-building which his father, President George H. W. Bush, had skillfully undertaken before the 1991 Gulf War. Instead, Bush simply announced: "You are with us, or you are with the terrorists." By contrast, his secretary of state, Colin Powell—the one administration official Europeans hoped would restrain Bush—tried eagerly to win United Nations support for a tough resolution that would place weapons inspectors in Iraq and would call for "serious consequences" if Iraq did not fully comply with this disarmament mission. Resolution 1441 of 8 November 2002, unanimously approved by the Security Council, declared Iraq in breach of previous UN resolutions and gave it a "final opportunity" to disarm. But the resolution, at the insistence of France and Russia, did not specify what would happen if Iraq did not do so.

Now began a high-stakes debate at the United Nations about what precisely Saddam Hussein would have to do to avoid war. He allowed the inspectors back into Iraq in November, but they did not turn up much. The American position was that since Saddam possessed chemical and biological weapons, the fact that the inspectors failed to find them meant that they were incompetent or that Saddam was hiding them, and probably both. Thus, inspections were a farce and it was time to move to all-out war. For the majority of the fifteen-member Security Council, however, the absence of any major new discoveries in Iraq seemed to argue in favor of prolonging the inspections until weapons could be found and destroyed. Either that, or Iraq had no banned weapons to begin with. The positions began to harden. The French foreign minister, the silver-haired, stylish Dominique de Villepin, became the voice and the face of the growing opposition to the United States within the United Nations. On 20 January 2003, he blurted out in a news conference that whatever the wording and intention of Resolution 1441, the French "will not associate ourselves with military intervention that is not supported by the international community. Military intervention would be the worst possible solution." Powell took this to be a betrayal of the diplomatic negotiations still under way in New York, and he never forgave the Frenchman.[11]

Although the Americans believed that Resolution 1441 gave them the right to resort to war, America's ally Britain wanted a second resolution specifically approving the use of military force to disarm Iraq. Indeed, polls showed 77 percent of Britons opposed a war without such approval. Colin Powell and Tony Blair, eager to make the strongest case possible, dressed up partial and inconclusive intelligence information to depict Saddam's Iraq as an imminent threat. In a dramatic speech on 5 February 2003 at the UN, Powell said American and British intelligence had evidence that Iraq possessed hundreds of tons of chemical weapons, including anthrax and VX nerve gas, had placed such facilities on trucks and railcars to avoid detection, and most worrisome, had given sanctuary to an al-Qaeda terrorist ring operating out of Baghdad. It was a grave bill of particulars, but it was not new information, nor did it necessarily militate for war. France, Russia, China, and Germany (which then occupied a rotating seat on the Security Council) all responded that if Powell was right, it was all the more imperative that inspections be continued—indeed, significantly expanded. There was not yet a reason for rushing to war. Powell was stymied.[12]

He was winning some converts in Europe, however. In one of the more fascinating subplots in this tale, a number of European states had moved in America's direction in the early weeks of 2003. This became strikingly apparent on 30 January, when eight governments published a joint declaration in support of a tough, unified position on Iraq. The governments of Britain, Spain, Italy, Portugal, Denmark, Poland, Hungary, and Czech Republic drew attention to the values America and Europe shared, called on all Europeans to stand by the United States, and urged Saddam Hussein to comply with disarmament resolutions. This was a political bombshell in Europe, because it shattered the idea that Europe was unified in its opposition to war. (Public opinion in these eight countries, however, was running strongly against American policy.) The American secretary of defense, Donald Rumsfeld, now asserted that Europe had split between a dynamic, forward-looking "new" Europe that wished to cooperate with Washington and a sclerotic, cynical, and envious "old" Europe—France, Germany, Belgium, perhaps Russia—that resented American leadership. That Vaclav Havel—the poster child of non-violent revolution—was a signatory and had spoken eloquently of the need "to protect human life, human freedom, and human dignity" from tyranny, struck a crashing blow to the antiwar forces.[13]

But back at the UN, this show of support did not win the United States any new votes. On 7 March 2003, the US, Britain, and Spain proposed a resolution to the Security Council that Iraq give up its weapons or face war. The fifteen members of the Security Council remained deadlocked, though a majority of them privately stated their opposition to the resolution. Yet a vote was never held. On 10 March, the French and Russian foreign ministers made it clear that even if the United States could persuade a majority of the Security Council, they would use their veto privilege to reject a resolution approving war. This was a tragic and ill-tempered act by the French and Russians, since it allowed the Americans to throw up their hands at the whole diplomatic process and blame them for obstructing the will of the United Nations. The resolution was withdrawn, and on 17 March, President Bush gave Saddam Hussein forty-eight hours to leave his country or face war. Absent any reply from the Iraqi dictator, on 20 March the United States launched cruise missiles on Baghdad, while American and British tanks thundered across the Iraqi border.

Iraq was defeated in a matter of weeks, but in another sense, Europe also lost this war. The year 2003 was supposed to have been a year of enhanced unity on the continent: ten new Eastern European states received approval for entry into the EU, and the EU launched a Constitutional Convention to define the new rights and duties of the union. Instead, the war drove Europe apart. By the spring of 2003, major leaders such as Blair, Aznar, Schroeder, and Chirac were scarcely on speaking terms. The writing of the constitution, which should have engendered a continent-wide debate about the future of Europe, was largely overshadowed by the Iraq crisis, and when it did emerge in June 2003, it was a bloated, colorless, jargon-laden document that could not possibly inspire any passion for the European project.

Another casualty was the long-hoped-for but elusive common European foreign policy. The EU had been working for years to develop institutions in which members states would work together to hammer out common positions. Instead, Britain, Spain, and Italy pursued their own agenda in cooperation with the United States, while France and Germany pulled in the opposite direction, bolstered by polls that showed that a huge majority of Europeans opposed war in Iraq.[14] To make matters worse, the antiwar states tended to play to the gallery, decrying American imperialism while failing to offer a coherent, substantive policy to counter the very real threats posed by Islamic radicalism. Chris Patten, a British Conservative and European Commissioner for External Relations who had worked diligently to forge a common European position on Iraq, was despondent. "Some Europeans think that grumbling about America is the same thing as having a foreign policy," he quipped.[15]

The only European leader who lent both moral and military support to the war was Britain's Tony Blair, and he paid a heavy price for his loyalty to America. This marked an important evolution in British politics. In the 1940s, Labour leaders Clement Attlee and Ernest Bevin helped found the NATO alliance and made the Marshall Plan a success. After the Suez debacle of 1956, the new prime minister Harold Macmillan immediately worked to improve relations with the United States, and everyone breathed a sigh of relief that the crisis did not permanently harm Anglo-American relations. Margaret Thatcher suffered no political damage from her close ties to the Reagan White House. Yet for Blair, his support of Bush's policy in Iraq nearly destroyed him politically. Although he survived a series of difficult votes in the House of Commons in early 2003, once the war actually ended in April, Blair faced a massive backlash at home. This was in large part because the British and American invasion forces failed to turn up caches of chemical and biological weapons which, Blair had assured the public, were weaponized and ready to be launched "within forty-five minutes." Six months after the end of the war, with American and British troops in occupation of the country, virtually no evidence could be found that Saddam Hussein had possessed usable weapons of mass destruction. High-profile investigations were launched by Parliament into Blair's alarmist claims, and though the committees found no deliberate campaign of misinformation, Blair's handling of the intelligence information he possessed came in for severe public condemnation. Blair's communications director, Alastair Campbell, was forced to resign, and Blair's popularity ratings plunged to an all-time low. Clearly, the days when the special relationship between Britain and the United States could be used as a political asset by British leaders were over.

Perhaps the greatest casualty of this transatlantic dispute, however, was the reputation of the United States in Europe. For fifty years, Europeans and Americans had been partners. They had not always agreed on policy, and anti-Americanism had always been present in the political discourse of some European countries, but in practice, Europeans and Americans had worked together to achieve great things: to rebuild the continent, to restore peace and prosperity where there had been war and genocide. They had made common cause against a repressive Communist bloc and finally, together, forged a post–Cold War Europe, united and free. But the Iraq war caused millions of Europeans to look anew at the US and to conclude that they no longer could accept what they saw. It wasn't just Iraq: it was the whole range of American excesses that many European voices now cited. A best-selling book by Will Hutton, the former editor of the newspaper *The Observer*, depicted America as a rogue state, with an economic and social model that had increased inequality, failed to deliver social justice and fairness, worsened the environment, and alienated friends across the world. America offered a model, Hutton argued, that Europeans should reject and defy. For the first time in fifty years, one could imagine the venerable European-American friendship turning into an ugly rivalry.[16]

Such an outcome would be terrible both for Europe and the United States. The great achievements of the post-1945 order, as this book has shown, were accomplished by Europe and America working together as partners. The creation of the UN, the institutions of the Marshall Plan and NATO, the establishment of the World Bank and IMF, the containment and final defeat of Communism, the massive expansion of foreign aid and humanitarian relief—these have been European and American successes. Naturally, time moves on: the Atlantic alliance no longer faces the same kinds of threats that brought it into existence in the mid-1940s. Yet other frontiers beckon: the challenges of global poverty, disease, weapons proliferation, religious fundamentalism, terrorism, failed states—the list goes on. Now more than ever, the world needs the concerted leadership of both the United States and Europe. This is no longer just Europe's struggle, but a struggle for humanity.

Wellesley, Massachusetts
September 2003

NOTES

.

INTRODUCTION

1. In its broadest definition, Europe has forty-eight political units: Albania, Andorra, Armenia, Austria, Azerbaijan, Belarus, Belgium, Bosnia, Bulgaria, Croatia, Cyprus, Czech Republic, Denmark, Estonia, Finland, France, Georgia, Germany, Greece, Hungary, Iceland, Ireland, Italy, Latvia, Liechtenstein, Lithuania, Luxembourg, Macedonia, Malta, Moldova, Monaco, Netherlands, Norway, Poland, Portugal, Romania, Russia, San Marino, Serbia, Slovakia, Slovenia, Spain, Sweden, Switzerland, Turkey, Ukraine, United Kingdom, and Vatican City.

2. For example, see Mark Mazower, *Dark Continent: Europe's Twentieth Century* (New York: Knopf, 1999); Tony Judt, *A Grand Illusion? An Essay on Europe* (New York: Hill and Wang, 1996); and John Newhouse, *Europe Adrift* (New York: Pantheon, 1997).

3. Winston Churchill, 19 September 1946, at Zurich University, in Brent F. Nelsen and Alexander Stubb, eds., *The European Union: Readings on the Theory and Practice of European Integration* (London: Lynne Rienner, 1998), 7–11.

PART ONE: AFTERMATH

1. Simone de Beauvoir, *Force of Circumstance* (London: Penguin Books, 1968), 132, 265, 242.

CHAPTER ONE: GERMAN MIDNIGHT

1. For a discussion of the difficulty of determining Soviet casualty figures, see Richard Overy, *Russia's War* (London: Penguin, 1997), 287–89; and B. V. Sokolov, "The Cost of War: Human Losses of the USSR and Germany, 1939–1945," *Journal of Slavic Military Studies* 9 (1996), 156–71.

2. Cited in Alfred-Maurice de Zayas, *A Terrible Revenge: The Ethnic Cleansing of the East Germans, 1944–1950* (New York: St. Martin's Press, 1993), 45.

3. Norman Naimark, *The Russians in Germany: A History of the Soviet Zone of Occupation, 1945–1949* (Cambridge: Harvard University Press, 1995), 133, and see chapter 2 for an extended discussion of the rapes and their impact on postwar East Germany.

4. Ruth Andreas-Friedrich, *Battleground Berlin: Diaries, 1945–1948*, trans. by Anna Boerresen (New York: Paragon, 1990), 16–17.

5. F. S. V. Donnison, *Civil Affairs and Military Government, North-West Europe, 1944–1946* (London: HMSO, 1961), chapter 19, and 355–56 for quotation; and see George Woodbridge, *UNRRA: The History of the United Nations Relief and Rehabilitation Administration*, vol. 2 (New York: Columbia University Press, 1950), table, 498, for numbers of DPs under UNRRA care.

6. Douglas Botting, *In the Ruins of the Reich* (London: Allen and Unwin, 1985), 121–30; Overy, *Russia's War*, 303.

7. The best English-language work on the issue of the *Vertriebenen*, or expellees, is Alfred-Maurice de Zayas, *Nemesis at Potsdam: The Expulsion of the Germans from the East*, 3rd ed. (Lincoln,

Neb.: University of Nebraska Press, 1988); for the numbers of dead, see his *A Terrible Revenge*, 151–52, and Statistisches Bundesamt, ed., *Die deutschen Vertreibungsverluste* (Stuttgart, 1958), 38, 45–46. For supporting data, see Eugene M. Kulischer, *Europe on the Move: War and Population Changes, 1917–1947* (New York: Columbia University Press, 1948), 274–311; and Michael R. Marrus, *The Unwanted: European Refugees in the Twentieth Century* (New York: Oxford University Press, 1985), 296–345. There is a vast amount of published evidence available on the saga of the expellees: see Theodor Schieder et al., *Dokumentation der Vertreibung der Deutschen aus Ost- und Mitteleuropa*, 8 vols. (Bonn: German Federal Ministry for Expellees, 1953–61). Victor Gollancz, a British journalist and publisher, traveled in Germany in late November 1946 and wrote a searing account of what he found: *In Darkest Germany* (Chicago: Henry Regnery Co., 1947); and for the grim personal experiences of a Prussian doctor and aristocrat under Russian and Polish rule, see Hans Graf von Lehndorff, *Token of a Covenant: Diary of an East Prussian Surgeon, 1945–1947*, trans. by Elizabeth Mayer (Chicago: Henry Regnery Co., 1964).

8. See the memoir of the US secretary of state, Edward R. Stettinius, *Roosevelt and the Russians: The Yalta Conference* (New York: Doubleday, 1949), 79–83; and Winston Churchill's account, *The Second World War*, vol. 6, *Triumph and Tragedy* (Boston: Houghton Mifflin, 1953), 346.

9. There is a large literature on Roosevelt and his foreign policy. Among the most useful works, see Robert Dallek, *Franklin D. Roosevelt and American Foreign Policy, 1932–1945* (New York: Oxford University Press, 1979), esp. 503–25; Herbert Feis, *Churchill, Roosevelt, Stalin: The War They Waged and the Peace They Sought* (Princeton: Princeton University Press, 1957), 489–558; Daniel Yergin, *Shattered Peace: The Origins of the Cold War and the National Security State* (Boston: Houghton Mifflin, 1977), 42–68. Especially good on Yalta is Lloyd C. Gardner, *Spheres of Influence: The Great Powers Partition Europe, from Munich to Yalta* (Chicago: Ivan Dee, 1993), 207–65.

10. For an assessment of Churchill's role at Yalta, see Fraser Harbutt, *The Iron Curtain: Churchill, America, and the Origins of the Cold War* (New York: Oxford University Press, 1986), 53–90; and Warren Kimball's excellent article "Naked Reverse Right: Roosevelt, Churchill, and Eastern Europe from Tolstoy to Yalta—and a Little Beyond," *Diplomatic History* 9, no. 1 (winter 1985), 1–24.

11. For a penetrating analysis of Stalin's postwar goals, based on recently released Russian archives, see Vladislav Zubok and Constantine Pleshakov, *Inside the Kremlin's Cold War: From Stalin to Khrushchev* (Cambridge: Harvard University Press, 1996), esp. 13–35. New material has also been well used by Vladimir O. Pechatnov, "The Big Three After World War Two: New Documents on Soviet Thinking About Postwar Relations with the United States and Great Britain," Cold War International History Project, Working Paper #13, July 1995 (available at http://www.cwihp.si.edu), who shows that there was a strong current of opinion in the Kremlin that favored a limited cooperation with the West, so as to consolidate Soviet security in Eastern Europe. An excellent earlier study is Vojtech Mastny, *Russia's Road to the Cold War: Diplomacy, Warfare, and the Politics of Communism, 1941–1945* (New York: Columbia University Press, 1979), 267–306.

12. The records of the conference are extensive. See *Foreign Relations of the United States: The Conferences at Malta and Yalta, 1945* (Washington, D.C.: Government Printing Office, 1955). The conference's final agreement, including the Declaration on Liberated Europe, appears on 968–75.

13. Dallek, *Franklin D. Roosevelt*, 520; and for a discussion of the role at Yalta of James F. Byrnes, FDR's close adviser, see Robert L. Messer, *The End of an Alliance: James F. Byrnes, Roosevelt, Truman, and the Origins of the Cold War* (Chapel Hill: University of North Carolina Press, 1982), 31–70.

14. For a concise summary of Truman's ideas about the Soviets in the first months after taking office, see Melvyn Leffler, *The Specter of Communism: The United States and the Origins of the Cold War, 1917–1953* (New York: Hill and Wang, 1994), 33–63; and Randall B. Woods and Howard Jones, *Dawning of the Cold War: The United States' Quest for Order* (Chicago: Ivan Dee, 1991), 33–72.

15. Churchill, *The Second World War*, vol. 6, *Triumph and Tragedy*, 630–31; and David McCullough, *Truman* (New York: Simon & Schuster, 1992), 407–15.

16. For a persuasive argument to this effect, based on East German sources, see R. C. Raack, "Stalin Plans His Postwar Germany," *Journal of Contemporary History* 28 (1993), 53–73.

17. On Potsdam, see Herbert Feis, *Between War and Peace: The Potsdam Conference* (Princeton: Princeton University Press, 1960); and for a fresh look at the conference, Carolyn Eisenberg, *Drawing the Line: The American Decision to Divide Germany, 1944–1949* (Cambridge: Cambridge University Press, 1996), 89–120.

18. Milovan Djilas, *Conversations with Stalin* (New York: Harcourt Brace, 1962), 114.

19. Soviet policy in Germany and the establishment of Communist rule in the Soviet zone have been treated in the following works: above all, see Norman Naimark, *The Russians in Germany;* and for earlier, still valuable studies, Gregory W. Sandford, *From Hitler to Ulbricht: The Communist Reconstruction of East Germany, 1945–1946* (Princeton: Princeton University Press, 1983); Henry Krisch, *German Politics Under Soviet Occupation* (New York: Columbia University Press, 1974); David Childs, *The GDR: Moscow's German Ally* (London: Allen and Unwin, 1983), 1–37; Hermann Weber, *Geschichte de DDR* (Munich: Deutscher Taschenbuch Verlag, 1985), esp. 1–186; and Vojtech Mastny, *The Cold War and Soviet Insecurity: The Stalin Years* (New York: Oxford University Press, 1996), 20–29.

20. Wolfgang Leonhard, *Child of the Revolution* (London: Ink Links, 1979), 321.

21. Good introductions to the US occupation administration in Germany are Harold Zink, *The United States in Germany, 1945–1955* (New York: D. Van Nostrand, 1957); and John Gimbel, *The American Occupation of Germany: Politics and the Military, 1945–1949* (Stanford: Stanford University Press, 1968). These have been superseded by Eisenberg's new account, *Drawing the Line,* which stresses the American initiative in dividing Germany.

22. The text of JCS 1067 is reprinted in Beate Ruhm von Oppen, ed., *Documents on Germany Under Occupation, 1945–1954* (London: Oxford University Press and the Royal Institute of International Affairs, 1955), 13–27.

23. International Military Tribunal, *Trial of the Major War Criminals Before the International Military Tribunal: Proceedings and Documents,* 42 vols. (Nuremberg, 1947–49). For works on the trials themselves, see Telford Taylor, *The Anatomy of the Nuremberg Trials: A Personal Memoir* (New York: Knopf, 1992); and Joseph E. Persico, *Nuremberg: Infamy on Trial* (New York: Penguin, 1994).

24. For a summary of the debate over de-Nazification, see Dennis L. Bark and David R. Gress, *A History of West Germany,* vol. 1, *From Shadow to Substance, 1945–1963* (Oxford: Blackwell, 1993), 74–89.

25. The comment was made by Lewis Douglas, Clay's financial adviser. See Robert D. Murphy, *Diplomats Among Warriors* (Garden City, N.Y.: Doubleday, 1964), 16.

26. The importance of US business circles in German reconstruction has been established by Volker Berghahn, *The Americanization of West German Industry, 1945–1973* (Cambridge: Cambridge University Press, 1986), 84–110. See also Eisenberg, *Drawing the Line,* 139–51.

27. For an overview of political reconstruction, see Zink, *The United States in Germany, 1944–1955,* 169–92; and Bark and Gress, *History of West Germany,* 93–107.

28. Cited in Melvyn Leffler, *A Preponderance of Power: National Security, the Truman Administration, and the Cold War* (Stanford: Stanford University Press, 1992), 70–71.

29. Anne Deighton has shown how significant British hostility toward the Soviet Union was in pushing the division of Germany: *The Impossible Peace: Britain, the Division of Germany, and the Origins of the Cold War* (Oxford: Clarendon Press, 1990). For an excellent portrait of Bevin's tenure at the Foreign Office, see Alan Bullock, *Ernest Bevin: Foreign Secretary, 1945–1951* (London: Heinemann, 1983).

30. Telegram to US State Department, February 22, 1946, in George F. Kennan, *Memoirs 1925–1950* (Boston: Little, Brown, 1969), 583–98.

31. Harbutt, *Iron Curtain,* 180, and for a careful examination of the speech itself, 183–208. The speech may be found in Brian MacArthur, ed., *The Penguin Book of Twentieth-Century Speeches* (London: Penguin, 1992), 229–31.

32. For the text of Byrnes's speech, see Ruhm von Oppen, *Documents,* 152–60; and for an analysis of its origins and impact, Lucius D. Clay, *Decision in Germany* (Garden City, N.Y.: Doubleday, 1950), 78–82; and Eisenberg, *Drawing the Line,* 244–48. On the hardening of US views in 1946, see Leffler, *Preponderance of Power,* 116–21, 130–40.

33. The Novikov telegram, 27 September 1946, Cold War International History Project, http://www.cwihp.si.edu.

CHAPTER TWO: BUILDING JERUSALEM

1. Martin Gilbert, *Winston S. Churchill,* vol. 8, *Never Despair, 1945–1965* (Boston: Houghton Mifflin, 1988), 106–7.

2. Mary Soames, *Clementine Churchill: The Biography of a Marriage* (Boston: Houghton Mifflin, 1979), 508–10.

3. Lord Moran, *Churchill: Taken from the Diaries of Lord Moran: The Struggle for Survival, 1940–1965* (Boston: Houghton Mifflin, 1966), 308. For the account of another who was with Churchill that day, see John Colville, *The Fringes of Power: 10 Downing Street Diaries, 1939–1955* (London: Norton, 1985), 612.

4. The Liberal Party had twelve seats and the independents had twenty-two. Predictions about Tory victory were widespread. The Gallup poll, however, showed Labour with a commanding lead throughout the election. Paul Addison, *The Road to 1945* (London: Cape, 1975), 266–67; and Anthony Howard, "We Are Masters Now," in Michael Sissons and Philip French, eds., *Age of Austerity* (London: Hodder and Stoughton, 1963), 17.

5. Angus Calder, *The Myth of the Blitz* (London: Cape, 1991), 33–37, 42; A. J. P. Taylor, *English History, 1914–1945* (London: Oxford University Press, 1965), 498–503; Arthur Marwick, *The Home Front: The British and the Second World War* (London: Thames and Hudson, 1976), 75–82; Angus Calder, *The People's War: Britain, 1939–1945* (London: Granada, 1971), 40–58, 212. The blitz saw the second major evacuation effort. Over 3 million people had been shipped out of cities in September 1939 in anticipation of a bombing campaign that never came.

6. Cato [Michael Foot, Frank Owen, Peter Howard], *Guilty Men* (London: Victor Gollancz, 1940).

7. Calder, *Myth,* 129; Marwick, *Home Front,* 68–75.

8. Ian Taylor, "Labour and the Impact of War, 1939–1945," in *The Attlee Years,* ed. by Nick Tiratsoo (London: Pinter, 1991), 7–28.

9. On the making of the report and its reception, see José Harris, *William Beveridge: A Biography* (Oxford: Oxford University Press, 1977), 378–451; and Addison, *The Road to 1945,* 211–28.

10. Kenneth Harris, *Attlee* (London: Weidenfeld and Nicholson, 1982); and C. R. Attlee, *As It Happened* (London: Viking, 1954).

11. Alan Sked and Chris Cook, *Postwar Britain: A Political History* (London: Penguin, 1990), 25; and Harold Nicolson, *Diaries and Letters,* vol. 3, *The Later Years, 1945–1962* (New York: Atheneum, 1968), 113.

12. Bernard Donoughue and G. W. Jones, *Herbert Morrison: Portrait of a Politician* (London: Weidenfeld and Nicolson, 1973); Alan Bullock, *The Life and Times of Ernest Bevin,* vols. 1 and 2 (London: Heinemann, 1960, 1967).

13. Stephen Brooke, ed., *Reform and Reconstruction: Britain After the War, 1945–51* (Manchester: Manchester University Press, 1995), 37.

14. Brooke, *Reform,* 38–39; and Gilbert, *Churchill,* 32.

15. Brooke, *Reform,* 39, and Harris, *Attlee,* 256–58; Gilbert, *Churchill,* 35; Moran, *Diaries,* 272.

16. Soames, *Clementine Churchill,* 504–5; Harold Macmillan, *Tides of Fortune, 1945–1955* (New York: Harper and Row, 1969), 32.

17. Harris, *Attlee,* 269.

18. "Our Overseas Financial Prospects," 13 August 1945, in *The Collected Writings of John Maynard Keynes,* vol. 23, *Activities, 1944–1946, The Transition to Peace,* ed. by Donald Moggridge (Cambridge: Macmillan and Cambridge University Press, 1979), 398–411; and for an excellent survey of Britain's financial picture at war's end, see both L. S. Pressnell, *External Economic Policy Since the War,* vol. 1, *The Postwar Financial Settlement* (London: HMSO, 1986), 1–12, and Alec Cairncross, *Years of Recovery: British Economic Policy, 1945–51* (London: Methuen, 1985), 3–16.

19. Randall Bennett Woods, *A Changing of the Guard: Anglo-American Relations, 1941–1946* (Chapel Hill: University of North Carolina Press, 1990), 332–62; R. F. Harrod, *The Life of John Maynard Keynes* (New York: Harcourt Brace, 1951), 595–623; Richard N. Gardner, *Sterling-Dollar Diplomacy in Current Perspective* (New York: Columbia University Press, 1980), 188–207.

20. *Economist,* 8 December 1945.

21. Morgan, *Labour in Power,* 151.

22. Richard Clarke, *Anglo-American Economic Collaboration in War and Peace, 1942–1949* (Oxford: Clarendon Press, 1982), 712–81.

23. Clarke, *Anglo-American Economic Collaboration,* 187–89; and for other surveys of the crisis, see Morgan, *Labour in Power,* 330–50; Henry Pelling, *The Labour Governments, 1945–51* (New York: St. Martin's Press, 1984), 165–76; Harris, *Attlee,* 332–47; and John Killick, *The United States and European Reconstruction, 1945–1960* (Edinburgh: Keele University Press, 1997), 72–75.

24. Addison, *Road to 1945,* 190–210; Morgan, *Labour in Power,* 359–63; Eric Estorick, *Stafford*

Cripps: Prophetic Rebel (New York: John Day, 1941), 150–76; David Marquand, "Sir Stafford Cripps," in Sissons and French, *Age of Austerity,* 167–87.

25. *Economist,* 14 February 1948 and 25 December 1948.

26. IMF, *Balance of Payments Yearbook: 1948* (Washington, 1950), 387; and IMF, *Balance of Payments Yearbook,* vol. 3, *1949–1950* (Washington, 1951), 397.

27. For all of these subjects, from the convertibility crisis to devaluation, planning, and controls, see the relevant chapters of Alec Cairncross, *Years of Recovery,* which is authoritative.

28. Susan Cooper, "Snoek Piquante: The Trials and Tribulations of the British Housewife," in Sissons and French, *Age of Austerity,* 35. This is a brilliantly evocative essay on living with rations in postwar Britain.

29. T. E. B. Howarth, *Prospect and Reality: Great Britain, 1945–1951* (London: Collins, 1985), 162.

30. Paul Addison, *Now the War Is Over: A Social History of Britain, 1945–51* (London: Jonathan Cape, 1985), 53.

31. Cripps, *Times,* 28 October 1946, cited in Brooke, *Reform,* 52–53.

32. Pelling, *Labour Governments,* 110.

33. Cited in John Campbell, *Aneurin Bevan and the Mirage of British Socialism* (New York: Norton, 1987), 162.

34. Bevan in the House of Commons, 9 February 1948, cited in Michael Foot, *Aneurin Bevan,* vol. 2 (New York: Atheneum, 1974), 191.

35. Addison, *Now the War Is Over,* 104.

36. Morgan, *Labour in Power,* 160, and in general, 151–63; Campbell, *Bevan,* 165–85; Peter Jenkins, "Bevan's Fight with the BMA," in Sissons and French, *Age of Austerity,* 233–54; Peter Hennessy, *Never Again: Britain, 1945–1951* (New York: Pantheon, 1992), 132–44.

37. A good survey of recent work in the field is David Reynolds, "Great Britain," in Reynolds, ed., *The Origins of the Cold War in Europe: International Perspectives* (New Haven: Yale University Press, 1994), 77–95.

38. The best work on Bevin in this period is the massive and exhaustive study by Alan Bullock, *Ernest Bevin: Foreign Secretary, 1945–1951* (London: Heinemann, 1984)—a book as large as its subject.

39. Bullock, *Bevin,* 196.

40. Bullock, *Bevin,* 214. For a full treatment of the issues, see Bruce R. Kuniholm, *The Origins of the Cold War in the Near East* (Princeton: Princeton University Press, 1980); and William Roger Louis, *The British Empire in the Middle East* (Oxford: Clarendon Press, 1984).

41. Frank Roberts to Foreign Office, 14, 17, and 18 March 1946, reprinted in Kenneth M. Jensen, ed., *Origins of the Cold War: The Novikov, Kennan, and Roberts "Long Telegrams" of 1946* (Washington, D.C.: United States Institute of Peace, 1991), 33–67.

42. Felix Chuev, *Molotov Remembers: Inside Kremlin Politics,* ed. by Albert Reiss (Chicago: Ivan Dee, 1993), 74. On the Iran crisis, Randall Woods and Howard Jones, *Dawning of the Cold War: The United States' Quest for Order* (Chicago: Ivan Dee, 1991), 111–12; for the US military preparations, see Eduard Mark, "The War Scare of 1946 and Its Consequences," *Diplomatic History* 21, no. 3 (summer 1997), 383–415.

43. On Bevin's pressure for a fusion of the US and British zones of occupation, see Anne Deighton, *The Impossible Peace: Britain, the Division of Germany, and the Origins of the Cold War* (Oxford: Clarendon Press, 1990), 93–134.

44. Louis, *British Empire,* 428.

45. Message of the president to the Congress on 12 March 1947, Department of State *Bulletin,* 23 March 1947, 534–37.

46. National radio broadcast, 28 April 1947, in Department of State *Bulletin,* 11 May 1947, 919–24.

47. *Foreign Relations of the United States [FRUS], 1947* (Washington, D.C.: GPO, 1972) 3: 237–39; and for a review of the origins of the speech, see Michael J. Hogan, *The Marshall Plan: America, Britain, and the Reconstruction of Western Europe, 1947–1951* (New York: Oxford, 1987), esp. 35–45.

48. Bullock, *Bevin,* 405.

49. Nikolai V. Novikov to Foreign Minister Molotov, 24 June 1947, cited in Scott D. Parrish, "The Turn Toward Confrontation: The Soviet Reaction to the Marshall Plan, 1947," Cold War International History Project Working Paper #9 (1994).

50. *FRUS, 1947,* 3: 297–99; 301–3.

51. *FRUS, 1948,* 3: 1; 4–6.

52. *FRUS, 1948,* 3: 32–33; 34–35; 46–48.

53. On Britain's role in the origins of NATO, see Martin H. Folly, "Breaking the Vicious Circle: Britain, the United States, and the Genesis of the North Atlantic Treaty," *Diplomatic History* 12, no. 1 (winter 1988), 59–77; Bert Zeeman, "Britain and the Cold War: An Alternative Approach. The Treaty of Dunkirk Example," *European History Quarterly* 16 (1986), 343–67; and John Baylis, "Britain, the Brussels Pact, and the Continental Commitment," *International Affairs* 60, no. 4 (autumn 1984), 615–29.

54. Bullock, *Bevin,* 90.

55. Margaret Thatcher, *The Downing Street Years* (New York: HarperCollins, 1993), 6–7.

56. Correlli Barnett, *The Pride and the Fall* (orig. *The Audit of War*) (New York: The Free Press, 1986), 304.

57. Kenneth O. Morgan, *The People's Peace: British History, 1945–1990* (London: Oxford University Press, 1992), 510; and for a similar view see Peter Clarke, *Hope and Glory: Britain, 1900–1990* (London: Penguin, 1996), 401–4.

CHAPTER THREE: DEMOCRACY EMBATTLED

1. Alexander Werth, *De Gaulle: A Political Biography* (New York: Simon & Schuster, 1965), 101.

2. Winston Churchill, *The Second World War,* vol. 2, *Their Finest Hour* (Boston: Houghton Mifflin, 1949), 182, 215.

3. Charles de Gaulle, *The War Memoirs of Charles de Gaulle,* vol. 2, *Unity, 1942–1944,* trans. by Richard Howard (New York: Simon & Schuster, 1959), 3.

4. Speech of 25 August 1944, in Charles de Gaulle, *The War Memoirs of Charles de Gaulle: Unity, 1942–1944. Documents,* trans. by Joyce Murchie and Hamish Erskine (New York: Simon & Schuster, 1959), 409–10.

5. Albert Camus, in his newspaper *Combat,* 25 October 1944, in Alexandre de Gramont, ed., *Albert Camus: Between Hell and Reason. Essays from the Resistance Newspaper Combat, 1944–1947* (Hanover, N.H.: University Press of New England, 1991), 72–73.

6. Jean-Pierre Rioux, *The Fourth Republic, 1944–1958* (Cambridge: Cambridge University Press, 1987), 29–42; and Peter Novick, *The Resistance Versus Vichy: The Purge of Collaborators in Liberated France* (New York: Columbia University Press, 1968).

7. On the idea of the betrayal of the resistance by de Gaulle and by the parties, see the various memoirs of key resistance figures, like Henri Frenay, *La Nuit finira* (Paris: Opera Mundi, 1973); Pierre Hervé, *La Libération trahie* (Paris: Grasset, 1946); and Claude Bourdet, *L'Aventure incertaine: De la résistance à la restauration* (Paris: Stock, 1975). For recent reflections on these themes, see Olivier Wieviorka, *Nous entrerons dans la carrière: de la résistance à l'exercice du pouvoir* (Paris: Seuil, 1994).

8. Rioux, *Fourth Republic,* 18–23.

9. William I. Hitchcock, *France Restored: Cold War Diplomacy and the Quest for Leadership in Europe, 1944–1954* (Chapel Hill: University of North Carolina Press, 1998), 32.

10. There is a large literature on the Monnet Plan, but the best work is Philippe Mioche, *Le Plan Monnet: Genèse et élaboration, 1941–1947* (Paris: Publications de la Sorbonne, 1987).

11. Norman Lewis, *Naples '44* (New York: Pantheon, 1978), 46–47.

12. C. R. S. Harris, *Allied Military Administration of Italy, 1943–1945* (London: HMSO, 1957), 85–91; 167–70; 193; Appendix IV, 419–28.

13. Richard Lamb, *War in Italy, 1943–1945: A Brutal Story* (New York: Da Capo Press, 1993), 56–68.

14. Paul Ginsborg, *A History of Contemporary Italy: Society and Politics, 1943–1988* (London: Penguin, 1990), 21; David Ellwood, *Italy, 1943–1945* (New York: Holmes and Meier, 1985), 75–78; G. Quazza, "The Politics of the Italian Resistance," in Stuart J. Woolf, ed., *The Rebirth of Italy, 1943–1950* (London: Longmans, 1972), 1–29.

15. There is a large literature on the *dopoguerra* (postwar period) in Italy. For a useful introduction, see G. Bertolo et al., *Il dopoguerra italiano, 1945–1948: Guida bibliografica* (Milan: Feltrinelli, 1975). Good surveys include Ennio Di Nolfo, *Le paure e le speranze degli Italiani, 1943–1953* (Milan:

Mondadori, 1986); Giuseppe Mammarella, *Italy After Fascism: A Political History, 1943–1965* (Notre Dame: Notre Dame University Press, 1966); Norman Kogan, *A Political History of Postwar Italy* (New York: Praeger, 1966); James Edward Miller, *The United States and Italy, 1940–1950: The Politics and Diplomacy of Stabilization* (Chapel Hill: University of North Carolina Press, 1986); John L. Harper, *America and the Reconstruction of Italy, 1945–1948* (Cambridge: Cambridge University Press, 1986). Many useful contemporary documents have been collected in Massimo Legnani, *L'Italia dal 1943 al 1948: Lotte politiche e sociali* (Turin: Loescher Editore, 1973). For a superb collection of photographs, see Andrea Nemiz, *La ricostruzione, 1945–53* (Rome: Editori Riuniti, 1998).

16. Joan Barth Urban, *Moscow and the Italian Communist Party: From Togliatti to Belinguer* (Ithaca: Cornell University Press, 1986), esp. 148–224; and chapters by Lawrence Gray, Ennio Di Nolfo, and Simon Serfaty in Simon Serfaty and Lawrence Gray, eds., *The Italian Communist Party: Yesterday, Today, and Tomorrow* (Westport, Conn.: Greenwood Press, 1980). For recent research on Soviet control of the PCI at this time, see Elena Aga-Rossi and Victor Zaslavsky, "The Soviet Union and the Italian Communist Party, 1944–1948," in Francesca Gori and Silvio Pons, *The Soviet Union and Europe in the Cold War, 1943–1953* (New York: St. Martin's Press, 1996), 161–84.

17. Ginsborg, *Contemporary Italy,* 50.

18. Harper, *America and the Reconstruction of Italy,* 99–104; Donald Sassoon, *Contemporary Italy: Politics, Economy, and Society Since 1945* (London: Longman, 1986), 15–27; FRUS 1946, 5: 930–32.

19. FRUS 1946, 5: 934–36, 946.

20. FRUS 1947, 3: 838–41, 845–50.

21. FRUS 1947, 3: 877–78; 880; 886–87.

22. FRUS 1947, 3: 889–92; 893–94.

23. FRUS 1947, 3: 904–13; for further discussion, see Miller, *The United States and Italy,* 213–35; and Alberto Tarchiani, *Dieci anni tra Roma e Washington* (Milan: Rizzoli, 1955); Ilaria Poggiolini, "Italy," in David Reynolds, ed., *The Origins of the Cold War in Europe: International Perspectives* (New Haven: Yale University Press, 1994), 121–43.

24. For persuasive evidence on this subject, see Scott Parish, "The Marshall Plan, Soviet-American Relations, and the Division of Europe," in Norman Naimark and Leonid Gibianskii, eds., *The Establishment of Communist Regimes in Eastern Europe, 1944–1949* (Boulder, Colo.: Westview, 1997), 268–90; and Vojtech Mastny, *The Cold War and Soviet Insecurity: The Stalin Years* (New York: Oxford University Press, 1996), 23–29.

25. For an excellent account of Stalin's thinking in the summer of 1947, based on new research in Soviet archives, see Vladislav Zubok and Constantine Pleshakov, *Inside the Kremlin's Cold War: From Stalin to Khrushchev* (Cambridge: Harvard University Press, 1996), 110–37. For new evidence on Stalin's ideas about the Cominform, see Csaba Békés, "Soviet Plans to Establish the Cominform in Early 1946: New Evidence from the Hungarian Archives," CWIHP *Bulletin* 10 (March 1998), 135–36.

26. "On the International Situation," Andrei Zhdanov's report, 25 September 1947, in *The Cominform: Minutes of the Three Conferences: 1947/1948/1949,* ed. by Giuliano Procacci (Milan: Feltrinelli Editore, 1994), 215–51. The nine countries represented were Bulgaria, Czechoslovakia, France, Hungary, Italy, Poland, Romania, the USSR, and Yugoslavia.

27. Ibid., 259, 351, 277, 319. For an earlier account of the founding of the Cominform, written without access to any documents, see Lilly Marcou, *Le Kominform* (Paris: Fondation Nationale des Sciences Politiques, 1977), esp. 39–72.

28. Rioux, *Fourth Republic,* 129–30; Frank Giles, *The Locust Years: The Story of the Fourth French Republic, 1946–1958* (New York: Carroll and Graf, 1991), 81–87; FRUS 1947, 3: 804–6.

29. FRUS 1947, 3: 727–29.

30. "Review of the World Situation as It Relates to the Security of the United States," CIA 1, 26 September 1947, reproduced in *The CIA Under Harry Truman* (Washington, D.C.: Central Intelligence Agency, 1994), 139–50; and NSC 4-A, 17 December 1947, reproduced ibid., 173–75.

31. FRUS 1947, 3: 819–20.

32. On US labor in France, see Irwin Wall, *The United States and the Making of Postwar France, 1945–1954* (Cambridge: Cambridge University Press, 1991), 96–113; and Ted Morgan, *A Covert Life: Jay Lovestone, Communist, Anti-Communist, and Spymaster* (New York: Random House, 1999), 177–89.

33. FRUS 1947, 3: 807–8; FRUS 1948, 3: 757–62, 765–69; and CIA report ORE 47/1, 16 February 1948, "The Current Situation in Italy," in *The CIA Under Harry Truman,* 181–89.

34. Miller, *The United States and Italy*, 236–49; and his article "Taking Off the Gloves: The United States and Italian Elections of 1948," *Diplomatic History* 7, no. 1 (winter 1983), 35–55; Ginsborg, *Contemporary Italy*, 115–18.

35. Anne Karalekas, *History of the Central Intelligence Agency* (Laguna Hills, Calif.: Aegean Park Press, 1977), 29–32. This study was originally prepared for the Senate Select Committee to Study Governmental Operations with Respect to Intelligence Activities, in April 1976. On NSC 10/2 and the CIA in this period, see also Peter Grose, *Gentleman Spy: The Life of Allen Dulles* (New York: Houghton Mifflin, 1994), 285–329; and the text of NSC 10/2 in *CIA Under Harry Truman*, 213–16.

36. Carolyn Eisenberg, *Drawing the Line: The American Decision to Divide Germany, 1944–1949* (Cambridge: Cambridge University Press, 1996), 363–410.

37. Jean Edward Smith, *The Papers of General Lucius Clay* (Bloomington: Indiana University Press, 1974), 2: 568–69.

38. On the impact of the Prague coup in Washington, see Daniel Yergin, *Shattered Peace: The Origins of the Cold War and the National Security State* (Boston: Houghton Mifflin, 1977), 350–65.

39. Milovan Djilas, *Conversations with Stalin* (New York: Harcourt Brace, 1962), 153.

40. On the role of intelligence in the blockade, see David E. Murphy, Sergei A. Kondrashev, and George Bailey, *Battleground Berlin: CIA vs. KGB in the Cold War* (New Haven: Yale University Press, 1997), 62–70. On Stalin's motives, which remain murky, see John Lewis Gaddis, *We Now Know, Rethinking Cold War History* (Oxford: Clarendon Press, 1997), 46–48, 118–21; Michail M. Narinskii, "The Soviet Union and the Berlin Crisis," in Gori and Pons, eds., *Soviet Union and Europe*, 57–75; and Caroline Kennedy-Pipe, *Stalin's Cold War: Soviet Strategies in Europe, 1943–1956* (Manchester: Manchester University Press, 1995), 124–38.

41. The origins and course of the blockade are treated in Ann and John Tusa, *The Berlin Airlift* (New York: Atheneum, 1988), and Avi Shlaim, *The United States and the Berlin Blockade, 1948–1949* (Berkeley: University of California Press, 1983). See also the account of the US military governor: Lucius D. Clay, *Decision in Germany* (Garden City, N.J.: Doubleday, 1950), 358–92. Many in the US government were at first opposed to sticking it out in Berlin. It was considered risky and strategically unnecessary to protect West Germany, and an airlift would dangerously weaken American air capacity elsewhere around the world. Marc Trachtenberg, *A Constructed Peace: The Making of the European Settlement, 1945–1963* (Princeton: Princeton University Press, 1999), 81–82. At the same time, the French were actually against the idea of turning Berlin into a showdown with the Russians. Initially, they favored giving the city to the Russians. Hitchcock, *France Restored*, 104–5.

42. Ernst Reuter, 24 June 1948, in Carl-Christoph Schweitzer et al., *Politics and Government in Germany, 1944–1994: Basic Documents* (Providence, R.I.: Berghahn Books, 1995), 11.

43. Tusa, *Berlin Airlift*, 336.

44. I have been greatly helped in understanding the diplomacy of the Berlin blockade by an unpublished essay by my former student Cameron MacDougall: "Acting in Concert: Anglo-American Strategy, Diplomacy and Cooperation During the Berlin Blockade, 1948–1949" (Yale College Senior Essay, 1998).

CHAPTER FOUR: BEHIND THE IRON CURTAIN

1. Hugh Seton-Watson, *The East European Revolution* (New York: Praeger, 1956), 169–71.

2. The most important early interpretations—which still have much value today—are Zbigniew Brzezinski, *The Soviet Bloc: Unity and Conflict* (Cambridge: Harvard University Press, 1960); Adam Ulam, *Titoism and the Cominform* (Cambridge: Harvard University Press, 1952); and François Fejto, *Histoire des démocraties populaires* (Paris: Seuil, 1952).

3. Jan T. Gross, "Social Consequences of War: Preliminaries to the Study of the Imposition of the Communist Regime in East Central Europe," *Eastern European Politics and Societies* 3 (spring 1989).

4. There is a large literature on the subject, but I have found most useful the following works: Krystyna Kersten, *The Establishment of Communist Rule in Poland, 1943–1948*, trans. by John Micgiel and Michael H. Bernhard (Berkeley: University of California Press, 1991); John Coutouvidis and Jaime Reynolds, *Poland, 1939–1947* (Leicester: Leicester University Press, 1986); and Antony Polonsky and Boleslaw Drukier, eds., *The Beginnings of Communist Rule in Poland* (London: Routledge and Kegan Paul, 1980), which contains a wealth of documentary material. Two autobiographical accounts that

give detailed narratives and a good insight into the postwar atmosphere in Poland are Stanislaw Mikolajczyk, *The Rape of Poland: Pattern of Soviet Aggression* (New York: McGraw-Hill, 1948), and Arthur Bliss Lane, *I Saw Poland Betrayed* (New York: Bobbs-Merrill, 1948). Lane was the US ambassador to Poland from 1944 to 1947.

5. J. K. Zawodny, *Death in the Forest: The Story of Katyn* (New York: Hippocrene, 1988). Mikhail Gorbachev first acknowledged Soviet responsibility in April 1990, but not until October 1992 did the Yeltsin government release the relevant files, showing that the murders were carried out on Stalin's orders. Celestine Bohlen, "Russian Files Show Stalin Ordered Massacre of 20,000 Poles in 1940," *New York Times,* 15 October 1992; and Nicholas Bethell, "Stalin's Final Solution," *Times,* 23 October 1992.

6. Winston S. Churchill, *The Second World War,* vol. 5, *Closing the Ring* (Boston: Houghton Mifflin, 1951), 361–62, 394–97. Stalin's remarks are in "Meeting of the PKWN [Polish Committee of National Liberation] Delegation with Comrade Stalin, 9 October 1944," in Polonsky and Drukier, *Beginnings,* 297–98. For the inter-Allied debate on Poland, see Edward J. Rozek, *Allied Wartime Diplomacy: A Pattern in Poland* (New York: Wiley, 1958); Richard C. Lukas, *The Strange Allies: The United States and Poland, 1941–1945* (Knoxville: University of Tennessee Press, 1978); Coutouvidis and Reynolds, *Poland, 1939–1947,* esp. chapter 4.

7. For Poland during the war, the work of Jan T. Gross is indispensable: *Polish Society Under German Occupation: The Generalgouvernement, 1939–1944* (Princeton: Princeton University Press, 1979) and his *Revolution from Abroad: The Soviet Conquest of Poland's Western Ukraine and Western Belorussia* (Princeton: Princeton University Press, 1988). Also Jozef Garlinski, *Poland in the Second World War* (New York: Hippocrene, 1985), and Richard C. Lukas, *The Forgotten Holocaust: The Poles Under German Occupation, 1939–1944* (New York: Hippocrene, 1990). Komorowski published his own memoir: *The Secret Army* (New York: Macmillan, 1951). One of the first accounts of the underground by a participant to reach the West was the gripping book by Jan Karski, *Story of a Secret State* (Boston: Houghton Mifflin, 1944).

8. Stalin sought to avoid any connection with the prewar Polish Communist Party, which he had ordered disbanded in 1938 because he thought it had become too independent of Soviet control. Hence the name "Polish Workers' Party."

9. Jan M. Ciechanowski, *The Warsaw Rising of 1944* (London: Cambridge University Press, 1974); J. K. Zawodny, *Nothing but Honor: The Story of the Warsaw Uprising, 1944* (Stanford: Hoover Institution Press, 1978).

10. Speech by Gomulka to Communist activists, 10 October 1944, in Polonsky and Drukier, *Beginnings,* 306–24.

11. "Minutes of the PPR [Polish Workers' Party] Central Committee, 9 October 1944," in Polonsky and Drukier, *Beginnings,* 299–302.

12. John Micgiel, "Bandits and Reactionaries: The Suppression of the Opposition in Poland, 1944–1946," in Norman Naimark and Leonid Gibianskii, eds., *The Establishment of Communist Regimes in Eastern Europe, 1944–1949* (Boulder, Colo.: Westview Press, 1997), 93–110. Gomulka's remarks are in his speech to Communist activists, 10 October 1944, in Polonsky and Drukier, *Beginnings,* 306–24.

13. "Conversation Between Gomulka and Stalin, 14 November 1945," found in Gomulka's private papers and translated by Anna Elliot-Zielinska, CWIHP *Bulletin* 11 (winter 1998), 134–39.

14. Kersten, *Establishment,* 128–29; Coutouvidis and Reynolds, *Poland,* 273–74.

15. In a fascinating interview given in the early 1980s, Jakub Berman, one of the leading Polish Communists between 1945 and 1956, gave an impassioned defense of Communist goals for postwar Poland. "The Case for Stalinism," in Gale Stokes, ed., *From Stalinism to Pluralism: A Documentary History of Eastern Europe Since 1945* (Oxford: Oxford University Press, 1996), 44–50.

16. Kersten, *Establishment,* 118.

17. Nicholas Bethell, *Gomulka: His Poland, His Communism* (New York: Holt, Rinehart and Winston, 1969); and Gomulka's speech of 20 May 1945, in Polonsky and Drukier, *Beginnings,* 424–28.

18. Bela Zhelitski, "Postwar Hungary, 1944–1946," in Norman Naimark and Leonid Gibianskii, eds., *The Establishment of Communist Regimes in Eastern Europe, 1944–1949* (Boulder, Colo.: Westview, 1997), 75, 77.

19. *The Cominform: Minutes of the Three Conferences, 1947/1948/1949,* ed. by Giuliano Procacci (Milan: Feltrinelli Editore, 1994), 309. The other Hungarian representative, József Révai, elaborated on the various means the Communists had used to assert power, which he viewed as largely complete by September 1947. See ibid., 201–15.

20. For useful surveys of Hungary in this period, see Seton-Watson, *East European Revolution*, 190–202; Rothschild, *Return to Diversity*, 97–104; Charles Gati, *Hungary and the Soviet Bloc* (Durham, N.C.: Duke University Press, 1986); Stephen D. Kertesz, *Between Russia and the West: Hungary and the Illusions of Peacemaking, 1945–1947* (Notre Dame: Notre Dame University Press, 1986); Bennett Kovrig, *Communism in Hungary: From Kun to Kádár* (Stanford: Hoover Institution Press, 1979); and the account of Ferenc Nagy himself, *The Struggle Behind the Iron Curtain* (New York: Macmillan, 1948).

21. As told to his old friend the British diplomat Sir R. H. Bruce Lockhart, in *Jan Masaryk: A Personal Memoir* (New York: The Philosophical Library, 1951), 39.

22. Karel Kaplan, *The Short March: The Communist Takeover in Czechoslovakia* (New York: St. Martin's Press, 1987), 1–17.

23. Igor Lukes, "The Czech Road to Communism," in Naimark and Gibianskii, *Establishment*, 249.

24. Lukes, "Czech Road," 249–50.

25. *Cominform*, 131, 135, 143; and see Josef Korbel, *The Communist Subversion of Czechoslovakia, 1938–1948* (Princeton: Princeton University Press, 1959), 134–70; and Kaplan, *Short March*, 133–38.

26. *FRUS 1947*, 4: 200–203; 212–13.

27. Stalin's remark is from Karel Krátký, "Czechoslovakia, the Soviet Union, and the Marshall Plan," in Odd Arne Westad, Sven Holtsmark, and Iver Neumann, eds., *The Soviet Union in Eastern Europe, 1945–1948* (London: St. Martin's Press, 1994), 9–25. This account is based on extensive new Czech sources. See also Kaplan, *Short March*, 70–74. The Masaryk quote is in Lockhart, *Masaryk*, 66.

28. Radomir Luza, "Czechoslovakia Between Democracy and Communism, 1945–1948," in Victor S. Mamatey and Radomir Luza, eds., *A History of the Czechoslovak Republic, 1918–1948* (Princeton: Princeton University Press, 1973), 387–415; Korbel, *Communist Subversion*, 198–235; and Kaplan, *Short March*, 162–86.

29. There is a grisly debate on these figures. Robert Conquest has suggested 1 million executed in the Terror and another 2 million deaths in camps in the 1937–38 period. Robert Conquest, *The Great Terror* (New York: Oxford University Press, 1990 ed.), 485–86. Other scholars offer slightly lower figures: Robert Service, *A History of Twentieth-Century Russia* (Cambridge: Harvard University Press, 1997), 210–34; Robert C. Tucker, *Stalin in Power: The Revolution from Above, 1929–1941* (New York: Norton, 1990), 441–78; and Stéphane Courtois et al., *The Black Book of Communism: Crimes, Terror, Repression* (Cambridge: Harvard University Press, 1999), 9–10, 159, 190, 206–7. A recent attempt to synthesize the available evidence is given in J. Arch Getty and Oleg V. Naumov, *The Road to Terror: Stalin and the Self-Destruction of the Bolsheviks, 1932–1939* (New Haven: Yale University Press, 1999), 587–94.

30. Tucker, *Stalin in Power*, 474–78.

31. John Keep, *Last of the Empires: A History of the Soviet Union, 1945–1991* (New York: Oxford University Press, 1995), 9–14; Courtois, *Black Book*, 216–31.

32. Leonid Gibianskii, a Russian scholar, has unearthed considerable new evidence on the origins of the Soviet-Yugoslav crisis, from which this account is drawn. See his "The Soviet-Yugoslav Split and the Cominform," in Naimark and Gibianskii, eds., *Establishment*, 291–308; "The 1948 Soviet-Yugoslav Conflict and the Formation of the 'Socialist Camp' Model," in Westad, Holtsmark, and Neumann, eds., *Soviet Union in Eastern Europe*, 26–46; "The Soviet-Yugoslav Conflict and the Soviet Bloc," in Gori and Pons, eds., *Soviet Union and Europe*, 222–45. The Yugoslav minutes of the 10 February 1948 meeting have recently been published in CWIHP *Bulletin* 10 (March 1998), 128–34, from which Stalin's remarks are drawn. For a nearly contemporaneous and still excellent account, see Ulam, *Titoism and the Cominform*, esp. 96–134.

33. Royal Institute of International Affairs, *The Soviet-Yugoslav Dispute: Text of the Published Correspondence* (London, 1948). These letters were released by the Yugoslavs shortly after their expulsion from the Cominform.

34. For the minutes of these meetings, including Zhdanov's report castigating the Yugoslavs, see *Cominform*, 507–641.

35. Adam Ulam, *Titoism and the Cominform*, sees Gomulka's 3 June speech as a conscious attempt to "increase his personal control over the party by an appeal to nationalist sentiment" (164–65), whereas Nicholas Bethell sees no evidence of a direct challenge and puts Gomulka's speech in the context of his long-standing interest in the theoretical questions of party history. Bethell, *Gomulka*, 144–62.

36. Bethell, *Gomulka*, 157.

37. George H. Hodos, *Show Trials: Stalinist Purges in Eastern Europe, 1948–1954* (New York: Praeger, 1987), 13–23; Ulam, *Titoism and the Cominform*, 200–218.

38. See George Hodos's account of his imprisonment, in *Show Trials*, 40–43, 51–58, 67–72, 89–91; and from the Czech experience, see Eugene Loebl, *Sentenced and Tried: The Stalinist Purges in Czechoslovakia* (London: Elek Books, 1969); and Artur London, *On Trial* (London: Macdonald, 1970). For a memorable fictional account of the Stalinist trials from the 1930s, see Arthur Koestler, *Darkness at Noon* (New York: Macmillan, 1941).

39. In Stokes, ed., *From Stalinism to Pluralism*, 69–70.

40. In 1968, in the wake of the Prague Spring, the Czech government allowed a commission to examine documents relating the Czech show trials of the early fifties. The commission's report revealed in an unprecedented way the mechanics behind the show trials, and remains an invaluable source: Jiri Peilkán, ed., *The Czechoslovak Political Trials, 1950–1954* (Stanford: Stanford University Press, 1971), esp. 69–147. One member of that commission, Karel Kaplan, has published two important and well-researched volumes on the Prague trials: *Dans les archives du Comité Central: 30 ans de secrets du bloc soviétique* (Paris: Albin Michel) and *Report on the Murder of the General Secretary* (Columbus: Ohio State University Press, 1990).

41. Peter Meyer, *The Jews in the Soviet Satellites* (Syracuse, N.Y.: Syracuse University Press, 1953), 98–112; 153–91; 247–53. For the persistence of these feelings in Eastern Europe, see Jonathan Kaufman, *A Hole in the Heart of the World: The Jewish Experience in Eastern Europe After World War II* (New York: Penguin, 1997).

42. Meyer, *The Jews in the Soviet Satellites*, 183. For slightly different rendering of the prosecutor's words, see Loebl, *Sentenced and Tried*, 234.

43. London, *On Trial*, 50.

44. Igor Lukes, "The Rudolf Slansky Affair: New Evidence," *Slavic Review* 58, no. 1 (1999), 185.

45. Loebl, *Sentenced and Tried*, 18–19.

46. George Orwell, *1984* (New York: Signet, 1950), 210.

PART TWO: BOOM

1. A term coined by Charles Maier, "The Politics of Productivity: Foundations of American International Economic Policy After World War II," in *In Search of Stability: Explorations in Historical Political Economy* (New York: Cambridge University Press, 1987), 121–52.

CHAPTER FIVE: THE MIRACULOUS FIFTIES

1. B. R. Mitchell, *International Historical Statistics: Europe, 1750–1993* (London: Macmillan, 1998), 260–317; 329; 382; 386; 389.

2. Statistical Office of the European Communities, *Basic Statistics for Fifteen European Countries* (1961), 82–99.

3. Mitchell, *International Historical Statistics*, 735–43; 775–80. For a provocative look at the impact of the automobile on French culture, see Kristin Ross, *Fast Cars, Clean Bodies: Decolonization and the Reordering of French Culture* (Cambridge: MIT Press, 1995).

4. "For European Recovery: The Fiftieth Anniversary of the Marshall Plan" can be viewed at http://lcweb.loc.gov/exhibits/marshall.

5. Charles Kindleberger, *Marshall Plan Days* (Boston: Allen and Unwin, 1987), 247.

6. There is now a large literature on the subject. The best general surveys, which come to divergent conclusions, are Michael Hogan, *The Marshall Plan: America, Britain, and the Reconstruction of Western Europe* (Cambridge: Cambridge University Press, 1987); and Alan Milward, *The Reconstruction of Western Europe, 1945–1951* (Berkeley: University of California Press, 1984). See Imanuel Wexler, *The Marshall Plan Revisited* (Westport, Conn.: Greenwood Press, 1983), for a positive appraisal based on detailed statistics. For the larger context, see Charles Maier's thoughtful essays in *In Search of Stability: Explorations in Historical Political Economy* (Cambridge: Cambridge University Press, 1987). For specific countries, see Gérard Bossuat, *La France, l'aide américaine, et la construction*

européenne, 1944–1954 (Paris: Comité pour l'Histoire Économique et Financière de la France, 1992); Irwin Wall, *The United States and the Making of Postwar France, 1945–1954* (Cambridge: Cambridge University Press, 1991); Frances Lynch, *France and the International Economy: From Vichy to the Treaty of Rome* (London: Routledge, 1997); Werner Abelshauser, *Wirtschaftsgeschichte der Bundesrepublik Deutschland, 1945–1980* (Frankfurt: Suhrkamp, 1983); and his article "Wiederaufbau vor dem Marshallplan, Westeuropa Wachstumschancen und die Wirtschaftsordungspolitik in der zweiten Hälfte der vierziger Jahre," *Vierteljahreshefte für Zeitgeschichte* 29 (1981), 545–78; Gerd Hardach, *Der Marshall-Plan: Auslandshilfe und Wiederaufbau in Westdeutschland, 1948–1952* (Munich: Deutscher Taschenbuch, 1994); Charles Maier and Günter Bischoff, eds., *The Marshall Plan and Germany* (Oxford: Berg, 1991); and the important collection of articles on various countries in *Le Plan Marshall et le relèvement économique de l'Europe* (Paris: Comité pour l'Histoire Économique et Financière de la France, 1993).

7. Milward, *Reconstruction*, 96. For industrial figures, see United States, *Tenth Report to Congress of the Economic Cooperation Administration* (1951), 98–101.

8. See, in addition to *Reconstruction*, Milward's essay "Was the Marshall Plan Necessary?" *Diplomatic History* 13, no. 2 (spring 1989), 231–53.

9. John Killick, *The United States and European Reconstruction, 1945–1960* (Edinburgh: Keele University Press, 1997), table 5.2, 45. Killick's book contains many useful tables and offers a concise summary of the Marshall Plan experience.

10. William I. Hitchcock, *France Restored: Cold War Diplomacy and the Quest for Leadership in Europe, 1944–1954* (Chapel Hill: University of North Carolina Press, 1998), 64–66, 82–84.

11. For a useful breakdown of US aid under the Marshall Plan, see United States Department of Commerce, *Statistical Abstract of the United States, 1952,* 836–37. For an interim assessment of French recovery efforts, see European Recovery Program, *France: Country Study* (Washington, D.C., 1949).

12. Richard Clarke, *Anglo-American Economic Collaboration in War and Peace, 1942–1949* (Oxford: Clarendon Press, 1982), 176–77.

13. For a critical assessment of Italy's progress, see Economic Cooperation Administration, *Italy: Country Study* (Washington, D.C., 1949), esp. 2–3, 12–13, 23. Chiarella Esposito has made a detailed study of these issues: *America's Feeble Weapon: Funding the Marshall Plan in France and Italy, 1948–1950* (Westport, Conn.: Greenwood Press, 1994). Ennio di Nolfo argues that Italy's participation in the plan was motivated far more by domestic political considerations than by economic ones: "L'Italie et le Plan Marshall: Aux origines de la participation italienne," in *Le Plan Marshall*, 59–68. For an excellent collection of essays that treats Italy in a European context, see Elena Aga Rossi, ed., *Il Piano Marshall e l'Europa* (Rome: Istituto della Enciclopedia Italiana, 1983); and a useful short survey may be found in Vera Zamagni, "Betting on the Future: The Reconstruction of Italian Industry, 1946–1952," in Josef Becker and Franz Knipping, eds., *Power in Europe? Great Britain, France, Italy and Germany in a Postwar World, 1945–1950* (Berlin: de Gruyter, 1986), 283–301.

14. Paul Ginsborg, *A History of Contemporary Italy* (London: Penguin, 1990), 214.

15. Ginsborg, *History of Contemporary Italy*, 150–52, 163–64, 213–14, 283–85.

16. For an introduction to Erhard's thinking, see Alan Peacock and Hans Willgerodt, eds., *Germany's Social Market Economy: Origins and Evolution* (London: Macmillan 1989), 1–14; Jeremy Leaman, *The Political Economy of West Germany, 1945–1985* (London: Macmillan, 1988).

17. Abelshauser, *Wirtschaftsgeschichte*, 46–54; Alan Kramer, *The West German Economy, 1945–1955* (New York: Berg, 1991), 134–48; Dennis L. Bark and David R. Gress, *From Shadow to Substance, 1945–1963: A History of West Germany*, vol. 1 (Oxford: Blackwell, 1993), 198–203.

18. Erhard's book was published in English as *Prosperity Through Competition*, trans. by Edith Temple Roberts and John B. Wood (New York: Praeger, 1958); see xii, 186, 61, 190.

19. Ludwig Erhard, speech at a CDU rally on 14 May 1957, in Erhard, *The Economics of Success* (New York: Van Nostrand, 1963), 191–92; and *Prosperity Through Competition,* 116.

20. Erhard, *Prosperity Through Competition,* 14–15.

21. Karl Hardach, *The Political Economy of Germany in the Twentieth Century* (Berkeley: University of California Press, 1980), 165.

22. Charles Maier, "Conditions for Stability," 173. For further work on the Marshall Plan in Germany, a subject that has raised some controversy, see the essays by Werner Abelshauser, Knut Borchardt and Christoph Buchheim, and Alan Milward in Maier and Bischoff, eds., *The Marshall Plan and Germany;* Kramer, *West German Economy,* 148–56; and Herbert C. Mayer, *German Recovery and*

the Marshall Plan (Bonn: Atlantic Forum, 1969), esp. 80–95, on counterpart funds. Werner Abelshauser has tried to puncture the Erhard "myth": see "The Economic Policy of Ludwig Erhard," European University Institute, Florence, Working Paper 80, January 1984.

23. Abelshauser, *Wirtschaftsgeschichte,* 95; Karl Hardach, *Political Economy,* 171; Gustav Stolper et al., *The German Economy, 1870 to the Present* (New York: Harcourt, Brace, 1967), 292–95.

24. Erhard, *Prosperity,* xii. For foreign trade figures, Kramer, *West German Economy,* 182–89.

25. Konrad Adenauer, *Memoirs, 1945–1953,* trans. by Beate Ruhm von Oppen (Chicago: Regnery, 1966), 195. I have learned much about Adenauer's policies in this period from Thomas Schwartz's excellent book *America's Germany: John J. McCloy and the Federal Republic of Germany* (Cambridge: Harvard University Press, 1991). In addition, see the massive biography by Hans-Peter Schwartz, *Adenauer,* vol. 1, *1876–1952,* trans. by Louise Willmot (London: Berghahn Books, 1995), esp. 475–503.

26. 30 October 1949, *Foreign Relations of the United States [FRUS] 1949,* 3: 622–25. John L. Harper has written a thoughtful assessment of Acheson's policy: *American Visions of Europe: Roosevelt, Kennan, Acheson* (New York: Cambridge University Press, 1994), 281–91; and see James Chace, *Acheson: The Secretary of State Who Created the American World* (Cambridge: Harvard University Press, 1998), chapters 19 and 22.

27. For the British view, see 26 April 1950, "Re-Establishment of German Armed Forces," *Documents on British Policy Overseas,* series 2, vol. 2, ed. by Roger Bullen and M. E. Pelly (London, 1986), 138–41. For the American discussion, see 7 March 1950 and 27 March 1950, *FRUS 1950,* 3: 34, 638–42. For further material on this debate, Pierre Guillen, "La France et la question de la défense de l'Europe occidentale," *Revue d'histoire de la deuxième guerre mondiale* 144 (1986), 79–98; David Clay Large, *Germans to the Front: West German Rearmament in the Adenauer Era* (Chapel Hill: University of North Carolina Press, 1996); and Saki Dockrill, *Britain's Policy for West German Rearmament, 1950–55* (Cambridge: Cambridge University Press, 1991), 8–14.

28. There is an extensive literature on Monnet, Schuman, and the origins of European integration. See Monnet's own *Mémoires* (Paris: Fayard, 1976); Hitchcock, *France Restored;* Douglas Brinkley and Clifford Hackett, eds., *Jean Monnet: The Path to European Unity* (London: Macmillan, 1991); John Gillingham, *Coal, Steel, and the Rebirth of Europe, 1945–1955* (Cambridge: Cambridge University Press, 1991).

29. Derek Urwin, *The Community of Europe* (London: Longman, 1991), 46.

30. Ibid., 76.

31. Simone de Beauvoir, *Force of Circumstance* (London: Penguin, 1968), 150; 264–67.

32. *FRUS 1952–54,* 6: 1372–75, 1405–7, 1614–17, 1763–73; Sartre quoted in Richard Kuisel, *Seducing the French: The Dilemma of Americanization* (Berkeley: University of California Press, 1993), 50.

33. For poll numbers, *A Survey of Public Opinion in Western Europe* (published in 1952 by the high commission in Germany), 24, 109, 34; and Frank Costigliola, *France and the United States: The Cold Alliance Since World War II* (New York: Twayne, 1992), 83–84; Harold Nicolson, *The Later Years, 1945–1962,* vol. 3 of *Diaries and Letters,* ed. by Nigel Nicolson (New York: Atheneum, 1968), 243.

34. Pierre Milza, "La Guerre froide à Paris: Ridgway la peste!" *L'Histoire* 25 (July–Aug. 1980), 38–47.

35. Robert S. Norris, William M. Arkin, and William Burr, "Where They Were," *Bulletin of Atomic Scientists* 55, no. 6 (November/December 1999), 26–35.

36. Lawrence S. Wittner, *Resisting the Bomb: A History of the World Nuclear Disarmament Movement, 1954–1970* (Stanford: Stanford University Press, 1997), 44–51, 85–96; J. B. Priestley, "Britain and the Nuclear Bombs," *New Statesman,* 2 November 1957, 554–56.

37. Wittner, *Resisting the Bomb,* 61–67; Bark and Gress, *Shadow to Substance,* 406–10. For the German effort to gain atomic weapons, see Marc Trachtenberg, *A Constructed Peace: The Making of the European Settlement, 1945–1963* (Princeton: Princeton University Press, 1999), chapters 5 and 7.

38. Edward A. McCreary, *The Americanization of Europe* (Garden City: Doubleday, 1964), 4; and Jean-Jacques Servan-Schreiber, *The American Challenge,* trans. by Ronald Steel (New York: Atheneum, 1969), 12–13.

39. Richard Pells, *Not Like Us: How Europeans Have Loved, Hated, and Transformed American Culture Since World War II* (New York: Basic, 1997), 212–20. For quotations, and an excellent treatment of the Coca-Cola debate in France, see Kuisel, *Seducing the French,* 52–69.

40. Peter Coleman, *The Liberal Conspiracy: The Congress for Cultural Freedom and the Struggle for the Mind of Postwar Europe* (Free Press: New York, 1989), 1.

41. *Encounter,* October 1953, vol. 1, no. 1; and *Encounter,* January 1954, vol. 2, no. 1.

CHAPTER SIX: WINDS OF CHANGE

1. The best short survey of the British colonial experience is Bernard Porter, *The Lion's Share: A Short History of British Imperialism, 1850–1983* (London: Longman, 1984).

2. Cited in Porter, *Lion's Share,* 312–13.

3. There is some debate about the economic value of colonies and the degree to which economic factors contributed to decolonization. For a useful summary, see John Darwin, *The End of the British Empire: The Historical Debate* (Oxford: Blackwell, 1991), 40–55; D. K. Fieldhouse, *Black Africa, 1945–1960: Economic Decolonization and Arrested Development* (London: Allen and Unwin, 1986); Michael Barrat Brown, *After Imperialism* (New York: Humanities Press, 1970); and for France, Jacques Marseille, *Empire colonial et capitalisme français: Histoire d'un divorce* (Paris: 1984).

4. Winston Churchill, 6 March 1947, *Parliamentary Debates of the House of Commons,* vol. 434, 678.

5. Among a large literature on decolonization, a handful of works stand out: Rudolf von Albertini, *Decolonization: The Administration and Future of the Colonies, 1919–1960* (New York: Holmes and Meier, 1982); R. F. Holland, *European Decolonization, 1918–1980* (New York: St. Martin's, 1985); and Franz Ansprenger, *The Dissolution of the Colonial Empires* (New York: Routledge, 1989).

6. Attlee in the House of Commons, 4 July 1947, cited in von Albertini, *Decolonization,* 195.

7. For an excellent survey that covers both the French and British cases, see John D. Hargreaves, *Decolonization in Africa* (London: Longman, 1988).

8. Cited in Henri Grimal, *Decolonization,* trans. by Stephan De Vos (Boulder, Colo.: Westview Press, 1978), 298.

9. John D. Hargreaves, "Toward the Transfer of Power in British West Africa," in Prosser Gifford and Wm. Roger Louis, eds., *The Transfer of Power in Africa: Decolonization, 1940–1960* (New Haven: Yale University Press, 1982), 117–40.

10. A thoughtful survey is offered in Alain Ruscio, *La Décolonisation tragique, 1945–1962* (Paris: Messidor, 1987), which covers Africa and Asia; and Raymond F. Betts, *France and Decolonization, 1900–1960* (New York: St. Martin's, 1991).

11. Here the literature is vast, but useful works devoted to the French (rather than the later, American) experience in Vietnam include Jacques Dalloz, *The War in Indochina, 1945–1955* (Dublin: Gill and Macmillan, 1990); Ellen J. Hammer, *The Struggle for Indochina, 1940–1955* (Stanford: Stanford University Press, 1954); Donald Lancaster, *The Emancipation of French Indochina* (London: Oxford University Press, 1961); and Joseph Buttinger, *Vietnam: A Political History* (New York: Praeger, 1968), which is especially good on the prewar period.

12. The British cabinet took the threat to the canal and the British oil supply very seriously. See, for example, a cabinet memo of 13 October 1955 on "Middle East Oil," in which the cabinet agreed that Britain's dependence on oil required a long-term strategic commitment to the region and a larger amount of aid for friendly regimes there. A. N. Porter and A. J. Stockwell, eds., *British Imperial Policy and Decolonization, 1938–1964,* vol. 2 (London: Macmillan, 1989), 385–92.

13. Alistair Horne, *Harold Macmillan,* vol. 1, *1894–1956* (New York: Viking, 1988), 395.

14. Keith Kyle, "Britain and the Suez Crisis, 1955–1956," in *Suez 1956: The Crisis and Its Consequences,* ed. by Wm. Roger Louis and Roger Owen (Oxford: Clarendon Press, 1989), 117, 123.

15. Horne, *Macmillan,* 396.

16. Robert R. Bowie, "Eisenhower, Dulles, and the Suez Crisis," in Louis and Owen, eds., *Suez 1956,* 201.

17. For a fully documented and superbly written history of the Suez affair, see Keith Kyle, *Suez* (New York: St. Martin's, 1991).

18. For an analysis of the financial aspects of the crisis, see Diane B. Kunz, *The Economic Diplomacy of the Suez Crisis* (Chapel Hill: University of North Carolina Press, 1991).

19. *Documents Diplomatiques Françaises, 1956,* vol. 3, 6 November 1956, doc. 138: 231–38. The French foreign minister, Christian Pineau, gives a lively rendering of the meeting: Christian

Pineau and Christiane Rimbaud, *Le Grand Pari: L'Aventure du Traité de Rome* (Paris: Fayard, 1991), 221–23.

20. Kyle, *Suez*, 514.

21. Alan Sked and Chris Cook, *Postwar Britain: A Political History* (London: Penguin, 1990), 176.

22. Maurice Vaisse, "Post-Suez France," in Louis and Owen, eds., *Suez 1956*, 335–40.

23. *Le Monde*, 14 November 1954. Leading studies of colonial Algeria are Charles-Robert Ageron, *Histoire de l'Algérie contemporaine, 1830–1964* (Paris: PUF, 1964); and Benjamin Stora, *Histoire de l'Algérie coloniale* (Paris, 1991).

24. John Ruedy, *Modern Algeria: The Origins and Development of a Nation* (Bloomington: Indiana University Press, 1992), chapter 5; and John Talbott, *The War Without a Name: France in Algeria, 1954–1962* (London: Faber and Faber, 1980), 22.

25. Ruedy, *Modern Algeria*, 162–67.

26. For this and many other details of the war, see Alistair Horne, *A Savage War of Peace: Algeria, 1954–1962* (New York: Penguin, 1987), 185–86. For a superbly researched account of the war that places the conflict in its international perspective, see Matthew Connelly, *A Diplomatic Revolution: Algeria's Fight for Independence and the Origins of the Post–Cold War Era* (New York: Oxford University Press, 2002).

27. Henri Alleg, *The Question* (New York: George Braziller, 1958). Alleg's account squared with other investigations: Paul-Henri Simon, *Contre la torture* (Paris: 1957), and Pierre Vidal-Naquet, *L'Affaire Audin* (Paris, 1958). These have recently been confirmed by a former French officer in Algeria: Paul Aussaresses, *Services spéciaux: Algérie, 1955–1957* (Paris: Perrin, 2001).

28. Jacques Bollardière, in *L'Express*, 29 March 1957. Servan-Schreiber's book is *Lieutenant in Algeria* (New York: Knopf, 1957).

29. Talbott, *War Without a Name*, 124.

30. For an authoritative account of his return to power, see Jean Lacouture, *De Gaulle: The Ruler, 1945–1970* (New York: Norton, 1991), 164–229.

31. For a good assessment of De Gaulle's evolving views on Algeria, see Michel Winock, "De Gaulle and the Algerian Crisis, 1958–1962," in Hugh Gough and John Horne, eds., *De Gaulle and Twentieth Century France* (Routledge: London, 1994), 71–82.

32. Charles Williams, *The Last Great Frenchman: A Life of General de Gaulle* (New York: Wiley, 1993), 402.

33. In Andrew Shennan, *De Gaulle* (London: Longman, 1993), 100.

CHAPTER SEVEN: HOPE BETRAYED

1. Nikita Khrushchev, *Khrushchev Remembers*, ed. and trans. by Strobe Talbott (Boston: Little, Brown, 1970), 323. On Beria's motives, see Amy Knight, *Beria: Stalin's First Lieutenant* (Princeton: Princeton University Press, 1993), 176–80. For further accounts, see Svetlana Alliluyeva, *Twenty Letters to a Friend*, trans. by Priscilla Johnson McMillan (New York: Harper and Row, 1967), 6–23; Edvard Radzinsky, *Stalin* (New York: Doubleday, 1996), 566–78; Dmitri Volkogonov, *Autopsy for an Empire*, trans. by Harold Shukman (New York: New Press, 1998), 171–77.

2. Knight, *Beria*, 3–10; this excellent book sheds much light on Beria's personality and background.

3. Knight, *Beria*, 180–91.

4. For figures, see Federal Ministry for All-German Questions, *The Flights from the Soviet Zone and the Sealing-Off Measures of the Communist Regime of 13 August 1961 in Berlin* (Bonn, 1961), 15 and Annex.

5. Cold War International History Project (CWIHP), *Bulletin* 10 (March 1998), 79–81; and Christian Ostermann, " 'This Is Not a Politburo but a Madhouse': The Post-Stalin Succession Struggle, Soviet *Deutschlandpolitik* and the SED," ibid., 61–72.

6. Sokolovski, Semenov, and Yudin, Report to the Soviet Leadership, 24 June 1953, CWIHP *Bulletin* 5 (spring 1995), 18.

7. Grechko and Tarasov to Bulganin, 17 June 1953 and 18 June 1953, in CWIHP *Bulletin* 10: 88–91. For further material on the uprising, see Armin Mitter and Stefan Wolle, *Untergang auf Raten* (Munich: Bertelsmann, 1993), chapter 1; and Torsten Diedrich, *Der 17 Juni 1953 in der DDR: Bewaffnete Gewalt gegen das Volk* (Berlin: Dietz Verlag, 1991).

8. Christian Ostermann, "New Documents on the East German Uprising of 1953," CWIHP *Bulletin* 10 (March 1998). For Soviet interpretation, see the illuminating document prepared by the Soviet commanders in Berlin, "Report to the Soviet Leadership"; and Allen Dulles, National Security Council Meeting, 18 June 1953, *FRUS 1952–1954*, 7:1587.

9. *Khrushchev Remembers*, 336–37; Knight, *Beria*, 194–200. There has always been uncertainty about the specifics behind Beria's demise. For some theories, see Tadeusz Wittlin, *Commissar: The Life and Death of Lavrenty Beria* (New York: Macmillan, 1972).

10. These themes have been ably examined by Mary Fulbrook, *Anatomy of a Dictatorship: Inside the GDR 1949–1989* (New York: Oxford, 1995), 177–87.

11. For an excellent portrait, see Vladislav Zubok and Constantine Pleshakov, *Inside the Kremlin's Cold War: From Stalin to Khrushchev* (Cambridge: Harvard University Press, 1996), 174–82; and Volkogonov, *Autopsy,* 181–261. Nixon quoted in Harry Hanak, "Foreign Policy," in Martin McCauley, ed., *Khrushchev and Khrushchevism* (Bloomington: Indiana University Press, 1987), 180.

12. John Keep, *Last of the Empires: A History of the Soviet Union, 1945–1991* (Oxford, 1995), 76, 84, 86, 99, 103, 118.

13. Text of speech in Bertram D. Wolfe, *Khrushchev and Stalin's Ghost* (Praeger: New York, 1957).

14. For an important new interpretation of these events, see the essay (with accompanying documents) by L. W. Gluchowski, "Poland 1956: Khrushchev, Gomulka, and the Polish October," CWIHP *Bulletin* 5.

15. Nikita Khrushchev, *Khrushchev Remembers: The Last Testament,* trans. and ed. by Strobe Talbott (Boston: Little, Brown, 1974), 199–200.

16. Gomulka reported this to the meeting of the Politburo of the Polish Workers' Party, 19 October 1956, CWIHP *Bulletin* 5: 39–40.

17. Meeting of the Central Committee of the Communist Party of the Soviet Union, 24 October 1956, CWIHP *Bulletin* 5: 54.

18. Nikita Khrushchev, *Khrushchev Remembers: The Glasnost Tapes,* trans. and ed. by Jerrold L. Schechter and Vyacheslav Luchkov (Boston: Little, Brown, 1990), 115.

19. There is now a considerable literature on the 1956 revolution in Hungary. Older works that remain excellent include Ferenc A. Váli, *Rift and Revolt in Hungary: Nationalism Versus Communism* (Cambridge: Harvard University Press, 1961), and Paul E. Zinner, *Revolution in Hungary* (New York: Columbia University Press, 1962). For a collection of contemporary sources, mostly from the world press, see Melvin J. Lasky, ed., *The Hungarian Revolution* (New York: Praeger, 1957). To these works must be added the impressive scholarship based on new archival sources. See in particular Csaba Bekes, "The 1956 Hungarian Revolution and World Politics," CWIHP Working Paper #16; and Mark Kramer, "The Soviet Union and the 1956 Crises in Hungary and Poland: Reassessments and New Findings," *Journal of Contemporary History* 33, no. 2 (1998), 163–214. For an important collection of material on Soviet actions, there is Jeno Gyorkei and Miklos Horvath, eds., *1956: Soviet Military Intervention in Hungary* (Budapest: CEU Press, 1999). Numerous new documents have been published in the CWIHP *Bulletin,* especially issues 5 (1995) and 8–9 (1996).

20. Kramer, "1956 Crises," 181.

21. From notes made by Vladimir Malin of the Presidium meeting, 28 October 1956, in CWIHP *Bulletin* 8–9: 391.

22. Ivan Serov to Presidium, 29 October 1956, CWIHP *Bulletin* 5: 31.

23. Mikoyan-Suslov Report to Presidium, 30 October 1956, CWIHP *Bulletin* 5: 32.

24. The drafting of this memo may be followed in the Malin notes of the 30 October Presidium meeting, CWIHP *Bulletin* 8–9: 392–93.

25. Khrushchev's thinking can be followed in the Malin notes of the 31 October Presidium meeting, CWIHP *Bulletin* 8–9: 393–94.

26. Kàdàr met with the Presidium on 2 and 3 November; see CWIHP *Bulletin* 8–9: 395–98 for the Malin notes on these talks.

27. Gyorkei and Horvath, *Soviet Military Intervention,* 106; and for further details on the Soviet military, see 109–14.

28. Zhukov to Presidium, noon, 4 November 1956, CWIHP *Bulletin* 5: 33–34.

29. Government radio broadcast, 4 November, in Lasky, *Hungarian Revolution,* 236–37.

30. Free Radio Petofi broadcast, 4 November 1956, in Lasky, *Hungarian Revolution,* 239.

31. UN Verbatim Record, Security Council, 4 November 1956, in Lasky, *Hungarian Revolution*, 232.

32. Cited in Gyorkei and Horvath, *Soviet Military Intervention*, 114.

33. *Khrushchev Remembers* (1970), 428.

34. Csaba Bekes, "New Findings on the 1956 Hungarian Revolution," CWIHP, cwihp.si.edu. Slightly different figures are given in Gyorkei and Horvath, *Soviet Military Intervention*, 187, 192; and Kramer, "1956 Crises," 210.

35. *Flights from the Soviet Zone*, 19.

36. Marc Trachtenberg, *History and Strategy* (Princeton: Princeton University Press, 1991), 187–88; Vladislav Zubok, "Khrushchev and the Berlin Crisis, 1958–1962," CWIHP, Working Paper no. 6, 3–4. For a number of important documents from the East German and Soviet archives, as well as a long interpretive essay, see Hope M. Harrison, "Ulbricht and the Concrete Rose: New Archival Evidence on the Dynamics of Soviet-East German Relations and the Berlin Crisis, 1958–1961," CWIHP, Working Paper no. 5. Other accounts of the crisis include Norman Gelb, *The Berlin Wall: Kennedy, Khrushchev and a Showdown in the Heart of Europe* (New York, Dorset Press, 1986); Michael R. Beschloss, *The Crisis Years: Kennedy and Khrushchev, 1960–1963* (New York: HarperCollins, 1991); A. James McAdams, *Germany Divided: From the Wall to Reunification* (Princeton: Princeton University Press, 1993), esp. chapter 2. I have also drawn on the superb summary of the crisis by John Lewis Gaddis, *We Now Know: Rethinking Cold War History* (New York: Oxford, 1997), 138–49.

37. *Khrushchev Remembers* (1970), 453.

38. Dean Rusk, *As I Saw It* (New York: Norton, 1990), 227.

39. For the ultimatum, see United States Department of State, *Documents on Germany, 1944–1985* (Washington, D.C., 1986), 552–59.

40. *Khrushchev Remembers* (1970), 453.

41. Quoted in Jack Schick, *The Berlin Crisis, 1958–1962* (Philadelphia: University of Pennsylvania Press, 1971), 121–22.

42. *Flights from the Soviet Zone*, 15–17.

43. Harrison, "Ulbricht and the Concrete Rose," Appendix A, record of meeting between Khrushchev and Ulbricht, 30 November 1960; and Appendix B, Ulbricht to Khrushchev, 18 January 1961.

44. Text available at www.cnn.com/coldwar.

45. Trachtenberg, "Berlin Crisis," 219.

46. Harrison, "Ulbricht and the Concrete Rose," 47–48.

47. *Khrushchev Remembers* (1970), 456.

48. Beschloss, *The Crisis Years*, 278.

49. Brian MacArthur, ed., *The Penguin Book of Twentieth-Century Speeches* (London: Penguin, 1992), 325–27.

CHAPTER EIGHT: THE GAULLIST TEMPTATION

1. De Gaulle's early life is treated admirably by Jean Lacouture, *De Gaulle: The Rebel, 1890–1944* (New York: Norton, 1990). An excellent short introduction is Andrew Shennan, *De Gaulle* (London: Longman, 1993).

2. The only issue on which de Gaulle did not immediately get his way concerned the election of the president. The 1958 constitution provided for the election of the president by 80,000 *notables*, or elected officials from across the country, right down to local mayors and municipal councilors. In 1962, in order to enhance his mandate, de Gaulle proposed a constitutional amendment that would allow for direct election of the president. A referendum was held on 28 October 1962 and the change was approved by 62 percent of the voters.

3. Charles de Gaulle, *Memoirs of Hope: Renewal and Endeavor* (New York: Simon & Schuster, 1971), 137.

4. Fernand Braudel and Ernest Labrousse, eds., *Histoire économique et sociale de la France*, vol. 4, part 3 (Paris: PUF, 1982), 1012.

5. De Gaulle, *Memoirs of Hope*, 305.

6. Hans Peter Schwartz, *Konrad Adenauer*, vol. 2, *The Statesman, 1952–1967* (Oxford: Berghahn, 1997), 331.

7. De Gaulle, *Memoirs of Hope*, 178.

8. Maurice Vaïsse, *La Grandeur: Politique étrangère du général de Gaulle, 1958–1969* (Paris: Fayard, 1998), 228–335; Lacouture, *de Gaulle*, 215–16; Schwartz, *Adenauer*, 354–69.

9. Memorandum of 30 July 1960, in Charles de Gaulle, *Lettres, notes, et carnets*, vol. 8 (Paris: Plon, 1985), 382.

10. Press conference of 5 September 1960, cited in F. Roy Willis, *France, Germany, and the New Europe, 1945–1967* (Stanford: Stanford University Press, 1968), 296.

11. Schwartz, *Adenauer*, 476; and on Rambouillet, Vaïsse, *La Grandeur*, 238–41.

12. Lacouture, *de Gaulle*, 340.

13. On the Skybolt and Polaris controversies, see Alistair Horne, *Harold Macmillan*, vol. 2, *1957–1986* (Penguin, 1989), 428–43; and Marc Trachtenberg, *A Constructed Peace: The Making of the European Settlement, 1945–1963* (Princeton: Princeton University Press, 1999), 359–67.

14. Peter Flora, ed., *State, Economy, and Society in Western Europe, 1815–1975*, vol. 2 (Frankfurt: Campus Verlag, 1987).

15. Horne, *Macmillan*, vol. 2, 239.

16. N. F. R. Crafts and N. W. C. Woodward, *The British Economy Since 1945* (Oxford: Clarendon Press, 1991), 261.

17. Diary, 9 July 1960, in Harold Macmillan, *Pointing the Way, 1959–1961* (New York: Harper and Row, 1972), 316.

18. Horne, *Macmillan*, vol. 2, 256.

19. Macmillan, *Pointing the Way*, 410.

20. Diary, 29 January 1961, in Macmillan, *Pointing the Way*, 327.

21. Horne, *Macmillan*, vol. 2, 260.

22. Diary, 29 November 1961, in Macmillan, *Pointing the Way*, 428.

23. Harold Macmillan, *At the End of the Day, 1961–1963* (London: Macmillan, 1973), 353–54.

24. On de Gaulle's concern about the agricultural dimension, see Andrew Moravcsik, "De Gaulle Between Grain and Grandeur: The Political Economy of French EC policy, 1958–1970," parts 1 and 2, *Journal of Cold War Studies* 2, no. 2 (2000), 3–43, and no. 3 (2000), 4–68.

25. Press conference, 14 January 1963, in Charles G. Cogan, *Charles de Gaulle: A Brief Biography with Documents* (New York: St. Martin's/Bedford Books, 1996), 199–202; and Horne, *Macmillan*, vol. 2, 446.

26. Macmillan, *At the End of the Day*, 367.

27. A good survey of de Gaulle's views toward Britain and America is John Newhouse, *De Gaulle and the Anglo-Saxons* (New York: Viking, 1970); and a brief, lucid account may be found in Serge Berstein, *The Republic of de Gaulle, 1958–1969* (Cambridge: Cambridge University Press, 1993), esp. 153–83. For exhaustive treatment, see Vaïsse, *La Grandeur*. De Gaulle's perception of the United States is superbly handled by Richard Kuisel, *Seducing the French: The Dilemma of Americanization* (Berkeley: University of California Press, 1993), chapters 6 and 7.

28. De Gaulle quoted in Frank Costigliola, *France and the United States: The Cold Alliance Since World War II* (New York: Twayne, 1992), 142; and for a recent look at the US-French wrangle on Vietnam in 1964, see Fredrik Logevall, *Choosing War: The Lost Chance for Peace and the Escalation of War in Vietnam* (Berkeley: University of California Press, 1999), esp. 173–89.

29. Cited in Alfred Grosser, *The Western Alliance: European-American Relations Since 1945* (Vintage: New York, 1982), 214.

30. Costigliola, *France and the United States*, 144–45; Vaïsse, *La Grandeur*, 381–90.

31. Kuisel, *Seducing the French*, 171–76; and Grosser, *The Western Alliance*, 217–37.

32. The text may be found in Cogan, *De Gaulle*, 211–13.

CHAPTER NINE: EUROPE AND ITS DISCONTENTS

1. The work of Hervé Hamon and Patrick Rotman captures the intellectual origins of the student movement in France: *Génération: Les Années de rêve* (Paris: Seuil, 1987). For a massive collection of largely impenetrable documents, see Alain Schnapp and Pierre Vidal-Naquet, eds., *Journal de la Commune étudiante* (Paris: Seuil, 1969). A lively survey is Patrick Seale and Maureen McConville, *Red Flag/Black Flag: French Revolution 1968* (New York: Putnam, 1968).

2. Daniel Cohn-Bendit, *Obsolete Communism: The Left-Wing Alternative* (New York: McGraw-Hill, 1968), 27.

3. Julien Besançon, ed., *Les Murs ont la parole: Mai '68* (Paris: Tahou, 1968).

4. Jean Lacouture, *De Gaulle: The Ruler, 1945–1970* (New York: Norton, 1991), 531.

5. Lacouture gives a detailed account in *De Gaulle*, 543–52.

6. For an essay that captures the discontent felt by many centrist French people toward the students and goes far to explain this sudden burst of support for the Fifth Republic, see Raymond Aron, *The Elusive Revolution: Anatomy of a Student Revolt* (Praeger: New York, 1969).

7. This account has drawn chiefly on Paul Ginsborg, *A History of Contemporary Italy: Society and Politics, 1943–1988* (London: Penguin, 1990), chapter 9.

8. Fiorella Farinelli recalling her experiences, in Luisa Passerini, *Autobiography of a Generation: Italy 1968* (Hanover, N.H.: Wesleyan University Press, 1996), 29, 34.

9. Gerd-Rainer Horn, "The Rise and Fall of the New Working Class," in Carole Fink et al., eds., *1968: The World Transformed* (London: Cambridge University Press, 1998), 355.

10. The definitive work on the topic is Sidney Tarrow, *Democracy and Disorder: Protest and Politics in Italy, 1965–1975* (Oxford: Clarendon Press, 1989).

11. In fact, his company built workers' barracks at the Peenemünde rocket testing plant, where slave laborers were employed.

12. Harold Marcuse, "The Revival of Holocaust Awareness in West Germany, Israel, and the United States," in Fink et al., *1968*, 421–38.

13. Andrei Markovits and Philip Gorski offer an excellent brief account of the RAF in *The German Left: Red, Green, and Beyond* (New York: Oxford University Press, 1993), 59–78. Also Peter H. Merkl, ed., *Political Violence and Terror: Motifs and Motivations* (Berkeley: University of California Press, 1986). Figures on casualties are in Walter Althammer, *Gegen den Terror* (Stuttgart: Verlag Bonn Aktuell, 1978), 57. For deeper analysis, see Stefan Aust, *The Baader-Meinhof Group: The Inside Story of a Phenomenon* (London: Bodley Head, 1987); and Bernhard Rabert, *Terrorismus in Deutschland: Zum Faschismusvorwurf der deutschen Linksterroristen* (Bonn: Bernard and Graefe, 1991).

14. For a detailed account of the far right, see Franco Ferraresi, *Threats to Democracy: The Radical Right in Italy After the War* (Princeton: Princeton University Press, 1995).

15. A full history is given in Robert C. Meade, *Red Brigades: The Story of Italian Terrorism* (New York: St. Martin's, 1990); and Richard Drake, *The Revolutionary Mystique and Terrorism in Contemporary Italy* (Bloomington: Indiana University Press, 1989). For portraits of some key leaders of the Red Brigades, see Alessandro Silj, *Never Again Without a Rifle: The Origins of Italian Terrorism* (New York: Karz, 1979).

16. Claire Duchen, *Women's Rights and Women's Lives in France, 1944–1968* (London: Routledge, 1994), 201.

17. Gisela Kaplan, *Contemporary Western European Feminism* (New York: New York University Press, 1992), 161–77; and Duchen, *Women's Rights*, 190–211.

18. On Italy, see Kaplan, *Contemporary Western European Feminism*, 229–58; Susan Bassnett, *Feminist Experiences: The Women's Movement in Four Cultures* (London: Allen and Unwin, 1986), chapter 3; and Lucia Birnbaum, *Liberazione della Donna: Feminism in Italy* (Middletown, Conn.: Wesleyan University Press, 1986). For figures on women in the workforce, see "The Position of Women on the Labour Market," *Women of Europe* no. 36 (1992).

19. Kaplan, *Contemporary Western European Feminism*, 107–28; and Markovits and Gorski, *The German Left*, 87–94.

20. Speeches and writings of two founders of the German Greens can be found in Petra Kelly, *Thinking Green: Essays on Environmentalism, Feminism, and Non-Violence* (Berkeley: Parallax, 1994); and Rudolf Bahro, *Building the Green Movement* (Philadelphia: New Society, 1986).

21. Useful surveys include Eva Kolinsky, ed., *The Greens in West Germany* (Oxford: Berg, 1989); and Charlene Spretnak and Fritjof Capra, *Green Politics* (Santa Fe: Bear, 1986).

22. Markovits and Gorski, *The German Left*, 106–12; and Jill Liddington, *The Road to Greenham Common* (London: Virago, 1989).

CHAPTER TEN: SOUTHERN RENAISSANCE

1. J. P. Fusi, *Franco: A Biography* (New York: Harper and Row, 1987), 1–18.

2. On the difficulties of accounting for the casualties, see Stanley G. Payne, *The Franco Regime, 1936–1975* (Madison: University of Wisconsin, 1987), 218–20.

3. Payne, *Franco Regime*, 223–28.

4. Joseph Harrison, *The Spanish Economy: From the Civil War to the European Community* (Cambridge: Cambridge University Press, 1995), 7–12; Joan Esteban, "The Economic Policy of Francoism: An Interpretation," in Paul Preston, ed., *Spain in Crisis: The Evolution and Decline of the Franco Regime* (New York: Barnes and Noble, 1976), 82–100.

5. Jean Grugel and Tim Rees, *Franco's Spain* (London: Arnold, 1997), 112–23.

6. Payne, *Franco Regime*, 543–63, 588–90; Paul Preston, *The Triumph of Democracy in Spain* (London: Methuen, 1986), 18–52.

7. Preston, *Triumph*, 138–39; and "Abortion Legislation in Europe," International Planned Parenthood Federation, vol. 28, no. 2 (2000), at www.ippf.org.

8. John Sullivan, *ETA and Basque Nationalism: The Flight from Euskadi* (London: Routledge, 1988); Mark Kurlansky, *The Basque History of the World* (New York: Walker, 1999).

9. Preston, *Triumph*, 195–202.

10. David Birmingham, *A Concise History of Portugal* (Cambridge: Cambridge University Press, 1993), 156–59.

11. Tom Gallagher, *Portugal: A Twentieth-Century Interpretation* (Manchester: Manchester University Press, 1983), 173–75.

12. *New York Times*, 31 May 1961.

13. Kenneth Maxwell, *The Making of Portuguese Democracy* (Cambridge: Cambridge University Press, 1995), 16–29.

14. Maxwell, *Making*, 155–67.

15. Mario Murteira, "The Present Economic Situation," in Lawrence S. Graham and Harry M. Makler, eds., *Contemporary Portugal* (Austin: University of Texas Press, 1979), 336.

16. Scott B. MacDonald, *European Destiny, Atlantic Transformations: Portuguese Foreign Policy Under the Second Republic, 1974–1992* (New Brunswick, N.J.: Transaction Publishers, 1993), 69.

17. Mark Mazower, *Inside Hitler's Greece: The Experience of Occupation, 1941–1944* (New Haven: Yale University Press, 1993), 23–41, 123–43.

18. Richard Clogg, *A Concise History of Greece* (Cambridge: Cambridge University Press, 1992), 120–43; Yorgos A. Kourvetaris and Betty A. Dobratz, *A Profile of Modern Greece* (Oxford: Clarendon Press, 1987), 47–51; and Haris Vlavianos, *Greece, 1941–1949: From Resistance to Civil War* (New York: St. Martin's Press, 1992), which focuses on the Communist strategy.

19. Loy Henderson to Secretary of States, 9 January 1948, *FRUS 1948*, 4: 12; and NSC 5, Report to the National Security Council, 6 January 1948, *FRUS 1948*, 4: 2–7.

20. William H. McNeill, *Greece: American Aid in Action, 1947–1956* (New York: Twentieth Century Fund, 1957), 229. These were large sums, amounting by 1953 to roughly $285 per capita; by contrast, France received about $125 per capita in US aid between 1944 and 1952.

21. Margarita Dritsas, "National Integration and Economic Change in Greece During the Twentieth Century," in Alice Teichova et al., eds., *Economic Change and the National Question in Twentieth Century Europe* (Cambridge: Cambridge University Press, 2000), 216–19.

22. Clogg, *Greece*, 150–55; Tozun Bahcheli, *Greek-Turkish Relations Since 1955* (Boulder: Westview, 1990), 30–71; Nancy Crawshaw, *The Cyprus Revolt: An Account of the Struggle for Union with Greece* (London: Allen and Unwin, 1978).

23. Richard Clogg, *A Short History of Modern Greece* (Cambridge: Cambridge University Press, 1979), 186–99; C. M. Woodhouse, *The Rise and Fall of the Greek Colonels* (London: Grafton, 1985). For the allegations of torture and abuse, see Council of Europe, European Commission of Human Rights, *The Greek Case* (Strasbourg, 1969), 4 vols.

24. Harry J. Psomiades, "Greece: From the Colonels' Rule to Democracy," in John H. Herz, ed., *From Dictatorship to Democracy: Coping with the Legacies of Authoritarianism and Totalitarianism* (Westport: Greenwood, 1982), 251–73. Papadopoulos was sentenced to death in August 1975. Karamanlis commuted the sentence, and Papadopoulos spent the rest of his life in prison. He died in June 1999.

25. Jean Siotis, "The Politics of Greek Accession," in G. Minet et al., eds., *The Mediterranean Challenge: Spain, Greece, and Community Politics* (University of Sussex Research Centre, 1981), 87–118.

26. Loukas Tsoukalis, *The New European Economy Revisited* (Oxford: Oxford University Press, 1997), 16–18; Michael P. Marks, "Moving at Different Speeds: Spain and Greece in the European Union," in Peter J. Katzenstein, ed., *Tamed Power: Germany in Europe* (Ithaca: Cornell University Press, 1997), 142–66; and Loukas Tsoukalis, "Greece: Like Any Other European Country?" *National Interest* 55 (spring 1999), 65–74.

CHAPTER ELEVEN: CRACKS IN THE WALL

1. The still-excellent standard account is H. Gordon Skilling, *Czechoslovakia's Interrupted Revolution* (Princeton: Princeton University Press, 1976); this can be supplemented with a work that uses newly available Czech and Slovak sources: Kieran Williams, *The Prague Spring and Its Aftermath: Czechoslovak Politics, 1968–1970* (Cambridge: Cambridge University Press, 1997).

2. Proceedings of the Fourth Czechoslovak Writers' Congress, excerpts, in Jaromir Navratil, ed., *The Prague Spring, 1968* (Budapest: Central European University Press, 1998), 9. This is an invaluable collection of 140 documents from Czech and Soviet archives on the events of 1968.

3. Resolution of the Czechoslovak Communist Party Central Committee Plenum, in Navratil, ed., *Prague Spring*, 34.

4. Report to the Presidium on Dubcek's visit to Moscow, 29–30 January, 1968, in Navratil, ed., *Prague Spring*, 42.

5. For an excellent account based on new archival findings, see Mark Kramer, "The Czechoslovak Crisis and the Brezhnev Doctrine," in Carole Fink et al., ed., *1968: The World Transformed* (New York: Cambridge University Press, 1998), 111–71.

6. Minutes of the Dresden meeting, 23 March 1968, in Navratil, ed., *Prague Spring*, 65–66.

7. The full text is in Paul Ello, ed., *Dubcek's Blueprint for Freedom* (London: William Kimber, 1969), 123–212.

8. Vaculik's text is printed in Gale Stokes, *From Stalinism to Pluralism: A Documentary History of Eastern Europe Since 1945* (New York: Oxford University Press, 1996), 126–30.

9. Transcript of Warsaw meeting, 14–15 July 1968, and Warsaw letter, 15 July 1968, in Navratil, ed., *Prague Spring*, 212–38.

10. Text in Stokes, *From Stalinism to Pluralism*, 132–34.

11. Willy Brandt, *My Life in Politics* (New York: Viking, 1992), 73–126. For a lively and sympathetic portrait, see David Binder, *The Other German: Willy Brandt's Life and Times* (Washington, D.C.: New Republic Books, 1975).

12. On the origins of *Ostpolitik*, see A. James McAdams, *Germany Divided: From the Wall to Reunification* (Princeton: Princeton University Press, 1993), 56–79; and for Bahr's account, his memoir *Zu meiner Zeit* (Munich: Karl Blessing Verlag, 1996).

13. Useful accounts of Brandt's policy are given in W. R. Smyser, *From Yalta to Berlin: The Cold War Struggle over Germany* (New York: St. Martin's Press, 1999), 225–64; Dennis L. Bark and David R. Gress, *A History of West Germany*, vol. 2, *Democracy and Its Discontents, 1963–1991* (Cambridge: Blackwell, 1993), 151–223. A more idiosyncratic account is in Timothy Garton Ash, *In Europe's Name: Germany and the Divided Continent* (New York: Basic, 1993), chapter 3.

14. Ulbricht's view of *Ostpolitik* is subtly treated by McAdams, *Germany Divided*, 71–79 and 87–93. For an analysis of the East German attitude, based on new archival materials, see M. E. Sarotte, *Dealing with the Devil: East Germany, Détente, and Ostpolitik, 1969–1973* (Chapel Hill: University of North Carolina Press, 2001).

15. Willy Brandt, *People and Politics: The Years 1960–1975* (Boston: Little, Brown, 1976), 399. This autobiography is an excellent source for Brandt's thinking on *Ostpolitik*.

16. McAdams, *Germany Divided*, 102–5, and Henry A. Turner, Jr., *Germany from Partition to Reunification* (New Haven: Yale University Press, 1992), 148–63.

17. Markus Wolf, *Man Without a Face* (New York: Public Affairs, 1997), 189. Wolf is also the source of information on the East German bribe to the CDU deputy Julius Steiner, 172. Christopher Andrew presents further evidence on the East German penetration of Brandt's government: *The Sword*

and the Shield: The Mitrokhin Archive and the Secret History of the KGB (Basic Books: New York, 1999), 440–59.

18. Vojtech Mastny, *Helsinki, Human Rights, and European Security* (Durham, N.C.: Duke University Press, 1986). The full text of the Final Acts and other useful materials is in John J. Maresca, *To Helsinki: The Conference on Security and Cooperation in Europe, 1973–1975* (Durham, N.C.: Duke University Press, 1987), 249–305.

19. The full text, along with many other documents and excellent commentary, is in H. Gordon Skilling, *Charter 77 and Human Rights in Czechoslovakia* (London: Allen and Unwin, 1981), 209–12.

20. Full text in Stokes, ed., *From Stalinism to Pluralism*, 168–74.

21. Jan Jozef Lipski, *KOR: A History of the Workers' Defense Committee in Poland, 1976–1978* (Berkeley: University of California Press, 1985); and Peter Raina, *Political Opposition in Poland* (London: Poets and Painters Press, 1978). A lively survey of events is given in Neal Ascherson, *The Polish August: The Self-Limiting Revolution* (New York: Viking, 1982). A good summary is in Gale Stokes, *The Walls Came Tumbling Down* (New York: Oxford, 1993), 25–45.

22. Lech Walesa, *A Way of Hope* (New York: Henry Holt, 1987), 27–39, 43–44, 46–47, 50–51.

23. Walesa, *A Way of Hope*, 131–33.

24. Session of the Communist Party of the Soviet Union Central Committee Politburo, 29 October 1980, in Mark Kramer, ed., "Soviet Deliberations During the Polish Crisis, 1980–1981," Cold War International History Project, Special Working Paper No. 1, April 1999, 44–54.

25. Session of the Politburo, 31 October 1980, and Brezhnev letter to East German leader Erich Honecker, 4 November 1980, in Kramer, ed., "Soviet Deliberations," 55–61.

26. Session of the Politburo, 22 January 1981, in Kramer, ed., "Soviet Deliberations," 79–85.

27. Session of the Politburo, 2 April 1981, in Kramer, ed., "Soviet Deliberations," 92–102.

28. "The Solidarity Program," October 1981, in Stan Persky and Henry Flam, eds., *The Solidarity Sourcebook* (Vancouver: New Star Books, 1982), 205–25.

29. Brezhnev conversation with Kania, 11 September 1981, in Kramer, ed., "Soviet Deliberations," 141–45.

30. Text in Stokes, *From Stalinism to Pluralism*, 214–15.

CHAPTER TWELVE: RULE, BRITANNIA

1. For explanations of British economic woes, see Isaac Kramnick, ed., *Is Britain Dying? Perspectives on the Current Crisis* (Ithaca: Cornell University Press, 1979); Tom Nairn, *The Break-up of Britain* (London: Verso, 1981); Robert Bacon and Walter Eltis, *Britain's Economic Problems: Too Few Producers* (New York: St. Martin's, 1976); Michael Surrey, "United Kingdom," in Andrea Boltho, ed., *The European Economy: Growth and Crisis* (London: Oxford University Press, 1982), 528–53. For the cultural explanation, see especially Martin Wiener, *English Culture and the Decline of the Industrial Spirit, 1850–1980* (Cambridge: Cambridge University Press, 1981).

2. On the political history of this period, see Paul Foot, *The Politics of Harold Wilson* (London: Penguin, 1968); Robert Rhodes James, *Ambitions and Realities: British Politics, 1964–1970* (New York: Harper and Row, 1972); and Wilson's own account, Harold Wilson, *The Labour Government, 1964–1970: A Personal Record* (London: Weidenfeld and Nicolson, 1971). For the 1970s, see James Callaghan, *Time and Chance* (London: Collins, 1987); Kathleen Burk and Alec Cairncross, *"Goodbye, Great Britain": The 1976 IMF Crisis* (New Haven: Yale University Press, 1992).

3. Margaret Thatcher, *The Downing Street Years* (New York: HarperCollins, 1993), 6–8. This is a plodding defense of her years in office but contains much useful detail. There are numerous biographies of Thatcher; the best so far is Hugo Young, *The Iron Lady* (New York: Farrar, Straus, Giroux, 1989).

4. Thatcher, *Downing Street Years*, 10.

5. Margaret Thatcher, *The Path to Power* (New York: HarperCollins, 1995), 5, 11.

6. Thatcher, *Downing Street Years*, 12.

7. For a careful analysis of the 1979 election, see David Butler and Dennis Kavanagh, *The British General Election of 1979* (London: Macmillan, 1980). A thoughtful analysis of the origins of Thatcherism is given in Peter Jenkins, *Mrs. Thatcher's Revolution: The Ending of the Socialist Era* (Cambridge: Harvard University Press, 1988), esp. chapters 1–4.

8. Thatcher, *Downing Street Years*, 122.

9. Thatcher, *Downing Street Years*, 143–47. For more sustained analysis, see Martin Holmes, *The First Thatcher Government, 1979–1983* (Brighton: Wheatsheaf, 1985), and William Keegan, *Mrs. Thatcher's Economic Experiment* (London: Allen Lane, 1984).

10. Lawrence Freedman has written two well-informed accounts: a brief survey, *Britain and the Falklands War* (London: Basil Blackwell, 1988), and a more detailed study with Virginia Gamba-Stonehouse, *Signals of War: The Falklands Conflict of 1982* (Princeton: Princeton University Press, 1991).

11. Freedman, *Britain and the Falklands*, 46.

12. For these and other examples, see Robert Harris, *Gotcha! The Media, the Government, and the Falklands Crisis* (London: Faber and Faber, 1983); more detail is offered in Valerie Adams, *The Media and the Falklands Campaign* (London: Macmillan, 1986).

13. Young, *Iron Lady*, 281.

14. Sked and Cook, *Postwar Britain*, 434–35.

15. Young, *Iron Lady*, 371.

16. Thatcher, *Downing Street Years*, 339.

17. Peter Wilsher, Donald Macintyre, and Michael Jones, *Strike: Thatcher, Scargill, and the Miners* (London: Andre Deutsch, 1985), 5–8, 30. For accounts more sympathetic to the miners' plight, see Geoffrey Goodman, *The Miners' Strike* (London: Pluto, 1985); and Huw Beynon, *Digging Deeper: Issues in the Miners' Strike* (London: Verso, 1985).

18. Thatcher, *Downing Street Years*, 378.

19. Thatcher, *Path to Power*, 467. There are a number of audits of the Thatcher years, including Dennis Kavanagh, *The Reordering of British Politics: Politics After Thatcher* (Oxford: Oxford University Press, 1997); Dennis Kavanagh and Anthony Seldon, *The Thatcher Effect* (Oxford: Clarendon Press, 1989); Charles Delheim, *The Disenchanted Isle: Mrs. Thatcher's Capitalist Revolution* (New York: Norton, 1995); and perhaps the best, Peter Riddell, *The Thatcher Decade: How Britain Has Changed During the 1980s* (Oxford: Blackwell, 1989).

20. Riddell, *Thatcher Decade*, 14–42.

21. Riddell, *Thatcher Decade*, 87–112; Alan Murie, "Housing and the Environment," in Kavanagh and Seldon, *Thatcher Effect*, 213–25.

22. Riddell, *Thatcher Decade*, 160.

23. Ivor Crewe, "Values: The Crusade That Failed," in Kavanagh and Seldon, *Thatcher Effect*, 239–50; polls cited on 242 and 246.

24. Kavanagh, *Reordering*, 169–93; and Jenkins, *Mrs. Thatcher*, chapters 6, 10, 14.

25. There is a huge literature on the Northern Ireland conflict. A very good, up-to-date summary is given by Jack Holland in *Hope Against History: The Course of Conflict in Northern Ireland* (New York: Henry Holt, 1999). For a broader scope, see Thomas Hennessey, *A History of Northern Ireland, 1920–1996* (London: Macmillan, 1997); and broader still, though brief, is Paul Johnson, *Ireland: A Concise History from the Twelfth Century to the Present Day* (Chicago: Academy Chicago, 1980). Padraig O'Malley offers a careful examination of each of the main groups in the conflict in *The Uncivil Wars: Ireland Today* (Boston: Beacon Press, 1997).

26. Sabine Wichert, *Northern Ireland Since 1945* (London: Longman, 1991), 213.

27. Thatcher, *Downing Street Years*, 385–86.

28. Thatcher, *Downing Street Years*, 393.

29. Extensive official documentation on the peace negotiations can be found at the Web site of the British Northern Ireland Office: www.nio.gov.uk.

30. For more analysis, see "Why Peace Is Now Possible," *Economist*, 16 April 1998.

CHAPTER THIRTEEN: THE EUROPEAN REVOLUTIONS, 1989–1991

1. Timothy Garton Ash has used the term "refolution" to suggest that the fall of Communism was at least as much the result of internal reforms by Communist regimes as of revolution. *In Europe's Name: Germany and the Divided Continent* (New York: Vintage, 1993), 344.

2. Mikhail Gorbachev, *Memoirs* (New York: Doubleday, 1995), 22–40. The best account of the Gorbachev years is David Remnick, *Lenin's Tomb: The Last Days of the Soviet Empire* (New York: Vintage, 1994).

3. For Gorbachev's rise to power, see the excellent and detailed analysis of Archie Brown in *The Gorbachev Factor* (Oxford: Oxford University Press, 1996), 24–88; and Robert G. Kaiser, *Why Gorbachev Happened: His Triumphs and His Failure* (New York: Simon & Schuster, 1991), 21–92. A general survey of the whole period is Stephen White, *After Gorbachev* (Cambridge: Cambridge University Press, 1993).

4. Kaiser, *Why Gorbachev Happened*, 75–80.

5. Gorbachev, *Memoirs*, 171.

6. For discussion about the divergent statistics on Soviet growth, see Anders Aslund, *Gorbachev's Struggle for Economic Reform* (Ithaca: Cornell University Press), 15.

7. Seweryn Bialer, *The Soviet Paradox* (New York: Knopf, 1986), 47–50, 57–71; Paul R. Gregory and Robert Stuart, *Soviet Economic Structure and Performance* (New York: Harper and Row, 1986), 321–62; John Keep, *Last of the Empires* (London: Oxford University Press, 1995), chapters 11–13; and Marshall Goldman, *The USSR in Crisis* (New York: Norton, 1983).

8. For chilling evidence of the Soviet misperceptions, see Christopher Andrew and Oleg Gordievsky, *Comrade Kryuchkov's Instructions: Top Secret Files on KGB Foreign Operations, 1975–1985* (Stanford: Stanford University Press, 1993), 67–90.

9. Grigori Medvedev, *The Truth About Chernobyl* (New York: HarperCollins, 1991); and International Atomic Energy Agency, *Summary Report on the Post-Accident Review Meeting on the Chernobyl Accident* (Vienna, 1986).

10. Gorbachev, *Memoirs*, 191–93.

11. White, *After Gorbachev*, 102–42. Aslund, *Gorbachev's Struggle*, provides an authoritative account of the first years of reform; and see Ed A. Hewett, *Reforming the Soviet Economy* (Washington, D.C.: Brookings, 1988), 303–64.

12. Kaiser, *Why Gorbachev Happened*, 153.

13. The letter was titled "Polemics: I Cannot Waive My Principles" and is reprinted in Isaac J. Tarasulo, ed., *Gorbachev and Glasnost: Viewpoints from the Soviet Press* (Wilmington: SR Books, 1989), 277–90; and see Remnick, *Lenin's Tomb*, 70–85.

14. For the text of the resolutions and Gorbachev's closing speech, see Mikhail Gorbachev, *Perestroika* (London: William Collins, 1987), 257–310.

15. White, *After Gorbachev*, 46–56.

16. Gorbachev, *Memoirs*, 401–3.

17. The US-Soviet negotiations are superbly covered by Don Oberdorfer, *From the Cold War to a New Era: The United States and the Soviet Union, 1983–1991* (Baltimore: Johns Hopkins Press, 1998), chapters 4, 5, and 6. A still more detailed account is Raymond Garthoff, *The Great Transition: American-Soviet Relations and the End of the Cold War* (Washington, D.C.: Brookings, 1994).

18. Associated Press, 7 December 1988.

19. Gorbachev, *Memoirs*, 459.

20. Gale Stokes, *The Walls Came Tumbling Down: The Collapse of Communism in Eastern Europe* (New York: Oxford University Press, 1993), 78–101; Laszlo Bruszt and David Stark, "Remaking the Political Field in Hungary," in Ivo Banac, ed., *Eastern Europe in Revolution* (Ithaca: Cornell University Press, 1992) 13–55.

21. Stokes, *Walls*, 126, and 102–30.

22. "A New Social Contract," January 1987, in Gale Stokes, ed., *From Stalinism to Pluralism: A Documentary History of Eastern Europe Since 1945* (Oxford: Oxford University Press, 1996), 233–36.

23. Garton Ash, *In Europe's Name*, 108; and Gorbachev, *Perestroika*, 199–200.

24. John Tagliabue, "Poland Flirts with Pluralism Today," *New York Times*, 4 June 1989.

25. There is now a vast number of books on the fall of the Berlin Wall and the unification of Germany. One of the clearest is Konrad H. Jarausch, *The Rush to German Unity* (New York: Oxford, 1994); also outstanding is Charles Maier, *Dissolution: The Crisis of Communism and the End of East Germany* (Princeton: Princeton University Press, 1997).

26. On the GDR's economic performance, see Maier, *Dissolution*, 78–97.

27. A thoughtful exploration of the history of the GDR is Mary Fulbrook, *Anatomy of a Dictatorship: Inside the GDR, 1949–1989* (New York: Oxford University Press, 1995). For the Stasi, see David Childs and Richard Popplewell, *The Stasi: The East German Intelligence and Security Service* (New York: NYU Press, 1996), esp. 82–111.

28. "Stasi Report on Motives for Emigration," 9 September 1989, in Konrad H. Jarausch and

Volker Gransow, *Uniting Germany: Documents and Debates, 1944–1993* (Oxford: Berghahn Books, 1994), 36–39. For an excellent discussion of the emigration crisis, see Norman Naimark, " 'Ich will hier raus': Emigration and the Collapse of the GDR," in Banac, ed., *Eastern Europe*, 72–95.

29. Founding Appeal of New Forum, 9 September; Appeal for a Social Democratic Party, 12 September; Appeal for Democracy Now, 12 September, in Jarausch and Grasnow, *Uniting Germany*, 39–48. For more detail and texts, see Gerhard Rein, ed., *Die Opposition in der DDR* (Berlin, 1989).

30. Gorbachev, *Memoirs*, 523–24.

31. Craig Whitney, "How the Wall Was Cracked," *New York Times*, 18 November 1989. There is still some dispute over the decision to avoid the use of force. For Krenz's account, see his memoir *Wenn Mauern Fallen: Die friedliche Revolution* (Vienna: Paul Neff, 1990), 136–38; and for further Stasi documents, Armin Mitter and Stefan Wolle, eds., *"Ich liebe Euch doch alle!" Befehle und Lageberichte des Mfs* (Berlin: Basis Druck, 1990).

32. Serge Schmemann, "East Germany Removes Honecker," *New York Times*, 19 October 1989.

33. Bill Keller, "Gorbachev in Finland," *New York Times*, 26 October 1989.

34. Krenz, *Wenn Mauern Fallen*, 161–95; Pond, *Beyond the Wall*, 132–34.

35. Timothy Garton Ash, *The Magic Lantern*; Tony Judt, "Metamorphosis: The Democratic Revolution in Czechoslovakia," in Banac, ed., *Eastern Europe in Revolution*, 96–116.

36. For the diplomacy of unification, one work stands out above the rest: Philip Zelikow and Condoleeza Rice, *Germany Unified and Europe Transformed: A Study in Statecraft* (Cambridge: Harvard University Press, 1995). The authors were closely involved in the negotiations, and what follows is based largely on their account. Other excellent studies of this process include Robert L. Hutchings, *American Diplomacy and the End of the Cold War* (Washington, D.C.: Wilson Center Press, 1997), and Elizabeth Pond, *Beyond the Wall: Germany's Road to Unification* (Washington, D.C.: Brookings, 1993). More anecdotal, but insightful, is Michael R. Beschloss and Strobe Talbott, *At the Highest Levels: The Inside Story of the End of the Cold War* (Boston: Little, Brown, 1993).

37. Kohl speech, 8 November 1989, in Jarausch and Gransow, eds., *Uniting Germany*, 74–77.

38. Kohl's Ten Point Plan, Jarausch and Gransow, eds., *Uniting Germany*, 86–89.

39. Pond, *Beyond the Wall*, 160.

40. See Democracy Now's platform for unity, which called for Germany to be neutral and insisted on major economic reforms—in *West* Germany; 14 December 1989, in Jarausch and Gransow, eds., *Uniting Germany*, 94–95.

41. Gorbachev, *Memoirs*, 528. On the roundtable talks, see Jarausch, *Rush to German Unity*, 101–7.

42. Jarausch and Gransow, *Uniting Germany*, "Kohl Campaign Promises, March 1990," 122–24.

43. The elections are followed carefully in Jarausch, *The Rush to German Unity*, 115–32.

44. The treaty is in Jarausch and Gransow, eds., *Uniting Germany*, 154–61.

45. Maeve Kennedy, "Thatcher's German Angst," *Guardian*, 16 July 1990; and *Independent*, 16 July 1990. The meeting took place at Chequers on 24 March 1990.

46. Kaiser, *Why Gorbachev Happened*, 336–56.

47. The Kohl-Gorbachev meeting stirred up much enthusiastic comment at the time. For the "miracle in Moscow," see Serge Schmemann, "Evolution in Europe," *New York Times*, 16 July 1990; and Gary Lee, "Gorbachev Drops Objection to United Germany in NATO," *Washington Post*, 17 July 1990.

48. On the coup, see Gorbachev, *Memoirs*, 626–45; Brown, *Gorbachev Factor*, 294–300; and Remnick, *Lenin's Tomb*, 433–90.

CHAPTER FOURTEEN: THE BONES OF BOSNIA

1. An excellent survey is Fred Singleton, *A Short History of the Yugoslav Peoples* (Cambridge: Cambridge University Press, 1985). For a short introduction, see Istvan Deak, "The One and the Many," *New Republic*, 7 October 1991, reprinted in Nader Mousavizadeh, ed., *The Black Book of Bosnia* (New York: Basic Books, 1996), 5–19.

2. On Yugoslavia during the war, see especially F. W. D. Deakin, *The Embattled Mountain* (New York: Oxford, 1971), and the memoir of Tito's close adviser Milovan Djilas, *Wartime* (New York: Harcourt Brace Jovanovich, 1977).

3. Tim Judah, *Kosovo: War and Revenge* (New Haven: Yale University Press, 2000), 44.

4. The following day, Milosevic gave a speech to the Serbs in Kosovo that railed against the "injustice and humiliation" being done to them by the Albanians, and declared that Serbia would "change the situation" in Kosovo. Address of 25 April 1987, in Philip E. Auerswald and David P. Auerswald, eds., *The Kosovo Conflict: A Diplomatic History Through Documents* (The Hague: Kluwer Law International, 2000), 10–16. On his visit to Kosovo, see Laura Silber and Allan Little, *Yugoslavia: Death of a Nation* (London: Penguin, 1997), 37–47. This is probably the best single volume on its subject.

5. Ivo Banac, "Nationalism in Southeastern Europe," in Charles A. Kupchan, ed., *Nationalism and Nationalities in the New Europe* (Ithaca: Cornell University Press, 1995), 107–21.

6. International Criminal Tribunal for the Former Yugoslavia (ICTY), Milosevic "Croatia" Indictment, 9 October 2001; and ICTY, Mrksic, Radic, and Sljvancanin Indictment, 26 October 1995.

7. For the broader background and the origins of the war, see Noel Malcolm, *Bosnia: A Short History* (New York: New York University Press, 1996), esp. 213–33.

8. Silber and Little, *Death of a Nation*, 215. Karadzic was born in 1945 in Montenegro. He was a founding member of the Serbian Democratic Party in Bosnia, the party that led the Bosnian Serbs into secession. He became president of the Bosnian Serb republic in 1992, and exercised control over the Bosnian Serbs throughout the war.

9. There are no reliable figures of deaths in the conflict. The number 200,000 is that used by the United Nations Mission in Bosnia-Herzegovina.

10. See Article 4 and Article 5 of the Statute of the International Criminal Tribunal (available at www.un.org/icty).

11. Malcolm, *Bosnia,* 252; and for an excellent analysis of how the Serbs manipulated the media, see Stuart J. Kaufman, *Modern Hatreds: The Symbolic Politics of Ethnic War* (Ithaca, N.Y.: Cornell University Press, 2001).

12. General Mladic was born in Bosnia in 1943 and had been a career soldier in the JNA. In 1991, Milosevic appointed him commander of the Ninth Corps of the JNA in Croatia, which helped Serbs wrest control of this breakaway province from the Croatians. In May 1992, Milosevic gave him control over JNA units in Bosnia, which became the Bosnian Serb army. Richard Holbrooke, who negotiated with him the cease-fire that ended the war, described him as "a charismatic murderer." Holbrooke, *To End a War,* 149.

13. ICTY, Sikirica Indictment, 24 August 1999; and ICTY, Meakic et al. Indictment, 2 June 1998. Due to the courageous reporting of *Newsday* reporter Roy Gutman, many of these atrocities became widely known in Europe and the United States, and the Omarska camp was closed down by Serb authorities in August 1992. Others remained open. See Roy Gutman, *A Witness to Genocide* (New York: Macmillan, 1993).

14. Human Rights Watch, "War Crimes in Bosnia-Hercegovina," June 1994, vol. 6, no. 8; and Human Rights Watch, "Northwestern Bosnia," February 1996, vol. 8, no. 1.

15. ICTY, Gagovic et al. Indictment, 26 June 1996; and Human Rights Watch, "Bosnia and Hercegovina: 'A Closed, Dark Place': Past and Present Human Rights Abuses in Foca," July 1998, vol. 10, no. 6. Gagovic was killed on 9 January 1999 during an attempt by NATO forces to arrest him on behalf of the war crimes tribunal.

16. Cited in Richard Holbrooke, *To End a War* (New York: Random House, 1998), 23.

17. David Owen, a former British foreign minister, was a prickly, often self-righteous, but tireless diplomat who after four years of effort failed to secure a viable peace plan. See his memoir, *Balkan Odyssey* (New York: Harcourt Brace, 1995).

18. UN Resolution 819, passed on 16 April 1993, declared Srebrenica a safe area; Resolution 824, passed on 6 May 1993, extended the safe-area guarantee to Sarajevo, Zepa, Tuzla, Gorazde, and Bihac—all cities held at the time by Bosnian government forces.

19. The role of the Dutch troops remains controversial. Could they have done more to hold off the Serbs? For a detailed examination, see Jan Willem Honig and Norbert Both, *Srebrenica: Record of a War Crime* (London: Penguin, 1996), esp. 3–27. In April 2002, the Netherlands Institute for War Documentation confirmed that Dutch peacekeepers did little to prevent Serb forces from rounding up Muslims in Srebrenica. The report led to the resignation of the Dutch government of prime minister Wim Kok, who was in office at the time of the massacre.

20. Human Rights Watch, "Bosnia-Herzegovina: The Fall of Srebrenica and the Failure of UN Peacekeeping," October 1995, vol. 7, no. 13, 44. Also ICTY, Karadzic and Mladic Indictment, 14 November 1995.

21. Richard Holbrooke gives a detailed account: *To End a War*, 231–312. The text of the agreement is available at www.ohr.int.

22. This section owes much to the superb account by Tim Judah, *Kosovo: War and Revenge*.

23. OSCE, *Kosovo/Kosova: As Seen, As Told*, part 1 (October 1998–June 1999), 100–101. This volume contains detailed accounts of the Serb assault on Kosovo before and during the NATO bombing.

24. OSCE, *Kosovo/Kosova*, part 1, 99. About 445,000 went to Albania, 237,000 to Macedonia, 64,000 to Montenegro, 22,000 to Bosnia, and 96,000 to other European countries. For casualties, see US Department of State, "Ethnic Cleansing in Kosovo: An Accounting," December 1999.

25. OSCE, *Kosovo/Kosova: As Seen, As Told*, part 2 (June to October 1999), xvii. And see US Department of State, "Erasing History: Ethnic Cleansing in Kosovo," May 1999.

26. I have relied on the superb reporting of these events by Timothy Garton Ash, "The Last Revolution," *New York Review of Books*, 16 November 2000.

27. European Stability Initiative, "Interim Evaluation of Reconstruction and Return Task Force," 15 September 1999.

28. Quoted in Nicholas Lemann, "The Provocateur," *New Yorker*, 13 November 2000.

CHAPTER FIFTEEN: WHO IS EUROPEAN?

1. Marc Fisher, *Washington Post*, 1 June 1993. On Mölln, Tyler Marshall, *New York Times*, 24 November 1992.

2. Akil Miah, quoted in "The Summer of Rebellion," *CARF* 63 (August/September 2001); and "The Fuse That Lit," *Manchester Evening News*, 28 May 2001.

3. European Union Monitoring Centre on Racism and Xenophobia, Annual Report 1999; "French Jews Concerned After Sharp Rise in Anti-Semitic Attacks," www.adl.org.

4. "Xenophobia and Racism in Europe: In Light of Public Opinion 1989–1997," EUMC, December 1998.

5. "Attitudes Toward Minority Groups in the European Union," EUMC, Vienna, March 2001, 37–49.

6. Extract from a Cabinet Memorandum, 2 September 1955; Extract from Minutes of a Cabinet Meeting, 3 November 1955; and Lord Salisbury to Lord Swinton, 20 March 1954, in A. N. Porter and A. J. Stockwell, eds., *British Imperial Policy and Decolonization, 1938–1964*, vol. 2 (London: Macmillan, 1989), 383, 399, 300.

7. Kathleen Paul, *Whitewashing Britain: Race and Citizenship in the Postwar Era* (Ithaca: Cornell University Press, 1997), 155–69.

8. Powell speech, 20 April 1968, in *The Penguin Book of Twentieth Century Speeches*, ed. by Brian MacArthur (Penguin: New York, 1992), 376–83.

9. Peter Clarke, *Hope and Glory: Britain 1900–1990* (Penguin: New York, 1996), 324.

10. Cited in Paul, *Whitewashing Britain*, 183.

11. Ceri Peach, "Postwar Migration to Europe: Reflux, Influx, Refuge," *Social Science Quarterly* 78, no. 2 (June 1997), table 2, 274.

12. In 1998, total net migration to the UK stood at 133,000 people, of whom 37,700 were from Europe, 19,000 from Oceania, and 14,000 from the United States; 26,300 came from Africa and 30,000 from Asia. Of the 2.2 million foreign citizens living in Britain in 1999, 1 million were from Europe (of whom 450,000 were Irish), 559,000 were from Asia, 265,000 from Africa, and 264,000 from the Americas. Council of Europe, *Recent Demographic Developments in Europe* (Strasbourg, 2000), 638–44. For useful statistical reports and surveys, see Robin Cohen, ed., *The Cambridge Survey of World Migration* (Cambridge: Cambridge University Press, 1995); OECD, *Trends in International Migration* (1998); and International Organization for Migration, *World Migration Report 2000* (New York, United Nations, 2000).

13. The police and immigration service began using mobile X-ray scanners, heartbeat sensors, and thermal imaging devices to search cars and trucks crossing from Europe for illegal immigrants. "Measures Announced to Improve Immigration Control," Home Office News Release, 19 September 2001.

14. Respectively, *Sun*, 7 March 2001; *Daily Star*, 7 December 2000; *Sunday People*, 4 March 2001. For further information, see the Refugee Council's Web site: www.refugeecouncil.org.uk.

15. "Fairer, Faster, and Firmer: A Modern Approach to Immigration and Asylum," British Home Office white paper, July 1998, Cm 4018.

16. Refugee Council, UK Statistics 2000.

17. A pathbreaking work on the history of citizenship law is Rogers Brubaker, *Citizenship and Nationhood in France and Germany* (Cambridge: Harvard University Press, 1992). See also Alec G. Hargreaves, *Immigration, Race, and Ethnicity in Contemporary France* (London: Routledge, 1995).

18. Hargreaves, *Immigration*, 14, 5; Philip E. Ogden, "Immigration to France Since 1945: Myth and Reality," in *Ethnic and Racial Studies* 14, no. 3 (1991), 294–317.

19. Jorgen Nielsen, *Muslims in Western Europe* (Edinburgh: Edinburgh University Press, 1992), 8–22; Robert Sole, *Le Monde*, 29 October 1989; Anne Corbett, *Guardian*, 1 December 1989; Agence France Presse, 27 October 1994.

20. Jean-Claude Barreau, cited in *Economist*, 16 November 1996.

21. *Economist*, 3 August 1996, 45. A useful survey is James F. Hollifield, "Immigration and Integration in Western Europe: A Comparative Analysis," in Emek M. Uçarer and Donald J. Puchala, eds., *Immigration into Western Societies: Problems and Policies* (London: Pinter, 1997), 28–69.

22. Alfred Rinaldi, "No Turks, Please: We're German," *New Statesman*, 1 January 1999.

23. Excellent surveys are Barbara Marshall, *The New Germany and Migration in Europe* (Manchester: Manchester University Press, 2000); Rainer Münz et al., *Zuwanderung nach Deutschland: Strukturen, Wirkungen, Perspektiven* (1997); and Ralph Rotte, "Immigration Control in United Germany: Toward a Broader Scope of National Policies," *International Migration Review* 34, no. 2 (summer 2000), 357–89.

24. Anthony Richter, " 'Blood and Soil': What It Means to Be German," *World Policy Journal* 15, no. 4 (winter 1998–99), 91–98; Ralph Rotte, "Immigration Control in United Germany," 357–89.

25. Brubaker, *Citizenship*, 114–37.

26. Christian Joppke, *Immigration and the Nation State: The United States, Germany, and Britain* (London: Oxford, 1999), 186–222.

27. United States Council on Refugees, *Germany: Country Report 2000* (www.refugees.org); Marshall, *New Germany*, 86–96; Joppke, *Immigration*, 85–94.

28. Cited in Jonathan Fenby, *France on the Brink* (Arcade: New York, 1998), 233; Michalina Vaughan, "The Extreme-Right in France: Lepenisme or the Politics of Fear," in Luciano Cheles et al., eds., *Neo-Fascism in Europe* (London: Longman, 1991), 211–30. There is a large literature on Le Pen, but for an excellent case study of far right politics in France, see Françoise Gaspard's account of the city of Dreux: *A Small City in France*, trans. by Arthur Goldhammer (Cambridge: Harvard University Press, 1995).

29. Voting results from the Ministry of the Interior, reported in *Le Monde*, 23 April 2002 and 6 May 2002.

30. Gerry Gable, "The Far Right in Contemporary Britain," in Cheles, ed., *Neo-Fascism in Europe*, 245–63; Cas Mudde, "Going to Extremes," *Guardian*, 29 June 2001; campaign slogans on the BNP's Web site, www.bnp.org.uk.

31. David Childs, "The Far Right in Germany Since 1945," in Cheles, ed., *Neo-Fascism in Europe*, 66–85; Roger Cohen, "Odd Couple of German Politics," *New York Times*, 8 September 2000; *Deutsche Presse-Agentur*, 31 January 2001.

32. Anna Pukas, "Taste of Power for a Wolf in Sheep's Clothing," *Daily Mail*, 9 March 1993.

33. Tyler Marshall, "Extreme Right Makes Gains in German Vote," *Los Angeles Times*, 8 March 1993.

34. Leon Mangasarian, "Biggest Post-1945 Win for a Far-Right Party Stuns Germany," *Deutsche Presse-Agentur*, 26 April 1998; Jack Thompson, "Odin's Legion on the March," *World Today* 2 (February 2001), 25–27.

35. William Hall, *Financial Times*, 16 November 1999; Imre Karacs, *Independent*, 4 October 1999; Anti-Defamation League, "Jörg Haider: The Rise of an Austrian Extremist," 2001. For poll numbers, *Eurobarometer* 54 (autumn 2000).

36. Elizabeth Olson, *International Herald Tribune*, 26 October 1999; *Economist*, 30 October 1999; Linda Grant, *Guardian*, 5 November 1999.

37. In a 1997 poll, 68 percent of EU citizens declared their support for "a world where people live by traditional values." European Commission, "How Europeans See Themselves" (Brussels, 2001), 8.

38. Ellie Vasta, "Rights and Racism in a New Country of Immigration: The Italian Case," in John

Wrench and John Solomos, eds., *Racism and Migration in Western Europe* (Oxford: Berg, 1993), 83–98; John W. P. Veugelers, "Recent Immigration Politics in Italy: A Short History," in Martin Baldwin-Edwards and Martin A. Schain, eds., *The Politics of Immigration in Western Europe* (London: Frank Cass, 1994), 33–49; Giovanna Campbell, "Immigration and Racism in Southern Europe: The Italian Case," *Ethnic and Racial Studies* 16, no. 3 (July 1993), 507–33.

39. For background, see Roberto Chiarini, "The 'Movimento Sociale Italiano': A Historical Profile," in Cheles, ed., *Neo-Fascism in Europe*, 19–42.

40. James Blitz and Edward Mortimer, "Italians Will Curb Asylum Seekers," *Financial Times*, 10 February 1998.

41. A well-informed review of European Union policies on immigration is Demetrios G. Papademetriou, *Coming Together or Pulling Apart? The European Union's Struggle with Immigration and Asylum* (Washington, D.C.: Carnegie Endowment, 1996).

42. *Economist*, 6 May 2000.

43. Roger Cohen, "Illegal Migration Increases Sharply in EU," *New York Times*, 25 December 2000.

CHAPTER SIXTEEN: THE ELUSIVE EUROPEAN UNION

1. "What Is Europe?" *Economist*, 12 February 2000, 15–16.

2. Desmond Dinan, *Ever Closer Union? An Introduction to the European Community* (Lynne Rienner: Boulder, Colo., 1994), 69–98. This is an excellent survey.

3. John Pinder, *The Building of the European Union* (New York: Oxford University Press, 1998), 142–59. Perhaps the most detailed study of the monetary system in its historical perspective is Andrew Moravcsik, *The Choice for Europe: Social Purpose and State Power from Messina to Maastricht* (Ithaca: Cornell University Press, 1998), esp. 238–313. More accessible is Kathleen R. McNamara, *The Currency of Ideas: Monetary Politics in the European Union* (Ithaca: Cornell University Press, 1998); and a useful historical survey is given in Daniel Gros and Niels Thygesen, *European Monetary Integration* (London: Longman, 1992).

4. Margaret Thatcher, *The Downing Street Years* (New York: HarperCollins, 1993), 79.

5. Thatcher, *Downing Street Years*, 81.

6. Pinder, *European Union*, 85–90.

7. Moravcsik, *Choice for Europe*, 379–471; and Paul de Grauwe, *The Economics of Monetary Integration* (London: Oxford University Press, 1997), 52–84.

8. John Grahl, *After Maastricht: A Guide to European Monetary Union* (London: Lawrence and Wishart, 1997), esp. 108–28.

9. For a sampling of this pessimism, see the special report on the EU by the *Economist* called "A Rude Awakening," 3 July 1993.

10. Eurostat, *Yearbook 2001*, 23.

11. For details on the agreement, see the various articles in the *New York Times*, 15 December 1993.

12. Pinder, *European Union*, is an excellent introduction to the history of the EU, as is Derek Urwin, *The Community of Europe: A History of European Integration Since 1945* (London: Longman, 1995). Also see Dick Leonard, *Guide to the European Union*, 7th ed. (London: Profile Books, 2000); and Desmond Dinan, ed., *Encyclopedia of the European Union* (London: Lynne Rienner, 1998).

13. European Commission, "The Budget of the European Union," Brussels, 2000.

14. Eurostat, News Release no. 117/2001, 8 November 2001.

15. Details on the CFSP may be obtained at www.europa.eu.int.

16. European Commission, "How Europeans See Themselves," 2001; *Eurobarometer* 52 (Autumn 1999); and *Eurobarometer* 54 (Autumn 2000).

17. For assessment of the thirteen candidate countries, see European Commission, *Bulletin of the European Union*, Supplement 3/2000, "Agenda 2000: Enlargement Strategy Paper"; and European Commission, "European Union Enlargement: A Historic Opportunity." The EU's research branch, Eurostat, maintains detailed statistics on all EU applicants. Also, see Deutsche Bank Research, at www.dbresearch.com. A useful overview is Heather Grabbe and Kirsty Hughes, *Enlarging the EU Eastwards* (London: Royal Institute of International Affairs, 1998).

18. Two useful assessments of Yeltsin are Roy Medvedev, "Boris Yeltsin Resigns," *Russian Politics*

and Law 38, no. 4 (July/August 2000), 82–88; and Michael McFaul, "Yeltsin's Legacy," *Wilson Quarterly* 24, no. 2 (spring 2000), 42–47.

19. World Bank, *World Bank Development Indicators 2000;* CIA, *World Factbook,* 2001; Transparency International, *Corruption Perceptions Index,* 2001; *Economist,* "Putin's Choice: A survey of Russia," 21 July 2001; and Martin Nicholson, "Putin's Russia: Slowing the Pendulum Without Stopping the Clock," *International Affairs* 77, no. 4 (2001), 867–84.

20. Romano Prodi, 28 February 2002, speech to the European Parliament during the opening session of the Convention on the Future of Europe.

21. *Financial Times,* 11 June 2001; *Economist,* 8 June 2001; *Agence France-Presse,* 9 June 2001; *Guardian,* 10 June 2001; *Financial Times,* 18 June 2001.

22. *Eurobarometer* 56 (autumn 2001), at europa.eu.int/comm/public_opinion/

23. *The Economist Pocket Europe in Figures* (London: Profile, 2000).

24. For an excellent discussion of this problem in the French case, see Jonathan Fenby, *France on the Brink: A Great Civilization Faces the New Century* (New York: Arcade, 1999), 95–119.

25. Dominique Moïsi, "Europe–Etats-Unis: vers un vrai découplage," *Politique étrangère,* avril-juin 2001, 255.

26. For a superb rumination on this topic, see Larry Siedentop, *Democracy in Europe* (New York: Columbia University Press, 2001).

AFTERWORD: EUROPE AND AMERICA AFTER SEPTEMBER 11

1. Jean-Marie Colombani, "Nous Sommes Tous Américains," *Le Monde,* 13 September 2001.

2. Deutsche Presse-Agentur, 11 September 2001; Agence France Presse, 12 September 2001; *Daily Mail,* September 14, 2001.

3. William Drozdiak, *Washington Post,* 13 September 2001; Deutsche Presse-Agentur, 14 September 2001; Bush address to joint session of Congress, 20 September 2001, www.whitehouse.gov.

4. For detailed polling, see Pew Research Center poll of 15 August 2001: "Bush Unpopular in Europe."

5. This line of reasoning, however, was often taken to extremes. Just one egregious example: Dario Fo, the Italian playwright and satirist who won the Nobel Prize for literature in 1997, said of 9/11: "The great speculators wallow in an economy that every year kills tens of millions of people with poverty—so what is 20,000 dead in New York? Regardless of who carried out the massacre, this violence is the legitimate daughter of the culture of violence, hunger and inhumane exploitation." Steven Erlanger, *New York Times,* 22 September 2001. Some Europeans indulged a taste for conspiracy theories. In France, a book called *L'Effroyable Imposture* (The Terrible Fraud) by Thierry Meyssan, which argued that the 9/11 attacks were staged by right-wing military officials in the US government in order to justify war on Afghanistan, hit the best-seller lists in May 2002.

6. In France, 64 percent approved of the Afghanistan invasion; in Germany, 61 percent did so. 73 percent of Britons polled supported the war. "Americans and Europeans Differ Widely on Foreign Policy Issues," Pew Research Center, 17 April 2002. EU foreign policy chief Javier Solana called the US-led military invasion "a legitimate act to find those responsible" for the September 11 attacks. "It has the support of the European Union and it has the understanding of the European people," he said. AFP, 8 October 2001.

7. A majority of Europeans believed that American foreign policy was in part responsible for the attacks of September 11. See Worldviews 2002, poll of 4 September 2002, at www.worldview.org.

8. AFP, 28 February 2002; *Daily Mail,* 8 April 2002; and Hugo Young, "The Terrifying Naivete of Blair the Great Intervener," *The Guardian,* 30 April 2002.

9. Bush UN speech at www.whitehouse.gov; Associated Press, 5 August, 13 September, 21 September, 2002. The election result was extremely close. Schroeder remained Chancellor only with the help of his Green Party allies.

10. Thomas Friedman, "Vote France Off the Island," *New York Times,* 9 February 2003. The most persistently anti-European journalists were Charles Krauthammer, George Will, and William Safire, all syndicated columnists. Robert Kagan, a conservative analyst and writer, coined the phrase that became the standard explanation for the US-European divide: "Americans are from Mars, Europeans are from Venus," which was meant to suggest that Americans understood that military force was a legitimate

tool of statecraft, while Europeans had come to believe that armed conflict was illegitimate. His book became a best-seller: *Of Paradise and Power: America and Europe in the New World Order* (New York: Knopf, 2003).

11. *Financial Times*, 27 May 2003.

12. *New York Times*, 6 February 2003, "France, Backed by Germany, Calls for Stronger Inspections, but the U.S. Is Unmoved."

13. *Financial Times*, 30 January 2003; Havel quoted in *Washington Post*, 2 December 2002. An additional ten European states—Slovenia, Slovakia, Romania, Bulgaria, Lithuania, Latvia, Estonia, Albania, Croatia, and Macedonia—later issued a second declaration of support for American policy. These ten states were all candidates for membership in NATO and had an incentive to support Washington. Virtually none of them gave any military or economic aid to the war effort. For an excellent review of the diplomatic wrangling on the eve of the Iraq war, see the four-part series by the *Financial Times*, 27–30 May 2003.

14. On the eve of war, opinion in the major states was running strongly against the war. In Italy, Spain, Poland, and Britain—all countries that officially supported the United States—81 percent, 81 percent, 73 percent, and 51 percent of the public, respectively, opposed the war. In France and Germany, 75 percent and 69 percent of the public opposed the war. Pew Research Center, 18 March 2003.

15. *Manchester Guardian Weekly*, 25 September 2002; and see his speech of 20 March 2003 to the European Parliament at http://europa.eu.int/comm/external_relations/news/patten/sp03_148.htm.

16. Will Hutton, *The World We're In* (Little, Brown: London, 2002).

INDEX

.

Hume, John, 336, 338–39, 341
Hungarian Communist Party, 108–10, 206, 212, 360
Hungarian Workers' Party, 110, 206
Hungary, 4, 18, 21, 58, 88, 98, 120, 121–22, 128,
219, 288, 296, 299, 303, 343, 347, 359–60,
363, 364, 454–55
 anti-Soviet rhetoric in, 208
 Communist takeover of, 108–10
 dissident movement in, 360, 362
 1956 uprising in, 206–13, 348
 purges in, 206
 Soviet invasion of, 161, 181, 208–13
 Soviet policy toward, 107
 West Germany agreements with, 295
hunger strikes, 337–38
Husak, Gustav, 367

IG Farben, 34–35
illegal immigration, 433, 434
Il Progresso, 92
Implementation Force (IFOR), 401
India, 51, 58, 60, 128, 165, 168, 169, 177
 divisions within, 166
 Muslim-Hindu violence in, 167
 partition of, 166–67
Indochina, 128, 162, 163, 164, 168, 172–77, 184, 425
Indochina War, 173–77
Indonesia, 163, 165
infant mortality, 352
influence, spheres of, 19, 21
Institute for Industrial Reconstruction (IRI),
140
intellectuals, 10–11, 156
Intermediate-Range Nuclear Forces (INF)
Treaty (1987), 358
International Criminal Tribunal, 393, 394, 400,
401, 408
International Independent Commission on
Decommissioning, 340
International Monetary Fund (IMF), 181, 182,
273, 280, 314, 359, 361, 408
International Red Cross, 101, 281, 400
Investment Fund for Economic and Social
Development (FIDES), 164
Ioannidis, Dimitrios, 285–86
Iran, 58, 59, 178, 282, 357
Iraq, 58, 178
Ireland, 334, 433, 437, 445, 460–61
Irish National Liberation Army, 337
Irish Republican Army (IRA), 332–41
Israel, 123, 243
 Suez crisis and, 180
Italian Communist Party (PCI), 79, 80–81,
84–85, 86, 87, 88, 89–90, 253, 259, 261,
431–32

 response to Marshall Plan of, 90
 strategy of, 81
Italian Socialist Party (PSI), 81, 84
Italian Social Movement (MSI), 254, 260, 432
Italian Social Republic, 78
Italian Women's Center, 264
Italian Women's Union, 264
Italy, 2, 10, 65–66, 67, 77–88, 89, 114, 132, 135,
136, 153, 154, 156–57, 159, 229, 256, 265,
380, 424, 459
 Allied occupation of, 78–79
 anti-immigrant sentiment in, 432–33
 Communist response to Marshall Plan in, 90
 currency devaluation in, 254
 economic policy of, 84–85
 exports of, 140
 far right in, 428
 first postwar government of, 82–83
 gas industry of, 140–41
 GDP of, 223
 German occupation of, 79–80
 immigration policy in, 430–44
 industrial cartels in, 140–41
 industrial production in, 131
 inflation in, 140
 liberation of, 77–78
 Marshall Plan in, 136, 138–41
 neo-Fascist formations in, 259–60
 public investment in, 139–40
 purges in, 83
 quasi-national sector in, 140
 resistance movement in, 79–80
 stationing of nuclear weapons in, 158
 strikes in, 85, 146
 student protests in, 251–54
 terrorist violence in, 259–62
 UNRRA aid package to, 83
 US role in 1948 elections, 11, 91–92
 US support for anti-Communists in, 86–88
 women's movement in, 264
Ivory Coast, 172
Izetbegovic, Alija, 391–92

Japan, 22, 163, 173
Jaruzelski, Wojciech, 307, 308, 309, 360–61, 362
Jasenovac, 382
Jaspers, Karl, 160
JCS 1067, 32, 33, 34
Jenkins, Roy, 437, 438–39
Jews, 60–61, 102, 116, 123, 412, 417
Jinnah, Mohammed Ali, 166
John Paul II, Pope, 361
Johnson, Lyndon B., 220, 238, 239
Jordan, 58, 178
Joseph, Keith, 318